THE DIGEST OF JUSTINIAN

THE
DIGEST OF
JUSTINIAN

TRANSLATION EDITED BY
ALAN WATSON

VOL. 3

PENN

UNIVERSITY OF PENNSYLVANIA PRESS

PHILADELPHIA

10   9   8   7   6   5   4   3   2   1

Published by
University of Pennsylvania Press
Philadelphia, Pennsylvania 19104-4011

Library of Congress Cataloging-in-Publication Data

Digesta. English.
    The digest of Justinian / translation edited by Alan Watson. —
Rev. English language ed.
        p.   cm.
    ISBN 978-0-8122-2035-3 (alk, paper)
    1. Roman law—Sources.   I. Watson, Alan.   II. Title.
    KJA1112.2   1998
340.5'4—dc21   97-42802
                                                       CIP

CONTENTS

BOOK THIRTY-SEVEN

BOOK THIRTY-EIGHT

BOOK THIRTY-NINE

BOOK FORTY

PREFACE TO THE
PAPERBACK EDITION

This is a corrected edition, minus the Latin text, of the four-volume *The Digest of Justinian*, Latin text edited by Theodor Mommsen with the aid of Paul Krueger, English translation edited by Alan Watson, published by University of Pennsylvania Press in 1985.

This edition incorporates a number of corrected translations. I am grateful to all who called suggested changes to my attention, and in particular to Tony Honoré and Olivia Robinson.

The biggest change has been a new translation by Sebastian and Olivia Robinson of the *Dédoken*, the Greek version of the preface, "The Confirmation of the *Digest*." The previous edition repeated the translation of the rather different Latin preface.

A note about the appearance of the pages. The pagination of the Mommsen edition has been maintained, as was done in the original four-volume hardcover edition. As a result, the pages of the translation vary in length.

ALAN WATSON

GLOSSARY

Abolitio. See Accusatio.

Acceptilatio (Formal Release). The method by which a creditor freed a debtor from his obligation under a verbal contract [*stipulatio* q.v.] producing the same effects as performance. *See D.*46.4.

Accessio (Accession). A general term for the acquisition of ownership by joining property to or merging it with something already owned by the acquirer. *See D.*41.1.

Accusatio (Accusation). The bringing of a criminal charge. Normally (exclusively until the early empire) this was left to the initiative of a private citizen acting as accuser [*delator*]. If a magistrate accepted the charge, he ordered its registration [*inscriptio*] on an official list. It could be removed from the list and so annulled [*absolutio*] during a public amnesty, or where the accuser withdrew the charge with the permission of the court. Unjustified withdrawal was a crime in itself [*tergiversatio*]. *See D.*48.2,16.

Actio Arbitraria. An action in which the judge could order the defendant to restore or produce the property at issue. If he failed to do so, the final judgment penalized him in various ways. *See D.*6.1.35.1; *D.*4.2.14.4.

Actio Civilis. See Ius Civile.

Actio Confessoria. See Servitus.

Actio Contraria. An action given to certain persons in particular legal situations where the normal direct action lay against them. *See* tutors [*tutor* q.v.] *D.* 27.4; depositees *D.*16.3; borrowers for use *D.*13.6.; creditors in the contract of *pignus* [q.v.] *D.*13.7.

Actio Famosa. See Infamia.

Actio in Factum. An action given originally by the *praetor* [q.v.] on the alleged facts of the case alone, where no standard civil law [*ius civile* q.v.] action was directly applicable. The expression *actio utilis* is also found, referring to a praetorian action which extended the scope of an existing civil law action, for example, by means of a fiction. The exact difference, if any, between this and the *actio in factum* is not known. *See D.*9.2.

Actio in Personam (Personal Action). An action based on an obligation of the defendant, whether this arose from a contract, delict, or other legal circumstance. Such an action lay only against the person under the obligation. Cf. *Actio in Rem.*

Actio in Rem (Real Action). An action asserting ownership of property, or other related though more limited rights over it, for example, a servitude [*servitus* q.v.]. Such an action lay against anyone withholding the property. Cf. *Actio in Personam.*

Actio Negatoria. See Servitus.

Actio Popularis. A penal action which could be brought by any person to protect the public interest in certain circumstances. The penalty was often paid to the complainant. *See D*.47.23.

Actio Praescriptis Verbis. An action given to a person after he had performed his part of the bargain under a contract which was not one of the standard types recognized by Roman law. *See D*.19.5.

Actio Utilis. See Actio in Factum.

Addictio in Diem. An agreement allowing a seller to set the sale aside if he received a better offer within a certain time. *See D*.18.2.

Ademptio (Ademption). The revocation, express or implied, of any disposition, usually a legacy. *See D*.34.4.

Adiudicatio (Adjudication). The order given by a judge [*iudex* q.v.] to settle certain proceedings between claimants over common property or between neighbors over boundaries. *See D*.10.2–3.

Adoptio (Adoption). A type of adoption where a dependent person [*alieni iuris* q.v.] was transferred from one family to another. This involved a change of *paterfamilias* [q.v.]. Adopted children were normally in the same legal position as natural children. Cf. *adrogatio* though the term *adoptio* is sometimes used to cover both. *See D*.1.7.

Adrogatio (Adrogation). A type of adoption where an independent person [*sui iuris* q.v.] joined a family, coming under parental power [*patria potestas* q.v.]. This could only be done to save a family from extinction and many restrictions were placed upon it. *See D*.1.7.

Adulterium (Adultery). This was made a criminal offense for a married woman by statute. Her husband was required to divorce and prosecute her, and her father could kill her and her partner with impunity in certain circumstances. *See D*.48.5.

Aedilis (Aedile). A magistrate of the republic whose duties were connected with the general management of daily life in the city, including some police work and the supervision of streets and markets. One type, the curule aediles, issued an edict [*edictum* q.v.] in connection with the latter which greatly influenced the law on sale and delictal liability for animals. The duties of the aediles were gradually taken over by the various types of prefect [*praefectus* q.v.] during the empire. *See D*.1.2.2.26; *D*.21.1.

Aestimatum. A transaction in which one person receives property from another on the basis that, within a specified time, he will either return the property or pay an agreed price. *See D*.19.3.

Agnatus (Agnate). A person related through the male line, whether by birth or adoption, to a common male ancestor. This is an important relationship throughout Roman law, especially in connection with the law of succession. Cf. also *paterfamilias.*

Alieni Iuris (Dependent). Subject to the legal power of someone else, either parental power [*patria potestas* q.v.] in the case of a son-in-power [*filiusfamilias* q.v.] and other descendants or the power of a master where slaves were concerned. Various legal disabilities were involved in either case. *See D*.1.6.

Aureus. See Solidus.

Bonae Fidei Iudicia (Actions of Good Faith). Certain contractual actions, for example, on sale, and certain quasi-contractual ones where the judge [*iudex* q.v.] had to take account of what ought to be done or given in good faith (*bona fides*) by the parties. This gave the judge wide discretion as to the amount of damages he could award. He could also take account of any defense [*exceptio* q.v.] even where it had not been expressly stated by the defendant.

Bonorum Possessio. A type of possession granted originally by the *praetor* [q.v.] giving rise to an extended or sometimes alternative system of succession, both testate and intestate, to that provided by the civil law [*ius civile* q.v.]. It was protected by an *interdictum* [q.v.] and an action. *See D.*37.1.

Calumnia. (a) In private law, vexatious litigation or receiving money for this purpose. (b) In criminal law, the offense of maliciously or recklessly bringing a false criminal charge. *See D.*3.6.

Capitalis (Capital). A criminal matter where the penalty is death, loss of liberty, or loss of citizenship.

Capitis Deminutio (Change of Civil Status). A loss of or change in one or more of the three basic elements of civil status, that is, freedom, citizenship, and membership of a family. *See D.*4.5.

Castigatio (Corporal Punishment). This took a number of forms: *flagellatio* was generally a whipping for slaves; *fustigatio* was beating with a rod or club, mainly a military punishment; *verberatio* involved multiple lashes and seems to have been severe.

Cautio. (a) A guarantee, either real or personal, that certain duties will be fulfilled. (b) A written document providing evidence of a contract, usually *stipulatio* [q.v.].

Census (Census). A public register of citizens, which estimated their property holdings and so assigned them to the various social classes. *See D.*50.15.

Codex. A collection, official or unofficial, of imperial enactments rather than a complete statement of the law as in a modern "code." *See* preface.

Cognitio. (a) A type of civil procedure, often referred to as *extra ordinem*, signifying its distinctness from the Formulary System [*formula* q.v.] of classical times, which it replaced in the third century A.D. The main difference was that under the *Cognitio* System the whole proceedings took place before an imperial magistrate. (b) The term is also used in a more general way in administrative and crimnal proceedings to cover the competent area of a judicial inquiry, or the investigation itself.

Collatio Bonorum. A contribution in respect of prior gifts which was required of emancipated [*emancipatio* q.v.] children who wished to benefit by intestate succession to their father. *See D.*37.6.

Collegium (Association). Any association, public or private, for religious, professional, or other purposes. Legal restrictions were placed on such associations to prevent subversive activities. *See D.*47.22.

Compensatio (Set-Off). The reduction of any claim by taking into account the defendant's counterclaim based on another transaction. *See D.*16.2.

Concubinatus (Concubinage). A legally and socially recognized monogamous relationship short of marriage. *See D.*25.7.

Condictio. A type of action alleging a civil law [*ius civile* q.v.] debt without mentioning any cause of action, available not only as a contractual remedy, but also on a quasi-contractual basis, where unjustified enrichment could be shown. Although its form was always the same, its name varied according to the situation involved, for example, the *condictio* for money not due [*indebiti*], that is, money paid in error. *See D.*12.4–13.3.

manumitted [*manumissio* q.v.] for this purpose. An *extraneus heres* was someone not subject to the deceased's parental power at time of death, either being unrelated or, for example, emancipated [*emancipatio* q.v.]. A *heres legitimus* was a person who succeeded in accordance with the civil law [*ius civile* q.v.] rules on intestacy. *See D.*28.5.

Honestiores. See Humiliores.

Humiliores. Persons of low social status, in contrast to the upper classes, the *honestiores.* The main legal difference was that only the former were liable to certain kinds of punishment, for example, crucifixion, torture, and corporal punishment.

Hypotheca. A contract of pledge in which the creditor obtained neither ownership nor possession of the property pledged. *See D.*13.7.

Imperium (Authority). The power of the higher republican magistrates, including the *praetor* [q.v.], and later the emperor to issue orders and enforce them, in particular the right to administer justice and to give military commands.

Impubes. A person under the age of puberty, which was eventually fixed at twelve years of age for girls and fourteen for boys. Such persons lacked full legal capacity, and those who were independent [*sui iuris* q.v.] had to be in tutelage [*tutela* q.v.] *See D.*26.

Incola. A person domiciled in a city or community other than the one in which he was born. *See D.*50.1.

Infamia. A condition of disgrace resulting from certain types of immoral or wrongful conduct. It followed, for instance, on conviction for a crime, or condemnation in delictal actions and those involving breach of trust called *actiones famosae.* Many legal disabilities resulted from this condition. *See D.*3.2.

Infans. A child under the age at which rational speech was possible, later fixed at seven years old. Such persons were a type of *impubes* [q.v.] with few legal powers.

Inscriptio. See Accusatio.

Institor. See Procurator.

Interdictum (Interdict). An order issued originally by the *praetor* [q.v.] or other magistrate in an administrative capacity, giving rise to further proceedings if disregarded. Many interdicts in private law were concerned with the protection of possession against unlawful interference in various circumstances. At times, interdicts were a procedural device for awarding interim possession, the party who acquired this becoming the defendant in a subsequent action. But they were also for many other private law and also public law purposes, for example, the interdict from fire and water was a form of banishment pronounced on a voluntary exile [*exilium* q.v.]. The complicated procedure required under the Formulary System [*formula* q.v.] for the use of interdicts became obsolete under the *Cognitio* [q.v.] System, and they were replaced by ordinary actions, although the issues and much of the terminology of the older system remained. *See D.*43.

Iudex (Judge). In the private law Formulary System [*formula* q.v.], the judge was a private individual chosen by the parties to decide the case on its facts, the legal issues having already been defined by the *praetor* [q.v.]. Under the later *Cognitio* [q.v.] System and in public and criminal matters, the term was used of any imperial official with jurisdiction, for example, a provincial governor [*praeses* q.v.]. *See D.*2.1.

Ius Civile (Civil Law). The original basic rules, principles, and institutions of Roman law, deriving from the various kinds of statute [*lex, senatus consultum, constitutio* qq.v.] and from juristic interpretation. They were applicable directly only to Roman citizens, but in 212 A.D. the *constitutio Antoniniana* conferred citizenship on most of the inhabitants of the empire. The expression is sometimes used in a more philosophical sense to mean the law peculiar to any community or people, whatever its source. Cf. *ius gentium* and *ius honorarium*. See D.1.1.

Ius Gentium. The original meaning of this term was probably the body of rules, principles, and institutions developed in the late republic to cover commercial dealings with peregrines [*peregrinus* q.v.] and other noncitizens, who could not use the civil law [*ius civile* q.v.]. Its development may be connected with the peregrine praetor [*praetor* q.v.]. Less formalistic and more sophisticated than the civil law, it came to have a more philosophical sense of the law which was common to all peoples and communities, although its detailed provisions were Roman in character and treated as ordinary rules of law. Cf. *ius civile*. See D.1.1.

Ius Honorarium (Praetorian Law). The law introduced by magistrates, especially the praetor [*praetor* q.v.] by means of his Edict [*edictum* q.v.], to aid, supplement, or correct the existing civil law [*ius civile* q.v.]. It provided a large number of remedies which were often preferable to the civil law ones, for example, in the field of succession. *See bonorum possessio.* In juristic writings it was commonly treated as distinct from the civil law, although both were simply parts of Roman law as a whole. Cf. *ius civile*.

Iusiurandum (Oath). Oaths were used in a number of contexts. (a) In general, a party could choose to swear an evidential oath before a judge [*iudex* q.v.]. But certain oaths were compulsory, for example, as to the value of the property claimed and that *calumnia* [q.v.] was absent. *See D.12.2, 3.* (b) In certain actions, the parties could challenge each other to swear oaths as to the validity of their cases. If the challenge was refused, the person refusing lost his case, bringing the trial to a speedy conclusion. This type of oath was called "necessary." *See D.12.2.* (c) In any action, a party could offer to swear or challenge the other party to swear to the validity of his case. The challenge need not be accepted, but if it was, an action or defense of oath was allowed in any subsequent proceedings. Here the oath was called "voluntary." *See D.12.2.* (d) An oath was required of a slave about to be manumitted [*manumissio* q.v.] that he would promise to perform certain services for his former master [*patronus* q.v.]. *See D.38.1.7.*

Ius Naturale (Natural Law). A vague expression in Roman law. At times it was merely a synonym for the term *ius gentium* [q.v.]. It often means that the rule or principle in question was thought of as based on everyday experience, referred to as "natural reason" [*naturalis ratio*]. Sometimes it refers to the justice or fairness of a rule, but the view of natural law as a universal ideal order in any way contrasted with positive law is almost entirely absent. *See D.1.1.*

Legatus (Legate). A term with a number of meanings. (a) An ambassador. Such a person on an imperial mission was called a *legatus Augusti (Caesaris)*. See D.50.7. (b) The deputy of a provincial governor [*proconsul* q.v.] with special delegated jurisdiction. *See D.1.16.* (c) A type of provincial governor was called a *legatus Augusti (Caesaris) pro praetore*. See D.1.18.1. (d) The commander of a legion.

Legitimus Heres. See Heres.

Lenocinium. See Stuprum.

Lex. (a) A statute passed by one of the popular assemblies of republican times. It normally took the gentile (middle) name of the proposer or proposers, the subject matter of the legislation sometimes also being indicated in the title, for example, the *Lex Cornelia* on Guarantors, the *Lex Fufia Caninia*. In the early empire some legislation was passed in this way, but the practice was obsolete by the end of the first century A.D. Thereafter, *lex* is often used of any piece of imperial legislation. *See D*.1.3,4. (b) The term also occurs in connection with the *Twelve Tables* [*lex duodecim tabularum*], a collection of early rules traditionally dating from c. 450 B.C., and drawn up by ten commissioners, the *decemviri*. It is not extant, but there are many references to its supposed provisions in the *Digest* and other legal and literary sources. *See D*.1.2.4.–6. (c) A special clause in a contract, for example, the *lex commissoria*, which allowed a seller to call off the sale if the price was not paid by a certain time. *See D*.18.3.

Libertinus, Libertus (Freedman). A former slave who, on manumission [*manumissio* q.v.], became a freeman and a Roman citizen, though with extensive public law disabilities. He had many duties toward his former master, his patron [*patronus* q.v.]. An imperial freedman [*libertus Caesaris*] manumitted by the emperor, often obtained high governmental office in the early empire. *See D*.38.1–5.

Lictor (Lictor). An attendant of a higher magistrate with *imperium* [q.v.], whose main duty was to escort him during public appearances.

Maiestas. This term was applied to a number of criminal offenses including treason, sedition, and desertion. In the empire it covered any action which endangered the emperor or his family. The earlier crime of betrayal to an enemy, *perduellio*, was eventually held to be merely a way of committing this offense. *See D*.48.4.

Manumissio (Manumission). The release of a slave by his master during the latter's lifetime or in his will. *See D*.40.1–9.

Metallum (Mine). Condemnation to work in a mine was a capital punishment [*capitalis* q.v.] only slightly less serious than the death penalty. There was a milder form known as *opus metalli*. *See D*.48.19.

Minor. A person over the age of puberty [*impubes* q.v.] but under the age of twenty-five. Such persons who were independent [*sui iuris* q.v.] had in classical times full legal capacity, though they could be protected by a grant of *restitutio in integrum* [q.v.]. In later law, the development of the institution of *cura* [q.v.] gave them more protection but some disabilities. *See D*.4.4; *D*.26.7,8.

Missio in Possessionem. A remedy granted originally by the *praetor* [q.v.] allowing a person to take over in whole or in part the property of another with various legal results. It had many uses, for example, to protect a creditor's interest after judgment or where property was threatened by the ruinous state of that of a neighbor. *See D*.42.4; *D*.39.2.

Munera. Certain public services which every person was bound to perform on behalf of his community or state. Some services were personal, for example, tutelage [*tutela* q.v.], others were burdens on property. Certain taxes were included under this term, and money payments could often be made in lieu of actual labor, for example, in maintaining public roads. The grounds for exemption [*excusatio*] from most of these services were limited. *See D*.50.4.

Naturalis Ratio. *See Ius Naturale*.

Negotiorum Gestio (Unauthorized Administration). The performance of some service on behalf of another person, without his request or authorization. If the action was reasonable in the circumstances, there was an action for compensation. *See D*.3.5.

Novatio (Novation). The extinction of one or more obligations by replacing it or them with a new obligation in the form of a stipulation [*stipulatio* q.v.]. *See D*.46.2.

Noxae Dare (To Surrender Noxally). To hand over a slave or animal as compensation to the victim of a delict committed by him. This alternative was open to an owner only where there had been no complicity on his part in the delict. *See D*.9.1,4.

Obsequium. See Patronus.

Occupatio (Occupation). The acquisition of ownership by taking possession of a thing not previously owned, such as a wild animal, or a thing which has been abandoned by its owner. *See D*.41.1.

Opus Metalli. See Metallum.

Opus Publicum. Forced labor on public works. This criminal punishment could only be imposed on *humiliores* [q.v.]. Condemnation for life meant loss of citizenship, but lesser terms did not affect status. *See D*.48.19.

Oratio (Oration). A proposal put forward by the emperor for legislation by means of a *senatus consultum* [q.v.]. The approval of the senate became a mere formality, so that the term came to mean a piece of direct imperial legislation, a type of *constitutio* [q.v.].

Pactum (Pact). Any agreement which did not come within one of the recognized categories of contract. Such an agreement was not generally actionable, but was accepted as a defense [*exceptio* q.v.]. However, pacts added to a recognized contract in order to modify its normal obligations were enforceable, as were certain pacts unconnected with any contract, for example, *constitutum debiti* [q.v.]. *See D*.2.14.

Paterfamilias (Head of the Household). The oldest ascendant male agnate [*agnatus* q.v.] in any family was its legal head. He exercised considerable powers over his sons, daughters, and other descendants, that is, those dependent [*alieni iuris* q.v.] on him. They were subject to his control in many matters relating to their persons, for example, marriage, and were incapable of owning property. Apart from certain kinds of *peculium* [q.v.] and some special categories of property in later law, all they acquired passed to their *paterfamilias*. The powers of a *paterfamilias* did not cease when the person subject to them reached majority. Often the word "father" [*pater*] is used in this sense.

Patria Potestas (Parental Power). The power of a *paterfamilias* [q.v.] over those dependent [*alieni iuris* q.v.] on him. In private law, the expression "in power" [*in potestate*] refers either to someone subject to this or the power of master over his slave. *See D*.1.7.

Patronus (Patron). The former master of a slave, who after manumission [*manumissio* q.v.] has become his freedman [*libertus* q.v.]. A patron had many rights over his freedman, particularly with regard to the performance of certain agreed services [*opera*] and in connection with succession. A freedman had to show respect [*obsequium*] to his patron and could not bring criminal proceedings against him or actions involving *infamia* [q.v.]. *See D*.37.14,15; *D*.38.1–4.

Pauperies. Damage done by an animal, without fault on the part of its owner. An action was given for the value of the damage done with the alternative of noxal surrender [*noxae dare* q.v.]. *See D*.9.1.

Peculatus. The misappropriation of public money or property by theft, embezzlement, or any other means. *See D*.48.13.

Peculium. The sum of money or property granted by the head of the household [*paterfamilias* q.v.] to a slave or son-in-power [*filiusfamilias* q.v.] for his own use. Although considered for some purposes as a separate unit, and so allowing a business run by slaves to be used almost as a limited company, it remained technically the property of the head of the household. From the early empire onward, special kinds of *peculium* came into existence, the "military" [*castrense*] and the "quasi-military" [*quasi castrense*] *peculium*, which were considered for many legal purposes to be the property of a son-in-power himself. *See D.*15.1; *D.*49.17.

Perduellio. See Maiestas.

Peregrinus (Peregrine). In classical times this term usually meant a member of a non-Roman community within the empire, who was subject to the law of his own state and had few of the public or private law rights of a Roman citizen, for example, *conubium* [q.v.]. A special *praetor* [q.v.] dealt with peregrines' transactions. After the *constitutio Antoniniana* [*see ius civile*], the expression came to be applied to foreigners living outside of the empire.

Pignus. A contract of pledge under which the creditor obtained possession of the property pledged, but ownership remained with the debtor. The expression was sometimes used as a general one for any form of real security, including *pignus* and *hypotheca* [q.v.]. *See D.*13.7.

Pollicitatio (Unilateral Promise). A promise made to city or community to make a gift of money or to erect a public building or monument. Such a promise was legally binding in most cases as a matter of public law. *See D.*50.12.

Postliminium. The regaining of most of a person's private and public law rights on returning from capture by the enemy. The main exception in classical law was that a marriage usually did not automatically revive. *See D.*49.15.

Potestas. See Patria Potestas.

Praefectus (Prefect). The title of various kinds of high officials and military commanders in the empire. The most important of these were the praetorian prefects [*praefecti praetorio*], the chief military and civil advisors of the emperor and governors of the four great prefectures into which the later empire was divided. They also had extensive private law and (from the the third century A.D.) criminal law jurisdiction, the courts over which they presided being the highest in the empire. But the two urban prefects [*praefecti urbi*], one at Rome and later one at Constantinople, exercised independent criminal and civil jursidiction over their respective territories. Many of the lesser prefects in charge, for example, of the corn supply [*praefectus annonae*] or the city guard [*praefectus vigilum*], served under the urban prefect and their legal decisions could be appealed to him. The prefect of Egypt [*praefectus Augustalis* or *Aegypti*] was in a special position in a number of ways. *See D.*1.11,12,15,17.

Praelegare. To make a legacy of a specific thing to an heir [*heres* q.v.] in addition to his share of the inheritance.

Praeses (Governor). The general name for any provincial governor, who had judicial as well as administrative powers. *See D.*1.18.

Praetor (Praetor). In the republic, an important magistrate second only to the *consules* [q.v.], in charge of the administration of private law. As well as the urban praetor [*praetor urbanus*], probably the most important, there was also a peregrine praetor [*praetor peregrinus*] dealing with foreigners [*peregrinus* q.v.] and later there were a number of other judicial praetors dealing with specific issues [for example, *fideicommissum* q.v.]. However, because of the growth of a standard body of praetorian law [*ius honorarium* q.v.] leading to the consolidation of the Edict [*edictum* q.v.], these officials are referred to collectively in the texts as "the praetor." The praetor greatly extended and modified the civil law [*ius civile* q.v.] by means of his control over the Formulary System [*formula* q.v.] of civil litigation. Praetors continued to be appointed during the empire, but gradually their legal functions were taken over by other officials such as the various kinds of prefect [*praefectus* q.v.] and the office became largely honorary. *See D*.1.2.27–34; *D*.1.14.

Praevaricatio. Collusion between the accuser [*accusatio* q.v.] and accused in a criminal trial to secure acquittal, or between a lawyer and his client's enemy. *See D*.47.15.

Precarium. A grant of the possession and general use of property made gratuitously and revocable at any time. *See D*.43.26.

Proconsul (Proconsul). A kind of provincial governor with civil and criminal jurisdiction. *See D*.1.16.

Procurator (Procurator). This term has a number of meanings. (a) The representative of a party in a civil trial. (b) A general manager of another person's business or other affairs. This position was often given to a freedman [*libertinus* q.v.] or a slave. Occasionally, the term was applied to an agent for a single transaction. An earlier type of business manager [*institor*] came to be considered a kind of procurator. *See D*.3.3; *D*.14.3. (c) Many imperial officials were called procurators, for example, a *procurator Caesaris*, originally a fiscal agent but later given many administrative duties. *See D*.1.19.

Quaestiones Perpetuae. Permanent criminal courts, each dealing with one class of offense, the penalty for it being fixed by the relevant statute [*lex* q.v.], which also usually set up the court itself. They had large juries, from whose verdict there was no appeal. The *Cognitio* [q.v.] System was sometimes an alternative. *See D*.48.18.

Quaestor (Quaestor). A magistrate whose office was created in the republic, whose duties were mainly connected with public finances and provincial administration. Their importance declined during the empire. *See D*.1.13.

Rei Vindicatio. *See Vindicatio*.

Relegatio (Relegation). A form of banishment either for a fixed period or in perpetuity. It did not necessarily involve loss of citizenship or confiscation of property, but merely exclusion from a specified territory. *See D*.48.22.

Repetundae. Extortion or unlawful acquisition of money or property by a person in an official position, such as a provincial governor. *See D*.48.11.

Rescriptum (Rescript). A written answer, issued by the imperial civil service on behalf of the emperor, to legal and administrative questions. These were sent in by officials and private individuals. In principle, such decisions were only binding in the case at issue, but they often came to be considered as of general application.

Restitutio in Integrum. A remedy granted originally by the *praetor* [q.v.] annulling the normal civil law [*ius civile* q.v.] effect of some event or transaction which had unfairly prejudiced a person's position. It had many uses as a remedy against fraud, or even, in the case of a *minor* [q.v.], a bad bargain in certain circumstances. *See D*.4.1,2,3,6.

Senator (Senator). A member of the senate [*senatus*], the most important assembly of the republic, with enormous and undefined advisory, deliberative, judicial, and later legislative powers [*senatus consultum* q.v.]. It was largely composed of ex-magistrates. During the empire the political importance of the senate declined, but senators and their families were considered to belong to the privileged senatorian class [*ordo senatorius*]. But certain legal disabilities were also involved, for example, marriage with a freedman [*libertus* q.v.] or woman was prohibited. *See D*.1.9.

Senatus Consultum. A decision of the senate [*senator* q.v.], which during the republic technically took the form of advice to a high magistrate, for example, the

BOOK THIRTY

1

LEGACIES AND *FIDEICOMMISSA*

1 ULPIAN, *Edict, book 67:* Legacies are held to be equal to *fideicommissa* in all respects.
2 ULPIAN, *Fideicommissa, book 1:* It should be known that only those with the right to make wills may leave *fideicommissa.*
3 ULPIAN, *Sabinus, book 4:* The testator's words "whoever of the above-written shall be my heir," or "if Seius shall be my heir," or "if he shall accept the inheritance," do not make the appended legacy or *fideicommissum* conditional.
4 ULPIAN, *Sabinus, book 5:* If someone has made a mistake in the name of a farm and has named the Cornelian instead of the Sempronian, then the Sempronian will be due; but if he has made a mistake with respect to a tangible object, it will not be due. In the case of someone who, wishing to bequeath clothing, has written "household goods," while thinking clothing to be included under the term household goods, Pomponius writes that clothing is not due, just as if someone were to think electrum or brass to be included under the term gold, or more foolishly still, silver to be included under the term clothing. For the names of things are unchangeable, but those of men are changeable. 1. If someone appoints heirs and leaves a legacy in these terms, "whoever shall be heir to my property in Gaul, let him be condemned to give," this legacy is taken as a charge upon all the heirs, since the property in Gaul belongs to them all.
5 PAUL, *Sabinus, book 1:* Where the right to select a slave has been bequeathed, we may choose once only. 1. Labeo says: When a certain thing or person is bequeathed as follows, "let my heir give him who shall be mine when I die," and he is held in common, then all of him is due. But according to Cassius, Trebatius replied that part is due; and that is the better opinion. 2. When a farm owned in common has been left as a legacy without mention of the testator's portion, but he has named it "mine," then it is settled that the portion is due.
6 JULIAN, *Digest, book 33:* "Let my heir give Stichus, who shall be mine when I die." It appears that the head of the household wished rather to impose a condition on the legacy than apply a description, because if this expression were provided for description, the wording would have been "Stichus who is mine," not "who shall be mine." The condition must be taken to mean "insofar as he shall be mine", so that if the testator has relinquished the ownership of all of him, the legacy is extinguished; if of a part, then what is due is the part owned by the testator at the time of his death.

7   PAUL, *Sabinus, book 2:* A legacy left to a slave may be repudiated by his master.

8   POMPONIUS, *Sabinus, book 2:* If from a whole farm that has been bequeathed the testator has alienated a part, it is held that the remaining part only is due, since, if he had added something to that farm, the increase would pass to the legatee. 1. If it is written, "let my heir Lucius Titius, or my heir Maevius, give ten to Seius," Seius is to sue whichever of the two he wishes, so that if one is sued and pays, the other will be released, just as if two promissors had been liable in full for a debt. What then if he should have claimed a part from the one? Then he will certainly be at liberty to claim the residue from either. It will be the same if the other has paid a part. 2. If a legacy reads "eight litter-bearers, or instead of these a certain sum of money for each one of them, whichever the legatee chooses," then the legatee cannot vindicate a part of the slaves and demand cash for the rest, because it has been a single legacy in either case in the same way as if fifty pounds weight of oil, or a sum of so much per pound, had been bequeathed. Were we to hold otherwise, a division would be allowable even when a single man had been bequeathed. It makes no difference whether the sum is stated as so much for each person or a lump sum. Certainly, if a legacy has been bequeathed of eight slaves or a certain sum of money for all of them, the heir cannot be made against his will to owe a part in money and a part in slaves.

9   POMPONIUS, *Sabinus, book 3:* What is in enemy hands can, as Octavenus wrote, be left as a legacy which holds good by right of *postliminium.*

10   PAUL, *Sabinus, book 2:* Julian thinks that a son-in-power cannot choose without his father's command, nor before the inheritance has been accepted; which is true.

11   PAPINIAN, *Questions, book 9:* When a legacy or inheritance is given to a son-in-power or to the slave of another, a *fideicommissum* may be charged on the father or master, but this *fideicommissum* takes effect as charged on them personally only when it is left to those through whom the benefit of the inheritance or legacy is obtained for the father or master. And Julian, moved by no unsubtle reasoning, replied

that a father, whose son has been appointed heir, may take the benefit of the *lex Falcidia* when he restores the inheritance to a stranger, since he was bound through his son, but must restore to the son himself without taking the *lex Falcidia* into account, because his son could not be personally bound to him, and the father is held to be asked not as heir but as father. And, therefore, if the father is asked to restore to his son after his death what has come to him from a legacy or inheritance left to the son, and the son dies in his father's lifetime, the father will certainly retain it, since the *fideicommissum* took effect as charged on him personally.

12 POMPONIUS, *Sabinus, book 3:* If the same thing shall have been left as a legacy to me and to you and then after the legacy falls due I become your heir, Labeo says that I am at liberty to acquire it under my legacy or on the ground that I am your heir. If I should wish, I may claim it under my legacy, so that the whole may belong to me; but I may also claim it under the legacy that goes with the inheritance. 1. Proculus says: If anyone were to make a will while dying at Rome, and in it condemn the heir to give to me within three days after his death slaves he had at Gades, this is a ratified legacy, and the narrow space of time does not hurt the legacy in any way. 2. There is a rule of civil law which ensures that if we can leave legacies to any persons, we can also leave legacies to their slaves. 3. In legacies, what is written last is valid; for a preceding legacy may be modified by the addition of a day of payment or of a condition or by complete ademption. But if a legacy is adeemed upon two different conditions, the last ademption is the one to be respected. At times, however, in legacies not what is last but what is first written is valid; for if I write, "what I shall have given to Titius below, that I neither give nor bequeath," the legacy left below will not be valid. And that clause too by which the payment of immediate legacies is deferred to a future date is held to apply to legacies subsequently written. So it is intention that validates what is written in a will.

13 POMPONIUS, *Sabinus, book 4:* When an unspecified slave was bequeathed to you and the heir delivered Stichus to your slave, Neratius replied that if he delivered him by the intention of the master or the master had ratified the choice, then the master is released just as if it had been Stichus who was bequeathed.

14 ULPIAN, *Sabinus, book 15:* If a clause has been inserted in a will as follows, "if I should make a bequest to anyone twice, let my heir pay him once," or "let one payment be due," and the testator then makes to the same person in writing a bequest of two sums or two farms, are both of them due? Aristo said that it appears that only one was bequeathed; for what has been adeemed is judged not to have been given according to the opinion of Celsus and Marcellus; which is true. 1. But Papinian, in the nineteenth book of his *Questions*, says that even after legacies that have been frequently inserted, if the testator adds that he wishes only one to be paid and does this before completing the will, the other bequests are thereby held to be adeemed. But which one is adeemed rather than another? That is not evident. But Papinian says it can be held that the smallest should be paid.

15 PAUL, *Sabinus, book 3:* A testator intended to bequeath a fourth part of his goods, but wrote a half; Proculus rightly said the fourth part could be maintained to have been bequeathed, because it is contained in the half. The same will apply if his

intention was to bequeath fifty and a hundred are written; for fifty will be due. And even if he intended to bequeath more and wrote less, the legacy will be valid. 1. If anyone bequeaths a sum to "his daughters" expecting a posthumous daughter and if she is not born, then the whole sum will be due to the surviving daughter.

16 POMPONIUS, *Sabinus, book 5:* If a thing is bequeathed jointly to two persons, though one of them is not in existence, then I think it true that only a part is due to the other. 1. An heir who is condemned to pay conjointly with a person named who is not an heir owes the whole legacy; for equally if someone had condemned two of his heirs by name to pay and one of them had not accepted the inheritance, the other who did accept it would owe the whole sum, if the share of the one who had not accepted had passed to the one who had. 2. If a legacy has been left to Titius and the posthumous children of the testator and no posthumous child is born, Titius shall vindicate it all. Even if the testator had intended equal shares to be given to Titius and the post-humous children and even if he expressly stated this intention, the whole legacy is due to Titius if no posthumous child is born.

17 ULPIAN, *Sabinus, book 15:* If anyone who has made a legacy to his daughters mentions a posthumous daughter in any part of his will, he is held to have meant to include in the legacy to his daughters the posthumous daughter also. 1. If anyone makes a legacy thus, "should any daughter be born to me, let my heir give her a hundred," then if several are born, he is held to have bequeathed this much to each of them, which must be so accepted unless the wish of the testator to the contrary is evident. 2. If a legacy has been made to one of the heirs, it is clearly the duty of the judge in an action for the division of the inheritance to award it to him. Even if he has refused to accept the inheritance, it is established that he may recover this legacy.

18 JULIAN, *Digest, book 31:* And, indeed, he may demand the whole legacy, although it would have been void if charged in his favor upon himself.

19 ULPIAN, *Sabinus, book 15:* Papinian, in his book of *Questions*, thinks that legacies ineffectively given are confirmed by repetition, that is, by a subsequent deposition in these terms, perhaps in a codicil, "and in addition, let my heir give him this." He thinks the case is different with this subsequent clause: "Let my heir be condemned to pay in three annual installments these moneys that I have bequeathed for which no day for payment has been named"; for the testator here was not intending to confirm invalid legacies but to defer the day of payment of valid ones. 1. The same author wrote in the same context, when treating of substitution for an *impubes,* that if a leg-acy has been ineffectively charged upon an *impubes,* it is due from the substitute if the legacy has been charged on him with the words "and in addition," but the *impubes* has not become his father's heir and has died. 2. In a legacy left to several people, if por-tions are not assigned, they are to be kept equal.

20 POMPONIUS, *Sabinus, book 5:* If a person owning two slaves has bequeathed one of these without making it clear which one he has bequeathed, the legatee may choose.

21 ULPIAN, *Sabinus, book 15:* If a herd has been bequeathed, any subsequent accessions belong to the legatee.

22 POMPONIUS, *Sabinus, book 5:* If a herd has been bequeathed and some herd animals die in the testator's lifetime and are replaced by others, it is taken to be the same herd. And if the livestock from this herd is diminished and only one ox survives, the legatee may vindicate it, although the herd has ceased to exist, just as when a tenement building has been bequeathed and is burned down the site may still be vindicated.

23 PAUL, *Sabinus, book 3:* If anyone bequeaths a part of his goods, it is usual today to restore it without the fruits unless delay on the part of the heir has intervened.

24 POMPONIUS, *Sabinus, book 5:* It is established that what is not yet in existence can be bequeathed, for instance, "whatever offspring may be born to such a female slave," or if a bequest is made thus, "let him give from the wine that is produced in my farm" or "only the young of my animals." 1. If I have a usufruct and bequeath it, unless I subsequently obtain the property from which it derives, the legacy is invalid. 2. If anyone after making his will and bequeathing the Titian farm had added to it any part which he intended to belong to the Titian farm, the addition can be exacted by the legatee, and the same applies in the case of alluvion, and especially if the part added was from another field which was his when he made his will. 3. But if, after making his will, he took something from the Titian farm and added it to another farm, it must be seen whether the legatee is to claim that part also or whether he should lose it on the grounds that it has ceased to be part of the Titian farm, since the names and delimitation of farms are established by our intention and not by nature. And it is the better view that what has been annexed to another property should be held to have been adeemed. 4. If I bequeath a ship and specifically describe it as mine, and then rebuild it all piecemeal, it would, if the same keel remains, be rightly vindicated by the legatee all the same.

25 PAUL, *Sabinus, book 3:* A son who is an heir may be charged unconditionally with a legacy in favor of his father, and it is immaterial whether he is in his father's power on the day when the legacy falls due. So even if the inheritance has been accepted by his father's command, the legacy will count toward his Falcidian share.

26 POMPONIUS, *Sabinus, book 5:* No one should be held to have received more in legacies than the balance remaining after deducting what has been given to fulfill a condition. 1. If the heir has been condemned to give a certain article and it is not his fault that he has failed to deliver it in the place where it was, then if it should afterward perish without the heir's fraud or fault, the legatee must suffer the loss. 2. When part of an estate has been bequeathed and it is doubtful whether a share of the things or the value is due, Sabinus and Cassius held that the value has been left, Proculus and Nerva a share of the things. But it is necessary to come to the relief of the heir, so that he himself may choose whether he prefers to give a share of things or the value. However, an heir is permitted to give a part of such things as may be divided without loss. If they are by nature undivided or cannot be divided without loss, the value must be paid by the heir in all cases.

27 PAUL, *Plautius, book 9:* But the heir may give the legatee the remaining part by giving fewer things or one only, with the consent of the legatee or by the judge's assessment, so that the legatee need not be obliged to vindicate a share of all the things.

28   ULPIAN, *Sabinus, book 19:* If I, being protected against my creditor by a defense, bequeath to him what I owe him, it is a valid legacy, because the defense is held to have been withdrawn. Similarly, Aristo says that a bequest to me of what is due to me by a praetorian action is a valid bequest, because a civil action is thereby granted me instead of a praetorian. 1. Marcellus, in his twenty-eighth book, thinks that if you bequeath to me a thing that you owe me under a stipulation, the legacy is valid, so as not even to be diminished under the *lex Falcidia.*

29   PAUL, *Lex Julia et Papia, book 6:* But if the debt is not modified either in manner, time, condition or place, the legacy is invalid.

30   ULPIAN, *Sabinus, book 19:* A clause of this sort, "let the moneys I have bequeathed, for which a day of payment has not been fixed, be paid by my heir after one, two, or three years," does not apply to tangible objects that have been bequeathed, but only to what can be weighed, numbered, and measured. 1. And it applies only to those legacies for which no day is fixed; so if a legacy should have been bequeathed unconditionally, it will be prorogued by this addition. 2. What if it should happen that a bequest is made to me of a hundred at once? Shall they be paid after one year or at once? Servius and Labeo say that they are due at once. So although the addition is superfluous as far as concerns the force and effect of the legacy, it will be of advantage in ensuring that the legacy is due straight away. 3. But if a legacy has been left payable after intervals of specified years or months, this clause will lose effect, because the legacy [already] has a beginning and end. 4. If a legacy has been left under a condition, a clause requiring payment after one year loses validity, because a condition means an uncertain day of payment. 5. With this, Trebatius's opinion agrees, that if a legacy is left to someone to be paid when he is twenty years old, this common clause does not apply. 6. Again, if money is bequeathed which is in a safe, or wine which is in a cellar, the clause must be said to be inapplicable, since, as stated above, it does not apply whenever individual things are bequeathed. 7. Gallus Aquilius, Ofilius, and Trebatius replied that this clause applies not only to preceding legacies but to all that are mentioned in the will; which is true.

31   PAUL, *Sabinus, book 3:* This clause applies to subsequent legacies that are confirmed by codicil.

32   ULPIAN, *Sabinus, book 20:* If somebody should charge a legacy upon a son, who is a *pupillus* and has been appointed heir "when he comes into his own tutelage" and has repeated the charge upon the substitute heir, then if the son dies while *impubes,* the legacy will not be due from the second heir. Both Sextus and Pomponius think this to be true provided that the repetition of the legacies has been drafted in such a manner as, for instance, "let my heir pay within so many days the legacy with which I have charged my son and which I have ordered him to pay in the event of his becoming my heir." But if the legacies are repeated thus, "let my heir pay the legacies with which I have charged my son," the legacies shall be held to have been repeated unconditionally and named only by way of designation. Consequently, the legacy in question shall be due at once. 1. If someone bequeaths Stichus when he owns several persons named

Stichus and it is not evident which Stichus he meant, the heir must deliver the one whom the legatee chooses. 2. If anything is left as a share to a *civitas*, for the benefit and ornament of the *res publica*, it will certainly be due.

33   PAUL, *Rules, book 3:* If the same thing has been left to several persons and it has been left to them jointly, then if one of them seeks to vindicate it and the other brings an action under the will, he who brings his action under the will shall have no more than his share. If it was left to them separately and if it is quite evident that the testator deprived the first legatee of it and went over the second legatee, it is held that only the latter accedes to the legacy. But if this is by no means apparent, all the legatees are entitled to equal shares of the legacy, unless, to be sure, the testator made it perfectly clear in writing that he wished each of them to receive the whole legacy. In that case, one is assigned the value and the other the thing itself with the choice of the thing or the value reserved to him who first joined issue with respect to the legacy or *fideicommissum* on the understanding that he does not have permission after choosing the one to go over to the other.

34   ULPIAN, *Sabinus, book 21:* It is evident that where the testator wished to transfer the legacy to the last-named legatee, it will not be due to the earlier one even if the last-named is a person not entitled to the legacy. But if the legatees are joint or were separated and are now commingled, they jointly qualify as one person. 1. If the same thing is bequeathed several times in the same will, it cannot be claimed more than once, and it suffices if either the thing or the value of the thing is acquired. 2. But if the same thing is bequeathed to me by two wills, I shall be able to claim twice, so as to obtain the thing by one will and the value by the other. 3. But if it is not a bequeathed article, but an identical quantity that is several times mentioned in the same will, the deified Pius ruled in a rescript that the heir must then pay the sum several times, if from quite evident proofs it is shown that the testator wished to multiply the legacy. He made the same rule for *fideicommissa.* The reason for this is evident, namely that the same thing cannot be delivered several times, but the same sum can be multiplied if the testator wishes it. 4. But this is to be understood as applicable where it is not a specific sum of money that has been left several times, as where the testator has several times left, say, the hundred that he has in his safe. In that case, I believe it is comparable to the [repeated] bequest of a farm. 5. But if a weight of gold or silver has been bequeathed several times, Papinian replied that this is rather to be compared to the bequest of a sum; rightly, as no specific thing appears to have been bequeathed. 6. And so if anything else is left several times that can be weighed, numbered, or measured, the same is to be said, that is, that it is due several times if that is what the testator wished. 7. If I have bought a thing that has been bequeathed to me, an action under the will lies in my favor up to the price that I have dispensed. 8. And this is to be said all the more if the same thing has been bequeathed to me by two different wills, but one of them requires me to restore this thing [to another person] or something in its stead, or if the testator has bequeathed it under the condition of my giving something in its stead, for it appears that I am deprived of the thing to the extent that I shall be paying. 9. If a thing is bequeathed jointly, it is agreed that it is apportioned from the beginning. The shares are due in

proportion not only to those who are personally entitled to the legacy but also to those who are not personally entitled, as, say, if a bequest is made to Titius and to his own slave without grant of freedom.   10. But if in a will made for a son who is a *pupillus*, a testator bequeaths to another the same thing that he bequeathed in his own will to me, Julian writes that we have concurrent shares. So in the meantime the one to whom he bequeathed the thing in his own will shall have his share.   11. If a thing is bequeathed to two persons of whom one has been appointed heir, a legacy charged upon the heir in his own favor is held to be ineffective, and consequently what is charged on him for himself will belong to the co-legatee.   12. Hence, it is said that if there are two heirs, one to a twelfth and the other to eleven twelfths, and a farm is bequeathed to them, the heir to a twelfth will have eleven twelfths of the farm and the other a twelfth.   13. Clearly, if one of the legatees is appointed heir of the heir upon whom the legacy has been charged, the heir will nonetheless render to his co-legatee his share; for he will retain the share of the legacy to which he is entitled.   14. If a bequest is made to Titius in these terms, "let him have the Seian farm or its usufruct for himself," these are two legacies, and it is for Titius to decide whether or not he wishes to vindicate the usufruct.   15. But if somebody makes a bequest to Titius as follows, "I give and bequeath a farm, that he may have it as his due share," I hold that it can be said that he will have a part. For it is held that by designating the farm he designates not all but a part of it; for a part of a farm is rightly called a farm.

35   PAUL, *Sabinus, book 3:* If the heir has been condemned to give a man belonging to another and this man has been manumitted by his master, nothing is due from this legacy.

36   POMPONIUS, *Sabinus, book 6:* "To Titia I bequeath all my weavers except for those I have bequeathed to another in my will. To Plotia I bequeath all my home-bred slaves except for those I have bequeathed to another." Since some slaves were both home-bred and weavers, Labeo says that because there is no way of discerning which weavers he did not bequeath to Titia other than if it were known which of them he had bequeathed to Plotia, and again no way of knowing which home-bred slaves he did not bequeath to Plotia other than if it were known which of them he bequeathed to Titia, the slaves in question are excepted from neither legacy and are therefore common to both. For this is the rule if something has not been expressly excepted from either of two legacies.   1. But if something has been bequeathed in this way, "all weavers except home-bred slaves" and again "all home-bred slaves except weavers," he who is both a home-bred slave and a weaver has been bequeathed to neither.   2. It makes no difference whether the legacy is worded "to Titius and Marcius" or "to Titius with Marcius"; for in each case, the legacy is held to have been bequeathed conjointly. 3. If the heir was condemned to give Stichus to two legatees and gives him to one, and before he is sued by the other, Stichus dies, then the heir is not liable, because it is understood that he has not been at fault.

37   ULPIAN, *Sabinus, book 21:* When a bequest has been left in general terms, like that of a man, Gaius Cassius wrote that care must be taken that neither the best nor the worst should be received. This opinion is strengthened by a rescript of our emperor

and of the divine Severus who decreed that when a man has been bequeathed, an estate manager cannot be chosen.   1. If the testator had a certain farm in mind but it is not evident which he meant, the heir shall choose to give which one he wishes, but if the intention is clear, that very farm shall be vindicated. Again, if he bequeathed a piece of silver plate and it is not evident which, the heir will equally have the choice to give which one he wishes.

38   POMPONIUS, *Sabinus, book 6:* The legatee cannot acquire a part of the legacy and repudiate the rest. His heirs can, so that one of them may acquire, and the other reject, his part.   1. If we decide to refuse a legacy left to us, it will be as if the legacy had never been bequeathed; and so we say that if it so happen that what was left to me were lands charged with servitudes in favor of my lands, the servitudes are not confused. And an action for theft will be unimpaired, if the bequest is of a slave on account of whom the legatee can bring an action for theft.

39   ULPIAN, *Sabinus, book 21:* When a slave who has been bequeathed is in flight, or is required when a long distance away, the heir must take pains to recover and deliver that property; and so Julian writes. For Africanus, in the twentieth book of his *Letters on Julian*, raises the question and thinks that the heir should go to expense, a view which I consider should be followed.   1. The fruits to be deducted in claiming the legacy are not those which the heir has collected but those which the legatee has been able to collect; and this is to be said of the work of slaves, transport by draft animals, or carriage by ships. What is said of fruits is to be understood to apply to the rents of town buildings. In assessing interest, the custom of the region is to be followed; the judge will, therefore, estimate the rate of interest and fix it. The heir will be liable for the destruction of the thing if he has delayed delivery, just as in a stipulation, if the thing has perished after delay, its value is paid. Similarly, the heir must surrender the offspring of female slaves; and if a slave has been bequeathed and the heir has acquired through him an inheritance or a legacy or anything, then the heir must surrender it.   2. If Titius had bought a thing from me and had bequeathed it to me before I delivered it to him and then I delivered it to him and received the price, it appears on first sight that he bequeathed my own property to me, and so the legacy is not valid. But as I am released from liability to an action on sale, I shall be able all the same to vindicate what I delivered by virtue of its being a legacy. But if the price has not yet been paid to me, Julian writes that I may bring an action on sale to recover the price and, under the will besides, to recover the thing that I sold and delivered. He adds that even if the price was paid to me and I had not yet delivered the thing, I would by an action under the will obtain freedom from liability.   3. Julian also writes: "If the testator has bequeathed to me a farm which he had bought from another, the heir should be compelled to assign to me the action on sale in the event of the thing not yet having been delivered to the deceased or the heir."   4. If anyone has bequeathed to another the right to quarry stone, does this legacy also pass to his heir? Marcellus maintains that it does not pass to the heir unless the name of the heir is added to the legacy.   5. The heir is compelled to pay on lands that have been bequeathed any

undischarged tax or tribute or ground rent or sewage charge or water rate. 6. I know that the following case has actually been investigated: A certain man had two farms of the same name and bequeathed the Cornelian estate. One was worth more than the other, and the heir said the less valuable farm had been bequeathed, the legatee the more valuable one. It will generally be admitted that he bequeathed the less valuable farm if the legatee cannot prove that he meant the more valuable one. 7. It is agreed that even the property of another can be bequeathed, as long as it can be acquired, even if its acquisition should be difficult. 8. But if someone should bequeath the gardens of Sallust, which are the emperor's, or the Alban estate which is for imperial uses, the addition of such legacies would be the act of a lunatic. 9. Similarly, it is agreed that the Campus Martius, the Roman forum, or a sacred building cannot be bequeathed. 10. And if a bequest should be made of estates of Caesar which form part of his patrimony and are under a procurator of the patrimony, their value should not be paid either, because there can be no commerce in them without the emperor's consent, as it is not the custom to sell them.

40   ULPIAN, *Fideicommissa, book 2:* But if the property of another over which the legatee has no commercial entitlement and which he has no right to possess is left by way of *fideicommissum,* I think its value is due.

41   ULPIAN, *Sabinus, book 21:* So let us consider other things beside these. 1. All bodies and rights and servitudes can be bequeathed. But things that are joined to buildings cannot be bequeathed, because of a *senatus consultum* to that effect dating to the consulship of Aviola and Pansa. 2. However, the question may arise whether, if at some time marbles or columns became separated from buildings, the legacy becomes valid. Well, if the legacy is not valid from the beginning, it does not become valid after the event, just as the bequest of my own property to me, if it is alienated after the will has been made, remains invalid because it had no effect in the first place. But if it is bequeathed under a condition, the legacy may be valid if at the time when the condition is fulfilled the property is not mine, or the thing is not joined to buildings, according to those who hold that I can buy my own property under a condition and that it can be promised and bequeathed to me under a stipulation. The rule of Cato will therefore prevent an unconditional legacy but not a conditional one, because it does not apply to conditional bequests. 3. Again, it may be asked, if anyone has two houses and bequeaths one of them, and makes a bequest of something joined to the other house to the person whom he bequeathed the [one] house, whether the legacy will be valid. What gives rise to the question is that by *senatus consultum* and imperial *constitutiones* we are permitted to transfer material from our house to another house of which we shall be the possessors, that is, which we are not going to sell. This has been stated in rescripts by our emperor and the deified Severus. So surely I can bequeath it to the person to whom I bequeath my one house? But this is to be denied, because the legatee is not the future possessor [of both]. 4. If someone has bequeathed the Sempronian house to two persons and marbles from it to one of them for improving the Seian house which he has also bequeathed to him, it may reasonably be asked whether the bequest is valid, because the legatee is the owner of both houses. And what if someone bequeaths the house after deducting the marbles, which he wishes his heir to have for improving a house which he has retained in the inheritance? The better opinion will be that neither deduction is valid; but the legacy will be valid in that the value must be paid. 5. But if someone has made such a bequest for

constructing some public work, I think the bequest valid; for Papinian, in the eleventh book of his *Replies*, relates that our emperor and the deified Severus ruled that those who have promised to erect some public work might remove material from their town and country houses and use it for that work, because it was not for a commercial purpose. But let us see: May the legacy be only to the *civitas* in whose territory it is, or may he transfer the material from one *civitas* to another? I think this is not to be permitted, although it is established that anyone is permitted to transfer material from his house in one *civitas* to his house in another.   6. This *senatus consultum* applies not only to Rome but also to other *civitates*.   7. But there is a rescript of the deified brothers in answer to a petition of Proclianus and Epitynchanus requesting permission to remove material on account of a public debt in which they denied them the right to remove it.   8. This *senatus consultum* extends not only to houses but also to baths or any other building or porticos apart from houses or taverns or cookshops. 9. The same *senatus consultum* forbids bequests of articles that cannot be delivered other than by removing or withdrawing them from a building, such as marbles and columns. The senate held it to apply to tiles, beams, and doors, and also bookcases attached to walls.   10. But if they are railings or awnings, they may be bequeathed, not, however, water pipes or tanks.   11. But automatic machines and basins for fountain jets may be bequeathed, especially if they are detachable.   12. What then is to be said of statues? If they are fixed to the walls, their removal will not be allowed; but if they stand elsewhere, there is room for doubt. But the intention of the senate is best taken as fully as possible, so that if any statues were there permanently, they should be treated as a part of the house and not be removed.   13. Furthermore, it must be said that pictures fixed and joined to the walls and individual images flush with the walls cannot be bequeathed either.   14. But if the testator prepared some of these with a view to transferring them to another house and bequeathed them, there may be doubt whether the bequest is valid, and I think it is.   15. But if he fixed to the house what he bequeathed, the legacy will be extinguished.   16. However, if the heir has fixed them, I think it is not extinguished,

42   ULPIAN, *Fideicommissa, book 2:* regardless of whether or not he has done so while aware of the bequest.

43   ULPIAN, *Sabinus, book 21:* For the senate allowed those things which are not part of a house to be bequeathed. But these at the time of death were not part of the house; so the heir will pay their value. But if he detaches them with a view to delivery, he will

be subject to penalties, even though he detached not for sale but to discharge his liability.   1. Marcellus also writes that if a husband builds an annex in his wife's gardens that he had received as a dowry, he may remove such materials as may be of future use to him without detracting from his wife's property, and that the *senatus consultum* will offer no hindrance to this. So if there is no objection to his removing them, it must be said that he may bequeath what he may remove.   2. The bequest can be made dependent on the will of others but not on that of the heir.   3. One who has been ransomed from the enemy may be bequeathed to himself, and the bequest will serve to free him from the bond of his pledge to the ransomer.

44   ULPIAN, *Sabinus, book 22:* A father may bequeath a slave who belongs to his son's *castrense peculium;* and if the son dies in his father's lifetime and the *peculium* remains with his father, the legacy holds good. For when the son makes no use of his right, the father is held retrospectively to have owned the slave who was part of the *peculium.*   1. If someone has bequeathed a thing while unaware that it has been bequeathed to himself and later discovers this and is willing that it should belong to him, the legacy will be valid, because where the legatee has not repudiated a bequest, it is held to have been his retrospectively from when the inheritance was accepted. But if he repudiates it, the repudiated thing is held retrospectively to belong to the heir.   2. If someone has bequeathed drinking cups and they have been turned into bullion or vice versa and again if wool is bequeathed and clothing is made of it, Julian, in his thirty-second book, wrote that the bequest of all the above things is valid and that they are due as they now are; an opinion I think true, as long as the testator did not change his intention.   3. And if he bequeathed a dish and it is melted down and turned into a drinking cup, the cup will be due provided that the testator did not change his intention.   4. If a house is built on a plot that has been bequeathed, it will be due to the legatee, always provided that the testator's intention remains unchanged.   5. He who bequeaths a note-of-hand bequeaths the claim, not just the document itself, as is proved by sale. For when they sell notes-of-hand they are held to have sold the claim for debt.   6. But if the claim is bequeathed, the debt must be construed benevolently so that actions may be assigned against the debtor.   7. If the same slave is both bequeathed and given his freedom, for the time being only the legacy can proceed, so that, suppose freedom has been given him to defraud a creditor, or if he is a slave who has been sold into perpetual servitude, it will be the same, or if the slave should by any chance have been given as a pledge.   8. If an heir bequeaths a *statuliber,* it will be expedient for the heir's heir to deliver the *statuliber* rather than the value; for he would have to deliver the true value. If he gives the man himself and the condition is fulfilled, he will suffer no loss; for he cannot afterward be sued for the value of a freeman.   9. If the testator has two farms and bequeaths the one to Titius and the usufruct of the other to me, the legatee will not owe me access, but the heir is compelled to purchase and assign the right of access.

45   POMPONIUS, *Sabinus, book 6:* If I have charged upon the substitute of a *pupillus* a legacy of female slaves to you and you have bought them from the *pupillus* and before learning that they had been bequeathed to you have alienated them, Neratius, Aristo,

and Ofilius affirm that the legacy is valid.   1. An heir who is charged in general terms to deliver a slave is not obliged to promise that he is healthy, but shall have to promise that he is free from charges for theft and injury, because he should deliver such a slave as the legatee may legitimately retain. The health of a slave has nothing to do with the right to own him; but on account of the theft or injury committed by a slave, the owner's right to retain him may be jeopardized, just as on account of a farm's being encumbered it may happen that the owner may not be allowed to retain it. But if a specified man is bequeathed, he should be delivered such as he is.

46   POMPONIUS, *Letters, book 9:* What has been said about a legacy can be applied to a person who has promised that either Stichus or another man is to be delivered.

47   ULPIAN, *Sabinus, book 22:* When a thing has been bequeathed, if it belonged to the testator, and he has control of it, the heir must not delay but deliver it. But if the thing is elsewhere than where it is sued for, it is settled first of all that it should be delivered where it has been left, unless the testator wished this to be done elsewhere; for if he did wish it to be delivered elsewhere, this must be done where the testator wished or where it is most likely that he wished. So Julian wrote concerning bequests both of things owned by the testator and of those owned by others. But if it has been left in one place but transferred to another by the heir with fraudulent intention, unless it is delivered where it is demanded, the heir will be condemned on account of his fraud. If, however, the transfer was not fraudulent, it shall be delivered in the place to which it was transferred.   1. But if what is claimed can be weighed, numbered, or measured and if a certain quantity has been bequeathed, such as corn from a certain granary or wine from a certain storeroom, it will be delivered where it was left, unless the testator's intention was otherwise. But if it was not a certain kind of thing, it is to be delivered where it is claimed.   2. Therefore, if Stichus is bequeathed and does not appear through the fault of the heir, he will have to pay his value. But if the heir is not at fault, he must provide a *cautio* for the restoration of the slave instead of paying his value. But if the slave of another is in flight through no fault of the heir, the same can be said; for one can be held to blame in the case of another man's slave. But the heir shall give a *cautio* so that if the slave is apprehended, either the slave or his value shall be delivered. This is also settled in the case of a slave captured by the enemy.   3. But if Stichus or Pamphilus is bequeathed and one of them is in flight or in the hands of the enemy, it is held that either the slave who is present must be delivered in person or the value of the one who is absent must be paid. The choice of these alternatives is entrusted to the heir whenever he shall not be causing delay to the legatee. For this reason it is settled that if one slave should die, the other must by all means be delivered, or perhaps the price of the dead slave instead. But if both are in flight, the stipulation must be not "if both of them return into his power," but "if one of them," and

"that he himself or his value must be delivered." 4. Again, if a thing belonging to another or to the inheritance should perish without the fault of the heir or is not produced, he need do no more than give a *cautio*; but if it has perished through the fault of the heir, he must be condemned straight away. 5. But let us consider how the fault of the heir can be assessed. Is it not only what comes close to fraud, but carelessness also? Surely care must be required from the heir. This is the better opinion. 6. Again, if a farm is engulfed in an earthquake, Labeo says its value is not due. This is correct, provided that the earthquake did not occur after delay caused by the heir in which case the legatee could have received the land and sold it.

48 POMPONIUS, *Sabinus, book 6:* If the heir's slave has taken away and sold, unbeknown to his master, a thing that has been bequeathed, Atilicinus says that an *actio in factum* is to be granted, so that the master must either hand over the slave to make good the damage or pay out of the slave's *peculium* what he received from the sale of the thing. 1. If one of the heirs has killed a slave who has been bequeathed, I hold that the co-heir must on no account be held responsible, if it was not his fault that the property had ceased to exist.

49 ULPIAN, *Sabinus, book 23:* If a legacy is left to someone when he becomes fourteen years old, we are certainly right in ruling that he becomes fourteen upon completing fourteen years; and Marcellus wrote that the emperor has so decreed. 1. When, therefore, the bequest has been made in these terms, "when he reaches his fourteenth year, let him be paid in three annual installments" and at the time of the testator's death he is found to be seventeen years old, the whole legacy will be payable at once; if sixteen, it will be due after a year; if there are some months to go to the seventeenth year, it will be due when these remaining months are over. This is so if the testator thought that the legatee's age was less than fourteen years when he left the bequest, though it was already more. If he knew the truth, we shall number the three years to the delivery of the legacy from the day the will was made. 2. This legacy is conditional and with a fixed date of payment. It is conditional upon the completion of the fourteenth year; subsequently it has a fixed date. 3. But if at the time the will was made the son is found to have been less than fourteen years old, I think that the period of three annual installments begins from the day of his completing his fourteenth year, unless it is clearly proved that the testator's intention was otherwise. And, therefore, if he should die before his fourteenth year, nothing passes to his heir; if afterward, he certainly transmits his legacy. 4. If I bequeath to Titius ten that I owe, and then I request him to pay them to my creditor, the *fideicommissum* is invalid as far as concerns the creditor personally, because he gains nothing from it. But the heir may bring an action against the legatee, because it is in his interest that my creditor be paid so that the creditor does not sue him. On this account, the legacy will be valid. 5. But if the testator owed me ten guaranteed by a surety, not only the heir but also the surety is entitled to demand the discharge of the legacy; for it is in the surety's interest that I be paid rather than that he should be sued and then bring an action on mandate. Whether or not the surety is solvent makes no difference. 6. Julian, in the thirty-ninth book of his *Digest*, writes: "If a surety bequeathed to a creditor what he owed him, is the legacy valid?" He says it makes no difference to the creditor, but the debtor has a right to an action under the will; for it is in his interest to be freed from the debt, although he will not be liable to suit by the surety's heir. 7. But if the same surety

makes a bequest to Titius and charges on him as a *fideicommissum* the payment of the creditor, both the debtor and the surety's heir will be able to bring an action against Titius by virtue of the *fideicommissum*, because it is in the interest of both of them that the legatee should pay. 8. It should furthermore be remembered that he who is condemned simply to "sell a farm" is not condemned to deliver it free of charge, but only to sell it at its true price. 9. But if he is condemned to do this for a fixed price, he is obliged to sell it for that price.

50 ULPIAN, *Sabinus, book 24:* If a slave is owned by several masters, he acquires a legacy that has been left to him for each master in proportion to the share of those owning him. 1. If a judge in an inheritance case pronounces against the heir for not conducting his case or for conducting it collusively, this will in no way harm the legatees. So what happens if the judge has pronounced an unfair verdict and the heir has not appealed? The injury done to him will not hurt the legatees, as Sabinus indicates. Let us, however, consider whether, if the judge pronounces in favor of the substitute, the substitute shall be liable to the legatees. Since this pronouncement provides justice for the substitute's person, he surely must be liable to the legatees; for nobody can be so impudent as to resort to the plea that the judgment in his favor was from partiality. He, therefore, will be as liable to the legatees as to the creditors. 2. If someone accepts an inheritance before the household slaves have been put to the question or if he does not avenge the killing of the testator, the legatees have the right of action against the imperial treasury. But what if the treasury does not accept the property? Then the burden of discharging the legacies will fall back on the heir. But if he has suborned an accuser against himself, so that the inheritance may be adjudged to the accuser and so be free of burdens, or if he defends his case inadequately, he does not free himself any more than does anyone who has litigated collusively about an inheritance. 3. If a number of coins has been bequeathed and it is not evident what coins are meant, then before all else the head of the household's custom is to be investigated, and then that of the region in which he has lived. But regard must also be paid to the intention of the head of the household and the legatee's rank, the affection in which he has been held and his wants, and also to the terms in which the preceding and following sums are written.

51 PAPIAN, *Questions, book 4:* But if he bequeaths certain coins, for example, those he has in a safe, or a certain piece of plate, then it is not a sum of money but the pieces themselves of coin or of the bequeathed thing that are meant; and these do not allow of change, but are to be treated in the same way as any other tangible object.

52 PAUL, *Sabinus, book 4:* If a bequest is made to anyone of all the slaves with their *peculium*, then even those slaves are due who have no *peculium*. 1. If a legacy is charged on a son who is *impubes* under a condition, and the son becomes heir and then dies, it can be said that the head of the household who charged the legacy on the son under a condition, and charged the same legacy on a substitute unconditionally, wished it to be discharged by the substitute at once if the son were to die while the condition was unfulfilled.

53 ULPIAN, *Sabinus, book 25:* What, then, if he left a larger amount to be paid by the substitute? The amount in excess will be what has been charged upon the substitute. The money up to the sum that was written in the former will be due on that account. 1. But if he repeats the legacy with the addition of another legatee, for example, if he charged the *impubes* with the legacy of a farm to me and has repeated this legacy charging the heir of the *impubes* to deliver it to me and Seius, then the effect of the repetition will be that a part is due to me. 2. If someone appoints two heirs and

condemns each one to deliver a thing entire to the legatee, it is the same as if the legacy had been bequeathed by two wills. For even if a legacy had been made to me and to my son or slave in the same will, the bequest of each would undoubtedly be valid, as Marcellus also observes in his work on Julian. 3. If the heir kills a man who has been bequeathed on account of a crime, that is, deservedly, then it will undoubtedly be held that he is not liable under the will. 4. But if he has surrendered him noxally, will he be liable because he can redeem him? I think he will be liable. 5. But if he has killed a bequeathed animal, I think he is liable not to deliver the flesh or the other remains, but to pay the value it would have if alive. 6. Similarly, if he has allowed a bequeathed house to be possessed [by another] because of threatened damage, I think he is liable; for he ought to have given a *repromissio*. 7. But if he has brought in a corpse and has made the bequeathed place religious, he will not be liable under the will if it is the head of the household whom he brought in and he could not inter him elsewhere or could not do so as conveniently. But will he be liable to pay the price of the land? If the head of the household himself wished to be buried there, he will not be liable under the will; but if the heir brought him in by his own decision, he will be liable to pay, if the inheritance is enough to provide the price; for the testator who made the bequest wished either to be buried elsewhere or that the value of the land should be paid to the legatee. 8. Again, if he did not kill a slave himself, but forced him to commit an offense, so as to incur killing or execution at the hands of another, it will be entirely fair that he should pay his price. But if the slave went into this of his own evil intent, the obligation to pay will lapse. 9. A bequeathed slave who has been captured by the enemy without the fraudulent intent of the heir will not be due; if with the fraudulent intent of the heir, he will be due.

54   POMPONIUS, *Sabinus, book 8:* Shameful bequests, which are inserted to bring disgrace rather than benefit to the legatee, are held, on account of the odium of the writer, to be unwritten. 1. If a legacy has been left to Titia on condition of her marrying by the wish of Seius and Seius has died in the testator's lifetime and she has married, then the legacy is due to her. 2. But if the death of a slave has prevented his manumission, when a legacy has been made to you on condition that you manumit him, the legacy will be due to you all the same. For it is not your fault that he did not obtain his freedom. 3. If a part of the heirs are named in a bequest, the heirs are liable equally; but if all are named, they are liable in proportion to their share of the inheritance.

55   POMPONIUS, *Sabinus, book 9:* Nobody can ensure in his will that the laws do not apply to it, because the obligation of the heir cannot on account of legacies be restricted by time, place, or condition.

56   POMPONIUS, *Sabinus, book 14:* If a legatee stipulates, when a slave has been bequeathed to him, that it must not be a runaway slave who is delivered, this stipulation will be ineffectual, because such a slave is due as is mentioned in the will, and the heir will not be understood to be injuring the legacy.

57   ULPIAN, *Sabinus, book 33:* If a thing that has been pledged has been left by *fideicommissum* and the testator knew it had been pledged, it is to be redeemed by the heir unless the testator intended otherwise; but if he did not know, by the beneficiary (unless the testator would have left either this or another thing if he had known it to be pledged), where something may be left over after the debt has been paid. But if the testator was so minded that although he did not wish the burden of disencumbering his estates to be borne by his heirs, he did not openly and clearly declare how this

was to be done, the beneficiary will be able to secure through a defense of fraud an action for production from the creditors who bring an action on mortgage against him. Even if he has not done this at the right time, it will, nevertheless, be accorded him through the jurisdiction of the provincial governor.

58 PAPINIAN, *Replies, book 9:* When a house belonging to an inheritance has been burned and rebuilt at the heir's expense and is to be restored after the heir's death on account of a *fideicommissum,* I have replied that with an upright man as arbitrator the expenses of rebuilding should be deducted, taking the age of the buildings into account,

59 ULPIAN, *Edict, book 33:* provided that no blame attaches to him for the fire.

60 JULIAN, *Digest, book 39:* If he has delivered the house without making any deduction, an action for recovery of an unspecified sum lies in his favor for having paid more than he owed.

61 PAPINIAN, *Replies, book 9:* But expenses necessarily incurred for repairing the house by the legatee when he claims the legacy upon the subsequent fulfillment of the condition are in my opinion not to be included in the calculation.

62 PAUL, *Edict, book 41:* If a female slave has been bequeathed with her children, the female slave only is due if there are no children, and the children only if there is no female slave.

63 CELSUS, *Digest, book 17:* If the testator bequeathed all his female slaves and their offspring and one has died, Servius denies that her offspring is owed, because this was bequeathed by way of addition. I hold this to be false. This opinion accords with neither the words nor the wishes of the deceased.

64 GAIUS, *Provincial Edict, book 15:* Writings procured by legacy-hunters are similarly invalid both in inheritances and in legacies.

65 GAIUS, *Praetor's Edict, Legacies, book 1:* If a legacy has been made thus, "I give Seius ten slaves, except for the ten I have bequeathed to Titius," and if only ten are left in the inheritance, the legacy is void. If more than ten are found, then after Titius has made his selection, the legacy takes effect for the remainder, but not for more than the ten who have been bequeathed. If they are less than ten, it takes effect for as many as may be found. 1. "To such a one, if he wishes, I give Stichus." This legacy is conditional and is not charged on the heir unless the legatee does so wish, although otherwise what is bequeathed without the addition "if he wishes" is charged on the heir. For it is one thing in law if something is included by implication, and another if expressed in words. 2. If a house has been bequeathed, even if it has been repaired piecemeal, so that none of the original building material survives, we shall, nevertheless, hold the bequest to remain valid. But if that house has been destroyed and the

testator has built another on the same site, we shall say the legacy has lapsed, unless it is proved that the testator's intention was otherwise.

66   GAIUS, *Provincial Edict, book 18:* If a testator has ordered his heir to buy or sell at a fair price, the legacy is still valid. But what if the legatee for whom the heir has been ordered to buy a farm is compelled to sell it through necessity and can find no buyer? Or, on the other hand, what if it is greatly in the legatee's interest to buy that farm and the heir would not be selling it unless the testator had so ordered?

67   GAIUS, *Praetor's Edict, Legacies, book 1:* A slave bequeathed to one of the heirs, if he is said to have done anything maliciously to damage the inheritance (for example, falsifying accounts by abstraction), is not to be adjudged to anyone before he has been put to the question if that is the wish of the co-heirs. The same applies if he is bequeathed to an outsider.   1. If the same thing is left as a legacy to two out of several heirs instituted in different shares, the heirs ought to have the legacy in equal shares, not according to their shares in the inheritance.

68   GAIUS, *Provincial Edict, book 18:* When a legacy is made to a son after the death of his father, there is no doubt that the legacy belongs to the son after his father's death, and it makes no difference whether or not he has been appointed his father's heir. 1. But when a legacy is left to a slave after his master's death, if he remains in the condition of slavery, it should belong to his master's heir. The same rule applies if he has been ordered to be free in his master's will; for the legatee becomes entitled to the legacy before any heir to the master appears; hence, any legacy added to the inheritance, when an heir subsequently appears, belongs to him. An exception is if someone has been made *suus heres* or a necessary heir to his master by the same will; for then, as the heir is instituted and the legacy vests at the same time, it is held with greater probability that the legacy belongs to the person to whom it has been left rather than to the heir of him from whom the slave obtains his liberty.   2. If a slave has been bequeathed unconditionally and ordered to be free under a condition, then if the condition cannot be fulfilled, the bequest is valid. Therefore, if it is fulfilled the legacy is annulled, whereas, failing this, he will belong to the legatee. So if the legatee dies, while it is still uncertain whether or not the condition of liberty can be fulfilled, the legacy will not belong to the heir of the legatee.   3. But if the same man is bequeathed unconditionally and ordered to be free after a certain time, the legacy is ineffective, because it is certain that the appointed day will come. Julian, too, was of this opinion; which is why he says that if a slave has been bequeathed to Titius and also ordered to be free after Titius's death, the legacy is ineffective, because it is certain that Titius will die.

69   GAIUS, *Praetor's Edict, Legacies, book 2:* It is accepted that a legacy can be made to a bequeathed slave; for when the inheritance has been accepted, the slave is at once acquired by the legatee, and then the legacy will follow.   1. If the heir alienates a slave bequeathed under a condition and the condition is subsequently fulfilled, the slave, nonetheless, can be vindicated by the legatee, and the legacy is not extinguished. 2. If the testator should order certain of his heirs to pay a debt, the creditors will not be entitled to an action against them, but the co-heirs will in whose interest it is that this should be done. It is not only in this instance that entitlement to an action belongs to someone other than the person to whom the testator ordered payment to be made, but in other cases too, for instance, when he has ordered a dowry to be paid in his daughter's name to his son-in-law or her fiancé: Here neither the son-in-law nor the fiancé will be entitled to an action, but the daughter, who has the greatest interest in not being undowered, will be so entitled.   3. If a bequeathed farm is charged with a servitude, it must be delivered such as it is; but if the terms of the bequest are that it

should be "on the best and greatest terms" [free from easements and of the size affirmed], it must be delivered unencumbered.   4. When a slave is bequeathed who has been engaged in business, he must not be handed over before he renders his accounts; and if it comes to judicial proceedings, it is for the judge to ensure this.   5. If there is doubt whether a bequeathed thing is in existence, for example, if it is doubtful whether a bequeathed man is living, it has been accepted that an action based on the will can be brought, and it belongs to the duty of the judge to oblige the heir to furnish a *cautio* that he will search for the thing and if he secures it, deliver it to the legatee.

70   GAIUS, *Provincial Edict, book 18:* If Titius's slave should steal from me and then Titius should appoint me as his heir and bequeath the slave to you, it is only fair that such a slave should be delivered to you as he was when he was Titius's, that is, that you should indemnify me for the theft he committed while he was Titius's.   1. For if a farm, which was under a servitude to my farm, has been bequeathed to you, it should be delivered by me to you in no other way than subject to the original servitude in my favor.   2. The case is not dissimilar to one where someone buys a slave by the mandate of another or returns a slave whom he has bought. They are all compelled to restore a slave only when account is rendered for any theft committed by that slave either before or after the purchase was effected.   3. Therefore, if after acceptance of an inheritance a bequeathed slave steals from the heir, the slave must be delivered on the understanding that the legatee will pay the heir on account of the offense the equivalent of assessed damages.

71   ULPIAN, *Edict, book 51:* If a house is simply bequeathed to someone without it being stated which house, the heirs will be obliged to give any house they please from those which the testator had. But if he left no house, the legacy is derisory rather than effectual.   1. Let us consider whether a person who delivers a slave because of a legacy should give a *cautio* against eviction. As a rule, it is to be said that whenever a bequeathed thing is delivered out of court and the recipient is evicted, it can be sued for under the will. But if it has been demanded in court, it is the judge's duty to require a *cautio*, so that an action on stipulation may lie.   2. Where money has been bequeathed and the heir admits it, a reasonable time must be given for payment and pressure should not be brought for taking the matter to court. The praetor must determine the length of time in accordance with what is fair and equitable.   3. Whenever someone admits that something is due from him but adduces a just cause why he cannot deliver it, the plea is to be heard, for instance, if property belonging to someone else has been bequeathed and he says the owner will not sell it, or declares that he is demanding an exorbitant price, or if he says that he is not obliged to deliver a slave belonging to the estate such as, say, his father, mother, or natural brothers. The most equitable course in this case is for the judge to allow him to pay the value instead.   4. When a cup was bequeathed to someone and the heir wished to pay its value, saying that it was unfair that he should be parted from it, he could not win the praetor's consent. For the case of persons is one thing, and that of things, another. An indulgent attitude is accepted in the case of persons, as we have shown above.   5. If a farm under long lease from a municipality is bequeathed to the municipality itself, let us

consider whether the legacy is valid and can be claimed. Julian, in the thirty-eighth book of his *Digest*, wrote that even though the farm under long lease belongs to the municipality, the legacy is valid all the same, because the person who left the legacy had some degree of right in it. 6. But if he bequeathed a farm under long lease not to the municipality but to someone else, the ownership of the thing appears not to have been bequeathed, but such rights as we have as leaseholders of such farms.

72   PAUL, *Edict, book 48:* If someone has bequeathed the Cornelian farm with the exception of such vineyards as there shall be at the time of his death, and there are no vineyards, nothing is deducted from the legacy.

73   GAIUS, *Praetor's Edict, Legacies, book 3:* If the heir has been ordered to arrange that Lucius may have a hundred, the heir is compelled to give a hundred; for nobody can arrange that I have a hundred unless he gives them to me. 1. Villages may receive legacies as may *civitates*, according to a rescript of our emperor.

74   ULPIAN, *Disputations, book 4:* It is true that our emperor ruled in a rescript with his father that where the testator laid a charge on an appointed heir, it should be held that he meant it to apply to the substitute. This, however, must be taken to be the case where it is clear that the testator had no different intention. It will be gathered from many indications whether a testator was unwilling that a legacy or *fideicommissum* charged on the heir should be due from the substitute. And what if he has left charged on the substitute the delivery to the fideicommissary or legatee of another thing, which he had not left charged on the appointed heir? Or if there was a definite reason why he should leave a legacy charged on the heir, which did not apply to the substitute? Or if he chose as partial substitute a beneficiary to whom he had left a *fideicommissum* charged on the appointed heir? It must therefore be said that the rescript applies where the testator's intention is obscure.

75   ULPIAN, *Disputations, book 5:* If a legacy or *fideicommissum* has been left in these terms, "if my heir should see fit," "if he should approve," "if he should think it right," then the legacy and *fideicommissum* will be due, since it has been left to his good faith rather than to his mere whim. 1. If what Titius owes has been bequeathed to me and Titius owes nothing, it should be understood that the bequest is void. And, furthermore, if the amount is not added, it is manifestly clear that nothing will be owed, because it is not evident how much was bequeathed. For if I leave to Titius whatever I owe him without adding how much, it is settled that the bequest is void; whereas if I bequeath ten that I owe to Titius and I owe Titius nothing, the false description does not annul the bequest, as Julian replied in the case of a bequest of a dowry. 2. But if he added, "I bequeath the ten that Titius owes me," undoubtedly there will be nothing in the bequest; for there is a great difference between a false description and a false condition or cause. Moreover, if I bequeath to Titius ten that Seius owes me, the legacy will be void; for [to make it valid] he must be my debtor. For if I exacted the debt in my lifetime, the legacy would be extinguished. If he were still my debtor, my heir would only be compelled to assign the rights of action against him. 3. If anyone had

stipulated, "Stichus or ten, whichever I may wish," and bequeaths what was owed to him, his heir will be obliged to assign the action to the legatee, who will then have the choice of suing either for Stichus or for the ten. 4. Furthermore, if he bequeaths Stichus, when the debtor owed him either Stichus or ten, an action for an undefined object lies in favor of the legatee against the heir, as Julian has written in the thirty-third book of his *Digest*; through which action he may compel the heir to sue the debtor; and if he recovers Stichus, the heir will deliver him to the legatee, but if ten, the legatee will get nothing. Accordingly, it will depend on the debtor whether the person to whom Stichus is bequeathed shall be a legatee.

76 JULIAN, *Digest, book 34:* But if someone has stipulated for Stichus or Pamphilus and bequeaths Stichus to Sempronius and Pamphilus to Maevius, the heir will be understood to be burdened with the obligation to give to the one legatee his right of action, and to the other the value of Stichus or Pamphilus.

77 ULPIAN, *Disputations, book 5:* If money was deposited with anyone and he has then been charged to pay that money as a *fideicommissum*, the *fideicommissum*, according to a rescript of the deified Pius, will be due, as though the heir had been asked to remit the deposit to the debtor; for the debtor, if he is sued by the heir, can avail himself of an action for fraud, which renders the *fideicommissum* effective. That being so, every debtor can be charged with a *fideicommissum*.

78 ULPIAN, *Disputations, book 8:* When a *fideicommissum* is charged on a legatee, it is only due from him if the legacy has come into the hands of the legatee.

79 JULIAN, *Digest, book 5:* If anyone in his will directs that ten are to be given to Titius and Seius, these words admit of no ambiguity; he who said ten is taken to have meant ten each.

80 MARCELLUS, *Notes on Julian, Digest, book 32:* A man who left only thirty bequeathed thirty to Titius, twenty to Seius, ten to Maevius. Massurius Sabinus holds that Titius shall get fifteen, Seius ten, Maevius five, always provided that proportionate deductions are made from each bequest to ensure that the heir gets his Falcidian share.

81 JULIAN, *Digest, book 32:* If an heir, who was charged with the bequest of a farm under a condition, had, while the condition was pending, bequeathed it to another under another condition, and after fulfillment of the condition prescribed in the former will, the condition under which the heir had bequeathed the farm was then also fulfilled, the ownership does not pass from the first legatee. 1. If a thing has been bequeathed to a slave owned in common, then one master may accept and the other reject the legacy; for in this case a common slave is like two slaves. 2. "I give and bequeath Stichus to Sempronius. If Sempronius has not manumitted Stichus within a year, I give and bequeath Stichus to Titius." What is the law here? I replied that Sempronius is to have him entirely in the meantime and, if he does manumit him within the year, he will effect his liberty; but if not, he will belong entirely to Titius. 3. He who bequeaths a farm except for the building means by "building" either the edifice or in addition the land on which the building stands. If he has excepted only the edifice, then the whole farm, nonetheless, will be vindicated by right of the legacy. But the heir will, by bringing a defense of fraud, obtain the right of living in the house, which

will include the right of entry to it in person or with cattle. But if the land was excepted, the farm with the exception of the house will have to be vindicated and a servitude will by reason of this attach to the house, just as if the owner of two farms had bequeathed the one subject to a servitude to the other. But one must incline to the assumption that the testator meant to include the land without which the building cannot stand. 4. If a freedman should appoint his patron as heir to seven twelfths and others to the remainder and make a bequest as follows, "I charge whoever else of the above-written shall be heir with my patron to deliver to Titius such and such slaves, whom I value at twenty aurei each," it is to be understood that the legacy is charged only upon the co-heir of the patron and that Titius, therefore, cannot vindicate more than five twelfths of the slaves. That addition, "whom I value at twenty aurei each," does not alter the condition of the legacy, if the *lex Falcidia* is to be taken into account. Nevertheless, the true price of the slaves must be deducted when estimating the Falcidian portion. 5. "To Titius I give and bequeath a farm, if he shall give ten to my heir." If he has owed ten to Titius and Titius gives him a receipt for them, he can vindicate the farm. 6. If Titius to whom Stichus had been bequeathed died before he knew the bequest belonged to him and bequeathed Stichus to Seius and the heir does not repudiate Titius's legacy, Seius will vindicate Stichus. 7. If the head of a household charges the bequest of a farm to Titius on a son who is *impubes* and should charge a substitute with the same bequest to the same person and the *minor* becomes his father's heir, then whether Titius vindicates the legacy or repudiates it, even though the son may die as an *impubes*, he will not be able to vindicate it from the substitute. For what is charged again as a legacy on the substitute is to be taken just as if it were a repeated legacy. Therefore, even if the legacy had been charged on the son unconditionally and on the substitute under a condition, it is all to be treated just as if the legacy had been charged only upon the son. But, on the other hand, if the legacy had been charged on the son under a condition and on the substitute unconditionally and the son had died a *minor* while the condition was pending, the legacy will be valid by virtue of the substitution alone. 8. A bequest made in these words, "I give and bequeath a farm to Lucius and Titius or to one of them," is valid, and will be due, if both of them live, to both, and if only one, to him. 9. When a *statuliber* has been bequeathed under a condition and, while the condition of the legacy is pending, the condition upon which he was to be freed should fail, the legacy is valid; for just as an intended manumission annuls the legacy when it takes effect, so also the legacy cannot be annulled before the time of its falling due has arrived. 10. A slave bequeathed as a charge on a son who is *impubes* and directed to be freed by the substitute will, if the *pupillus* comes of age, be vindicated by the legatee, but will gain his liberty if the *pupillus* dies first. There will be much more reason for this to be observed if the same slave has been charged as a legacy on the *impubes* and the son should die before coming of age while the condition was pending.

82 JULIAN, *Digest, book 33:* It is not in every respect that if the bequeathed thing comes into the hands of the legatee on the day prescribed, the obligation of the legacy is extinguished, but only if it becomes his in such a way that he cannot be deprived of it. Let us suppose that a thing, which has been bequeathed to me unconditionally, is delivered to me on the day the legacy falls due by an heir who was also charged with the legacy of the same thing to another person under a condition. I can certainly bring an action under the will, because the situation is such that if the condition is fulfilled I lose the ownership. For if Stichus is due to me under a stipulation, and he has been bequeathed under a condition to another, he will have become mine gratuitously, despite which I shall be able to bring an action on stipulation if the condition is fulfilled.

1. If from the goods of someone who is absent on public business I acquire a thing by right of use and, before I am evicted from it, it is bequeathed to me and I am evicted subsequently, I shall be right to sue for it to be given to me under the will. 2. A farm is bequeathed to me; I have purchased the ownership of this farm without the usufruct; subsequently, the vendor has suffered change of civil status and the usufruct has fallen to me. If I bring an action based on the will, the judge will have to give me judgment in a sum of money equivalent to what I have expended. 3. MARCELLUS: The same applies if I buy a part and that part is bequeathed or given to me. I shall then be able to sue for that part only. 4. JULIAN: If a bequest is made to me of the offspring of Pamphila, and I have bought Pamphila and she has given birth while in my possession, I cannot be held to have acquired her child gratuitously, because I purchased the child's mother. This is proved by the fact that if I am evicted from it, I am entitled to an action on sale. 5. A testator who had Gaius and Lucius as debtors for the same money and made a bequest in these terms, "let my heir be condemned to pay to Sempronius what Gaius owes me, and let my heir be condemned to pay to Maevius what Lucius owes me," has imposed on his heir a condition requiring him to assign his rights of action to the one, and the value of the claim due to the other. If, however, the testator has in his lifetime given a receipt to Gaius, the legacy to Sempronius and Maevius necessarily becomes ineffective. 6. When Stichus and Pamphilus have been bequeathed to me under the wills of two persons and I have sued for Stichus under the one will, I may sue for Pamphilus under the other, because if Stichus and Pamphilus had been bequeathed to me in one will and Stichus had become mine for nothing, nevertheless, I would be entitled to sue for Pamphilus.

83   MARCELLUS, *Digest, book 13:* Titius has bequeathed a share in Stichus to you. Seius has bequeathed a share in the same Stichus to you. You may claim him under both wills.

84   JULIAN, *Digest, book 33:* A legacy after this manner, "if Titius gives a *cautio* to my heir that he will give a hundred to Maevius, let my heir also give a hundred to Titius," is an effective legacy, just as when something has been bequeathed to someone so that it may be paid to another as a *fideicommissum.* 1. In the same way, this legacy, too, is effective: "If Titius gives a *cautio* to my heir that he will construct a public work in the municipality for a hundred aurei, let my heir be condemned to pay him a hundred aurei." 2. If Sempronius appoints Titius as his heir and directs him to deliver a farm to Maevius after two years and Titius has then directed his heir to deliver the same farm to Maevius immediately and Maevius accepts the price of the farm from Titius's heir, then if he wishes to sue for the farm under Sempronius's will, he will be barred by a defense, if he is not content with the price of the farm. 3. If a man had been bequeathed to someone and it was the fault of the legatee that he did not accept Stichus when the heir was willing to deliver him, then if Stichus dies, the heir will be able to have recourse to a defense of fraud. 4. A house, in favor of which the heir's house

was charged with a servitude, was bequeathed and delivered to the legatee without the servitude. I said that the legatee could bring an action based on the will, because he had not received the legacy in full; for anyone who received a slave from the heir in a disabled state may also rightly bring an action based on the will. 5. A person who bought a slave bequeathed to him, not knowing that he had been bequeathed to him, from the heir, and having discovered the bequest sues under the will and recovers the slave, must be absolved from an action on sale, because this judgment is in good faith and contains in itself a defense of fraud. If, having paid the price, he institutes an action based on the will, he shall obtain the man and recover his price by an action on sale, as he would have done if he had lost the man through eviction. If an action on sale has been initiated and the plaintiff then learns that the man was bequeathed to him and brings an action based on the will, the only way the heir can be absolved is if he repays the price and surrenders the slave to the plaintiff. 6. When a father had promised a hundred for his daughter's dowry and afterward bequeathed to her the same hundred, the heir will be safeguarded by a defense of fraud, if the son-in-law brings an action based on the promise and the daughter one on the will. For they ought to agree between themselves, so as to be content with one or the other action. 7. If a bequest has been made to anyone in this way, "if he returns the note-of-hand to my heir, let my heir give him a hundred," a condition of this sort has the force of "if he releases my heir from the debt." Therefore, if the note is in existence, the creditor will not be taken to have satisfied the condition unless he hands it over to the heir; and if the note is not in existence, he will be held to have fulfilled the condition if he releases the heir. It will make no difference whether the note had perished when the will was being made or afterward or even after the testator's death. 8. If Stichus, who was Titius's, has been bequeathed to Titius and Maevius, then [only] part of Stichus will be due to Maevius; for Titius, though receiving nothing from the legacy, will have his share. 9. "Let my heir give Stichus or Pamphilus, whichever he wishes, to Titius." If the heir says he wishes to give Stichus, he will be released by Stichus's death. But when the heir has once stated whom he wishes to give, he will not be able to change his mind. 10. A legacy was made as follows: "Let my heir give to Titius the Cornelian farm and the slaves which shall be in that farm and shall be mine when I die." A female slave who used to be in that farm was in flight at the time of the testator's death and gave birth. Is she or her offspring included in the legacy? I replied: The female slave, even if in flight, is held to have been bequeathed and, though a fugitive, is treated just as if she had been on the farm when the head of the household died. It follows that the offspring goes with the mother and belongs to the legacy just as if it had been born on the farm. 11. If Stichus or Pamphilus, whichever he may prefer, has been bequeathed to Titius, and the testator has subsequently given Pamphilus to Titius as a gift, he remains obliged to deliver Stichus. 12. When a legacy is made in these terms, "I give and bequeath to Titius and Maevius a slave each," it is agreed that they shall not both be claiming the same slave, just as they do not when the legacy reads "to Titius I give and bequeath a slave, to Maevius I give and bequeath another slave." 13. If a legatee before deciding what action to employ should die leaving two heirs, they cannot come together at the same time and receive the legacy unless they agree; for as long as the one wishes to vindicate a thing, the other cannot take a personal action. But if they agree, they shall have the thing in common; for they must agree either of their own accord or under pressure from the judge.

85 PAUL, *Plautius, book 11:* A farm was bequeathed to two persons conjointly. One of them obtained the value of his part through a personal action. Should the other wish to vindicate the whole farm, he is barred by a defense of fraud from the half because the deceased wished the legacy to come to them once only.

86 JULIAN, *Digest, book 34:* If a man whom you had given as pledge has been bequeathed by you to someone else, you will have an action based on the will against the heir so that the pledge may be released.   1. If in a will Stichus has been charged on one of the heirs as a legacy to Maevius and in a codicil the same Stichus has been charged on all the heirs as a legacy to the same person and, before the codicil is opened, Maevius obtains a judgment for the appraised value, then Stichus cannot lawfully be vindicated by virtue of the codicil, because the testator wished the legacy to come to Maevius once only.   2. When a slave is bequeathed, the status of that slave and of everything that relates to him is in suspense. For if the heir should refuse the legacy, the slave will be taken never to have been his; if he does not refuse, the slave will be taken to be his from the day the inheritance is accepted. According to this rule, a decision will be made on the rights to what the slave may have received by delivery or stipulation and on what has been bequeathed or given to him, so that he will be held to have made the individual transactions as the slave of the heir or the legatee, as the case may be.   3. If all the heirs should be charged with the legacy of a farm which belonged to one of the heirs, he whose farm it was shall deliver no more than his share, and the others shall be liable for the other shares.   4. If *superficies* has been bequeathed to the person on whose land it is, even if he is the owner of the land, the legacy will be valid. For he will get freedom from this servitude and the profit from the *superficies.*

87 PAPINIAN, *Questions, book 18:* A father, having appointed as part heir a son whom he retained in power, also left him a legacy. There is excessive severity in the opinion of those who hold that he should be forbidden to sue for the legacy if he has not accepted his father's inheritance. For the judgment [of the testator] is not impugned by one who for just cause refuses to be involved in the affairs of an inheritance.

88 MARCIAN, *Institutes, book 6:* But if the father wished him to have the legacy on no other terms than if he retained the inheritance, then it is agreed, following the opinion of Aristo, that an action is not to be granted to him even against his co-heir, since the son himself considered the estate to be insolvent. This applies even if the testator expressed no condition, but it is clearly proved that this was his intention.

89 JULIAN, *Digest, book 36:* For even an emancipated son, if he does not accept the inheritance, is not prevented from claiming a legacy. The praetor, in permitting those who were in power to refrain from their paternal inheritance, makes it plain that he grants them personally the same right that they would have had if they had free discretion to accept the inheritance.

90 PAPINIAN, *Questions, book 18:* But what if he has left a legacy "in addition, to my son"? Here it will certainly be a question of the intention, but the case is not dissimilar to the former one about the prudence [allowed to] the son, unless there is evident proof of the father's wish having been otherwise.   1. Plainly, if he appointed several

sons as heirs and divided his goods among them in terms of legacies on the grounds of his intention, an action for recovering legacies will be refused to a son who did not accept the inheritance.

91   JULIAN, *Digest, book 36:* May a son-in-power, who had a son and was appointed heir while both of them were in the power of another, be charged with a legacy in favor of his son? I replied that since the son can be charged with a legacy in favor of his father, it follows that he may be charged in favor of his own brother or son or even his father's slave.   1. Where freedom is given to a slave at once, a legacy may be bequeathed to him unconditionally or under a condition. But when freedom is given him conditionally, an unconditional legacy will sometimes be effective, sometimes ineffective. For if the condition of his freedom is such that it can be fulfilled immediately on the death of the head of the household before the inheritance is accepted, for example, "let Stichus be free if he gives ten to Titius (or if he mounts to the Capitol)," the legacy is effective. But conditions, such as "if he gives ten to the heir," "if after the inheritance is accepted he mounts to the Capitol," render the legacy ineffective.   2. Having appointed two heirs, a man bequeathed Stichus to the one and ten to the same Stichus. If Stichus had attained his freedom in the lifetime of the testator, the whole legacy will be due to him. For that the entire legacy vests in him personally is proved by the fact that if the heir to whom Stichus had been bequeathed had not accepted the inheritance, Stichus could have claimed the entire legacy from the other heir.   3. A legacy was given to a slave who had himself been bequeathed. If the testator had alienated the slave, the legacy will belong to the purchaser.   4. When a slave is bequeathed to Titius and something is bequeathed to the same slave, Titius can be charged with the *fideicommissum* of delivering to someone either the slave or what has been bequeathed to the slave. In addition, a *fideicommissum* can be charged on Titius in favor of the same slave when he shall become free.   5. If someone should bequeath Stichus and has alienated or manumitted him and then gives him a legacy by codicil, the legacy will be due to the manumitted slave or to the purchaser.   6. When a slave has been bequeathed to me as a charge on you as heir and someone makes a bequest to the same slave and, in the lifetime of the person who bequeathed the slave to me, the day of the legacy given to the slave falls due, then this legacy is at once acquired by the estate. Therefore, even though the person who bequeathed the slave to me should subsequently die, the legacy made to the slave will not belong to me.   7. When a man has been claimed on the grounds of a will, he must be delivered to the plaintiff in the condition in which he was at the time that the suit was contested, and just as the offspring of female slaves as well as the fruits of farms collected in the meantime are included in the claim, so whatever has come to the slave by way of legacy or inheritance is to be delivered to the plaintiff.

92   JULIAN, *Digest, book 39:* If one of the heirs has bought a farm left as a *fideicommissum* at a price settled according to the revenue from that farm on account of the debt due from the inheritance and in the presence and with the consent of the beneficiary of the *fideicommissum*, then in my opinion not the farm but its value should be

delivered. MARCELLUS notes: if the heir should prefer to deliver the farm, I think he should be heard. 1. JULIAN: If money has been bequeathed to Titius and he is charged with the *fideicommissum* of freeing the slave of another, but the slave's owner is unwilling to sell him, he will nevertheless receive his legacy, because it is not his fault that he cannot discharge the *fideicommissum*. For if the slave had died, he would not be deprived of the legacy. 2. Just as anyone is permitted to charge a *fideicommissum* on whoever shall succeed him as *legitimus heres* or by *bonorum possessio*, so *fideicommissa* will rightly be charged on him who shall succeed as *legitimus heres* or by *bonorum possessio* to a son who is *impubes*.

93   ULPIAN, *Fideicommissa, book 1:* Such a *fideicommissum* will only be valid when the son dies while *impubes*; but if he dies after coming of age, the *fideicommissum* becomes void.

94   JULIAN, *Digest, book 39:* Plainly, if a father should have disinherited his son while *impubes*, the *legitimus heres* cannot be compelled to deliver the *fideicommissum*, unless he is at the same time the father's heir.   1. A man was asked to restore an inheritance to which his own slave had been appointed heir. He sold the slave to someone else. The question was whether the obligation to restore the inheritance will fall on the person to whom the inheritance has come by the purchase of the slave who was heir. I said that the man who had sold the slave who had been appointed heir should be compelled to restore the *fideicommissum*, since he would have the price of the inheritance which he was asked to restore. But the person to whom the inheritance would have come through the purchase of the slave appointed as heir, could, in certain circumstances, be compelled to deliver the *fideicommissum*, that is, if the owner of the slave who has been appointed heir is insolvent. 2. If either Stichus or Dama had been bequeathed to someone and the choice of which one had been given to the legatee and he had been charged with a *fideicommissum* to deliver Stichus to someone else, then if he prefers to vindicate Dama, he will be obliged to deliver Stichus all the same on account of the *fideicommissum*. If Dama is worth more, the legatee will be compelled to buy Stichus; or if he is worth less, it will be equally fair that the legatee should deliver Stichus, since it was his own doing that he has received less from the will than the *fideicommissum* is worth. 3. He who is manumitted by will and receives no legacy and no inheritance is not to be compelled to deliver a *fideicommissum*. The same is true of anyone who has been asked to manumit a slave bequeathed to him; for someone can [only] be compelled to deliver money by virtue of a *fideicommissum* if he receives something of the same or similar kind under the will.

95   ULPIAN, *Fideicommissa, book 1:* However, it should be considered whether, if the testator has asked him to give something in lieu of services, this *fideicommissum* can be valid. This is by no means to be admitted, because services cannot be imposed on a freedman in this way, nor if imposed can they be exacted, even if the testator so provided.

96   JULIAN, *Digest, book 39:* A certain man in a will or codicil made a bequest in these

terms: "I wish four hundred aurei to be paid to Pamphila as is written below: so many from Julius my estate manager, so many that I have in camp, and so many that I have in cash." After many years, without changing his intention, he died, when all the sums had been transferred to other uses. I ask whether the *fideicommissum* is due. I have replied that it is much more likely that the head of the household wished rather to point out to his heirs where the four hundred aurei could be collected without inconvenience to the estate than that he had imposed a condition on the *fideicommissum* which had originally been unconditional. Therefore, the four hundred will be due to Pamphila.   1. Whenever under the *lex Julia* goods without an owner fall to the imperial treasury, those legacies and *fideicommissa* shall be discharged which the heir to whom they were left would have been compelled to pay.   2. If a slave had been bequeathed to you and you had been asked to deliver to Titius the equivalent of the slave and the slave has meanwhile died, you will not be compelled to deliver anything by virtue of the *fideicommissum*.   3. If an heir appointed for part of the inheritance is asked to advance money and to distribute it among those who have been given legacies in the will, he will have to advance what was bequeathed conditionally only when the condition is fulfilled; meanwhile, security must be given either to him or to the legatees.   4. A person to whom a *statuliber* has been directed to pay money can be asked to restore the same money to another. For since the testator can grant freedom unconditionally by codicil and by this means extinguish the condition, why should he not also have the power of taking away this money by a *fideicommissum*?

97   JULIAN, *Digest, book 42:* If Stichus was bequeathed to me and I should be charged with a *fideicommissum* of delivering either Stichus or my slave Pamphilus and I have lost something from my legacy in Stichus on account of the Falcidian law, I shall be obliged to give either my slave Pamphilus entirely to Titius or that part of Stichus which I shall have received by virtue of the legacy.

98   JULIAN, *Digest, book 52:* A slave captured by the enemy can rightly be bequeathed. For by right of *postliminium* it comes about that just as we may appoint as heir a slave who is in enemy hands, we may also bequeath him.

99   JULIAN, *Digest, book 70:* If Stichus was bequeathed to his master and a choice given to a slave of the master, I say that half of Stichus belongs to the master, because the slave when manumitted could choose the same Stichus.

100   JULIAN, *Digest, book 77:* If Sempronius charged his heir Titius with a legacy to me and Titius bequeathed the same thing to me under a condition, then if the condition is fulfilled, I may claim the legacy under Sempronius's will.

101   JULIAN, *Digest, book 78:* If Stichus was bequeathed to my slave by will and I repudiated the legacy and afterward a codicil is produced showing that Stichus has been bequeathed to me also, I can vindicate him all the same.   1. If a legacy has been

bequeathed to someone in enemy hands and he dies there, it will be of no effect even though it could have been confirmed by *postliminium*.

102   JULIAN, *Digest, book 81:* If a master under twenty years old manumits a slave without proving good cause and afterward bequeaths a legacy to him and the slave has been alienated and has obtained his liberty, he does not receive the legacy. For the legacy is of no effect, just as if it had been given him while he was not free.

103   JULIAN, *Digest, book 83:* A secret *fideicommissum* is held to be a fraud against the law whenever someone is not asked by will or codicil, but binds himself by a private *cautio* or note-of-hand to deliver a *fideicommissum* to a person who is not entitled to it.

104   JULIAN, *Urseius Ferox, book 1:* All the heirs were charged with a legacy as follows: "Whoever becomes my heir, let him be condemned to pay Titius a hundred." Afterward a clause was included below that one of the heirs should not pay him. The question arises whether the remaining heirs must give the entire hundred or whether a deduction should be made in proportion to that one person's share in the inheritance. He replied that the better opinion was that the remaining heirs owed the entire hundred, since the meaning of the words does not militate against this opinion and the intention of the testator agrees.   1. In a will, it was written thus: "Lucius Titius, if he gives my heir the document in which I had promised him money, let my heir give a hundred." Titius subsequently died before returning the document to the heir. The question arises whether the legacy is due to Titius's heir. Cassius replied that if the document had existed, it was not due, because the legacy does not vest if it is not returned. JULIAN notes: if at the time of making the will there was no document, for this one reason it can be said that the legacy is due to Titius, because a condition that cannot be fulfilled counts as unwritten.   2. Even a thing belonging to the enemy can be bequeathed, according to Sabinus, if it can under any circumstances be bought.   3. If a bequest has been made to Attius as follows, "let whoever becomes my heir be condemned to give ten to my heir Attius," Attius may claim ten after deducting his share.   4. Again, if the heir has been directed to give ten and have a farm for himself, he will give ten after deducting his share.   5. Finally, it is settled that when a legacy has been left as follows, "let whoever shall be my heir be condemned to give ten to my heir," all the heirs' shares are made equal, because each is held to be condemned to give to himself and his co-heir.   6. When someone appointed an heir for the event of his mother's death, and afterward a second heir was appointed and legacies charged on him in favor of the heir appointed under the condition and this first heir died in the mother's lifetime, then, after the bequest had fallen due, the question was whether the legacies were due to the first heir's heir. The better opinion is that they were, whether the legacy to the first heir was charged on the substitute unconditionally or under the condition "if he does not become heir," because with his death that condition is fulfilled.   7. If a son-in-law has appointed his father-in-law as heir and has left a

part of the inheritance as a legacy to someone else, Sabinus replied that after deduction of the dowry the father-in-law would be liable for that part of the inheritance, just as, if money had been due to the father-in-law on account of a loan, he would after deducting it have been liable to give that part of the inheritance.

105   JULIAN, *From Minicius, book 1:* A legacy was left as follows: "What Lucius Titius owes me, let my heir be condemned to pay to Cornelius." Under this bequest, the heir is bound to do no more than assign his right of action.

106   PAUL, *Epitome of the Digest of Alfenus Varus, book 2:* If in a will the wording is "let my heir be condemned to a hundred to Licinius," omitting the word "give," it is settled that the legacy is due.

107   AFRICANUS, *Questions, book 2:* If legacies have been charged on several heirs and one of these is directed to discharge them in advance, he says it is in the power of the legatees whether they will claim from the individual heirs or the one directed to advance the legacies. The latter, therefore, must give a *cautio* to his co-heirs to ensure their indemnity.   1. If someone has left a legacy to his slave without conferring freedom on him and, when the slave himself dies, bequeaths him, there can scarcely be a doubt that the legacy will be effective, since it is clear that on the death of a slave a legacy left to him will go to the person to whom the slave was bequeathed.

108   AFRICANUS, *Questions, book 5:* If a bequeathed slave is said to have run away in the testator's lifetime, he must be delivered at the expense and risk of the legatee, because the heir's obligation is to deliver a bequeathed thing in the place where it was left by the testator.   1. If what you owe me under a will has been given by someone else to my slave, an action under the will still lies in my favor, especially if I should be unaware that the thing had become mine. Otherwise, it would follow that if you yourself give it to my slave, you will be released without my consent, which is quite unacceptable, when you will not be released even by paying me its value without my consent.   2. When a man was bequeathed to Titius, the question arose whether the choice of the slave to be given would be the heir's or the legatee's. I replied that the better opinion was that the right to select belonged to him who had the power to make use of what action he wished, that is, the legatee.   3. A legacy "to this or that person, whoever should first mount to the Capitol" he says is confirmed as valid by clear proof, because it is settled that where a usufruct has been left to several freedmen and ownership to whoever outlives the rest, the legacy is valid. He held that the same principle applied to the appointing of heirs.   4. Titius charged you as heir with a legacy to me of Stichus, who was due to me from you under a stipulation. It was held that if the stipulation was for value, the legacy was valid, but if I was to have him gratuitously on two different grounds, the better view is that the legacy is not effective, because nothing is lost and the same thing cannot be delivered twice.   5. But if, when you owed me Stichus by virtue of Titius's will, Sempronius bequeathed this same Stichus to me as a charge on you as heir and charged me with a *fideicommissum* that I should deliver him to someone else, the legacy will be effective, because I am not to keep him. The same rule applies if he has bequeathed money as a charge on me, and all the more if it was a *fideicommissum* in the former will. Again, if there was scope for the *lex Falcidia* in the former will, I shall obtain from the following will what I have lost on

account of the *lex Falcidia*.   6. Again, if I become the heir of an owner who is not solvent, whose farm you were directed to give to me, your obligation will remain, just as it would if I had bought the farm.   7. If a clause reads, "in addition to what I have bequeathed to Titius, let my heir give ten to Seius," Titius will undoubtedly keep his legacy and nothing beyond ten will be due to Seius. For the usual practice is to leave a legacy in terms something like these, "to Lucius Titius so much, and in addition so much to his wife and children."   8. If someone to whom nothing was bequeathed is left a legacy prefaced by "in addition," it can scarcely be doubted that what the testator so bequeathed is due. There is even less doubt, if I should stipulate from someone who owes me nothing, "do you promise to give me ten in addition to what you owe me," that ten are due.   9. If a slave belonging to another is directed to be free and bequeathed, he says he may be claimed under the legacy; for since the grant of freedom is void, it is absurd that it should invalidate a legacy that would otherwise be valid, if the slave had only been bequeathed.   10. Someone who had five in his safe bequeathed or promised under a stipulation "the ten I have in my safe." Both the legacy and the stipulation will be valid, but so that five only shall be due under the stipulation or the will. That the outstanding five should be claimed seems hardly reasonable; for it is, so to speak, a certain tangible object which is not in existence that is held to have been bequeathed. But if at the time of death the full sum had been there and afterward something had disappeared from it, the heir alone must undoubtedly stand the loss.   11. If a slave is bequeathed and the heir has caused delay, the slave's life and deterioration is at the risk of the heir, so that the heir, if he should hand him over disabled, nonetheless, will be liable.   12. When something has been bequeathed to you or charged on you as a *fideicommissum* to deliver it to me, then if you should receive nothing else under the will, he held that you will only be liable to me for fraud in exacting that legacy, but otherwise for negligence also, just as in contracts of good faith the law is that if the contract is for the benefit of both parties, you will be liable for negligence also, but if for the benefit of one only, for fraud alone.   13. A man who had given pearls to Titius as a pledge appointed his son heir and disinherited his daughter and then provided as follows: "I request you, Titius, and charge on you as a *fideicommissum* that you sell the pearls I left you as a pledge and after deduction of all that is due to you deliver all the residue to my daughter." On the grounds of this writing, the daughter can sue her brother for the *fideicommissum*, so that he deliver to her his right of action against the debtor; for in this instance the former creditor must be understood to be a debtor, because the price of the pledge exceeds the sum of the debt.   14. It is no wonder if one person is sued for a *fideicommissum* when another is bound by it; for similarly when a will reads as follows, "I ask you, Titius, to receive a hundred and manumit that slave," or "remit something to Sempronius," this is to be understood, however inadequately expressed, as a *fideicommissum* charged on the heir to deliver money to Titius; and, therefore, Titius himself can take an action against the heir and compel him to give the slave his freedom or Sempronius what he was asked.   15. Avidius charged his son with the *fideicommissum* of lending a certain sum to four of his freedmen and fixed a low rate of interest; it was held that this *fideicommissum* was fully valid.

109   AFRICANUS, *Questions, book 6:* If someone should bequeath to his wife what he had given her in the ordinary way during his lifetime, he says that the testator appears to have meant no other gifts than those which would not be valid by law. Otherwise, he would be making an ineffectual bequest, as though he had expressed himself as follows: "I bequeath to my wife what gifts I shall have legally made to her," or "what I shall have given to her for the purpose of manumission"; for these bequests would be void.   1. An heir charged with the *fideicommissum* of giving me a farm or a hundred sold the farm to Titius. Since he is left, the choice of which he prefers to give, provided that he delivers the money in full, I hold it to belong to the praetor's duty to bar an action for recovery of the farm if Titius offers the money. For in that way the same situation would arise as would have come about if the farm had not been alienated, since even in an action against the heir himself the praetor or arbitrator would have the duty of providing that if the farm were not delivered, Titius's obligation would not be assessed at more or less than a hundred.

110   AFRICANUS, *Questions, book 8:* If an heir, directed in general terms to deliver the slave he wishes, knowingly gives a thief and the thief steals from the legatee, he says an action will lie for fraud. But since it is rightly held that the heir is only obliged not to give the worst slave, he will be obliged to deliver another man and leave the first in noxal surrender.

111   MARCIAN, *Institutes, book 2:* If a tutor excuses himself from even a part of the property, for instance, of things in Italy or the provinces, he will lose everything that has been given to him by a will; and so the deified Severus and Antoninus ruled in a rescript.

112   MARCIAN, *Institutes, book 6:* If anyone bequeaths laborers tied to the soil without the lands to which they belong, the legacy is invalid. But the deified Marcus and Commodus ruled in a rescript that it must be established according to the intention of the deceased whether their value is due.   1. When an heir condemned to give a slave manumits him, he will be obliged to give his value, and it makes no difference whether or not he knew of the legacy. Even if the heir gave the slave away and the recipient manumitted him, the heir will be liable, although he may have been unaware that the slave had been charged on him as a legacy.   2. If a legacy has been made as follows, "I give and bequeath to Titius with Seius," the legacy is to both, just as, when the Formian farm has been bequeathed with the house, both have been bequeathed.   3. If anyone wrote in his will that something should be done contrary to law or sound morals, it is invalid just as if someone had written something against a statute or against the praetor's edict, or something disgraceful.   4. The deified Severus and Antoninus ruled in a rescript that an oath against the force of statutes and the authority of law, when written in a will, is without effect.

113   MARCIAN, *Institutes, book 7:* A legacy may be made to the slave of another "for as long as he is a slave," or "if he should be Titius's slave," as Marcellus also says.   1. If anyone should grant freedom to his slave after a time and meanwhile request the heir

to give him board until he attains his freedom, the deified Severus and Antoninus stated in a rescript that the wish of the testator is to be observed.   2. If anyone bequeathed a hundred to someone as a charge on his first heir and two hundred to the same person as a charge on the second heir and subsequently repeats the legacy in general terms, he is held to have meant three hundred by the repetition.   3. But if a father appointed a substitute for a son who is *impubes* and repeated the legacies as a charge on the substitute and if the *pupillus* becomes heir and dies before coming of age, the repetition is invalid, because the intention of the deceased was that the legacies should be due once only.   4. If a legacy was charged on an *impubes* under the condition "if he comes of age" and was repeated as a charge on the substitute, the legacy is due from the substitute also, and the condition invalidating the legacy is not held to have been repeated.   5. Inept wishes of the deceased about their burial, such as clothing or other unnecessary expenses for the funeral, are invalid, as Papinian wrote in the third book of his *Replies*.

114   MARCIAN, *Institutes, book 8:* A son-in-power who is a soldier or veteran, even if he dies intestate, can impose a *fideicommissum* on his father, since he is also entitled to make a will.   1. If a freedman dies intestate, he can leave a *fideicommissum* charged on his patron up to the share due to him, because, if he made a will, he would be allowed to leave him that share only.   2. A person who dies intestate and knows that his property will pass to the imperial treasury in the absence of an heir may impose a *fideicommissum* on the treasury.   3. Marcellus discusses the following question in the twelfth book of his *Digest*. A man charged someone to whom he had bequeathed a farm with a *fideicommissum* to deliver that farm after his death to Sempronius. He imposed on the same person a *fideicommissum* to give a hundred to Titius. The question arises: What is the law? Marcellus says that if the testator left Titius a hundred out of the fruits which the legatee could collect in his lifetime and the legatee died after the period of time required for collection, Titius should receive the hundred. But if the legatee should die immediately after receiving the legacy, the *fideicommissum* is extinguished, because it is settled that nobody can be required to deliver more than has been left to him.   4. But if the *fideicommissum* in favor of Titius has not been assigned to the time of the legatee's death, Marcellus says that it is to be given to Titius at once, but in return for a *cautio* that Titius will refund anything received in excess. This *cautio* will be payable if the legatee should die before having collected a hundred from the fruits. But it can hardly be the case that the testator wished the legatee to pay from the profits before the legatee had collected the fruits. The legatee must certainly be heard if he wishes to deliver the whole farm, provided that a *cautio* is given for restitution. For it is absurd that he should pay a hundred of his own money, especially if the farm is worth a hundred or not much more. This is the rule we follow.   5. If a bequest has been made to someone of something or of some right which he cannot have on account of a bodily defect or some other justifiable reason, but which another person can have, the legatee shall receive its resale value.   6. A person cannot be asked to appoint another as his heir. The senate has plainly decreed that this is to be treated like a request to restore an inheritance.   7. What then if the heir has been asked to restore a fourth part of his inheritance after his death? I hold the better opinion to be what Scaevola notes and Papirius Fronto writes that the *fideicommissum* is valid as though he had been asked to restore his inheritance; and it is to be restored in

common form of law so far as the testator's inheritance permits.   8. But if he has been asked to emancipate his children, he is not compelled to do so; for parental power does not permit of valuation.   9. Houses to be demolished can neither be bequeathed nor left as a *fideicommissum*, and the senate has so decreed.   10. If a *fideicommissum* was left to someone else's slave without grant of freedom, and he has gained his freedom, it must be said that he may be permitted to take it.   11. The deified Severus and Antoninus stated in a rescript that when a man has been asked to remit to his brother's children, he may not do so before the *fideicommissum* falls due, even with their consent, while they are under paternal power, since, when it falls due, it may have to be remitted to them after they have won their independence, or not to all of them if one of them should have died previously.   12. The same emperors stated in a rescript that a mother's inheritance need not be restored to her sons before the day of an expected legacy, but that the heir may provide a *cautio* in common form or, if he is unable to do this, put the sons into possession for the sake of preserving the *fideicommissum*, so that they may possess it as a pledge, not as owners or with the right of alienation. . . that they may have it as a pledge so that the son may collect the fruits through his father or the slave through his master.   13. When someone is asked to make restitution under a *fideicommissum* if he dies without offspring, the condition will be held to have failed if children survive the father, and no inquiry is made whether they have been appointed as heirs.   14. The deified Severus and Antoninus stated in a rescript that in the case of those who forbid by will that something should be alienated and do not explain the condition of nonalienation, the writing is of no effect, unless a person is found in respect of whom this disposition has been made, just as if the testators had left a bare precept, because they may not lay down a law of this kind in a will. But if it was in favor of children or descendants or freedmen or heirs or other specific persons that they expressed a wish of this kind, it is to be respected, provided it is not to defraud creditors or the imperial treasury. For if the goods of the heir are sold on account of the testator's creditors, the fideicommissaries are also subject to the common misfortune.   15. When a father charges a son who has been appointed heir by whom he has three grandchildren with a *fideicommissum* not to alienate a farm and to keep it in the family, and the son on his decease has appointed two as heirs and disinherited the third and bequeathed the farm to an outsider, the deified Severus and Antoninus ruled in a rescript that the son has indeed failed to comply with his father's wish.   16. And again, if he had disinherited two and appointed one as heir and bequeathed the farm to an outsider, Marcellus thinks that the disinherited grandsons may claim the *fideicommissum*. This also is the case if he emancipated his sons in his lifetime and afterward alienated the farm.   17. But if all the sons are appointed heirs to unequal shares, those who have been appointed to smaller shares cannot sue for the *fideicommissum* so as to have equal instead of hereditary shares. For he is held to have left the farm in the family even if he left it to one of them.   18. Again, if he appointed one as heir and bequeathed no legacy, the disinherited can claim nothing so long as the property is in the family.   19. Sometimes it is profitable to the heir if a slave who has been bequeathed or left by *fideicommissum* dies, for instance, if it is the slave of someone else or even his own, left individually to several people so that each one may claim him in full, provided that the slave dies through no fault of the heir.

115   ULPIAN, *Institutes, book 2:* Even an expression such as "I want you to give," "I desire you to give," "I believe that you will give," is a *fideicommissum.*

116   FLORENTINUS, *Institutes, book 11:* A legacy is a deduction from an inheritance by which a testator wishes something to be transferred to somebody out of the total that would belong to the heir.   1. An heir cannot be left a legacy charged on himself, but he can be left one charged on a co-heir. So if a farm should be bequeathed to someone appointed heir to half the estate and to two strangers, the heir to whom the bequest was made will get a sixth of the farm. For he cannot vindicate what is charged on himself, but from the co-heir to the other half he can vindicate not more than a third [of half the farm] since the two outsiders are concurrent claimants. The two strangers for their part will vindicate half the farm from the heir to whom the bequest was made and a third of the farm from the other heir.   2. Another person's slave who has been appointed heir cannot be left as a legacy charged on himself either in full or in part.   3. A legacy can properly be bequeathed to a slave who belongs to an inheritance, even if the inheritance has not been accepted, because the inheritance takes the place of the person of the deceased who left it.   4. A bequeathed farm must be given in the state in which it was left. So if the farm owed a servitude to the heir's farm or the heir's farm to it, even should the servitude have been extinguished through confusion of ownership, the original right must be restored. And if the legatee will not suffer a servitude to be imposed, his claim to the legacy can be barred by a defense of fraud; but if a servitude is not restored to a bequeathed farm, an action based on the will remains in the legatee's favor.

117   MARCIAN, *Institutes, book 13:* If anything is left to *civitates,* it is all valid, whether it be for distributions or for public works or for the maintenance or education of boys or anything else.

118   NERATIUS, *Rules, book 10:* A *fideicommissum* left in terms such as "I require," "I desire that you give" is valid, and even if worded "I wish my inheritance to be Titius's," "I know that you will remit my inheritance to Titius."

119   MARCIAN, *Rules, book 1:* If a slave has been directed by the testator not to give an account, it does not follow that he need not deliver what he has in his hands and so make a profit. The object is to prevent a scrupulous examination, so that he need not be called to account for negligence but only for fraud. Consequently, the fact that a manumitted slave is directed not to give an account does not imply that he has had the *peculium* bequeathed to him.

120   ULPIAN, *Replies, book 2:* There is no reason why an heir should be prevented from selling away from the inheritance buildings from which the income has been left for doles to dependents, provided that the rights of the legatees remain unimpaired.

1. If all those who have been left a *fideicommissum* agree to this sale, no claim to the *fideicommissum* will remain.   2. The fruits of a farm bequeathed unconditionally, when collected by the legatee after the inheritance is accepted, belong to him. But a tenant has the right to an action under the lease against the heir.

121   MARCIAN, *Rules, book 3:* If anyone makes a bequest to Titius with Maevius, either can be admitted to the bequest without the other. For similarly, when the praetor says, "I order the unborn child with the other children to have possession," the unborn child is placed in possession even when there are no other children.

122   PAUL, *Rules, book 3:* Legacies can be made to *civitates* that are conducive to the honor or ornament of the *civitas*. Legacies for ornament are, for example, those left for building a forum, theater, or stadium. Legacies for honor include those left for giving a gladiatoral spectacle, a wild beast show, theatrical performances, or chariot races, a largesse among individual citizens, or a banquet. In addition, what has been left for the maintenance of those of infirm age, such as senior citizens or boys and girls, is held conducive to the honor of the *civitas*.   1. "Let Lucius Titius and Gaius Seius be condemned to give ten to Publius Maevius." Gaius Seius did not become heir. Sabinus says that Titius alone will owe the legacy: for Seius is to be taken as unwritten. This is the correct opinion, and so all ten will be due from Titius. When a farm has been bequeathed to someone on condition that he give a hundred to the heir, then if the value of the farm is as much as he has been directed to give to the heir, the legatee is not to be compelled to deliver the *fideicommissum* imposed on him, since one who dispenses as much as he receives cannot be said to have gained anything by the will.

123   MARCELLUS, *Replies, sole book:* Lucius Titius, when he left two sons as heirs, provided as follows in his will: "On whoever of my children becomes my heir I charge as a *fideicommissum* that if any of them dies without issue, he restore at his death two thirds of my inheritance to his brothers." A brother died and made his brother heir to three quarters. Did he comply with the *fideicommissum*? Marcellus replied that what the testator owed to his brother under the will of Lucius Titius could be claimed by another who had become heir in proportion to his share, unless it were proved that the testator's intention was otherwise. For there is little difference between this kind of case and any other where a creditor is appointed heir to his debtor. But the co-heir must plainly be heard if he can prove that the testator intended to appoint his brother as heir, so that he should be content with his appointment and refrain from the *fideicommissum*. 1. A will contained the following clause: "To Gaius Seius let my heir give this and that. And I ask you, Seius, and commit to your trust to discharge all the above-written without any delay to him to whom you will discharge in person." Query: Is this a tacit *fideicommissum*, when the testator has not named in his will the person to whom he wishes discharge to be made? Marcellus replied: If Seius had given a secret promise in fraud of the law, it will not help him if the head of the household addressed him in these words. For he is not to be held to have circumvented the laws

any the less because it remains uncertain whom the testator wished to benefit.

124 NERATIUS, *Parchments, book 5:* If the heirs are mentioned by name as condemned to give something, it is more proper that they should be liable in equal portions, because the enumeration of persons has the effect of imposing equal shares in payment of a legacy upon those who, had they not been named, would have been liable proportionately to their share in the inheritance.

125 RUTILIUS MAXIMUS, *Lex Falcidia, sole book:* If an heir has been directed to take in advance a hundred, and restore the inheritance, and the testator's patron sues for *bonorum possessio* against the provisions of the will, then both the legacies and the amount received will be diminished in proportion to what the patron takes away.

126 PAUL, *Secundae Tabulae, sole book:* A legacy charged on the substitute of a disinherited son is ineffective. Consequently, it will not be possible to leave a *fideicommissum* as a charge on the *legitimus heres* of a disinherited son; for *legitimi heredes* are obliged to deliver according to the rules that would have applied had they been appointed heirs. But if when one of the children invokes the praetor's edict by which *possessio bonorum* is promised against the terms of the will, a son who was appointed heir also sues for *bonorum possessio* against the terms of the will, his substitute will deliver the legacies as far as the patrimony which has come to the son allows, just as if the son had received from the father what he has secured by *bonorum possessio*. 1. When a legacy is charged on a posthumous son "if he becomes heir" but no posthumous son is born and substitutes come forward, then they are held to owe the legacies which he would have owed if he had lived.

127 PAUL, *Law of Codicils, sole book:* A *fideicommissum* may be charged on the posthumous son of a brother. For only intention is respected in *fideicommissa*, and Gallus's opinion has prevailed that the posthumous sons of others may also become *legitimi heredes* to ourselves.

128 MARCIAN, *Institutes, book 2:* If a tutor has married his *pupilla* contrary to the *senatus consultum*, she may take under the will, but he cannot; and deservedly so. For those who contract prohibited marriages are delinquents and deserve to be penalized. But this blame does not attach to a woman who has been deceived by her tutor.

BOOK THIRTY-ONE

1

LEGACIES AND *FIDEICOMMISSA*

1 ULPIAN, *Sabinus, book 9:* To make a legacy subject to someone else's discretion is like imposing a condition. For what difference is there between bequeathing something to me "if Titius should mount to the Capitol" and "if he should wish?" 1. But a legacy to a *pupillus* or *pupilla* "subject to their tutors' discretion" implies no condition or delay, since in wills it is settled that a legacy subject to someone else's discretion is taken as subject to the discretion of an upright man. Now what delay is there in the discretion of an upright man, imposed on the legacy just as if the testator had expressed the bequest of a fixed sum "as far as the resources of the inheritance allow?"

2 PAUL, *Edict, book 75:* Whenever several things are expressed by name in a legacy they are several legacies. But if furniture or silver or *peculium* or equipment is bequeathed, it is one legacy.

3 PAUL, *Plautius, book 4:* A legacy worded "let my heir be condemned to give, if he does not mount to the Capitol" is valid, even though it is in his power to mount or not to mount.

4 PAUL, *Plautius, book 8:* The better opinion is that nobody should accept part and refuse part of the same thing that has been bequeathed to him.

5 PAUL, *Questions, book 7:* But when two legacies are left, it is held that one may be repudiated and the other welcomed. 1. But if one of the legacies implies a burden and this is refused, the same cannot be said. Take the case of one to whom ten and Stichus have been bequeathed, with the requirement of manumitting Stichus. If the *lex Falcidia* applies here, a fourth of each legacy will be deducted from the ten. So the burden of deduction will not be escaped if the slave is repudiated, but the legatee will relinquish two fourths of the money.

6 PAUL, *Lex Falcidia, sole book:* When a flock has been bequeathed, some sheep cannot be rejected and others vindicated; for this is one legacy and not several. We shall say the same when *peculium* is bequeathed or clothing or silver or the like.

7 PAUL, *Plautius, book 8:* If ten are bequeathed to Titius and to someone who may not take, then because the heir is condemned to give to two persons and one cannot take, only five are given to Titius.

8   PAUL, *Plautius, book 9:* If anyone bequeaths the slave of the heir or of another and
he has taken flight, *cautiones* must be furnished for bringing him back. But if he has
taken flight in the lifetime of the testator, he is brought back at the cost of the legatee;
if after his death, at the cost of the heir.   1. Should a bequest be worded, "to Sempronius I bequeath ten, or if he refuses, the man Stichus"; in this case there are two
legacies, but he must be content with one.   2. If anyone has bequeathed ten flagons
from the same cask, then even if not ten can be found but less, the legacy is not extinguished, but the legatee receives only what is found.   3. If there is doubt to whom
the same legacy should rather be given, as, for example, if it has been left to Titius,
and two friends of the testator answering to that name come and claim the legacy and
the heir is prepared to pay it and then both are prepared to defend the heir, the heir
must choose whom to pay on condition of being defended by him.   4. If a certain sum
of money that has been bequeathed is claimed by both the legatee and substitutes of
the legatee and the heir is prepared to pay, then if both are prepared to defend the
heir, the heir must choose which one to pay on condition of being defended by him; and
if it is clear that neither is acting in bad faith, he should rather pay the one to whom
the bequest was made first.   5. If I have bequeathed a legacy to someone of a fixed
share of the inheritance, the deified Hadrian ruled in a rescript that neither the price
of manumitted slaves nor the cost of the funeral should be deducted.

9   MODESTINUS, *Rules, book 9:* But when a share of my goods is left as follows, "of my
goods which there shall be when I die," then the dowry and the price of manumitted
slaves is to be deducted from the total.

10   JAVOLENUS, *From Plautius, book 1:* When a farm has been bequeathed by name, if
anything has been added to it after the will was made, that too passes with the legacy,
even if the words "which shall be mine" have not been added, provided that the testator did not possess that part separately, but added it to the whole of the previous farm.

11   POMPONIUS, *From Plautius, book 7:* Labeo says that a *statuliber* cannot receive a
legacy from the testator's heir without his freedom, even when he has a doubtful freedom under the will, because he would be the heir's slave. But if the heir inserts the
same condition into the legacy as was prefaced to the freedom granted by the testator,
the legacy is good. For even if the slave had been ordered to be free on the death of the
heir, it is certain that a legacy can rightly be left to him by the heir without grant of
freedom, because it is superfluous to give him the freedom which he is not to receive
under the will of the heir, but has under that of the testator.   1. "Let my heir give
Stichus or Pamphilus, whichever he chooses, to Titius, provided that on the day when
my will is read he says which he wishes to give." If the heir does not say whether he
prefers to give Pamphilus or Stichus. I think he will be liable, just as though he was
charged to give either Pamphilus or Stichus, to give the one the legatee chooses. If he
says he wishes to give Stichus, he is released by Stichus's death. If before the day that
the legacy falls due, one of the slaves should die, he will remain obliged to give the one

who survives. When the heir has once said whom he wishes to give, he will not be able to change his mind. And so Julian also decided.

12   PAUL, *Vitellius, book 2:* If money that has been bequeathed is not among the goods of the person who left the legacy, but the inheritance is solvent, the heir will be compelled to give the money bequeathed either out of his own resources or from selling things that have been inherited or from wherever he wishes.   1. A legacy left in these terms, "let my heir give at his death ten to Lucius Titius," since it has been left for an uncertain day, will not belong to the heirs of the legatee if he dies in the lifetime of the heir.

13   POMPONIUS, *From Plautius, book 7:* A man who had two debtors for the same money, Titius and Maevius, left a legacy in these terms: "What Titius owes me, let my heir give to Maevius. What Maevius owes, let him give to Seius." With these words he burdens the heir. For by the fact of the heir's transferring his right of action against Titius to Maevius, Maevius is held to be released, and consequently the heir will be liable to Seius.   1. If someone who has one debtor leaves, separately to two people, the whole sum that the debtor owes him, the heir is obliged to satisfy both, by ceding to the one his right of action, and by paying money to the other.

14   PAUL, *Vitellius, book 4:* If the same slave has been left as a legacy and directed to be free, the grant of freedom will prevail. But if he has been left as a legacy in a later writing and his freedom is clearly shown to be revoked, this later legacy will prevail on account of the intention of the deceased.   1. To someone else's slave appointed heir after the death to his master who has acquired the inheritance, it is settled that freedom can be given as a *fideicommissum.*

15   CELSUS, *Digest, book 6:* If anyone after appointing two heirs leaves a legacy worded, "let my heirs give Stichus or ten," it is not possible for one to give five and another a part of Stichus, but it is necessary for each of them to pay the whole of Stichus or ten.

16   CELSUS, *Digest, book 16:* If a legacy is left to Titius or Seius, whichever the heir wishes, the heir by giving to one is released from liability to each. If he gives to neither, each can claim as if the legacy were to himself alone. For just as two people can become creditors under a stipulation, so they can under a will.

17   MARCELLUS, *Digest, book 10:* If someone bequeathed ten to Titius and asked him to restore them to Maevius and Maevius has died, the benefit accrues to Titius, not the heir, unless he merely chose Titius as an agent. The same applies if you suppose a usufruct to have been bequeathed.   1. If an heir has been condemned to give ten to one of the freedmen and the testator did not indicate to which, the heir will be compelled to pay the ten to all the freedmen.

18   CELSUS, *Digest, book 17:* I can make my heir liable to you in such a way that if at my death Stichus is not your slave, my heir may be condemned to give him to you.

19   CELSUS, *Digest, book 18:* If a person to whom Stichus or Pamphilus was left as a legacy vindicates Stichus, thinking it was Stichus who was bequeathed to him, he does not have the right of changing his vindication afterward, just as, if the heir had been

condemned to give either of them and gave Stichus, being unaware that he was permitted to give Pamphilus instead, he could not take him back.

20   CELSUS, *Digest, book 19:* Proculus held and I also had it from my father that a legacy left to a slave held in common, if one master should refuse it, will not accrue to the other. For it is not a joint legacy, but parts are bequeathed; because, if both vindicated it, each would have a part of the legacy in proportion to his share in the slave.

21   CELSUS, *Digest, book 20:* When a man had given back to his wife her dowry, wished to leave her a legacy of forty, and, knowing that the dowry had been restored, left that sum as a legacy under pretext of restoring the dowry, I hold that the forty are due. For the word "restore," though it means "to give back," can also be used in the sense of giving outright.

22   CELSUS, *Digest, book 21:* Lucius Titius in his will left to Publius Maevius a commission or whatever money could be made from selling it with its perquisites. But Lucius Titius lived on after making the will, sold the commission, exacted its price, and gave it to the man to whom he had wished in his will that the commission or its price should be given. After the death of Lucius Titius, Publius Maevius again demanded from the heirs the commission or its price. CELSUS: I think the price of the commission should not be given, unless the legatee can prove that the testator had, even after the payment, wished the legatee to receive the price of the commission once again. But if the testator in his lifetime gave the legatee not the whole price of the commission but a part, the rest may still be claimed, unless the heir can show that the testator departed from his intention. The burden of proof that he changed his mind belongs to him who refuses to discharge the *fideicommissum.*

23   MARCELLUS, *Digest, book 13:* "I bequeath to Lucius Titius the Seian farm or the usufruct of the Seian farm." The legatee can vindicate the farm or the usufruct, which cannot be done by one to whom only the farm has been bequeathed.

24   ULPIAN, *Fideicommissa, book 2:* When someone had left a *fideicommissum* in these terms, "I ask that you restore to those of my freedmen whom you wish," Marcellus held that the heir could prefer even an unworthy freedman. But if the terms should be "to those whom you think worthy," he says only those may claim who have committed no offense. He also says that if the heir chooses nobody, all may be admitted to claim the *fideicommissum* as for immediate payment, when it has been left "to those whom you wish" and he does not offer it to anyone. Plainly, if the others are dead, it must be given to the survivor or to the survivor's heir if he died before claiming. But Scaevola objects: If all can claim when it is offered to nobody, why should not all those who have died transmit the claim to their heirs, so that the heir should not, with one claimant only, be without a choice of beneficiary? For Marcellus seems to hold

that when a *fideicommissum* if left "to anyone of my freedmen you wish," unless the heir offers it to one whom he wishes and makes the offer at once and with no delay, the claim is immediately open to all. So he rightly incurs the objection: Why should he think the legacy due to the survivor alone, unless it should happen that the others have died before a reasonable time had elapsed for the heir to choose to whom he would prefer to make the offer?

25   MARCELLUS, *Digest, book 15:* If, however, in the absence of certain freedmen, those who are present claim, when the *fideicommissum* has been left for immediate payment, then, upon cause being shown, it should be determined and explored whether there are others too entitled to claim.

26   MARCELLUS, *Digest, book 16:* A person who had bare ownership of a slave without usufruct, having appointed as heir the owner of the usufruct, bequeathed the slave to another. The heir cannot have recourse to a defense of fraud if the legatee wishes to vindicate the slave without leaving the usufruct to the heir.

27   CELSUS, *Digest, book 34:* If this or that thing is bequeathed, it is one legacy. If this or that thing has been bequeathed under contradictory conditions, we hold it to be one legacy. It makes no difference if the heirs and the legatee are different persons, for example, if the legacy reads, "if Nerva becomes consul, let my heir Titius give Attius a farm; if Nerva is not made consul, let my heir Seius give Maevius a hundred."

28   MARCELLUS, *Digest, book 29:* A patron appointed heir to the share due to him is not compelled to deliver a *fideicommissum* charged on him. If, therefore, he rejects the inheritance, do those who vindicate the share keep it in the same way or must they deliver the *fideicommissum*? The better opinion is that the *fideicommissum* is due, because what was conceded to the patron personally should by no means apply to anyone else.

29   CELSUS, *Digest, book 36:* My father used to tell how, when he was in the council of the consul Publius Ducenius Verus, his opinion was endorsed in the case of Otacilius Catulus's legacy of two hundred to his freedman, which he had asked him to give to his concubine. Catulus had appointed his daughter heiress to his entire estate, and, the freedman having died in the testator's lifetime, what had been left to him remained with the daughter. My father held that the daughter should be compelled to restore the *fideicommissum* to the concubine.   1. Where a *fideicommissum* is charged on someone who is named as heir, it can be held that the testator wished it to be given only if he became heir.   2. If my son is heir and there accrues to him the share of a person on whom a legacy had been charged by name, he will not deliver the legacy, which he takes by ancient right.

30   CELSUS, *Digest, book 37:* [A woman] wrote in [her] will: "To the state of Gravisca I leave a legacy for the supervision of the repairs of the road in that colony which runs as far as the Aurelian Way." The question was whether the legacy was valid. Juventius Celsus replied: The writing is indeed somewhat defective, because the sum bequeathed is not stated. But it can be held that as much was bequeathed as would be enough for the work. Provided that it does not appear that the intention of the deceased was otherwise, either because of the great extent of the cost or of the moderate

means which the testatrix left, then it is the duty of the judge to fix the size of the legacy in proportion to the value of the inheritance.

31   MODESTINUS, *Rules, book 1:* If anyone should bequeath for manumission persons he was not entitled to manumit, neither the legacy nor their freedom is good.

32   MODESTINUS, *Rules, book 9:* Everything that is written in a will without fixed day or condition shall be delivered as soon as the inheritance is accepted.   1. A farm not transferred by the heir pending fulfillment of a condition, but taken into possession by the legatee, may be vindicated by the heir with its fruits.   2. A legacy in these terms "to such a one in addition that farm with all the things that shall be in the said farm" also includes the slaves.   3. When a legacy is worded "whatever shall be in my barn" and the legatee has, unbeknown to the person who left the legacy, brought unbe-queathed things into the barn for the sake of increasing his legacy, what has been brought in is held not to have been bequeathed.   4. What the legatee has been asked to restore to another must, if the legatee dies, be delivered by the legatee's heir. 5. Specifically named articles, if they are not found and are not proved to be missing through the bad faith of the heir, cannot be claimed under the will which named them.   6. Where a *fideicommissum* is left to a family, those who are named are al-lowed to claim it, or after the death of all of them, those who were of the name of the deceased at the time of the testator's death and those born from them in the first de-gree, unless the deceased should have specifically extended his intention to those at further remove.

33   MODESTINUS, *Replies, book 9:* He replied: The claim for legacies against heirs lies in proportion to their several shares in the inheritance, and co-heirs are not to be bur-dened on behalf of those heirs who are insolvent.   1. Someone appointed several heirs and in his will charged legacies on some of them by name and afterward wrote a codicil to all his heirs. What legacies do they owe? Modestinus replied that since the testator clearly expressed in his will which heirs he wished to discharge legacies, then even if he wrote a codicil to all of them, it is evident that what he gave in the codicil must be delivered by those whom the testator in his will required to perform the duty.

34   MODESTINUS, *Replies, book 10:* Titia, after making her will, died, having appointed as heirs in equal shares Maevia and Sempronius, her children. She asked Maevia to manumit her slave Stichus in these words: "I ask you, my dearest daughter Maevia, to manumit your slave Stichus, since I shall have left you by codicil a legacy of so many slaves to minister to you." But she left no such legacy. What should be held to have been left by these words, when as has been observed above, the fact is that the testa-trix died with two heirs appointed, the slaves inherited belonged to two persons, and nothing was left in the codicil about delivery of slaves; and the *fideicommissum* could not be thought good since nothing was given when she said she had left a legacy, and she had added no specification of the legacy and had not asked her heir that the slaves should be delivered? Modestinus replied that upon the case as put Maevia had no claim for a legacy or *fideicommissum*, but was not compelled to grant freedom to her

slave. 1. Lucius Titius provided in his will as follows: "To Octaviana Stratonica, my dearest daughter, greeting. I wish her to receive from herself my estate of Gaza with all its appurtenances. To Octavianus Alexander, my dearest son. I wish him to have exclusively from himself the joint estate Comiana with its osier-beds and all its appurtenances." Should a writing of this kind be held to give an intact estate to each of them or only the part each one had inherited, since he had expressed the ineffectual wish that each should receive from himself the part he already had? Modestinus replied that the writing in question should not be so interpreted as to render the *fideicommissum* ineffectual. Again, if an intact estate is held to have been left, is the price of the portion to be paid by the brother and his co-heir, assuming that by virtue of requiring him to receive it from himself the testator wished him to have it by throwing in the price? Modestinus replied that he was by no means to be compelled to pay the price. 2. Lucia Titia who died intestate left a house to the slave of another as a *fideicommissum* charged upon her sons. After her death, her sons, who also became her heirs, when dividing their mother's inheritance, also divided the house at which division the master of the slave fideicommissary was present as a witness. Now should it be held that because he was present at the division, the master lost the right of claiming the *fideicommissum* acquired for himself through his slave? Modestinus replied that the *fideicommissum* was not automatically lost, because it could not even be repudiated; and the master could not be barred by a defense of fraud either, unless it appeared evident that he had acted in this way with a view to letting go the *fideicommissum*. 3. Gaius Seius had his own house and had moved to his wife's country seat. He transferred certain things from his house into this country seat, and after many days died there, leaving in his will his wife as heiress with several others. In his will, he signified the words written below: "First, let my heirs take note that there is no money in the hands of my wife, nor anything else; on this account, therefore, I do not wish her to be disturbed." Now can what he transferred to the country seat of his wife be vindicated by virtue of the common inheritance, or can the co-heirs be barred by prescription on the part of the deceased's wife according to the wording of the will? Modestinus replied that if what the deceased transferred to his wife's country house had been intended by him to belong to her in advance, nothing as put prevented his intention from standing. The wife, therefore, needs to prove that such was the intention of the testator. Unless this was so, these things must remain in the husband's inheritance. 4. If a *fideicommissum* has been left to a freedman on condition of his not leaving the testator's children and their tutors have prevented him from fulfilling the condition, it is unjust that since he is blameless he should forego the profit from the *fideicommissum*. 5. A man, who had brought an action for his daughter's dowry against her wishes, died having disinherited the daughter and appointed his son as heir and charged the son with a *fideicommissum* to give to his daughter for the dowry. How much should the daughter recover from her brother? Modestinus replied that what is of first importance is that the action for the dowry is not lost to the woman, as she had not consented to her father's action though not unaware of it. The business works out in this way. If the greater sum was in the original dowry, the woman should be content with claiming that only. But if in the sum of the legacy for the dowry there is more than in the original dowry, she should be compensated to the extent of the original dowry, and only the excess in the subsequent sum can be claimed under the will. For it is improbable that the father should have intended to burden his son and heir with a double payment of the dowry, when moreover he thought he had effectively, though without the consent of his daughter, instituted an action for the dowry against his son-in-law. 6. Lucius Titius, having left two children of different sex as appointed heirs, added a general clause that these heirs should discharge the legacies and grants of freedom. But in a certain part of his will, he asked his son to take on himself the whole burden of the legacies in this manner: "Whatever I have directed to be left or given in advance as legacies, I shall require my son and heir Attianus to give and discharge." Then he added in the legacy to be left in advance to his daughter these words: "Anything that I have given in my lifetime to my dearest daughter Paulina, I direct that she have for herself and forbid any inquiry into this matter. And I ask you, my beloved daughter, not to be angry because I shall have left a more substantial inheritance to your brother, who, as you know, will be sustaining great burdens and will be discharging the legacies I have made above." Now should we take it that the effect of these last words in which the father spoke to his daughter in his will is that he burdened his son with answering for actions against the inheritance, that is, all of them, or should he be held to have spoken in this way only with respect to the legacies, whereas the right of suing the inheritance should be given to the creditors against either heir? Modestinus replied that the case as put did not imply that the testator had directed that the son alone should answer for the actions of the creditors. 7. Titia on her marriage to Gaius Seius gave lands for her dowry and certain other things and afterward at death provided in a codicil as follows: "I commend Gaius Seius my husband to you, my daughter. I wish him to be given for life the usufruct of my share in the village of Naklenoi, which I have already given him for dowry. He should in no way be troubled about the dowry; for after his death, it will belong to you and your children." Besides this she bequeathed to him many other things, which he was to have as long as he lived. Now apart from what was left him by codicil other than the dowry, could an action on the *fideicommissum* lie in favor of the daughter and heiress for those things which Gaius Seius received as dowry? Modestinus replied: Though the words cited give no grounds for the daughter of the testatrix to claim a *fideicommissum* from Gaius Seius, after he has discharged what had been bequeathed in the will, nothing, however, forbids a claim for a *fideicommissum* after the death of Gaius Seius on account of the intention of the testatrix.

35　MODESTINUS, *Replies, book 16:* He replied that when a legacy is made to a wife of what has been acquired for her use, those slaves who were acquired not for herself personally, but for common use, do not belong to it.

36　MODESTINUS, *Encyclopaedia, book 3:* A legacy is a gift left by will.

37　JAVOLENUS, *From Cassius, book 1:* A person invalidly manumitted by will may be bequeathed by the same will. For a grant of freedom takes precedence over a legacy only when it is a valid grant.

38　JAVOLENUS, *From Cassius, book 2:* What a bequeathed slave has acquired before the inheritance has been accepted, he acquires for the inheritance.

39　JAVOLENUS, *From Cassius, book 3:* If a plot of land has been bequeathed and after the will a building is erected on it, the ground and the *superficium* will both be due.

40　JAVOLENUS, *Letters, book 1:* If the same thing is bequeathed to two of my slaves and I do not wish it to belong to me by virtue of the legacy to one of the two slaves, the whole will belong to me, because I acquire the share of the one slave through the other, just as if the legacy were to my slave and someone else's slave.

41　JAVOLENUS, *Letters, book 7:* "To Maevius I bequeath half my farm, to Seius half; and I bequeath the same farm to Titius." If Seius should have died, his part accrues to each, since as the parts of the farm and the whole have been bequeathed separately, it is necessary that the part that loses its owner should be added to each of those to whom the farm has been bequeathed separately in proportion to their share in the legacy.　1. A legacy has been charged on me as heir for my wife as follows: "Whatever has come into the hands of Seius for Titia as her dowry, let my heir Seius give the same sum as Titia." I ask whether deductions of expenses are allowable, as they would have been in an action for dowry. He replied: I have no doubt that when a legacy to a wife is worded, "I ask you, my heir, to give her whatever has come into your hands," the whole dowry, without taking account of the deduction of expenses, is due to the woman. But the same right cannot be maintained in the case of the will of a stranger as in that of the will of a husband who made a *relegatio* of dowry to his wife. For in this case, "whatever has come into your hands" takes the place of a valuation, but in the former, where a husband makes a *relegatio* of dowry to his wife, it is held that he bequeaths as much as the wife would be able to claim in a judgment for the dowry.

42 JAVOLENUS, *Letters, book 11:* When a legacy was made to someone entitled to take [only] a part, for him to restore it to someone else, it is settled that he may take it in full.

43 POMPONIUS, *Quintus Mucius, book 3:* A bequest worded, "I wish as much to be given to Tithasus as my heir will have," amounts to the same as if it were written, "as much as all my heirs will have." 1. But if the terms were, "I wish my heirs to give to Tithasus as much as one heir will have," then the smallest share that comes in the legacy is to be received. 2. Pegasus used to distinguish, if a *fideicommissum* was left with a fixed day of payment, for example, in ten years' time, the difference it made for whose benefit the time was extended, whether for that of the heir, in which case the heir should retain the fruits, or that of the legatee, for example, if a *fideicommissum* should have been left for an *impubes* when he should come of age, because then the fruits of the preceding time should be delivered. These principles are to be understood to apply unless it was specifically added that the heir should discharge the *fideicommissum* with the increment. 3. If it is written, "let my heir give ten or fifteen," that amounts to the same as if ten only were bequeathed. Or if it is written, "a year or two years after I die, let my heir give," that is held to be a legacy after two years, because the heir is empowered to choose.

44 POMPONIUS, *Quintus Mucius, book 4:* If, when several heirs have been appointed, it is written as follows, "let my heir be condemned to give five aurei," it is not just any heir, but all the heirs together who are held to be condemned to give five between them. 1. If a bequest reads, "let my heir Lucius Titius be condemned to give to Tithasus five aurei," and then in another place reads, "let Publius Maevius my heir be condemned to give to Tithasus five aurei," then, unless Titius can show that the bequest was charged on Publius in order that the charge should be lifted from himself, the legatee will receive five aurei from the one and five from the others.

45 POMPONIUS, *Quintus Mucius, book 8:* If it is written, "I give a hundred aurei to my daughters," does the legacy appear to have been given to children of both the male and female sex? For if it had been written, "I assign these tutors to my sons," the received opinion is that the tutors were also assigned to the daughters. But this is not to be held applicable the other way round so as to include males under the designation of females. For males to be included under a word describing females would set a very bad precedent. 1. If a legacy has been left to us under a condition or with a fixed day of payment, we cannot repudiate it before the condition is fulfilled or the day falls due. For before that time the legacy does not belong to us. 2. If a father has directed his heir by will to pay so many aurei to his daughter, when he marries her, then if the girl was married at the time the will is made, but unbeknown to her father and in his absence, the legacy, nonetheless, will be due. But if he was not unaware of this, he is held to have meant another marriage.

46 PROCULUS, *Letters, book 5:* If a person making a legacy wrote, "whatever Lucius

Titius has to give and do for me, I bequeath to Sempronius," but did not add, "immediately or after an interval," then I would not doubt, as far as concerns the meaning of the words, that such money as was not yet due at the time of the testator's death was not included. But by adding the words "immediately or after an interval," it seems to me obvious that he showed that he wished to bequeath that money also.

47   PROCULUS, *Letters, book 6:* Sempronius Nepos to Proculus, greeting. Two documents of the will of the same head of the household, made at the same time, as is the common practice, for the sake of having a copy, are produced. In one a hundred, in the other fifty, aurei are bequeathed to Titius. The question is whether he is to have a hundred and fifty, or only fifty aurei? Proculus replied: In this case it is better to deal lightly with the heir. Therefore, both legacies are by no means due, but only fifty aurei.

48   PROCULUS, *Letters, book 8:* Licinnius Lucusta to Proculus, greeting. When a husband makes a condition in repaying a dowry by legacy that his wife should, if she prefers, receive the slaves she had given him as dowry instead of a sum of money, I ask: Will those slaves who have been subsequently born from the slaves given as dowry also be due to the wife? Proculus to Lucusta, greeting. If the wife prefers to take slaves rather than dowry money, then the slaves themselves that she gave, valued for the purpose of dowry, shall be due to her, but not also the offspring of the slaves. 1. Where *bonorum possessio* has been granted to the curator of a lunatic, legacies may be claimed from the curator who represents the lunatic. But the claimants must give a *cautio* that in the event of the inheritance being lost by eviction, what has been given as legacies will be returned.

49   PAUL, *Lex Julia et Papia, book 5:* When a bequeathed ox has died neither the hide nor the flesh will be due.   1. If a ticket for the corn-dole is bequeathed to Titius and he has died, some think that the legacy is extinguished. But this is not true; for when a ticket or a commission is bequeathed to someone, what is held to have been bequeathed is the value.   2. Labeo reports that according to a reply of Trebatius, a field which you have no right to buy or sell may be bequeathed to you. This Priscus Fulcinius rightly said is false.   3. Proculus says that if someone had ordered his heir to give a farm, which that heir had no right to buy and sell, to someone who did have that right, the heir is bound to give the property itself, if it was among the goods of the testator, or if not, its value; and this is the better opinion.   4. If the testator had ordered something to be given or a work to be carried out or a show to be provided, it is held that those to whom a share of the estate has accrued should give in proportion to their share, just as they should the other legacies.

50   MARCELLUS, *Digest, book 28:* As substitutes may be appointed for heirs, let us see if the same can be done for legatees also and for recipients of gifts *mortis causa,* so

that the donor may promise them to another, if [the recipient] cannot himself take. It can, the more so because the gift is bestowed personally, too, on the second [recipient].   1. If Titius owes me Stichus or ten and I bequeath to you Stichus whom he owes to me, it is held that if ten are paid instead, the legacy is extinguished. If my legacies should be to different people, ten to one and Stichus to another, [one or other] legacy is good depending on how the payment falls out.   2. When a legacy has been made in these terms, "let my heir give to Maevius as much money as he shall have exacted from Titius," if the legacy is under a condition, the legatee cannot take an action before the money is exacted. But if the legacy falls due at once, as Publicius rightly thinks, the legatee can bring suit so that the rights of action may be transferred to him.

51   ULPIAN, *Lex Julia et Papia, book 8:* If anyone has provided in his will as follows, "to such a one I wish to be given the maximum he may accept according to the law," it is to be understood as left to him for the time when he will be entitled to take. If he said, "let my heir be condemned to give him the largest share that I am allowed to give," the same is to be said.   1. A man to whom a third part has been left for when he has children will certainly not be able to obtain the third part by resorting to adoption.

52   TERENTIUS CLEMENS, *Lex Julia et Papia, book 3:* It is not proper that inquiries should be made about a person's condition before an inheritance or legacy applies to him.

53   TERENTIUS CLEMENS, *Lex Julia et Papia, book 4:* When one heir has been charged with a legacy to a woman with a view to compensating her for her dowry and she prefers to receive her dowry rather than the legacy, the question arises whether an action for the dowry should be given her against all the heirs or against only the one on whom the legacy was charged. Julian holds that the action should be given first against him on whom the legacy was charged; for since she ought to be content either with her right or with her husband's judgment, it is just that he whom the husband charged with the legacy in compensation for the dowry should bear the burden of this debt up to the full sum of the legacy, but that, with respect to the remaining part of the dowry, all the heirs should be responsible for delivery.   1. The same must be said if she is appointed heiress instead of receiving her dowry, but lets go the inheritance, so that an action may be given her against the substitute; which is correct.   2. On legacies and the calculation of the *lex Falcidia*, there is a nice point in dispute: whether the person against whom alone an action for dowry is granted should owe the entire legacies personally, just as if all the heirs were paying the dowry, or whether to compute the whole dowry as a debt [of the inheritance], because the action for it is given against him alone, which certainly seems more reasonable.

54   TERENTIUS CLEMENS, *Lex Julia et Papia, book 13:* If a person is bequeathed a farm worth a hundred on condition of giving a hundred to the heir or anyone else, there are times when such a legacy is held valid. For sometimes it is in the interest of the legatee to have a farm rather than a hundred, since it is often in our interest to acquire neighboring farms for more than their just value.

55   GAIUS, *Lex Julia et Papia, book 12:* If the same thing has been bequeathed to Titius and me and on the day the legacy falls due he has died leaving me as heir, and I repudiate the inheritance, I see that the more commonly adopted view is that part of the legacy has lapsed.   1. If an heir has been appointed who is entitled to take nothing or not the whole inheritance and a legacy is made to a slave of the estate, we must, in treating of capacity to inherit, see whether regard should be paid to the person of the heir or of the deceased or neither. And after considering a variety of views, we conclude that as there is no master whose person is open to inquiry about his capacity to inherit, the legacy is acquired with no hindrance for the estate and on this account belongs in every respect to the person who shall subsequently become heir according to what he is entitled to take. The rest goes to those who are designated by law.

56   GAIUS, *Lex Julia et Papia, book 14:* A legacy to an emperor who is taken from mankind before the day of its falling due is, according to a *constitutio* of the deified Antoninus, due to his successor.

57   JUNIUS MAURICIANUS, *Lex Julia et Papia, book 2:* If you have left a legacy to the empress and she ceases to sojourn among mankind, the legacy is void, as the deified Hadrian ruled in the case of Plotina, and his successor the Emperor Antoninus in that of Faustina Augusta, when she ceased to sojourn among mankind before the death of the testator.

58   GAIUS, *Lex Julia et Papia, book 14:* If a thing has been bequeathed to someone and he only wishes to have a part of it, he acquires it all.

59   TERENTIUS CLEMENS, *Lex Julia et Papia, book 15:* If the same thing is bequeathed to me unconditionally and to my slave either unconditionally or under a condition and I repudiate the legacy given to me and afterward when the condition is fulfilled wish the legacy made to my slave to belong to me, the received opinion is that [only] part of the legacy has lapsed; unless anyone should doubt that on fulfillment of the condition in the slave's lifetime, the legacy would in any event become mine if I once expressed the wish it should belong to me; which is held to be the more equitable. It is the same if the identical thing should be bequeathed to two of my slaves.

60   ULPIAN, *Lex Julia et Papia, book 16:* Julian says that if a legacy is charged on a son and heir in favor of Seius, and a *fideicommissum* is charged on Seius under a condition to give to Titius, and Titius should die while the condition is pending, the unfulfilled *fideicommissum* remains with Seius and not with the son and heir, because the senate's wish is that in questions of *fideicommissa* the person to whose trust they have been committed should have the better case.

61   ULPIAN, *Lex Julia et Papia, book 18:* If a testator, having appointed Titius and Maevius as heirs, leaves four hundred and bequeaths two hundred as a charge on Titius and one hundred on whoever shall be his heir and Maevius does not accept the inheritance, then Titius shall owe three hundred.   1. Julian indeed says that if one of the *legitimi heredes* repudiates his share, when *fideicommissa* were left as a charge on him, the co-heir is not to be compelled to deliver the *fideicommissa*; for the share

belongs to the co-heir unencumbered. But in consequence of a rescript of Severus, according to which *fideicommissa* left charged on the appointed heir are due from his substitutes, a co-heir too, like a substitute, will get the accruing share with its encumbrance.

62   LICINNIUS RUFINUS, *Rules, book 4:* If the slave of another has been appointed heir, a *fideicommissum* can be left charged on his master. But the master will only be obliged to discharge it if he is made heir through his slave. If, however, the slave is manumitted, before the inheritance is accepted, at his master's direction, the master will not owe it, because he has not been made heir; nor will the slave, because he has not been asked. Therefore, in this case an effectual action will lie to compel the person to whom the profit of the inheritance shall have come to discharge the *fideicommissum*.

63   CALLISTRATUS, *Monitory Edict, book 4:* If the heir disposes of a thing, not knowing it to have been bequeathed, for the funeral expenses, he will not be liable to an action for its production, because he does not possess it and did not dispose of it with fraudulent intent. But the legatee may be furnished with an action on the fact, so that the heir may pay him an indemnity.

64   PAPINIAN, *Questions, book 15:* When it was put that in writing the terms of a *fideicommissum*, which was left to several persons under a condition, the mutual substitution of the fideicommissaries had been accidentally left out, but the testator expressed it in a second will when he substituted the same persons, the deified Emperors Marcus and Commodus ruled in a rescript that the intention of making mutual substitution appeared evident. For in the case of a *fideicommissum*, where in any case it is a question of intention expressed by request, inference may be admitted.

65   PAPINIAN, *Questions, book 16:* A legacy of *peculium* may be increased and diminished, if things began or ceased to belong to it afterward. The same is true of a staff of slaves, if a testator bequeaths an entire staff or a specific one, such as his city or country staff, and afterward changes the offices or duties of his slaves. The same applies when litter-bearers or footmen are bequeathed. 1. When a four-in-hand is bequeathed and a horse subsequently dies, some believe that the legacy is extinguished if it is the leading horse that has died. But if the loss is meanwhile made up, the four-in-hand will belong to the legatee. 2. Stichus, bequeathed to Titius, was to receive his freedom after Titius's death. Here the legacy is due on the acceptance of the inheritance, and his freedom after the death of Titius. The same applies if he was directed to be free when Titius was dying. 3. But if, when Titius was appointed part heir, a slave was bequeathed to him and directed to be free after his death, then whether or not Titius, after whose death freedom was given the slave, accepts the inheritance, the slave gets his freedom on Titius's death.

66   PAPINIAN, *Questions, book 17:* Maevius bequeathed a farm to me and Titius under a condition, but his heir bequeathed the same farm to me under the same condition.

Julian says it is to be feared that on fulfillment of the condition the same part may be due to me from both wills. But it will be a question of intention. For it appears incredible that the heir acted in this way so that the same part should be due twice to the same person; but it is probable that he was thinking of the other part. The imperial *constitutio* which holds that an article several times bequeathed to the same person should not burden the heir applies only to one will. A debtor in bequeathing what he owes does not always bequeath lawfully, but only when there is more [than the debt] in the legacy. For if the same is bequeathed under the same condition, what profit will there be in the legacy?   1. In the wills of two persons, Maevius's share of a farm was bequeathed to Titius. It was judged, not inelegantly, that when one heir had delivered Maevius's share of the farm, obligation under the other will was lifted, and that afterward if the share was alienated, the right of action once extinguished could not be revived.   2. But if what is bequeathed should be not Maevius's share but a share of the farm unconditionally, the earlier delivery does not prevent an action for the other bequest, and the other heir will be able to deliver even this same share if in some way it has become his. For several persons may have ownership of one farm as understood by law and without dividing it up physically.   3. The same view will not hold when one man is bequeathed in general terms by two wills. For he who is made the property of the legatee through delivery by the one heir, although he may later be alienated, cannot be delivered by the other heir. The same principle holds for a stipulation. For the bequest of a man, to put it briefly, implies individual men, and just as the bequest cannot be valid from the beginning if it consists of persons who belong to the legatee, so the delivery of someone whose ownership the legatee has subsequently acquired is void, even if he has ceased to be the master.   4. If the heir has buried a corpse in a bequeathed farm, a valuation must be made of the whole price of the farm as it would have been assessed before the burial. Hence, if the place of burial should be detached, it is reasonable that an action under the will should still lie for the alienated ground. 5. When a legatee had obtained from one of the heirs who had alone been burdened a judgment in a sum of money on account of a thing bequeathed, and afterward a codicil was opened leaving the same thing charged on all the heirs, I said he was not to claim ownership. For he who uses different legal methods does not bequeath the same thing more than once but expresses the same wish more than once.   6. If the usufruct of a bequeathed farm is another's, it is to be claimed from the heir all the same. For usufruct, even if lawful, does not consist of a part but implies the benefit of the thing. So when the farm has been left, actions will lie for the other payments that follow the bequest, for example, if the farm has been given by way of pledge or is in the possession of another. The same does not apply to other servitudes. But if my own thing is bequeathed to me, the legacy will be invalid for the reasons given.   7. Members of a municipality who have been appointed heirs may bequeath a property without the usufruct, because they can lose the usufruct by making no use of it.

67   PAPINIAN, *Questions, book 19:* On account of a *fideicommissum* left by him while dying the heir must choose one of a staff of slaves; to him whom he chooses he leaves ineffectively by his will what, after he has been chosen, he may sue for under another will. Is the bequest, therefore, invalid, as though it had been left to a creditor, or is the analogy with a creditor incorrect as long as the intention may be changed? If the choice is maintained, he indeed appears to have become a creditor. If it is changed, it is permissible to sue under neither will.   1. If a question of the Falcidian share arises, everything will be taken into consideration in the same way, even if the *fideicommissum* in the first will was left by name to the person subsequently chosen. For the exercise of a necessary choice is not a benefit conferred by personal liberality; for what can he be held to have conferred who was under an absolute obligation to give it up?   2. Certainly, when there should happen to be three of the family of the person who has left the *fideicommissum,* related in the same or unequal degree, it will be enough to have left it to one of them. For after the intention of the testator has been obeyed, the others fail.   3. But if one of the family has been appointed heir and the farm is left to a stranger, then the *fideicommissum* can be claimed under the will as if nobody from the family had been appointed heir. But he who is appointed heir is understood to be able by a defense of fraud to deduct his share from others claiming the *fideicommissum.* For the principle that admits others to the claim also implies an understood right to compensation.   4. If the testator appoints two of his family as heirs to unequal parts and bequeaths a legacy of, say, a fourth of the same farm to an outsider, the *fideicommissum* cannot be claimed as far as concerns the parts which they retain by right of inheritance, any more than if he had bequeathed the farm to another to take in advance. But in respect of the other part, which has been conferred on the outsider, the members of the family will claim portions, compensation in equal shares having been admitted on behalf of the heirs.   5. But if he left the farm to one of his family and charged on him as a *fideicommissum* that he should restore it to an outsider, the question arises whether this *fideicommissum* can be claimed. I have said it can be claimed only if the claim is for the price of the farm. But if the previous testator had left a *fideicommissum* in these terms, "I ask that you leave the farm to the person or persons of your choice from the family," there will be no difficulty. However, if his words were to this effect, "I request that the farm does not go out of the family," the heir's heir is understood to be burdened on account of the second *fideicommissum,* which is conferred on an outsider, while claims will be forthcoming from the others for the *fideicommissum* under the first will, after the death, that is to say, of the person chosen first.   6. Therefore, if when one [family member] is chosen, the *fideicommissum* is not to be conferred on an outsider, the *fideicommissum* will not be delivered to the chosen person other than with the furnishing of *cautiones* "that the farm, when he dies, if it is not validly left within the family, shall be restored [to all the family]."   7. "I ask that when you die you restore the farm to whichever freedman you wish." As far as these words are concerned, the choice will be his own, and nobody will be able to claim as long as another can be preferred. But if he dies before making a choice, all will claim. Thus, it will come about that what is given to one cannot, while several are living, be

claimed by one, but all may claim what is not given to all; and so in the end, one will be able to claim if he alone survives the heir's death.   8. If I bequeath your thing, thinking it to be mine, to Titius as a charge on you my appointed heir, there is no room for the opinion of Neratius Priscus or for the *constitutio* which provided that the heir should not be compelled to deliver the legacy. For relief is [in any case] provided for heirs, so that they should not be compelled to purchase what the testator, believing it to be his own, has left; for testators are much more inclined to bequeath their own things than to burden their heirs with the purchase of those of others; which does not arise in this kind of case, when the ownership of the thing is with the heir.   9. If words of a *fideicommissum* have been left out but the rest that is read agrees with what should have been written, then it is lawfully given and what is inadequately written is understood, following the example of institution of heirs and of legacies. This opinion has also been followed by our excellent Emperor Severus.   10. Again, the Emperor Marcus ruled in a rescript that the words in which a testator had provided "that he did not doubt that his wife would deliver to the children whatever she had taken" should be taken as a *fideicommissum.* This rescript is highly salutary to ensure that the honor of a well-conducted marriage, and confidence that children are held in common, does not deceive a husband who thought too highly of the mother. And, therefore, that most far-sighted and scrupulously law-observing emperor, when he observed that the words of a *fidei-commissum* were omitted, ruled that the language should be taken as establishing one.

68   PAUL, *Questions, book 11:* The next question is whether the things the testator conferred by gift to his wife in his lifetime can be included in a claim for a *fideicom-missum.* I replied that they should be computed separately from the goods of the deceased and are not included in the *fideicommissum* on the grounds that she should have them even if another had been appointed heir. But if he names them, the husband can certainly leave them as a *fideicommissum* charged on his wife for her to deliver them.

69   PAPINIAN, *Questions, book 19:* "I ask you, Lucius Titius, to be content with a hundred aurei." It is held that the *fideicommissum* is good, and there is a rescript to that effect. What, then, if he should have appointed a part heir and expressed himself as follows: "I ask you, Lucius Titius, for your part to be content with a hundred aurei?" The co-heirs will be able to sue for his part of the inheritance, while he will retain or take in advance the sum with which the deceased wished him to be content. It will undoubtedly be easier to adopt this opinion than it was to adopt the previous one where the *fideicommissum* is claimed by persons whom the testator had not addressed. We shall say the same when a testator has appointed an heir to the entire estate for the benefit of his future *legitimus heres* and addresses him in these terms: "I ask you that in place of the inheritance which I have left to you and which should go to my *legitimus heres*, you should be content with a hundred aurei."   1. Lands that have been left within the family may, in the event of the heir's goods being disposed of under a forced sale, be retained by the buyer for as long as the debtor would have had them if the goods had not been sold. After his death he will not retain what an outside heir would be compelled to give.   2. A mother, having appointed her son who was *im-pubes* as heir, named a tutor for him and charged on the tutor as a *fideicommissum* that if her son should die before the age of fourteen, he should restore the inheritance to Sempronius. The *fideicommissum* is not understood to have been any the less

rightly given because the mother could not formally appoint the tutor. For even if a father had charged a *fideicommissum* on a tutor in a will not rightly drawn up, it will be discharged just as if the will had been drawn up rightly. For it is enough for a *fideicommissum* to be held to be charged on an *impubes* that it should be charged on him whom the donor had appointed as tutor, or even him who the donor thought would be the tutor. The same must be held in the case of a curator of an *impubes* or a *minor*. It is immaterial whether the tutor rightly appointed dies, or is excused on account of some privilege, or cannot be tutor on account of age of the person to whom he had been appointed tutor. In these cases, the *fideicommissum* is certainly not annulled, because it is held to be charged on the *pupillus*. In accordance with this reason, it has furthermore been decided that a *fideicommissum* cannot be charged in favor of the *pupillus* on a tutor who has received nothing, because what is left charged on him in favor of an outsider is due from him not on his own account but in the name of the *pupillus*.   3. A testator appointed his brother as heir and asked that the house should not be alienated but remain in the family. If the heir does not obey his wish, but alienates the house or dies having appointed an outsider as heir, all members of the family will claim the *fideicommissum*. What if they are not of the same degree? The ruling should be that whoever is next of kin should be considered as invited in first place. However, the cause of those further removed should not be prejudiced for the future on account of those who came before them; but the next of kin in each case should be admitted on terms of providing a *cautio* that he will restore the house to the family. But if a *cautio* has not been demanded from him who was admitted in first place, no *condictio* will arise on this account; but if the house should at some time come into the hands of an outsider, a suit for the *fideicommissum* will lie in favor of the family. I think a *cautio* can rightly be required to forestall a defense of fraud, even though no further member of the family survives.   4. If certain members of the family are subsequently emancipated, it can be debated whether these too are entitled to claim the *fideicommissum*. I think they will be right to claim, because under the term "family" these persons too are understood to be indicated.

70   PAPINIAN, *Questions, book 20:* The Emperor Antoninus ruled in a rescript that a legatee, if he receives nothing from the legacy, may cede his rights of action to the person to whom he owes a *fideicommissum* and is not to be compelled to discharge it. What, then, if he has been asked to restore not all, but part of a legacy left to him, and abstains from it? Is he to be compelled to withdraw from all his rights of action or only to the extent of the sum contained in the *fideicommissum*? This last seems reasonable. If he does receive the legacy, he is not to be compelled to pay by reason of the *fideicommissum* more than he received.   1. If a hundred have been bequeathed and he is asked to restore double, his liability will be held to have been fixed as the sum of the bequest. But if the *fideicommissum* has been left for payment after a certain time, the addition of interest only will be allowed. This opinion will not be subject to change if it should happen that he made a great profit by some business upon receiving the legacy or escaped the imminent penalty due under a stipulation. It applies when sums [of money received] are compared with sums [to be dispensed]. But if after accepting money he is asked to restore a thing of [the testator's] own, even if it is of greater value, the legatee is not to be heard if he wishes to reckon it against the legacy received. For here equity does not allow approval of a legatee's offering [only] what he

has received as a legacy.   2. A certain man appointed his son as part heir, gave him his uncle as co-heir and asked the uncle to appoint the son as co-heir in equal shares to the uncle's own sons. If such an equal share proves less than what the uncle got from the inheritance of his brother, nothing more can be claimed. But if more, it has been decided that the fruits also, which the uncle collected or failed to collect, through bad faith, when he could have done so, must be taken into account, just as when, if a hundred have been left, the recipient is asked after a time to restore a greater sum. 3. But when someone is asked to restore what is left over from the inheritance after his death, and sells things and buys others with the proceeds, the inheritance is not held to have been diminished by the sale.

71   PAPINIAN, *Replies, book 8:* But what has been bought in this way will be restored instead of the property that has been exchanged for it.

72   PAPINIAN, *Questions, book 20:* The same principle is to be observed if he paid off his own creditors from that money. For what is retained in the whole estate is not spent.

73   PAPINIAN, *Questions, book 23:* If Pamphila's future offspring is bequeathed to me and I buy Pamphila and she gives birth while with me, it has been most reasonably decided that the offspring is not understood to have become mine for payment and, therefore, can be claimed under the will as though I had bought the offspring itself, so that I should obtain from the contribution of its price as much as a judge assigned in the case of a legacy would have estimated the boy to be worth after deducting the value of the mother [from the total paid].

74   PAPINIAN, *Questions, book 27:* "Let my heir give a hundred aurei to Titius immediately." Afterward he prolonged the time for payment of the legacy. Alfenus's statement that the hundred are due immediately is not true; for they [now] have their own time for payment.

75   PAPINIAN, *Replies, book 6:* A soldier wrote a letter to his sister with instructions that it should be opened after his death, to this effect: "I wish you to know that I am giving you eight hundred aurei." It is settled that the *fideicommissum* is due to the sister; nothing else could be held if these were the last wishes of anyone else. For it is settled that a *fideicommissum* still holds good if the deceased addresses directly the person whom he is proposing to remunerate by a request [to the heir]. 1. A person appointed as part heir to whom legacies were left to be taken in advance died while the legacies were not yet due, before accepting the inheritance. It was held that his share of the inheritance belonged to the substitute co-heirs, but that the portions of the legacies to be taken in advance with which the co-heirs had been charged would be transmitted to his own heirs.

76   PAPINIAN, *Replies, book 7:* When a son had brought actions for an undutiful will of his mother before separate tribunals and, therefore, there were various decisions

of the judges, it was agreed that the heir who had superseded the son would not obtain the legacies given to him to be taken in advance, as far as concerns the shares of which the son deprived the co-heirs, anymore than the other actions on the legacy. But it was held that the grants of freedom under the will were valid when the son had brought a case on the mother's will for his share. This rule is not to be extended to servitudes, which cannot be partly diminished. Plainly, the entire servitude will be claimed by the person who superseded the son, but the value of the son's share will be delivered; or if the son is prepared to surrender the servitude on receiving the price, the legatee will be barred by a defense of fraud if he does not offer the value of the share, following the example of the *lex Falcidia.*   1. "To Lucius Sempronius I bequeath all the inheritance of Publius Maevius." Sempronius, then, will take up those burdens which belonged to the Maevian inheritance and have continued with it to the day of the death of the person who has become Maevius's heir, just as conversely those actions will be assigned to him that can [still] be assigned.   2. The owner of a farm, having appointed as heir the person entitled to the usufruct, bequeathed the farm [to a third person] under a condition. The intention of the testator provides no reason why the heir should retain the profit from the usufruct. A different view has obtained in the case of other lands whose servitudes were held by the heir, because usufruct amounts to a share of the property.   3. "Let my heir give to Titius what is due to me under the will of Sempronius." Sempronius's legatee, now the testator, had effected a novation by virtue of which the legacy was not due under the will. It was held that the false description did not damage the legatee and that what was originally true should not be held as totally false.   4. A slave manumitted unconditionally, who cannot obtain his freedom after the inheritance is accepted on account of a legal obstruction, because his status is in suspense through outside circumstances such as, for instance, a court case of adultery, cannot hope for legacies or *fideicommissa* given absolutely under the same will, because the day of payment falls due without effect.   5. A father, having appointed his daughter heiress to half his estate, addressed her in his will as follows: "I ask you when you die, even if you have had other sons also, to give a larger share to my grandson Sempronius in honor of my name." The first necessity is held to be that of restoring equal shares to the [other] grandsons, but the assessment of the greater share that he wished to be conferred on the person of the one grandson is left to the daughter's choice.   6. A mother left a legacy to a tutor not legally appointed. If he consents to be confirmed by the praetor's decree, and the praetor does not consider him suitable, he will not be refused an action for the legacy.   7. A legatee who has given a Mucian *cautio* that he would not do something and afterward does it must also restore the fruits of the legacies, which must [therefore] be promised from the beginning.   8. The legatee cannot use different action for legacies at the same time because a legacy given cannot be divided into parts. It is not with this intention that the legatee is granted the right of making use of several actions, but to give him greater scope for pleading so that he may claim a legacy by means of the one among them that he chooses. 9. Power is given to recover legacies paid under a will that has been found to be void subsequent to the deceased suffering *damnatio memoriae*, provided that an accusation of *perduellio* was brought after the legacies had been paid.

77   PAPINIAN, *Replies, book 8:* A father appointed his sons as heirs and wrote as follows: "I ask you, my daughter, that, having accepted from my inheritance as your portion a hundred aurei and my Tusculan lands, you restore to your mother your share of the inheritance." I replied that the daughter would have the hereditary lands, by the judgment of division, as from the common inheritance, but have the money as her own share.   1. Those to whom a gift has been made *mortis causa* can be charged with a *fideicommissum* for any length of time. The heirs shall deliver this *fideicommissum* while deducting the Falcidian fourth, which it is settled applies to these donations too, after the model of legacies. If a part of the gift is burdened with a *fideicommissum*, the *fideicommissum* shall also be subject to the Falcidian deduction. If, however, he wished maintenance to be provided, it must be held that the whole burden of the deduction will fall on the residue left after the gift according to the intention of the deceased, who undoubtedly wished that it should be provided intact out of the greater sum of money.   2. A mother allowed a stipulation to be made for her dowry as a gift *mortis causa* to her children born out of wedlock. She then appointed other heirs and asked her children that her dowry should be restored to her husband. The whole *fideicommissum* of the dowry is due to the husband, if a Falcidian deduction has not come into effect. Therefore, it was held that the husband could retain the dowry. Otherwise, the Falcidian fourth would have to be restored from the dowry to the heirs by the children through an *actio in factum* against the husband under the stipulation.   3. A deaf-mute who receives a legacy can rightly be directed to restore it after his death. For *fideicommissa* are even binding on persons charged without their knowledge, if they have profited under a will without their knowledge.   4. A son was asked to restore his inheritance after his death to his sons or to the one son whom he wished. Meanwhile, he was deported to an island. It was held that his power to choose had not been extinguished by the penalty and that the condition of the *fideicommissum* would not be fulfilled before the death of the son and heir. But restoration [to all the sons] would have to be in equal shares to those living at the time [of deportation], since he had no power of choosing from others.   5. A man who sold a landed estate belonging to the dowry, contrary to the *lex Julia*, gave a legacy to his wife and left a *fideicommissum* charged on the purchaser that he should in addition restore the price to her. It was agreed that the purchaser was not bound by the *fideicommissum*; but if the woman by accepting the legacy annulled the sale, it was held that after being offered the price she could be barred by a defense of fraud.   6. A creditor instructed his debtor Maevius to pay the money he owed him to Titius to whom he was making a gift *mortis causa*. If Maevius, knowing that the owner was dead, then paid the money, it is settled that he did not free himself. Nor is an action for the entire amount, or under the *lex Falcidia*, to be granted against Titius, because he is not held to have taken *mortis causa*. The case would be different if Maevius had been unaware that the owner had died and had paid the money in error, for then a portion would be reclaimed under the *lex Falcidia*.   7. A father owed his daughter a *fideicommissum* of lands under the will of her mother. He appointed her as his part-heiress so that he might compensate her for the *fideicommissum* with an inheritance and wished to give the lands in question to his disinherited son. It was held that even if the daughter did not wish to accept the father's inheritance, the heirs to whom the portion of the inheritance intended for the daughter fell must deliver the *fideicommissum* to the son. If he substituted another person for his daughter, that person must deliver the *fideicommissum* to the son.   8. If a son is evicted from lands which his father, believing himself to be the owner, had left to him by the terms of a *fideicommissum*, he will have no right of action against his brothers and co-heirs. If, however, the father made a

division among the sons, the arbitrator on presumption of the father's intention will not allow him to restore to the co-heir the part bequeathed to be taken in advance, unless they too are prepared to see that their father's intention is carried out in favor of their brother.   9. A father left a certain sum of money to his disinherited daughter under the terms of a *fideicommissum* and wished it to be given to her for dowry when she married, the son stipulating for the dowry. When the son gave a smaller dowry, it was agreed that he should pay the balance to the daughter. If a divorce should follow, the daughter will be right to claim the *fideicommissum*, so that an action on the stipulation should be furnished her, because it was improbable that the father should have wished the stipulation to result in her becoming undowered after her first marriage. But if she should marry again, the *cautio* should not be extended to the second marriage.   10. A father asked his daughter that she should restore lands when she died to whichever of her children she chose. She donated the lands while living to one of her children. It was held that this was no choice, because the date of the donation was certain but that of the *fideicommissum* was uncertain. For the choice can only be made of a person who is to have the *fideicommissum* among others if the mother's right of choice was not applicable.   11. "I charge as a *fideicommissum* on my heirs that they should not alienate the Tusculan farm and that it should not pass out of the family to those not of my name." According to his intention it is to be understood that the invitation extends to those to whom the heirs outside the family have given freedom under *fideicommissa*.   12. "I charge you, my wife, with the *fideicommissum* of restoring to my daughter, when you die, whatever of my goods have come into your hands in whatever way." Even those things which he gave to his wife afterward by codicil shall be included in the *fideicommissum*. For the order in which the writings were made does not stand in the way of right and intention. But a dowry bequeathed to be taken in advance will be retained, because it is held to be restored rather than given.   13. "I wish that lands be given to my freedmen. If one of them dies without issue, I wish his share to belong to the rest." It was held that the substitution intended by the testator excludes a father's fellow freedman who is himself a son.   14. A *fideicommissum* charged by someone on his curator that he should give an account of business conducted to the brother and heir was held to be void. Although it had been provided in the will that when the brother eventually came of age he should receive payment, it was nevertheless held that the brother acting under another curator could rightly bring an action, since by these words the testator was considered to be rather taking thought for his brother than delaying payment that could rightly be made. 15. A testator charged an heir appointed outside the family with the *fideicommissum* of leaving lands on his death to freedmen and asked that they should not be alienated from the family bearing his name. I replied that the substitute owed them according to the intention of the deceased, but whether at once or under the same condition depended on his intention. But by inference of the intention of the testator, the death of the appointed heir was to be awaited first.   16. Where the business of a bank has been taken up on account of a *fideicommissum* and the heirs indemnified by a *cautio*, this is held to resemble a purchase, and no inquiry is therefore to be made whether the debts are greater than the assets.   17. A father wished that the slaves whom he gave his daughter on her marriage should be delivered to her under the terms of a *fideicommissum*. I replied that the offspring, even though the mothers should have died before the will, were to be delivered under the *fideicommissum*. The same observation has been made earlier in the case of donations confirmed to a wife.   18. Those asked to restore an inheritance on their death are not liable to the risk of losing what they have obtained by division between co-heirs when directions have been interposed that debtors should pay third parties, any more than they are liable to lose lands when exchange of property has divided what was owned in common. 19. "I wish my daughter to take in advance and have for herself the property of her mother." The fruits, which the father shall have gathered in the meantime and not kept separate, but has consumed or invested within his own patrimony, are not held to have been left to the daughter. 20. "To my dearest brothers, your uncles, I wish that whatever is left to me in Pamphylia or Lycia or elsewhere of my mother's property shall be given, so that you may have no controversy with them." All corporeal things belonging to the mother's inheritance that have remained in the same condition of ownership are meant to be included in this *fideicommissum*. Money that has been collected from this property and invested within his own patrimony, and similarly things that have been appropriated by right of division, shall not be delivered, since he intended to appease the discord of relatives which property owned in common usually excites. 21. A father, having appointed several children as heirs, at his death handed his keys and signet ring to his eldest daughter for safe keeping, and ordered a freedman who was present to assign to her the things he had under his care. It was understood that this measure was taken for all the children in common and that on this account the daughter was not to have any preference before the arbitrator for division. 22. When a clause is found incomplete, the wording of a legacy or *fideicommissum* that precedes or follows it can be brought to bear, if what is written fits the clause. 23. A son appointed his mother as heiress, and in his will asked her to bind herself by a solemn oath to deliver the *fideicommissum*. The will was found to be legally invalid, but I replied that the mother as *legitima heres*, nevertheless, should be compelled to deliver the *fideicommissa*. For urgent expressions of a wish were held to apply to every sort of succession. 24. "I direct my daughter, out of concern for her safety, not to make a will until she bears children; for in this way she will be able to live without danger." It was apparent that a fideicommissary inheritance could not be held to have been left to her sister and co-heiress, because the testator wished not to make a testamentary disposition of his money, but by offering advice to derogate from her rights by forbidding her to make a will. 25. "I ask you, my daughter, in due course to distribute all your goods among your children, according to how each has deserved of you." It appears that a *fideicommissum* has been left to all the children, even if they have not deserved equally. In the absence of a choice by the mother, it will be enough if they have given no offense. If the mother chose some, I held that these would have preference, assuming that they alone had deserved especially well. But if she chose nobody, only those who have given offense are not to be admitted. 26. A mother deposited in a temple without the knowledge of her son a letter giving lands, but not in terms of a *fideicommissum*; and she wrote a letter to the temple warden to this effect: "I wish this instrument of my wishes to be handed over to my son on my death." When she died intestate, leaving several heirs, I replied that it was to be understood that a *fideicommissum* had been left to her son; for it is proper to ask not whom someone addressed about his last wishes, but toward whom the intention of his wishes was directed. 27. A man left a landed estate to his freedmen and asked that they should not alienate it, but keep it in the family of freedmen. If, with the exception of one, the others sell their portions, then he who did not sell will be able to claim the entire portions of the rest to whom the testator gave no freedom of alienation. For it is held that he invited those to the *fideicommissum* who obeyed his wishes. Otherwise, it would be absurd if each could in turn file a claim against the other, so that one man could claim the portion of another, when he has himself lost his own portion by alienating it. But this procedure only applies if they have alienated their portions at the same time. Insofar as one has alienated earlier, he will have no share in the rights of those who do so later; but he who has sold later is understood to be liable to the one who has not sold at all for the portions of the earlier sellers. But if no one has sold and the last dies without issue, no claim for the *fideicommissum* will be outstanding. 28. When among freedmen a freedwoman also has been admitted to the legacy of a landed estate, despite the request of the patron that the estate should not go out of the family bearing his name, it was held that the son and heir of the freedwoman should retain the part of the estate which his mother had accepted. 29. A person who thought his property would go to his cousin, and to her alone, made a codicil and left several *fideicommissa* charged on her. His possessions descended by right of succession to two cousins of the same degree. For reasons of equity and following the example of the Perpetual Edict, I replied that the woman should be relieved of half the *fideicommissa*, but that the grants of freedom should all be executed, because it seemed hard that they should lapse on account of her loss. 30. A father who had appointed his son heir to half his estate and his daughters, being *impuberes*, to a fourth each, gave their brother to them as tutor and addressed him as follows: "You, my son, will be content for your half with two hundred aurei, and you, my daughters, for your fourths with a hundred aurei each." He was held not to have imposed *fideicommissa* on his children in favor of one another, but to have made a valuation of his patrimony, as thrifty parents commonly do. For this reason the brother will not, in an action for tutelage, be able to rule out his giving an account of his good faith on the grounds that the exact sum to be given had at some time been prescribed. 31. Maevius was appointed heir by Seius and asked by him to restore after his death the inheritance of Seius to Maevius's brother Titius. He appointed the same Titius as heir and asked Titius on his death to restore his and Seius's inheritance to Sempronius. In the meantime, Titius collected the sum due from the fruits of the *fideicommissum*. I replied that the *fideicommissum* could not be deducted as a debt, because Titius was held to have collected what was due to him by reason of compensation. Plainly, if Maevius were to appoint Titius heir on condition that he was not to retain the *fideicommissum* under the will of Seius, the Falcidian share would be enough for compensation, and to make up for any inequity. But Titius would do better to repudiate the inheritance under his brother's will and to accept possession on grounds of intestacy. He would not be held to have acted fraudulently, but to have excluded fraud. 32. "I ask you, my husband, if you have any children, to leave lands to them, or if you have none, to your or my relatives or even to our freedmen." I replied that no choice had been given here, but that the writing had set out the order of substitution.   33. A *civitas* had villages with their own territories left to it. It was held that they would be no less due under the *fideicommissum* because the testator had promised that he would define their boundaries and would set out in another writing the plan of a contest which he wishes to be celebrated each year, but then did not do so because he was forestalled by death.

78   PAPINIAN, *Replies, book 9:* If someone should have been unsuccessfully claiming an entire *fideicommissum*, while the heir was adducing the *lex Falcidia* as an objection and, in the meantime, requests that a part should be paid him and does not receive it, he is understood on this account to be the victim of delay.   1. Our best and greatest Emperor Severus Augustus ordered that a sale of public property should be rescinded after the death of the buyer and the price restored to his heirs. In the matter of the money due to the legatee to whom the buyer had made a legacy of part of the public land possessed in this way, I replied that following the conjectured intention of the testator, the appropriate part of the value should be paid.   2. A *res publica* too must pay interest on a *fideicommissum* after delay, but any loss that so ensues will have to be made good by those who, after judgment has been given, neglect to pay what has been adjudged. The same applies to the costs of litigation if there was no reason for it. Incompetence is no excuse and deserves no hearing. The same holds good for tutors. 3. A father forbade lands to be alienated from the family under the terms of a *fideicommissum*. The last of his children who could claim the *fideicommissum* is held to have left no less right to action in his estate because he died without issue leaving an outsider as heir.   4. If a creditor receives a house by right of pledge from a testator and sells it, no judgment can be given against him on the grounds of a *fideicommissum*, even if he was not unaware of the intention of the deceased.

79   PAPINIAN, *Replies, book 11:* A widow, who owed lands left as *fideicommissa* to her husband's freedmen on her death, left the fruits of these lands to her own freedmen also. Her husband's freedmen, who should have claimed the lands under the husband's will but were unaware of their rights, for a long time collected the fruits among the other freedmen. It is settled that they should not on this account be held deprived of their claim to the first *fideicommissum*.

80   PAPINIAN, *Definitions, book 1:* A legacy confers ownership of a bequeathed thing on the legatee, just as inheritance does of individual things on the heir. This means that if a thing is left unconditionally and the legatee has not repudiated the wish of the deceased, its ownership, which was in the inheritance, passes directly to the legatee and never becomes the heir's.

81   PAUL, *Questions, book 9:* If anyone makes a will and leaves *fideicommissa* charged on his sons, whom he has appointed as heirs on the assumption that these are

appointed heirs and not *legitimi heredes*, and the will for some reason becomes void, the sons who obtain the estate on grounds of intestacy cannot be compelled to deliver the *fideicommissa*.

82   PAUL, *Questions, book 10:* A debtor bequeathed to his creditor ten which he owed him in a year's time against a pledge. It is not, as some think, only the interest in the meantime that is due under the will, but the ten can be claimed in their entirety. Nor is the claim barred if a year has elapsed; for it is enough that the effective day of payment has arrived. But if a year goes by in the lifetime of the testator, it must be said that the legacy is rendered ineffective, although it was valid originally. In the case of the legacy of a dowry, to be taken in advance, it has also been replied that the whole can be claimed under the will. Otherwise, if we follow the opinion that only the intermediary interest is included in the legacy, what shall we say if a farm is bequeathed that is due on a certain day? For neither can money be claimed that was not bequeathed, nor would a part of the farm easily be found that could be claimed in lieu of the profit.   1. If Primus, Secundus, and Tertius are appointed as heirs and legacies are given as follows, "if Primus will not be my heir, let Secundus give ten to Titius; if Secundus will not be my heir, let Primus give to Seius the Tusculan farm," then in the event of both Primus and Secundus letting the inheritance go, will the substitutes he gave them be obliged to deliver legacies and to whom? The legacies will be due from both substitutes.   2. Valens wrote that a legacy could be made to another man's slave of his master's thing and also of what is owed unconditionally to his master. For when we give the slave of another something in a will, the person of the master is considered only in respect of whether he is entitled to take under a will, and for the rest the legacy holds good for the person of the slave. And, therefore, Julian very rightly defines what can be bequeathed to the slave of another as that which the same slave could take if he were freed. For the observation that a legacy can also be made to a slave for as long as he remains a slave is most misleading, because this legacy too derives its force from the person of the slave. Otherwise, we could note that there are certain slaves who, though they cannot obtain their freedom, may nevertheless acquire a legacy and inheritance for their master. From this precept, therefore, namely that, as we have said, it is the person of the slave that is considered in wills, it has been ruled that a legacy can be made to a hereditary slave. Therefore, it is no wonder that the master's property and what is due to him unconditionally can be bequeathed to a slave, although they could not be effectually bequeathed to his master.

83   PAUL, *Questions, book 11:* Latinus Largus: Recently, the following case occurred. A freedman appointed his patron heir to half his estate and his own daughter as heiress to the other half. He charged his daughter with the *fideicommissum* of making restoration to certain female slaves of his patron on their manumission, and in case his daughter should not become heiress he substituted these female servants for her. Because the daughter did not wish to accept the inheritance, the female servants at the direction of their master, that is, the patron, accepted the inheritance of the deceased. After some time, they were manumitted by him and inquired if they could claim the *fideicommissum* from their patron. Therefore, I ask you to write to me what you

think of this. I replied that the *fideicommissum* did not seem to have been repeated in this case, but one or the other had been given, either the *fideicommissum* or the inheritance itself. But it would be better to say that they were made substitutes for the same eventuality under which they would have been entitled to the *fideicommissum*, and were therefore called to the substitution. For when a *fideicommissum* is charged on one of the heirs in favor of the slave of another, on condition of his freedom, and this same slave is substituted for that heir, even if the substitution is unconditional, he is held to have been substituted on the same condition under which he was entitled to the *fideicommissum*.

84   PAUL, *Questions, book 21:* When someone has left a grant of freedom to his slave by means of a *fideicommissum* and added something else, there are people who say that because the testator wished that the slave should be manumitted by the heir, it should follow that he will not be admitted to the *fideicommissum*. But this is unjust. For with a person of this kind somehow the [same] day falls due for claiming both his freedom and the money, so that I think that if there is delay in giving him his freedom, a delay is also held to have occurred in delivering the *fideicommissum* and a burden of interest accrues. For a reply has besides been very rightly given that what the master has acquired in the meantime, while delaying his grant of freedom, ought to be restored to him.

85   PAUL, *Replies, book 4:* A creditor to whom a thing pawned by way of pledge has been bequeathed is not prevented from claiming the money he has lent, if an intention of the testator to compensate him has not been evidently shown.

86   PAUL, *Replies, book 13:* "Let Gaius Seius my great-grandson be heir to half my property with the exception of my house and my father's in which I live, with all that is in them, all of which you should know does not belong to the share of the inheritance which I have given you." My question is whether, since in these houses there are debt claims, silver, furniture, and slaves, all those things that are found there should belong to the other appointed heirs. Paulus replied that debt claims are not included, but are common to all, whereas the great-grandson is not entitled to the rest. 1. Titius, when he left to his brother's son farms and city property, included in these a legacy of the Seian farm which the head of the household himself in his lifetime had had entirely under one name. But so as to find a tenant more easily, he let it out in two parts, calling, from the nature of the ground, the higher part the Upper Seian and the lower part of the Lower Seian. Should the whole of this farm belong to his brother's son? Paul replied that if the testator had possessed the entire Seian farm under one name, although he had let it out in separate parts, the whole should be delivered by virtue of the *fideicommissum*, unless the heir could bring clear proof of what part the testator had in mind.

87   PAUL, *Replies, book 14:* Titia wished a ticket for the corn dole to be bought for Seius thirty days after her death. Since Seius in the lifetime of the testatrix had acquired for

payment a ticket for the corn dole and may not claim what he already has, does an action lie in his favor? Paulus replied that the price of the ticket should be paid to the person in question, because a *fideicommissum* of this kind consists more of a sum of money than of a tangible object. 1. I replied that the interest on a *fideicommissum* was due to a girl over twenty-five years old from the time that delay had been caused. For although it is settled that interest must in any event be paid to girls younger than twenty-five years, this is not, however, to be taken to be on account of delay which need only have set in once for interest to be due continuously. 2. Seia bequeathed a farm to her freedmen and charged them with the following *fideicommissum*: "I commit to your trust, Verus and Sapidus, that you do not sell this farm and that the one of you who dies last should at his death restore it to my freedmen Symphorus and Successor and Beryllus, whom I have manumitted below, or to those of them who shall still be living then." My question is: As she did not substitute them in the first part of her will in which she made the bequest of the farm to be taken in advance, but added in the second part the words "who dies last" should the portion of the one who dies first belong to the other? Paul replied that the testatrix appeared to have established two degrees of succession in the *fideicommissum* in question: one, that the first of the two to die should restore to the other; the other, that the last to die should restore to those whom she later listed by name. 3. The Emperor Alexander Augustus to Claudianus Julius, urban prefect: "If you are satisfied, my dearest Julianus, that the grandmother has exhausted her patrimony by making grants to her grandson with a view to frustrating a charge of undutifulness, reason demands that half of what has been donated should be revoked." 4. Lucius Titius had five sons. He emancipated them all and endowed one son, Gaius Seius, with ample means through donations. He reserved a moderate residue for himself and appointed all his children heirs with his wife. In the same will, he gave a legacy to be taken in advance to the said Gaius Seius of two possessions which he had retained and asked him that from the revenues of the lands which he had given him in his lifetime he should give so many aurei to Lucius's daughter Maevia and another sum of so many to another brother. Sued by his sister Maevia, Gaius Seius invoked the *lex Falcidia*. My question: Since our most sacred emperor, as has been written above, ruled that against the intention of the donor grants should be revoked, should Gaius Seius be compelled to deliver the *fideicommissum* to the heiress his sister in accordance with his father's intention? Paul replied that following the letter of our emperor there should be no doubt that in the case in question assistance should also be rendered to the children whose share has been diminished on account of donations made to one son, especially since our emperor came to their help against the intention of the father, but in the case as put the intention of the father has intervened in favor of those claiming the *fideicommissum*. Thus, even though the *lex Falcidia* should be applicable, the *fideicommissa* are to be paid entire on account of the immoderate extent of the donations.

88 SCAEVOLA, *Replies, book 3:* Lucius Titius provided in his will as follows: "What I have given to any of my children or presented or ceded for their use and what anyone has acquired for himself or has been given him or left him by someone let him take in

advance, have, and hold." He had kept an account book of debts in his son's name. Afterward a judgment was given and it was held that what under the name of the son himself had remained in the debt book was due to him, but not also what had been exacted and had been converted to the father's own account. Question: Should what the father had exacted under the son's name before the will was made and had then after the will was made invested in his son's name again belong to the son according to the judgment? I replied that what had belonged to this class of exactions and had returned to the same class would be due.   1. "I ask you, Titius, and charge on you as a *fideicommissum* that you should take the responsibility for my burial, and for this you shall take in advance so many aurei from my estate." Question: If Lucius Titius spends less than the ten *aurei*, will the remaining sum go to the heirs? I replied that upon the case as put they would go to benefit the heirs.   2. A woman who had become heiress to her husband provided in her will as follows: "Maevius and Sempronius, my dearest sons, you are to take in advance everything that has come into my hands of the inheritance and goods of Titius, my lord and your father, at the time of his death, but on condition that you acknowledge the burden of this inheritance with respect to both past and future, not excepting anything imposed subsequently to the death of my lord Titius." Question: If she had paid off anything after her husband's death, after taking and selling the fruits, would it still belong to the burden? I replied that upon the case as put, she had imposed on the legatees only those burdens that still remained. 3. "To whoever shall become my heir or heirs: Lucius Eutychus, in addition to being appointed my heir, is to take from the inheritance and have for himself with Pamphilus, whom I direct to be free, the equipment of my blacksmith's shop, so that you may carry on the business." Lucius Euthychus died in the lifetime of the testatrix, and his share of the inheritance passed to his co-heir. Question: May Pamphilus who was manumitted by this will be admitted to claim part of the equipment, even if he cannot carry on the shop as the testatrix wished? I replied that he may.   4. Sempronia, the substitute of an appointed heir, was to receive legacies in the event of not becoming heiress. She brought an action against the instituted heir, saying it was on account of his bad faith that the testatrix, who had in the first place wished to appoint her heiress, had changed her will. She lost her case. Question: Is her right to sue for the legacy intact? I replied that upon the case as put it was.   5. A testator forbade that the legacies should be claimed and delivered before five years, but the heir of his own accord paid some before the five years had expired. It was asked whether he could take into account the profit of what he had paid before the date prescribed, when paying the rest of the legacy? I replied that nothing less had been left for due payment because something had been paid before the prescribed date.   6. Lucius Titius provided as follows in his will: "I wish my small holding to be given to my freedmen and freedwomen and to those I have manumitted by this will and to Seia, my foster daughter, so that it shall not pass to anyone not bearing the family name, until the property comes into the hands of one person." Question: Does Seia have a share in common with the freedmen, or can she vindicate for herself half of the small holding? I replied that it was clearly the intention of the testator to call all to equal shares.   7. A testator appointed his *impubes* son as heir. He bequeathed to his wife her dowry to be taken in advance and also her jewelery, slaves, and ten aurei; and in the event of the death of the *impubes*, he substituted heirs on whom he charged a legacy as follows: "Everything I have given in my first will, I wish to be given twice over by the heirs of my heir." Question: Is the dowry due a second time from the substitute when the *impubes* has died? I replied that the testator did not appear to have meant to double the legacy of the dowry. A further question: If tangible objects are bequeathed that are already possessed for value, can they be claimed from the substitutes? I replied that they cannot.   8. "To my fellow citizens I give and bequeath the note-of-hand of Gaius Seius." Subsequently, he forbade exaction to be made from Seius, and he asked his heirs that he should give to the *res publica* from the debt of another debtor whom he named in a codicil. Question: If the last-named debtor should be unable to pay, should the heirs deliver the entire sum? I replied that the heirs should deliver to the *res publica* their right of action against only that debtor who had, upon the case as put, been designated by the latest codicil.   9. A testator appointed his daughter heiress to his entire estate, substituted his grandson for her, and provided as follows: "If, which I pray may not happen, neither my daughter nor my grandson shall be my heirs, I wish my half of such a farm to belong to my freedmen." Question: When the daughter and grandson have predeceased the testator, and his property has passed to his great-grandson by reason of intestacy, will the *fideicommissum* belong to the freedmen? I replied that upon the case as put, if no heir has been appointed and substituted other than the daughter and grandson, the delivery of the share should be held charged as a *fideicommissum* on the *legitimi heredes*.   10. "Whoever shall be my heir, let me know that I owe Demetrius my uncle three denaria and that Seleucus my uncle has deposited with me three denaria, which I direct to be immediately handed over and paid to them." Question: If they were not owed, would there be an action? I replied that if they were not owed, there would be no action on the debt, but there would be on the *fideicommissum*.   11. Lucius Titius dismissed Dama and Pamphilus his freedmen from his house two years before his death and stopped providing them with their board which he had been giving. Soon after he made his will and left a bequest as follows: "Whoever shall be my heir is to give a certain sum of money for their maintenance each month to all my freedmen whom I have manumitted in this will, to those which I have had earlier and to those whom I have asked to be manumitted." Question: Should the *fideicommissum* be due to Dama and Pamphilus? I replied that upon the case as put it was due, provided that the claimants could clearly show that the patron, when he made his will, had begun to be of such a mind about them as to wish that the legacy should be given to them also. Otherwise, nothing shall be provided for them.   12. To Dama and Pamphilus whom the testator had manumitted by will he gave a farm on condition that they restored it to their daughters after their death. In the same will, he asked his heirs to manumit Pamphila, who was the natural daughter of Pamphilus. This same Pamphilus had, after the day the legacy fell due, appointed by will Maevius as his heir and had charged on him as a *fideicommissum* that he should restore to Pamphila his daughter, as soon as she became free, his inheritance, that is, half of the above-written farm, which was the only part of his property that he had from the will of his patroness. Question: Can Pamphila, once manumitted, claim this share under the first will, that of the patroness of her father, or under the will of her natural father on the grounds of the *fideicommissum* with due regard to the *lex Falcidia?* I replied that on the facts as put it should be held that Pamphila could only claim the *fideicommissum* under the first will, CLAUDIUS: because it is believed that the term sons includes natural sons also, that is, those born in slavery.   13. SCAEVOLA: A testator in a codicil left a legacy of a hundred to Gaius Seius and charged on him as a *fideicommissum* that he should give them to a female servant of the testator. Question: Is a *fideicommissum* which the legatee has been directed to give to a female slave of the testator valid? I replied that it was not. Second, if it is not valid, is the legatee to be compelled to restore it to the heir to whom the female servant belongs? I replied that he is not compelled, but the legatee himself cannot claim the legacy.   14. A testator bequeathed a tenement building to his freedmen of both sexes on condition that from its revenues the males should receive doubly and the females singly and forbade its alienation. With the consent of all it was sold by the heir. Question: Should the males take doubly and the females singly from the price? I replied that there was no right to sue for the *fideicommissum* with respect to the price, unless they consented to the sale with the intention that the males should similarly receive doubly and the females singly from the price.   15. A testator, having appointed his son as heir and emancipated his son's children, provided as follows: "And I wish my houses not to be sold or mortgaged by my heirs, but to remain unencumbered for them and their children and descendants forever. But if anyone of them should wish to sell his share and take up a mortgage on it, let him be empowered to sell it or mortgage it to his co-heir. If anyone contravenes these terms, let his transaction be ineffectual and void." Question: Since a son of the deceased borrowed money from Flavia Dionysia and made over to her as creditor his share of the income from the house that had been let, should the condition of the will be held to have been fulfilled, so that he should be held responsible to his sons under the terms of the *fideicommissum?* I replied that upon the case as put it had not been fulfilled.   16. A testator appointed his mother and wife as heirs and provided as follows: "I ask you, my dearest wife, that you should not leave anything after your death to your brothers. You have sons of your sisters to whom you may leave property. You know that one of your brothers killed our son while robbing him; and another, too, has done me injury." Question: Now that the wife has died intestate and her inheritance belongs to the brother as *legitimus heres,* can the sister's sons claim the *fideicommissum* from him? I replied that it could be argued that the *fideicommissum* is due.   17. "I, Lucius Titius, have written this my will without the aid of anyone learned in the law, following the promptings of my own heart rather than excessive and small-minded pedantry. And if I have done anything that falls short of legal or learned form, the wishes of a sane man should be taken as valid in law." Thereupon he appointed heirs. It was asked, when a claim was made for *bonorum possessio* on the grounds of his intestacy, whether the parts assigned to *fideicommissa* could be claimed? I replied that upon the case as put they could.

89   SCAEVOLA, *Replies, book 4:* A man appointed his son and wife heirs in his will. Afterward he is said to have written a letter in which he donated to his son whatever he had by way of *peculium* and added that he wished him to take it in advance when attaining independence after his father's death. Question: As he indicated in his will that if he left anything sealed it should be valid in lieu of a codicil, but this letter was not sealed, should what was in the letter belong to the son? I replied that if the letter that had been left was agreed to be genuine, then what he indicated in it that he wished to give should be due.   1. A man had property jointly with his brother. He appointed his daughters as heiresses and provided as follows: "With respect to the property that I have in common with my brother such a one, your uncle, all of which is agreed to be worth two thousand aurei, I charge you with the *fideicommissum* of accepting as your share one thousand aurei from Lucretius Pacatus your uncle." He survived this will for five years, and left the patrimony much increased. It was asked whether the heirs of Lucretius Pacatus would be carrying out the *fideicommissum* by offering a thousand aurei. I replied that upon the case as put it was not the intention of the testator that the whole should be restored for these thousand aurei, but that an offer of the value of the property at the time of the testator's death should be made.   2. To Seius, whom he had substituted for the heir, someone made the following legacy: "To Seius, if he shall not become my heir, and to his wife Marcella I wish fifteen pounds of silver to be given." Question: Seius has become heir, so should half the legacy be due to Marcella? I replied that on the facts as put it should.   3. Lucius Titius before dying intestate inserted these words into a codicil: "This codicil applies to my wife and daughter. First, I ask that you should so arrange matters between you as you did when I was alive, and, therefore, I ask that whatever I leave or you have yourselves be held by you in common." The daughter received *bonorum possessio* from her father's intestacy. Question: Is some part of the inheritance of Lucius Titius due from the daughter to the mother under the *fideicommissum*, and, if so, how much? I replied that on the facts as put half is due, provided that the wife is prepared to bring her own goods into common ownership.   4. Someone appointed four sons as heirs to equal shares, and bequeathed a farm, to be taken in advance, to each of them. The sons, since all the property of their father was encumbered, borrowed money and paid the creditor of the inheritance and mortgaged the property to the second creditor, who

when his debt was not paid sold all the lands by right of pledge to one of the heirs. Question: Since the son in question possesses them by right of purchase, do his brothers and co-heirs have a claim on the *fideicommissum*, or was the claim extinguished when the lands were all jointly mortgaged to the second creditor? I replied that an action on the *fideicommissum* still lay open to all of them in turn against the relevant person, but that the *fideicommissum* could not be restored unless the earlier debt was paid by them to the purchaser and co-heir.   5. Someone charged a *fideicommissum* on his daughter in these words: "I ask you, my daughter, to change the *cautio* for your dowry after my death, and so to renew it that your brothers may stipulate for the dowry on condition that if you should die while married without one or more children, the dowry may come to them." After the death of her father, her husband died before the *cautio* for the dowry had been renewed, and afterward she married another and died, leaving no children, while one of her brothers, Titius, was still living. The question was whether Titius had a right to claim the dowry property. I replied that the *fideicommissum* could be claimed by the sister's heirs, if it was her fault that her brother had not stipulated for the dowry.   6. Someone appointed his son and daughter heirs and gave legacies to his freedmen, charging a *fideicommissum* on them in these words: "I ask you that you should be content in your lifetime with what I have bequeathed to you, so as to restore it after you to my children." The testator's daughter Maevia died, and then a freedman died having appointed his patroness's son as heir to the usual patron's share and an outsider to the rest. The question was whether, on accepting the inheritance, the patroness's son can claim from his co-heir the part of what under his mother's will had gone to the freedman Maevius. I replied that the part of what was due to him, if he did not accept the inheritance, could be claimed from the co-heir.   7. A husband appointed his wife heiress to his whole estate and made a codicil which he directed to be opened after her death. The wife sold a piece of land, belonging to the inheritance, which she thought was useless for her purposes. The purchaser asked whether this sale could be revoked after the death of the woman by those to whom the inheritance had been found to be left under a *fideicommissum* by the codicil or if only the sum paid would be due to the beneficiaries of the *fideicommissum* from the wife's heir. I replied that on account of the excusable ignorance of both the woman and the purchaser, he should give the price of the farm to the beneficiary of the *fideicommissum*, so that the farm may remain with the purchaser.

BOOK THIRTY-TWO

1

LEGACIES AND *FIDEICOMMISSA*

1 ULPIAN, *Fideicommissa, book 1:* If someone is uncertain whether he is a prisoner of war or held by robbers or is ignorant of his status in law and mistakenly believes that because he has been captured by robbers he is their slave as if they were the enemy, or if he is an envoy who thinks he is in no way different from a prisoner of war, it is certain that he cannot leave a *fideicommissum*. For no one can make a will either, if he is in doubt whether he is entitled to do so. 1. If a son-in-power or a slave leaves a *fideicommissum*, it is invalid. But if it is represented that they have died after being manumitted, we shall be consistent in saying that a *fideicommissum* is held to have been left, as though it had been given at the moment of death, always provided that the intention has evidently persisted after manumission. Nobody, however, should suppose that in our view this rule applies to wills, since nothing in a will is valid unless the will itself is valid. The rule applies if the *fideicommissum* has been left in some other way. 2. Those who have been interdicted from fire and water and those who have been deported may not leave *fideicommissa*, because being stateless they have no right to make wills either. 3. We must consider as deported those to whom the emperor has assigned residence on an island or whom he has banished in writing. Otherwise, before the emperor confirms the decision of a governor, the person concerned is held not yet to have lost his citizenship. If he dies first, he is held to have died a citizen, and a *fideicommissum* left before sentence will be valid. Even if he dies after sentence but before the emperor's confirmation, what has been done will be valid, because he had an assured status up to then. 4. But those deported by the praetorian prefect, or by his deputy who has cognizance of cases by the emperor's mandate, or by the urban prefect (for he too has been granted the right to deport by a letter of the deified Severus and our emperor) are held to lose their citizenship immediately and, therefore, to have the right neither of making wills nor of leaving *fideicommissa*. 5. Should anyone definitely deported to an island make a codicil there and after being restored by the indulgence of the emperor die with the codicil still in being, it can be maintained that the *fideicommissum* is valid, provided that he persisted in the same intention. 6. It should be known that a person may charge a *fideicommissum* on those to whom something will come on his death, if it is either given to them or not adeemed from them. 7. We may charge a *fideicommissum* not only on the nearest *bonorum possessor* but also on one at further remove. 8. And even someone as yet unborn may be entrusted with a *fideicommissum*, provided that when born he succeeds us. 9. It can be stated without any doubt at all that if someone who dies intestate has left a *fideicommissum* charged on someone who could have succeeded him in the next degree and if that person repudiates the succession and it passes to the following degree, the *fideicommissum* is not due; and so our emperor has ruled in a rescript. 10. The same applies if a *fideicommissum* is left charged on a patron and on

his death one of his children is admitted to *bonorum possessio.*

2   GAIUS, *Fideicommissa, book 1:* A *fideicommissum* cannot be charged on a son who has been passed over in a will, even though he should be *suus heres.*

3   ULPIAN, *Fideicommissa, book 1:* If a woman has stipulated for her dowry and released it to her husband for the purpose of his giving a *fideicommissum*, it must be said that the *fideicommissum* is due; for he is held to have received something from his wife. This is so if a woman has formally released her husband with a view to making him a gift *mortis causa*. And if she increases the dowry for her husband in view of death or returns to matrimony with him *mortis causa*, it may be said that the *fideicommissum* is due from him.   1. Julian writes that if a slave has been bequeathed to me and I am asked to manumit him, a *fideicommissum* cannot be charged on me, if I am asked unconditionally. If I am asked under a condition or after a stated period, I can be bound on account of the intermediary profit, nor would Julian doubt it.   2. If someone owes a thing under a stipulation to the person to whom he has bequeathed it, he will not be able to charge a *fideicommissum* on him, although leaving it as a legacy to him would benefit him, because he gets ownership at once and need not wait for an action on stipulation. One might perhaps say that he saves the expense of the suit he would have to sustain if he took the case on stipulation to court. But it certainly cannot be said that it may be charged on him as a *fideicommissum*.   3. But if I cede to you *mortis causa* the usufruct of a property which is yours, it may be said that I can charge it on you as a *fideicommissum*. Nobody should be influenced by the fact that a usufruct is normally extinguished by death; for we shall take into consideration the intermediary profit during the lifetime of the donor.   4. But if I release my debtor's pledge *mortis causa* and charge a *fideicommissum* on him, the *fideicommissum* will not be valid.

4   PAUL, *Sentences, book 4:* A *fideicommissum* left charged on a father or master can, if the inheritance is not acquired by him, be claimed from his emancipated son or manumitted slave by appropriate actions. For it is with them that the profit of the acquired inheritance remains.

5   ULPIAN, *Fideicommissa, book 1:* If a legacy was left to a municipality, a *fideicommissum* may be charged on those who conduct the public administration.   1. If anyone should leave a *fideicommissum* charged not on an heir or legatee, but on the heir of the heir or legatee, it is benevolent to consider it valid.

6   PAUL, *Fideicommissa, book 1:* If I charge a *fideicommissum* on my heir as follows, "I ask you, Lucius Titius, to request your heir to give to Maevius ten aurei," the *fideicommissum* will be valid, so that on Titius's death it will be possible to claim it from the heir. And so Julian replied.   1. But it is not possible for a *fideicommissum* to be given in this way, "if Stichus should become Seius's and should accept the inheritance at Seius's direction, I ask Seius to give," since he who acquires an inheritance by chance and not by the decision of the testator should not be burdened, and it is inadmissible that you should by asking him place an obligation on someone to whom you have given nothing.

7   ULPIAN, *Fideicommissa, book 1:* If a *fideicommissum* is left to the slave of a deportee, it is to be said that it belongs to the imperial treasury, unless the deportee has alienated him in the lifetime of the testator or has been restored in which case it should belong to him.   1. If a soldier leaves a *fideicommissum* in favor of a deportee, the better opinion is, as Marcellus confirms, that he may take it.   2. If anyone bequeaths to his creditor what he owes him, he cannot charge him with a *fideicommissum*, unless he gets some benefit from the legacy, as, for instance, when he feared a defense, or if it was something due on a fixed date or under a condition.

8   PAUL, *Fideicommissa, book 1:* If a legatee on whom a *fideicommissum* has been

charged sues for the legacy, he will be compelled to deliver to the fideicommissary only what he exacts through the judge, or if he does not exact anything, to assign to him his right of action. For if it is not the legatee's fault that the suit has failed, it is unfair that the risk of an action should fall on him.   1. A *fideicommissum* left to a slave of the heir is void unless the heir is charged with the *fideicommissum* of manumitting the slave.   2. When a testator asked his father to restore to his daughter such of his goods as had come into the father's hands in addition to what she was to have from the father's goods, the deified Pius ruled in a rescript that it was evident that the testator meant the time after the father's death.

9   MAECIANUS, *Fideicommissa, book 1:* If a *fideicommissum* is left "to whoever inherits under my will or through intestacy," or "to whoever receives my property by whatever right," by this wording the *fideicommissum* is held to be chargeable also on one who is born or enters the family subsequently, on a person first becoming a relation subsequently, and on a woman not yet married [to the testator] but married subsequently, in the event of the husband's goods coming to the wife under the edict by reason of intestacy.

10   VALENS, *Fideicommissa, book 2:* If I bequeath a hundred aurei to you and to such of my three children as shall come to my funeral and nobody comes, the legacy to you personally is not diminished.

11   ULPIAN, *Fideicommissa, book 2: Fideicommissa* may be left in any language, not only Latin or Greek but Punic, Gallic, or that of any other nation.   1. When someone prepares the draft of a will and dies before he ratifies it, what is written in the draft is not valid, as if it were a codicil, even if the draft is in terms of a *fideicommissum*. So Maecianus writes that the deified Pius decreed.   2. If anyone has written, "I commend such a one to you," the deified Pius ruled in a rescript that a *fideicommissum* is not due; for it is one thing to commend a person and another to intimate to one's heirs the intention of leaving a *fideicommissum*.   3. When someone was asked to relinquish his portion of an inheritance upon receiving a fixed sum, it was replied that he could himself of his own accord claim the *fideicommissum* from the heir. But whether he should choose to claim and on taking the money restore the portion or whether he should refuse and be compelled to restore the portion on receipt of the fixed sum is a matter for his own decision. Certainly, when a man is asked to accept a certain sum and restore his portion, the *fideicommissum* is double. It entitles him to claim the sum if prepared to cede the portion; alternatively, if he does not claim, he nonetheless may be compelled to restore the portion to the fideicommissary, if the fideicommissary is prepared to pay the sum.   4. If somebody has written, "let the vineyards, or farm, be enough for you," it is a *fideicommissum*, since we also hold "let him be content with such a thing" to be a *fideicommissum*.   5. A *fideicommissum* left in these terms, "unless my heir refuses, I wish him to pay ten to such a one," is like a conditional *fideicommissum* and requires that the heir should be once willing. After he has been once willing the heir is not free to say that he refused.   6. The term "when he wishes," however, could mean prolongation for as long as the person on whom the *fideicommissum* is charged remains alive. But if he dies before paying, his heir must pay. But if the fideicommissary should die before the heir decides, he is held to have transferred nothing to his heir; for nobody can doubt that the legacy was conditional and that the fideicommissary died while the condition of the legacy was pending.   7. But although a *fideicommissum* worded, "if you should wish," may not be due, it will be due if the wording is "if you judge it good," "if you think it suitable," "if you hold it," or "shall hold it advantageous." For here he has not left full discretion to the heir, but has committed a trust to him as an upright man.   8. Moreover, if a *fideicommissum* is left "to such a one, if he has deserved well of you," the *fideicommissum* will certainly be due provided that the fideicommissary has behaved in a way that an upright man would think deserving. And if left to him "if he does not offend you," it will equally be due,

and the heir will not be able to justify a claim that the fideicommissary is undeserving, if another man who is upright and not antagonistic would admit him as deserving. 9. The words "I ask you, my son, that you cherish with all your diligence the estates that will come to you, and so look after them that they may pass to your children," though they do not adequately express a *fideicommissum*, but advice rather than obligation, will on the death of the father be held to have the force of a *fideicommissum* in favor of the grandchildren.   10. If the father be instituted heir, a *fideicommissum* given to the son, even if not left expressly "when the father dies," could be so understood. For example, where a *fideicommissum* has been left in these terms, "I wish him to have it," or "I wish it to belong to him, so that he may leave it to his son," it could be argued that it was left for the time when the son shall become independent.   11. If a *fideicommissum* is worded, "if he shall have become independent by the death of his father," and he has become independent by emancipation, the condition is not held to have failed. When the death of his father also occurs, he will be admitted to the *fideicommissum* as though the condition had been fulfilled.   12. If a testator bequeaths a thing that is his and then alienates it through urgent need, the *fideicommissum* may be claimed unless it is proved that the testator wished to deprive him of it. But it is for the heirs to produce proof that he changed his intention.   13. Therefore, if a testator has called in a debt which he had left as a *fideicommissum*, but not with the intention of extinguishing the *fideicommissum*, it may be said to be due, unless there should happen to be a difference between this and the previous case. For in this, the debt itself is extinguished, whereas in the previous case the thing remains, though alienated. But when a testator has called in a debt and deposited the money, I held that the claim for the *fideicommissum* remains, especially when he did not exact the debt himself, but the debtor offered it to him personally and could not be refused. Therefore, by degrees we shall be admitting that even if the testator has purchased a thing with part of the money, if he did not call in the money with the intention of depriving the fideicommissary of the *fideicommissum*, the *fideicommissum* may still be claimed.   14. If someone has built unlawfully, that is, a building which the *constitutiones* order to be demolished, let us see whether he could leave any *fideicommissum* from it. I think he may; for when it is necessary to demolish the building, there is no doubt that the *senatus consultum* offers no hindrance. 15. If an heir is asked to lend a sum of money at a fixed rate of interest, the *fideicommissum* is valid. Maecianus held that he can only be compelled to lend if furnished with a suitable *cautio*. But I incline to the view that a *cautio* need not be exacted. 16. If a commission is left to the slave of someone else, does his master acquire the legacy? Either the testator knew him to be a slave in which case I say its value is due, or he did not in which case the suit for the *fideicommissum* must be rejected, because he would not have left it to him had he known he was a slave.   17. From these instances it is evident that when something is left as a *fideicommissum*, it must itself be delivered; but when this cannot be done, its value must be paid.   18. If someone left ten to somebody as a *fideicommissum* and left the same sum to him again if he should have lost what was left to him by the will, the question was whether the second *fideicommissum* was valid or whether the heir should demand a *cautio* to safeguard the ten and whether, if the beneficiary should lose it several times, the *fideicommissum* should be replaced several times. The deified Pius ruled in a rescript that no *cautio* should be demanded, and that replacement of loss should be once only. For the heir is not to be burdened with the obligation of replacing every loss indefinitely; but by virtue of this *fideicommissum* the legacies are held to be doubled, and the heir should not be at any additional risk if the beneficiary dissipates anything after the second *fideicommissum* is paid.   19. Again, if someone leaves a certain sum to somebody and adds that this sum can easily be offset, because the fideicommissary is his debtor by reason of the inheritance of Gaius Seius and the fideicommissary does not wish to accept Gaius Seius's inheritance but claims the *fideicommissum*, our emperor has ruled in a rescript that he is claiming the *fideicommissum* against the wishes of the testator, whereas in *fideicommissa* the wishes of the testator are especially to be considered and respected. 20. It often happens that many have an interest in what was left, but the testator wished to pay respect to one only; this opinion of Marcellus is very true. 21. It happens that at times, if the testator wished to pay respect to several persons and had several in mind, although it is only one legacy, several are allowed to claim it all the same. For example, if one thing were due to ten persons under a stipulation, and the heir or fideicommissary were asked to pay them, then here, if all are interested and the testator had all in mind, all may claim the *fideicommissum* that is left. But let us see whether they can bring an action for part or the whole. I believe that what they will obtain will be according to the interest of each one. The one, therefore, who first brings the action gets the whole, provided that he gives a *cautio* to the person who discharges it so that he will be defended against the other fideicommissaries whether or not they are in partnership. 22. At times the name of one person is written in the will, but the right to claim the *fideicommissum* or legacy belongs to another. For instance, if the heir is charged with the *fideicommissum* of paying a tax on behalf of Titius, it will not be the tax farmer who will sue for the *fideicommissum* or legacy, even if it is assigned to him, but the person on whose behalf the legacy was left. I think it makes a great difference whom the testator wished to benefit and whom he had in mind when leaving the *fideicommissum*. Generally, however, it is to be understood that he made it to benefit a private person even if the payment goes to the tax farmer. 23. In the case of a bequest for a public work for a *civitas*, the deified Marcus and Lucius Verus ruled in a rescript to Procula that each heir is severally liable for carrying it out fully. But they allowed time for the co-heir during which he might send for what was needed to do the work, after which time they required Procula to carry it out alone, and to charge her co-heir with his share of the expense. 24. Therefore, the deified Marcus ruled in a rescript that the same applied to a statue, a servitude, and other things not admitting division. 25. If some one ordered to erect a structure is ready to give money to the state so that the state erects it, when the testator wished him himself to erect it he will not be listened to: and thus the deified Marcus ruled in a rescript.

12   VALENS, *Fideicommissa, book 1:* "Let Stichus be free. And I ask that my heir should teach him a craft to support himself." Pegasus says that the *fideicommissum* is ineffective, because the kind of trade is not added. But the praetor or arbitrator shall decide in accordance with the intention of the deceased and the age, condition, disposition, and ability of the beneficiary, which craft it is best that the heir should teach him at his expense.

13   MAECIANUS, *Fideicommissa, book 2:* If the testator's words were, "let my heir give a farm to such a one, and to Seius ten in addition," Seius must undoubtedly receive both his portion of the farm and ten under the will.

14   GAIUS, *Fideicommissa, book 1:* Undoubtedly if a legacy is bequeathed to a wife "if she does not remarry," and she is asked to restore it to someone else, she will be compelled to make restoration if she does remarry. 1. An heir who has been released from the condition that he should take an oath is still liable for legacies and *fideicommissa*. 2. But a person to whom a legacy has been left so that he should buy or deliver a thing belonging to someone else should, if he cannot buy it because the owner will not sell or will only sell at an unreasonable price, pay its correct value.

15   MAECIANUS, *Fideicommissa, book 2:* Things of a testator which have been bequeathed and are said to be in the deep must be delivered in the event of their recovery.

16   POMPONIUS, *Fideicommissa, book 1:* A legacy will often be restored to the fideicommissary more fully than it was left, for instance, land augmented by alluvion

or when islands have been formed.

17   MAECIANUS, *Fideicommissa, book 2:* Even what is future can be bequeathed, such as an island formed in the sea or in a river.   1. A servitude can also rightly be bequeathed to the person who has the land.

18   POMPONIUS, *Fideicommissa, book 1:* If in a will made according to law I leave you a *fideicommissum* and afterward make another will not according to law in which the *fideicommissum* left to you is either other than what it was in the earlier will or is omitted altogether, then it is to be seen whether my intention when making the later will was that what I left you in the earlier will should not be ratified, because *fideicommissa* are annulled by bare intention. But this will hardly hold, because it could happen that it was my wish that what was written in the earlier will should be withdrawn only if the later one was going to be valid; and now the *fideicommissum* from the later will shall not be due to you, even if the same heirs were appointed by both wills and became heirs under the first.

19   VALENS, *Fideicommissa, book 5:* If a legacy or *fideicommissum* has been left to you so that you might do a certain thing, then even if it is not in the interest of the heir that it should be done, Nerva and Atilicinus rightly held that you should be denied an action unless you give a *cautio* to the heir that what the deceased wished will be done.

20   ULPIAN, *Fideicommissa, book 6:* If a thing left to me by *fideicommissum* has also been left as a legacy or *fideicommissum* to you with a view not to our holding it in common, but to our each getting it in full, then undoubtedly if it is delivered to one of us, the other has no right to the thing itself, but has an unimpaired right to an action for its price.

21   PAUL, *Sentences, book 4:* A *fideicommissum* can even be left by a nod, provided that the person who so leaves it is someone who can also speak or is hindered from speaking by a disease which has attacked him.   1. It is settled that a *fideicommissum* found to be in the hands of the person to whom it was left without his having paid for it is extinguished, unless the deceased wished that its value should also be paid.   2. When columns or timbers of a house have been left as a *fideicommissum*, the most honorable senate has decided that only those may be delivered which can be removed without injury to the house, and their value is left out of account.

22   HERMOGENIAN, *Epitome of Law, book 4:* If someone has written at the beginning of a will, "whatever I bequeath to anyone twice, I wish to be due only once," and afterward knowingly later in the same will or in a codicil makes several bequests to the same person, then his last intention is held to prevail. For nobody can prescribe a law to himself that will prevent him from withdrawing from his earlier intention. But this will only apply if he specifically states that he repents his earlier intention and wishes the legatee to accept several legacies.   1. A soldier, when a capital sentence has been pronounced against him for a military offense, may, by permission of him who condemned him, expressed in the sentence itself, obtain the power of leaving a *fideicommissum* as also of making a will.   2. Loss by death of a slave left by *fideicommissum*, in advance of any delay in delivery, must be borne by the fideicommissary alone, even if it is someone else's slave who was bequeathed.

23   PAUL, *Sentences, book 5:* For the emperor to vindicate legacies or *fideicommissa* under an imperfect will is shameless. For it is proper that so great a majesty should observe the laws from which he is deemed to be himself exempt.

24   NERATIUS, *Replies, book 2:* A bequest may be made to a creditor so that what is not owed should not be demanded back from him.

25   PAUL, *Neratius, book 1:* "This or that heir is to pay a hundred to Seius." Seius may claim from whichever he wishes.

26   PAUL, *Neratius, book 2:* He who owes a *fideicommissum* and has caused delay is compelled not only to deliver the fruits but also to make good all the loss incurred by· the fideicommissary.

27   PAUL, *Decrees, book 2:* Paula, having appointed Callinicus part heir, in her will bequeathed ten to his daughter Juventiana when she married into the family. Then after a time she made a codicil in which she left a hundred to the same Callinicus without adding "in addition." [The emperor] pronounced both sums due, especially as nothing had been bequeathed to Callinicus's daughter in the codicil.   1. Pompeius Hermippus appointed his son Hermippus heir to three quarters and his daughter Titiana heiress to a quarter of his estate. And he left them each legacies, to be taken in advance, of certain lands. Besides this, he directed that if Hermippus were to die without issue, another possession should be given to his daughter. After making his will he drew up a codicil in which he gave his daughter certain lands and required her to be content with these in place of her whole inheritance together with the lands he had left her in his will. Hermippus's property passed to the imperial treasury. Titiana his sister claimed the legacy. The question was whether her father had wished her to accept what he had left by codicil in place of her inheritance only, or also in place of what her brother had been asked to restore after death. I considered that the father had entirely revoked his first intention. The more humane view was that she should be held to have been deprived only of what she would have received in her brother's lifetime and not of what he had left her after her brother's death if her brother should die without issue. This was what [the emperor] decided.   2. Julianus Severus on his decease, having appointed certain heirs, bequeathed fifty to his foster son and wished these to be paid by Julius Maurus his tenant out of the farm rent that he owed him. He also left certain legacies to Maurus. The imperial treasury raised a question about the inheritance; and by order of the procurator, Maurus paid the money into the treasury. Afterward the appointed heir won against the treasury. But the foster son had died and his heir claimed the *fideicommissum* from Maurus's heir. The emperor decided that this should be held to be not a *fideicommissum*, but an indication of where the money could be found, and, therefore, the heir of Severus must make this payment.

28   PAUL, *Senatus Consultum Tertullianum, sole book:* If it is charged on me as a *fideicommissum* that I should restore to another what has been left to me beyond what I am entitled to take, it is settled that I may take it.

29   LABEO, *Posthumous Works, Epitomized by Javolenus, book 2:* A man who had a concubine gave her the clothing of his former concubine for her use. Then he left her a legacy as follows: "the clothing which I have purchased and acquired for her." Cascellius and Trebatius say that what was acquired for the previous concubine is not due, because in the case of a wife there would be another provision. Labeo does not approve this, because in this kind of legacy we should not follow the law applying to wives, but interpret the words, and the same rule would hold good for a daughter and any other person. Labeo's opinion is correct.   1. A legacy was left in these terms: "Titia my wife should have a share just as great as what little share has been left to one of my heirs." If the heirs do not have equal shares, Quintus Mucius and Gallus thought that the greatest share had been bequeathed, because the smaller is contained in the greater; and Servius and Ofilius the smallest, because since the heir had been condemned to give, it would be in his power to decide what share to give. Labeo approves this last, the true opinion.   2. When a legacy had been left in these terms, "let my heir give to Seia as much money as has come to me from the inheritance of Titius," Labeo thinks that the bequest amounts to what the testator entered in his accounts as received from that inheritance. Furthermore, he says that the legatee need not give the heir a *cautio* for the event of the heir's being later condemned to give anything on account of this inheritance. I hold the contrary opinion, because it cannot be held that what he is to deliver on account of this inheritance has come to the heir. Alfenus Varus writes that Servius was of the same opinion, which is the correct one.   3. If an heir,

when a slave has been bequeathed to you in general terms, delivers Stichus to you and you lose him by eviction, Labeo writes that you have an action under the will, because the heir cannot be held to have given anything if he gave it in such a way that you cannot keep it. This I hold to be correct. But he adds that you must notify the heir of the eviction before taking the matter to court; for if you do not, a defense of fraud will bar your action based on the will.   4. "If Stichus and Dama, my slaves, are in my power when I die, then let Stichus and Dama be free and have such a farm for themselves." If after making his will the master has alienated or manumitted one of them, Labeo thinks that neither will be free. But Tubero thinks that the one who remained in power will be free and will take the legacy. The opinion of Tubero in my view better fits the intention of the deceased.

30   LABEO, *Posthumous Works, Epitomized by Javolenus, book 2:* The owner of four cups of olive-wood made the following bequest: "two *paria* [similar] cups of olive-wood." I replied that one pair had been bequeathed; for the wording was not "two *paria* [similar] cups each," nor yet "two *paria* [pairs] of cups." Trebatius is of the same opinion.   1. A man who had rented public gardens from the *res publica* left the fruits of those gardens to Aufidius up to the end of their five-year lease and condemned his heir to pass on to him the lease of those gardens and allow him to use them and take the fruits. I replied that the heir was bound to let him take the fruits, and besides to pay to the *res publica* the rent of the gardens.   2. When a will read, "let my heir give five to my slave Stichus, and if Stichus serves my heir for two years, let him be free," I think this legacy is due after the two years, because both his freedom and the legacy should be referred to that time. This was also Trebatius's reply.   3. If you are condemned to sell me a farm at a fixed price, you will not be free to except any fruits of the property from the sale, because the price is for everything belonging to the farm.   4. A person who, mandated by me, had bought a farm in partnership for myself and himself, afterward divided it by a boundary and before delivery to me bequeathed it to you in these terms, "I give my farm to such a one." I held that more than a part was not due, because it was unlikely that the head of the household had made his will with a view to his heir being condemned by an action on mandate.   5. "To my wife, while she is at Capua with my son, let my heir give two hundred." The son moved away from his mother. But if both had lived at Capua, even if not together, I held that the legacy would have been due to the mother. But if he had moved to another town, Trebatius says that the legacy would only have been due for one year in which they had lived together however briefly. Let us see: Can it be that the words "while she is at Capua with her son" do not imply a condition, but should be held as superfluous? I do not think they should. But if it is not because of the woman's delay that she does not live with her son, the legacy is due to her.   6. If you should be condemned to give the house of someone else and cannot buy it on any condition, Ateius wrote that the judge must value the house so that the heir may be released by paying its price. The same rule applies even if you could have bought the house but did not do so.

31   LABEO, *Plausible Views, Epitomized by Paul, book 1:* If a house is bequeathed to someone, he will have the whole building as far as its site extends. PAUL: This is false only when the owner of two adjoining houses converts a room which is above the vault of one house to the use of the other and has used them in this way. Under these circumstances, the room is taken from the one house and added to the other.

32   SCAEVOLA, *Digest, book 14:* A testator appointed his daughter Sextia heiress to a quarter of his estate and Seius and Marcius, his daughter's sons, heirs to the rest. He substituted Sextia for Marcius, and Marcius for Sextia. But he bequeathed certain specific things for Marcius to take beforehand. Marcius rejected the part of the inheritance to which he was appointed heir. When he died intestate his property went to his legitimate brother Seius. The question was: Could Sextia as substitute vindicate for herself from the legitimate heir of the deceased, by right of substitution, what had

been bequeathed for Marcius to take beforehand? He replied that upon the case as put, Sextia had not been substituted in respect of the legacy bequeathed to Marcius.

33   SCAEVOLA, *Digest, book 15:* A man bequeathed to his wife, among other things, the following legacy: "and that part of the house in which we used to stay." Since he had the whole house in use both at the time of making the will and at the time of his death, and no part of it was let out, is he taken to have bequeathed only the room in which they used to sleep? He replied: every part in which he used to stay with his family. 1. A man bequeathed to his wife, among other things, the following legacy: "Whatever I have given, presented, or acquired for your use in my lifetime I wish to be granted to you." Is what was presented to her after the will was made also to be taken as granted? He replied that the words stated had no reference to future time. 2. Seius paid a hundred aurei on behalf of his wife to a creditor and released jewelry she had deposited as a pledge. Later, after making his will, he bequeathed to her whatever he had paid her or had paid to discharge her stipulations and in addition twenty aurei a year. The question was: Might the man's heirs reclaim the hundred aurei from the wife or the wife's heirs? He replied that if Seius had paid the creditor as a gift to his wife, the heirs would be bound by the *fideicommissum* if they got them back and that if they sued for them, they could be barred by a defense. It must be presumed that the payment was a gift unless the heir can prove the contrary.

34   SCAEVOLA, *Digest, book 16:* [A woman] bequeathed a debt due to her in these words: "I wish Titius in addition to be given ten aurei, which the heirs of Gaius Seius owe me. I wish the right of action against them to be transferred to him and their pledges to be delivered to him." Should the heirs transfer to him the ten only or the whole debt, that is to say, the interest too? He replied that the whole debt appeared to have been bequeathed. And since, unbeknown to the *materfamilias*, her agents in the province had stipulated for ten with the interest added to the capital, does the increment added to the debt also belong to Titius by reason of the above-mentioned *fideicommissum*? He said that it does. 1. A man bequeathed to a son appointed as part-heir among other things a legacy to be taken beforehand in these words: "Let them be condemned to give without fraud to Titius my son twenty claims out of my debt book which my son is to choose for himself." To the same son he made over the administration of all his affairs in his lifetime. After the will was made and for ten years before his father's death in which he was acting for his father, he lent new debtors large sums of money contrary to his father's old practice in managing the debt book, and to his father's previous debtors of small means he gave more credit, so that almost the whole contents of the debt book consisted of twenty debts. Should this son take beforehand the loans he made himself? He replied that he should have the choice of those which the testator had in his debt book at the time of making the will. 2. A woman left as a legacy to be taken beforehand to one of her heirs what had come down to her from the patrimony of her husband Aretho. She charged him with the *fideicommissum* of delivering this to her great-grandson when he reached the age of sixteen. She added these words: "I also ask you to pay the remaining debts that are due from the estate of Aretho to all the creditors out of the income from that property, and to satisfy them in full." The question was: If the heir can prove that the income from the property is not enough for discharging the whole debt, must he, nonetheless, himself acknowledge the burden of the debt? He answered that it was clearly stated that he should pay the debt out of the income from the property and not from his private resources. 3. A father who had appointed his son and daughter heirs left each of them a *praelegatum* of certain lands and debt entries, providing as follows: "I ask you, moreover, my dearest son, to deliver whatever legacies I have bequeathed, and if any debt should accrue from what I have meanwhile received and borrowed, I wish you to pay it so that what I have left to your sister may come into her hands intact." Must the

son, it was asked, pay whatever debt the father has incurred for any reason? He replied that the daughter could claim relief under the *fideicommissum* so that the testator's gift should come into her hands intact.

35   SCAEVOLA, *Digest, book 17:* A patron had asked that a place in a tribe should be bought at once for his freedman. The freedman suffered a long delay by his patron's heir and died, leaving as his heir a man of high rank. It was asked whether the value of the place in a tribe was due to the heir? He replied that it was. The heir also asked whether the benefits and imperial largesses, which the freedman would have obtained to the day of his death if that place in a tribe had been acquired for him according to his patron's intention, were due to the heir or only the interest on the value. I replied that the freedman transmitted to his heir the right to what he would have obtained.   1. A testator made a bequest to Sempronius as follows: "Let Sempronius take all my lands, as far as the estate called Gaas, in the territory of Galatia, under the charge of my manager Primus, together with all their appurtenances." It was asked whether, since in this tract of lands there was one estate in the territory not of Galatia but of Cappadocia, though under the charge of the same manager, that estate also should belong with the rest to Sempronius. He replied that it also was due.   2. A testator bequeathed in these terms to freedmen whom he named: "The Trebatian farm which is in the district of Atella, and the Satrian farm in the district of Niphana, together with the shop, I wish to be given." It was asked whether, since there was indeed a farm called Satrian among those bequeathed above, but not in the district of Niphana, it was due to the freedmen. He replied that if there was no Satrian farm in the district of Niphana but the testator certainly meant one that was elsewhere, the farm was not any the less due because there had been a slip in designating the district.   3. A person made the following provision in a confirmed codicil: "To my kind friends, my fellow citizens of the municipality of Tibur, [I leave] the Julian bath which you know adjoins my house, so that at the expense and by the diligence of my heirs, it may be made publicly available free of charge." It was asked whether the heirs must provide the necessary expenses of repair. He replied that upon the case as put, the testator appeared to have had in mind, over and above the burden of heating and service, the usual expenses of daily maintenance for the equipment of the baths or for their preparation and cleaning during the usual closing times to render them fit for washing.

36   CLAUDIUS, *Note on Scaevola, Digest, book 18: Fideicommissa* are not due on grounds of intestacy when given by someone whose will has been declared undutiful. Because he is believed to have been unable to make a will, like a lunatic, therefore nothing else belonging to his last dispositions is valid.

37   SCAEVOLA, *Digest, book 18:* A man when dying bequeathed to his mother Seia a farm which already belonged to her and asked her to restore it on her death to Flavia Albina his wife. After the death of the testator, his mother declared before the magistrate that she would do nothing against the wishes of her son and was prepared to transfer the farm to Flavia Albina, if her annuity were doubled in compensation for the farm income. But she did not transfer possession or receive the doubled annuity. It was asked whether she could rightfully sell the farm to another. He replied that as far as concerned the law of legacies and *fideicommissa*, upon the case as put, the legacy of her own property to the mother had not been valid, nor could the burden of the *fideicommissum* have been validly imposed if the mother had received nothing besides.   1. A man who had appointed an heir by will bequeathed two hundred to Maevius and charged on him as a *fideicommissum* to give a hundred to Glauce and fifty to Tyche and Elpis. Afterward Maevius by the wish of the testator sent letters to them that he would pay them their legacies according to the intention of the testator. Afterward the testator made a codicil in which he included a clause that if anything

were produced other than the codicil it would not be valid. It was asked whether Maevius who took two hundred could be sued by the women on account of the *fidei-commissum*, although the testator had changed his intention about that letter. He replied that upon the case as put Maevius would be sued in vain, whether he received the two hundred, or a landed estate in their place.   2. A man appointed Seia and Maevius his freed slaves as his heirs in equal shares. For Maevius he substituted his *pupillus* Sempronius. Afterward he confirmed a codicil by a *fideicommissum*. In his codicil he provided as follows: "Lucius Titius to his heiress Seia, whom I have appointed to half my estate, greeting. I forbid Maevius my freedman, whom in my will I appointed heir to half my estate, to receive that share of the inheritance. In his place or share, I wish my master Publius Sempronius to be heir." To Maevius to whom he did not wish the share of the inheritance to come he left a *fideicommissum* with this clause: "to Maevius my freedman, who has deserved nothing from me, one hundred and fifty jars of the oldest wine." It was asked whether, since the intention of the testator was that the share of his inheritance should in any case come to the *pupillus* Sempronius, the *fideicommissum* from the above-written words should be understood to be valid, and from whom Sempronius might claim it, since the testator addressed the codicil to a certain person. He replied that the *fideicommissum* could be claimed from Maevius.   3. A father gave, not *mortis causa*, his entire property to his emancipated son, except for two slaves. He stipulated with his son in these words: "As for the slaves and lands which I have delivered and ceded to you by way of gift, no act or bad faith by you, or by him to whom this property shall belong, shall prevent these slaves with their offspring, and these lands with their equipment, when I wish or when you die—whichever of them shall exist or through fraud or bad faith by you or by him to whom this property shall belong shall have ceased to exist or to be in power—from being returned and restored, if I live, to me or to anyone I wish. This stipulation was made by Lucius Titius the father; Lucius Titius the son gave the *sponsio*." The same father on his decease wrote a letter charging a *fideicommissum* on his son in these words: "To my son Lucius Titius, greeting. Convinced of your sense of duty, I charge on you as a *fideicommissum* that you give and discharge a certain sum of money to this and that person; and I wish my slave Lucrio to be free." The question was whether, since the son of the father had received neither *bonorum possessio* nor become his heir, he should discharge the *fideicommissa* and grants of freedom under the letter. He replied that even though he had not accepted the inheritance or claimed *bonorum possessio*, and possessed nothing by way of inheritance, he should be liable all the same not only to an action on stipulation by his father's heirs but also to an action on the *fideicommissum* by those having interest, as if he were a debtor, especially following the *constitutio* of the deified Pius, who introduced this principle.   4. A woman about to marry gave a mandate to her two sons by a previous husband that they should stipulate for the twenty she was giving as dowry, for the event of any possible dissolution of the marriage, on condition that the whole dowry should be paid to one or other of them. While the marriage was still in being, one of the sons died. The wife wrote a letter to the surviving son, asking him that in due course he should exact only half the dowry and be content with that and allow the other half to remain with her husband. The question was when the woman subsequently died still married, whether the husband, if sued for the whole dowry by the son, could protect himself with a defense of fraud or whether he was entitled on his own account to an action under the *fideicommissum* so as to obtain release from part of the obligation. He replied that the defense would be effective and that he could himself claim under the *fideicommissum*. The husband also asked if an action on the mandate for the remaining half would be effective for the heirs of the woman against her son. He replied that upon the case as put and especially after the letter to the son, it would be ineffective, CLAUDIUS: because she wrote in it that he should be content with half the dowry. With these words, he held that a *fideicommissum* had been adequately left to the son.

5. Someone wrote in a codicil: "I wish all that is written below to be valid. To my master Maximus I wish to be restored the fifteen thousand denaria which I took as a deposit from his uncle Julius Maximus to give to him on his reaching puberty. These with the interest come to three hundred thousand. I made this promise on oath to his uncle." The question was whether the words of the codicil are adequate for a claim for the deposited money, when the claimant has this proof only and no other. I replied: Upon the case as put, since the testator in addition declared that he had sworn an oath, the writing must be believed.   6. Titia, a lady of the highest respectability, had in her business affairs always made use of the services of Callimachus, who was not entitled to take under a will. When making her will she provided in her own handwriting as follows: "I, Titia, have made this will, and wish that Callimachus be given ten thousand denaria as wages." Question: Can this money be exacted from Titia's heirs as wages? I replied that this being in writing does not make it possible to exact what was left in fraud of the law.   7. "To all men and women whom I have manumitted or shall manumit, either in this testament or in any other, I wish that their sons and daughters may be granted." Because of these words in a will, the question was whether the sons of those whom he manumitted in his lifetime were due to them. He replied that by virtue of the *fideicommissum* those men and women whom he had manumitted before making his will should also receive delivery of their sons and daughters.

38   SCAEVOLA, *Digest, book 19:* A father had forbidden his son and heir to alienate or pledge his lands, but had charged him with the *fideicommissum* of keeping them for his legitimate children and other relatives. The father had left lands encumbered. The son paid off the creditor of the inheritance with money from a new creditor, and transferred the lands from the first creditor to the second by way of *pignus* or *hypotheca*. The question was whether the contract for the pledge had been rightly made. He replied that upon the case as put, it was. The same person asked whether, since the son had removed by sale certain lands belonging to the inheritance to pay off the creditors of the inheritance, the purchasers who had been unaware of the *fideicommissum* had made a purchase that was good. He replied that according to the case as put, their contract was valid, if there was nothing else in the inheritance from which the debt could have been paid.   1. A man appointed two freedmen, Stichus and Eros, as heirs and provided as follows: "I forbid the Cornelian farm to pass to those not of my name." Stichus, one of the heirs, in his will directed the female slave Arescusa to be free and bequeathed to her his share of the farm. Question: May Eros and the other fellow freedmen of Stichus claim the share of the farm from Stichus's heiress under the *fideicommissum*? I replied that there was nothing to prevent them.   2. A testator appointed his daughter as heiress and provided as follows: "I forbid this building to pass to those not of my name, but I wish it to belong after you to my home-bred slaves whom I have named in my will." The question was whether after the death of the heiress and the other home-bred slaves the whole of the *fideicommissum* would belong to the one surviving freemen. He replied that upon the case as put the equal share would belong to him.   3. A testator forbade that his son should in his lifetime sell, give, or pledge a farm, and added these words: "But if he attempts to flout my wishes, the Titian farm is to belong to the imperial treasury; for this will ensure that the Titian farm never passes to anyone not of your name." The question was: When the son had kept the farm in his lifetime according to his father's wish, would it on his death go, not to the heirs appointed by the son, but to members of his family? He replied that it could be gathered from the intention of the deceased that the son could not in his lifetime alienate or pledge the farm, but would be entitled to include the farm in his testamentary dispositions, and even leave it to heirs who were outsiders.   4. Julius Agrippa, the senior centurion, provided in his will that his heir should by no means pledge or alienate in any way the suburban plot where he was buried or the main house. His daughter who was appointed heiress left as heiress her own daughter, the senior centurion's

granddaughter, who remained in possession of these properties for a long time and on her death appointed outsiders as heirs. The question was whether the outside heir should have these estates or whether they should belong to Julia Domna, the great-niece of Julius Agrippa. I replied that since this had been a bare precept, nothing upon the case as put had been done against the wishes of the deceased, so as to prevent the estates from belonging to the heirs. 5. To fifteen freedmen, whom he named, a testator bequeathed a plot of land with a shop, adding these words: "I wish them to have and hold [it] for themselves on the strict condition that none of them shall attempt to sell, give, or make any other disposition of his share to another. But if anything is done contrary to this, then I wish those shares or the plot of land with the shop to belong to the *res publica* of Tusculum." Certain of these freedmen sold their shares to two fellow freedmen of theirs from the same body, and the purchasers on their deaths left Gaius Seius, an outsider, as their heir. The question was: Did the shares that had been sold belong to Gaius Seius or to their surviving fellow freedmen who had not sold their shares? He replied that upon the case as put, they belonged to Gaius Seius. The same person asked whether the parts that had been sold belonged to the *res publica* of Tusculum. I replied that they did not, CLAUDIUS: because regard must be had not to the person of the possessor, who is now a stranger, but to that of the purchasers, who following the intention of the deceased were among those to whom the testatrix had permitted sale; and the condition on which the *fideicommissum* was given to Tusculum had not been fulfilled. 6. A testator charged a *fideicommissum* on a man to whom he had bequeathed two thousand in these words: "I ask you, Petronius, to restore these two thousand solidi to the priestly *collegium* of a certain temple." The question was whether, since this *collegium* had subsequently been dissolved, the legacy should belong to Petronius or remain with the heir. He replied that Petronius could rightly claim it, as it had not in any case been in his power to obey the wish of the deceased. 7. A mother had appointed her sons as heirs and added: "The lands which are to come to them from my property should on no account be alienated by them, but they are to keep them for their successors and give *cautiones* to one another in this matter." From these words the question arose whether the lands should be held left by *fideicommissum*. He replied that there was no evidence of a *fideicommissum*. 8. A testator left to an heir, whom he had appointed to a half share, the legacy of a farm to be taken in advance and made a request to him as follows: "I ask you, please, to accept as your co-heir in my Julian farm, which I have directed you to take in advance additionally, my grandson and your relative, Clodius Verus." The question was, whether a share of the farm was due to the grandson by virtue of a *fideicommissum*. He replied that it was.

39 SCAEVOLA, *Digest, book 20:* "To Pamphilus, my freedman, in addition to what I have left him by codicil, I wish a hundred to be given. I know that everything I leave to you, Pamphilus, will come to my sons, since I have clear evidence of your affection for them." Question: Did the testator by the words above-written impose a *fideicommissum* on Pamphilus to restore the hundred after his death to the sons of the deceased? He replied that, upon the case as put, he could not be held to have imposed a *fideicommissum* on Pamphilus, as far as concerns the words of the testator; but since it would be quite heartless that the deceased should be cheated of his intention by his freedman, the hundred left to him should be restored to the sons of the testator, since this was the ruling of our emperor, the deified Marcus, in a similar case. 1. The case put was that a childless man with no relatives in danger of his life through sickness summoned his friends and told his comrade Gaius Seius that he wished to leave him lands which he named. Gaius Seius drew up a document attesting to this statement. He asked the testator if this was what he had said and entered his reply, "certainly." The question was whether the lands which were intended for him should belong to Gaius Seius by *fideicommissum*. He said that upon these facts there could be no doubt but that the *fideicommissum* was valid. 2. A testator had made two daughters heiresses in equal shares. To one he had bequeathed a farm as a *praelegatum*, and he had asked her to give twenty to her sister; he asked the same daughter to restore half the farm to the same sister. The question was whether the twenty should not be paid.

I replied that they should not.

40   SCAEVOLA, *Digest, book 21:* A daughter born after her father's emancipation had asked her paternal uncle, as her *legitimus heres,* to give a part of her inheritance to her maternal uncle together with two fields. But the succession passed to both of them as next of kin through *bonorum possessio.* The question was whether, since the *fideicommissum* did not hold good for the part of the inheritance which the maternal uncle was to have on his own account through *bonorum possessio,* it would, nonetheless, hold good for a share of the fields. In that event, Titius would have two shares of the fields, one on his own account through *bonorum possessio,* the other which he should claim by virtue of the *fideicommissum.* He replied that he could claim it. The same person asked whether, if the testator had given a *fideicommissum* to others also charged on the paternal uncle, it would have to be paid by him in full or in part. He replied that it should be paid in full.   1. A testator appointed Maevius heir to a quarter of his estate and Seia to three quarters. He imposed a *fideicommissum* on Seia in these words: "I ask you and charge on you as a *fideicommissum* that you restore to your son whatever comes to you of my inheritance, keeping my gardens for yourself." The question was whether, since by a general clause he had committed to the trust of "whoever became his heir," with respect to his whole inheritance, that they should deliver what he had bequeathed, or ordered to be delivered or to be done for each legatee, Seia, after restoring the three quarters of the estate, should vindicate the gardens in their entirety. He replied that he held the *fideicommissum* to be charged on the co-heir also to the effect that he should restore to Seia the quarter share he had in these gardens.

41   SCAEVOLA, *Digest, book 22:* A testator appointed as heirs his wife and their son and charged a *fideicommissum* on his wife in these words: "I ask you, my lady wife, not to vindicate a part from the Titian farm for yourself, since you know that I purchased this entire farm myself, but held this purchase, bought with my own money, in common with you so that you should benefit from the affection and duty I owed you." The question was whether he wished this farm to be wholly the son's. He replied that the person in question wished the farm to be treated just as if the whole of it belonged to the inheritance, so that the wife and son should each inherit half the land.   1. A clause in a will read as follows: "I wish my house with the adjoining garden to be surrendered to my freedmen." Another clause read: "To Fortunius, my freedman, I wish my heir to surrender the annex in which I used to live that belongs to the house which I have given my freedmen, and also the storeroom connected with this annex." The question was whether the testator's heir should be burdened with the delivery of the legacy to Fortunius, although the whole house had been bequeathed in advance to the freedmen. He replied that he should not be so burdened.   2. Someone provided as follows in a confirmed codicil: "To all my freedmen whom I have manumitted both in my lifetime and in this codicil or shall manumit in future, I bequeath their partners and their sons and daughters, with the exception of such persons of either sex that I have desired in my will to belong to my wife, or have bequeathed or shall bequeath to her by name." The same testator afterward asked his heirs to restore to his wife, their coheir, the territory of Umbria Tuscia in Picenum together with all that was in it, and the rural and urban slaves with their managers, except for those manumitted. The question was whether Eros and Stichus, who had managed the testator's affairs in Umbria in Picenum to the last day of his life, should be delivered by the heirs, by virtue of the wording of the codicil, to Dama, because they were his natural sons and Dama had been manumitted by the testator in his lifetime, or should they belong to the testator's wife Seia by virtue of the wording of the letter. He replied that they should belong to their father, following the codicil, out of respect for natural loyalty.   3. A woman bequeathed to Felicissimus and Felicissima to whom she had granted their freedom the Gargilian farm with a cottage. In another clause, she left a legacy, to be taken in advance, to her son Titius, whom she had appointed heir to a quarter share, in these words: "You, my son Titius, are to take in addition out of my inheritance my legacies, which your father Praesens and Coelius Justus, your father's

brother, left to me." The question was whether the Gargilian farm, which had been a legacy to the testatrix from her husband, that is, from the father of her son Titius, to whom the farm was due by virtue of the *fideicommissum*, should go only to the son Titius or to Felicissimus and Felicissima or to all three. He replied that it was improbable that the testatrix, who had bequeathed nothing to Felicissimus and Felicissima other than this specific legacy, had wished to transfer the legacy by a general clause to her son to whom she had also left a share of the inheritance.   4. A testator made a legacy of slave boys as follows: "To Publius Maevius, my dear young master, I wish my heirs to give five boys out of my household, but only such as are under seven years old." The question was how old should the slaves due to Maevius be. Should they be slaves under seven years old at the time the will was made, or slaves found to be under that age at the time of the testator's death? He replied that the age meant should be held to be their age when they were left by the testator.   5. A testator had left a legacy among others to his concubine in these words: "I wish her to be given my farm in Appia with its manager and his partner and their children." The question was whether the testator had wished the grandson of the manager and his partner to belong to the concubine also. He replied that there was no reason given why they should not. 6. Someone had left a legacy by *fideicommissum* to the Maevii as follows: "and whatever I possess in Gades, my native city." The question was whether any adjacent suburban possessions that he might have would also be due to the Maevii by virtue of the *fideicommissum*. He replied that the sense of the words could be extended to include this. Another question was whether, if he had left in the house which he had in his native city the documents belonging to the debt book of the transactions of the deceased in his native place or within its territories, that debt book too, on account of the words written above, would be due to the Maevii by virtue of the *fideicommissum*. He replied that they were not due. A further question was whether the money found in his safe in his house in Gades, exacted from various debtors and deposited there, would be due by virtue of the *fideicommissum*. He replied as above.   7. In a will by which he appointed his son and wife as heirs, a man bequeathed by *fideicommissum* a hundred to his daughter when she married within the family and added these words: "I charge on you, my daughter, as a *fideicommissum*, that when you marry within the family, and as often as you marry, you allow your brother and your mother Seia to stipulate that a half share of the dowry that you shall give be paid to them in equal portions in the event of your death while still married to your husband, or after divorce before the dowry is returned or satisfaction given for it, if you leave no son or daughter by him." The father arranged a marriage for his daughter as a virgin and gave her a dowry on that account. After her divorce, he took it back and gave her in marriage to another with the dowry and stipulated that this dowry should be returned to him or his daughter. He died while his daughter was still married to her second husband, leaving the same will, and his son and wife became heirs. Then her husband died, and the girl received back her dowry and married again in the presence and with the consent of her brother and mother, who also increased the dowry. Neither of them stipulated for the dowry. He replied that, on the case as put, he was not liable. 8. Seius as heir or legatee was asked to adopt a certain person with the addition of whether, since the girl had not received the money for her dowry by way of legacy from her father's heirs, but on the death of her second husband had become a *mater-familias* and recovered the dowry, her heir was liable to the brother of the deceased because of the *fideicommissum* for the money which he could have obtained, if he had stipulated for the dowry. He replied that on the case as put, he was not liable. 8. Seius as heir or legatee was asked to adopt a certain person with the addition of these words: "If he does otherwise, he is to be disinherited," or "he is to lose the legacy." The question was whether, if he failed to adopt, the person not adopted had a right to an action on the *fideicommissum*. He replied that a *fideicommissum* requiring someone to adopt was not ratified.   9. "I wish the tract of land which is in such a region to be conveyed to Publius Maevius and Gaius Maevius, at a price fixed at the discretion of an upright man and paid into the inheritance, and with a promise from the remaining heirs of double in the event of eviction, provided that on penalty of a hundred they promise that neither that tract of land nor any part of it shall come to Seius or his successors on any account whatever." The question was whether the legacy was valid when Publius wished to buy it but Maevius did not. He replied that the one who wished the *fideicommissum* to be delivered to him could claim half of the land bequeathed to him, even if the other did not wish to proceed with his claim. Another question was how to apportion the *cautio* which should be furnished, following the testator's intention, to each heir. He replied that it should be in proportion to what was delivered by virtue of the *fideicommissum*.   10. A testator bequeathed to his sister men whom he named in his will and charged on her as a *fideicommissum* that when she died she should restore these slaves to his sons. The question was whether their offspring should be restored to the heirs of the deceased after the death of the legatee, or remain with her heirs. He replied that subsequent offspring was not included in the words of the *fideicommissum*.   11. A father was in debt to his natural daughter under a *fideicommissum* charged by her husband's will. The woman married again, and without her mandate, the father gave a dowry to her husband and stipulated that it should be returned to him, if his daughter died without issue. The woman gave birth to a daughter. The question was whether the *fideicommissum* could be exacted from the father. He replied that if she had not confirmed the dowry given, she still had a claim to the *fideicommissum*. The same person asked whether, if the father was willing to give a receipt for the stipulation, the woman could be barred from suing for the *fideicommissum*. He replied as above, saying that if the father had made the gift provided that the woman confirmed it, he could proceed by *condictio*.   12. A woman appointed her husband Seius as heir, substituted her foster daughter Appia for him, and charged on her heir as a *fideicommissum* that he should restore the inheritance to this foster daughter after his death or if before that anything had happened to the foster daughter, that he should restore the inheritance to Valerianus, her brother's son. The question was whether, if Seius in his lifetime had restored to the foster daughter anything that had come to him from that inheritance, he should be held to have followed the testator's intention by doing so, especially since the foster daughter was his substitute. He replied that if Appia had died in Seius's lifetime, he was not released from the *fideicommissum* left to Valerianus.   13. Scaevola replied: If an appointed heir has been asked to restore the inheritance to another when he pleases, he cannot, in the meantime, be compelled to discharge the *fideicommissum*. CLAUDIUS: For it is in any case taken to be given [for discharge] after [the heir's] death.   14. A testator had imposed as a *fideicommissum* on his appointed heir, that he should restore the whole inheritance to Seia his wife, and charged a *fideicommissum* on his wife in these words: From you, Seia, I ask that you return and restore whatever comes to you from my inheritance, all but what I have bequeathed to you above, to our dearest infant Maevia. I forbid the exaction of security from the said Seia, for I know that she would sooner increase than detract from the property." The question was whether Maevia can claim the *fideicommissum* from Seia immediately. He replied that there was no reason stated why she should not.

42   SCAEVOLA, *Digest, book 33:* Titius appointed Seia his wife heiress for a twelfth share and Maevia for the rest. He provided for the moment he wished to be raised to himself as follows: "I wish my body to be handed over to my wife for burial in such an estate, and a monument to be erected for up to four hundred aurei. Question: Not more than one hundred and fifty aurei having come to the wife as her twelfth share from her husband's property, does this clause show that the testator wished the monument to himself to be erected by her alone? He replied that the monument was to be built by both heiresses in proportion to their shares of the inheritance.

43   CELSUS, *Digest, book 15:* If a father had directed that a dowry should be given to his daughter at her tutor's discretion, Tubero says this is to be taken just as if it had been bequeathed at the discretion of an upright man. Labeo asks: How can you tell how much dowry ought to be provided for the daughter of this person or that, at the discretion of an upright man? He says it is not difficult to estimate from the rank,

means, and number of children of the person making the will.

44 POMPONIUS, *Sabinus, book 2:* If a farm should be bequeathed with what is in it, what is temporarily in it is not held to have been bequeathed. Consequently, monies which were in it to be loaned at interest are not bequeathed.

45 ULPIAN, *Sabinus, book 22:* A bequest of "what has been acquired for the wife" is general and includes both clothing and silver, gold and jewelry, and other things acquired for the wife's sake. But what should be held to be acquired for the wife's sake? Sabinus, in his books on *Vitellius,* wrote: The very frequent addition of the term "what has been acquired for the wife" to legacies for wives has come to be interpreted as what might be acquired more for the wife herself than to be used in common and indiscriminately. It is held to make no difference if the head of the household acquired it before or after marrying the wife, or even if he assigned something to the wife from the things he was in the habit of using himself, as long as it was made over to the wife's personal use.

46 PAUL, *Vitellius, book 2:* This addition, however, sometimes reduces and sometimes increases the legacy. It is increased when the clause reads, "*and* what has been acquired for her"; for this means the addition of anything else, *beyond* what has been said above, that was acquired for this purpose. It is decreased when the conjunction "and" is removed, because then out of all that is comprised above, *only* those things are designated which were acquired for this purpose.

47 ULPIAN, *Sabinus, book 22:* If he acquired any of those things before he married the wife and handed them over to her for her use, it is just as if he had acquired them afterward. But by virtue of this legacy everything belongs to the wife that has been bought, acquired, and kept for this purpose; this includes what belonged to a previous wife, daughter, granddaughter, or daughter-in-law. 1. What is the difference between things bought and acquired? The answer is that what is acquired is not always bought, but what is bought is always acquired. For example, if a man bought something for a previous wife and then handed it over to a subsequent wife, it is agreed that he acquired but did not buy it for the subsequent wife. So even if the husband bought nothing for his subsequent wife, by handing over to her what the previous one had, he is held to have acquired it for her. Things may be given under this legacy, even if they were not made over to the wife. But what was acquired for the previous wife is due to the subsequent wife only if they had been made over to her; for when they were acquired, the subsequent wife was not in his thoughts.

48 PAUL, *Sabinus, book 4:* For not even what was handed over, if it was subsequently taken back, will pass with the legacy.

49 ULPIAN, *Sabinus, book 22:* Again the legacy includes: slaves such as litter-bearers who only carried the *materfamilias;* also draft animals or mules, litter or sedan; also other slaves such as girls whom women dress up with long hair for themselves. 1. But even if he should happen to have given her some things intended for men, they will be held to have been somehow acquired for her. 2. Furthermore, if some things were used by them in common, but he was in the habit of lending them, as it were, for her use, it must be said that they are held to have been acquired for her. 3. Again, it makes a difference whether the legacy to her is of things acquired for her or things bought. For things acquired include everything intended for her use, but things bought are only those which the husband has bought for her. So in legacies of things bought only, nothing is included that the head of the household acquired in some other way and intended for her. But each legacy will include what the husband gave a mandate to be bought, or bought himself, even if he had not yet made them over to her, but would have made them over if he had lived. 4. It makes little difference if it is to a wife or a concubine that someone makes a legacy of things bought and acquired for her. The only difference is that of rank. 5. If gold acquired for a wife was bequeathed and later melted down but the material remains, it is due to her. 6. But for the legacy

to be valid, Proculus wrote that she must have been a wife at the time of death; which is true; for separation extinguishes the legacy.   7. A son or daughter may also be left this legacy: "what has been acquired for his [or her] sake." So may a male or female slave. And it will include what was apportioned to them or intended for them.

50   ULPIAN, *Sabinus, book 23:* If a legacy is left to a son-in-power, "when he enters under his own tutelage," it means the time of puberty. Certainly, if the legacy is to a son-in-power who is *impubes*, it is mostly to be understood, as Sabinus says, as coming to him not when he becomes a *paterfamilias* but when he reaches puberty. However, a woman who entertained suspicions of the life of her husband from whom she was divorced and made a legacy to her son, though *impubes*, is not held to have meant the time of puberty, but the time when he will have reached puberty and also become head of the household. (If he had already reached puberty, we should say all the more that she meant his becoming head of the household.) It is just as if she had said "under his own tutelage and in his own power."   1. But if someone should make a bequest to a head of the household who is *impubes* "when he comes under his own tutelage," it means puberty. Sometimes it also means the age of twenty-five, where the testator's intention is clear. For if he has left him the legacy when he is already of the age of puberty but under twenty-five years, it is beyond doubt that twenty-five years will have been fixed.   2. Again, if a legacy in these terms has been left to a lunatic or spendthrift or to someone to whom the praetor has assigned a curator for just cause, I think he had in mind the event of his release from the curator.   3. From these and similar examples, it appears that Sabinus interpreted the question as one of intention; and he would, in any event, not have doubted that if a legacy in these terms were left to someone of the age of puberty and much more than twenty-five years, the testator was thinking of his being under his own power.   4. So varied is the meaning of this form of words, implying a question of intention, as also is the formula, "when he shall have become independent," for this is taken in different ways at different times. In many instances, it means release from power; in many others, puberty or the twenty-fifth year.   5. I myself think that if someone makes a bequest to a person who has reached puberty but is less than twenty-five years old, he meant the age at which he can no longer avail himself of *restitutio in integrum* [to a *minor*].   6. The same applies if someone has written, "when he becomes of age." One may dispute about the intention, whether puberty or the age of twenty-five is meant, no less than when the wording is "when he becomes of due age" or "of mature age" or "when he grows up."

51   PAUL, *Sabinus, book 4:* A legacy to a daughter-in-power "when she comes under her own tutelage" will be due when she becomes marriageable.

52   ULPIAN, *Sabinus, book 24:* Under the term books are included all rolls, whether of papyrus or parchment or any other material. And even if they are of the rind of the lime or linden tree (as made by some) or of some other bark, the same must be said. But are they due if they are in codex-form, either of parchment or papyrus or ivory or some other material, or of waxed tablets? Let us see. Gaius Cassius wrote that [loose] parchments are due also, when books have been bequeathed. Therefore, it follows that the others too will be due, unless this is contrary to the testator's intention. 1. If someone has been bequeathed one hundred books, we shall give him a hundred rolls, not a hundred of what someone has measured out by his own ingenuity to suffice for writing a book. For instance, if he should have the whole of Homer in one roll, we shall not count this as forty-eight books, but shall take the whole roll of Homer to be one book.   2. If Homer's works are bequeathed and the set is incomplete, as many cantos as can be found will be due.   3. In a legacy of books, the bookcases are not included, as Sabinus writes. So does Cassius; for he says that parchments with writing

on them are due, but added that neither boxes nor cases nor other receptacles for books are due.   4. But what Cassius writes of blank parchments is true. For neither are blank papyri due in a legacy of books, nor when papyri are bequeathed will books be due, unless by any chance we should here be impelled by the testator's wishes, for instance, if someone should happen to have left papyri in these terms, "my entire papyri," when he had nothing other than books, as one scholar to another; for then nobody will doubt that books are due, because many people commonly call books papyri. What then if someone has bequeathed blank papyri? Parchments will not be included, nor any other writing material, nor yet books that have begun to be written.   5. This brings us to what is no bad question: If books have been bequeathed, are unfinished books to be included? I think they are not, any more than what is not yet fully woven is included in the description of clothes. But books fully written out, though not yet hammered or ornamented, will be included. So will books not yet glued together or corrected; and even parchments not yet bound together will be included. 6. A legacy of papyri will include neither papyrus plants acquired for making them, nor papyri not yet perfected.   7. But if someone has bequeathed a *bibliotheca*, is this one bookcase only, or bookcases, or are books included too? Nerva elegantly says that what makes the difference is the sense in which the testator meant the word. For *bibliotheca* can mean a place, as, when we say: "I am going to the *bibliotheca* [library]." At other times, it can mean a case, as when we say: "He bought an ivory *bibliotheca*." At other times, it can mean books, as, when we say: "He bought a [Greek] *bibliotheca*."   7a. So what Sabinus writes, that books do not follow a *bibliotheca*, is not true in every case; for sometimes the cases are also due, which many call *bibliothecae*. Plainly, if you put it to me that the cases are attached or fixed to a room, then they will undoubtedly not be due, since they are a part of the building.   8. What we have discussed in the case of a *bibliotheca* has also been treated by Pomponius in the sixth book of *Sabinus* in the case of the bequest of a ring-casket. He says that the rings are also included, not only the casket which was acquired for the sake of the rings. He concludes this from the fact that someone bequeathed "my ring-casket and any rings I may have besides." And he says Labeo thought the same.   9. However, there are some things that invariably follow a legacy. The legacy of a bed includes the bedposts, and keys and locks pass with cases and caskets.

53   PAUL, *Sabinus, book 4:* When silver is bequeathed, it is accepted that the boxes do not belong to the legatee.   1. In like manner, when rings are bequeathed, the ring-caskets are equally not included.

54   POMPONIUS, *Sabinus, book 7:* If I have left the legacy unconditionally and then later write as follows, "in addition, if my ship arrives from Asia, let my heir give him a farm," the better opinion is that by the words "in addition" what was written above is repeated, as when we say, "Lucius Titius gave five each to the plebs, and in addition Seius gave a distribution of meat." Here we understand Seius to have given five each too. By "Titius accepted five, Seius in addition a farm," we understand that Seius accepted five too.

55   ULPIAN, *Sabinus, book 25:* Wood is a general name, but one distinguishes between timber, which is one thing, and firewood, which is another. Timber is what is needed for building and supporting; firewood is what is acquired for burning. But is it firewood only if it is cut up, or even if it is not? Quintus Mucius, in his second book, states

that if a legacy has been left of the firewood which is in a farm, trees felled for timber are not due. He did not add that they would belong to the legatee if felled not for building but for burning, but it follows that this must be understood.   1. Ofilius, in the fifth book of his *Classification of Law*, wrote: If a bequest of firewood is made to anyone, all firewood is to belong to him which is not called by any other name, such as twigs, charcoal, and olive stones, which are only good for burning, and also acorns and other kernels.   2. In his second book, Ofilius says that trees which are not yet felled, unless they are being cut up, are not held to be included in a legacy of firewood. But my view is that the term firewood comprises what has not yet been cut up, but has already been marked out for cutting up. So if the testator marked out a copse for this purpose, the copse will indeed not pass with the legacy; but the trees which are lying felled will be included under firewood, unless the testator meant otherwise.   3. In a legacy of firewood, what has been acquired for burning is included, whether normally used for warming baths, annexes or hypocausts, or burning lime or anything else. 4. Ofilius wrote in the fifth book of his *Classification of Law* that prunings are not included in the term firewood. But if the testator's wishes are not against it, twigs, brushwood, prunings, chips from timber, and the stems and roots of vines will be included.   5. In certain regions such as Egypt, where reeds are used instead of firewood, the term firewood will include reeds and papyrus plants and certain kinds of grasses and thorns or briars. This is not surprising, since they call it by the Greek word for wood, and call the boats, which bring it from the marshlands, "wood transports."   6. In certain provinces they use cow dung for this purpose.   7. If firewood has been acquired for charcoal-burning, Ofilius, in the fifth book of his *Classification of Law*, says that material of this kind is not included under the term charcoal. But is it firewood? Someone may say that it is not firewood either, since the testator did not have it for this purpose. And should we count wood prepared for firebrands, or treated to make smokeless fuel, as firewood or charcoal or as in categories by themselves? The better course is to classify them separately.   8. Sulphur matches of wood are held distinct in the same way.   9. Wood acquired for torches will also not be included under the term firewood, unless this was the testator's intention.   10. Whole pinecones will be included under the term "firewood."

56   PAUL, *Sabinus, book 4:* Stakes and poles are counted as timber and so are not included under the term "firewood."

57   POMPONIUS, *Sabinus, book 30:* Servius replied that a legacy of the entire timber does not include chests and cases.

58   ULPIAN, *Disputations, book 4:* When a man had bequeathed to his wife all that he had acquired for her and afterward, in his lifetime, purchased purple garments in a province, but had not yet brought them back, it was ruled in a rescript that the purple garments belonged to the woman.

59   JULIAN, *Digest, book 34:* A testator who bequeaths a note-of-hand has in mind not so much the document as the right of action which the document confirms. It is well known that we use the term "bond" for the action itself, since when a note-of-hand is sold we understand that the debt has been sold. And indeed if anyone bequeaths the name of a debtor, this is understood to be a legacy of what is to be had from the actions.

60   ALFENUS, *Digest, Epitomized by Paul, book 2:* In the case of a bequest of lambs, the question was up to what age they are lambs. Some said a lamb was no more than six months old. But the better opinion is that those less than one year were included in the legacy.   1. When a testator's urban slaves, male and female, had been bequeathed,

I replied that the legacy did not include his groom and muleteer; for that number should be held to comprise only those whom the head of the household had about him for his personal care and maintenance. 2. When a legacy had been left to a wife of the wool, linen, and purple acquired for her and the testator had left a quantity of wool of all kinds, the question was whether it was all due. He replied that if he had intended none of it for the wife's use but all was mixed together, the discussion was not unlike that concerning a legacy of victuals, when the head of the household had left a quantity of victuals from which he had been accustomed to sell. For if he had bottled off wine for the use of himself and his heir, it would still all be counted as victuals. But when it was proved that the testator had been accustomed to sell part of the victuals, it was ruled that the heirs should give from them to the legatee what he would need for a year's supply. I consider that the same ruling should apply to the wool; so let the woman take from it what is enough for a year's supply. For the legacy left to the wife was not the residue after deduction of what the husband would need for his personal use, but what he had acquired for hers. 3. A legacy of lands and of what has been bought and acquired for cultivating them includes neither an ornamental gardener nor a gamekeeper. For the ornamental gardener is acquired to adorn, the gamekeeper to look after and protect the farm rather than to cultivate it. A donkey that drives the mill is held to be included, as are sheep acquired for manuring the land and the shepherd who looks after this kind of sheep.

61   ALFENUS, *Digest, Epitomized by Paul, book 8:* A testator bequeathed all the weavers which should be his when he died. The question was whether one of them whom he had later made a door-keeper was included in the bequest. He replied that he was, because he had been transferred not to another craft but to another use.

62   JULIAN, *Ambiguities, sole book:* A man who had two mules left a legacy as follows: "Let my heir give two *muli* [he-mules] which shall be mine when I die." He left no he-mules but two *mulae* [she-mules]. Servius replied that the legacy was due, for she-mules are included under the term *muli*, just as *servae* [female slaves] are mostly included under the term *servi* [male slaves]. This comes from the usual practice of including the feminine in the masculine.

63   JULIAN, *Urseius Ferox, book 1:* When legacies are repeated, the common addition, "let him also be condemned to give," refers to conditions and dates of payment also, as Sabinus replied.

64   AFRICANUS, *Questions, book 6:* A man who appointed his son as heir gave to his grandson by *fideicommissum* certain lands, and what would be in them at the time of his death, except for his debt book. At the time of his death, the safe which held the documents and *cautiones* of his debtors was found to contain some ready money. Most held it very unlikely that the testator had meant the ready money. But I thought it worth noting whether, when someone wished his debt book to be delivered to anybody, he wished only the claims in the debt book to be delivered, or any money too which had been exacted from these debtors but intended for the same debt book. I should rather think that just as the change of debtors' names should not extinguish or reduce the *fideicommissum* if the money had been exacted and reinvested, the money itself, if still intended for the debt book, that is, for lending, should belong to the same *fideicommissum*. I should think that one could go even further and defend the view that not only money exacted from debtors but that obtained from any source whatever, if intended for the same account, should belong to the *fideicommissum*.

65   MARCIAN, *Institutes, book 7:* When a legacy was left of slaves, with the exception of traders, Labeo wrote those should be held to be excepted who had been entrusted with the exercise of some trade, such as those in charge of buying, letting, and hiring. But valets, caterers, or overseers of fishermen should not be held to be included under

the term traders. And I think Labeo's view is correct.   1. If someone is transferred from an office to a craft, as when a litter-bearer later becomes a cook, some rightly think the legacy is extinguished because the office is replaced by the craft. But this does not apply in reverse.   2. If one slave knows several crafts and cooks have been bequeathed to one person, weavers to another, the slave must be said to go to the one to whom the practitioners of the craft with which he is mos₊ familiar have been bequeathed.   3. When women have been bequeathed as dressers, Celsus wrote that those who have been only two months with an instructor shall not belong to the legacy. But others say that these too should belong, ʟo forestall a situation where none may do so, since all of them could still learn and every craft allows of improvement. This opinion should be preferred, as it accords with human nature.   4. A legacy of *pecora* (herd animals), Cassius wrote, includes all four-footed creatures that feed gregariously. Pigs, too, are included under the term *pecora*, for they also feed in herds, as Homer says in the *Odyssey*:

> You'll find him where his pigs are foraging
> By Raven's Crag and Arethusa's Spring.

5. Oxen are not included among draft animals, nor vice versa.   6. But a legacy of horses includes mares.   7. Lambs are not included in a legacy of sheep. How long they are to be considered as lambs depends on the custom of each place; for in certain places, they are counted as sheep after the first shearing.

66   PAUL, *Sentences, book 3:* In a legacy of birds, geese, pheasants, hens, and cages of birds are due. Keepers of pheasants and geese are not due, unless the testator expressed that wish.

67   MARCIAN, *Institutes, book 7:* A testator who bequeathed summer pastures and in addition the things usually kept there is not held to have meant the herd animals which spend the winter on winter pastures and the summer on summer pastures, but he meant those which are there all the time.

68   ULPIAN, *Replies, book 1:* To Junianius he replied that a testator by adding "all the Seian estate" was held to have left by *fideicommissum* that part of the farm above-written which he had acquired as a pledge, as though it belonged to him, while safeguarding the rights of the debtor.   1. From the words "look after the fields carefully, and in this way it will come about that my son will grant you your sons as a favor," a *fideicommissum* cannot be claimed.   2. Slaves owned in common, left by Seia "if they shall be mine when I die" are not due, provided that the testatrix meant that they should only be due if they were wholly hers.   3. When lands have been left "with such appurtenances as were in these possessions," the estate slaves shall pass if they were there at the time of making the will. And so shall those that were added later, provided that the testator expressed clearly the wish that they should.

69   MARCELLUS, *Replies, sole book:* One ought only to depart from the sense of the words when it is clear that the testator meant something else.   1. Titius provided in his codicil as follows: "To Publius Maevius I wish to be given all the young men in my service." Question: By what upper and lower limit of age are young men to be defined? Marcellus replied that it was for the person taking *cognitio* of the matter to decide whom the testator wished to indicate by the words stated. For in the case of wills, one

surely must not stoop to definitions, since most people speak carelessly and do not employ the right names and words. But one could hold that a young man is one who has passed adolescence and has not yet begun to be counted among the older men.

70   ULPIAN, *Sabinus, book 22:* If wool is bequeathed, the legacy is held to be of what is not yet dyed, but is in its original state.   1. This, whether processed or not, is included under the term "wool."   2. It has been asked whether the term "wool" includes only unspun or also spun wool such as the warp and the weft. Sabinus said that spun wool was included, an opinion that we follow.   3. It is held that the term "wool" may be extended to when it is on the loom.   4. And it should be noted that wool with its natural oil is included, and washed wool also so long as it is not dyed.   5. The term "wool" will not include upholstery.   6. Neither will it include the wool from which someone has made any kind of covering against ill-health or for special comfort.   7. Nor will the term "wool" include what has been acquired for the sake of poultices or treatment of the sick.   8. But should fleeces be included? Yes, they clearly pass with wool.   9. A legacy of wool may, I believe, even include the hair of goats and hares, the feathers of geese, and the product of wood which in Greek they call "tree-wool" [cotton].   10. But flax will not in any event be included.   11. A legacy of flax includes both finished and unfinished linen, what is spun and what is on the loom but not yet fully woven. So flax is treated differently from wool. And if there is any dyed linen, I think it will be included under flax.   12. Let us consider colored stuffs. It was settled by the old jurists that colored stuff is not included under the term wool. But [in a legacy of colored stuff] everything is included that has been dyed, and spun, and is not fully woven and finished off. A further question is whether purple is included in colored stuff. For my part, I think that what is not dyed is not to be counted as colored stuff, and, therefore, what is white or naturally black or of any other natural color is not included. But purple and scarlet, because they are not natural colors, I think must be included, unless the testator intended otherwise.   13. Under the term "purple," I think purple of every kind is included. Scarlet will not be included, but *fucinum* (the dye of the orchella-weed) and violet will be. Purple-dyed weft will undoubtedly be included, but not wool that was intended for purple-dying.

71   ULPIAN, *Sabinus, book 20:* When in a will someone writes of "his" male or female slaves, he is held to mean those whom the head of the household had in the number of his household.

72   PAUL, *Sabinus, book 4:* The same is to be said in the case of all things which someone has bequeathed as "his."

73   ULPIAN, *Sabinus, book 20:* But "his" male or female servants we take to be those who are his in the full legal sense among whom those in whom he has a usufruct will not be included.   1. But it is preferable that those who serve the testator in good faith should be included under the term "his," so long as he wished those to be included whom he had in the number of his household.   2. But slaves pledged by anyone as *pignus* or *hypotheca* will be held as undoubtedly bequeathed as "his" by the debtor, certainly not by the creditor.   3. Moreover, if someone had slaves of his own but has

hired out their services as bakers or players or the like, should he be held to have bequeathed them as "his" slaves? Yes, this should be presumed, unless the testator evidently intended the contrary. 4. A man who was earning his living as a slave-dealer would not, I think, readily wish slaves of this kind to be included in the number of his own slaves, unless he gave evidence of intending this to be his meaning. For when someone has bought slaves for immediate disposal by sale, he is to be considered as having had them as merchandise rather than as "his" household. 5. *Vicarii,* Pomponius wrote in his fifth book, are not included among the number of the testator's household.

74 POMPONIUS, *Sabinus, book 6:* If anyone has bequeathed "his" slaves, then slaves held in common and those in whom another person has a usufruct are included.

75 ULPIAN, *Sabinus, book 20:* Where coins have been left without distinction, it is accepted that the less valuable ones should be held to have been bequeathed, if the denomination does not appear from the custom of the head of the household, the practice of the region where he was, or the context of the will.

76 ULPIAN, *Edict, book 2:* Nobody will say that written sheets and finished books should pass with a legacy of papyri. The same applies to tablets.

77 JAVOLENUS, *From Plautius, book 1:* When legacies are repeated as a charge on the substitute, grants of freedom are included.

78 PAUL, *Vitellius, book 2:* The question concerned the slave Stichus who had been taken from the farm a year before the testator's death and handed over for instruction and had not afterward returned to the farm. Was he due? The reply was that if the testator had sent him for study, but not with a view to transferring him away from the farm, he was due. 1. "My son Maevius, as I have given to you the greatest part of my means, you should be content with the Sempronian farm with its inhabitants, that is, the estate slaves, and what will be there." The question was: What of the debt claims and the cash? The same testatrix sent a letter in these terms: "All the silver and household goods that I may have I give to you and whatever I may have in the Sempronian estate." Would the household goods in the other estates or houses belong to Maevius? And would this be true of the slaves of the Sempronian farm which she had bequeathed to others? The reply was that the debt claims and the cash were not held to be due, unless it could be proved that the deceased clearly intended them to be bequeathed too. Slaves from the Sempronian farm given to others would diminish the son's legacy. The assessment of the silver and household goods elsewhere should be left to the person responsible for judging the case, so that the intention of the deceased, as proved by the legatee, should hold good. 2. A certain person left lands, adding these words, "as possessed by me, and whatever shall be in them when I die." The question was about the slaves who had stayed on these lands to do farm labor or some other service and about the other things that were there at the time of death: Would they belong to the legatee? He replied that all the things in question were held to have been bequeathed. 3. "I ask you, my heirs, to convey to my foster daughter Genesia my Campanian farm for two hundred aurei, just as it is." The question is whether the tenants' arrears and any slaves that were in the farm at the time of death should go with the farm. He replied that the tenants' arrears were indeed not bequeathed, but the rest should be held to be given by the words "just as it is." 4. Someone may perhaps ask why, under the term silver, silversmith's work is included, whereas when marble is bequeathed nothing beyond the raw material can be held to have been intended. The accepted reason is that objects whose nature is such that they can repeatedly be reduced to their original state are subsumed under the property of the raw material and do not achieve an identity of their own. 5. Scarlet is

called by a proper name, but no one will doubt that it passes with colored stuff. And have raven-black, crimson, or Melian gray any less distinct names than scarlet or purple? 6. When a man had left a legacy in these terms, "what has been acquired for my wife, I give and bequeath to her," I claimed, before the praetor responsible for *fideicommissa*, those things taken at a valuation whose price was in the dowry. I did not obtain them on the grounds that the testator did not have these things in mind. But if they were given for her use, it makes no difference whether they were bought from her or from someone else. Afterward I found the following case described in Aburnius Valens: A woman gave certain things at a valuation by way of dowry. Afterward the husband made her a bequest in these words: "what was acquired or purchased for her." He said that the term "acquired or purchased" did not include what had been given by way of dowry, unless the husband, after they had become his, had converted them to his wife's use. 7. To a legacy of things in a farm, those which are not there will be added if they are usually there, but those which are there by chance are not held to be bequeathed.

79 CELSUS, *Digest, book 9:* If a choir or staff of slaves should be bequeathed, it is just as if individual men were bequeathed. 1. The words "such movables of mine as shall be there, I give and bequeath" do not, Proculus says, imply that cash which has been kept there for loans has been bequeathed. But monies kept there for safe-keeping, as some people were in the habit of doing during the civil wars, are included in the legacy. As he says he had heard aged country folk saying that "no reliance could be placed on money without *peculium*," meaning by *peculium* what was put aside for safety. 2. An open space that was bequeathed, if built on in the meantime and now an open space once more, could not be claimed while built on but will now be due. 3. A bequeathed slave, if manumitted in the meantime and afterward reduced to slavery again, can be claimed.

80 CELSUS, *Digest, book 35:* Appointing heirs jointly or leaving legacies jointly means that the whole inheritance and the whole of the legacies are given severally but shared concurrently.

81 MODESTINUS, *Distinctions, book 9:* Certain authorities rightly think that under a legacy of *servi* (male slaves), *ancillae* (female slaves) are also due, because a common name includes both sexes. But nobody doubts that under a legacy of *ancillae* males are not due. Again, when boys are bequeathed, girls will be due; but boys are not equally held to be included under girls. 1. Where women are bequeathed, virgins are also due, just as, when men are bequeathed, it will be held that boys are due. 2. Where *pecudes* (farm animals) are bequeathed, oxen, and other draft animals, are included. 3. Where a herd is bequeathed, it is settled that cattle are included, but not flocks of sheep and goats. 4. Where sheep are bequeathed, certain authorities rightly think that male lambs and rams are not included. 5. But where a flock of sheep is bequeathed, nobody doubts that male lambs and rams are both due.

82 MODESTINUS, *Rules, book 9:* If a slave who used to stay in the farm takes to flight, then, even if he is caught after the death of the testator, he passes with the bequest of the farm with its equipment.

83 MODESTINUS, *Replies, book 10:* When a bequest is made in these words, "I ask you to restore, when you die, whatever comes to you from my inheritance or my goods," it is held that the fruits collected by the heir in his lifetime, and what is in lieu of fruits does not pass. Nor has anything been stated from which the testatrix can be proved to have asked that these too should be restored. 1. MODESTINUS: A testator, who was leaving a *fideicommissum* in favor of his freedmen, substituted them one for another and expressed the wish that after the death of the last one it should belong to their descendants. Question: Since there is no one except a freedman of the one who died, should he be admitted to the *fideicommissum*? He replied that it is absolutely certain that under the term "descendants," only children and not freedmen also were included among those to whom the *fideicommissum* was left.

84   JAVOLENUS, *From Cassius, book 2:* In a bequest of what was at Rome, what was stored for safe keeping in warehouses outside the city will also be due to the legatee.

85   POMPONIUS, *Quintus Mucius, book 2:* It was recently decreed by the emperor that where the word "my" is not added to a legacy of an article, it should be valid, provided that the testator meant it to be delivered if it should be his. So it appears that preference is given to considering the meaning of the legator, not the word "my." This gives rise to an elegant distinction to the effect that whenever a specific article is bequeathed, the addition of the word "my" with reference to present time does not make a condition, but if an unspecified thing is bequeathed, such as "my wines," "my clothing," the word "my" is taken as a condition that those things should be taken as bequeathed if they are his. This I do not think can be defended strongly, but here too it is preferable that the bequest should be of the clothing or wine which he had counted as his. In this way, it was replied that even wine which had gone sour should pass with the legacy, if the testator had counted it as his. Plainly, when referring to the time of death, the expression "the clothing which shall be mine" must undoubtedly, I think, be taken as a condition. But "Stichus who shall be mine" should also, I believe, be taken as a condition, and it makes no difference if it is "who shall be mine" or "if he shall be mine"; it is a condition in either case. Labeo admittedly writes that this form of words applied to future time is to be taken as a description, but we follow a different rule.

86   PROCULUS, *Letters, book 5:* Where a legacy has been left as follows, "the house and what of mine shall be in it when I die," I do not think that cash exacted when due from debtors, so as to be lent to others, is included. And I warmly approve of Labeo's distinction in writing that what was accidentally missing is bequeathed nonetheless, and what was accidentally present none the more.

87   PAUL, *Lex Julia et Papia, book 4:* The term "legacy" includes both a *fideicommissum* and a gift *mortis causa*.

88   PAUL, *Lex Julia et Papia, book 5:* When wool has been bequeathed, it is settled that clothes made of wool are not due.   1. Again, when timber has been bequeathed, a ship or a cupboard made from timber is not to be vindicated.   2. When a ship that was bequeathed has been broken up, neither the timber nor the ship will be due.   3. But when a mass of metal has been bequeathed, cups made out of it can be exacted.

89   PAUL, *Lex Julia et Papia, book 6:* Legatees are held to be joint in deed but not in word, when the same thing is bequeathed to them severally. Again, they are joint in word but not in deed where the bequest reads, "I give and bequeath to Titius and Seius a farm in equal shares," when both legatees have had shares from the beginning. So in all cases the legatee who is joint both in word and deed has the preference. One who is only joint in word is held to have no priority. Where one is joint in deed, not word, it is a question whether the joint legatee is preferable; and the better opinion is that he is preferred here also.

90   PAUL, *Lex Julia et Papia, book 7:* A legacy is to be taken as being charged on a named person, when it is understood on whom it is charged, even if the name is not expressed.

91   PAPINIAN, *Replies, book 7:* Where lands have been given to a daughter to take in advance together with the arrears from the managers and tenants, the legacy is held to be of such residue as comes from the revenue of the lands and has remained for the purpose of the lands. On the other hand, it will readily be agreed that money exacted from the tenants and turned into the debt book for lending out at interest in the same region is not included in the arrears from the tenants and managers, even if the testator named the managers as intended by him to belong to his daughter.   1. From these words "to Lucius Titius my lands with the country house, as I possessed them on the day of my death," it is agreed that the farm equipment and everything that was there for the better equipment of the master was due; but the arrears from the tenants are not.   2. A father bequeathed to his son a purple shop, with the slave factors and the purple that was in it on the day of his death. It was held that the legacy included

neither the price set aside to buy purple nor the debts nor the arrears. 3. "To Titius I give and bequeath the Seian lands, as they were purchased." Since the Gabinian lands were also purchased at the same time for the same price, I replied that the proof of purchase was not enough by itself, but that examination should be held into whether the Gabinian lands were also included under the term Seian in letters and accounts, and whether the revenue from both possessions had been put together and entered under the rubric of the Seian. 4. It was settled that a legacy of a house would include a bathhouse. If the bathhouse had been made available to the public, it would be held a portion of the house, provided that access to it had been through the house, it had often been used by the head of the household and his wife, the income from it had been entered under the same account with the other letting income from the house, and house and baths had been bought for one payment or built at common expense. 5. A person who possessed a house bought a garden adjoining the house and later bequeathed the house. If he bought the garden for the house, so as to make the house he possessed more convenient and healthy, and had access to the garden through the house and the garden was an addition to the house, the garden will be included in the legacy. 6. Under the term "house" is included a tenement building joined to a house, if they were bought with the house by one payment, and the rents from both were entered in the accounts together.

92 PAUL, *Replies, book 13:* "If Maevia and Negidia become my heirs, then let Maevia take from my estate as an advance legacy and keep for herself this farm and that farm with the cottages and keepers of all these farms, and with all such fields as have been joined to them by purchase or in any other way, and with all the slaves, herd animals, draft animals, and the whole of all the other things that shall be in these farms or in one of them, when I die, on the best and greatest terms, and as I possessed them on the day of my death, and to put it more fully with all that is in their enclosures." Now in one of these farms left to be taken in advance, there is a deed box containing the purchases of several slaves, deeds of farms and various contracts, and debt claims besides. Question: Are these documents the common property of the heirs? I replied that upon the case as put, the documents of purchases and loans which had remained in the farm left in advance were not to be included in the legacy. 1. Where houses were left in these words, "I charge on my heirs as a *fideicommissum* that they allow him to have my houses in which I live with nothing excepted whatever and with all their equipment and contents," the testator is not to be held to have meant cash or documents of debtors.

93 SCAEVOLA, *Replies, book 3:* Lucius Titius provided in his will that his heir should in no way alienate his suburban estate or house. He appointed his daughter as heiress. She left as heiress her own daughter, who possessed these properties for a long time and died, appointing outsiders as heirs. The question was whether the estates belonged to Julia, the great-niece of Lucius Julius the testator. He replied that nothing had been stated that had been done against the wishes of the deceased to prevent the estates from belonging to the heir, since this had been a bare precept. 1. "To Sempronia, my wife, I direct my heirs to pay a hundred aurei which I had borrowed from her." The question was whether, if Sempronia had sued for this money as a debt and had lost, it could be claimed as a *fideicommissum.* He replied that on the case as put, the money could be claimed under the *fideicommissum,* since it appeared that it was not due on any other account. 2. A certain person bequeathed lands to his freedmen with the addition of these words: "as possessed by me and with whatever shall be there when I die." The question was whether the slaves who had stayed on these lands to the day of the head of the household's death for farm labor or other work, and the other things there, would belong to the legatees. He replied that they would. 3. It was asked whether what the heirs had been asked to restore to the brothers would

also belong to the sisters. He replied that they would, unless the testator were proved to have meant otherwise.   4. Someone left a farm with the woods that usually went with it on the best and greatest terms to a *collegium* of smiths. Would the things which were there on the day of his death, that is, hay, fodder, and straw, the mill, wine vessels, that is, casks and vats fixed to the cellar, and granaries be bequeathed? He replied that what was not bequeathed could not rightly be claimed.   5. A testator bequeathed a farm to take in advance to one whom he had appointed heir to a half share and asked him: "I ask you, please, to accept as co-heirs in my Julian farm, which I have directed that you should receive in addition, my grandson and your kinsman Clodius Verus." Should a share of the farm be due to the grandson by virtue of the *fideicommissum*? He replied that it should.

94   VALENS, *Fideicommissa, book 2:* A man who left numerous freedmen bequeathed a farm to three of them and had asked that they should see to it that it did not pass to those not of his name. The question was whether the first of these three to die should leave his share to one or both of his co-legatees or whether he could leave it to another fellow freedman of his. It was held that despite this being a question of intention, he would satisfy the terms if he left it to another. But if he gave it to no one, there was doubt whether the claim for the *fideicommissum* would lie in favor of the first to take action, or of all the freedmen, or only of those to whom the legacy had equally been bequeathed. And Julian rightly thought that it was due to all.

95   MAECIANUS, *Fideicommissa, book 2:* "Whoever shall be my heir, let him be condemned to give, and I charge him with the *fideicommissum* of giving, sums of the quantity that I shall prescribe and give." Aristo says that tangible objects are also included here, such as lands, slaves, clothing, and silver, because the word "quantity" does not refer only to cash, as appears from the rebequeathing of dowry, and stipulations for purchase of inheritances; and the term "sums" should be taken in a similar way, as is shown by the proofs adduced. Besides, the intention of the deceased, which is of the greatest weight in *fideicommissa*, supports this opinion. For after this preface the testator would not have gone on to add tangible objects, if he had only wished cash to be delivered.

96   GAIUS, *Fideicommissa, book 2:* If Titius, a part-heir, has been asked to restore the inheritance to Maevius and his co-heir has, in turn, been asked to restore his part or part of his part to Titius, should Titius restore to Maevius the part which he received from his co-heir under a *fideicommissum*? The deified Antoninus was consulted and ruled in a rescript that he should not restore it; for neither legacies nor *fideicommissa* are included under the term inheritance.

97   PAUL, *Judgments, book 2:* A certain Hosidius, having appointed his daughter Valeriana as heiress, granted his freedom to his manager Antiochus, and bequeathed to him certain lands and *peculium* and the arrears, both his own and those of the tenants. The legatee brought forward a note in the handwriting of the head of the household of arrears both on his own and his tenants' account. This writing had the following addition: "item of what he must give account," namely of what the head of the household had in store of corn, wine, and other things. The freedman had sued for these things too and said they were part of the arrears and had won his case before the governor. On the other side, it was argued that what was being claimed was neither the tenants' arrears nor his own, but the case of the things in store was different. The emperor asked the legatee's side: "Suppose, for the sake of argument, that there were a hundred aurei in store for regular use, would you say that everything in the safe was due?" And he upheld the heiress's appeal. On the legatee's side, it was suggested that

some arrears had been exacted from the tenants after the father's death. He replied that what had been exacted after death should be returned to the legatee.

98   PAUL, *Form of a Will, sole book:* If there are several degrees of heirs and the will reads, "let my heir give," these words apply to all degrees, as do the words "whoever shall be my heir." So if someone should wish not to charge all the heirs with payment of the legacies, but only some of them, he must condemn these to give by name.

99   PAUL, *Meaning of Documents, sole book:* Where town slaves have been bequeathed, some authorities distinguish them not by their place but by their work, so that even if they are on country estates but do not do country work they are held to be town slaves. But it should be said that town slaves must be understood to be those whom the head of the household used to count as his town slaves, which is best gathered from the list of his staff and also from his ration allowances.   1. There may be doubt whether huntsmen and fowlers should be included under town or country slaves, but it should be said that where the head of the household used to maintain them and they stayed is where they should be counted as belonging.   2. Muleteers belong to the town service, unless the testator intended them for country work.   3. Some maintain that the child of a female town slave who has been sent to the farm to be nursed is for the time being in neither category. But let us see whether it should not be taken to belong to the town slaves. That is more acceptable.   4. If the litter-bearing slaves have been bequeathed and one of the litter-bearers is a cook, he will pass with the legacy.   5. If the home-bred slaves have been bequeathed to one person and the runners to another and some home-bred slaves are runners too, they will pass with the runners. For the particular always takes precedence over the general. If both legacies tally in both general and particular, they will mostly be owned in common.

100   JAVOLENUS, *From the Posthumous Works of Labeo, book 2:* "Let my heir be condemned to restore to Lucius Titius my slave Stichus," or as follows: "Let him restore such a slave to such a person." Cascellius says the legacies are due, and Labeo does not impugn this view, since whoever is directed to restore is directed to give.   1. Two marble statues were bequeathed to a certain person by name and also all the marble. Cascellius thinks no marble statue is due beyond two; Ofilius and Trebatius are against this. Labeo approves Cascellius's opinion, which I think true, because by specifying the legacy of two statues, the testator can be seen not to have thought of including any statues in the legacy of marble.   2. "To my wife I give and bequeath the clothing, lady's toilet articles, all the jewelry, gold, and silver which has been made or acquired for her." Trebatius thinks the words "made and acquired for her" apply only to the gold and silver; Proculus, to everything, which is correct.   3. In the case of a legacy of Corinthian vases, Trebatius replied that the bronze bases, which had been acquired as stands for these vases, were also due. But Labeo does not approve this, unless the testator counted these bases among his vases. Proculus, however, rightly says that if they are bronze, but not Corinthian bronze they are not due.   4. In the case of a legacy of tortoise-shell articles, Labeo and Trebatius replied that tortoise-shell couches with silver-plated feet were also due, which is correct.

101   SCAEVOLA, *Digest, book 16:* Someone who had lands of his own and others pledged to him for debts in the province where he was born wrote in a codicil as follows: "To my dearest native city I wish to be given for its share, and I allot to it all the places I possess in Syria with all the cattle, slaves, fruits, stores, and equipment that are in them." The question was whether the lands which the testator had by way of pledge should also be held to have been left to his native city. He replied that, upon the case as put, they should not be held to have been left, provided that they had not been included in his own patrimony, which generally happens when the debtor fails to pay.   1. "I ask that my farm should be given, as it is, to my foster daughter." The question was whether any arrears from the tenants and slaves that were in that farm at the

time of death should be due. He replied that the arrears from the tenants were indeed not bequeathed, but the rest was to be held given by the words "as it is."

102   SCAEVOLA, *Digest, book 17:* A legacy was left in these words: "To my wife, my saddlebags and whatever shall be stored in them, anything that shall be contained in parchment leaves written in my own hand if not exacted when I die, even if entered in my accounts and even if I have handed the *cautiones* to my manager." This man stored the notes-of-hand of debtors and money in his saddlebags when about to set off to the city, and, after exacting the debts due and expending the money, returned to his native place after two years, and stored other notes-of-hand for lands which he had subsequently bought and money in the saddlebags. The question was whether he was to be held to have bequeathed to his wife only those debts which he stored in the saddlebags after his subsequent return. He replied that, upon the case as put, only that was due which was in the saddlebags at the time of death, and was contained on parchments written in his handwriting. The same person asked whether, as he had stored the deeds of land purchases in the saddlebags, the lands also went with the legacy. He replied that it did not clearly appear what he had intended about the lands, but if he had stored the deeds there with the intention of giving them to the legatee with the ownership of the lands, it could be argued that the lands were also due. 1. A head of a household made the following bequest: "I wish him to be given two unchased dishes which I bought in the market for little images." He had not bought unchased dishes in this market, but he did have dishes which he had bought there and had dictated his will three days before his death. The question was whether the dishes he had bought in the image market should pass with the legacy, since he had not bought any other dishes there or bequeathed them. He replied that upon the case as put the dishes he had bought in the image market should be due. 2. Someone directed that a commission should be bought for his foster son in these words: "To Sempronius, my foster son, this and that; and when he is old enough I wish such a commission to be bought for him, with the admission fee, and with all that goes with it intact." The question was whether, if Sempronius bought the commission for himself, its price, and the customary admission fee, could be claimed from the heirs by virtue of the *fideicommissum.* He replied that, upon the facts as put, it could. 3. The same testator bequeathed a commission to his freedman in these words: "To Seius, my freedman I give and bequeath such a commission." This commission the testator had himself. The question was whether all the burdens and the admission fee should be paid by the heir. He replied that they should.

103   SCAEVOLA, *Questions Publicly Debated, sole book:* If a father had disinherited his son and substituted a stranger as heir and then this outsider appointed this son as heir and he, having becoming heir, dies before puberty, I think the substitute for this son need not deliver the legacies at all, since the inheritance has of the father has come to the son not directly but through succession. 1. In the case of a brother who, when he became heir to his father, appointed his disinherited brother heir, I have taken it that his substitute does not owe a legacy, not even if he succeeds his brother by reason of intestacy, since the father's goods will have come to him not directly but through succession. 2. If a son has been appointed heir to a twelfth of the estate and legacies given by him and he has a substitute and, because another son has invoked the edict, he has

received *bonorum possessio* of half, should his substitute pay all or half the legacies? The better opinion is that he should pay half to children and parents.   3. On the other hand, if he has been appointed heir to three quarters and the edict is invoked and he receives *bonorum possessio* of half, the legacies will be due from the substitute for that half only. For the more there is in the *bonorum possessio*, the more they are increased; and similarly, the less there is, the more they are reduced.

BOOK THIRTY-THREE

1

ANNUAL LEGACIES AND *FIDEICOMMISSA*

1 POMPONIUS, *Sabinus, book 5:* When a legacy is to be paid annually and nothing is added about the place where payment is to be made, it should be paid wherever it is demanded, as in the case of a stipulation or a debt.
2 POMPONIUS, *Sabinus, book 6:* When an heir is charged by legacy (*sinendi modo*) to allow me the annual usufruct of a farm, if he causes a delay at the beginning of a year in which I should cultivate it, then, although he afterward allows me to do so, nevertheless, he will be liable to me for the entire year, because I have been prevented from cultivating it. Similarly, if he is charged by legacy (*per damnationem*) to make the daily labor of Stichus available to me, and does so not from the morning but from the sixth hour of the day, he is liable for the whole day.
3 ULPIAN, *Sabinus, book 24:* If a legacy, for example, of thirty, is left payable after one, two, and three years, ten are owed each year, even though "in equal payments" is not added. 1. Likewise, if "by payments" is added, though "equal" is not inserted and likewise, if "equal" is written but "payments" not added, it must be said that the payments are to be equal. 2. But if "by unequal payments" is added, unequal payments will be owed: Let us, therefore, see what payments are due. I think those are owed (unless the testator has specifically given the choice to the heir) which a good man judges consistent with the resources of the deceased and the situation of the property. 3. But if "in accordance with the judgment of a good man" has been added, we shall follow the principle that it should be made with regard for the situation of the property and without trouble and inconvenience to the heir. 4. What if the wording is "by whatever payments the legatee thinks fit?" Let us see whether he may demand the whole. I think that the whole must not be demanded at once, just as in the case where the choice is granted to the heir. For the testator wanted more than one payment to be made and placed only the amounts of those payments in the control of the heir or the legatee. 5. But if the legacy is made in these terms, "let my heir give ten to Titius in three years," would the sum be owed in installments or at the end of three years? I think it is to be understood as if the head of the household were shown to have intended payments after one, two, and three years. 6. If a certain amount is legated to someone and the testator has ordered a certain fixed sum to be paid by way of interest every year until the legacy is paid, the legacy is valid, but in the matter of the interest, it should be valid only insofar as it does not exceed the acceptable rate of interest.
4 PAUL, *Edict, book 62:* If a legacy is made to be paid annually to someone, Sabinus, whose opinion is correct, says that several legacies have been made and that the legacy for the first year is unconditional, while those for the following years are conditional; for the condition "if he lives" is regarded as included, and, therefore, when he is dead, the legacy does not pass to his heir.
5 MODESTINUS, *Replies, book 10:* "Of you also, my other heirs, I request that you provide for my wife, as long as she lives, ten aurei a year." The wife survived her husband by five years and four months. I ask whether the legacy is owed to her heirs for the whole of the sixth year. Modestinus replied that the legacy is owed for the whole of the sixth year.
6 MODESTINUS, *Replies, book 11:* A man left an annual sum of money to his city for games at which he wanted his heirs to preside. The successors of the heirs deny that they are

liable on the ground that the testator wanted it to be paid only as long as the heirs presided. I ask, therefore, whether, since he mentioned presiding, he wanted the *fideicommissum* to be paid for a period or in perpetuity. Modestinus replied that the *fideicommissum* must be paid to the city each year in perpetuity.

7   POMPONIUS, *Quintus Mucius, book 8:* Quintus Mucius says that if a man has written as follows in his will, "let my sons and daughters reside where their mother wishes them to reside and let my heir be charged to give ten aurei each year to each boy and girl by way of subsistence," but the tutors are unwilling to give that money to the person at whose house the boys and girls reside, there is no ground of action under the terms of the will. For the object of that clause is that the tutors may know what the testator's wishes were, so that they may pay the money without risk. POMPONIUS: Some things are written in wills which merely indicate the testator's wishes and do not create an obligation. The following are of this kind: if I institute you my sole heir and write that you should erect a monument to me for a fixed sum; for that clause involves no obligation, but you can, if you desire, put it into effect in order to carry out my wish. It will be otherwise if I write the same clause after giving you a co-heir; for if I charge you alone to erect the monument, your co-heir will be able to bring an action for dividing the inheritance to make you do so, since it is in his interest. Moreover, if you are both ordered to do it, you will both be entitled to the action against each other. It is also a matter of the testator's wishes when a man has ordered statues to be placed in a municipality; for if he did this to honor not the municipality but himself, nobody is entitled to an action on that ground. So the clause, cited by Quintus Mucius, "let my children reside where their mother wishes them to reside," creates no obligation, but it will be a matter of the upholding of the wishes of the deceased that they should reside where he ordered. Nevertheless, his wish or instruction should not always be upheld, as, for instance, if the praetor is informed that it is not in the interest of the *pupillus* for him to reside where his father ordered on account of some vice, which the father chanced not to know was present in those persons with whom he ordered him to reside. But if ten aurei a year have been left for their subsistence, the legacy will be valid, whether it be taken to refer to those with whom the mother wished the *pupilli* to reside or whether we take it that the legacy is owed to the children themselves, the more so, as he appears to have done this out of forethought for his children. And in all cases where the testator's wishes alone are concerned, they must neither be entirely disregarded nor entirely upheld. But all these things ought to be put into effect by the intervention of the judge, if they do not relate to any dishonorable cause.

8   GAIUS, *Lex Julia et Papia, book 5:* A legacy left annually is similar to a usufruct, since it is terminated by death. It is not of course terminated by change of civil status, although a usufruct is so terminated. A usufruct too may be legated as follows: "I legate to Titius the usufruct of the farm, and however often he suffers change of civil status, I give him the same usufruct." This legacy is certainly more extensive in that if the legatee dies at the beginning of any year, he leaves that year's legacy to his heir, which is not the case with a usufruct, since the usufructuary, even if he dies when the fruits, though ripe, nevertheless have not been gathered, will not leave those fruits to his heir.

9   PAPINIAN, *Replies, book 7:* A farm, which a head of a household wanted to be a pledge to his freedmen for the legacies which he left to them annually, may be rightly claimed on the strength of the *fideicommissum* in order to preserve the property. PAUL notes: this is to be admitted also in the case of other items in an inheritance, so that the legatee may be given possession of them too.

10   PAPINIAN, *Replies, book 8:* "To my faithful friend Seius, if he is prepared to engage in my children's affairs in the same way as he engaged in mine, I wish to be given six aurei a year and the right of habitation he enjoys." It was decided that an annual sum in proportion to her share of the inheritance was owed to Seius by the surviving daughter, despite the fact that of the three children of Titia two had died and other heirs had been instituted, since both the labor and the money could be divided. 1. "I want my doctor Sempronius to be given what I gave him during my lifetime"; those sums appear to be left which took the form of a definite annual payment, not a vague

intention of liberality.   2. "I want my wife to be given a hundred aurei apart from what she received from me during my lifetime as an annual allowance"; it appears that an annuity and a single sum of a hundred aurei have been bequeathed.   3. "I want my freedmen to be given what I gave them during my lifetime"; the right of habitation will also be provided, but expenses for beasts of burden, which the mistress was accustomed to give to her agent for her own convenience, will not be owed. Therefore, a freedman doctor cannot rightly claim the purchase price of medicines, which he received in order to treat his patroness and her family.

11   PAUL, *Questions, book 21:* When a legacy is made payable annually, it is held that several legacies have been made and that the right to take is to be investigated for each legacy. Likewise, in the case of a slave, the capacity of the master is to be investigated.

12   PAUL, *Replies, book 13:* Gaius Seius legated estates in various places to Maevia and Seia and provided as follows: "I further want three hundred thousand reeds and one thousand pounds of clean osier to be supplied each year from the Potitian estates to the Lutatian estates." I ask whether that legacy is extinguished by the death of the legatee. Paul replied that no servitude, either personal or real, appeared to have been legitimately created, but that an action on the ground of the *fideicommissum* was available to the person to whom the Lutatian estates were legated, and, therefore, since the legacies were annual, the legacy appeared to be terminated by the death of the legatee.

13   SCAEVOLA, *Replies, book 4:* Maevia instituted as her heir her adult grandson born to Maevius and made a legacy to Lucius Titius as follows: "To Lucius Titius, a good man, for whose *obsequium* I offer thanks, I want to be given ten aurei a year for as long as he lives, if he attends to the affairs of my grandson and takes the full administration of them under his care." I ask, when Lucius Titius has for some time managed the affairs of Maevius and has made no objection to continuing to do so, but Publius Maevius is unwilling for him to administer them, whether the *fideicommissum* need be paid. I replied that if it was not on account of fraud or any just cause for criticizing his services that he had been removed from affairs which he was willing to administer in accordance with the wish of the deceased, he should receive the legacy.   1. A man appointed his wife as his heir and provided as follows: "I want twelve denarii a year each to be given to all my freedmen for maintenance, if they remain with my wife." I ask, since the head of the household was reluctant to leave the town of his own accord, whereas she traveled constantly, whether the freedmen should accompany her. I answered that no unconditional reply was possible, since many considerations might arise which should be judged on their merits; therefore, these various possibilities should be settled by the arbitration of a good man. Likewise, it is asked whether the legacy is owed when on setting out she offered them nothing extra and, therefore, they did not accompany her. He replied that this too should be judged with regard to the length or brevity of the journeys and the amount of the legacy.

14   ULPIAN, *Fideicommissa, book 2:* If an annual legacy is left to someone without the addition of the sum, Mela says the legacy is void; but the opinion of Nerva is more correct that that amount appears to have been left which the testator was accustomed to provide. Otherwise, the decision must be made in accordance with the standing of the person.

15   VALENS, *Fideicommissa, book 7:* Javolenus replied that a man who was asked to hand over a sum of money after ten years but handed it over before the due day is in no way released from liability if the *fideicommissum* is proved to have been left at the end of that period on account of the character of the recipient, because he was unable to look after his property, and the heir restored it to him before the date in the expectation that he would waste it. But if the period was protracted for the sake of the heir, so that he himself might benefit in the interim, it is understood that he is released; for, indeed, he has paid more than he need have.

16   PAUL, *Neratius, book 3:* A slave was ordered to be free after ten years and an annual legacy was left to him from the day of his master's death. The legacy will be due in those years in which he is already free; in the meantime, however, the heir is compelled to provide him with maintenance.

17   LABEO, *Posthumous Works, Epitomized by Javolenus, book 2:* A legacy was made as follows: "Let my heir be charged to give Attia fifty until she marries," and "each year" was not added. Labeo and Trebatius think that the legacy is owed immediately, but it is better

to say that the legacy is owed annually.   1. "Let my heir give to Attius every year two measures a year of the Falernian wine produced on my estate." Two measures are due also for any year in which no wine was produced, provided that they can be supplied from the vintage of other years.

18   SCAEVOLA, *Digest, book 14:* A man, in a codicil confirmed by his will, left a farm to his freedmen and prohibited its alienation but wanted it to belong to the children and grandchildren of the freedmen. Then he added these words: "By whom I want ten each year to be paid to my heir from the revenue of that farm for thirty-five years from the day of my death." It was asked, since the heir instituted by Titius died before the thirty-five years had elapsed, whether the *fideicommissum* was owed to the heir's heir for the remainder of the period on the strength of the words cited above. He replied that it was owed, unless it was shown by the freedmen that the testator was referring to the heir's thirty-fifth year.   1. A man wanted Stichus, his foster child, to be given a hundred, and ten a month, and a hundred a year, and charged Sempronia, whom he had instituted heir to a third share, as follows: "I commit to your faith, Sempronia my sister, to take from the inheritance the legacies I have left to my foster children and to keep the children by you as long as they are entrusted to your care." It was asked, since Sempronia, on whom the *fideicommissum* was imposed, had refused the inheritance before taking the money left to the foster children in accordance with the wish of the deceased, whether an action on the legacy would be available to Stichus even before his twenty-fifth year. He replied that it would.

19   SCAEVOLA, *Digest, book 17:* Titia appointed Seia her heir and left the usufruct of a farm to Maevius and imposed a *fideicommissum* on him in these words: "I want you, Maevius, to pay from the income of the Speratian farm six hundred a year to Arrius Pamphilus and Arrius Stichus from the day of my death every year as long as they live." It was asked, when Maevius had provided the annual allowance but after his death the farm had returned in accordance with law to Titia's heir, whether subsistence was owed to Pamphilus and Stichus on the strength of the *fideicommissum.* I replied that no reason had been brought forward why the allowances should be paid by Titia's heirs, since they had been left as a charge on the usufructuary. The same man asked whether the allowances should be paid by the heirs of the legatee Maevius. He replied that there was no obligation on the legatee's heirs, unless it was plainly proved that the testator wished payment to be made even after the usufruct had terminated, provided that the yield of the usufruct was sufficient for the purpose.   1. A man who paid Marcus, a learned man, a fixed annual sum provided in his will: "Most revered lady, I know that you will see to it that my friends want for nothing, but, nevertheless, let eight hundred be given to Marcus." It was asked whether Marcus, once the eight hundred have been paid to him by the terms of the legacy, should also receive the annual payment. He replied that no reason had been shown why, on the facts cited in the consultation, the payments should not be owing.   2. "To Lucius Titius three pounds of gold, which I used to give him while I was alive." I ask, when the testatrix, as long as she lived, gave Titius the fixed sum of forty as salary and further gave him on feast days a fixed weight of silver or its cash value, whether the same should be paid to Titius by the heirs on the strength of the legacy or the *fideicommissum.* He replied that no reason had been shown why they should not be paid.

20   SCAEVOLA, *Digest, book 18:* A man left an annual legacy in these words: "if they reside with my mother, whom I have instituted as part heir." It was asked whether, if the mother died, the condition imposed was held to have failed, so that no allowances for food or clothing were owed to them. He replied that according to the facts stated they were owed.   1. Attia left a *fideicommissum* in these words: "Whoever shall be my heir, I impose on him a *fideicommissum* that after my death he shall give to the priest, the guardian, and the freedmen in that temple, on the day of the festival which I established there, ten denarii from the income of my attic and my warehouse." I ask whether the legacy is owed only to those who were alive and in office at the time that the legacy was made or also to their successors. He replied that according to the facts set before him, the office of specific individuals had been designated, but the gift had been made to the temple. Likewise, I ask whether the ten are owed under the *fideicommissum* for only one year or whether ten also have to be paid every year in perpetuity. He replied in perpetuity.

21   SCAEVOLA, *Digest, book 22:* He left a legacy to his freedman as follows: "I want to be given to Philo, as long as he lives, one fiftieth of all the revenues which accrue from my estates from the tenants or the purchasers of the fruits according to the custom of my house. The heirs sold the estates from the revenue of which the fiftieth was left; it was asked whether a fiftieth of the interest on the price, which was paid according to the custom in the province, was owed. He replied that only a fiftieth of the income had been legated, although the estates had been sold.   1. He had given ten a year to Pamphila by a *fideicommissum* imposed on a freedman to whom he had legated a farm producing sixty a year. It was asked whether, if the *lex Falcidia* diminished the legacy to the freedman, the annual *fideicommissum* for Pamphila would also be held to be diminished, since the legacy was made from revenue which covered the annual payment to Pamphila, even if the *lex Falcidia* removed half the farm. He replied that according to the facts stated it did not appear to be diminished, unless the testator's intention was proved to be otherwise.   2. A man instituted as heirs his son to three quarters and his wife to one quarter and imposed on his son a *fideicommissum* that he should hand over his inheritance to his stepmother. Of her, however, he asked that she should take thought for the youthful infirmity of his son and pay him ten aurei a month until he reached his twenty-fifth year, but that when he had reached that age she should hand over to him half the inheritance. The son deducted a quarter of the portion to which he had been appointed, delivered the inheritance to his stepmother, and eventually attained his twenty-fifth year. It was asked whether, since the stepmother had thirteen sixteenths of the entire inheritance, she should restore half of that to her stepson. He replied that according to the facts as stated she should restore only enough to make up a half along with the sum which the son had deducted in accordance with the *lex Falcidia.* The same man asked whether, because the father wanted her to care for his son's youthful infirmity, the stepmother should also return to him the fruits for the intervening period. He replied that according to the facts stated she should.   3. In his will, Lucius Titius left a hundred to his hometown Sebaste, so that from the interest on the sum games might be celebrated in his name in alternate years, and added these words: "But if the city of Sebaste refuses to accept the money legated to it on the condition stated above, I do not want my heirs to be under obligation to it in any way, but to have the money for themselves." Subsequently, the governor of the province selected suitable items from the list of debts owed to the estate and adjudged them to the city as payment of its legacy. After his decision the city collected the money from the majority of those named in the judgment. It was asked whether, if the city subsequently failed to comply with the conditions laid down in the will, the legacy would belong to the sons who were the heirs. He replied that the city should be compelled to comply with the testator's wish and that if it did not do so, the heirs should be helped to recover those claims which had been settled either in cash or by novation. Moreover, in the case of those debts which had neither been paid to the city nor been released from the original obligation by novation, they should not be prevented from demanding payment [of the debt].   4. Largius Eurippianus sought a consultation when a patron had legated a fixed sum of money to a foster child in his will and had provided as follows in the will concerning the matter: "The money which I have legated to my freedman and foster child Titius I want to remain in the hands of Publius Maevius until his twenty-fifth year and interest on it at three percent to be calculated with him. However, the amount to be fixed for his expenses you, Publius Maevius, will calculate, since you should show him a father's affection." It was asked whether the heirs should take security from Publius Maevius when paying him that money. He replied that since no mention of demanding security was made in the will, it was sufficient for the heirs to pay the money to Publius Maevius in accordance with the wish of the deceased. Therefore, neither the foster child Titius nor his heirs should be heard if they brought an action against the patron's heirs because they had not demanded security; for by paying the money the aforesaid heirs had been freed of obligation both toward Titius and likewise toward his heirs, unless Publius Maevius had ceased to be solvent during the testator's lifetime. For in that case a *cautio* should be

demanded from him. 5. A father instituted as heirs in equal shares two sons, the older and the younger, who was still below the age of puberty. Toward his share he left certain estates and legated to him, when he reached the age of fourteen, a fixed sum of money, and made this a *fideicommissum* on his brother, whom he charged in the following words: "I ask of you, Seius, that from the time he reaches the age of twelve, you should pay an annual sum to his mother for your brother's education, until he reaches the age of fourteen; moreover, that you should pay your brother's taxes in accordance with his census until you hand over the property. The revenues of those estates are to belong to you until your brother attains fourteen years." It was asked whether, since the elder brother had died leaving a third party as his heir, the entire condition of receiving the revenue of the farms, so that the annual allowances, which Seius would have made if he were alive, might be paid, passed to his heir, or whether the entire legacy should be handed over at once to the *pupillus* and his tutors. He replied: According to the facts as stated, the testator is understood to have addressed the tutor, as it were, so that at the time when the tutorship was to be given up, the payments which he had ordered to be made annually in return for the collection of the fruits should cease, but since the elder brother had been overtaken by death, all that had been left passed to the *pupillus* and his tutors immediately after the brother's death.

22   ALFENUS VARUS, *Digest, Epitomized by Paul, book 2:* "Let my heir give a hundred each year to my daughter, every time she is widowed." It is asked whether, if the daughter had been a widow for less than a year, the hundred, nevertheless, were owed to her. He replied that he thought they were, notwithstanding the fact that a full year had not yet elapsed.

23   MARCIAN, *Institutes, book 6:* When a man had wanted distributions to be made to the decurions on his birthday, the deified Severus and Antoninus stated in a rescript that it was not plausible that the testator should have been thinking about a single year, but rather about a perpetual legacy.

24   MARCIAN, *Institutes, book 8:* When a fixed sum of money, namely a hundred, had been left to the city of Sardis for the quadriennial games of Chrysanthus, the deified Severus and Antoninus stated in a rescript that the testator appeared to have left a sum to be paid every four years in perpetuity, not merely after the first four years.

25   VALENS, *Fideicommissa, book 2:* Ten a year can be given to a son-in-power for as long as he is in his father's power.

2

RIGHT OF USE, USUFRUCT, INCOME, RIGHT OF HABITATION, AND SERVICES GIVEN BY LEGACY OR *FIDEICOMMISSUM*

1   PAUL, *Sabinus, book 3:* Neither the right of use nor the usufruct of a right of way in person or with cattle or by a road or of a right of aqueduct can be legated, because a servitude of a servitude cannot exist. Nor will it be valid under the *senatus consultum* which provides that the usufruct of everything included in the property may be legated, because it is neither included in nor excluded from the property. But an action for an indeterminate amount will lie against the heir to make him grant the legatee, as long as he lives, a right of way in person or with cattle or a right of aqueduct or the servitude may be established under the proviso that it should be restored if the legatee dies or suffers a major change of civil status.

2   PAPINIAN, *Questions, book 17:* If a man's services are legated, they are not lost by change of civil status or lack of use. And since the legatee can draw profit from the

man's services, he can also rent them out, and if the heir prevents him from receiving the services, he will be liable. The same is true if a slave rents himself out. Because the legatee is not a usufructuary, he transmits the legacy of services to his own heir; but if the slave is acquired by usucapion, the legacy is extinguished.

3   PAUL, *Sabinus, book 3:* The services of a freeman can also be legated, just as they can be rented out and made the subject of a stipulation.

4   ULPIAN, *Sabinus, book 18:* If the ownership is legated unconditionally, it will pass to the legatee, although the usufructuary is instituted heir.

5   PAUL, *Sabinus, book 3:* I cannot validly stipulate for a usufruct "when I die"; the same is true of a legacy, because even an established usufruct is normally extinguished by death.

6   POMPONIUS, *Sabinus, book 15:* If a usufruct is legated to me for two successive years from the death of the testator and I am prevented from receiving it by the heir, he is no less liable when the two years have elapsed (just as he would be liable if an object legated, which someone owed and did not deliver in time, had ceased to exist), in that the usufruct which was legated cannot indeed now be claimed, because it will be different from that which was legated, but its value over two years, nevertheless, should be calculated.

7   ULPIAN, *Edict, book 26:* When should the right to services left in a will vest: from the time the legatee demands them or from the time the inheritance is accepted? And who should bear the loss for those days on which the slave is ill? I think the right vests from the day the services are demanded; therefore, if the slave subsequently falls ill, the legatee will bear the loss.

8   GAIUS, *Praetor's Edict, Legacies, book 3:* If a usufruct is legated to the citizens of a municipality, it is asked to what extent they are to be protected in that usufruct. For if anyone protects it for them in perpetuity, there will be no value in the bare ownership, if the usufruct is always separated from it. Therefore, it is agreed that one hundred years, which would be the longest term of life, should be accepted.

9   ULPIAN, *Disputations, book 8:* If a *fideicommissum* is imposed on a man to whom a usufruct has been legated, although the usufruct does not come into the hands of the legatee, nevertheless, the heir, in whose hands the usufruct remains, is to execute the *fideicommissum*. This will also apply to a military will, if the legatee on whom the *fideicommissum* is imposed should refuse the legacy or die during the testator's lifetime.

10 JULIAN, *Digest, book 78:* If a farm and the usufruct of the same farm are legated to Titius, it will be up to him whether he prefers to claim the farm or the usufruct. And if he chooses the farm, he will of necessity have full ownership, although he has rejected the usufruct; if, however, he prefers to have the usufruct and rejects the ownership of the farm, he will have only the usufruct.

11 JULIAN, *From Minicius, book 1:* It is agreed that a legacy of an annual right of habitation is owed from the beginning of the year.

12 ALFENUS VARUS, *Digest, Epitomized by Paul, book 2:* The heir built a villa on a farm, the usufruct of which had been legated; he cannot demolish it against the wish of the usufructuary, any more than if he wanted to uproot a tree on the farm, which he had planted. But if he demolishes it before the usufructuary prohibits it, he will incur no liability.

13 PAUL, *Plautius, book 13:* When a usufruct is legated for alternate years, not one, but several things are legated. It is different in the case of a servitude of water and of a right of way; for the servitude of a right of way is single, because by its nature it is subject to interruption.

14 CELSUS, *Digest, book 18:* An heir who was charged by legacy (*sinendi modo*) to allow a usufruct to two persons separately allowed it to them jointly; it was asked whether he was liable to both under the will. I replied that he was liable, if the testator wished each to enjoy the entire usufruct; for it is the heir's responsibility to deliver the entire legacy to individuals. Therefore, whatever part the heir allowed one of the two to enjoy he could not allow to the other, and therefore, he is bound to estimate the value of the deficiency and make it good to each of them.

15 MARCELLUS, *Digest, book 13:* "Let my heir be obliged to allow Titius to live in that house, as long as he lives"; one thing appears to have been legated. 1. A man who had two farms legated one and left the usufruct of the other to another man. I ask, if the usufructuary had no other access to the farm except by way of the farm which was legated, whether a servitude is owed to the usufructuary. He replied that just as, if the farm through which the right of way could be granted to the usufructuary had been part of an inheritance, it is regarded as being required of the heir according to the wish of the deceased, so too in this case the legatee should not be permitted to claim the farm unless he previously granted to the usufructuary the right of crossing it, so that the same arrangement would be preserved with regard to the lands as obtained during the testator's lifetime, either as long as the usufruct remained or until it returned to the ownership.

16 MODESTINUS, *Replies, book 9:* A legacy was left to a town, so that from the revenues each year a spectacle should be celebrated in that town to keep alive the memory of the deceased, but it was not permitted to celebrate it there; I ask what you think about the legacy. He replied that since the testator wanted a spectacle to be celebrated in the town, but of such a kind as could not legally be celebrated there, it was unfair that the sum which the deceased had intended for the spectacle should fall to the profit of the heirs. Therefore, the heirs and the chief men of the town should be summoned to discuss how the *fideicommissum* could be transformed so that the testator's memory would be celebrated in some other legal way.

17 SCAEVOLA, *Replies, book 3:* A man left estates to a town, from the income of which he wanted games to be put on each year and added: "I ask and beg, decurions, that you do not attempt to convert these legacies to any other form or use." For four years in succession the town did not put on the games; I ask whether the town should restore to the heirs the income which it received during those four years or set it off against a legacy of another kind from the same will. He replied that if possession had been taken against the will of the heirs, the profits collected must be returned and that what was not spent in accordance with the deceased's wishes should be set off against other legacies owed.

18 MODESTINUS, *Replies, book 9:* A man who had several freedmen said in his will that he left a right of habitation to those whom he had designated in a codicil. Since he subsequently designated none, I ask whether all should be admitted. He replied that, if the patron, who promised that he would designate the individual freedmen, subsequently designated none, the legacy of the right of habitation appeared to be imperfect, since nobody existed to whom it could be understood to have been given.

19 MODESTINUS, *Advice on Drafting, sole book:* If a testator leaves to one man a farm, to another the usufruct of that same farm; if he did it with the intention that one should have only the bare ownership, he falls into error. For he should leave the ownership with the usufruct reserved as follows: "I leave to Titius the farm with the usufruct reserved, or let my heir give the usufruct of that same farm to Seius." Unless he does this, the usufruct will be shared between them, because sometimes what is written has more force than was intended.

20 POMPONIUS, *Quintus Mucius, book 8:* If I order a slave to be free subject to a condition and legate the usufruct of him to you, the legacy is valid.

21 PAUL, *Lex Julia et Papia, book 7:* The usufruct of Stichus is legated to Titius or, if a ship comes from Asia, ten. He cannot claim the usufruct before the condition concerning the ten is either fulfilled or fails, so that the heir is not prevented from giving whichever he pleases.

22 ULPIAN, *Lex Julia et Papia, book 15:* "I want the income from my patrimony every year to be given to my wife." Aristo replied that this did not pass to the wife's heir, because it was similar either to a usufruct or to a legacy "to be paid annually."

23   JUNIUS MAURICIANUS, *Lex Julia et Papia, book 2:* It is legitimate for a testator to
repeat the legacy of a usufruct, so that it may be owed even after a change of civil
status; this was recently confirmed by the emperor Antoninus in a rescript to a petition. Nor do I think that this constitution operates only when a legacy is to be paid
annually.

24   PAPINIAN, *Replies, book 7:* If the profits of property are legated to a wife, the interest on the capital sums which the deceased has loaned will also be paid after a *cautio*
has been furnished in accordance with the *senatus consultum*. Therefore, it is necessary for the interest on the debts left as part of the inheritance, which was due before
the *cautio* had been given, to be included in the *cautio* just like the capital sums. The
same rule will not apply to loans made by the heir; for then only the capital sums will
be given to the legatee, or, where it has also been decided that on account of delay the
interest too should be paid over, no *cautio* will be required for this interest.   1. "I
want my slave Scorpus to be the slave of my concubine Sempronia." Not the ownership, but the usufruct, of the slave is held to have been bequeathed.

25   PAPINIAN, *Replies, book 8:* A man who left the fruits of his landed estates to his wife
wanted the estates, together with the income, to revert to his heirs after her death.
He erred through inexperience; the owner did not impose any *fideicommissum* that
the ownership or the profits should revert to the heir, for future income, not past,
appeared to be meant.

26   PAUL, *Questions, book 10:* Sempronius Attalus ordered a farm in Italy to be given
after ten years by his heir to Gaius with reservation of the usufruct. I ask, if the heir
dies during this period of ten years, whether the farm belongs immediately to the
legatee when the ten years have elapsed. For I am moved by the fact that the right to
this legacy or *fideicommissum* has vested, and so it could also belong to the legatee's
heir, and therefore, just as if the case involved a legacy that was already due when the
heir died, the usufruct has been extinguished and cannot belong to the heir's heir. I
replied: Certainly, the *fideicommissum* or legacy vests at once, when the heir is asked
or ordered to deliver after a fixed time, but the usufruct does not yet belong to the heir
except when he hands over the ownership while reserving the usufruct; and therefore,
it cannot perish with change of civil status or death because he has not yet had it. The
same is the case, if ownership with reservation of the usufruct is legated subject to a
condition and the heir dies before the condition has been fulfilled; for then the usufruct
begins with the heir's heir and will end with his life. But in these cases, the intention of
the testator must be investigated; for he certainly meant the usufruct which was
vested in the person of the heir to be reserved, and on the heir's death, he wanted full
ownership to belong to the legatee and nothing to be transmitted to a successor who
had not yet begun to enjoy the usufruct, any more than if he had already begun to
enjoy it.   1. If a farm is legated to two men and the usufruct to another, the usufruct
is divided into two parts, not three; the same is true in the opposite case, if there are
two usufructuaries and ownership is legated to another. The right of accrual exists
only between them.

27   SCAEVOLA, *Replies, book 1:* A husband made a *praelegatum* by *fideicommissum* to
his wife of a usufruct, other things and her dowry. The heirs granted her the usufruct.
After two years her marriage was declared to have been illegal. It was asked whether
what she had received in the preceding period could be demanded back from her. He
replied that what she had taken under the heading of fruits could be demanded back.

28   PAUL, *Replies, book 13:* I ask what the legal situation is, if the usufruct of a farm is
legated and temporary taxes are imposed on the same farm. Paul replied that it is the
same in those cases where taxes are imposed afterward as in the matter of ordinary
taxes; therefore, this burden falls on the usufructuary.

29   GAIUS, *Fideicommissa, book 1:* If a man is asked to hand over to another a usufruct
which was left to himself and has installed him on the farm so that he may enjoy it,
although by the civil law the usufruct perishes with the death or change of civil status
of the legatee, because it was acquired by him under that very law, nevertheless, the
praetor should use his jurisdiction to ensure that the right is preserved as it would

have been if it had been acquired under the terms of a legacy by him to whom it was handed over by *fideicommissum*.

30 JAVOLENUS, *From the Posthumous Works of Labeo, book 2:* If a woman has been legated a usufruct until her entire dowry has been made good to her, when one heir has given her security for his share, although the rest have not done so for theirs, nevertheless, Labeo says the woman ceases to have that proportion of the usufruct; it is the same if the woman is responsible for delay in her receiving security. 1. An owner had legated to his tenant the usufruct of the farm which he worked; the tenant should bring an action against the heir so that the judge may compel the heir to free him from an action on the lease.

31 LABEO, *Posthumous Works, Epitomized by Javolenus, book 2:* A man who shared the ownership of a farm with you had legated the usufruct of the farm to his wife; after his death the heir had applied for an arbitrator for dividing the common property. Blaesus says Trebatius replied that if the arbitrator divided the farm into fixed areas, the usufruct of that part which fell to you is in no circumstances owed to the woman, but she should have the usufruct of the whole of that portion which fell to the heir. I think this is false; for since, before the arbitrator's division, the woman had had the conjoined usufruct of a *pro indiviso* half share of the whole farm, the arbitrator had no power in deciding between other parties to change the rights of a third. This has been accepted.

32 SCAEVOLA, *Digest, book 15:* After placing a general clause at the head, a man made the following addition to his will: "To Felix, whom I ordered to be free, I legate the usufruct of my Vestigian farm. I think that you will secure the ownership of this, if you do not contend with my heir, but rather establish friendly relations with him. But do you too, my heir, do everything to ensure that you are friends; for this is in both your interests." It was asked whether Felix could claim the ownership of the farm while the heir was alive. He replied that no reason had been given why the ownership of the farm might appear to have been legated to Felix. 1. A woman instituted as heirs to equal shares her sons by Seius and her daughter by another husband and made a legacy to her mother as follows: "To Aelia Dorcas, my mother, I want to be given, as long as she lives, the usufruct of my property on condition that after her death it may belong to my children or to whichever of them is alive." The sons had died after accepting the inheritance. It was asked, when the mother died and the daughter of the testatrix survived, whether the usufruct belonged to the daughter alone or only in proportion to her share of the inheritance. He replied that it returned to those in whom the ownership reposed. CLAUDIUS: He did not believe that the usufruct itself had been divided among the children in accordance with their shares of the inheritance after the grandmother's death, especially as they had been instituted heirs to equal shares. 2. A man had legated to his wife the usufruct of houses and of all the things that were in those houses except the silver, likewise, the usufruct of farms and salt-pans. It was asked whether the usufruct of wool of various colors intended for sale, likewise, of purple which was in the houses, was owed to her. He replied that with the exception of the silver and those things which were intended for sale, the legatee had the usufruct of everything else. 3. The same man asked, when a considerable amount of salt was found in the saltpans of which the usufruct had been legated, whether the usufruct of it belonged to the wife by the terms of the *fideicommissum*. He replied that the testator had not intended to legate those things which were there to be sold. 4. The same man asked, since he had provided in the same will: "I ask of you, my wife, that from the usufruct, which I want to be given to you for fifteen years, you should be content with four hundred a year, and that the surplus should be paid to the account of my heir or heirs," whether this appeared to be a retraction of the earlier clause, so that the wife should not have more than four hundred a year from the usufruct. He replied that the words cited made the answer to the question sufficiently clear. 5. In his will, Lucius Titius left his Tusculan farm to Publius Maevius and imposed on him a *fideicommissum* that he should give to Titia the usufruct of half the said farm. Publius Maevius rebuilt a villa dilapidated with age which was necessary

for the collection and storing of the fruits. I ask whether Titia must accept part of the expense in proportion to her share of the usufruct. He replied that if it was necessary for him to build before he could supply the usufruct, he could not be compelled to pay up unless account was taken of his expenditure. 6. A man instituted as heirs two daughters and a mentally afflicted son, and legated the usufruct of the share given to the mentally afflicted son in the following words: "Publia Clementina, furthermore, will take as a *praelegatum* the usufruct of the fourth part of my estate to which I have instituted my son Julius Justus heir. And I ask of you, Publia Clementina, that you should nourish and protect your brother Julius Justus and handle his financial affairs, in consideration of which I have left you the usufruct of his share, until he becomes of sound mind and recovers his health." It was asked, since the son died after remaining insane until the day of his death, whether the usufruct perished. He replied that the legacy persisted given the words as cited, unless it was very clearly proved that the testator intended otherwise. 7. A woman imposed on her instituted heir a *fideicommissum* to pay ten a year to her son or to buy estates which would produce an income of ten a year and assign the usufruct to him. The son rented out the farms which were delivered to him by the heir in accordance with his mother's wish. It was asked whether, when he died, the arrears due from the tenants would belong to the heir of the usufructuary son or to the heir of the testatrix Seia. He replied that no reason had been shown why they should belong to the heir of Seia. 8. A man had legated the usufruct of a third of his property to one of his heirs; it was asked whether a third of the money obtained when the property was divided in accordance with a valuation was to be handed over. He replied that the heir could choose whether he wished to pay over the usufruct of the property or of the estimated sum. 9. Likewise, it was asked whether in addition the taxes, which were bound to be demanded and paid either on the estate or on the movables, should be deducted from the amount, so that payment would have to be made only on the remainder of the money, if the heir chose this option. He replied that a third of the remainder of the money should be paid over.

33   SCAEVOLA, *Digest, book 17:* "I want to be given to Sempronius what I paid during my lifetime"; he also lived in the testator's house, which had been bequeathed as a *praelegatum* to one of the heirs. It was asked whether a right of habitation was also owed. He replied that no reason had been shown why it should not be owed. 1. Concerning these words of a will, "To my freedmen to whom I have left nothing by name I want to be given what I provided during my lifetime," it was asked whether a right of habitation also appeared to have been left to those freedmen who were living with their patron up to the day of his death. He replied that it did. 2. In a codicil, a woman wrote as follows: "I ask that you allow my elderly and infirm freedmen Negidius, Titius, and Dio to grow old in the places which they now occupy." I ask whether by this clause the aforementioned freedmen should receive by *fideicommissum* the fruits of the places in which they dwell, when they have received without argument other things which were legated to them specifically. He replied that according to the words cited what was asked was that the heirs should allow them to remain where they were on the same terms as she herself allowed it.

34   SCAEVOLA, *Digest, book 18:* In a codicil, a man imposed *fideicommissa* in the following words: "To my freedmen and freedwomen and those whom I manumitted in the codicil I want to be given the farm where I wish to be buried on condition that if one of them dies, his portion shall accrue to the remainder, so that it will all belong to the last survivor; after the death of that last survivor, I want it to belong to the city of Arelate. In addition, to my freedmen and freedwomen the right of habitation in my house as long as they live, and to Pactia Trophima all the rooms which she was accustomed to use. After their deaths, I want the house to belong to the city." It was asked whether the *fideicommissum* for the city was imposed on the heirs or on the freedmen. He replied that according to the facts as stated the words could be taken to mean that the *fideicommissum* devolved on the last surviving legatee. The same man asked

whether, when some of the freedmen to whom the right of habitation had been bequeathed had died, their shares of the house in which they had lived now belonged immediately to the city. He replied that as long as any one of them was alive, the *fideicommissum* was not owed to the city.   1. A man who had instituted as heirs Sempronia to a tenth, Maevia to a tenth, and his foster child to the remainder gave a curator to the foster child, thinking that he was acting legally and imposed on the curator a *fideicommissum* that he should not allow the farm to be sold but should enjoy the revenue of it together with his nurses Sempronia and Maevia. And at the end of the will, he made the following addition: "I make all my wishes a *fideicommissum* on my heirs." It was asked whether under the *fideicommissum* the nurses could demand third shares in the usufruct of the farm, although the curator, whom he could not legally appoint for the foster child, had not been admitted. He replied that according to the facts as stated, the testator had validly confirmed his wishes by the *fideicommissum* and, therefore, had given the same to each, so that the nurses should receive the income of the farm along with the foster child.

35   SCAEVOLA, *Digest, book 22:* A man legated to his wife the usufruct of a villa for five years from the day of his death, then added these words: "And when the five years have elapsed and the usufruct has ceased to exist, then I want that farm to be given to my freedmen 'X' and 'Y.'" It was asked, since the wife died within the five years, whether a claim to ownership would lie for the freedmen immediately or only when the full five years had elapsed, given that the testator had legated the ownership "when the five years have elapsed." He replied that the farm belonged to the freedmen after the completion of the five years.

36   SCAEVOLA, *Digest, book 25:* The usufruct of a farm had been legated to Stichus, who had been manumitted in the will, and, when he ceased to enjoy the usufruct, the testator imposed a *fideicommissum* on his heirs that they should give that farm to Lucius Titius. But Stichus in his will legated the ownership of the same farm to his grandsons, and Stichus's heirs delivered the farm in accordance with the will to the grandsons who were the legatees. It was asked, since the grandsons had been unaware of the condition imposed on the said farm in the earlier will and had possessed it for more than the prescribed time, whether they had acquired ownership of the farm. He replied that according to the facts stated the legatees had acquired it.   1. The same man asked, if in any circumstances the land could be taken from the legatees, whether Stichus's grandsons could bring an action for recovery against his heirs. He replied that he had already answered about the acquisition of the land; but if for some reason the acquisition had failed, it appeared that Stichus, if he had made his will after the deaths of those to whom the ownership had been legated, had legated something which he believed he owned, rather than that he had wished to place a burden on his heirs.

37   SCAEVOLA, *Digest, book 33:* "To my wife I legate the usufruct of my property until my daughter reaches the age of eighteen years." It was asked whether the usufruct of estates both rural and urban and of slaves, of furniture, and likewise of the account book belonged to the wife. He replied that according to the facts stated the usufruct of everything belonged to her.

38   SCAEVOLA, *Replies, book 3:* "I want the income of my Aebutian farm to be given to my wife as long as she lives." I ask whether the heir's tutor may sell the farm and offer to the legatee the annual sum which had customarily been brought in by the renting out of the farm during the lifetime of the head of the household. He replied that he may. Likewise, I ask whether she can without liability be prevented from living there. He replied that the heir was not bound to provide a right of habitation. Likewise, I ask whether the heir is to be compelled to keep up the estate. He replied that if the revenues have been diminished by the act of the heir, the legatee may rightly claim whatever loss has been incurred on that account. Likewise, I ask how this legacy differs from a usufruct; he replied that the difference can be discerned from the replies given above.

39   SCAEVOLA, *Replies, book 6:* A man instituted his sons as heirs, legated to his wife

clothing, female toiletries, wool, flax, and other things, and added: "However, I want the ownership of the items listed above to revert to my daughters or to whichever of them are living at the time." It was asked whether the usufruct or the ownership of those things had been given. He replied that the ownership appeared to have been legated.

40   ALFENUS VARUS, *Digest, Epitomized by Paul, book 8:* "I legate a right of habitation to 'X' along with 'Y'; it is as if he had legated "to 'X' and 'Y.'"

41   JAVOLENUS, *From the Posthumous Works of Labeo, book 2:* When a legacy has been made as follows, "I give and legate the annual fruits of my Cornelian farm to Publius Maevius," Labeo thinks that it should be taken as if the usufruct of the farm had been similarly legated, because this appears to have been the testator's intention.

42   JAVOLENUS, *From the Posthumous Works of Labeo, book 5:* Fruits are understood to include what is gathered for the use of man; for it is not the time of natural ripening that is to be considered here, but the time at which it is most expedient for the tenant or owner to gather those fruits. So, since olives bring greater revenue unripe than if they are gathered when ripe, it cannot be held that if they are gathered when unripe, they do not count as fruits.

43   VENULEIUS, *Actions, book 10:* It makes no difference whether someone legates a usufruct of a third of his property or of his things; for if a usufruct of the property is legated, debts will still be deducted from it and rights of action will be included. But if the usufruct of specific things is legated, the same rule will not be observed.

3
LEGACIES OF SERVITUDES

1   JULIAN, *From Minicius, book 1:* A man who had two adjoining shops legated them separately to two persons. It was asked, if any part of the upper shop was built on to the lower, whether a servitude imposed on the lower to maintain the burden was included in the legacy of the shop. He replied that the servitude appeared to have been imposed. JULIAN notes: Let us see whether this is true only if either this servitude is specifically imposed or the legacy is given in the form: "I give and legate my shop as it now is."

2   MARCELLUS, *Digest, book 13:* A right of way can be legated to persons having a farm in common, since a jointly owned slave can legally stipulate for a right of way and the stipulation is not invalidated when the man who himself stipulated for the right of way has two heirs.

3   MARCELLUS, *Digest, book 29:* If a man legated to Maevius a farm and a right of way to it through another farm and to Titius the same farm without a right of way and both claimed the farm, the farm will go to the legatee without the right of way, because the existence of the other legatee is an impediment to claiming sole ownership of the farm together with the right of way, and a servitude cannot be acquired partially. But if Maevius claims the farm first while the other legatee is deliberating, it is possible to wonder whether, if Titius later gave up his claim, the legacy of the right of way might be preserved, and this seems the better view. However, if anyone legated a farm under a condition and a right of way unconditionally or a farm in part unconditionally, in part under a condition, and a right of way without any condition, and the legacy had vested before the condition had been fulfilled, the legacy of the right of way would be annulled. A similar answer has been given, when a man legated to one of two neighbors who had a farm in common a right of way under a condition, to the other a right of way unconditionally, and died before the condition was fulfilled.

4   JAVOLENUS, *Letters, book 9:* If a man who had two houses legated one to me, the other to you, and there was a party wall separating the two houses, I think it belongs to us in common just as if the wall alone had been legated jointly to the two of us.

Therefore, neither you nor I will have a right to prevent the other from inserting a beam; for it is agreed that if a partner owns something jointly, he has all the rights pertaining to it, and so an arbitrator for dividing common property must be appointed in the matter.

5 PAPINIAN, *Questions, book 16:* Although *testamenti factio* with other persons' slaves depends chiefly on the status of their owners, nevertheless, legacies to slaves are valid if they would be potentially valid if left to free persons. Thus, a legacy to a slave of a right of way to his owner's farm is void.

6 PAPINIAN, *Replies, book 7:* A father legated a house to his daughter and wanted a right of passage through the buildings belonging to the inheritance to be made available to her. If the daughter lives in her own house, the right of passage will also be made available to her husband; otherwise, it will not appear to have been made available to the daughter. But if anyone takes it that this is not a right of passage granted to an individual, but a complete legacy of a servitude, then the same right will also be transmitted to the heir. But this is in no way to be admitted here, lest what was given to the daughter as a mark of affection should be thought to pass to her heirs even if they came from outside the family.

7 PAUL, *Questions, book 21:* When a right of way is legated against several instituted heirs, the individual heirs, because the servitude is indivisible, are liable for the entire right, because the legacy can be claimed by vindicatio even if only one of the heirs accepts the inheritance.

4

PRAELEGATUM OF A DOWRY

1 ULPIAN, *Sabinus, book 19:* When a dowry is legated, it is true that everything is contained in the legacy of the dowry which would be included in a dotal action. 1. Therefore, if it had been agreed between a man and his wife that if the marriage was dissolved by the husband's death and a son of the marriage was born, then the dowry should remain with the husband's heir, and the dying husband legated the dowry, the pact must not stand because the dowry was bequeathed. But this must also be accepted when the dowry is not legated; for the principle that the condition of a dowry can become worse through the intervention of children applies whenever the wife herself dies during the marriage or divorce occurs. 2. And it is true that the legacy of a dowry carries the advantage of immediate payment, whereas a dowry would be paid annually. 3. It is also true that nowadays, since the *senatus consultum*, no demand is made for property donated, provided that the testator did not change his intention. 4. Expenses, however, diminish a dowry by operation of law. But what we have said to that effect is to be referred not to single items but to the whole. 5. The legacy of a dowry so far includes the dotal action that if a man pays the dowry to his wife in his lifetime (namely, in these cases in which it is permitted), the legacy will be void. 6. Moreover, if slaves whose value had not been estimated were included in the dowry and these died, the legacy of the dowry is void as far as they are concerned. 7. Moreover, if a woman promised a dowry but never gave it, and the husband when dying legated the dowry to his wife, the woman will have nothing more than a release from liability; for if someone makes a legacy, "the hundred which I have in my safe" or "which 'X' deposited with me," it is agreed that if they do not exist, nothing is owed. 8. If a man legated his Titian farm to his wife as follows, "for that farm came to me on her account," the farm is certainly owed; for whatever is added to clarify something already sufficiently clarified is superfluous. 9. Celsus writes in the twentieth book of his *Digest* that if a father-in-law legates her dowry to his daughter-in-law, then if he wanted to legate the right of dotal action, the legacy will have no force; for she is already married. But, he says, if he wanted her to receive the money she brought as dowry, the legacy will be valid. Nevertheless, if she

receives the dowry, the husband will still have the right to claim it by the action for dividing an inheritance if an heir has been instituted, by an *actio utilis* if one has not. I think, since the father-in-law did not want the heir to pay the dowry twice, that if the woman brings an action based on the will, she should give a *cautio* that the heir will be defended against the husband. Therefore, the husband too should give the same *cautio* that the heir will be defended against the wife, if he brings an action first.   10. On the other hand, the question is asked in Julian's thirty-seventh book what happens if a father-in-law legates his daughter-in-law's dowry to his disinherited son; and he says that she cannot bring an action against the disinherited husband for the dowry, whereas he himself can claim the dowry on the ground of the legacy. But he will acquire the legacy only if he gives a *cautio* that the heirs will be defended against the woman. He also distinguishes between the man to whom the dowry is legated and a freedman liberated by the will to whom his *peculium* is legated. For he says that the freedman can be sued in an action on the *peculium*, but the heir cannot, because he has ceased to have the *peculium* in his possession; but the dotal action lies nonetheless, even if he has ceased to have the dowry in his possession.   11. Julian also asks, if a father-in-law left the dowry to a husband, whether the husband's legacy is extinguished if the dowry is paid to the wife. And he says that it is extinguished, because there is nothing further which could be paid to the husband.   12. He also asks, if a dowry is legated to someone else and he is asked to restore it to the woman, whether the *lex Falcidia* applies to the legacy. And he says that it does, but that the woman will secure by the dotal action any shortfall in the *fideicommissum*. I ask whether the benefits of immediate payment are to be observed in this legacy just as if the dowry had been legated to the woman herself. And I think that they are.   13. Julian also asks, if a dowry is legated to a woman and she is asked to restore it, whether the *lex Falcidia* operates. And he says that it does not, since he also denies that the *fideicommissum* is valid. But if anything further is legated to the wife, he thinks that the *fideicommissum* should be paid from the residue; this undoubtedly will be paid to the woman subject to the operation of the *lex Falcidia*. But when the husband is also instituted heir to a part and the dowry is left to him as a *praelegatum* by the father-in-law, the legacy of the dowry will be subject to the *lex Falcidia*, that is, because the dowry legated is held not to be due while the marriage still exists. But the husband can recover preferentially what has been deducted under the *lex Falcidia* by the action for dividing the inheritance, just as he would recover preferentially the whole dowry if it had not been legated.   14. Mela wrote that if a farm is included in the dowry and is specifically legated, and then the dowry is legated in general terms, the farm will be due not twice but once.   15. Mela adds that if a farm included in the dowry had been rented out by the husband for a fixed term, the wife can receive the farm under the legacy only if she gives a *cautio* that she will allow the tenant to enjoy the farm, provided that she herself receives the rent.

2   ULPIAN, *Disputations, book 5:* When a man leaves her dowry to his wife and imposes a *fideicommissum* on her, this *fideicommissum* will be estimated according to the benefit that the woman receives from the legacy; thus Celsus also wrote in the twentieth book of his *Digest*. But if there have been necessary expenses, which diminish the dowry by operation of law, it can further be said that if the entire amount of the dowry which the husband received was left to her, the amount by which the dowry was diminished by operation of law can also be paid out under the *fideicommissum*; for nobody can doubt that the woman is a legatee. But even if not the dowry but something in lieu of the dowry was left to the wife, it is still treated as if the dowry had been legated. Julian has written further that even if it has not been added that the legacy is in lieu of dowry, but it was, nevertheless, left with that intention, it is still in the same case. Therefore, if the wife is asked to hand over either the dowry or what was legated in lieu of dowry or what was ascribed to her in lieu of dowry, she will not be compelled to hand it over except insofar as we have stated. Therefore, if she is instituted heir and asked to hand over a part of the inheritance, she will hand over only that which is in excess of her dowry and the benefit received from immediate payment. For even if a man, when he had received a dowry from his daughter-in-law, instituted his son as heir and asked him to restore whatever came to him from the inheritance and the son then obtained the dowry through the death of his wife, he would not restore what he obtained from the dowry, because he obtained it through his marriage, not

by his father's decision. 1. A woman promised a dowry of four hundred and gave two farms to the value of two hundred and debtors' notes to the value of the other two hundred. Then, when her husband died, he left to her in lieu of dowry two farms, not those which he had received as part of the dowry, and in addition the two received by him as part of the dowry, at valuation and imposed on her a *fideicommissum*, that when she died she should hand over to Seius whatever had come to her from his inheritance. It was asked how much was included in the *fideicommissum* when the woman died. I said that the position of the woman, who had been asked to hand over whatever had come to her from the will, was such that she was being asked to hand over only what had come to her after the amount of her dowry had been deducted; for she had recovered, rather than received, the dowry, with the exception of what could be made the object of the *fideicommissum* imposed on her as constituting benefit resulting from immediate payment. Therefore, she will not be compelled to hand over what the husband left to her in lieu of her dowry unless it amounts to more than the dowry; but she will be compelled to hand over the residue of what was left to her, along with the fruits. Therefore, she will have the dowry with its fruits as a *praelegatum*, but what was left to her apart from this, together with the fruits that have come to her, she will hand over.

3   JULIAN, *Digest, book 34:* A man who makes a legacy to his wife as follows, "Let my heir be charged to give Titia so many aurei over and above her dowry," has clearly legated the dowry as well.

4   AFRICANUS, *Questions, book 5:* When, as is usual, a date is fixed for the payment of legacies, he says that this has no effect on the legacy of a dowry, because that has its own due date.

5   MARCIAN, *Rules, book 3:* When a dowry has been legated, the heir is not to be heard if he wants to put off payment on account of donations made to the wife or other expenses, apart from those which diminish a dowry by operation of law; for it is one thing for a dowry to have been diminished through necessary expenses, another for a dowry to be retained as a pledge on account of sums which it is fair that the wife should pay in her turn.

6   LABEO, *Posthumous Works, Epitomized by Javolenus, book 2:* When it had been written, "as for that money, fifty, which came to me on account of my wife, let my heir give her so much in lieu of that dowry," although the dowry had been of forty, nevertheless, Alfenus Varus writes that Servius replied that he owed fifty, because the sum intended had been written in as fifty. 1. Likewise, a husband had made a legacy as follows to a woman who had no dowry: "However much money as dowry," and so forth, "in lieu of that let my heir give fifty." Ofilius, Cascellius, and likewise the pupils of Servius held that the legacy was due to her; it was to be treated in the same way as if a slave, who died, or a hundred in lieu, had been legated to someone. This is true, because by these words not the dowry itself but a sum in lieu of dowry appears to have been legated.

7   PAPINIAN, *Questions, book 18:* A father left the dowry he had received from his daughter-in-law to his disinherited son; the father's heir, by entering a defense of fraud, will not be compellable to pay the legacy until a *cautio* has been furnished to him that he will be indemnified if the marriage is dissolved. 1. But if, before the legacy is paid to the son, the woman has recovered her dowry, it will be vain for the son to bring an action for the legacy. 2. But if the *lex Falcidia* has operated on the legacy of the dowry against the disinherited son and the woman has ratified the payment, she will be given a dotal *actio utilis* for the amount which the heir retained. But if she does not ratify the payment, the heir must be defended by the husband, who promised that he would do so; but if the husband alone undertakes the whole defense, an *actio judicati* will be given against the heir for the amount which can legitimately be claimed under the *lex Falcidia*, if a *cautio* has not been given. 3. But if, before the legacy is paid to the son, the woman gets a divorce, although she herself cannot yet secure the dowry, the son's action, nevertheless, is not delayed on that account, because it was answered that the dowry should be paid to the son at the time when he became heir in part to his father, and he was admitted to receive the dowry, if the marriage was dissolved, after he became heir. 4. If it happens that the *cautio* for the defense has been omitted through error and the son has received the dowry

under a *fideicommissum*, the *fideicommissum* cannot be reclaimed as not having been due; for the necessity of providing a *cautio* delays payment, but does not make not due a debt that was due. But it will not be unjust to grant relief to the heir. 5. What, therefore, if the father's heir is not solvent? Will not a dotal *actio utilis* justly be given to the wife against her husband? For her dowry should not perish because the heir through a mistake did not give a *cautio*.

8 PAPINIAN, *Replies, book 7:* A husband had legated to his wife money in lieu of her dowry, which had consisted of slaves; the slaves died during the husband's lifetime, the wife died after her husband. The action for the legacy is rightly passed on to her heir, since the wish of the husband is to be respected.

9 PAPINIAN, *Replies, book 8:* "To my wife I want to be handed over the Cornelian farm and in kind whatever she brought as a bride at valuation." I replied that the estate given as dowry did not appear to be excepted, although it had not been valued, but that since the whole dowry had been legated, it was not the price of the valued articles which had been left, but the articles themselves, in whatever condition they were found.

10 SCAEVOLA, *Questions, book 8:* If a farm is legated to Seia in lieu of dowry of a hundred and the same farm to Maevius, the woman will claim in addition what the *lex Falcidia* takes from Maevius, as if they were not competing claimants, because there is more in the woman's dowry.

11 PAUL, *Replies, book 7:* When she married Lucius Titius, Seia gave a hundred aurei by way of dowry and brought in Quintus Mucius, who paid nothing but stipulated for the dowry, if the marriage was dissolved by the death of the wife. When dying, Seia made the following provision in her will: "To Lucius Titius, my husband, to whom I give my warmest thanks, I want to be given in addition to the dowry which I gave him so many aurei." I ask, when Quintus Mucius instituted an action on the stipulation against Lucius Titius, whether the husband could defeat him through the wording of the will. He replied that if Quintus Mucius made the stipulation on Seia's instructions but she did not intend to make a gift, he is liable to the wife's heirs, and, therefore, Quintus Mucius will be defeated by a defense. But if Seia, in order to make him a gift, had allowed him to stipulate for the situation arising from the death of the wife, then he appeared to have stipulated *mortis causa*, and, therefore, it must be said that a *fideicommissum* could in that case have been imposed on him.

12 SCAEVOLA, *Replies, book 3:* A man who had received a dowry in coin and in property at valuation made a legacy to his wife as follows: "To my wife, Seia, if she produces and hands over to my heir all the articles that are contained in the dotal inventory, I want to be given the sum total of her dowry, which her father paid over to me on her behalf, and a further ten denarii." It was asked, since several articles contributed to the dowry had been worn out by use and were not in existence when the husband died, whether the legacy was due, given that it had been made as it were under an impossible condition. I replied that the condition would appear to have been met, if whatever survived of the articles contributed to the dowry came into the hands of the heir.

13 LABEO, *Plausible Views, Epitomized by Paul, book 1:* PAUL: If a son-in-power, when he had a wife, received a dowry from her, then after becoming the head of the household legated the dowry to her as is customary, even if he is not his father's heir, nevertheless, the legacy will be due.

14 SCAEVOLA, *Digest, book 15:* Theopompus made a will, instituted his two daughters and son as heirs to equal shares, and in a codicil provided as follows: "Pollianus, knowing my intention, will take thought for the marriage of my daughter Crispina, whom I want to be married to whomsoever my friends and relations may deem fit on the same terms as I married her sister." Pollianus, called on to take an oath by the girl's husband, wrote that the father had wanted his younger daughter to receive the same amount for her dowry as the elder had received. I ask whether the co-heirs should give the younger daughter the same sum as dowry over and above her share of the inheritance. He replied that the magistrate with cognizance of the case should make a valuation, so that the same amount may be taken from the bulk of the inheritance and given to the younger daughter as dowry.

15   GAIUS, *Praetor's Edict, Legacies, book 2:* Although it is agreed that the heir, who is ordered to give it, must release property that has been pledged or mortgaged to the state, nevertheless, if a man who received such property as dowry has legated the dowry, the heir will not be compelled to release it, unless the testator has specifically stated otherwise.

16   PAUL, *Vitellius, book 2:* A man who had received a dowry from his wife's mother and had entered into a stipulation to repay it to her legated the dowry to his wife in his will. When it was asked whether the wife could obtain the sum total of the dowry, Scaevola replied that it did not appear that what had to be returned to the mother was being given to the wife. In other words, he replied that unless the wife had plainly demonstrated that such was the testator's wish, it did not appear that he wanted to burden the heir with a double payment of the dowry.

17   SCAEVOLA, *Replies, book 3:* A man made a legacy to his wife as follows: "Let my wife take for herself from the whole whatever I have obtained from her and what she gave me." I ask whether the dowry appears to have been legated. He replied that from the words cited it appears that he was speaking about a legacy of the dowry, unless it was proved that the testator intended something else.   1. "To my wife, Titia, the money which came to me as her dowry or has been stipulated for as such, which dowry is in two sealed dotal inventories of a hundred aurei each." It was asked whether she can secure both sums. He replied that, on the facts stated, there was no reason why she can not.

5
THE LEGACY OF AN OPTION OR CHOICE

1   ULPIAN, *Sabinus, book 2:* The deified Pius wrote in a rescript to Caecilius Proculus that a man to whom a choice of slaves had been legated could choose three.

2   ULPIAN, *Sabinus, book 20:* Whenever the choice or option of a slave is given, the legatee can opt for whom he wishes.   1. Also when a slave is legated in general terms, the choice of whom he will take again belongs to the legatee.   2. Therefore, if, when an option is given, a man opts for another's slave or a freeman, it must be considered whether he has used up his option; I think he has not.   3. The man to whom the choice of a hundred amphorae has been given does not use up his option by choosing vinegar, if he chooses that vinegar which the head of the household did not reckon as wine,

3   ULPIAN, *Sabinus, book 23:* provided that he chose the vinegar before it was produced, that is, before tasting it.

4   PAUL, *Sabinus, book 3:* Where the choice of a cup is given, if the legatee made his choice when not all the cups were produced, it is agreed that his option remains unimpaired (unless he had wanted to choose from those alone, although he knew that there were also others),

5   AFRICANUS, *Questions, book 5:* and not only if this happened through fraud by the heir but also if from any other cause.

6   POMPONIUS, *Sabinus, book 6:* A choice of slaves was legated. In order that a sale be not prevented while the legatee is making his choice, the praetor should decree that unless he chooses within a period defined by himself, he will not be entitled to an action on the legacy. What, then, if the legatee should want to claim after the time has elapsed but before the heir sells? Because the heir will not suffer loss by such a decision, the praetor is accustomed to allow it. And what if, when the period laid down by the praetor has elapsed, the heir manumits some or all of the slaves? Will not the praetor protect their freedom? Therefore, the action must not be refused whenever everything is intact. The same is true also if the heir has given some of these slaves as a pledge or sold them after the time has elapsed.

7   PAUL, *Questions, book 10:* Indeed, even if the heir has disposed of some slaves and kept some, the legatee is not to be heard, if he wants to choose from those kept by the heir, since the heir has already disposed of the household.

8   POMPONIUS, *Sabinus, book 6:* If the choice of a slave is legated to you and the rest are legated to me, the praetor must decree, if you have not exercised your option within a fixed time, that the right of action will not be given to you.   1. If out of four bracelets two,

which I may choose, are legated to me, the legacy is valid, whether only two are left or only two existed from the start.   2. The option of one man was given to you and me; when I had chosen and then you chose the same man, if I had not changed my mind, he will be our joint slave. But if I had died or gone mad first, he will not be our joint slave, because I am not held to consent, because I cannot have an opinion; it will, however, be more humane that in this case too he should become our joint slave once the choice has been made.   3. If a choice of articles deposited is left to me, I shall be able to bring an action both against the man with whom they were deposited for production and against the heir to make him give me the opportunity to choose by bringing an action on deposit.

9   JULIAN, *Digest, book 32:* When a legacy is worded as follows, "to Titius I give and legate Stichus, if he does not choose Pamphilus; and to the same Titius Pamphilus, if he does not choose Stichus," it is the same as if the legacy had been as follows: "To Titius I give and legate Stichus or Pamphilus, whichever of them he wishes."   1. It was asked what was the state of the law, if Stichus was ordered to be free under a condition and I had been given the option of a slave or a slave had been legated to me in general terms. I said that it was more convenient to decide that the man who gives his liberty to Stichus under a condition and the option of slaves is not thinking of Stichus, just as it is agreed that he is not thinking of a slave to whom he has given immediate freedom. Accordingly, if I opt for or choose Stichus, my act will be void and I will still have a choice from the others.   2. In the same case, it was asked, if the option of a slave is given and the condition on which his freedom depended has failed before I make my choice, whether I can choose Stichus. I think the opinion of Mucius is to be followed, whereby it is agreed that a legacy is annulled by freedom itself, not by the grant of conditional freedom. Therefore, if the condition on which freedom depends fails either during the testator's lifetime or after his death and before the inheritance is accepted, the legacy will be valid; for conditional freedom, like unconditional freedom, takes effect from the time when the inheritance is accepted. Therefore, I can choose Stichus.

10   JULIAN, *Digest, book 34:* If a slave was legated in general terms to Pamphilus, the slave of Lucius Titius, and Pamphilus's owner then had manumitted him after the legacy has vested, Pamphilus's legacy is extinguished if Titius claimed the slave, because there was no slave in the inheritance who could be chosen. But if Titius had rejected the legacy, it is agreed that Pamphilus can exercise his option; for although by the manumission of Pamphilus two persons, Titius and Pamphilus, were constituted, nevertheless, the legacy of a single thing is in issue between them, and if Titius claims it, the option is extinguished, but if he rejects it, Pamphilus can exercise the option.

11   JULIAN, *Digest, book 36:* If Eros is legated to Seius and a farm to Eros and the option of a slave is given to Maevius and he opts for Eros, the farm will belong to Seius alone, since at the time the inheritance is accepted, he will be the only person to whom the legacy can belong. For when one of the joint owners makes a legacy to a jointly owned slave, the whole legacy belongs to the joint owner alone, for the reason that when the legacy vests, he is the only person who can acquire through that slave. ·

12   JULIAN, *From Minicius, book 1:* When a slave is legated in general terms, it is more correct that all the heirs, if a choice is given them, should give the same slave; if the heirs do not agree, they are liable under the will.

13   PAUL, *Plautius, book 8:* If the option of a slave has been given to me and the testator has left something to Stichus without granting him freedom, the second legacy stands only when the entire household is reduced to one individual, namely Stichus, so that the legacy is valid just as if it had been made unconditionally. Cato's rule does not tell against this, if a *heres voluntarius* has been instituted, because the household can be diminished before the inheritance is accepted, even if the testator dies immediately. But if a *heres necessarius* has been instituted, the second legacy is invalid on

account of Cato's rule.   1. Pomponius writes that when the buyer of an inheritance demands that the person to whom the option of a slave has been legated should exercise it, it must be considered whether the praetor should compel the legatee to do so, just as if the instituted heir were making the demand, because the buyer can accomplish this through the heir. I do not see why he should not be able to.

14   JAVOLENUS, *From Cassius, book 2:* If, when the option of a slave from the entire household had been legated, the heir manumitted one before the option had been exercised, he cannot in the interim give him his freedom, but he, nevertheless, will lose the slave whom he has thus manumitted, because the slave will either constitute the legacy, if he is chosen, or become free, if he is passed over.

15   JAVOLENUS, *Letters, book 2:* I made a legacy to a slave without granting him freedom, then gave the option of slaves to Maevius; he opted for that same slave. I ask whether what was legated is also owed to him. He replied: I do not think that a legacy in the name of this slave belongs to the owner.

16   TERENTIUS CLEMENS, *Lex Julia et Papia, book 15:* When an option is legated, it is agreed that it cannot be exercised before the inheritance is accepted and that it is void if it was so exercised.

17   TERENTIUS CLEMENS, *Lex Julia et Papia, book 17:* When the option of two slaves is given to Titius and the rest are legated to Maevius, if the first legatee fails to make a choice, all belong to Maevius under the rubric "the rest."

18   SCAEVOLA, *Questions, book 13:* Neratius says that when a man is legated, the act is void if Pamphilus is excluded, and so Pamphilus himself can be chosen.

19   PAUL, *Views, book 3:* "'X' or 'Y,' whichever the legatee chooses"; if the legatee chooses nothing and dies after the time when the legacy vests, it is agreed that the choice passes to his heir.

20   LABEO, *Posthumous Works, Epitomized by Javolenus, book 2:* It is written in the first book of Aufidius's *Replies* that when a legacy is made as follows, "let him take and have for himself any couch-covers that he wishes," if he stated which ones he wanted, then, before he took them, said he wanted others, he cannot change his mind, so as to take others, because he has used up his entire right under the legacy by his first statement by which he said he was taking, since an article becomes his immediately, as soon as he has said that he is taking it.

21   SCAEVOLA, *Digest, book 22:* A man appointed his son and wife as heirs, disinherited his daughter, and gave her a legacy of a hundred, and added the following when she married within the family: "also, at the choice of her mother Sempronia, ten slaves, which I want to be chosen by my wife Sempronia as soon as my inheritance has been accepted; these slaves I want to be given when she has married into the family. And if, before she marries, any of the slaves dies, then I want another to be chosen by her mother Sempronia to be given in his place, so that the full number may come to her. But if her mother Sempronia does not make the choice, then let her choose which ones she likes for herself." It was asked, when the mother has made the choice, whether the children born from those slaves before the marriage would belong to the girl over and above the total of ten slaves. He replied that since the testator had postponed the legacy of slaves to the time of the marriage, the offspring produced by the slave-women in the meantime did not belong to the daughter. The same man asked whether the usufruct of these slaves belonged to the mother Sempronia before the marriage. He replied that no facts had been stated to explain why it should belong entirely to the mother.

22   SCAEVOLA, *Digest, book 17:* A husband gave landed estates to his wife in a codicil by a *fideicommissum*, also four plates which she might choose. It was asked whether she could choose from those plates which were found at the time of death. He replied that she could.

6

LEGACIES OF WHEAT, WINE, OR OIL

1   ULPIAN, *Sabinus, book 20:* When wine is legated, vinegar that the head of the household reckoned as wine is also included.

2   POMPONIUS, *Sabinus, book 6:* When stores are legated to one person, wine to another, all stores with the exception of wine will belong to the first legatee.   1. If a hundred amphorae of your choice are legated to you, by bringing an action based on the will you can obtain the right of tasting, or you can bring an action for production for the amount of your interest in being allowed to taste.

3   ULPIAN, *Sabinus, book 23:* If a hundred amphorae of wine are legated to someone, when the testator had left no wine, the heir shall buy and deliver wine, not vinegar which was reckoned as wine.   1. If wine is legated, let us see whether it is owed together with its containers. Celsus says that when wine is legated, even if it is not legated with its containers, the containers too appear to be legated, not because the containers are part of the wine, as the ornamentation is of silver (as it might be of cups or a mirror), but because it is credible that the testator's intention was such that he wished the amphorae to be an accession to the wine; thus, he said, we speak of having a thousand amphorae, referring to the amount of wine. Where casks are concerned, I do not think it true that when wine is legated the casks are also owed, especially if they are fixed in the wine cellar or are difficult to move because of their size. However, in the case of tuns or tubs I think it must be admitted that they too are owed, unless they are likewise immovably fixed in the land so as to be an *instrumentum* of the land. When wine is legated, wineskins will not be owed; I also say that leather bottles are not owed.

4   PAUL, *Sabinus, book 4:* When a certain weight of oil is legated without mention of quality, it is not usual to ask what kind of oil the testator was accustomed to use or what kind of oil the men of that region use; therefore, the heir is free to deliver to the legatee oil of whatever kind he wishes.

5   JULIAN, *Digest, book 15:* When a fixed number of amphorae of wine out of that produced on the Sempronian farm was legated and less was produced, it was agreed that more was not due and that the words "that produced" functioned, as it were, as a limitation.

6   PROCULUS, *Letters, book 5:* When an heir is charged by legacy *per damnationem* to give someone wine, what has been poured off in amphorae and jars must be given, even if no mention was made of containers. Likewise, even if it has been legated along with the containers and jars, nevertheless, that contained in casks also appears to be legated, just as, if a man legates all his slaves with the *peculium* of each of them, he appears also to have legated those who have no *peculium*.

7   JAVOLENUS, *From the Posthumous Works of Labeo, book 2:* A man charged his heir by legacy *per damnationem* to give to his wife wine, oil, grain, vinegar, honey, and salt fish. Trebatius said that of each item no more was owed than the heir wanted to give to the woman, since it was not stated how much of each thing was to be given. Ofilius, Cascellius, and Tubero think that all that the head of the household had left was legated; Labeo approves this and it is correct.   1. "Let my heir give to Lucius Titius a hundred measures of wheat, each weighing a hundred pounds." Ofilius thinks that the legacy is void, which Labeo also approves, since wheat of this kind does not exist. I think this is correct.

8   POMPONIUS, *Letters, book 6:* If an heir was charged by legacy *per damnationem* to give the wine which was in casks and it was the fault of the legatee that he did not receive it, the heir will put himself at risk if he pours off that wine, but it is agreed that

if the legatee demands the wine from the heir, he will be barred by the defense of fraud if he does not give compensation for the loss suffered by the heir on account of his delay.

9 ULPIAN, *Sabinus, book 23:* If a man legates wine, everything which originates from the vine and remains wine is included. But if mead has been made, it will not properly be included under the heading of wine, unless the head of the household chanced to have it too in mind. Certainly, zythum, which is made in some provinces from wheat, barley, or bread, will not be included; likewise, neither ale nor beer nor hydromel will be included. What about spiced wine? I think it too will not be included, unless the testator's intention was otherwise. Plainly honey-wine, that is, the sweetest wine, will be included, and raisin-wine will be included, unless the intention was otherwise; concentrated must will not be included, because it is prepared rather for preserving fruit. Wine made from dried grapes is obviously included in wine. Quince-wine and any other drinks not made from the vine will not be included under the name of wine. Likewise, vinegar will not be included under the name of wine. In short, all these things are not included under the name of wine, provided that they were not reckoned as wine by the testator. However, Sabinus writes that all things are included under the heading of wine, which the head of the household reckoned as wine; therefore, both vinegar which the head of the household reckoned as wine and zythum, ale, and the other things which are reckoned as wine according to the reckoning and usage of men. But if all the wine which the head of the household possessed has gone sour, the legacy is not extinguished. 1. If a man legated vinegar, vinegar which the testator reckoned as wine will not be included in the legacy; however, vinegar sauce will be included, because it was reckoned as vinegar. 2. Likewise, if a man legated the wine which he had, then this went sour, although it was subsequently reckoned as vinegar by the head of the household, it will be included in the legacy of wine, because that was designated which was wine at the time the will was made; and this is true unless the intention is otherwise. 3. However, when wine that belonged to the testator's father is legated, only that appears to be legated which the testator reckoned as wine, not what his father did. Yet if wine belonging to a *peculium* is legated, what the slaves reckoned as wine will be included. Why so great a difference? Because wine inherited from the father has already begun to be used by the testator himself, but wine belonging to a *peculium* remained in the use of the slaves. 4. Likewise, if old wine is legated,

10 HERMOGENIAN, *Epitome of Law, book 2:* the legacy will be estimated according to the usage of the testator, that is, what age of wine he treated as old. But if this is not known,

11 ULPIAN, *Sabinus, book 23:* what is not new will be accepted as old, that is, even wine of the previous year will be included under the appellation "old";

12 PAUL, *Sabinus, book 4:* for if other criteria are adopted, what terminal or initial limits could be taken to define old wine?

13 ULPIAN, *Sabinus, book 23:* "From the wine which is produced on that farm, let my heir give ten amphorae a year every year." In a year when none was produced, Sabinus thinks the heir should give that number of amphorae of the previous year from that farm. I too agree with this opinion, if the intention is not otherwise.

14 POMPONIUS, *Sabinus, book 6:* When wine is legated, only those vessels are included which have been drawn off in such a manner that the containers are not reserved for perpetual use, such as amphorae and jars.

15 PROCULUS, *Letters, book 2:* A man legated wine with containers. Trebatius denies that what was in casks was owed and thinks that the testator's intention was at variance with his words; further, that casks are not included among wine containers. Even if casks are not included among wine containers, I should not concede to Trebatius that wine which was in casks, which was not, that is, in containers, had not been legated. I think it is true that when wine with containers is legated to someone, the amphorae and jars in which we keep wine drawn off are legated to him; for we draw off wine into amphorae and jars with the intention that it remain in them until it is poured out for use, and we certainly sell it along with these amphorae and jars. We place it in casks, however, with a different intention, namely that we may subsequently either draw it off from these into amphorae and jars or that it may be sold without the casks themselves.

16 JAVOLENUS, *From the Posthumous Works of Labeo, book 3:* A man who had Surrentine wine drawn off in urns legated to you all his wine in amphorae. Labeo and Trebatius replied that the wine which had been in urns had also been legated. 1. When sweet things have been legated to someone, if there is no other indication in the will, all the following are legated: mead, raisin-wine, concentrated must, and similar drinks; likewise, grapes, figs, dates, and dried figs. 2. But if a legacy is made as follows, "wine in amphorae Aminaean and Greek and all sweet things," Labeo thinks that nothing is legated under "sweet things" except drinks, because of the conjunction with wine in amphorae. This opinion I do not reject.

7

THE LEGACY OF *INSTRUCTUM* OR *INSTRUMENTUM*

1 PAUL, *Sabinus, book 4:* Whether a farm is legated with its *instrumentum* or as *instructus*, two legacies are understood. 1. When a farm is legated with its *instrumentum* and sold, the *instrumentum* cannot be claimed by *vindicatio* on the strength of the deceased's intention.

2 PAPINIAN, *Replies, book 7:* When a father, after appointing several sons as heirs, gave to two of them a *praelegatum* of their grandmother's property in addition to their shares of the inheritance, it was agreed that the legatees should have equal shares in proportion to those of their co-heirs. 1. The accessories of landed estates which are called by the Greek term ἐνθῆκαι are not delivered to the legatee when the estates are not legated as *instructa*.

3 PAPINIAN, *Replies, book 8:* A patron legated to his freedmen in his will a *fundus instructus*; subsequently, he asked in a codicil that when they died they should hand over their shares of the farm to the survivors, but did not mention the *instructum*. It was decided that the farm should be brought under the *fideicommissum* in the condition in which it had been legated; moreover, the increase of animals and slaves in the meantime, likewise, losses caused by death, were included in the *fideicommissum*. 1. A person under twenty wanted estates to be given as *instructa* to his female cousin and during his lifetime manumitted certain slaves attached to the estates. Although they cannot attain their freedom, the manumitted slaves will not on that account be delivered. The law is the same when freedom is not obtained for any other cause.

4 JAVOLENUS, *From the Posthumous Works of Labeo, book 2:* When a man had two contiguous farms and the oxen used to return from one to the other when they had done their work, he legated both farms with their *instrumentum*. Labeo and Trebatius think the oxen will go with that farm where they worked, not that where they were habitually stalled; Cascellius holds the opposite view. I agree with Labeo.

5 LABEO, *Plausible Views, Epitomized by Paul, book 1:* If you want to legate to someone a farm and its *instrumentum*, it makes no difference whether you word the legacy "the farm with its *instrumentum*" or "the farm and the *instrumentum*" or "the *fundus instructus*." PAUL: On the contrary, for there is this difference between the legacies, that if the man who made such a legacy died after alienating the farm, by the form of words "the farm with its *instrumentum*" nothing will be legated, while by the other forms the *instrumentum* can be legated.

6 SCAEVOLA, *Digest, book 16:* A woman had legated to her grandson the estates she had in a certain region as *instructa*, with the wine, grain, and the account book, and had added these words: "whatever shall exist in that region at the time of my death, in whatever form it shall exist, that is mine." One of her debtors was condemned during the lifetime of the testatrix and did not pay up; it was asked whether what was owed as a result of the judge's decision belonged to the grandson. He replied that no reason had been shown why it should not be due.

7 SCAEVOLA, *Digest, book 22:* A man had left to Pardula, whom he manumitted in his will, a shop with an attic, together with the merchandise, *instrumenta*, and furniture which were there; likewise, a winestore together with the wine, vessels, *instrumentum*, and the managers whom he had been accustomed to keep with him. It was asked, since the block in which the attic that had been legated to him was situated had been burned down in the testator's lifetime and rebuilt in the same place two years later, and the store, which had been legated to him, had been sold by the testator, but the sale of the wine had been delayed so that it might be sold at a favorable price, whether Pardula could secure the whole legacy. He replied that those things concerning which the intention had changed were not due.

8 ULPIAN, *Sabinus, book 20:* Sabinus states plainly in his books on Vitellius that those things are included in the *instrumentum* of a farm which are provided for the producing, gathering, and preserving of the fruits. Thus, for producing, the men who till the soil and those who direct them or are placed in charge of them, including stewards and overseers, also domesticated oxen and beasts kept for producing manure, and implements useful in farming, such as plows, mattocks, hoes, pruning hooks, forks, and similar items. For gathering, such things as presses, baskets, sickles, scythes, grape-pickers' baskets in which grapes are carried. For preserving, such things as casks, even if not set in the ground, and tuns. 1. In certain regions, there are added to the *instrumentum,* if the villa is of the better equipped sort, such items as majordomos and sweepers, and, if there are also gardens, gardeners, and, if the farm has woods and pastures, flocks, shepherds, and foresters.

9 PAUL, *Sabinus, book 4:* With reference to a flock of sheep, the following distinction must be made. If it was assembled for the purpose of deriving profit from it, it is not owed; but if because the profit of the woodland can be gathered in no other way, the opposite will be the case, because the profits of the woodland are gathered by means of the flocks.

10 ULPIAN, *Sabinus, book 20:* If the revenue also consists of honey, the hives and bees are included.

11 JAVOLENUS, *From Cassius, book 2:* The same rule applies to birds, which are kept on islands in the sea.

12 ULPIAN, *Sabinus, book 20:* It was asked whether grain, which had been intended for the rations of farmhands, would be included in *instrumentum.* The majority hold that it would not, because it would be consumed, whereas *instrumentum* comprises things collectively of longer duration without which possession could not be exercised. An additional reason is that food is prepared for nourishment rather than for purposes of cultivation. But I think that both grain and wine intended as rations are included in *instrumentum,* and his pupils report that Servius replied in that sense. Likewise, some have held that grain which was set aside for sowing is included in *instrumentum,* I think because it is involved in cultivation and is consumed in such a way that it is always replaced; and the case of seed-corn is no different from that of food. 1. For preserving the fruits, items such as granaries, because the fruits are stored in these, pitchers, and coffers in which the fruits are collected; but it is also agreed that those things which are intended for the transport of the fruits count as *instrumentum,* such as pack animals, vehicles, ships, tuns, and leather bottles. 2. Alfenus says, however, that if a man legated some of his slaves to others, the rest, who were on the farm, are not included in the *instrumentum,* because he held that no living creature counts as *instrumentum.* This is not true; for it is agreed that those who are there for the sake of the land are included in the *instrumentum.* 3. It is asked whether a slave, who was in a position like that of a tenant on the land, is included in a legacy of the *instrumentum.* Both Labeo and Pegasus rightly denied this, because he had not been fulfilling the function of *instrumentum* on the farm, even if he had been accustomed to give orders to the household. 4. Moreover, Labeo also thinks that a forester is included only if he was intended to preserve the fruits, not if he was to guard the boundaries. But Neratius includes the latter too, and as the law stands, all foresters are included. 5. Trebatius further thinks that a baker and barber, intended to serve the needs of the rural household, are included; likewise, the mason, who is intended to repair the villa, and the women who cook bread and look after the villa; likewise, the millers, if they are intended for use on the estate; likewise, the kitchen maid and the steward's wife, provided she assists her husband in some duty; likewise, the woolmakers who make clothes for the rural household and those women who cook relishes for the rural slaves. 6. But it is asked whether *instrumentum* of the *instrumentum*

is included in a legacy of *instrumentum*; for those things that are intended for the use of the rural slaves, as woolmakers, shearsmen, fullers, and kitchen maids, are *instrumentum* not of the land but of its *instrumentum*. I think, therefore, that a cook is included and also woolmakers and the others enumerated above; and his pupils report that Servius replied to this effect.   7. It should also be held that the testator wanted the wives and children too of those enumerated above, if they live in the same villa, to be included in the legacy; for it is not credible that he would have imposed a harsh separation.   8. If beasts are pastured on the farm for part of the year and for part fodder is brought for them or if slaves cultivate the land for part of the year and are hired out for part, they, nonetheless, are included in the *instrumentum*.   9. It is agreed that the steward, that is, the man appointed to see that the accounts are in order, is included in the *instrumentum*; likewise, the doorkeeper and the muleteer. 10. Millstones, machinery, bales of hay, the ass that works the machine, grinding machinery, the bronze vessel in which new wine is boiled, concentrated must is made, and water for the household to drink and wash in is prepared are included in *instrumentum*, also sieves and wagons in which dung is taken out.   11. Cassius writes, however, that those things which are attached to the soil are not part of the *instrumentum* of a farm, such as reed beds and osiers, before they are cut, because a farm cannot be the *instrumentum* of a farm; but if they have been cut, I think they are included, because they serve in producing the fruits. The same must be said in the case of stakes.   12. If there is hunting on the land, I think that huntsmen, trackers, dogs, and the other items necessary for hunting are also included in the *instrumentum*, especially if the land has derived income from this.   13. And if there has been income from fowling, fowlers, nets, and the *instrumentum* of this activity will be included in the *instrumentum* of the land; nor is it surprising, since Sabinus and Cassius thought that birds were included in the *instrumentum* by analogy with bees.   14. If a man uses the same *instrumentum* on several pieces of land, it is asked of which piece it is the *instrumentum*. I think that if the wish of the head of the household, as to which piece of land he had intended it for, is apparent, it is the *instrumentum* of that piece; for the other pieces of land borrow, as it were, from this piece. If it is not clear, it will be reckoned as the *instrumentum* of none; for we should not divide up *instrumentum* in shares.   15. Furniture and whatever else was on the land so that the head of the household might be better equipped are not included in the *instrumentum* of the farm.   16. If the *instrumentum* of a house is legated, we must see what is included. Pegasus says the *instrumentum* of a house is what is intended to keep out the weather and fight fires, not what is for pleasure; thus, neither windows nor awnings, which are in the house to keep out cold or give shade, are owed. This was the opinion of Cassius, who said that there was a great difference between *instrumentum* and ornaments; *instrumentum* included those things which served to protect the house, ornaments those which were for pleasure, such as paintings.   17. However, Cassius held that Cilician awnings, which are set up so that the buildings may not suffer from wind or rain, are included.   18. Most authorities, including Pegasus, say that vinegar too, which is intended to put out fires, is included; likewise, rags, siphons, also poles and ladders, mats, sponges, buckets, and brooms.   19. Moreover, tiles and timbers intended for this purpose are included in the *instrumentum*, if the testator has timber intended for this purpose which does not serve any other use. Similarly, if he had any props necessary to this purpose, they too will be included in the *instrumentum* of the house.   20. Concerning awnings spread in open walks and those set up around columns, Celsus writes that they are rather to be reckoned with furniture and that Sabinus and Cassius think the same.   21. It is, however, agreed that conduits, grappling hooks, and buckets are included in the *instrumentum*.   22. Likewise, poles with which cobwebs are brushed away, sponges with which columns, pavements, and balconies are cleaned, and ladders which are set against ceilings are included among *instrumentum*, because they make the house cleaner.   23. Papinian also says in the seventh book of his *Replies*: Figures and statues fixed in place are not included in the *instrumentum* of a house but are part of the house. However, those which are not fixed are equally not included he says; for they are reckoned with the furniture, except for a bronze clock which is not fixed in place; for this, he thinks, is included in the *instrumentum* of the house, just as the vestibule of a house, if it is an awning, he says, is included in the *instrumentum* of the house.   24. However, gutters, conduits, basins, and whatever else is necessary for fountains, likewise, locks and keys, are rather a part of the house than *instrumentum* of the house.   25. Fixed panes of glass too I think are rather part of the house; for in buying a house the windows and shelves go with it, whether they are set in the fabric or temporarily removed. But if they are not in place, but have been set aside for the purpose of replacing any that are missing, they will rather be included in the *instrumentum*.   26. I think that lattices also are included in the *instrumentum*.   27. But if a farm is legated, not with its *instrumentum*, but as *instructus*, it has been asked whether more is included than if it were legated with its *instrumentum*. And Sabinus writes in his books on *Vitellius* that it must be said that more is included when a farm is legated as *instructus* than if it is legated with its *instrumentum*; and we see this opinion growing and gaining strength every day. Therefore, we must see in what degree this legacy is more extensive. Sabinus lays down, and Cassius, cited by Vitellius, notes that everything placed there in order that the head of the household may be better equipped will be included in *instructum*. Therefore, by this legacy he appears to have left not the *instrumentum* of the land, but his own personal *instrumentum*.   28. So if a farm is legated as *instructus*, the furniture which was there for his use will be included, and clothes, not only rugs but also what he was accustomed to wear there, also tables, ivory or other, glassware, gold and silver, also whatever wines were there for his own use, and all other utensils.   29. But whatever he had collected there not for his own use but for safekeeping will not be included; also wine contained in storerooms will not be included, and the law is that what the head of the household kept there, as it were, in store is not included.   30. Celsus also writes in the nineteenth book of his *Digest* that fruits stored there to be sold or put to some use other than that of the farm are not included in a *fundus instructus*.   31. Celsus again says in the same book that slaves who look after furniture and others of this kind are included, that is, those through whose services he had been equipped on that farm (apart from those who received their freedom) and who were accustomed to live on the country estates.   32. If he had legated a *fundus instructus*, trainee slaves, whom he kept there so that when he came there they might wait at table, are included in the legacy.   33. It is true that the companions and children of slaves are also included in a *fundus instructus*.   34. Moreover, it is agreed that a library and the books that were there for him to use whenever he came are included in a *fundus instructus*. But the opposite must be said if he used it, so to speak, as a bookstore.   35. Neratius also replied to Rufinus in his fourth book of *Letters* that furniture, wines, and slaves, not only those intended to cultivate and guard the villa but also those who were there to wait on the head of the household himself, are included in the legacy of a *fundus instructus*.   36. Only those pictures are held to be legated which were in some sense ornaments of the villa.   37. Papinian also holds that when estates are legated as *instructa*, those slaves are not included who were there for some temporary purpose and whom the head of the household did not take there with the intention of making them *instrumentum* either of the farm or of his own use.   38. Papinian replied that when landed estates were legated as *instructa*, an agent sent from them to a province, with instructions to return to his former occupation when his business was concluded, went with the legacy of the estate, although he had not yet returned.   39. Papinian also replied that when gardens were legated as *instructa*, the wines which were there so that the owner might be better equipped were included; it was otherwise if he had storehouses there from which to equip himself either in the city or on other estates.   40. Papinian also replied that when a house was left by *fideicommissum* together with its furniture to the highly respected Claudius Hieronymianus by Umbrius Primus, the tables and other furniture which the head of the household had placed in store for greater safety, when about to set out to his proconsulate, were included. 41. Papinian also replied that an antidote and other medicines, which the owner kept there for his visits, and clothes deposited there against his visits were also included in a legacy of a *fundus instructus*. 42. Papinian also replied that when a house is legated as *instructa* and with all legal rights pertaining to it, the urban household is not included in the legacy; likewise, craftsmen, whose skills were practiced also on other estates; doorkeepers; however, he says, or gardeners, valets, and water carriers who worked only in the house will be included. But what he says about craftsmen is false, if they were procured for the sake of that house, even though they were lent to other estates as well. 43. Papinian also replied that when a house is legated as *instructa*, ivory tables and books are not included; but this too is false, for everything that was in the house in order that the head of the household might be better equipped there will be included. Moreover, nobody doubts that the furniture of the head of the household is *instrumentum*. Finally, Neratius, in the fourth book of his *Letters*, replied to his brother Marcellus that clothes are also included in a legacy of a house as *instructa*, especially, he says, in the case proposed; for it was posited that the testator had excluded the silver and the accounts. For anyone, he says, who excluded these things must be held to have intended to include everything else that was in the house. But Papinian himself, in the same book of his *Replies*, says that a father who was a merchant and moneylender, and had instituted as heirs two sons and two daughters, had left a legacy as follows: "To my sons I give, legate, and order to be given my house as *instructa*." It could be asked whether merchandise and pledges are included; but it will be easy for the judge to divine the intention by examining the father's other property. 44. Celsus writes that when the slaves who reside on a farm are legated, their *vicarii* are not included, unless it appears that he also had *vicarii* in mind. 45. Papinian, too, in the seventh book of his *Replies*, answered that *cautiones* for debts and purchase vouchers for slaves did not appear to have been legated to a wife, to whom her husband wished his daughter as heir to deliver everything that was in the house, unless, he says, it appears on some other ground that he had the slaves too in mind, so that he might appear to have legated to her the purchase vouchers of those slaves whose persons he wished to belong to her. 46. If someone legated a farm as *instructus* and added "along with the furniture" or "the slaves" or some other single item mentioned by name, which was in it, it is asked whether or not he diminishes the legacy by adding the specification. And Papinian replied that it does not appear to be diminished; the addition rather appears to be tautologous. 47. Papinian also says in the seventh book of his *Replies*: After legating her gardens as *instructi* to her son, a mother legated to her daughter the silver intended for female use. He replied that that silver for female use, which she kept in the gardens in order that she might be better equipped there, also belongs to the daughter.

13   PAUL, *Sabinus, book 4:* Neratius thinks that the slave managers too are included in a legacy of the *instrumentum* of a wineshop; but we must see whether there is a difference between the *instrumentum* of a wineshop and the *instrumentum* of an inn, in that only the *instrumentum* of the place is included in that of a wineshop, such as casks, vessels, mugs, cups, ladles which usually circulate at table; likewise, bronze urns, flagons, beakers, and the like, whereas in the *instrumentum* of an inn, as the reference to "inn" covers the business carried on there, the managers are also included. 1. Neratius replied that the bath-attendant was also included in the legacy of the *instrumentum* of a bathhouse.

14   PAUL, *Vitellius, book 2:* Moreover, the stoker is also included.

15   POMPONIUS, *Sabinus, book 6:* If the following clause is written in a will, "I give and legate those things which were made and acquired to equip and carry on the business of my shops, mill, and inn," Servius replied that by these words both the horses which were in the mill and the millers, and in the inn the slave-managers and the cook, and the merchandise which was in these establishments, were regarded as legated. 1. It was replied that by *domus instructa* the furniture too is legated, not, however, wines, because a house cannot be understood to be equipped with wines. 2. A woman who was the permanent custodian of a villa will be included in a farm which is legated with

its *instrumentum* or as *instructus*, as will the forester. The reason is the same for both lands and villas require guardians, the one so that neighbors may not seize any of the land or its fruits, the other so that they may not seize any of the other things contained in the villa. Moreover, the villa is without any doubt considered as part of the farm.

16   ALFENUS, *Digest, Epitomized by Paul, book 2:* It is more correct that the furniture is not included in the legacy of the *instrumentum* of a villa.   1. When a vineyard and its *instrumentum* were legated, Servius replied that there was no such thing as the *instrumentum* of a vineyard; the man who consulted him said that Cornelius had replied that stakes, poles, rakes, and hoes are *instrumentum* of a vineyard; this is more correct.   2. A man legated to his wife the farm, as *instructus*, on which he himself lived. When consulted as to whether the wool-making women were included in the *instrumentum*, he replied that they were not indeed part of the *instrumentum* of the farm, but since the head of the household, who made the legacy, himself lived on that farm, it should not be doubted that the slave-women and other things, with which the head of the household was equipped on that farm, all appeared to have been legated.

17   MARCIAN, *Institutes, book 7:* Likewise, when the *instrumentum* of a painter is legated, waxes, colors, and similar things are included in the legacy; likewise, brushes, encaustic tools, and oil pans.   1. Aristo says that in the *instrumentum* of fishing are included boats which are provided for catching fish; moreover, it is more correct that the fishermen also are included.   2. It has been said that when the *instrumentum* of a bathhouse is legated, the bath-attendant is included in the *instrumentum*, just as the forester and gardeners are included in the *instrumentum* of a farm and the manager in the *instrumentum* of an inn, since baths cannot fulfill their function without bath-attendants.

18   PAUL, *Vitellius, book 2:* When the question of the *instrumentum* of a butcher is raised, we set aside the meat and leave as *instrumentum* tables, weights, and tools prepared for cutting up meat, that is, scales, knives, and cleavers.   1. When *instrumentum* is legated, it is sometimes also necessary to consider the person of the testator, as, when the *instrumentum* of a mill is legated, the millers themselves can be regarded as included only if the head of the household ran the mill. For it makes a very great difference whether the *instrumentum* was intended for the millers or for the mill.   2. Neratius denies that an ass employed in grinding and the millstone are included in the *instrumentum* of a farm.   3. Likewise, we say that pots and pans are included in the *instrumentum* of a farm, because without them relishes cannot be cooked. Nor is there much difference between pots and the cauldron which hangs over the fire; in the latter, water is boiled for drinking; in the former, relishes are cooked. But if the cauldron is included in the *instrumentum*, the pitchers too, with which water is poured into the cauldron, are placed in the same category, and so eventually each next item is linked to the one before to infinity. Therefore, Pedius says it is best not to scrutinize the precise meaning of the words but above all what the testator wanted to designate, and then the natural assumptions of those who reside in each region.   4. When it was asked whether a steward was included in the *instrumentum* and a doubt was raised, Scaevola, when consulted, replied that he was due if he cultivated the land on trust from his master and not in return for the payment of a fixed yield.   5. Scaevola also replied, when consulted about a lower millstone, that it too was owed if the grinding was done for the rural slaves of that farm. The lower millstone is called *meta*; the upper, *catillus*.   6. He also replied that a plowman was due, whether the question referred to one who plowed with the oxen there or one who fed the plow-oxen of that farm.   7. He also replied concerning pruners that if they were kept for the sake of that farm, they were included   8. and that shepherds and ditchers too belonged to the legatee.   9. Likewise, when a farm is legated as follows, "to Maevius the Seian farm, in best and fullest condition, with all its rural and urban *instrumentum* and the slaves that are there," and it was asked whether the seeds were owed, he replied that they were, more correctly, owed, unless the heir proved that the testator's intention was otherwise. He gave the same answer concerning corn set aside for the maintenance of slaves.   10. Cassius writes that eye lotions,

plasters, and other things of that kind are included in the *instrumentum* of a doctor. 11. A man had legated a *fundus instructus* to someone and legated some slaves to him by name; it was asked whether the rest of the slaves, whom he had not named, went with the *instrumentum*. Cassius says that an opinion had been given that although slaves are part of a *fundus instructus*, nevertheless, only those appeared to have been legated who had been named, as it was plain that the head of the household had not realized that slaves too were reckoned as *instrumentum*. 12. SABINUS: If a farm and whatever things are there are legated to someone, the farm, whatever is accustomed to be on it, whatever is accustomed to remain there for the greater part of the year, and those slaves who are accustomed to repair there to live appear to have been legated to him, but anything that has been deliberately collected on the farm or conveyed there in order to increase the legacy does not appear to have been legated. 13. When someone made a legacy as follows, "my villa, just as I possessed it myself, with the furniture, the tables, the slaves, both urban and rural who are sent there, the wines which are there on the day of my death, and ten aurei," it was asked, since on the day of his death he had there books, glassware, and a small garment, whether all these went with the legacy, given that he had enumerated certain things. Scaevola replied that only those things specially mentioned went with the legacy. 14. A man legated a *domus instructa* with all its attachments; it was asked whether the legatee could have the debtors' notes. He replied that according to the facts stated he could not.

19 PAUL, *Replies, book 13:* I replied that if slaves had been brought by the testator, after the making of the will, to a farm bequeathed to Seia and had been on that farm in order to cultivate it, they too were included in the *instrumentum* of the farm; for although the testator had designated those slaves who were there at the time he made the legacy, he, nonetheless, also mentioned the slaves not in order to diminish the legacy, but to increase it. Moreover, there is no doubt that slaves brought in to cultivate the land are also included in the *instrumentum* of a farm. 1. Paul replied that neither stored fruits nor a stud of horses are included in the *instrumentum* of a villa, whereas furniture goes with the legacy; but that a slave skilled in the craft of a smith, who brought in an annual wage, is not included in the *instrumentum* of a villa.

20 SCAEVOLA, *Replies, book 3:* To Seia, whom he instituted part-heir, a man had given, if she became heir, as a *praelegatum* farms as *instructi* with their stewards and the rent outstanding from the tenants, and he wrote as follows in a codicil: "It has subsequently come to my mind that I want Seia to have the farms I have bequeathed to her as *instructi* with the rural *instrumentum*, furniture, beasts, and stewards together with the rent outstanding from the tenants and the storehouse." It was asked whether those things which were on the farms for the daily use of the head of the household were also included in the legacy. He replied that in the will as cited there was a legacy to Seia over and above the farm but that no more was owed to her than what he had plainly shown he meant to be included under the heading of *instructum* in the codicil (which he had obviously made after forgetting what he had written in the will). 1. Someone legated landed estates to his freedman in these words: "I give and legate to my freedman Seius my farms 'X' and 'Y,' as *instructi*, together with accessories and rents due from tenants and the foresters with their companions, sons and daughters." It was asked whether the slave Stichus, who cultivated one of these estates and owed a large sum, was owed to Seius under the *fideicommissum*. He replied that if he had cultivated the farm not in trust from his master but for a rent, as extraneous tenants are accustomed to do, he was not owed. 2. "To Gaius Seius my foster child I want to be given my farms 'X' and 'Y,' as *instructi*, and the upper house." It was asked whether he wanted the house too to be given as *instructa*. He replied that according to the facts stated he appeared to have made the gift on those terms, unless the man from whom it was demanded showed plainly that the testator intended otherwise; but if he had legated the *instrumentum* of the dwelling, that is, of the building, slaves

intended for labor or any other purpose would not be included. 3. A man legated estates as *instructa* with accessories, payments outstanding from tenants and stewards, slaves, all cattle, *peculia*, and the agent. It was asked whether the rents outstanding from tenants who had on the expiry of their lease left their tenancy after giving a *cautio* should go with the legacy on the strength of the words cited above. He replied that he did not appear to have been thinking of these rents. 4. The same man asked, concerning the legacy of the agent, whether his wife and daughter went with the legacy, since the agent had lived, not on the estate, but in the town. He replied that no reason had been given why they should go with it. 5. The same man asked, since the testator, after making his will, had set out for a province, whether those slaves went with the legacy who had, after his departure or death, of their own accord without authority from anyone migrated to join relatives and acquaintances on the legated farms. He replied that those who had migrated there by chance, as it were in transit, had not been legated. 6. "To my freedwoman Pamphila I want to be given the Titian farm with its *instrumentum* and those slaves who are on it when I die." It was asked whether, if the slave Stichus had been removed from that farm a year before the testator's death and sent to be educated, and had not subsequently returned to the farm, he was owed. He replied that if he had sent him away to study and not in order to transfer him from the farm to some other place, he was owed. 7. "To my sister, Tyranna, I bequeath my Graecian farm with the stable and all the rural *instrumentum*." It is asked whether under the heading of the farm the pastures, which came to him at the same time as the farm and which he had always kept for the use of this possession, went with the legacy. He replied that, if he had joined the fields with the Graecian farm so that they were reckoned under the single heading of the farm, they too were owed. 8. When a house was legated as *instructa*, a bed covered with silver gilt was not found in the house at the time of Titia's death, but had been stored in the meantime in a warehouse; I ask whether it too is to be delivered. He replied that if it was customarily kept in the house and had been temporarily placed in the warehouse for safekeeping, it should be delivered nonetheless. 9. When the testator has added, "just as I possessed it," does this mean "as *instructa* on the day of my death," that is, with the slaves, cattle, and rural *instrumentum*? He replied: This is not a question of law.

21 POMPONIUS, *Fideicommissa, book 1:* When a farm is legated without its *instrumentum*, casks, olive mills, the press, and whatever is fixed or built in are included in the legacy of the farm, but none of those things that can be moved, with a few exceptions, is included under the heading of the farm. The question customarily arises concerning mills, when they are so fixed or built in as to appear to be part of the building.

22 PAUL, *Views, book 3:* When a farm is legated "in best and fullest condition," boar nets and other *instrumenta* of hunting will be included, which also belong to the *instrumentum* if the income of the farm is chiefly derived from hunting. 1. When a farm is legated with the slaves, cattle and all rural and urban *instrumentum*, the majority view is that the *peculium* of an agent who dies before the testator, if it was derived from the same farm, belongs to the legatee.

23 NERATIUS, *Replies, book 2:* When it is asked, what is the *instrumentum* of a shop, it makes a difference, what kind of business is habitually carried on in it.

24 PAUL, *Neratius, book 3:* A farm which had been rented out was legated with its *instrumentum*; the *instrumentum* which the tenant had on it goes with the legacy. PAUL: That which belonged to the tenant, or only that which belonged to the testator? We must rather say the latter, unless none of the *instrumenta* belonged to the owner.

25 JAVOLENUS, *From the Posthumous Works of Labeo, book 2:* When the *instrumentum* of a farm is legated, Tubero thought that such cattle went with the legacy as the farm could have supported; Labeo disagrees. For what will happen, he says, if, when the farm could have supported a thousand sheep, two thousand sheep were on it? Which sheep, in particular, are we to think will go with the legacy? Nor should it be asked how many beasts should have been procured to constitute the *instrumentum* of the farm, but how many were procured; for the calculation should not be made from the number or the amount legated. I approve Labeo's view. 1. When someone had

potteries on a farm and used the services of the potters for the greater part of the year for work on the estate, he then legated the *instrumentum* of that farm. Labeo and Trebatius say that the potters do not appear to be included in the *instrumentum* of the farm. 2. Likewise, when all the *instrumentum* was legated with the exception of cattle, Ofilius wrongly thinks that shepherds and sheepfolds are included in the legacy.

26 JAVOLENUS, *From the Posthumous Works of Labeo, book 5:* Labeo and Trebatius think that earthenware and leaden pots filled with earth, in which plants are set, are part of the house. I think that is true, provided that they are fastened to the fabric of the house in such a way as to be set there permanently. 1. Ofilius says that hand mills are part of the furniture, but mills worked by animals are part of the *instrumentum*. Labeo, Cascellius, and Trebatius think that neither is part of the furniture but that both rather belong to the *instrumentum*, and I think this is true.

27 SCAEVOLA, *Digest, book 6:* A man legated to the man who had reared him his maritime estates with the slaves who were there and all the *instrumentum* and the fruits which were there and the rents outstanding from tenants. It was asked whether slave fishermen, who were accustomed to attend on the testator and follow him everywhere, who were reckoned in with the urban accounts and had not been found on the legated estates at the time of the testator's death, appeared to have been legated. He replied that, according to the facts as stated, they had not been legated. 1. A woman made a legacy as follows to a relation by marriage: "I want my Cornelian farm to be given to Titius, as *instructus* with all the property and slaves and the rents outstanding from tenants." When coming to Rome from Africa for a lawsuit, the testatrix took some of the slaves from the above-mentioned farm away with her, so that she might make the journey more quickly during the winter. It was asked whether those slaves were included in the *fideicommissum*, since some had been taken from their rural duties for the period of the journey, leaving behind their companions and children, and some their mothers and fathers. He replied that, according to the facts stated, the slaves about whom the question was asked were owed on the ground of the *fideicommissum*. 2. The same man asked whether the fruits of that farm, which had been gathered up to the time of her death and remained there, went with the *fideicommissum*, when the very generous intention of the testatrix toward her relative was also manifested by the fact that she wished the rents outstanding from the tenants of the property to belong to him. He replied that it can be said that when the form of words is of this kind, it should only be asked whether it is quite clear that the deceased did not wish the item about which the query is made to be given. 3. To a freedman, whom he appointed part-heir, a man gave a farm as a *praelegatum* in these words: "Freedman Pamphilus, take as a *praelegatum* and have for yourself my Titian farm and the Sempronian plot with the *instrumentum* and those things which are on it when I die, and the household which resides on that farm, with the exception of those whom I shall manumit." It was asked, when the testator had some wine in casks on that farm, all of which he had sold during his lifetime and had received a third of the price for it, whether the wine remaining in the casks belonged to the freedman by the terms of the *praelegatum*. He replied that it was included by the words cited, unless the co-heirs prove a manifestly contrary intention. He left on that farm the records of his accounts and some cash. The answer concerning the cash too was as given above. 4. A legacy was made as follows: "To my sister, Septicia, I want to be given half of the Seian farm, which was my father's, as it is, the other half as it shall be on the day of my death." It was asked whether, on the strength of the words quoted, the beams and joists already in position and ready to be fitted into the building; likewise, the urban and rural *instrumentum* with the slaves who served the farm, would belong to the legatees. He replied: The words "as it is" can be referred to *instructum*. 5. A man legated farms as follows: "Further, to my brother Sempronius my Cassian and Nonian farms, as *instructi*, with their woods and willow groves." It was asked, since

the woods and willow groves were not on the aforesaid farms but on adjoining plots which the testator acquired at the same time, and the farms could not be cultivated without them, whether they went with the legacy. He replied that only those things which had been comprehended by the words went with the legacy.

28 SCAEVOLA, *Digest, book 23:* Lucius Titius had legated a farm as *instructus.* It was asked how a *fundus instructus* should be given: as it was *instructus* at the time of the death of the head of the household, so that any slaves born or taken to the farm in the meantime belong to the heir? Or should a *fundus instructus* be taken as at the time the will was made? Or rather as at the time when the farm is first claimed, so that whatever *instrumentum* is found at that time will benefit the legatee? He replied that, according to the wording of the legacy, those things which are in that category when the legacy vests are included in the *instrumentum.*

29 LABEO, *Plausible Views, book 1:* If you bought a ship with its *instrumentum*, the ship's boat should be delivered to you. PAUL: On the contrary. For the ship's boat is not *instrumentum* of the ship; for it differs from it in size, not in kind, whereas the *instrumentum* of any thing must be of a different kind from the thing, whatever it is. This is approved by Pomponius in his seventh book of his *Letters.*

8

THE LEGACY OF A *PECULIUM*

1 PAUL, *Sabinus, book 4:* If a slave is legated with his *peculium* and is alienated or manumitted or dies, the legacy of the *peculium* is also extinguished.

2 GAIUS, *Provincial Edict, book 18:* For those things which occupy the place of accessions are extinguished when the principal property is destroyed.

3 PAUL, *Sabinus, book 4:* But if a slave-woman is legated with her children, even if she dies or is alienated or manumitted, the children will belong to the legatee, because the two legacies are separate.

4 GAIUS, *Provincial Edict, book 18:* Moreover, if a slave is legated with his *vicarii*, the legacy of the *vicarii* endures even if the slave dies or is alienated or manumitted.

5 PAUL, *Sabinus, book 4:* When a *peculium* is legated, it is agreed that the heir can collect debts due to the *peculium* and, moreover, is obliged to render to the legatee anything he himself owes to the slave.

6 ULPIAN, *Sabinus, book 25:* If a *peculium* is legated and consists of tangible objects, such as farms or houses, these can be claimed entire, provided that the slave owes no debts to his owner, his fellow slaves, or his owner's children; if, however, he owes anything to his owner or the aforementioned persons, the individual items must be diminished *pro rata.* Both Julian and Celsus also think thus. 1. If a *peculium* has been legated without deduction of the debts, it is to be feared that the legacy may be void, because what is added is contrary to the nature of the legacy. But I think the truth is that this addition does not vitiate the legacy, but adds nothing to it; for the claim to the *peculium* cannot be increased by this addition. Obviously, if you assume that the legatee has gained possession of the property, he can use the defense of fraud against the heir, if he brings a *vindicatio*; for he holds in physical form the intention that the debts should not be deducted. Moreover, if the owner meant to indicate that he was releasing the slave from what he owed or that the slave owed him nothing, this addition is valid, because an owner can, by the mere expression of his wish, release a slave from what he owes him. 2. Moreover, if my *vicarius* has been legated to me, it is asked whether his *peculium* also belongs to me. We think that his *peculium* is contained in the legacy of the *vicarius*, unless the testator's intention is otherwise. 3. If a slave and his *vicarius* have been ordered to be free and their *peculia* have been legated to them, the words should be interpreted in accordance with the testator's intention, as if he had spoken about two separate *peculia*; consequently, the *vicarius*

of a *vicarius* will not be held jointly, unless this was the testator's intention. 4. However, just as a debt, one, that is, which is owed to the owner, diminishes the legacy of a *peculium*, so on the other hand, what the owner owes the slave should increase it. But opposed to this opinion is a rescript of our emperor and his father, which runs as follows: "When *peculium* is legated to a slave, he is not also given the right to claim money, which he says he has spent on his master's account." But what if this was the testator's intention? Why should he not be able to recover it? Certainly, what he has spent should be set off against what is owing to his owner. Will what the owner had stated in writing that he owed to the slave go with a legacy of the *peculium*? Pegasus says not, as does Nerva; and when Gnaeus Domitius legated to his daughter the *peculium* that was hers, and for two years had not given her the annual allowance which he was accustomed to give her, but had entered in his accounts that he owed his daughter fifty, Atilicinus thought that this did not go with the legacy, which is true, because it accords with the rescript. 5. Moreover, not only what is owed to the owner is deducted from the legacy of a *peculium* but also anything that is owed to the heir.

7   POMPONIUS, *Sabinus, book 7:* If a man has given himself in adrogation to his creditor and an action for the *peculium* is brought against the *adrogator*, I think the same is to be said as is said in the case of the heir.

8   ULPIAN, *Sabinus, book 25:* Finally, Pegasus replied that if an heir lends money in the meantime to a *statuliber* to whom his *peculium* has been legated, the amount will be deducted by operation of law and the individual items will also be diminished by this debt. 1. Likewise, if a slave receives his freedom unconditionally and the heir lends to the slave either during the owner's lifetime or before accepting the inheritance, the legacy of the *peculium* will be diminished, in Julian's opinion, although he was never the owner of the slave. 2. A man who had slaves, Stichus and Pamphilus, manumitted them in his will and legated to each his *peculium*. It is held that what one owes to the other is deducted from his *peculium* and added to the other's legacy. 3. Likewise, it is asked, if freedom was given to a slave if he had given ten to the heir and his *peculium* was legated to him, whether the ten which he would have given to the heir should be subtracted from the *peculium*. Sabinus's opinion is correct that they are to be taken from the legacy of the *peculium*. 4. Sabinus further says that if a *statuliber* has sold a slave to the heir, that slave ceases to be part of the *peculium*, just as if he had sold him to an outsider. 5. Consequently, it is asked, if a slave has made an agreement with his owner concerning his freedom and has paid a part of the money, and the owner dies before he has paid the rest and in his will orders him to be free with the legacy of his *peculium*, whether what he has paid to his owner should be reckoned as part of the *peculium*. Labeo says it is deducted from the *peculium*. Clearly, if he had not yet given it but it was in his hands as a deposit until he handed over the whole, it is agreed that it forms part of the *peculium*. 6. Likewise, if his *peculium* is legated to a slave and the heir is forbidden to collect from a debtor to the *peculium*, it is true that this amount is deducted from the legacy of the *peculium*, that is, what has been legated to the debtor must be subtracted. 7. Sometimes, although a *peculium* has not been legated, it is treated as if it had been, that is, in a case of this kind; a man had given his freedom to a slave, if he rendered his accounts and paid a hundred to the heirs. Therefore, our emperor with his father replied that the *peculium* was indeed owed only if it had been legated. "But," he said, "we take it that the owner wished the slave to retain his *peculium* if he complied with the conditions stated," that is, on the ground that it was from the *peculium* that he had ordered him to pay the hundred. 8. Moreover, do we take the *peculium* to be what it was at the time of death? Or do we rather add what has subsequently accrued or subtract what has been removed? Julian says that the legacy of a *peculium* is to be understood in one way if it is legated to the slave himself; in another, if to someone else; for if to himself, the time to be taken into account in the legacy is the day it vests, but if to an outsider, the time of death, with the proviso, however, that increments from the property in the *peculium* should come to him, such as the offspring of slave-women or the young of animals, but accessions from his own labors or any other property will not be owed, if the *peculium* is legated to someone other than the slave himself. Julian writes that both

these cases are in accordance with the testator's wish; for when his *peculium* is legated to the slave himself, it is likely that he wanted every increase to belong to him whose patrimony it would be when he was manumitted, but not when it is legated to another, with the proviso, however, that if it should appear that he intended this in the case of another, you should say the same.

9 PAUL, *Sabinus, book 4:* What is owed by a slave to a slave who is part of his own *peculium* is not deducted from the legacy of the *peculium*, even though he be his fellow slave. 1. If a slave wounds a fellow slave and diminishes his value, Marcellus says that there can be no doubt that the owner's interest is to be deducted from the *peculium* (For what difference does it make whether he wounds a fellow slave or tears, breaks, or steals some object in which case the *peculium* is undoubtedly diminished?), but not beyond the simple amount of the damage. 2. But if he wounds or even kills himself, nothing is to be deducted on this account; otherwise, we would have to say that if he runs away, the diminution in his value caused by his flight must be deducted.

10 POMPONIUS, *Sabinus, book 7:* If you wish to make a *praelegatum* of his *peculium* to a slave or son, so that what is owed to you may not be deducted, the items which constitute the *peculium* should be legated specifically.

11 ULPIAN, *Edict, book 29:* His *peculium* can also be legated to one who has none; for not only an existing but also a future *peculium* can be legated.

12 JULIAN, *Digest, book 37:* The legacy of a *peculium* becomes void, when the slave dies during the testator's lifetime; but if the slave was alive at the time of death, the *peculium* will go to the legatee.

13 CELSUS, *Digest, book 19:* It is different if the slave was legated with his clothing.

14 ALFENUS VARUS, *Digest, book 5:* A man had written in his will as follows: "When I die, let my slave Pamphilus have for himself his *peculium* and be free." He was asked whether the *peculium* appeared to have been correctly legated to Pamphilus, because he had been ordered to have his *peculium* before he was free. He replied that in conjoined provisions the order was of no account and that it made no difference which was uttered or written first; therefore, the *peculium* appeared to have been correctly legated, just as if he had been ordered first to be free and then to have his *peculium*.

15 ALFENUS VARUS, *Digest, Epitomized by Paul, book 2:* His *peculium* was legated to a manumitted slave; in another clause, he legated all his female slaves to his wife; there was a female slave in the *peculium* of the slave. He replied that she belonged to the slave and that it made no difference which legacy had been made first.

16 AFRICANUS, *Questions, book 5:* Stichus has Pamphilus in his *peculium*. Their owner defended Pamphilus in a noxal action, lost, and paid the amount assessed. Then he manumitted Stichus in his will and legated his *peculium* to him. It was asked whether what had been paid out on Pamphilus's account was to be deducted from the *peculium* of Pamphilus himself or from that of Stichus. He replied that the full amount should certainly be deducted from the *peculium* of Pamphilus, that is, even if it would have been expedient to surrender him noxally; for whatever is paid out on behalf of a slave, he becomes his owner's debtor in that amount. But if the *peculium* of Pamphilus did not suffice, then no more than the value of Pamphilus should be deducted from the *peculium* of Stichus. 1. It was asked, if Pamphilus had owed money to his owner on some other ground and it could not be kept back from his *peculium*, whether it could be deducted up to his value from the *peculium* of Stichus. He said: "No"; for this was not like the previous case. For there the value of the *vicarius* was to be deducted because Stichus became his owner's debtor in that amount on account of the defense of his *vicarius*, but in the present case nothing should be deducted from Stichus's *peculium*, because he owed nothing; only the *peculium* of Pamphilus should be diminished, and he can surely not be understood to be part of his own *peculium*.

17 JAVOLENUS, *From Cassius, book 2:* A man who had legated a slave's *peculium* had joined issue in an action in respect of it, then died. He held that the *peculium* should be paid on the ground of the legacy only if a *cautio* was given to the heir with regard to the action in which issue had been joined.

18 MARCIAN, *Institutes, book 6:* If his *peculium* has been legated to a manumitted slave, creditors of the *peculium* undoubtedly have no actions against him; but the heir must hand over the *peculium* only if he is given a *cautio* that he will be defended against the creditors of the *peculium*.

19 PAPINIAN, *Replies, book 7:* When a man wanted to manumit a slave, he ordered him to furnish an inventory of his *peculium*, and the slave received his freedom on those terms. It was plain that items omitted from the inventory of the *peculium* do not appear to have been tacitly granted to the manumitted slave. 1. After granting freedom by will he legated the *peculium* and subsequently manumitted the slave; the freedman will, by the testament, secure that the actions for debts to the *peculium* will also be made available to him. 2. A son-in-power to whom his father legated his *peculium* manumitted a slave of the *peculium* in his father's lifetime. He is the joint slave of all the heirs, being removed from the *peculium* on account of the son's intention, because the *peculium* which belongs to the legatee is that which is in that category at the time of the father's death;

20 MARCIAN, *Institutes, book 7:* and it makes no difference whether he was first legated, then invalidly manumitted, or vice versa.

21 SCAEVOLA, *Questions, book 8:* If Stichus is manumitted and his *peculium* legated to him and a slave of the *peculium* is legated to Titius, Julian says that the amount subtracted from the *peculium* on account of what is owed to the owner accedes to him to whom the *vicarius* is legated.

22 LABEO, *Posthumous Works, Epitomized by Javolenus, book 2:* An owner had manumitted a slave in his will and had legated his *peculium* to him; the slave had owed a thousand sesterces to his owner and paid these to the heir. I replied that all the property was due to the enfranchised slave, if he had paid the money which he had owed. 1. An owner had manumitted by will a slave, who held a *vicarius* jointly with him, then legated the jointly held *vicarius* by name to him and his freedwoman. I replied that a fourth share would belong to the freedwoman, the remainder to the freedman; thus, also Trebatius.

23 SCAEVOLA, *Digest, book 15:* An owner in his will had given freedom, if he rendered his accounts, to his slave Stichus, who had managed the affairs, including the account books, of a freedman of his, to whom, by his will, he had become heir to a half share, and he gave him his *peculium* by a *fideicommissum*. Stichus rendered an account of the sums which he owed, both according to the account book and on various grounds, while the debtors on whose behalf he had himself refunded money to his patron's heirs still remained liable, and having obtained his freedom he died. It was asked whether the patron's heirs should on the ground of the *fideicommissum* be compelled to assign to the heirs of Stichus the actions against the debtors on whose behalf Stichus had made payment to his patron's heirs, given that nothing else had been owed by Stichus to his patron. He replied that they should assign them. 1. A man manumitted slaves in his will or a codicil and legated their *peculia* and made the following provision concerning Stichus: "I want my slave Stichus to be free, and I want to be given to him ten aurei and whatever he has on account of my purse; however, I want accounts to be given to my heirs. To all those I have manumitted in this will I want their *peculia* to be granted." It was asked whether Stichus should receive from the heirs what he had spent from his *peculium* up to the day of death on account of the purse, given that it was the custom of the house that his owner's account was debited and paid to him whatever he spent from his own money on account of the purse. He replied that in accordance with the facts stated about the usual practice, what was debited to his owner's account and was habitually paid to him was also included in the legacy of the *peculium*. 2. He had given freedom and legacies to slaves and had written a condition as follows: "I do not want accounts to be required of those whom I have left free or of their legacies." It was asked whether their *peculia* would also appear to be legated to them. He replied that, according to the facts stated, they would not appear to be legated. 3. Likewise, it was asked whether, on the strength of the same words, they could retain sums that remained due to them as if they had been legated, if they had property of their owner's in their possession or their rent, if any of them were tenants of estates. He replied that he had already given the answer.

24 ULPIAN, *Sabinus, book 43:* If a slave has been legated, there is no need to except his *peculium*, because it does not follow him unless it is legated.

25 CELSUS, *Digest, book 19:* If a slave is ordered to be free and his *peculium* is legated to him, *vicarii* of his *vicarii* are included in the legacy.

26 SCAEVOLA, *Replies, book 3:* "Titius, my son, do you take as a *praelegatum* and have for yourself that house, likewise, a hundred aurei"; then, in another clause, he made a *praelegatum* of their *peculia* to his sons. It was asked whether the hundred aurei and the interest on them are owed in the *praelegatum* of the *peculium*, given that he had entered both the principal and the interest in his account books under debts among the rest of his creditors. He replied that if he had lent that money in his son's name and had credited the interest to the son in the manner stated, this too was owed in the legacy of the *peculium*.

9

THE LEGACY OF STORES

1 ULPIAN, *Sabinus, book 24:* The heir was ordered to give to his wife a quantity of stores every year and was charged by legacy *per damnationem*, if he did not, to give her money. It is asked whether the stores legated can be demanded or whether the heir has merely the option to provide them, and if they are not provided, the amount may then be demanded. And if indeed the stores are legated once, not annually, received law is certainly, as Marcellus notes in the thirty-ninth book of his *Digest* cited by Julian, that there is merely an option to provide stores, but the amount can be demanded. The heir, therefore, will have the right to offer the stores until issue is joined with him for the money, unless the testator's intention or words chance to have laid down another date. But if stores are legated annually, the stores can still be provided each year, or else the sums of money can be demanded each year. What, then, if a single sum was legated and the stores were not provided in the first year? It may be doubted whether the whole sum is owed on the basis that the entire legacy of the stores has been transformed or whether in fact only the amount of the estimated value for the first year is translated into money. Nevertheless, I think that the testator's wishes should be followed in that the whole sum should be paid at once, as soon as the heir has failed to give the stores to the wife, to punish the heir's lack of duty.

2 MARCIAN, *Rules, book 3:* When specified stores have been legated with specified vessels and consumed, the vessels, as in the case of *peculium*, do not go with the legacy.

3 ULPIAN, *Sabinus, book 22:* When someone legates stores, let us see what is embraced by the legacy. Quintus Mucius writes in the second book of his *Civil Law* that things intended to be eaten and drunk are included in a legacy of stores. Sabinus writes to the same effect in his books on *Vitellius*. Whatever of these, he says, [are kept for the use of] the head of the household, or his wife, or children, or the household which habitually surrounds them; likewise, of pack animals which are kept for the owner's use. 1. But Aristo notes that things which are not for eating and drinking are also included in the legacy, as, for instance, those things in which we are accustomed to eat things, such as oil, fish sauce, brine, honey, and other similar items. 2. Admittedly, he says, if edible stores are legated, Labeo writes in the ninth book of his *Posthumous Works* that none of these things goes with the legacy, because we are accustomed not to eat these things but to eat other things by means of them. In the case of honey, Trebatius states the opposite, rightly, because we are accustomed to eat honey. But Proculus correctly writes that all these things are included, unless the testator's intention should appear otherwise. 3. Did he legate as eatables those things which we are accustomed to eat or also those things by means of which we eat other things? The latter should also be considered to be included in the legacy, unless the intention of the head of the household is shown to be otherwise. Certainly, honey always goes with edible stores, and not even Labeo denied that fish too, along with their

brine, are included.   4. In drinkable stores, those things which the head of the household reckoned as wine will be included, but the items mentioned above will not be included.   5. Nobody doubts that vinegar also goes with stores, unless it was kept for putting out fires; for in that case it was not for eating and drinking. Ofilius writes to this effect in the sixteenth book of his *Actions*.   6. But our words "kept for his own use" must be understood to include his friends, clients, and all whom he kept about him, but not that part of his household which he did not keep about him or his, as, for instance, those who were employed in villas. Quintus Mucius defined those included as follows: He thought that the food of those who performed no work was included. But this gave Servius occasion to make a note to the effect that the food of male and female weavers was included; but Mucius intended to designate those who attend on the head of the household.   7. Similarly, the fodder of pack animals is included in stores, but only of those which serve the uses of the owner and his friends; on the other hand, the fodder of those animals which serve the lands or are hired out does not go with the legacy.   8. However, whatever grain or vegetables he kept in a storeroom will be included in a legacy of stores, as will barley for the use of his household or pack animals; and Ofilius writes to this effect in the sixteenth book of his *Actions*.   9. It is asked whether logs, charcoal, and the other things by means of which stores are prepared are included in a legacy of stores. Both Quintus Mucius and Ofilius denied it; they are not included, they say, any more than millstones are. They also denied that either incense or wax is included. But Rutilius says that both logs and charcoal, which are not kept for sale, are included. Moreover, Sextus Aelius writes that incense and wax too are included in the legacy if kept for domestic use.   10. Servius, cited by Mela, writes that unguents and writing paper are included in stores, and the better view is that all these things and also perfumes are included, and that paper kept for writing trivial accounts is also included.   11. There is no doubt that vessels in which stores are kept are also included. Aristo, however, writes that casks are not included, and this is true in accordance with the distinction we drew above concerning wine. Nor will receptacles for grain or vegetables (such as boxes or hampers) or any other containers which constitute the *instrumentum* of the storehouse or storeroom be included, but only those things without which stores cannot properly be kept.

4   PAUL, *Sabinus, book 4:* For liquid, because it cannot be kept without a container, carries with it as an accession that without which it cannot be kept. Vessels, however, are not legated but are an accession to the legacy of stores; the vessels are not owed when the stores have been consumed. Indeed, even if stores are specifically legated with the vessels, the vessels will not be owed when the stores have been either consumed or removed.   1. If the contents of the store room are legated to someone, not all the stores are legated.   2. Likewise, if a man who was accustomed to sell his fruits legates stores, he does not appear to have legated everything that he had for the purposes of trade, but only those things which he set aside for himself as stores. But if he was accustomed to use them indiscriminately, then the amount which would suffice for a year's use for him, his household, and the others who were about him will go with the legacy; this, says Sabinus, tends to happen in the case of merchants or whenever a store of oil and wine which were habitually sold is left in the inheritance.   3. Moreover, I am informed that the noun *penus* is used in all genders.   4. If a legacy is made as follows, "the stores, which are at Rome," do those stores which are within the suburbs appear to be legated, or rather only those which are within the walls? Generally, indeed, all cities are held to extend as far as their walls, but Rome as far as the suburbs, and "the city of Rome" equally so.   5. But if urban stores are legated, Labeo

says that all stores, wherever they are, appear to be legated, even if they are in villas or on the land, provided they are destined for urban use, just as we also call those who are accustomed to serve us outside the city "urban servants." Moreover, if they are outside the city but still at Rome, and indeed if they are in gardens adjoining the city, the same must be said. 6. If stores other than wine are legated to someone, all stores appear to be legated with the exception of the wine; but if the clause is written as follows, "all stores except the wine at Rome," only those stores which are at Rome appear to be legated. Pomponius too writes to this effect in his sixth book on *Sabinus*.

5 PAUL, *Sabinus, book 4:* Not everything which is drunk is reckoned as stores; otherwise, it would be necessary that all medicines which are drunk should be included. So only those things count as stores which are drunk as nourishment among which antidotes are not included, as Cassius of course rightly held. 1. But the view of some authorities that pepper, lovage, caraway seed, assafoetida, and other such items are not included in stores has been rejected.

6 PAUL, *Sabinus, book 10:* The *instrumentum* of a bakery and likewise all cooking vessels are not included in stores.

7 SCAEVOLA, *Replies, book 3:* "I want all my stores to belong to my mother and to my children, who are with my mother." I ask, if the tutors of a *pupillus* say that only those stores are owed which were in his dining room, while there are also amphorae in storehouses, whether these too are owed. He replied that all stores everywhere which he had had for his own use were owed.

10
THE LEGACY OF FURNITURE

1 POMPONIUS, *Sabinus, book 6:* Furniture is the domestic *instrumentum* of the head of the household, which is not reckoned with silver or gold articles or clothing,

2 FLORENTINUS, *Institutes, book 11:* that is, inanimate movable objects.

3 PAUL, *Sabinus, book 4:* The following are contained in a legacy of furniture: tables, table-legs, three-legged tables, benches, stools, beds including ones inlaid with silver, mattresses, coverlets, slippers, water jugs, basins, washbasins, candelabra, lamps, and bowls. 1. Likewise, common bronze vessels, that is, ones which are not specially attributed to a place, 2. moreover, bookcases and cupboards. But there are those who rightly hold that bookcases and cupboards, if they are intended to contain books, clothing, or utensils, are not included in furniture, because these objects themselves

to which they are subordinated do not go with the *instrumentum* of furniture.
3. Glass eating and drinking vessels are included in furniture just like earthenware
ones, and not only common ones but also those of great value; for there is no doubt
that silver basins and washbasins and silver-inlaid, gilded, and jeweled tables and
beds are included in furniture to the extent that the law is the same even if they are of
solid silver or gold. 4. Concerning murrine and crystal objects, it may be doubted
whether they should be reckoned with furniture because of their special use and value;
but concerning these too the same is to be said. 5. It makes no difference of what
material objects that are included in furniture are made. That neither a silver bowl nor
any silver vessel was included in furniture in accordance with the severity of an age
which did not yet admit silver furniture, but today, thanks to the practice of the un-
instructed, if a silver candelabrum is reckoned among silver, it is considered part of
the silver, and the error creates the law.

4   PAUL, *Meaning of Instrumentum, sole book:* Carriages and cushions are usually
reckoned with furniture.

5   PAUL, *Sabinus, book 4:* Concerning rugs with which armchairs are habitually covered, it may be asked whether they are included in clothing, like blankets, or furniture, like coverlets, which are different in kind from blankets. It was felt to be the
better view that they were included in furniture. 1. Concerning rugs or cloths which
are spread in vehicles, it may be doubted whether they are included in furniture. But
it must be said that they belong rather to the *instrumentum* of traveling, as do skins
in which clothes are wrapped, also the straps with which these skins are normally
tied up.

6   ALFENUS, *Digest, Epitomized by Paul, book 3:* I think that those things are furniture which are intended for the general use of the head of the household and have no
separate generic name of their own; therefore, those things which pertain to some
craft and are not adapted to the common use of the head of the household are not included in furniture. 1. Neither are writing tablets and ledgers included in furniture.

7   CELSUS, *Digest, book 19:* Labeo says that the origin of the word *supellex* was that it
was once the custom to hire to those who were setting out on an embassy those articles which would be of use to them in tents (*sub pellibus*). 1. Tubero attempts to
define furniture in this way: any *instrumentum* of the head of the household consisting
of articles intended for everyday use which do not fall into any other category, as, for
instance, stores, silver, clothing, ornaments, or *instrumentum* of the land or the
house. Nor is it surprising that the designation has changed along with the customs of
the state and the use of objects; for they used to use earthenware, wooden, glass, or at
most bronze furniture, whereas now they use furniture of ivory, tortoiseshell, and silver, and even of gold and jewels. Therefore, it is proper to consider the category to
which things belong, whether to furniture rather than to silver or clothing, rather
than the material of which they are made. 2. Servius admits that the opinion of the
testator should be considered, that is, the category in which he was accustomed to
place the objects. But if anyone was accustomed to ascribe to furniture those things
concerning which there is no doubt that they belong to another category, as, for instance, silver eating vessels or cloaks and togas, it should not on that account be held
that if furniture is legated, those things too are included; for words should not be interpreted according to the opinions of individuals but by common usage. Tubero says
that this is not quite clear to him; for what, he says, is the use of words, except to
indicate the wishes of the speaker? For my part I do not think that anyone says what
he does not intend, especially if he has used the word by which the object is commonly
called; for we use speech as our servant. Moreover, nobody should be thought to have
said what he had not considered in his mind. But although the argument and authority
of Tubero move me greatly, yet I must agree with Servius that nobody can be held to
have said that for which he did not use the correct word. For although thought is prior
to and more powerful than speech, yet nobody is reckoned to have spoken without the

use of speech, unless perhaps we also reckon that those who cannot talk speak by virtue of the mere attempt and their sounds and inarticulate cries.

8   MODESTINUS, *Replies, book 9:* When a man had legated to his wife a house with its full legal rights, *instrumentum* and furniture, it was asked whether silver eating and drinking vessels also appeared to be included in the legacy. He replied that whatever silver was among the furniture was owed; but silver eating or drinking vessels were not owed, unless the legatee showed that this was also the testator's intention.

9   PAPINIAN, *Replies, book 7:* In a legacy of furniture, when through ignorance the categories are enumerated in full, the general legacy is not impaired. If, however, categories containing a fixed number of objects have been specified, it is understood that a limit has been set on the kinds of objects in these categories. The same rule is observed if an estate is legated as *instructum,* if certain categories have been given a fixed number. 1. It is agreed that tables of whatever material are included in furniture, for instance, silver ones or ones encased in silver; for the present age has accepted that even silver beds, likewise, silver candelabra, go with furniture, since Homer claimed that even Ulysses adorned with gold and silver a bed made from the trunk of a living tree, which Penelope took as a sign whereby to recognize her husband. 2. In a legacy of all a man's furniture, silver accepted as a pledge will not be included, because he legated his own furniture, especially if the silver was not used, with the debtor's consent, by the creditor, but set aside in terms of his contractual duty and his obligation to restore the thing.

10   JAVOLENUS, *From the Posthumous Works of Labeo, book 3:* A man who was accustomed to set down in his accounts all his clothing and articles of many kinds as furniture legated his furniture to his wife. Labeo, Ofilius, and Cascellius rightly denied that the clothing would go with the legacy, because clothing cannot be held to be included under the term furniture.

11   JAVOLENUS, *From the Posthumous Works of Labeo, book 10:* Labeo and Trebatius think that bronze vessels placed in fountains, likewise, anything else that is intended more for pleasure than for practical purposes, are not included in furniture. However, murrine and glass vessels, which are intended for use in eating and drinking, are said to be included in furniture.

12   LABEO, *Plausible Views, Epitomized by Paul, book 4:* Just as an urban and a rural slave are distinguished not by their place of employment but by its nature, so urban stores and furniture are to be classified by their urban use, not by their urban or rural situation, and it makes a great difference whether urban stores and furniture or those which are in the city are legated or promised.

13   MODESTINUS, *Replies, book 9:* He replied: A husband is never held, because he legated furniture in his will, to have legated the right of habitation in the dwelling where the furniture was. Therefore, there is no doubt that in claiming the right of habitation for herself the wife is acting against the intention of the deceased.

14   CALLISTRATUS, *Judicial Examinations, book 3:* When a farm is legated, its *instrumentum* does not go with the legacy unless this is specifically stated; for also, when a house is legated, neither its *instrumentum* nor the furniture goes with the legacy, unless that fact has been expressly stated by the testator.

BOOK THIRTY-FOUR

1

ALIMENT OR LEGACIES OF PROVISIONS

1 ULPIAN, *All Tribunals, book 5:* If aliment has been left as a legacy, it is possible to hold that the legacy includes water, if the legacy were left in an area where it is usual to sell water.

2 MARCIAN, *Institutes, book 8:* If someone has left aliment to his freedmen and if slaves have been left as a legacy and the legatees have been asked to manumit them, they are included in the *fideicommissum*, as both the divine Severus and Antoninus have also ruled in a rescript. 1. And although the property from which the aliment is due has devolved on the imperial treasury, it is to be provided, just as if it had passed to any other successor.

3 ULPIAN, *Duty of Consul, book 2:* Wherever there are several heirs, judges in the case of aliment usually distribute the freedmen to prevent them having to apply for small measures of aliment from individual heirs; and this distribution should be observed, just as if the head of the household had himself distributed the freedmen. Normally, too, they choose one person to supply the aliment, either in accordance with the wish of the deceased or at their own discretion, as the annexed rescripts show: "I have sent to you a copy of the petition made to me by the freedmen of Silius, knowing that this matter is relevant as a precedent, because many persons direct in their wills that necessaries are to be provided for [their] freedmen, which, since the testators are of small means, are reduced to nothing when several persons fall to be heirs by succession. Wherefore, in my opinion, you will do rightly, if, having summoned the heirs of Favilla or their procurators, you have established to which of them money should be paid by the rest from the interest on which aliment is to be provided. But the person who will receive it will have to execute a *cautio* in favor of those who give it to the effect that as each freedman has died or has ceased to be a member of the community in some other way, he will return so much of the capital as the reckoning will permit in respect of [each one's] share. The deified Pius has ruled in a rescript [addressed] to a certain Rubrius Telesphorus: "The consuls, having summoned those from whom it has been established aliment is owed you by [way of] *fideicommissum*, will decide whether you are all to receive it from one of them or who is to receive [what] from whom on the basis of a proportionate allocation. For the imperial treasury, if anything should be due to you from it under this head, will follow [the same] example. For the present know that the shares of those who have ceased to be solvent are not attributable to the burden of the remaining heirs."

4 MODESTINUS, *Replies, book 10:* "And to my freedmen and freedwomen, whom I have freed or am about to free in my lifetime and by will and by codicil, I wish there to be given my lands in Chios for the provision of food and clothing for them to the extent that they received it in my lifetime." I ask what meaning [these words] have, whether that they themselves are to take aliment from the estates or, in fact, that, apart from the estates, they are to receive both provisions and clothing from the heir? And has the property been left [to them] or the usufruct? And if the property has been left [to them], but something is to be found in the returns over and above [what is expended on] the amount for provisions and clothing, does it belong to the patroness's heir? And if some of the freedmen have died, does their share belong to the surviving *fideicommissarii*? And are the shares of the freedmen who die before the day that the *fideicommissum* takes effect to devolve on their heirs or on those of the testator? Modestinus has given as his opinion: In my view, the estates

themselves have been left to the freedmen, to hold with full *dominium* and not merely for usufruct, and, for that reason, even if there shall be anything in the returns over and above that reflected by [the expenditure on] provisions, this is to belong to the freedmen. But also where a *fideicommissarius* has died before the day when the *fideicommissum* takes effect, his share belongs to the other *fideicommissarii*; but if any have died after the period, they will hand these on to their heirs. 1. Lucius Titius in his will directed that provisions and clothing be provided for his freedmen and freedwomen by his children, the same being his heirs without attaching any condition [to the provision]; I ask, where the same freedmen bring a case without their patron's children, whether they can receive provisions and clothing. Modestinus has given it as his opinion that there is no reason to prevent them suing for straightforward bequests by will.

5   MODESTINUS, *Replies, book 11:* The wording of a will [runs as follows]: "You will supply provisions for all our freedmen in accordance with your own judgment, being not unaware how many [of them] I have cherished." Likewise, in another part: "I commend [to your care] Prothymus, Polychronius, Hypatius; I ask you both to keep them with you and to supply them with provisions." I ask whether they are to supply provisions to all of them or for those whom he has [specially] commended and has required to reside with the heirs. Modestinus has given it as his opinion that the legacy of provisions is in favor of all the freedmen, the measure of which is to be determined by the judgment of a man of probity.

6   JAVOLENUS, *From Cassius, book 2:* Where aliment is left as a legacy, provisions, clothing, and housing will be due [to the beneficiaries], since the body requires all these things for its maintenance; other items pertaining to education are not comprised in the legacy,

7   PAUL, *Replies, book 14:* unless a contrary intention on the part of the testator is proved.

8   PAPINIAN, *Replies, book 7:* It has been resolved that one of the heirs who, in accordance with the deceased's wish, receives in advance of distribution capital money destined for the provision of aliment for freedmen is not to be compelled to execute a *cautio* to restore to his co-heirs the shares of the freedmen who die; on that basis, therefore, the *actio indebiti* is not available after the death of all the freedmen, nor will an *actio utilis* be granted. The person to whom the distribution of the legacies is entrusted is in a different case; for that enjoins a present duty of brief duration; but the requirement of supplying aliment is bound up by monthly and annual burdens which banish timidity too.

9   PAPINIAN, *Replies, book 8:* After appointing another person heir, [a testator] has written as follows: "I request you, Gaius Seius, to pay my *alumni* ten aurei each out of whatever you have received from my estate, and I intend you to have control of a like sum from the interest on which I wish you to provide aliment for them; the remainder you will restore to Numerius our fellow freedman." I have given it as my opinion that although Gaius Seius cannot alienate the property when another has been appointed heir, nevertheless, he will rightly make application under the [*lex*] *Falcidia* to preserve and restore the money legacy to the *alumni*; but this [procedure] cannot be approved of in respect of the excess. 1. It has also been my view that that freedman, too, [who is numbered] among those to whom a patroness has left the provisions and likewise the clothing which she was accustomed to provide in her lifetime, and who has received twenty aurei annually and a monthly supply of grain and wine, will probably apply for the *fideicommissum*.

10   PAPINIAN, *Replies, book 9:* When one of the heirs had been instructed to take in advance of distribution a sum certain from the capital of which he was to provide aliment for freedmen, it was resolved that the heir's heir should also be allowed to take in advance. If, however, the heir were to have several heirs, the intention of the deceased is indeed *prima facie* opposed [to such a decision], but no other [view] should be admitted. For what if, in the interests of his freedmen, he has shunned his other heirs and has preferred to charge a house that is peaceful and respectable and also solvent? And for that reason aliment will be provided by all the heir's heirs. 1. When a person has received his freedom solely in view of the words of the *fideicommissum*, even if he has received it at a later date, and the heir has not been a source of delay in granting it, aliment for the period that is past is also to be restored to him. For delay is to be investigated at the point when a question arises concerning the interest on the *fideicommissum* and not concerning *fideicommissa* themselves. 2. Where aliment has been left to a daughter at the discretion of a man of probity, charged

on a son who is the heir in proportion to the dowry left her by way of legacy and intended as the father's sole gift on marriage to the daughter he has disinherited, nevertheless, I have given it as my opinion that it is to be provided in relation to the years of her age, and not the resources of the estate.

11   PAUL, *Questions, book 10:* A person to whom aliment had been left was condemned to the mines and [subsequently] restored through the grace of the emperor. I have given it as my opinion that he had properly received aliment both in respect of the foregoing years and that it is due to him in the case of the subsequent years.

12   PAUL, *Replies, book 14:* Lucius Titius has left provisions and clothing to his freedmen [to be supplied] annually to the value of a certain sum, and in a later part of his will has provided as follows: "That such and such farms of mine have been mortgaged in their favor on account of the *fideicommissum,* so that from the return on them they may receive the aforementioned aliment." It has been asked, if at any point fewer returns have come in than envisaged by the amount of provisions and clothing, whether the heirs should not be burdened with supplying [the deficiency] or, where in another year the returns have exceeded [the amount required], whether the previous year's deficiency is to be supplied. Paul has given it as his opinion that the deceased's freedmen are owed their provisions and clothing in their entirety, and that the testator does not appear to have reduced or increased the extent of the legacy from the fact that he subsequently intended to mortgage his estates in their favor by right of pledge, so that they should receive aliment from the return on them.

13   SCAEVOLA, *Replies, book 4:* [A testator] has left Gaius Seius three hundred aurei for the provision of food and clothing which he had prescribed for his freedmen from the interest on that sum; but in a codicil, he has forbidden the sum in question to be given to Gaius Seius but has desired it to go to Publius Maevius; I ask whether Maevius is charged with the *fideicommissum* in favor of the freedmen. I have given it as my opinion that unless Maevius makes plain that the testator had enjoined upon him some other burden about which there was no doubt, he is regarded in accordance with the testator's wish as having taken on the burden attributable to the sum transferred to him in the codicil.   1. The Emperor Antoninus Pius to the freedmen of Sextia Basilia: "Although the wording of the will is [strictly] construed as follows, namely that aliment and clothing have been left to you for the duration of your residence with Claudius Justus, nevertheless, I interpret the deceased's intention as meaning that she wished the same items to be provided for you after Justus's death." [Scaevola] has given it as his opinion that phrasing of this kind is to be understood in the sense that the obligation to provide aliment is to continue in perpetuity.   2. Likewise, being consulted about a phrase such as the following, "and I wish them to reside with you for all time," I ask, when [slaves] manumitted by the heir have remained with him for a long period but have left him on account of oppressive servitude, whether there is owed to them the aliment that he refuses to provide unless he were to have the use of them in place of slaves. [Scaevola] has given it as his opinion that according to the facts as alleged it is due to them.

14   ULPIAN, *Fideicommissa, book 2:* Mela states that where aliment is left to a boy or girl it is due [to him or her] up to the time of puberty. But this is incorrect; for it will be due for the period intended by the testator, or if his intention is not clear, throughout their lifetime.   1. Obviously, where aliment has been left for the period up to puberty, if it is wished to observe the precedent of the aliment formerly given to boys and girls, it is to be understood that Hadrian established that boys are maintained up to the age of eighteen, and girls up to the age of fourteen, and our emperor has ruled in a rescript that the formula worked out by Hadrian is to be observed. And although in general puberty is not defined in this way, from considerations of duty it is not inequitable that solely in the case of aliment, this age should be adhered to.   2. But if the testator has left aliment which he was in the habit of providing in his lifetime, only that amount will be provided which he had been accustomed to provide at the time of his death. Therefore, if his distributions have chanced to vary [in amount], the distribution made nearest the time of his death will be looked to. What is the position, therefore, if he provided less at the time of making his will and more at the time of his death or vice versa? It will still have to be held that the most recent distribution must be followed.   3. A certain man had left not only aliment but also water to

his freedmen by way of *fideicommissum*. I was consulted about the *fideicommissum*. Since the matter was to be litigated in that area of Africa or possibly Egypt, where water is normally sold, I held therefore that it was a benefit of the *fideicommissum*, whether left by a person owning cisterns or not, so that the *fideicommissum* embraces the cost of the water to each of the beneficiaries; and that the *fideicommissum* is not regarded as ineffective, as though a servitude on an estate had been left to a person who was not the possessor of a neighboring property; for [the right] to draw water, like [the right] to drive cattle to water, is a servitude, but is an ineffective bequest to anyone not a neighbor. The [right] to carry [burdens over] or press grapes on your [land] will be in the same case or to make use of your threshing floor to thresh corn or other vegetable crops. For the water in question is left to the individual.

15 SCAEVOLA, *Digest, book 17:* [A testator] has left ten to Seia in a codicil, charged on his son who is the heir, and has made a bequest to his *alumnus* as follows: "I desire there to be given to the *infans* Maevius, my *alumnus*, forty, which I request you, Seia, to take charge of and to pay him five percent interest annually up to his twentieth year and to take charge of him and watch over him." It has been asked, where Seia, after receiving her legacy, is unwilling to take charge of the money left to the *alumnus* or has ceased to take charge of it, whether she is compelled to recognize the burden of aliment from the time of the testator's death. [Scaevola] has given it as his opinion that according to the facts as given, she is to be compelled to provide it, since it is a *fideicommissum*. The same person has asked whether Seia's heir, too, is obliged to provide aliment for twenty years. [Scaevola] has given it as his opinion that he is. 1. A testator has left to his concubine eight country slaves and has instructed her to supply them with provisions in the following words: "And it is my wish that those slaves whom I have left as a legacy above be supplied by my heirs with the provisions they received in my lifetime." Since in the testator's lifetime those slaves have always been lent out at harvest and threshing time, and during this period have never received provisions at their master's expense, save for the estate bailiff, it has been asked whether the heir should supply the concubine with provisions for the country slaves during that period too, that is, during harvest and threshing time. [Scaevola] has given it as his opinion that the person who has cognizance of the matter will decide. CLAUDIUS: Rightly, for if the testator has left the slaves to reside with the concubine on the same terms as they have resided with him, provisions were not due during the period in question; but if they shall be transferred by them for service in the city, they will be due. 2. Titia on her death provided in her will as follows: "I desire there to be given and supplied to all my freedmen and freedwomen the provisions and clothing that I provided in my lifetime." It has been asked, since, as was reflected by the accounts, she has supplied provisions and clothing for three alone in her lifetime, whether her heir can be sued by the other freedmen too or whether he is merely liable to the three who are found to have received provisions and clothing in her accounts. [Scaevola] has given it as his opinion that [he can be sued] by all [of them].

16 SCAEVOLA, *Digest, book 18:* A testator has given aliment and clothing to his freedmen; because he has expressly instructed them to be provided by Moderatus, one of the heirs, it has been asked whether they are due from Moderatus alone and not also from his heirs after his death. [Scaevola] has given it as his opinion that the heirs, too, are liable. 1. [A testatrix] had instructed that the aliment and benefits which she provided in her lifetime be given to her freedmen and freedwomen and likewise to slaves of either sex whom she had manumitted by will or codicil; likewise, [she had left] farms to all her freedmen and freedwomen. It was asked whether the freedman of her father's freedman to whom she used to write as follows, "to our freedman, son of Rufinus," would be admitted to that legacy. She had also requested by a letter sent to the *ordo* of the community where she had been born that he be paid a salary from the public purse (because he was a doctor), making it clear in her letter that he was her freedman. [Scaevola] has given it as his opinion that the person in charge of the

investigation will decide the merits of the case, so that, if, in fact, she was in the habit of providing for him, too, in her lifetime, he would nonetheless be admitted to the *fideicommissum*, but otherwise not. 2. [A testator] has left ten to his freedwoman Basilice, whom he intended to remain with his freedmen Epictetus and Callistus with the object that, when Basilice has reached the age of twenty-five, they would be restored to her together with five percent interest, so that she would be maintained from the interest in proportion to the increase in her age. It has been asked whether Basilice would also have a claim under another head, whereby the testator has left provisions and clothing and housing to his freedmen and freedwomen in general, [Scaevola] has given it as his opinion that, on the above facts, she has no claim, unless it were proved that this, too, had been given to her, CLAUDIUS: because he had destined for her aliment the interest on the money that he had specifically left to her as a legacy payable before distribution. 3. A man who has held all his property in partnership with his wife for more than forty years has left the same wife and the grandson fathered by his son heirs to equal shares in his will and has provided as follows: "likewise, for my freedmen whom I have manumitted in my lifetime those things which I was in the habit of supplying." It has been asked whether those [slaves] too, who were manumitted by both parties at the time when the partnership subsisted between them and who have become freedmen in common, can demand in their entirety from the *fideicommissum* those things which they received from [the testator] in his lifetime. [Scaevola] has given it as his opinion that no more is owed than the husband, for his part, was used to provide.

17   SCAEVOLA, *Digest, book 19:* [A testator] had left slaves as temple guardians, and had left a legacy to them charged on the heir in these words: "I request and impose on you a *fideicommissum* to give and supply in my memory each of my footmen whom I have left to take care of the temple with monthly provisions and a fixed amount of clothing *per annum*." It has been asked, since the temple had not yet been constructed, whether the slaves should receive the legacy from the date of death or from the time when the temple has been finished. [Scaevola] has given it as his opinion that the judge's duty is to compel the heir to supply the slaves with what has been left them until such time as the temple should be constructed.

18   SCAEVOLA, *Digest, book 20:* A testator had left to the freedman whom he had manumitted in his will a monthly payment of ten for the purpose of aliment; then, in a codicil, he has left a monthly payment of seven to all his freedmen without distinction and an annual payment of ten each for clothing. It has been asked whether the heirs are to be charged with the *fideicommissum* in favor of the freedmen both on the basis of the will and on that of the codicil. [Scaevola] gave it as his opinion that there was no reason why they should not be responsible for the gifts set out in the codicil; for [the testator] has abandoned the disposition he had made in his will in respect of provisions on account of the bequest he has made in the codicil. 1. [A testator] has left an annual provision to his manumitted [slaves] charged as a *fideicommissum* on condition that they shall reside with his mother; the mother has survived the son by three years but has not supplied them with provisions or clothing, since the freedmen failed to apply for the *fideicommissum*; but the daughter, too, who subsequently fell to be heir to her mother, although surviving fourteen years, has not been sued in respect of payment of the same. It has been asked whether, after the death of the daughter, they can apply to the most recent heir for the legacy left them in respect of provisions and clothing, both for the period that is past as well as for the future. [Scaevola] has given it as his opinion that if the condition had been fulfilled, there was no reason why they could not do so. 2. [A testator] desired that Stichus be manumitted by his heirs and, if he were to remain with Seius, be supplied with provisions and clothing by Seius; then he added these words: "But I request you, Seius, when you have reached the age of twenty-five, to obtain a commission in the army for him, provided that he has not left you before this." It has been asked, where Stichus has obtained his freedom immediately, but Seius has died before attaining the age of twenty-five, whether the commission is to be acquired for Stichus by the heirs on whom Seius's property has devolved. And, if it is resolved that it should be, whether it is to be acquired immediately or at the point when Seius would have completed his twenty-fifth year, had he survived. [Scaevola] has given it as his opinion that although it is resolved that it should be acquired, it is not due [to Stichus] before that period

had elapsed. 3. [A testator], having instituted *postumi* as his heirs together with his mother and father and having provided for substitute heirs, has manumitted his agents and left them their *peculia* and has also made annual provisions both for specified freedmen of his and for others who are outsiders, the latter to receive greater sums. Then, after making his will, on the birth of a daughter to him, he has made the following provision in a codicil: "If I have left anything in my will, which I made at an earlier date, to be given to anyone, I request them to restore a third share [of it] to my daughter Paetina." But by the pupillary substitution in the second document, he has expressed a wish that as much again be given to those freedmen who are *impuberes* to whom he had granted their freedom by the agency of their parents, as he had left in cash, apart from provisions and clothing. It has been asked, where the daughter had survived at the point when the will and codicil were opened but has subsequently died and had transferred to her heirs the *fideicommissum* in her favor relating to the restitution of a third share, whether third shares of the provisions and clothing, too, are regarded as having been granted her by way of *fideicommissum*. [Scaevola] has given it as his opinion that they are not so regarded. 4. The same person has inquired whether third shares of those bequests made by way of *fideicommissum* in the codicil should belong to the daughter. [Scaevola] has given it as his opinion that they ought not to. The same person has inquired whether the further sum left in the substitution is to be calculated after the amount of the legacies made by will has suffered deduction by a third, so as to make two thirds payable, apart from the [bequests by] codicil in which the testator expressed a wish that a third of the legacies made by codicil should belong to his daughter. [Scaevola] has given it as his opinion that the legacies made as a result of the substitution are due in their entirety. 5. [A testator] had left provisions and clothing by way of *fideicommissum* and has added the following words: "And I instruct those freedmen of mine to reside where I have been buried, so that, in the absence of my daughters, they may hold annual celebration of my memory at my tomb." It has been asked whether aliment is to be provided for one of the freedmen who, from the date of death, has never called on the heirs and has refused to reside near the tomb. [Scaevola] has given it as his opinion that it is not to be provided.

19 SCAEVOLA, *Digest, book 22:* It has been provided by a will: "I desire that my freedmen be supplied by my heirs with provisions and whatever else I was in the habit of providing." One of the freedmen has been absent with his patron's permission on his own business for four years preceding the death, and for that reason was not, at the time of the death, in receipt of the provisions that he had previously received; nevertheless, the patron had given this freedman a legacy of five in the same will, just as he had the other freedmen whom he had manumitted in his lifetime. It has been asked whether the provisions and other things left as a legacy to the other freedmen are due to him too. [Scaevola] has stated as his opinion: Why not?

20 SCAEVOLA, *Replies, book 3:* "Stichus, my nurse's grandson, is to be free, and I wish him to be paid ten aurei *per annum*"; then, having made other entries, [the testator] has left the same Stichus his wife and children and has left them the things he was accustomed to provide for them in his lifetime. Then, under another head, he has instructed that all his freedmen be supplied with the things he was accustomed to provide for them in his lifetime. I ask whether Stichus is able to take aliment in addition to the legacy. [Scaevola] has given it as his opinion that, according to the facts of the case, he cannot. 1. Likewise, since he had intended there to be given to his freedmen and freedwomen the aliment he has left charged on the state and the estates which he has left to it, I ask whether the food allowance and clothing which he used to provide for them in his lifetime should be provided by the instituted heir or by the estate to Stichus's wife and children. [Scaevola] has given it as his opinion that by a generous interpretation of the disposition, it can be held that they, too, are to be provided for by the state. 2. Titia has left the usufruct of a farm to Maevius and has given him a *fideicommissum* to pay Pamphila and Stichus an annual pension of one hundred sesterces from the return of the farm so long as they live; I ask whether, on Maevius's death, the heir is liable for aliment. [Scaevola] has given it as his opinion that there is no reason why it should be supplied by Titia's heir, but that it should not be provided by the legatee's heir either, unless the testator is clearly proved to have intended it to be supplied even after the usufruct has been extinguished, provided that what had been received from the usufruct would be sufficient to supply it. 3. A mother, after instituting her son heir, has granted his freedom to her slave Pamphilus by way of *fideicommissum* and has left him five aurei for provisions and fifty for clothing each year on condition that he remains with her son. I ask whether aliment is due on the son's death. He has given it as his opinion that if he had fulfilled the condition, it is due even after the son's death.

21 ULPIAN, *Fideicommissa, book 2:* It is clear that where an allowance of food or provisions has been left, neither housing nor clothing nor an allowance for shoes is due, since the testator has

expressed an intention only with regard to provisions.

22   VALENS, *Fideicommissa, book 1:* When aliment has been left by way of *fideicommissum* without reference to the amount, first of all we must look to see what the deceased had been accustomed to supply for him, then what he has left to others of the same standing; if neither has been capable of discovery, the measure will have to be determined in accordance with the deceased's resources and the charity of the person on whom the *fideicommissum* has been imposed. 1. A person who owed aliment to his brother's freedmen had left them vines in his will with the addition of the words, "to hold them for the purpose of maintenance." If he had left vines instead of aliment, they should only be provided for them in accordance with the *fideicommissum* on the terms that the heirs had been freed from the obligation imposed by the will; or if this had been neglected and they were later to sue on the will, the heir would be protected by the defense of fraud, that is to say, provided the vines are worth no less than the estimated cost of the aliment. But the addition, "to hold them for the purpose of maintenance," is really relevant to the case where the beneficiaries take in advance of distribution, rather than to the constitution of a usufruct.

23   PAUL, *Neratius, book 4:* You have been asked to bring up someone; you are to be compelled to provide him with the necessaries of life. PAUL: Why is a legacy of aliment fuller when it has been defined as including clothing and housing? In fact, both are to be equated.

2

LEGACIES OF GOLD, SILVER, TOILET EQUIPMENT, JEWELRY, PERFUMES, CLOTHING OR GARMENTS, AND STATUES

1   POMPONIUS, *Sabinus, book 6:* If one person has been left garments and a distinct legacy of women's clothing has been made to another, when the women's clothes have been extracted and assigned to the person to whom they have specifically been left, the remainder is due to the other. The same holds good when one person has been left women's toilet equipment and a second all the silver from that comprised in the toilet equipment. Likewise, if two marble statues had been left to you and then a bequest had been made of all marble items, aside from the two, no marble statue has been left to you. The same holds good where urban slaves have been left to you, if the steward has been left to me. 1. Where the heir has been directed to give a certain weight of silver to a person, he is *ipso jure* freed by giving him a sum of money, provided that the money has constituted the same value; and this is true if no specific type of silver has been left.

2   AFRICANUS, *Questions, book 2:* A person who had instructed you to purchase jewelry for his wife's use has left to the same wife, as is customary, "those things which shall have been acquired for her benefit"; subsequently, after the death of the *mandator*, in ignorance of the fact that he has died, you have purchased the articles. They will not be due to the woman, since those words are referred to the time of death. But if, in the testator's lifetime, you have purchased the items after the woman has died, it will not be out of place to hold that this legacy is ineffective, since it cannot properly be held that they are regarded as acquired for the benefit of a woman who has previously died. The same will also have to be held in the case where the woman is in fact alive, but has been divorced; and it is asked whether items purchased after [the divorce] are due to her in that they do not appear to have been acquired for the benefit of a wife.

3   CELSUS, *Digest, book 19:* [A testator] left his wife the articles acquired for her benefit, and divorced her before his death. Proculus says that [the articles] are not due, because they are regarded as adeemed. Doubtless it is a question of fact; for it is possible that he did not intend them to be adeemed even from a wife he had repudiated.

4   PAUL, *Edict, book 54:* Where a certain man had sent his freedman to Asia to purchase purple and had left his wife purple wool in his will, Servius has given it as his opinion that any purple purchased by the freedman in the [testator's] lifetime belongs to her.

5   AFRICANUS, *Questions, book 2:* The following occurs in the second book of *Questions* by Fufidius. If a woman has instructed you to buy for her large pearls for her use and you have

bought them after her death at a point when you thought she was alive, Atilicinus says that they have not been left to the beneficiary in whose favor the woman has made the following legacy: "jewelry which has been or will have been acquired for my benefit"; for those articles which have been purchased after her death are not regarded as acquired for her benefit.

6 MARCELLUS, *Replies, sole book:* Seia left a legacy charged on Publius Maevius, her heir, in the following terms: "I bequeath to Antonia Tertulla so much gold by weight and my large pearl with the hyacinths."[1] Subsequently, she lost the large pearl and left no large pearl among her jewelry at the time of her death. I ask whether the heir, as a result of the *fideicommissum*, is obliged to pay the value of an item not comprised in the estate. Marcellus has given it as his opinion that he is not. 1. Likewise, I ask, if it can be proved that Seia had altered the large pearl and some hyacinths into another item of jewelry, the value of which she subsequently increased by the addition of other gems and pearls, whether [the beneficiary] can sue for these large pearls or hyacinths and the heir be compelled to remove them from the later piece of jewelry and hand them over. Marcellus has given it as his opinion that it is not possible to sue. For how can it happen that a legacy or *fideicommissum* is thought to subsist when the subject matter of the bequest has not remained in its own form, for it has, in a certain sense, been extinguished— overlooking for the moment the fact that by disassembling and altering [it] in such a way, [the testatrix] appears to have changed her mind. 2. Lucius Titius has written in his will: "I desire and impose on my heir a *fideicommissum* to construct a public portico for my place of birth in which I desire silver and marble reliefs [of myself] to be set up." I ask whether the legacy is effective. Marcellus has given it as his opinion that it is and is understood as a legacy to his birthplace of the work and other objects the testator has desired to be placed there; for some embellishment could have [thereby] been added to the community.

7 PAUL, *Plautius, book 8:* If a legacy has been left in the following terms, "let my [heir] be obliged to make a gift of my clothing [and] my silver," the legacy is regarded as comprising property that existed at the time of his will, since the present time would always be understood, if nothing else had been included; for when he says, "my clothing," "my silver," by the description "mine" he indicates present, not future, time. The same is the case, too, if someone has left as a legacy "my slaves."

8 PAUL, *Plautius, book 9:* PLAUTIUS: A woman left a legacy in the following terms: "Whoever shall be my heir, let him be obliged to give my clothing, toilet equipment, and female jewelry to Titia." Cassius says, if her intention were not clear, all her clothing is regarded as having been left according to the wording of the will. PAUL: Javolenus makes the same observation; because it is probable, he says, that the testatrix had segregated from the whole of the jewelry only that to which she had applied the label "female"; there is also the fact that the description "female" cannot be applied to the clothing or toilet equipment without damaging the correct order of the language.

9 MODESTINUS, *Rules, book 9:* When a fixed weight of gold or silver has been left as a legacy without designation of type, it should be paid, not in specie, but at the rate of its current value.

10 POMPONIUS, *Quintus Mucius, book 5:* Quintus Mucius says: If the head of the household has left a vessel or clothing or anything else to his wife in the following terms, "which had been purchased or acquired for her benefit," he is regarded as having left what had been acquired for her use rather than for communal use. POMPONIUS: But this is true not only where there has been communal use between husband and wife but also where use has been in common with their children or some other party; for he is regarded as having indicated what has been acquired for his wife's specific use. But, as Quintus Mucius points out, "vessel or clothing, or anything else" renders our assumptions false; for it makes a great difference whether these legacies are of a general or specific nature. For if they are of a general nature, such as, "what has been acquired for the benefit of my wife," his definition is correct; but if [the bequest] has been expressed as follows, "that purple clothing," to indicate particular objects, whether there has been added, "which had been purchased or acquired for her benefit," [or] whether neither [the words] purchased nor acquired nor given to her for her use [have been added], the legacy is valid in every respect, because when a certain object has been left as a legacy, the addition of a false description does not destroy the legacy, for instance, if the following has been written, "Stichus, whom I bought at Titius's sale"; for if he did not buy him, or bought him at another sale, the legacy nonetheless is good. Obviously, if a legacy has been left in the following terms, "the vessel or garments or what

---

1. Evidently a type of gem similar to sapphire.

has been acquired for my wife's benefit," then Quintus Mucius's view will be equally true in which case it is to be understood that even if the property which the testator thought was his belonged to somebody else, the heir is bound to yield it up.

11   PROCULUS, *Letters, book 5:* If someone has left a legacy of gold [and] the gems and pearls set in the gold, that portion of the gold in which no gems or pearls were set is regarded as forming part of the legacy.

12   PAPINIAN, *Questions, book 17:* If, where a portrait has been left as a legacy, the heir has scraped off the paint and broken up the material on which it was painted, it can be held that an action on the will subsists, because the legacy was of the portrait, not of the material on which it was painted.

13   SCAEVOLA, *Digest, book 15:* A man left a legacy to his wife in the following terms: "In respect of all the women's toilet equipment, jewelry, and whatever I have given, donated, acquired, [or had] made for her benefit, all this I desire to be given to her." It has been asked whether the overnight traveling coach together with the mules are due to her since the wife has always had the use of them. [Scaevola] has given it as his opinion that if it had been held for the purpose of her use, it is due to her. The same person has asked whether the clothing [the testator] had acquired or had [had] made for the female slaves or litter-bearers of that same wife were to be provided for her in accordance with the same head [of the will]. [Scaevola] has given it as his opinion that they are to be so provided.

14   POMPONIUS, *Sabinus, book 5:* If I have bequeathed as a legacy a statue and have subsequently added to it the arm from another statue, there is no reason why the complete statue cannot be claimed by the legatee.

15   SCAEVOLA, *Digest, book 15:* [A testator] left gold and silver of a certain type to Seia and has made the following request to her: "I request you, Seia, that in respect of the gold and silver I have left specifically to you, you restore it on your death to such and such of the slaves born in my household; the usufruct of these articles will be adequate for your lifetime." It has been asked whether only the usufruct of the gold and silver is due to the legatee. [Scaevola] has given it as his opinion that by the wording as set forth, the legacy is one of property [in the gold and silver] encumbered by a *fideicommissum.*

16   SCAEVOLA, *Digest, book 18:* A mother appointed as heir the daughter who remained in her father's power; she appointed as substitute heir her father Maevius and added: "Whoever shall be my heir, I impose upon him a *fideicommissum* to prevent the sale of all my jewelry, gold, silver, [and] clothes, which I have used [in my lifetime], and to preserve them for my daughter." It has been asked, since the daughter renounced her interest and the father had fallen to be heir as a result of the substitution and had died intestate, but the daughter had failed to take his property, whether she can apply for the *fideicommissum.* [Scaevola] has given it as his opinion that, according to the facts given, there appears to be an effective *fideicommissum* charged on the father's estate. CLAUDIUS: Since, by [the use of] the word "preserving," the *fideicommissum* is regarded as having been prolonged to the time when the legatee would be *sui juris.*

17   ULPIAN, *Sabinus, book 21:* If a gem from a ring is left as a legacy or [stones] connected to other material, or superficial ornaments, the legacy is good; they are both separable and to be paid.

18   SCAEVOLA, *Digest, book 22:* A testator had left to his wife one tenth of his property and slaves and silver articles which he had specified, and requests the heirs to hand over to her rings and clothing, as if they had been the wife's own property. It has been asked, if they have not belonged to the wife, whether they should be paid her in accordance with the legacy. [Scaevola] has given it as his opinion that [the testator] is regarded as having made the gifts with the intention of leaving them as a bequest, unless the opposite is proved by the heir.   1. The same testator imposed a *fideicommissum* on his wife to restore to the *alumnus* they had in common whatever had come to her under his will; it has been asked whether those things too, which the testator knows to have been his wife's own property and has ordered to be handed over to her, are due to the *alumnus.* [Scaevola] has given it as his opinion that if they had been her own property, they are not due; if they were acquired as a legacy, they are due.   2. A woman has left by will and subsequent codicil, specifically by way of *fideicommissum,* many items of clothing and silver that she has indicated she had either made herself or holds [as her own]; it has been asked whether items [of the kind] other than those discovered in the estate should not go to the legatees. [Scaevola] has given it as his opinion that those forming part of the estate go [to them].

19   ULPIAN, *Sabinus, book 20:* When gold or silver has been left as a legacy, whatever gold or
silver has been left forms part of the legacy, whether it has been worked or remains in its raw
state; but it is resolved that what has been coined as money does not form part of the legacy.
1. Accordingly, if a certain weight of gold or silver has been left as a legacy, it is the amount that
is rather regarded as the legacy, and it will not be taken in the form of vessels.   2. But if a hundred by weight of worked silver has been left, the legacy will be due from silver that has been
worked. Therefore, we find the question in Celsus whether [the legatee] can also separate the
smaller vases; and he has observed that he need not separate the smaller vases, although the
option has been granted him.   3. Celsus also asks in the nineteenth book of his *Questions,* where
a hundred of silver has been left by weight, whether the lead content is to be removed for the
purposes of weighing it. Both Proculus and Celsus maintain that it should be weighed after the
removal of the lead. For they are reckoned to buyers less lead content; and thus, the weight of
the silver is entered in the accounts; and this opinion makes sense.   4. Obviously, if someone has
been left small silver vessels such as square dishes, he will also get the lead [base] which holds
them.   5. Similarly, there is the question whether a person to whom silver has been left obtains
the gold relief ornament on it. And Pomponius, in the fifth book of his *Sabinus,* makes the distinction that it is of great importance whether a fixed weight of worked silver is left to him or
simply worked silver; if the weight has been left, [the ornament] is not included; if worked silver
has been left, it is included, since an adjunct to a [particular] form of silver is subsumed under the
silver in the same way as gold stripes and purple form part of garments. Pomponius, in his
Letters, also [holds] that even if the stripes have not been sewn together with the garments, they,
nevertheless, are contained in a legacy of clothing.   6. Celsus, in the nineteenth book of his *Digest* and in the seventh book of his *Commentaries,* observes that where gold has been left as a
legacy, gilded items are not payable, nor are the gold relief ornaments found on silver dishes.
7. But it is questionable whether gold rings are included in the term gold; and Quintus Saturninus, in the tenth book of his *Edict,* observes that they are included.   8. Obviously, a silver bed
or any other furniture which was of silver is not included in the term silver, if it has not been
considered as forming part of the silver collection, as I know I decided in the case of a silver chain
on the ground that the head of the household did not keep it in his silver strongroom. But candelabra, silver lanterns, and small miniature figures that have been kept in the house, or por-
traits in silver, will not be included in the term silver either, nor a mirror, whether it is a fixture
or the kind a woman kept for her toilette, so long as they have not been considered part of the
silver collection.   9. Quintus Mucius says that silver vessels are included in a legacy of worked
silver, for instance, dessert dishes, cruets, ladles, basins, and the like, but not items of furniture.   10. But where a person has been left vessels, there are included not only those of the kind
capable of containing food or drink but also those which act as a support, and so salvers and trays
are included. Receptacles will also be included; for the term vessel is of a general nature; wine
flasks and ice buckets[2] are vessels.   11. But the term unworked silver embraces the raw material, that is, material that has not been worked. What is the position if the silver has begun to be
worked? It is questionable whether, not yet being completed, it is subsumed under the term
worked or unworked. But I submit [that it belongs] rather with worked silver. Obviously, if it had
already been worked, but was in process of being engraved, it will be included in the term
worked. But will what has begun to be engraved be included with engraved? And I submit that it
is included in a case where a person has left engraved silver.   12. If someone has been left silver
dining plate, only that will be due which [the testator] had in use at table, that is, for the purpose
of eating or drinking. As a result, there has been some doubt about a finger bowl; and I submit
that it is included, for this, too, is provided for the purpose of eating. Obviously, if the testator
had silver saucepans or a silver kettle or frying pan or some other item for the purpose of cooking, it will be capable of doubt whether it is included in a dining service. And these items are
rather cooking equipment.   13. Let us turn also to gems set in gold and silver. And Sabinus says
they are subsumed under the gold and silver; for an object gives way to that which is greater in
form; and he has stated [the situation] correctly; for when we inquire what gives way to what, we
always look to what is applied as ornament to an object with the result that an accessory gives
way to the main object. Therefore, gems mounted on saucers or dishes will give place to the gold

---

2. The meaning of *vasa navalia* is uncertain; an alternative translation is "ships' decanters."

or silver [of which the dishes are made].   14. But also, in the case of the rims of tables, gems will pass with the rims and the rims with the tables.   15. In the case of pearls too and gold, the same is true; for if the pearls have been added as decoration to the gold, they pass with the gold; if the opposite is the case, the gold will pass with the pearls.   16. The same is true of gems set in rings.   17. But gems are of a translucent material, and, as Sabinus reports in his books on *Vitellius*, Servius distinguished them from [precious] stones on the ground that gems were of a translucent material, like emeralds, chrysolites, and amethysts, but stones are of a different nature from the foregoing, such as the obsidian from Veii.   18. But in the same place, Sabinus says that there is sufficient authority to the effect that pearls are not included among gems or [precious] stones, because the pearl oyster grows and is formed in the Red Sea region.   19. But Cassius observes that a murrine vase is not numbered among gems.   20. Where gold has been left as a legacy, golden vessels are included and where gems have been left vessels [set with] gems. According to this doctrine, whether the gems are on gold or silver vessels, they will pass with the gold or silver, since we always look to this [question], which item has been applied for the purpose of embellishing the other, not which is more valuable.

20   PAUL, *Sabinus, book 3:* If gems have been set in gold to enable them to be worn more easily, then we hold that the gold passes with the gems.

21   POMPONIUS, *Sabinus, book 6:* In the case of a silver drinking vessel, it is open to doubt whether it is simply an item from which one may drink or also one acquired for the preparation of drink, such as a strainer filled with snow and pitchers. But it is more likely that these too are included.   1. Where unguent has been left as a legacy, the legacy is regarded as comprising not only those perfumes which are used for pleasure but also items for medicinal purposes, such as *commagenum, glaucium, crinum*, rose, *muracolum*, pure nard oil; in fact, women use this too to make themselves more decorative and attractive.   2. But, in respect of a finger bowl, Cassius says that on being consulted he gave it as his opinion, where one [beneficiary] had been left silver for drinking from and another silver dining plate, that it passed with the latter.

22   ULPIAN, *Sabinus, book 22:* A garment is something completely woven, even if it has not been severed, that is, if it has been completed. What is still on the loom and not fully woven or completely finished is said to be in process of weaving. Therefore, where a person has left clothing, warp and weft will not be included in the legacy.

23   ULPIAN, *Sabinus, book 44:* 1. It makes no difference whether clothing or clothes are left. All wool, linen, silk, and bombazine made up as clothes, belts, cloaks, covers, wraps, bed linen, and accessories subsumed under these terms, the embroidery incorporated in them, and the stripes which are sewn on to clothes, are counted as clothes. 2. All clothing is men's or children's or women's or that which may be worn by either sex or that worn by slaves. Men's clothing is that provided for the benefit of the head of the household, such as togas, tunics, cloaks, bedspreads, coverlets, and blankets, and the like. Children's garments are clothes used only for this purpose, such as *togae praetextae*, coats, *chlamydes*, and cloaks which we provide for our sons. Women's clothes are those acquired for the benefit of the matron of a household, which a man cannot easily use without incurring censure, such as robes, wraps, undergarments, head coverings, belts, turbans, which have been acquired more with a view to covering the head than for their decorative effect, coverlets, and mantles. Clothes adapted to the use of either sex are those which a woman shares in common with her husband, for instance, where a mantle or cloak is of the type that a man or his wife may use it without criticism, and other garments of this nature. Slaves' clothing is that acquired for dressing the household, such as blankets, tunics, mantles, bed linen, and the like.   3. Clothing will also consist of skins,

24   PAUL, *Sabinus, book 11:* since some people have both tunics and bed-coverings made of skins.

25 ULPIAN, *Sabinus, book 44:* This is also proved by certain tribes, such as the Sarmatae, who dress in skins. 1. Aristo says that felt items, too, pass with clothing, and seat coverings pass with a legacy of clothes. 2. Headbands made of pearls and brooches are items of jewelry rather than clothing. 3. Coverlets which are normally spread out or put over things are comprised in clothing, but I submit that horse blankets and coverings are not clothing. 4. Bindings for the legs and feet and felt shoes are considered clothing because they cover parts of the body. Socks are another case in point because they supply the need for shoes. 5. Pillows are also included under the heading of clothing. 6. If someone has added "his clothing," it is clear that his intentions concerned that which he himself had for his own use. 7. Cushions will also be clothing. 8. Likewise, goatskins and lambskins will be clothing. 9. Pomponius rightly observes in the twenty-second book of his *Sabinus*, that a legacy of women's clothes includes baby clothes, female children's clothes, and young girls' clothes; for all those of the female sex are classed as women. 10. Women's jewelry is of the kind with which a woman adorns herself, such as earrings, bracelets, small bangles, rings, with the exception of signet rings, and everything acquired for no other purpose than adornment. And the following, too, belong to this category: gold, gems, and [precious] stones, because in themselves they have no other use. Women's toilet equipment is employed to make a woman more attractive; under this head are included mirrors, jars, perfumes, perfume bottles, and anything that may be of like nature such as equipment for the bath [or] a chest. The following are classed as jewelry: headdresses, turbans and half turbans, a headcovering, a pearl hairpin which women are accustomed to possess, saffron colored [hair]nets. And just as a woman can also be clean without being dressed up, as normally happens in the case of those who have bathed, but not dressed up, the contrary is also true when a woman has been dressed up from the moment she got out of bed, but not completely clean. 11. Pearls, if they are not loose, or other stones (if in fact they are removable) are to be held classed as jewelry; but even if they have been removed for resetting they constitute jewelry. But if the stones or pearls or gems are in an unpolished state, they will not count as jewelry unless the testator's intention was otherwise, meaning those, too, which he had acquired for [use as] jewelry to be included in the category and term jewelry. 12. Unguents intended for medicinal purposes do not form part of toilet equipment.

26 PAUL, *Sabinus, book 11:* Although certain items of clothing are acquired more for the purpose of decoration than to cover the body, nevertheless, because they have been discovered under that head, they are to be considered as belonging to the category of clothing rather than that of jewelry. Similarly, it is established that there be classed as jewelry those items which women have begun to use to augment their charm and attraction and that it makes no difference if some of them supply another use too, such as turbans and headdresses; for although they cover the body, nevertheless, they constitute jewelry and not clothing.

27 ULPIAN, *Sabinus, book 44:* Quintus Mucius, in the second book of his *Civil Law*, gives the following definition, that worked silver is regarded as constituting a silver vessel. 1. It is asked whether, in the case where a person has been left all the silver, coins, too, are regarded as part of his legacy. And for my part I submit that they are not included; for cash is not readily reckoned as part of the silver. Likewise, where worked silver has been left as a legacy, I submit that unless there is clear evidence of a contrary intention on the part of the testator, cash is not included. 2. Where [the testator] has left a legacy of all the silver belonging to him, clearly what has been consigned on loan is not due for the reason that what he cannot claim as his is not regarded as his. 3. Where worked gold or silver has been left to someone, what has been broken or battered is not contained [in the legacy]; for Servius is of the opinion that that which can be advantageously used is regarded as worked gold or silver, but silver that is broken or battered does not fall within that definition, but is included with unworked silver. 4. Where a person has been left all the gold belonging to [a testator] when he died, he will receive all the gold the head of the household could

have claimed as his own when he died. But if the gold has been distributed, then it makes a difference how it has been left. If worked gold has been left, the legatee obtains all the gold from which anything had been made, whether it had been made for the testator's use or someone else's, for instance, gold vessels, ornaments, statues, women's gold [jewelry], and other things of a similar fashion. But if unworked gold has been left, such of it as has been so fashioned that you cannot use it for the purpose for which it was acquired without reworking, and whatever had been reckoned as unworked by the head of the household is regarded as included in the legacy. But if stamped gold or silver has been left, the head of the household is regarded as having left by will such of it as has been struck in a particular shape, such as Philippes d'or, similarly coins, and other like objects. 5. I do not believe that chamber pots are included in a legacy of silver, because they are not considered part of the silver collection. 6. Worked silver shall have been properly defined as excluding ingots, leaf, stamped silver, that used in the manufacture of furniture, toilet equipment, and jewelry.

28   ALFENUS VARUS, *Digest, book 7:* When a testator left as a legacy the silver which had been acquired for his use and likewise clothing or furniture, it was asked what was regarded as having been acquired for which purpose, whether the head of the household had acquired for his daily use the silver acquired for his table or if those silver tables and silver of that sort which he himself was not in the habit of making indiscriminate use, but was accustomed to provide for games and other shows [had also been acquired for his daily use]. And it is resolved rather that only that acquired for his table is included.

29   FLORENTINUS, *Institutes, book 11:* If material of another type has been introduced with the gold and silver, where worked gold or silver is left as a legacy, the added matter is due as well. 1. But which material is an accessory of the other is to be determined by its appearance and use and the use made of it by the head of the household.

30   PAUL, *The Assignment of Freedmen, sole book:* If someone has left a legacy in the following terms: "I give and bequeath to my wife her toilet equipment and jewelry or whatever I have acquired for her use," it is resolved that all the articles are due, just as when a legacy is left as follows: "I give and bequeath to Titius the wines I have in the city or in the harbor," all the wines are due; for the word "or" has been employed in a conjunctive and not a disjunctive sense.

31   LABEO, *Posthumous Works, Epitomized by Javolenus, book 2:* A person who left dishes of three sizes had made a legacy as follows: "I leave my smaller dish to so and so." The opinion was given that where it was not clear which of the dishes the head of the household had intended to indicate, the one of middling size was to be regarded as comprising the legacy.

32   PAUL, *Vitellius, book 2:* Small bronze figures that have been added to silver feet and other objects which can be treated as of a similar nature pass with worked silver. 1. Gems set in rings are reckoned with worked gold, since the gems are part of the rings, and likewise, silver drinking vessels encased with gold embossed work. Pearls which have been set in women's jewelry in such a manner that the gold predominates are reckoned with worked gold. Gold decoration present on stones on silver dishes, which could be detached and melted down, are due in Gallus's view, but Labeo disapproves [of this opinion]. Tubero, however, says that what the testator had reckoned to be part of his gold is due as the legacy; otherwise, that gilded vessels and vessels of another material encased in gold are not to be considered as part of the gold. 2. Where a silver vessel for the purposes of drinking or eating has been left as a legacy, the habit of the head of the household must be looked at in cases where it is not clear of which type the object is, but not in those too where it is clear it is not of that type. 3. A certain centurion had left his wife a silver dining service; it was asked, since the head of the household had among his silver vessels from which he was accustomed both to drink and eat, whether these vessels, too, were included in the legacy. Scaevola has given it as his opinion that they are part of it. 4. [Scaevola] was also

asked about a legacy of the following kind: "Further, let my dearest daughter take from the residue and have for herself all my women's jewelry, together with the gold and other female accoutrements." Since the testratrix was a business woman, do not merely the silver that was kept at home or in store for her own use but also the women's silver articles kept at her commercial premises pass under the legacy? [Scaevola] has given it as his opinion that if the testatrix had silver of her own acquired for her own use, the silver which she used to put up for sale in the course of business is not regarded as part of the legacy, unless the claimant proves that her intention had embraced this too.   5. Neratius reports that Proculus has given the following opinion where amber vessels have been left as a legacy: that the amount of silver or amber contained in the vessels in question makes no difference, but whether the silver passes with the amber or the amber with the silver; and this can be easily understood from the appearance of the vessels; but if it is not clear, we must look and see in which category the testator has ranked those vessels.   6. Labeo has expressly left by will to Neratia his wife clothing, all her toilet equipment, and all the women's jewelry, wool, linen, purple, dyed and undyed stuffs, and other things. But the multiplicity of superfluous words does not change the substance of the legacy, because Labeo has written in his will wool and then dyed stuffs, as if dyed wool ceases to be wool; and if we take away the word dyed, the dyed stuffs will nonetheless be due, unless it appears that the deceased had a contrary intention.   7. Titia has left women's toilet equipment to Septicia. She thought she had been left both the jewelry and the necklaces of gems and pearls too, and rings and clothing, including colored clothing; it has been asked whether all these are included under the head, toilet equipment. Scaevola has given it as his opinion that of all the above-mentioned articles only the silver ware pertaining to the bath is included in women's toilet equipment.   8. Likewise, when a testatrix had left her earrings in which there were [set] two pearls as pendants and emeralds and had subsequently removed the pendants from them, it was also asked whether the earrings were due, notwithstanding the fact that the pendants had been removed; he has given it as his opinion that they are due, if they still remain in the form of earrings, although the pearls have been taken away from them.   9. In another case he has given the same opinion where a testatrix had left a brooch of thirty-four *cylindri* and thirty-four circles of pearls, and had subsequently removed four of the *cylindri* and also six of the pearls.

33   POMPONIUS, *Quintus Mucius, book 4:* There is no difference between men's clothing and men's garments; but the intention of the testator makes for difficulty, if he himself had been in the habit of using certain clothing which is also suitable for women. And so, in the first place, it must be held that that clothing constitutes the legacy which the testator intended, not what is in fact female or male. For Quintus Titius also says that he knows that a certain senator was accustomed to use women's dinner dress, and if he were to leave women's clothing would not be regarded as having expressed an intention in respect of what he himself used as if it were men's clothing.

34   POMPONIUS, *Quintus Mucius, book 9:* Quintus Mucius observes that if a head of a household had left all his gold to his wife, the gold which he had given to the goldsmith to work, or what was due to him if it had not been repaid by the goldsmith, is not due to the woman. POMPONIUS: This is partly true and partly incorrect; for, in respect of what is due, it is without doubt true; for instance, if he has stipulated for so many pounds of gold, the gold owed him in accordance with the stipulation does not belong to the wife, since it has not yet become his; for he has left [gold] that was his and not [gold] in respect of which he had an action. In the case of the goldsmith, it is incorrect, where he has given him gold with the object that he should make something from it; for then, although the gold may be with the goldsmith, there, however, has been no change of ownership, but it remains the property of the person who gave it, and he is regarded only as having to pay for the work of the goldsmith, as a result of which we

reach the point that it is nonetheless due to the wife. But if he has given gold to the goldsmith, so that some small object should be made for him, not, however, from that gold, but from other gold, then, insofar as the ownership in that gold has passed to the goldsmith in that he is regarded as having effected an exchange as it were, this gold, too, will not pass to the wife.   1. Likewise, Quintus Mucius observes that if a husband, having five of gold by weight, had left it to his wife in the following terms, "that my heir give my wife whatever gold had been acquired for my wife," even if a pound of gold had then been sold and at the time of his death not more than four pounds were discovered, the heir is bound in respect of the whole five pounds, because the head containing the description relates to the present time. And it will properly be so held insofar as the legal obligation is concerned, that is, the heir is bound *ipso jure*. But it is to be understood that if the testator has subsequently alienated a pound of that gold for the reason that he intended to reduce his wife's legacy, then the deceased's change of intention will let in the defense of fraud, so that, if the woman has persisted in suing for five pounds, she may be rebutted by the defense of fraud. But if the testator has been activated by some compulsion, and not because he wished to reduce her legacy, then five pounds of gold will be due to the woman *ipso jure*, and the defense of fraud will not prejudice her suit.   2. But if he had made a legacy to his wife in the following terms, "gold which shall have been acquired for her benefit," then Quintus Mucius's observation that the phrase is both a description of the legacy and proof of it is perfectly correct. And so, where the pound of gold has been alienated, *ipso jure* the heir will not be liable for more than four by weight, and no distinction will have to be made in respect of the testator's reason for alienating it.

35   PAUL, *Replies, book 14:* "I intend five pounds of gold to be given to my mistress Titia with whom I have lived without hypocrisy." I ask whether the heirs are to be obliged to provide gold entirely in specie or to hand over the price and how much should be paid. Paul has given it as his opinion that either the gold or its market price should be handed over to the woman in question.   1. Likewise, I ask, if, after issue has been joined, the praetor has ruled that it is to be paid in specie, whether tutors are to be heard on the point when they desire that their *pupillus* against whom judgment has been entered be restored to his former position by the praetor's successor. Paul has given it as his opinion that the praetor who ruled in respect of the legacy of the gold that a certain weight should be paid in specie appears to have given the right judgment.

36   SCAEVOLA, *Replies, book 3:* "I impose on my heirs a *fideicommissum* to give my dearest Seia the gold cup of her choice." I ask, since there are only basins, goblets, small measures, and shallow drinking vessels in the estate, whether Seia can make her choice from these objects. [Scaevola] has given it as his opinion that since all drinking vessels are called cups, she may make her choice from them.

37   PAUL, *Replies, book 21:* I have given it as my opinion that women's clothing is not included under the head of adornment and that the heir's mistake had not served to change the law.

38   SCAEVOLA, *Replies, book 3:* Titia made specific bequests by way of *fideicommissum* by will and by codicil of many different kinds of silver and clothing. I ask whether other types too pass with the legacy or only those found in the estate. [Scaevola] has given it as his opinion that those found in the estate pass; concerning others, it should be guaranteed that if discovered, they are to be handed over.   1. "Further, I wish Sempronia Pia to be given my Tavian covers and three tunics with cloaks of her choice." I ask whether Sempronia can choose her separate tunics and cloaks from all the clothing, that is, whether from complete suits. Scaevola has given it as his opinion that if there were particular tunics left together with their [matching] cloaks, she can choose only from these; but if that is not the case, the heir will provide the tunics and cloaks, but from complete suits, or will pay her the value.   2. Seia has provided as follows in her will: "If it has fallen to me to be able to do so in my lifetime, I shall do it myself; but, if not, I wish it to be done by my heirs, and I direct them to set up a statue of the god of one hundred pounds in that sacred temple and in my birthplace under my name." It has been asked: Since there are only bronze and silver gifts in that temple, are Seia's heirs to be compelled to set up a gold or silver statue or one of bronze?

[Scaevola] has given it as his opinion that according to the facts as given a silver [statue] should be set up.

39 JAVOLENUS, *Posthumous Works of Labeo, book 2:* If women's toilet equipment had been left to a wife, Ofilius [and] Labeo have given it as their opinion that only that is due which had been handed over by the husband to his wife for her use; for other interpretations would induce the greatest abuse, if a goldsmith or silversmith had made such a legacy in favor of his wife. 1. Where a legacy had been left as follows, "the silver which shall be in my home when I die," Ofilius has given it as his opinion that silver deposited by the testator or loaned is not regarded as included in the legacy. Cascellius is of the same opinion in respect of that loaned. Labeo holds that what had been deposited is due, if it was so deposited for current and not for perpetual safekeeping, as where it had been deposited as treasure, because the words, "what shall be in my home," should be understood as "was normally in my home," and I approve of this view. 2. Ateius observes that Servius has given it as his opinion that the person to whom had been left the silver on the testator's Tusculan farm when he died should also receive what had been moved from the city to the Tusculan estate on the testator's instructions before his death; the contrary would be the case if it had been transferred without his instructions.

40 SCAEVOLA, *Digest, book 17:* A testator had left, *inter alia,* the following legacy to his doctor, who shared his quarters and accompanied him on their joint expeditions: "I desire him to be given my traveling monies." It has been asked, since the head of the household had been absent on state business on different occasions, what traveling money is regarded as having been comprised in this legacy. [Scaevola] has given it as his opinion that the traveling money he had at the time of making his will is due. 1. The testator has made a legacy to his wife in the following terms: "to Sempronia, my lady wife, in addition, the silver bathware." It has been asked whether the silver which he used to use in the bath on festal days passed with the legacy. Scaevola has given it as his opinion that all of it is regarded as [forming part of] the legacy. 2. A woman on her death had left her jewelry in the following terms: "I desire that my entire collection of jewelry be given to my friend Seia." In the same will, she had written: "I wish to be buried as my husband deems fit, and whatever I wear for the purpose of burial, I wish there to be put on me from my jewelry, two strings of pearls and my emerald bracelets." But neither the heirs nor the husband, when he buried the body, buried the jewelry which he had been ordered to put on the body; it has been asked whether it belongs to the legatee to whom all the jewelry had been left or to the heirs. [Scaevola] gave it as his opinion that it does not belong to the heirs, but to the legatee.

3

RELEASE BY WILL

1 ULPIAN, *Sabinus, book 21:* Debts can properly be left to all [types of] debtors, even if they are owners of the objects owed. 1. Julian has observed, if something given as a pledge is left to a debtor by the creditor, the legacy is good, and he has an action to recover his pledge, before paying the sum concerned. But Julian talks as if he should not recover his debt but if the testator's intention was otherwise, this too will be achieved on the analogy of payment.

2 POMPONIUS, *Sabinus, book 6:* The heir who has been obliged to refrain from suing the surety can nevertheless sue the principal debtor, but where he has been forbidden to sue the principal debtor, if he sues the surety, Celsus submits that he is liable to the principal in an action on the will. 1. Again, Celsus says that he has no doubt that where the heir is forbidden to sue the debtor, the heir's heir cannot sue him either.

3 ULPIAN, *Sabinus, book 23:* It is now certain that a debtor may be released by will. 1. But also where a man on his death has given the debtor a note [of release] in his own hand, I submit that a defense is available to him, as if a gift of this kind were valid as a *fideicommissum.* 2. Julian has also observed in the fortieth book of his *Digest* that if, on his death, a man has given a note [of release] to Titius in respect of [a debt owed by] Seius, to give to the latter after his death, or, in the case of his recovery, to return to him, then, [if] on the donor's death Titius has given it to Seius, and the donor's heir sues for the

debt, Seius has the defense of fraud. 3. Now let us look at the effect of such a legacy. Where release has actually been left to me when I am sole debtor, if I am sued, I can plead a defense; if I am not sued, I can sue for formal discharge. But also where I am debtor together with another, for instance, where both of us have been answerable as principals for the debt, and the testator has had only my interests at heart, by bringing suit I shall not gain release by receipt; for that releases my co-debtor too, contrary to the testator's intention, but I shall be released by covenant. But what if we have been partners? Let us see whether I ought not rather to be released by discharge; otherwise, when my fellow debtor is sued, I am put to trouble. And Julian has made the following observation in the thirty-second book of his *Digest*, that if, in fact, we are not partners, I should be released by covenant; if we are partners, by discharge. 4. Consequently, the question arises, whether that partner too is to be considered as a legatee whose name has not been mentioned in the will, although the benefit conferred by the will belongs to both, if they are partners. And it is true that not only the person who has been mentioned in the will but also the one who has not been mentioned is to be considered as a legatee, if release had been left with him in mind too. 5. Both are considered as legatees in the following case too. For if what I owe to Titius has been left to him on my account, so that I am released, no one will deny that I am a legatee, as Julian, too, observes, in the same book. And Marcellus remarks that the legacy belongs to both of us, and is as much mine as my creditor's, even if I have been solvent; for it is in the interest of the creditor to have two debtors to sue.

4   POMPONIUS, *Plautius, book 7:* What, therefore, is the position when the creditor will be in a position to sue on the will? The heir should only have judgment entered against him where a *cautio* has been given to the effect that he will be protected against the debtor. And if the debtor brings a case, the heir should have to do no more than defend him against the creditor.

5   ULPIAN, *Sabinus, book 23:* If a man has a debtor and a surety, and releases the debtor by will, Julian has observed in the same place that the debtor is to be released by formal discharge; otherwise, if a suit has been started against the surety, the debtor is being sued by another method. What, however, if the surety has undertaken the guarantee gratuitously, and he has no recourse against him? Or what if the money has come into the hands of the surety who has put up a principal on his own account and has gone surety himself? The debtor is to be released by covenant. But we are accustomed to hold that the defense of covenant which belongs to the debtor should be given to the surety; but where the testator has one intention, and the covenantor another, we by no means hold this. 1. But if release has been left to the surety, doubtless, as Julian has observed, the surety will have to be freed by covenant. But I submit that he, too, should sometimes be released by discharge, if he was either in fact principal debtor himself or with regard to this matter a fellow principal. 2. The same Julian has observed in the same book that if the son of the household were the debtor and release has been left to his father, the father is to be released by covenant, lest the son, too, should be released. And he says it makes little difference, if he has anything in his *peculium* when the legacy becomes due or not; for the father is secured as a result of this legacy; it makes every difference, he says, when his *peculium* is examined at the time of trial. Julian equates the father in this case with a husband in whose favor a divorced wife has left release from payment of dowry; for even if he is insolvent when the legacy becomes due, he is a legatee, and he says neither can recover what he has paid. But it is truer to say, as Marcellus remarks, that the father can sue (for he was not a debtor at the time he paid), but the husband cannot, because he paid what was owing. For even if the father were thought to be a debtor, yet there is no doubt that he is in the position of a conditional debtor who can recover what he has paid. 3. But if the heir has been obliged to release the son, Julian does not add whether the son is to be released by discharge or covenant; but he seems to hold the view that he should be released by discharge, which will also be of advantage to the father. And this view is to be maintained, unless it is clearly proved that the testator had a contrary intention, that is, so that the son is not troubled, and not that the father is not troubled; for, in that case, he will have to be released not by discharge but by covenant. 4. Julian has also observed that if the father has stood surety for the son and release has been left to him, he is to be freed by covenant as surety and not as father, and for that reason it is possible to bring an action on the *peculium*. He

submits that this happens only in the case where the testator wished him to be released merely as surety; however, if he also wished to release him in his capacity of father, he will have to be released in respect of the *peculium*.

6   JAVOLENUS, *Letters, book 6:* But after his son's emancipation, a father will have an action insofar as he is due to pay anything on the *peculium* or from benefit taken. For [only] that in which he shall have an interest will belong to the father on the ground of the legacies. 1. It may be asked whether the father can sue on the will under this head, too, so as to release the son from an action. Some authorities resolved that the action lies to this extent, because, where he had granted his *peculium* to the son after emancipation, it is regarded as an object of interest to the father to maintain the son's right intact. I am of the opposite opinion; I submit that nothing further is due to the father on the wording of that kind of will other than that he pay none of what he has been obliged to pay the heir.

7   ULPIAN, *Sabinus, book 23:* But release can be obtained not only from what is owed, but from part of it or from part of an obligation, as is discussed by Julian in the thirty-third book of his *Digest.*   1. If a person who has stipulated for Stichus or for ten has charged the heir not to sue for Stichus, it is established that there is a valid legacy, but we must see what it contains. And Julian observes that the action on the will appears to turn on the fact that the debtor is released by receipt; and this will equally release the debtor in respect of the ten, because discharge is comparable to payment, and just as the debtor would be freed if he had paid over Stichus, he is also released by discharge of Stichus.   2. But if the heir has been obliged to release a debtor for ten in respect of twenty, Julian has observed in his thirty-third book that he is nonetheless released in respect of ten; for even if twenty are entered in the receipt, he will be released in respect of ten.   3. But if two heirs have been instituted and the testator has obliged one of them to pay a creditor, the legacy is valid on the co-heir's account, and he will have an action on the will, so that the creditor is paid. 4. But where release has been left to a debtor, it is effective only if the debt was not collected in the testator's lifetime; otherwise, if it was collected, the legacy disappears. 5. Therefore, Julian asks, if release has been left charged on the substitute heir to an *impubes* and the *impubes* has then collected the debt, whether the legacy disappears. And since it is established that in respect of legacies charged on the substitute heir, the *pupillus* holds the position of one on whom they are conditionally charged, the substitute is consequently liable in an action on the will, if the *pupillus* has collected from the debtor.   6. And the same position holds good if the *pupillus* has not collected, but merely engaged in a lawsuit, that the substitute is bound to drop the action.   7. For, even if release had been left to the debtor conditionally and issue had been joined or [the debt] been collected while the condition was in suspense, an action on the will would subsist in respect of the release that had been left to him.

8   POMPONIUS, *Sabinus, book 6:* We may provide by will not only for the release of our own debtor but for that of the debtor of the heir or of anybody else.   1. The heir may be charged not to sue the debtor for a given period, but, without doubt, he ought not to release him within this period, and if the debtor has died, his heir will not be able to be sued within this period.   2. We must see whether the heir can sue for interest or a penalty during the period within which he has been forbidden to sue. And Priscus Neratius submitted that he contravened the will in a case where he had sued, which is true.   3. A legacy such as the following, "my heir is not to sue only Lucius Titius," does not pass to Lucius Titius's heir, if the heir has not infringed the provisions of the will in Lucius Titius's lifetime by attempting to exact the debt from him; for whenever a legacy is coupled with the person of the beneficiary, so to say, as a personal benefit, it does not pass to his heir; if it is not so coupled, it passes.   4. If the words of release were expressed *in rem*, they are taken as having forbidden the heir to sue the debtor or his heir, so that the addition of the heir is accordingly of no more validity than it would be if the person of the debtor had not been included.   5. A person who has been instructed to render accounts does not appear to have fulfilled the demand if he gives up the residue without producing accounts.   6. If the heir has been forbidden to sue the business administrator of the deceased, the obligation is not regarded as precluding him from suing in respect of activities of the administrator involving malpractice or fraud, and the testator is regarded as having had such intention. And so

if the heir had brought a case for unauthorized administration, a procurator who brings an action on the will in respect of an uncertain amount can be rebutted by the defense of fraud.   7. And release is properly left to one with whom I have made a deposit or to whom I have lent something, or given a pledge or to a person who is obliged to me on the basis of theft.

9   ULPIAN, *Sabinus, book 24:* If a person is forbidden to demand accounts, as has often been ruled in rescripts, he is not to be prevented from demanding the balance which has remained with the other party and anything the accountant has in respect of which he has committed a fraud. And if a person wishes to release this too, he should leave it in the following terms: "Let my heir be obliged to restore to him whatever he has exacted from him by such and such action" or "drop the action against him."

10   JULIAN, *Digest, book 33:* If the heir has been charged not to sue the surety, but to give what the principal debtor owes to Titius, he should convenant not to sue the surety and to grant the legatee his actions against the principal debtor; insofar as the heir has been charged not to sue the principal debtor and to hand over what the surety owes, he is compelled to give the principal debtor a receipt and to tender the legatee the value of the claim.

11   JULIAN, *Digest, book 36:* If a debtor has ordered his surety to be released by his heir, is the surety to be released? I have given it as my opinion that he should be. Likewise, it has been asked whether a legacy had been made without effect, where the heirs were liable in an action on mandate in the same way as a legacy from a debtor to his creditor is ineffective. I have given it as my opinion that whenever a debtor made a legacy to his creditor, it was thus ineffective, unless the creditor derived some new cause of action on the will as opposed to on the former obligation. For if Titius had given a mandate to Maevius to promise to pay money and has then ordered him to be released from the promisee, it is clear how important it is for the promisor to be released rather than pay money in accordance with the stipulation and then bring an action on mandate.

12   JULIAN, *Digest, book 39:* Lucius Titius who had an agent called Eros provided as follows in a codicil: "I desire that Eros be free and I wish him to give accounts of all transactions falling after my last signature." He subsequently manumitted Eros in his lifetime, kept him in the same employment, and signed the accounts up to a day shortly before he died. The heirs of Lucius Titius allege that Eros received certain sums, both while still a slave and subsequently when free without entering them in the accounts signed by Lucius Titius; I ask whether the heirs should demand nothing from Eros during the period when Lucius Titius signed the accounts. I have given it as my opinion that Eros cannot sue for release in respect of the above-mentioned circumstances, unless this, too, has been specifically permitted him.

13   JULIAN, *Digest, book 81:* If a creditor has left the amount of his debt to a debtor who could protect himself by a perpetual defense, the legacy will be of no importance. But if the same debtor has made a legacy in the creditor's favor, it will have to be understood that he intended to release the defense in the creditor's favor.

14   ULPIAN, *Fideicommissa, book 1:* The same is true whether the debt was payable on a day certain or under a condition.

15   ULPIAN, *Edict, book 64:* If someone has been charged by will not to demand a debt from Titius, he cannot sue him or his heir; for the heir's heir cannot sue for the debt, nor can the heir's heir of the debtor be sued; but the heir's heir can be obliged not to sue for the debt.

16   PAUL, *Plautius, book 9:* I have left to the person to whom I had leased a farm for a term of five years whatever he is, or will be, obliged to give or provide for me charged

on my heir. Nerva and Atilicinus say that if the heir were to prevent him enjoying this benefit, he would be liable on the lease; if he were to withhold anything in virtue of the law in respect of leases, he would be liable on the will, because it would make no difference whether a thing were sued for or he were to withhold it, since the whole lease is regarded as a legacy.

17   JAVOLENUS, *Posthumous Works of Labeo, book 2:* As to the rest, it comes into an action on the lease.

18   PAUL, *Plautius, book 9:* CASSIUS: Even if housing had been left in this fashion, the heir would have to provide free housing. And furthermore, it has been resolved that a *colonus* can bring a case on the will against the heir to gain release from his tenancy agreement. And this is most properly held to be the case.

19   MODESTINUS, *Rules, book 9:* When we make a will as follows, "let my heir be obliged to grant him his freedom, because he has conducted my business, and, if he is in the position of having to give or provide me with anything, [let my heir be obliged] not to demand it," the heir is obliged not to demand money that has been loaned to him either. But in a similar kind of legacy, it is hardly the case that the head of a household has intended to leave that too which is owed to his slaves by way of *peculium.*

20   MODESTINUS, *Replies, book 10:* "To Aurelius Sempronius, my brother, I want no one to be troubled on account of a debt, nor anything demanded from him in his lifetime either from the capital or on account of the interest on the debt. And I release him and free from its mortgage the house and the property known as Caperlata." Modestinus has given it as his opinion that where a case is brought, the debtor is protected by a defense; the position is different in respect of the person of his heir. 1. When he had reached puberty, Gaius Seius received as curators Publius Maevius and Lucius Sempronius. But when the same Gaius Seius died under legal age, he made the following provisions in his will in respect of his curators: "My curators are not to be questioned; for I have managed my affairs myself." I ask whether the heirs of the young man can ask the curators for an account in respect of their curatorship, since the deceased, as is clear from the words of his will, has acknowledged that he has administered all his property himself. Modestinus has given it as his opinion that if the curators have committed fraud in any way or if any property of the testator is in their hands, they can be sued in these respects.

21   TERENTIUS CLEMENS, *Lex Julia et Papia, book 12:* If I have left your debt to me to you or to another person and you have paid me or have been released by me in some other manner, the legacy is extinguished. 1. Therefore, it was resolved by Julian that even if the heir has fallen to be creditor of the debtor and the creditor has subsequently died, the legacy is extinguished; and this is true, because the obligation is extinguished by conflation just as it is by payment. 2. But if, where a legacy has been made conditional, the heir has anticipated the condition and has demanded the debt, it should be held otherwise, since it should not lie in the heir's determination that whenever the condition is fulfilled, the legacy is due neither to the legatee, so long as he is alive and can take it, nor to the person to whom this benefit falls if the heir cannot take it.

22   PAPINIAN, *Questions, book 19:* "I do not wish Sempronius's debt to me to be recovered"; the opinion has been given that the debtor not only has a defense but also can apply under the *fideicommissum* for his release.

23   PAPINIAN, *Letters, book 7:* The procurator from whom the heir has been prevented from demanding accounts and on that score has been obliged to release the procurator is compelled by the action on mandate to restore money due from a banker on a contract he has made as procurator or to hand over his rights of action.

24   PAPINIAN, *Replies, book 8:* When the heir is requested to release his own debtor, only
that part of the debt appears to be in contemplation which has remained an obligation; and
so, if anything has been paid before the will has been opened, it will not fall within the
scope of the *fideicommissum;* but whatever has been demanded after the will has been
opened, but before the estate has been accepted by an heir not unaware of the deceased's
disposition, will be equated with fraud and may therefore be recovered.

25   PAUL, *Questions, book 10:* I have left to Titius his debt to me, possibly adding a fixed
sum or the form in which it is owed or possibly without such addition, or in the opposite
case, I may employ the same distinction, for example, "what I owe Titius," or, as follows,
"the hundred I owe Titius." I inquire whether you submit that in all cases the question to
be asked is: "Has there been a debt?" And I ask you to touch on the matters affecting the
question in full; for they are everyday occurrences. I have given it as my opinion that if
Titius's creditor intended to remit the debt in full, it makes no difference whether he has
instructed his heir to release him or prevents him from demanding the debt; for in either
case the debtor is to be released and in either case he further has a right of action for release; but where [the testator] has made reference to a hundred aurei or a [specific] farm
that is due, if it is proved that he was the debtor, he is to be released; but if he owes
nothing, it will be possible to hold that he can also sue for what has been included by the
addition of a false description. But it will be possible to hold this where [the testator] has
left the legacy in the following terms: "the hundred aurei that he owes me" or "let my heir
be obliged not to recover Stichus, whom he owes me." But if he has provided as follows,
"let my heir be obliged to give Titius the hundred aurei that he owes me," it will be possible
to put this, too, to the test [to see if] he can sue on the ground that a false description has
been added, although I am by no means in favor of this view, since the testator has considered himself as referring the word "gift" to the debt. But, on the other hand, if the debtor is
making a legacy to his creditor, I see no point in it if he leaves the debt without reference to
a specified sum. But even if he were to indicate what he agrees he owes, there is no point
unless he states the form in which the benefit of the debt is increased. But if he has left the
hundred aurei which he has said he owes, if in fact he owes them, the legacy is ineffective,
but if he was not the debtor, it has been resolved that the disposition is effective; for a
certain amount of cash is on a par with a legacy of Stichus made with false description; and
the divine Pius has ruled that this is the case in a rescript where a sum certain has been left
in lieu of dowry.

26   SCAEVOLA, *Replies, book 4:* A tutor on his death, after appointing other heirs, has expressed his intention that his *pupillus* for whose tutelage he was responsible be given a
third share of his property on condition that he has not disputed the matter of the tutelage
with his heirs, but has released them all in that respect; the *pupillus* has taken the legacy
in advance of distribution and, nonetheless, has subsequently brought a claim to the effect
that something from the tutelage came into his tutor's possession as a result of sale or for
some other reason. I ask whether he is barred from these demands by the wording of the
will. [Scaevola] has given it as his opinion that if he had taken the *fideicommissum* before
obeying the condition and went on to claim something whereby he was contravening the
condition, the defense of fraud will be raised against him, unless he had been prepared to
restore what he had taken as a result of the *fideicommissum,* which he is to be allowed to
do as a concession to his age.

27   TRYPHONINUS, *Disputations, book 8:* Let us see whether release has been left by will to
one against whom there will be an action in respect of *peculium* or, if there is nothing in the
peculium on the day when the legacies take effect, whether he is to be considered as a
legatee. But he has not yet been a debtor, and no advantage accrues to him from the legacy
except through the expectation of a future *peculium.* Therefore is not his status as legatee
in suspense, just as if another reason were in some way to render his expectation of the
legacy uncertain?

28   SCAEVOLA, *Digest, book 16:* Aurelius Symphorus had gone surety for a certain tutor and
on his death left a legacy to the same *pupilli* in the following terms: "To Arellius Latinus
and Arellius Felix five each, when each of them has attained the age of fourteen years, up
to which time I desire them each to be provided in respect of aliment with a monthly allowance of six denarii and with a yearly allowance in respect of clothing of twenty-five

denarii. And you should be content with this legacy, since your tutelage has inflicted no little loss on my accounts. But I request you, my heirs, not to desire to exact anything from them by reason of the tutelage or to keep anything back from their legacy." It has been asked, if his heir has paid anything as a result of the suretyship, whether he can reclaim it from the heir of the sons of the person for whom he had stood surety. [Scaevola] has given it as his opinion that according to the above wording the heirs are regarded as charged only with a *fideicommissum* not to exact what was due to him from the Arellii by reason of the tutelage that Symphorus himself had administered. 1. In making his will, a testator left release to his debtors; subsequently, he cut the thread and reviewed the will and made another in which he repeated the legacy in these words: "And all the legacies made to the persons in the will which I had cut open I desire to be ratified and any appointments made therein." It has been asked, where the estate had been accepted in accordance with the second will, whether the debtors to whom release had been left in the former will can manage to acquire their release in respect of that sum too, which they had begun to owe after the first will was written, and if the heirs have commenced proceedings, whether they were to be rebutted by the defense of fraud. [Scaevola] has given it as his opinion that they are not released. 2. Titius had made a legacy to his debtor in the following terms: "I give and bequeath to Seius ten denarii, and I likewise give him whatever he owed me in respect of capital or interest." Further, he generally obliged the heirs and imposed on them a *fideicommissum* to give and make over to each what he had left him. Subsequently, Seius borrowed another sum from Titius. I ask whether this money, too, which had been handed over to Seius after the will was made, is understood as part of the legacy. [Scaevola] has given it as his opinion that since words referring to past time were employed, the later sum is not to be treated as a legacy. 3. Titius, after making his will and instituting his sons as heirs, made the following statement in respect of his father who had once been his tutor: "I desire my father Seius to be held released from an action on the tutelage." I inquire to what extent these words apply, that is, should he restore money from sales of property or foreclosure on debts, which he has converted to his own use or loaned out in his own name, to the testator's sons and heirs, being his own grandchildren? [Scaevola] has given it as his opinion that it will be decided by the [judge] in charge of the case. For there is a presumption in favor of the father's being released in all respects on the ground of natural affection, unless the heirs prove a contrary intention on the part of the testator. 4. Maevia desired to release one of her heirs by will from an action on tutelage in the following words: "I desire no statement of account to be demanded of the tutelage Julius Paulus administered with Antistius Cicero, and, on that score, I desire him to be held released from every action." I ask whether, in the case where money deriving from the tutelage has remained in his possession, he can be sued for it. He has given it as his opinion that there is no reason why money belonging to a *pupilla* that remained deposited with a tutor should be regarded as a legacy. 5. A testator has written as follows: "I desire my relative Titius to be released from whatever he owes me for whatever reason, and, in addition, I give him ten." In a codicil, he has written as follows: "I leave my kinsman and debtor Titius in addition the interest on the money he owes me charged on my heir so long as he lives; and if he has attempted to demand it in contravention of my wishes, I desire the interest on the capital to be paid to the same Titius by my heirs so long as he lives." It has been asked, since the testator has had the intention of increasing rather than diminishing his legacy, whether the heirs are liable to Titius as a result of the *fideicommissum*, so as to release him from the entire debt. [Scaevola] has given it as his opinion that, according to the facts, the legacy which he had given him in the first place is regarded as diminished. 6. A legacy has been made by will in the following fashion: "I wish there to be granted to Seius whatever sum he has owed me or the sum in which I have stood surety on his behalf." I ask whether only that sum has been left which was owed at the time of making the will, or if there were any later accretion to it by way of interest, whether this, too, passes with the legacy. [Scaevola] has given it as his opinion that he is regarded as having intended that the whole obligation of that debt be removed by the *fideicommissum*. 7. A testator left to Stichus, whom he manumitted by will, a fully equipped farm and other things and added the rider: "And I forbid him to give an account because he has the documents in his possession." It has been asked whether Stichus should give back those things that had become due as a result of his administration. I have given it as my opinion that Stichus is not liable on that count. CLAUDIUS: For no one is liable after manumission in respect of an act effected in servitude, and the advice had been sought in relation to the law of debt; therefore, the remainder can be kept along with the *peculium* or subtracted from it, if [the *peculium*] has been left as a legacy.   8. "I desire that the hundred, which I have on deposit with Apronianus, remain with him until my son has reached the age of twenty, and I forbid interest to be exacted on that sum." It has been asked whether Apronianus can sue on the *fideicommissum* to prevent the sum being demanded from him before the time prescribed by the testator. Scaevola has given it as his opinion that according to the facts as given he can.   9. A testator had appointed his daughters heirs and imposed upon them a *fideicommissum* in the following words: "not to demand from Gaius Seius accounts of his administration of my estate which he has administered through his bank or outside his bank to the date of my death, and release him in that respect." It has been asked, since he has had charge of the entire accounts up to the date of death, including those effected through his bank and those administered outside it, whether he is liable to account to the heirs. [Scaevola] has given it as his opinion that release has in fact been left to him according to the facts as given, but that the judge will decide how far it is to be afforded him from the nature of the argument.   10. A testator has appointed as his heirs the person who had administered his tutelage together with his brother and certain others and has left as a legacy to the tutor the ten he had expended upon him and his brother. It has been asked whether the *fideicommissum* was effective in the person of the tutor. [Scaevola] has given it as his opinion that if he was given by way of *fideicommissum* what was owing, it cannot be sued for.   11. The same person has asked, if it were ineffective with regard to the person of the tutor, whether it would be effective in the person of the brother, since it would benefit one whose tutelage he had also administered. He has given it as his opinion that it has been effectively left to the brother, since it would release him from his debt.   12. The same person has asked, if the tutor were to take up the *fideicommissum* in such a way that he wished to rely on certain words in the will but withdraws from others in that he alleges that a smaller amount of expenses is contained in the *fideicommissum* than he paid out, whether he should be heard. [Scaevola] has given it as his opinion that he is not hindered by the wording of the will from being able to sue for everything he had proved owing to him.   13. A [testator] has left a legacy as follows: "I instruct my heirs to restore to Sempronia my wife the fifty I had received as a loan by promissory note for the special purpose of my business." It has been asked whether, if he has in fact been his wife's debtor, a *fideicommissum* has come into existence. [Scaevola] has given it as his opinion that if the sum had constituted a debt, there is no *fideicommissum*.   14. The same person has asked, if she has brought a case to recover the debt and has lost, whether she can sue for the *fideicommissum*. He has given it as his opinion that, according to the facts as stated, she can bring suit on the ground of a *fideicommissum*, since it had become apparent that it had not been due for some other reason.

29   PAUL, *Lex Julia et Papia, book 6:* If a man with two debtors has obliged the heir to release both, where one of them is unable to receive release and they are not partners, the one who is incapable of receiving the benefit will have to be subrogated to the one to whom it belongs by law; and on the latter's petition two things happen: This benefit both falls to him and the one who takes it is released. But if they are partners, the one who is under an incapacity takes consequentially through the one who is under no incapacity, and the latter is released by discharge; for this would happen even where the heir had been instructed to release only the one who was not under an incapacity.

30   PAUL, *Questions, book 10:* The plaintiff or defendant has charged his heir not to have recourse to the centumviral court; the question arises: What is the effect of this legacy? And it has been held that it is regarded as an effective legacy only where the testator's opponent had a bad case, so that he must have lost if prosecuted by the heir. For in that case, the heir is obliged to pay the legatee not only the benefit of the action but also costs in cause. For where he has a good case, there appears to be no advantage in the legacy, not even on the grounds of costs as some have thought.

31   SCAEVOLA, *Replies, book 3:* A creditor has made a legacy in favor of his debtor in the following terms: "I desire there to be given to Gaius Seius whatever he owes me by way of mortgage of his gardens." I ask, when the testator has received something from Seius in his lifetime, whether it can be recovered on account of the legacy. [Scaevola] has given it as his opinion that according to the facts of the case it cannot. The same person has posed the question a second time and, likewise, says that the testator before making the codicil in which he has left the legacy had received back practically all the capital and interest so that only a small amount of capital and interest is owing, and he has asked whether he would be able to sue to recover it on account of the wording relating to past time, "whatever he owed me." [Scaevola] has given it as his opinion. The former opinion was in fact correct according to the facts as alleged, but as to the second, on account

of the words which were added in respect of the time, the judge will have to determine on an examination of the question whether he had done this overlooking the fact that money had been paid or whether it had been added to the accounts without his knowledge or whether he had done it deliberately, because he had wanted the bequest to reflect the amount that had at one time been due and not the right of release.   1. A [testator] has made a legacy to his freedman, *inter alia*, of the following: "And if he has managed anything for me in his lifetime, I forbid accounts to be demanded from him." It is asked whether he must give the heirs the papers on which the accounts have been written and, likewise, the balance reflected by income and expenditure. [Scaevola] has given it as his opinion that the heir may claim the items in question, but what he has entrusted to his fellow slaves who remain in the estate and what had been employed in the administration of his master's estate had ceased to be residuary sums in his possession.   2. Titia, who had had two tutors, has provided as follows: "I do not wish accounts of my tutelage which Publius Maevius administered with Lucius Titius to be required from him." It is asked, if any money from the tutelage has remained in his possession, whether it can be recovered from him. Scaevola has given it as his opinion that there is no reason why money that belonged to the *pupilla* and remained with the tutor should be regarded as a legacy.   3. Likewise, it is asked whether his co-tutor would be regarded as released. [Scaevola] has given it as his opinion that the co-tutor is not released.   4. "To Gaius Seius who is fully deserving I additionally leave and desire to be granted to him that whatever debts to me are reflected in [promissory] notes or accounts or whatever loan he has received from me or in respect of which I have stood surety is not to be recovered from him or his heirs." I ask whether only sums due at the time the will was made have been left to him or whether interest subsequently accruing on that sum passes with the legacy. [Scaevola] has given it as his opinion that, according to the facts as alleged, the testator is regarded as having intended to release in favor of Seius every obligation attaching to the debt by way of *fideicommissum*.   5. Likewise, it is asked, if he subsequently came to be indebted for an increased sum by novation, whether the sum owed in virtue of the old contract nonetheless subsists for the purpose of the legacy and whether, in fact, as a result of the novation, he may be summoned as a new debtor in a greater sum. [Scaevola] has given it as his opinion that the legacy is regarded only as comprising what had been owed at the time, but if the testator has remained of the same intention, what would then have been owed.

4

THE ADEMPTION OF LEGACIES AND *FIDEICOMMISSA*

1   PAUL, *Sabinus, book 3:* If anyone legates a right of way with cattle and then adeems the right of way in person, this ademption is ineffective, since a right of way with cattle can never exist without a right of way in person.

2   POMPONIUS, *Sabinus, book 5:* Where a piece of land has been legated, an ademption can be made in the following terms: "I neither give nor legate to him the piece of land, apart from the usufruct of it," so that what is left in the legacy is the usufruct.   1. The usufruct can also be adeemed, so that ownership is left.   2. Again, an ademption can be applied to part of a legated piece of land.

3   ULPIAN, *Sabinus, book 24:* If someone makes a legacy in the following terms, "I give and legate such-and-such a piece of property to Titius; in the event of Titius's death, let my heir be charged to give it to Seius," a correct transfer of the legacy is deemed to have occurred. But if the testator transfers the property in question when the legatee is already dead, the legacy should be delivered to Sempronius.   1. If someone makes a legacy to Titius in the following terms, "let my heir give it to Titius or, in the event of Titius dying before receipt, let him give it to Sempronius" and Titius dies after the *dies cedens* of the legacy, then according to absolutely strict interpretation, the heir would be regarded as being under obligation to each of two parties, that is, to Sempronius and to Titius's heir. However, if there was delay by the testator's heirs in paying to Titius, the right to demand the legacy is transmitted to Titius's heirs, Sempronius's claim being rejected. But if there was no delay involved, then it is Sempronius and not Titius's heirs who receives the legacy. If, on the other hand, Titius died before the *dies cedens* of the legacy, the latter should be delivered to Sempronius alone.   2. The same rule applies in the case in which an inheritance is given to a child by *fideicommissum* or in the event of his death before delivery is left to his mother. Consequently, if the child dies before the *dies cedens* of the legacy, the legacy is owed to his mother; but if he dies after the *dies cedens*, it is transmitted to the heirs of the *pupillus*, treating it as a case where the facts involve⋅delay in the execution of the *fideicommissum*.

3. But when someone has made a legacy in the following terms, "let my heir give it to Titius; and if he does not do so, let him give it to Sempronius," the legacy is also owed to Sempronius, only if it had not vested with reference to Titius.   4. If someone makes a legacy in the following terms, "let my heir give such-and-such a piece of land to Titius; and if Titius alienates that piece of land, let my heir give it to Seius," it is the heir who is liable, since the situation is not that Titius was charged with a *fideicommissum* in favor of Seius in the event of his alienating the property but that the heir was charged with the execution of the legacy in favor of Seius. Therefore, the heir will have to lodge a defense of fraud in order to protect his interests by securing a *cautio* from Titius against alienation of the property. 5. Where someone adeems more then he originally gave the ademption is valid (for example, if someone legates twenty and adeems forty).   6. If a testator legates the usufruct of a plot of land and then adeems the right of way in person over it, that ademption is not valid and the legacy is unaffected, just as anyone who legates ownership of a piece of land cannot diminish the legacy by adeeming the right of way in person over the land in question.   7. If someone makes separate legacies to two persons called Titius and then adeems the legacy from one of them but it is unclear to which of them that ademption applies, each of them should receive his legacy on the same principle by which, in the case of the grant of a legacy, if it is unclear which of two persons is the beneficiary, we hold that the legacy should be delivered to neither of them.   8. If a piece of land has been legated to Titius both absolutely and under condition and subsequently there is an ademption in the following terms, "let my heir not give to Titius that piece of land which I legated under condition," the legacy should not be delivered on the basis of either grant unless the testator specifically states that he wishes Titius to receive the legacy absolutely.   9. Let us consider whether a condition attached to a legacy, an inheritance, or a *statuliber* can be adeemed. Julian writes that in the case of a *statuliber* the removal of the condition does not *ipso facto* yield freedom. Papinian, in the seventeenth book of his *Questions*, also writes that as a general rule a condition cannot be adeemed since, as he says, a condition is not a grant but an ancillary provision and ademption cannot apply to such provisions but only to grants. But it is better to follow the sense rather than the letter and to hold that just as conditions can be introduced as an ancillary provision so they can be adeemed.   10. When a testator has legated one hundred to Titius in his will and in a subsequent codicil makes the same individual a legacy in the following terms, "let my heir give Titius just fifty and no more," the legatee will be entitled to claim no more than fifty.   11. It is not only legacies but also *fideicommissa* that can be adeemed, and that by a mere expression of the testator's wishes. Hence, the question arises of whether a *fideicommissum* is not owed in the event of enmity arising between the parties involved. If the enmity is mortal or very serious the *fideicommissum* which has been left is regarded as adeemed. But if the quarrel is trivial the *fideicommissum* remains in force. We also follow these principles in dealing with a legacy by lodging a defense of fraud.

4   ULPIAN, *Sabinus, book 33:* But if the parties become friends again and the testator repents of his previous ill will the legacy or *fideicommissum* which has been left resumes its force, since the deceased is entitled to change his mind up to the last moment of his life.

5   GAIUS, *Urban Praetor's Edict, book 2:* Just as a legacy can be adeemed, so it can be transferred to someone else as, for example, in the following terms: "That which I legated to Titius I give and legate to Seius," a formula which involves an implied ademption against Titius.

6   PAUL, *Lex Julia et Papia, book 5:* There are four ways in which a transfer of legacy can occur: where a legacy is transferred from one recipient to another; where it is transferred from the person who was instructed to deliver it so that someone else is to do so; where something is given in place of something else, for example, ten aurei instead of a piece of land; where an absolute gift is turned into a conditional one.   1. Although it is usually held that if I charge Maevius to deliver that which previously Titius had been charged to deliver they are both under an obligation to deliver the same thing, the more correct view is that in this case the legacy has been adeemed, the grounds being that when I say, "let Seius be charged to deliver that which previously I charged Titius to deliver," I am in effect saying that Titius should not deliver the legacy.   2. Again, some think that if ten are legated in place of a piece of land, the previous legacy has not been adeemed. But the more correct view is that it has, since it is the most recent expression of wishes that is upheld.

7   ULPIAN, *Sabinus, book 24:* But if something which has been given absolutely to one individual is then legated under condition to another, the first recipient is not considered thereby to have lost the legacy irrevocably but only if the condition imposed upon the second is fulfilled. However, if the testator's intention was that the first recipient be totally deprived of the legacy the view will have to be taken that the latter has been adeemed from the first recipient.

8   JULIAN, *Digest, book 32:* Consequently, if the person to whom a legacy has been transferred dies during the lifetime of the testator, the legacy in question will still not belong to the person from whom it was transferred.

9 ULPIAN, *Disputations, book 5:* Suppose that a testator left someone one hundred absolutely and then legated the same amount to the same person with a condition attached. If the testator wished the second sum of one hundred to count as a separate sum of money, then that which was left absolutely will be owed immediately and that which had a condition imposed upon it will be owed on the fulfillment of the condition. But if he had changed his mind and it was the same sum of money that he left under condition, then the previous absolute gift will be held to have turned into a conditional one. Therefore, if in the same will in which he has named the sum of one hundred, the testator later on leaves fifty then, if he wished these fifty to be distinct from the one hundred, a sum of one hundred fifty will have to be delivered, but if he wished only fifty to be delivered, that is all that has to be delivered. The same applies if this was done in a codicil.

10 JULIAN, *Digest, book 37:* If a legacy which was given absolutely to Titius is conditionally adeemed and Titius dies while the question of the fulfillment of the condition is pending, then even if the condition is not fulfilled, the legacy will not belong to Titius's heir, since when a legacy is conditionally adeemed the situation is exactly as if it had been given under the opposite condition. 1. When a legacy has been made in the following terms, "let my heir give ten to Titius; and if he does not do so, let him give the same amount to Sempronius," if Titius dies before the *dies cedens* of the legacy, Sempronius can properly lay claim to it, since the legacy will have to be regarded as having been transferred.

11 JULIAN, *Digest, book 54:* Anyone who legates "a slave" but adeems "Stichus" does not annul the legacy but only weakens it,

12 ULPIAN, *Sabinus, book 50:* to the extent that the legatee cannot elect to have Stichus.

13 MARCIAN, *Institutes, book 6:* The deified Severus and Antoninus stated in a rescript that where a testator is for some reason induced to add in a final provision that a particular freedman is of very bad character, that which was left to the latter under an earlier provision should be considered adeemed.

14 FLORENTINUS, *Institutes, book 1:* Legacies whose grant is invalid are not confirmed by ademption. An example would be a situation in which a man is appointed heir, an absolute legacy is given to his slave and this is then conditionally adeemed, since an absolute legacy, if conditionally adeemed, is regarded as a legacy given under the opposite condition and is, by virtue of that interpretation, confirmed. But the purpose of ademption is to prevent, not to lead to, a legacy being owed. 1. Whatever circumstances cause the gift of a legacy to be invalid also cause an ademption to be ineffective, for example, if you partially adeem a right of way or impose a partial veto on someone's freedom.

15 PAUL, *The Assignment of Freedmen, sole book:* Where a slave is legated by a testator and is then alienated and reacquired by the latter, the claim of the legatee can be defeated by the defense of fraud. Of course, if the legatee proves a renewed intention on the testator's part that he should have the slave he will not be debarred from receipt.

16 PAUL, *Law of Codicils, sole book:* There is no difference between the erasure and the ademption of a provision.

17 CELSUS, *Digest, book 22:* Nothing prevents the correction, alteration, or cancellation of an earlier provision by a later one.

18 MODESTINUS, *Distinctions, book 8:* If, during his lifetime, a testator gives someone property previously legated to someone else, the legacy is entirely extinguished. We make no distinction according to whether the gift was the result of financial constraints or of simple inclination such that in the former case the legacy is owed and in

the latter case is not, since such a distinction makes no allowance for generosity on the donor's part given that nobody in financial difficulties is liberal.

19   MODESTINUS, *Replies, book 11:* Modestinus replied that where the deceased, while adeeming a legacy which had been left to Maevius, did not wish to revoke a *fideicommissum* with which the latter had been charged, the view that the heirs could be sued on the basis of the *fideicommissum* was rightly approved.

20   POMPONIUS, *Quintus Mucius, book 1:* If I transfer a legacy to someone with whom we do not have *testamenti factio* or to one of my own slaves, making him the legacy without a grant of freedom, then, even though the legacy is not owed to these persons, it is not owed to the person from whom it was adeemed either.

21   LICINNIUS RUFINUS, *Rules, book 4:* A legacy cannot be adeemed from anyone other than the person to whom it was given. Consequently, if a legacy has been made to someone else's son or slave, it cannot be adeemed from the father or owner.

22   PAPINIAN, *Replies, book 6:* A man was appointed partial heir and also received a legacy. As a result of a serious personal quarrel, the testator omitted to mention him when he began, but was unable to complete making a new will. Actions in respect of the inheritance are not to be denied to him, but if he lays claim to the legacy, he can be resisted by means of a defense of fraud.

23   PAPINIAN, *Replies, book 7:* A man divided his goods among his sons but wished his daughter to receive a sum of three hundred aurei derived from his stipend as a *primipilus.* Subsequently, he used the money from the stipend to acquire a piece of property. The sons and co-heirs nonetheless will have to execute the *fideicommissum* in favor of their sister, because anything which is subsumed in the father's estate is not regarded as having been consumed. Since, however, after dividing his estate among his sons, his intention was that any undivided property should belong to all the co-heirs, it is agreed that the piece of property bought with the money from the stipend should be divided, so that the daughter may receive her hereditary portion from the money yielded by the sale. For this is what would happen if the cash had been left among the testator's goods.

24   PAPINIAN, *Replies, book 8:* When a legacy given under condition is transferred, it is regarded as having been transferred under the same condition, provided that the condition is not one that is tied to the person of the original legatee. For if someone makes a legacy to his wife, to be paid in the event of her having children, the condition, which applied to the person of his wife, is not deemed to be repeated in the event of the legacy being transferred to a sister or other related woman. 1. A man legated some gardens together with their appurtenances to his daughter. Subsequently, he gave some of the slaves belonging to the gardens to his wife. Whether or not he confirmed the gift his later wishes take precedence over the legacy to his daughter. In fact, even if the gift is invalid, he is regarded as having diminished his daughter's legacy.

25   PAPINIAN, *Replies, book 9:* A man made a legacy *per praeceptionem* of a piece of land to one of two heirs. Next, he directed that right of action against debtors up to the amount for which the land was bought should be granted to the other heir. Later the piece of land was sold without the heir who had received it as a legacy *per praeceptionem* having offended the testator and the money realized became part of the estate. I replied that the actions should not be granted to the co-heir.

26   PAUL, *Questions, book 9:* If a legacy is given to a slave along with his freedom and the slave is then alienated and his freedom adeemed then, although an ademption applied to someone else's property is void, nonetheless, the legacy will not pass to the purchaser. This is as it should be since the ademption stands because the slave can be repurchased, just as the grant of a legacy stands if that legacy was given to someone who at the time of the making of the will belonged to the testator but who was later alienated and granted freedom in a codicil. 1. What happens if, during his lifetime, a man manumits a slave whom, in his will, he had directed to be freed and whose freedom he then adeemed in a codicil? Let us consider whether the mere ademption of liberty annuls the legacy. Some think that it does. But the existence of a superfluous provision does not adversely affect a legacy.

27   PAUL, *Questions, book 21:* Suppose that a slave is both the object and the recipient of a legacy. If he is alienated and the legacy made to him is adeemed, that ademption is valid since the legacy can be effected if the slave is repurchased. 1. Suppose that a slave is given a legacy and is then manumitted during the lifetime of the testator. If the legacy is adeemed, that ademption is of no significance, and so he will get the legacy which was given to him since, even if he

reverts to servile status, his legacy will not be revived because he is considered to be a new slave.

28   VALENS, *Fideicommissa, book 5:* If I legate you a specific piece of property and ask you to deliver it to Titius and later leave you the same piece of property as a *fideicommissum* without asking you to give it to somebody else the question arises of whether, by virtue of the existence of the *fideicommissum,* it lies in your power to elect not to execute the charge laid upon you. The view which has been preferred is that we should respect the later testamentary provision.

29   PAUL, *Views, book 3:* If a freedman receives a legacy in the first part of a will and is then, later in the same document, described by the testator as ungrateful, the latter's change of mind means that the former has no right of action under the will.

30   SCAEVOLA, *Digest, book 20:* A testatrix legated a number of items to her foster daughter. Later she removed some of these items but requested her heir to see to the delivery of certain others, among which she wished to be included twenty. The provision ran: "I further give and legate and wish to be delivered twenty pounds of gold" to which she added: "I charge you, Attius, with a *fideicommissum* to protect and guide your sister Sempronia in accordance with your sense of duty toward her and, in the event of your considering her to have returned to a proper life-style, to give her twenty pounds of gold when you die. In the meantime, you are to provide her with the income from the twenty pounds of gold, to wit interest at one half-percent per month." In a subsequent codicil, she transferred the same twenty pounds of gold to Maevius and imposed a *fideicommissum* on him in the following terms: "I wish the twenty pounds of gold which, in my will, I left to my foster daughter, Sempronia, to be given to Maevius on the provision of *cautiones* that he, from that sum, will provide the said Sempronia with five denarii per month for as long as she lives as well as one hundred twenty-five denarii per month for clothing, and I charge this to you as a *fideicommissum.* I am sure, Maevius, that you will, in accordance with your sense of duty, request your heir to see to it that my wishes in respect of my foster daughter continue to be fulfilled after your death." The question arises of whether the legatee Maevius is to be compelled to deliver the twenty pounds of gold to Sempronia after his death as the heir Attius had been requested to do. He replied that, given the circumstances as outlined above, Maevius is not to be compelled to deliver the twenty pounds of gold but that the other charges made upon him in favor of the foster daughter should be executed by him and his heir so long as the foster daughter lives. 1. In her will, Titia appointed the freedwoman Seia, who was also her foster sister, as heir in the twelfth part and granted certain land to her freedman Pamphilus by *fideicommissum.* Among this land was a σύγκτησις of the pieces of land described as being "near Kolone." In a subsequent letter, she gave some other pieces of property to Pamphilus and in this letter she spoke of Seia and Pamphilus as follows: "Titia to my heirs, greetings. I wish all the provisions set out below which I have already made in respect of the person of Pamphilus to be ratified. In the event of my foster sister Seia not becoming heir in the proportion that I have laid down, I wish her to be given the σύγκτησις near Kolone." Seia chose to forego the share of the inheritance allotted to her in the will and elected to have the benefit of the *fideicommissum* in the codicil, that is, the σύγκτησις near Kolone. The question arises of whether, if Pamphilus makes a *vindicatio* of the same property on the basis of the *fideicommissum,* he should be resisted by means of a defense of fraud. He replied that the *fideicommissum* of the land, that is, the σύγκτησις near Kolone, should be regarded as having been transferred to the freedwoman Seia. 2. A testator requested his heirs, in the event of his death abroad, to give sixty to Lucius Titius for him to see to the return home of the body and added: "I wish any surplus from this sixty to be bestowed upon Titius." On the same day, he addressed a codicil to his heirs in the following terms: "In the event of my dying abroad or while on a journey, I request you to see to it that my body is brought back to my sons' tomb in Campania." The question arises of whether he had in effect adeemed the surplus of the sixty from Lucius Titius. He replied that such an ademption should be considered to

have occurred.   3. In one and the same will, a man appointed his daughters heirs in different proportions and made a division of almost all his goods. He then added: "All the rest of my goods together with any liabilities attaching to my estate are to belong to my two daughters Prima and Secunda alone or to whichever of them survives." In a subsequent codicil, he made a quite different division of his goods among the same daughters from that in his will. Some items, however, he did not specifically give to anybody. The question arises of whether the daughters Prima and Secunda could successfully claim on the basis of the wording of the will to be the sole owners of those items which were not specifically given to anybody in the more recent division made by their father. He replied that the testator should not be deemed to have changed his mind totally but only in relation to those matters which he reformulated.   4. A woman made the following provision in a letter concerning the legacy and hereditary portion of her son: "Since I understand that my son Priscillianus is at death's door, I consider it entirely just and dutiful to legate his hereditary portion in equal proportions to my brother Marianus and my husband Januarius. Similarly, in the event of Priscillianus's death, I give and legate to the same persons and wish to be delivered to them anything further that I have legated to my son." Priscillianus survived the opening of the will but later died of the same illness. The question arises of whether his legacy should also belong to Januarius and Marianus by virtue of the *fideicommissum*. He replied that if it was from the same illness that he died, she should certainly be deemed also to have transferred his legacy to the persons in question.

31   SCAEVOLA, *Digest, book 14:* A testator appointed his son partial heir and legated to him two pieces of land together with the slaves and all the appurtenances belonging to them. The same man also left his wife several legacies including the slaves Stichus and Dama. However, discovering that one of the pieces of land already legated to his son in addition to his hereditary portion had no bailiff, he sent Stichus to take charge of its cultivation and accounts. The question arises, does Stichus belong to the testator's wife or his son? He replied that since the testator knew what provisions he had made in his will, Stichus, as bailiff, belonged with the piece of land to which he had been sent and that the wife could not lay claim to him on the basis of the *fideicommissum*.   1. A man legated four pieces of land to his mother whom he had appointed as partial heir and charged her with a *fideicommissum* to deliver two of them to his father-in-law. In a later codicil, he adeemed the *fideicommissum* made in favor of his father-in-law. The question arises of whether the pieces of land still belonged to the mother on the basis of the earlier legacy. I replied that there was no reason in the circumstances stated why they should not do so.   2. In her will, Seia legated five pounds of gold to her stepson Titius. Titius accused her of having ordered the murder of his father. After the accusation was lodged, Seia made a codicil but did not adeem Titius's legacy. Then, before the hearing of the accusation had been completed, she died. At the conclusion of the case the judgment rendered was that the death of Titius's father had not been criminally procured by Seia. My question was whether, in view of the fact that Seia did not in her codicil adeem the legacy which she had given to Titius, that legacy was owed to him by Seia's heirs. He replied that, given the facts as stated above, it was not owed.   3. Among other things a man legated to his daughter-in-power her *peculium*. After the making of the will, he exacted some money from one of his daughter's debtors and treated it as his own. My question was whether the daughter could on this account bring an action against her father's heirs. He replied that she could do so, provided that she was able to prove that her father had not acted as he did with the intention of adeeming her legacy.

32   VENULEIUS, *Actions, book 10:* If all that is involved in a legacy is cash, it is a simple matter to make subtractions or additions. But when it is a question of physical objects, drafting becomes more difficult and the apportionment obscure.   1. Where a grant of freedom to some slaves is adeemed, there is no point in specifically adeeming any legacies left to them.

DUBIOUS CASES

1 PAPINIAN, *Replies, book 7:* A testator legated to Titius either the Maevian or the Seian farm. The treatment as a whole estate of several pieces of land under the name "Maevian farm" was demonstrated in his accounts. I replied that the deceased should not be regarded as having wished the inclusion of these other pieces of land in the legacy, provided that the values of the Seian and Maevian farms did not differ by any great amount.

2 PAPINIAN, *Replies, book 9:* A legacy or *fideicommissum* given to the citizens of a city is regarded as having been given to the city.

3 PAUL, *Questions, book 14:* Where a statement is ambiguous, the person uttering it is not saying both the things that it might be interpreted as meaning but only that which he intends to say. Thus, if someone says something different from what he intended, he neither says what the words mean, because that is not what he intends to say, nor says what he intends, because his formulation is wrong.

4 (5) PAUL, *Replies, book 19:* Paul replied: There is no doubt that when the name of the fideicommissary is not entered in the will the *fideicommissum* should not be deemed to have been given to any person defined or undefined.

5 (6) GAIUS, *Fideicommissa, book 1:* A man who had suffered relegation made a will and, after appointing an heir and granting legacies to certain individuals, added the following provision: "If any of my heirs or other friends whom I have mentioned in this will or any other person successfully petitions the emperor for my recall and I die before I can thank him, I wish such-and-such a sum to be given him by the other heirs." One of the persons whom the testator had put down as his heirs successfully negotiated his recall, but he died before learning of this. Consulted on the question of whether the *fideicommissum* should be executed, Julian replied that it should be, and that even if it was not an heir or legatee but some other friend who organized the testator's restoration, the *fideicommissum* should be executed in his favor as well. 1. Suppose that somebody requests the delivery of his inheritance to you and a posthumous child, either his own *suus heres* or the child of another,

6 (7) MAECIANUS, *Fideicommissa, book 3:* or appoints you and his posthumous child partial heirs or gives a legacy or a *fideicommissum* in a similar fashion.

7 (8) GAIUS, *Fideicommissa, book 1:* A question arises: does the posthumous child only get its share if it is born alive or does it also get it if it is not? I consider it more appropriate to hold that if the posthumous child is not born alive, it does not get its share and the whole sum in question belongs to you, just as if it had been left to you in the first place, but that if it is born alive, both parties should receive what was left to them, so that if there is one child, you will be entitled to half the estate; if two, to a third; if three, for triplets do occur, to a quarter. In our own time, in fact, an Alexandrine woman called Serapias was presented to Hadrian with the five children she had borne in one confinement. However, where more than three children are born at once, the event is regarded as almost sinister. 1. When a testator appoints several heirs and charges one of them with a *fideicommissum* by which, at his death, he is to pass that share of the inheritance which had come to him to whichever of the co-heirs he may choose, it is quite correct to hold the *fideicommissum* to be valid, since what is left to the discretion of the heir is not whether he should deliver his share at all, but rather to whom he should deliver it. For it makes a great deal of difference whether the testator leaves the person whom he is placing under an obligation a choice on the issue of delivery of the estate or constrains him to deliver it and concedes freedom only on the issue of how that delivery is carried out. 2. The question arises of whether, if someone is instructed to deliver his portion to his co-heirs and the latter are appointed

heirs in different proportions from one another, he must do so to each individual equally or in proportion to the shares of the inheritance they are put down as receiving. The decision was as follows: Suppose the testator directed the person in question to deliver his portion on condition that the co-heirs give him a sum of money. If the latter were instructed to contribute equal portions to that sum it appears logical that they should receive equal shares under the *fideicommissum*. But if the testator made it clear that the co-heirs should contribute unequal portions, matching their hereditary portions, it is logical that the *fideicommissum* should also be executed in proportion to their hereditary shares.

8   (9) PAUL, *Views*, book 2: If a gift has been made between man and wife and the recipient is the first to die, it reverts to the party who made the gift. If the party who made a gift at the time of marriage survives and is predeceased by the recipient, the gift remains with the donor. But if the recipient and the donor die at the same time, it is generally agreed that for the sake of settling the question then arising, the gift counts as valid, the chief reason being that a donor who could make a *condictio* for the property in question does not survive.

9   (10) TRYPHONINUS, *Disputations*, book 21: A man who had two sons who were *impuberes* appointed Titius as a substitute for whichever of them died second. Both of them died together in a shipwreck. The question arises of whether any inheritance should go to the substitute and, if so, to which of the two sons he succeeds. I said that if they had died one after the other the first to die would be succeeded by his brother as intestate heir and the second by the substitute, the latter's inheritance including the estate of the first brother to die. However, in the question before us, where the two brothers died at the same time, will the substitute be heir to both of them on the grounds that since neither brother survived the other both of them, as it were, died second and there was no succession of one by the other, or will he be heir to neither of them on the grounds that the existence of the "second to die" is dependent on one of them dying first? The former view, that he is heir to both, is more deserving of acceptance on the grounds that even if someone who has only one son appoints a substitute for the son who is last to die he is not considered to have made an invalid substitution; and a relative is considered the "nearest agnate" even if he is the only relative and there is no other one for him to take precedence over. In the present case, therefore, since neither brother survived the other, they are each regarded as having died both first and second.   1. In a case in which a man died in war together with his son and the mother made a *vindicatio* of her son's goods on the grounds that he died second, while the father's relatives made a similar *vindicatio* on the grounds that the son died first, the deified Hadrian took the view that the father was the first to die.   2. If a freedman dies at the same time as his son and without leaving a will, the inheritance passes to the freedman's patron as *legitimus heres*, unless it be proved that the son outlived his father. We hold to this view under the influence of the respect due to a patron.   3. If a man and his wife die at the same time, a stipulation concerning her dowry under the title, "if the wife dies during the marriage," will take effect, unless she be proved to have survived her husband.   4. If Lucius Titius dies at the same time as a son who is *pubes* and whom he has entered in his will as sole heir, the son is deemed to have survived his father and, under the terms of the will, to have been his heir, and the inheritance is passed to the son's successor unless the contrary be proved. But if a son who is still *impubes* dies at the same time as his father, the father is deemed to have survived him unless, in this case too, the contrary is proved.

10   (11) ULPIAN, *Disputations*, book 6: If a legacy has been left "to whichever of my cognatic relatives is the first to climb the Capitol" and two of them are reported to have done so at the same time without it being clear which one arrived first, will execution of the legacy be impeded? A similar question arises if the legacy was for the person who erects a monument and several persons do so; or if it was for "the oldest" and there are two persons of the same age; or if the legacy was left for the testator's friend Sempronius and he has two equally close friends of that name. Again, if a legacy is left to two people with the same name, for example, Sempronius, and is then adeemed from "Sempronius" without it being clear which Sempronius is meant, the

question can be asked whether the gift is invalidated in respect of both Sempronii or the ademption is void. There is a similar problem if freedom is legated to one or more of several slaves who bear the same name. In all these cases, the more correct opinion is that the execution both of legacies and of grants of freedom is impeded but that any ademption takes effect against neither party.   1. It is clear that if a female slave has received freedom on the following terms, "let her be free if the first child she bears is male" and she gives birth at the same confinement to two children, one male and one female, then, provided that it is certain which child was born first, there is no reason for doubt to arise either about her status, that is, whether or not she is free, or about that of the female child, since, if she was the second to be born she will be of free birth. However, if there is uncertainty as to the order of the births and no clarification can be secured even by careful judicial investigation, then, since the circumstances are controversial, the more humane view should be adopted whereby the slave obtains her freedom and her daughter the status of being freeborn on the presumption that the male child was the firstborn.

11   (12) JULIAN, *Digest, book 36:* Where the usufruct of a piece of property is legated to a number of freedmen and ownership of it to the last survivor of the group, the legacy is valid; for I regard ownership as having been given to all the freedmen under the condition "if he be the last survivor."

12   (13) JULIAN, *Digest, book 50:* Where a formulation is an action or defense is ambiguous, the most appropriate rule is rather to accept that interpretation which validates the instrument than that which nullifies it.

13   (14) JULIAN, *Ambiguities, sole book:* Suppose somebody who has deposited a sum of two hundred makes a legacy in the following terms: "I legate to Seius three hundred along with the two hundred I have deposited with him." The two sums of money taken individually each have a clear designation, but, taken together in this manner, they are liable to be the object of controversy. However, the view should be taken that it is not three hundred but five hundred that are to be delivered, the two sums being conjoined.   1. If a man makes a legacy in the following terms, "let my heir give the Seian farm to Attius with Dion the slave of Maevius," a doubt may arise as to whether Dion is the recipient of the legated farm along with Attius or the object of a legacy along with the farm. The preferable view is that it is not only the estate but also the slave Dion that is being legated, especially if the testator had no good reason for making a legacy to Dion.   2. When we formulate a stipulation in the following terms, "do you undertake in the event of your failure to deliver such-and-such a slave or such-and-such a piece of land to pay one hundred," both actions must be performed to prevent the stipulation becoming operative; that is, the stipulation will apply both in the event of neither of the actions being performed and in the event of only one of them being performed. Clearly, the same is true when we specify several actions we wish performed and make a stipulation on the basis "if any of this is not carried out," for example, if we say, "will you produce Stichus and Dama and Eros in court; do you undertake in the event of any of them not appearing to pay ten," it is necessary for all of them to appear for the stipulation to be satisfied. Or, to come closer to the matter in hand, let us imagine a stipulation formulated in the following terms: "Do you undertake in the event of your failing to produce Stichus and Dama and Eros to pay ten?" In that case, we shall be in no doubt that the obligation to appear applies to all of them equally.   3. Between the formulation "provided that this or that action is not performed" and the formulation "if any of the actions whose performance is herein included is not carried out," there is this difference: Although the performance of one or other action means that it is true that this one or that one has in fact been carried out, it does not follow that this one or that one has not been carried out. For the two propositions, though of contradictory form, can be simultaneously true since, when the sense depends not on the whole but only on part of a statement, any element of truth verifies the whole statement. The same applies in the opposite case of two state-

ments containing inconsistent elements which are both false. For example, if, out of a group of children, some die after attaining puberty and some die while still *impuberes*, then both the statement that all died as *minores* and the statement that all died after attaining puberty are false. This is because the sense depends on the whole of the statement, so that any element of falsehood falsifies the whole statement. Therefore, one must take care to identify the relevant question accurately. When I use the formulation, "provided that this or that action is not performed," the question is whether there is something that has not been done. But when I use the formulation, "if this and that action are not performed," the question is whether both actions have been performed. The effect of the former formulation is that neither action should be performed, that of the latter formulation that both actions should be performed. In the first case, it is of no advantage not to have performed one of the actions if the other has been performed; in the latter case, it is of no advantage to have performed one of them if the other has not been performed. 4. Accordingly, if someone asks, "did you perform any of the actions you were required to perform," and the person questioned says, "no," he means to say, "I did not perform any of the actions I was required to perform," that is, "I performed none of them." 5. But if one wishes to introduce several actions into a stipulation, one of which one wishes performed, it should be done as follows: "Do you undertake to perform this or that action? Will you pay such-and-such an amount in the event of neither of them being performed?" 6. Again, if a head of household makes the following provision in his will, "if a son or a daughter is born to me, let him or her be my heir; in the event of a son or daughter of mine not becoming my heir, let Seius be my heir," he has failed to make his intentions sufficiently clear, if what he meant was that there should only be an *extraneus heres* in the event of neither his son nor his daughter becoming his heir. The provision should be formulated as follows: "in the event of neither my son nor my daughter becoming my heir." Sometimes, however, the earlier formulation is what the situation requires, if a man who has a son and a daughter wishes to appoint both of them as his heirs but to add an *extraneus heres* in the event of only one of them becoming his heir and to substitute an *extraneus heres* in the event of neither of them doing so. But the preferable view is that the testator's words should be so interpreted that in the event of either a son or a daughter being born to him the *extraneus heres* will not be admitted as heir unless the testator has specifically stated otherwise.

14 (15) MARCIAN, *Institutes, book 6:* Trebatius considers that if somebody makes the following provision, "let my heir give ten to the persons who put their seals to my will," the legacy is valid. Pomponius thinks that this is the better view because the will itself is confirmed by using the witnesses and I agree.

15 (16) MARCIAN, *Rules, book 2:* There are circumstances in which doubt arises, but subsequent events clearly determine what happened. For example, suppose that a piece of property has been legated and, while the legatee is considering whether to accept the legacy, the heir delivers it to someone else. In that case, if the legatee decides that he wants the legacy, the delivery is null and void, but if he rejects the legacy, the delivery is valid. The same applies if an heir lends money from the inheritance which is the object of a legacy. If the legatee does not reject the legacy, the heir has made a loan of money that does not belong to him, but if the legatee does reject it, the heir is regarded as having loaned his own money. What if the money has been spent? A similar view will have to be taken, depending on the circumstances.

16 (17) MARCIAN, *Rules, book 3:* The questions that we discuss in relation to persons who die at the same time as one another can be raised in other contexts as well. For example, suppose that a mother stipulates that her daughter's dowry should be returned to her by the husband in the event of her daughter's death during marriage and that the mother dies at the same time as her daughter. Does an action under the stipulation pass to the mother's heir who would not be entitled to it if the daughter died after her mother? The deified Pius stated in a rescript that the stipulation does not

become operative because the mother did not outlive her daughter. 1. Again, the question arises of whether in the event of an outsider who has stipulated a dowry dying at the same time as the husband or as the woman on whose account he made the stipulation the said outsider can transmit a right of action to his heir.

17 (18) PAUL, *Plautius, book 12:* The case is the same if a dowry is legated to a woman and she dies at the same time as her husband.

18 (19) MARCIAN, *Rules, book 3:* In the case in which a *pupillus* and his brother, who had been appointed *heres necessarius* as his substitute, die at the same time the question arises whether one brother becomes the other's heir or not. Or if two persons are appointed *heredes necessarii* as each other's substitute and then die at the same time, are any heirs deemed to exist? Similar problems arise where two persons are requested to deliver an inheritance to each other. In such cases, if the two parties die at the same time and it is unclear which was the first to expire neither is regarded as having outlived the other. 1. For the purposes of the *lex Falcidia* also if a man dies at the same time as some of his slaves, the latter are not counted as being among his goods at the time of his death.

19 (20) ULPIAN, *Sabinus, book 25:* If a legacy is made to cognatic relatives of the testator and they then cease to be his relatives but do not emigrate, the view must be taken that the legacy is owed since they were relatives at the time of the making of the will. Of course, anyone who, at the time of the making of the will was not a relative but became one by *adrogatio* at the time of the testator's death secures his legacy quite easily. 1. If someone makes a legacy to his "cognatic kindred," this is the same as if he had made it to his "cognatic relatives."

20 (21) PAUL, *Plautius, book 12:* Given that during the reign of the deified Marcus the senate permitted the making of legacies to *collegia*, there is no doubt that provided the *collegium* in question is legal, the legacy should be delivered. If, however, the *collegium* is not legal, any legacy made to it will be invalid, unless it was made to the members individually; for in that case, they will be allowed to have the legacy not as a *collegium* but as defined individuals.

21 (22) PAUL, *Plautius, book 14:* Where there is a verbal ambiguity, for example, if I stipulate Stichus and there are several persons of that name or for a slave at Carthage and there are two places of that name, it is the interpretation that corresponds to the parties' intentions that is valid. 1. In cases of doubt, the principle that should always be followed is that except where a provision is patently contrary to the laws, any contract made in good faith should be accorded the maximum protection.

22 (23) JAVOLENUS, *From Cassius, book 5:* A woman died in a shipwreck along with her son who had attained puberty. Granted the impossibility of determining which of them died first, it is more generous to regard the son as having lived longer.

23 (24) GAIUS, *Lex Julia et Papia, book 5:* If a woman dies in a shipwreck along with a son who is *impubes*, the son is regarded as the first to have been killed.

24 (25) MARCELLUS, *Digest, book 11:* Where a testamentary provision is either ambiguous or incorrectly drafted, it should be interpreted generously, and any credible intention on the testator's part should be credited.

25 (26) CELSUS, *Digest, book 22:* "Let him whom I tell my heir I wish to be free be free. Let my heir be charged to deliver a legacy to him to whom I charge such a legacy to be delivered." If any line of reasoning can establish the identity of the person about whom the testator was speaking, the latter's wishes are to be carried out.

26 (27) CELSUS, *Digest, book 26:* Where a question arises about the intention of a stipulation, any ambiguity works against the stipulator.

27 (28) MODESTINUS, *Rules, book 1:* If a testator wishes one of a number of slaves to be manumitted but it is not clear which one he has in mind, the freedom granted under the *fideicommissum* does not take effect in favor of any of them.

28 (29) JAVOLENUS, *From the Posthumous Works of Labeo, book 3:* A man who owned a fuller called Flaccus and a baker called Philonicus legated "Flaccus the baker" to his wife. Is only one of them to be delivered and, if so, which one? Or are both to be delivered? It was decided that in the first instance that slave was legated whom the

testator thought he was legating, but that if this was not clear, the first thing to consider was whether the owner knew the names of his slaves. If he did, then it is the slave who is named that should be delivered, the error being supposed to lie in the description of his trade. But if he did not, then it is the baker who should be deemed to have been legated just as if no name had been given to him.

29 (30) SCAEVOLA, *Digest, book 18:* In his will, a testator manumitted several slaves, including Sabina and Cyprogenia, the manumission to take effect when each of them reached thirty years of age, and expressed the wish that when they became free, a specified sum of money should be given to them. In an adjoining clause, he also made the following provision: "When they reach the age laid down, I wish Sabina and Cyprogenia to be given ten plus an additional ten each per year for as long as they live for their maintenance." The question arises of whether provision for maintenance has to be given to all the slaves manumitted or only to Sabina and Cyprogenia. He replied that given the circumstances as stated above, provision of maintenance should be regarded as having been legated to all of them.

6

LEGACIES MADE BY WAY OF PENALTY

1 AFRICANUS, *Questions, book:* He replied that where a son-in-power or a slave has been appointed heir, any illegal or insulting legacy which will act as a penalty even against the father or owner is of no weight; for any testamentary provision based on the last wishes of a testator who intends to inflict a penalty is held to be of no weight, whether the provision relates to the heir's benefit or to that of some other party.

2 MARCIAN, *Institutes, book 6:* It is the intention of the testator that distinguishes a condition from a penalty and the question of whether a given clause is a penalty, a condition, or a transfer is decided on the basis of the wishes of the deceased. The deified Severus and Antoninus stated this in a rescript.

7

THE CATONIAN RULE

1 CELSUS, *Digest, book 35:* The Catonian Rule is as follows: "Any legacy which would have been invalid if the testator had died at the time of the making of the will is invalid whenever he dies." In some cases, this statement of the rule is misleading. 1. For suppose someone makes a legacy in the following terms: "If I die after the Kalends, let such-and-such a sum be given to Titius." Are we going to quibble about this? The more correct view is that in the event of the testator's immediate death, the situation is one in which the legacy does not take effect rather than one in which it was invalidly made. 2. Similarly, if a piece of land which at the time of the making of the will was your property is legated to you on the understanding that you will alienate it during the testator's lifetime, the legacy is owed to you, but would not have been owed in the event of the testator's immediate death.

2 PAUL, *Plautius, book 4:* But if someone makes a legacy on the condition that "my daughter will marry Titius," it has been held sufficient that she is shown to be married at the time of the testator's death, even if at the time of the making of the will she was *impubes.*

3 PAPINIAN, *Questions, book 15:* The Catonian Rule does not apply to inheritances or legacies whose *dies cedens* is not the time of death, but the acceptance of the inheritance.

4 ULPIAN, *Sabinus, book 10:* It is agreed that the Catonian Rule does not apply to conditional appointment of heirs.

5 ULPIAN, *Sabinus, book 22:* The Catonian Rule does not apply to new laws.

8

PROVISIONS DEEMED NOT TO HAVE BEEN WRITTEN

1   JULIAN, *Digest, book 78:* Suppose someone writes into a will an inheritance or a legacy to himself. The question arises of whether the inheritance or legacy should be deemed not to have been written. And what is the position if an appointment of this sort is subject to a substitution? I replied: "The portion of the inheritance about which you have sought my opinion belongs to the substitute; for when the senate fixed the penalties under the *lex Cornelia* against a person who writes in an inheritance or legacy to himself, it appears to have regarded such a procedure with the same disapproval as that shown to appointments of the following sort: "Let Titius be my heir in the same proportion as that in which he has read out that he has appointed me heir in his will"; consequently, both appointments are treated just as though they were never inserted into the will.

2   ALFENUS VARUS, *Digest, book 5:* Any testamentary provisions whose meaning is incomprehensible are treated just as if they were never made. But the rest of the will's provisions retain their validity independently.

3   MARCIAN, *Institutes, book 11:* Anything, apart from provision of maintenance, left to someone condemned to the mines is deemed not to have been written but does not belong to the imperial treasury, since the criminal is the slave of the penalty not of the emperor. The deified Pius states this in a rescript.   1. If an appointed heir or legatee is condemned to the mines after the making of the will, that which was left to him does not belong to the imperial treasury either.   2. Again, if something is legated to another person's slave and that slave is subsequently acquired by the testator, the legacy is extinguished since, if the circumstances affecting a provision become such that, had they obtained before, the provision could not have been made, the provision in question is deemed not to have been written.

4   ULPIAN, *Lex Julia et Papia, book 13:* If at the time at which a legacy was made the legatee was not alive, the legacy is deemed not to have been written.   1. If at the time of the making of the will the beneficiary in question was in the hands of enemies and if he fails to return from captivity, the provision will be deemed not to have been written. Julian writes to this effect.

5   PAUL, *Questions, book 12:* If anyone has written into a will that something be given to himself and has been instructed by the testator that he should deliver it to another person, it remains in the hands of the heir together with the attached fideicommissary obligation, even though the provision is deemed not to have been written. The same applies even in the case of a soldier's will.

9

LEGACIES TAKEN AWAY ON GROUNDS OF UNFITNESS

1   MARCIAN, *Institutes, book 6:* The deified Severus and Antoninus stated in a rescript that a freedman should be deprived of a legacy on *fideicommissum* left him under his patron's will on grounds of unfitness if he denounces the latter after his death for being engaged in illegal traffic, even if he earns a reward by so doing.

2   MARCIAN, *Institutes, book 11:* An inheritance is taken away in its entirety and belongs to the imperial treasury if, against the terms of his father's will, an emancipated son claims *bonorum possessio* on the grounds that he has been passed over and accepts the inheritance as a substitute for an *impubes*.   1. Again, the deified Severus and Antoninus stated in a rescript that if a man infringes imperial instructions by marrying a woman from a province in which he is performing some official function, he may not keep anything he acquires under his wife's will, just as a similar rule applies to the case of a tutor who marries his *pupilla* in contravention of senatorial decree. In both cases, even if the man was appointed sole heir and has accepted the inheritance, there is forfeiture to the imperial treasury, the inheritance being taken away on grounds of unfitness.   2. On the other hand, the preferable view is that the woman illegally married by a provincial official or by her tutor is allowed to receive property under their wills and should not be excluded as unfit.   3. The same rule will apply to anyone who makes a gift of all or part of the goods of a cognatic relative of his during the latter's lifetime but without his knowledge.

He too will be deprived as unfit.

3   MARCIAN, *Rules, book 5:* The deified Pius decreed, as Marcellus, in the twelfth book of his *Digest,* reports, that a man who is clearly demonstrated to have negligently and culpably caused the death of a woman by whom he had been appointed heir is unfit.

4   ULPIAN, *Edict, book 14:* Papinian, in the fifth book of his *Questions,* says that someone who lays an accusation that the appointment of one of the heirs is a forgery will not be deprived of a legacy left to him as a charge upon a co-heir whose standing he has not questioned.

5   PAUL, *Law of the Imperial Treasury, book 1:* Even when a legacy has been received, it will remain permissible not only to arraign the will as a forgery but also to assert that it was not lawfully made. But it is not permitted to claim that it was undutiful. 1. A person who asserts that a will was not lawfully made, but fails to win his case is not excluded from receipt of that to which he is entitled under its terms. A person who secures a legacy and later claims that the provision was a forgery will have to lose what he secured. However, on the subject of a person who receives a legacy but claims that the will was not lawfully made, the deified Pius made the following statement in a rescript: "Although the relatives of Sophron have received legacies from the appointed heir, if the latter's status appears to be such that he may not obtain the inheritance and this inheritance really belongs to the said relatives by the law of intestacy, they can lay claim to it under that law. Whether or not they should be prohibited from bringing this claim will have to be determined by a judge after the case has been examined and on the basis of the identity, status, and age of the parties involved." 2. It is agreed that anyone who is appointed a tutor but excuses himself from administering the tutelage should lose that to which he is entitled under the will. If, however, he has already received it he should not be permitted to excuse himself from administering the tutelage. The position is, I think, different in the case of someone who is only entitled to a legacy under the will, and who is asked by the mother of the *pupillus* to become his tutor but chooses not to do so, since such a person has done nothing contrary to the wishes of the deceased. A legacy thus denied to a tutor does not pass to the imperial treasury but is left to the son whose interests have been ignored. 3. If a father or owner contests a will, he will also be denied an action for any legacy left to his son or slave if the benefit from the property would go to him. But if it concerns them personally a different view must be taken. 4. If someone entitled to a legacy is requested to manumit one of his slaves or even if both legacy and manumission are given to the slave himself, the view should be taken that the owner's action ought not to prejudice the slave's interests and that the latter should be purchased by the imperial treasury for him to be manumitted, provided that the party who has spurned the wishes of the deceased is prepared to sell him (which he cannot be forced to do). 5. Let us consider whether in the event of a son-in-power contesting a will an action should be denied to his father. I think that if he contests it without his father's consent, the latter should not be denied an action. 6. If someone to whom I am directed to deliver a legacy claims that the will is a forgery, I shall have to deliver the legacy to the imperial treasury. 7. In the event of someone who has contested the genuineness of a will becoming heir to a legatee or appointed heir, the view should be taken that the fact of his having contested the will ought not to prejudice his interests. 8. The case is similar to that of someone who claims that a will is undutiful. 9. Allowance must be made for the age of a person contesting a will, especially if it is a tutor or curator who wishes to claim that the will is forged or undutiful. The Emperors Severus and Antoninus issued a rescript to this effect. 10. However, an action is to be denied to those who, by their evidence, support the accusation leveled by someone who contests a will. The deified Severus issued a decree to this effect. 11. There are those who hold rightly that an action should be denied to anyone who assists somebody in contesting a will or who acts as *fideiussor* for him. 12. Some consider that if a governor pronounces a will forged and, after appeal, the appointed heir obtains the inheritance, the said governor is unfit to take under the will. 13. A representative of the imperial treasury who pursues the accusation leveled by someone who has denounced a will is adequately excused in all respects by the obligations of his office. 14. Anyone who attacks the main will should be excluded from benefit under *secundae tabulae* and under any codicil to the will, even if it is not confirmed. But the same line is not to be adopted if his attack is on the *secundae tabulae* or the codicil since in this case he is not considered to have impugned the will as well. 15. Let us consider whether a slave who attempts to nullify a will by his testimony should be deprived of the freedom granted to him under it. He is certainly unfit to receive the *fideicommissum;* and, as to his liberty, the deified Pius judged that he should be deprived of it. 16. An accusation of forgery does not assist someone appointed a tutor to obtain release from administering the tutelage; but he is excluded from receipt of any legacy. 17. The recipient of a gift *mortis causa* from the testator is not in this context similar to

a legatee. 18. The situation is different with someone who under the terms of the will is directed to receive something from a legatee or *statuliber*; for he is excluded as unfit. 19. The deified Pius and Marcus also considered that any benefit under the *lex Falcidia* should be taken away from the appointed heir. 20. All persons who are rejected as unfit should be excluded from receipt of the reward which, under an edict of the deified Trajan, is given to those who report themselves to the imperial treasury.

6   MARCELLUS, *Digest, book 22:* The emperor stated in a rescript that an heir is not entitled to keep a quarter of any property which he has abstracted. Consequently, if someone who possesses four hundred legates the whole four hundred and the heir takes away one hundred of them, he will be entitled to keep a quarter of the remaining three hundred, that is, seventy-five aurei, and he will have to deliver two hundred twenty-five to the legatee. Of the one hundred aurei that he removed he will have to deliver seventy-five to the legatee and the remainder, that is, twenty-five aurei will go to the imperial treasury.

7   MODESTINUS, *Distinctions, book 6:* Anyone who claims that Titius's will is forged but fails to win his case is not forbidden to become heir to Titius's heir since he does not thereby succeed directly to Titius's inheritance.

8   MODESTINUS, *Rules, book 9:* When an heir is declared unfit after the acceptance of the inheritance, any merger of actions that has occurred is not to be reversed.

9   ULPIAN, *Lex Julia et Papia, book 14:* The preferable view is that if mortal hatred arises between legatee and testator and it becomes probable that the testator did not wish any legacy or *fideicommissum* to be executed in favor of the person to whom it was appointed or left, the legacy cannot be claimed by the latter. 1. The same view should be held if the legatee openly and publicly insults the testator and makes malicious remarks about him. 2. If it is the testator's status that is the cause of argument the legatee is denied the right to claim that which he was to receive under the will and it is immediately forfeit to the imperial treasury.

10   GAIUS, *Lex Julia et Papia, book 15:* Anyone who, whether by means of a written bond or by mere verbal undertaking, secretly promises delivery of an item left in a will or any other item to a person who is legally forbidden to receive anything under the will is making an undertaking in fraud of the law. 1. If someone is requested to deliver property to a person who, at the time of the request, was entitled to receive it but at the time of death is legally forbidden to do so, I do not doubt that although the *fideicommissum* fails, the property in question should remain in the hands of the person requested to deliver it, since no fraud on his part appears to be involved, unless he gave an undertaking for the future, that is, that he would deliver the property even in the event of the recipient becoming legally forbidden to receive it. 2. It has rightly been held that if the father of a son-in-power gives a secret undertaking, this should not prejudice his son since the latter was under constraint to obey.

11   PAPINIAN, *Questions, book 15:* An heir who gives a secret undertaking in contravention of the laws cannot make use of the *lex Falcidia* in connection with that part of the inheritance which was the object of his fraudulent behavior. The senate made a resolution to this effect. But if the extent of his appointment as heir is greater than that of his fraud then, as far as the *lex Falcidia* is concerned, a quarter can be retained of the balance between the two.

12   PAPINIAN, *Questions, book 16:* The senate long ago decided that when a man sets down as heirs persons whom he cannot appoint as such, although this appointment is not valid and an earlier will is not rendered void, nonetheless, those heirs who did not have the favor of the testator's final wishes should be deprived of the inheritance on grounds of unfitness. This is the judgment that the deified Marcus reached in the case of a man whose name the testator erased from his will after its completion, since he sent the case to the prefect of the imperial treasury. However, legacies charged upon that heir remained unaffected. As for legacies *per praeceptionem* given to him, the question of the testator's intentions will arise, and he will not be refused these legacies unless it is clear that the testator so wished.

13   PAPINIAN, *Questions, book 32:* "Claudius Selencus to his friend Papinian, greetings.

Maevius was condemned for adultery with Sempronia and later married the said Sempronia who had not been condemned. At his death, he left her as his heir. I ask: Was the marriage legal and should the woman be permitted to receive the inheritance?" I replied that such a marriage could not stand, that the woman should not profit by receipt of the inheritance, and that what was left should go to the imperial treasury. We also hold that if such a woman appoints her husband as heir, he should be deprived of the inheritance on grounds of unfitness.

14   PAPINIAN, *Questions, book 33:* I recently replied to you that a woman who lived with a soldier as his mistress should not be permitted to benefit under a military will, even if the soldier dies within a year of his discharge, and that what was left should belong to the imperial treasury.

15   PAPINIAN, *Replies, book 6:* An inheritance is not taken away from an heir who claims that a codicil is forged but fails to win his case; but if under the terms of the codicil he stands to receive something from one of the co-heirs, he will be denied an action to enforce such receipt. So, if the deceased used the codicil to make a division of his goods, the contesting heir will keep that share of the inheritance in respect of which a legacy could not operate but will not be able to benefit under the *lex Falcidia* if there is enough in the portions he has lost to stop the application of that law by equitable set-off.

16   PAPINIAN, *Replies, book 8:* In *secundae tabulae* a father named co-heirs and appointed his brother's sons as substitutes for his own son who was *impubes.* After the boy's death the substitutes, wishing to obtain their uncle's inheritance as *legitimi heredes,* arraigned the mother on a charge of introducing a supposititious child. I replied that if they lost the case, they should be deprived of that share of the inheritance due to them by virtue of the substitution, because they did not accept the inheritance in accordance with the will, following a decision in their favor.   1. Since it is agreed that a woman who allows herself to be the concubine of someone other than her patron cannot be the victim of *stuprum,* the man in question will not be denied an action for that which is left to him in the woman's will. This is the judgment that our best and greatest emperors reached in the case of the will of Cocceius Cassianus, a *vir clarissimus,* who treated the freeborn woman Rufina with the utmost respectful affection. It turned out that Rufina's daughter, whom Cassianus appointed as co-heir with his own granddaughter and referred to in his will as his "foster child" had been begotten illegitimately.   2. A head of household changed his mind about his will and, opening it, erased the name of one of the heirs. As a result, the benefit of that heir's portion was abjudicated to the imperial treasury. The deified Marcus decided that this circumstance should not prejudice the interests of the legatees who had kept the testator's favor and, therefore, that the imperial treasury should succeed to the said heir's portion together with the obligations attached thereto.

17   PAPINIAN, *Replies, book 13:* I held that an heir who knowingly makes light of securing redress for the death of the deceased should be compelled to give back all profits from the inheritance and cannot decently claim the right to request the restoration of any merged actions; but that if he was deceived by ignorance of what had happened, he should be able to advance the defense that he was possessor in good faith, at least if an accounting of the profits was made before the question was raised, and should not be forbidden to demand the restoration of merged actions.

18   PAPINIAN, *Replies, book 15:* I replied that someone who undertakes a secret *fideicommissum* in fraud of the law should also be compelled to give back those fruits which he gathered before the start of litigation since he cannot be regarded as a possessor in good faith of property which is instantly subject to *vindicatio* by the imperial treasury. I replied that once the issue of a secret *fideicommissum* has been raised, the value of the fruits together with any interest should be given back, this applying, of course, to all fruits for which a cash-value has been received; if the recipient has used the fruits, it is sufficient for their value to be returned. The deified Severus generously decreed that in the case of goods left secretly, no distinction of time should be made and only the fruits, and not any interest on them, should be paid back. We follow this ruling.   1. Where all the goods of an estate have been delivered to the imperial treasury on grounds of secret *fideicommissum,* it is reasonable that any debts should not concern the heir. Just the same rule is followed in the case of an unavenged death. However, the heir will not be entitled to the benefit of

restoration of any loss incurred by way of merger of actions or of servitudes resulting from acceptance of the inheritance.   2. A man appointed partial heir to an estate received the legacy of a piece of land and undertook privately to deliver it to someone not legally entitled to receive anything from the inheritance. Although, as far as the heir's share was concerned, the legacy was invalid and consequently he held that share of it as heir, nonetheless, I replied that he should be left the piece of land intact, since neither legal reasons nor variety of possession justified dividing up what was willed to pass as a whole.

19   PAUL, *Replies, book 16:* He replied that if an inheritance is taken away from the appointed heirs because the testator, having changed his mind, wished to make another will and was prevented from so doing by those heirs, the testator should be regarded as having entirely abandoned his earlier intentions.

20   HERMOGENIAN, *Epitome of Law, book 3:* A man who fails to seek redress for his wife's death is deprived of her dowry on grounds of unfitness.

21   PAUL, *Views, book 5:* The portions of those who fail to seek redress for the death of freedmen who have died in suspicious circumstances should also be subject to *vindicatio* by the imperial treasury since it is appropriate for all heirs and all those whose position resembles that of an heir to do their duty in the matter of avenging the deceased.

22   TRYPHONINUS, *Disputations, book 5:* It is entirely reasonable to hold the view that a tutor who, acting in the name of his *pupillus*, claims that a will is undutiful or forged should not lose his legacies in the event of his failing to win the case; and that, if a tutor, acting in the name of his *pupillus*, brings a capital charge against a freedman of the latter's father, he should not be excluded from *bonorum possessio contra tabulas*, since the duties of his office and his responsibility as tutor should excuse his actions. Nor will any judge convict of malicious prosecution a tutor who lays a charge in the name of his *pupillus* not because of any personal quarrel but, for example, at the insistence of the mother of the *pupillus* or the urgent request of the freedmen of the father of the *pupillus*. If a tutor lays a charge against someone in the name of the *pupillus* but does not prosecute the case because in the meantime the *pupillus* has attained puberty, it should not be held that he becomes liable to the terms of the *senatus consultum Turpillianum*, since legal rights are distinct entities, even if several of them are vested in one person; in this case, the rights of a tutor and those of a legatee are different things. So when a tutor lays a charge in pursuance not of his personal rights but of those of his *pupillus*, he must not be regarded as deserving punishment in his own person. Finally, anything left to the *pupillus* in the will in question is forfeit, unless the emperor determines otherwise, since it is very much the case that the *pupillus* is the real author of the charge while the tutor is his defender or, as it were, his *patronus*. Sabinus takes the same view in his *Vitellius*.

23   GAIUS, *Secret Fideicommissa, sole book:* If anyone who is an heir under someone's will is secretly asked to deliver the quarter part which he stands to keep under the *lex Falcidia* to a person not legally entitled to receive it, the *senatus consultum* will be applicable here as well, since there is not much difference between a *fideicommissum* of this sort and the case in which somebody is requested to deliver that which has passed to him under an inheritance.

24   PAPINIAN, *Questions, book 18:* Since a son who claims that his father's will was not lawfully made is not impugning his father's intentions or accusing him of any offense but is merely raising a question of law, he can retain what the deceased wished him to have.

25   PAPINIAN, *Replies, book 14:* If a son-in-law leaves his father-in-law as heir, considerations of paternal affection do not by themselves justify suspicions of the existence of a secret *fideicommissum*.

26   SCAEVOLA, *Digest, book 30:* CLAUDIUS notes: If a person who was left an illegal legacy dies during the lifetime of the testator, the legacy is not subject to *vindicatio* by the imperial treasury, but remains in the hands of the person charged with it.

BOOK THIRTY-FIVE

1

CONDITIONS, PARTICULARIZATIONS, EXPLANATIONS FOR AND MODALITIES OF PROVISIONS IN WILLS

1 POMPONIUS, *Quintus Mucius, book 3:* An uncertain vesting date or a condition may be ascribed to legacies bequeathed; if neither of these be effected, the legacies are presently due unless a condition be inherent by the very nature of the bequest. 1. When a specific vesting date is set down, the legacies can be discharged forthwith, although that date has not yet arrived, because it is certain that they will become due. 2. The day is nonspecific when it is written as follows: "Let my heir give ten when he dies"; for the date of no man's death is certain. Hence, if the legatee should die first, the legacy does not pass to his heir because the day does not come during the legatee's life, although it is certain that the heir will die. 3. Now a condition is inherent in a legacy when, for instance, we write: "Let my heir give what is born of Arescusa"; or "let my heir give the produce gathered from such-and-such field"; or "let him give to Seius the slave that I have not bequeathed to someone else."

2 ULPIAN, *Sabinus, book 5:* Some conditions can be satisfied at any time, even during the testator's life, for instance, "if the ship comes from Asia"; for, whenever the ship shall have arrived, the condition is seen to be satisfied; others can be satisfied only after the testator's death, for example, "if he shall have given ten," "if he goes up the Capitoline hill"; now for someone to be regarded as complying with such a condition, he must know of its insertion in the will; should he have done by chance what is requested, he is not deemed to have complied with the testator's wishes.

3 ULPIAN, *Sabinus, book 6:* The rule has prevailed that impossible conditions inserted in a will are treated as though they had not been written in.

4 POMPONIUS, *Sabinus, book 3:* If a legacy be made to those to whom a patron owes legacies, the praetor must ensure that the condition is obeyed so that proportionate advances are made to both the patron and the instituted heirs for the purpose of honoring the condition. 1. Suppose that it be written: "If a son be not born to Titius in the next five years, let my heir then give ten to Seia"; should Titius die earlier, the ten will not be due to Seia forthwith because the specification "then" denotes the very end of the five years' period.

5 PAUL, *Sabinus, book 2:* A *pupillus* can satisfy a condition even without the authority of his tutor. It should occasion no surprise that once the condition be satisfied, one can become a *necessarius heres* at any time; for this ensues by virtue of [paternal] power not by reason of compliance with the condition. 1. Similarly, a slave or son-in-power can satisfy a condition without authorization by his master or head of household, since no one comes to harm thereby.

6 POMPONIUS, *Sabinus, book 3:* A penalty imposed in a will is not incurred by the heir, legatee, or another who benefits under a last testament, if he be charged to erect a monument satisfactory to someone's judgment and that someone be dead or unable to be present or refuse to pass judgment. 1. A person was directed to be heir, on

manumitting certain slaves. If some of them were already dead, Neratius replied that the condition failed, and he did not think that the condition could be complied with. Servius, however, was of opinion that when it was written, "if my daughter and mother be alive" and one of them was already dead, the condition did not fail. The same is written in Labeo. Sabinus and Cassius also say that virtually impossible conditions written into a will are to be treated as though not written; and that is the view to be accepted.

7 ULPIAN, *Sabinus, book 18:* The advantage of the *cautio Muciana* pertains to conditions positing inactivity, for example, "if he does not go up the Capitoline hill," "if he does not manumit Stichus and the like." This was the view of Aristo, Neratius, and Julian, and it is endorsed by a constitution of the deified Pius: "It has been accepted that the same relief shall be admitted not only in respect of legacies but also in relation to inheritances." 1. Hence, if a wife were to write in as part-heir the husband, to whom she had promised a dowry, in the following terms, "if he neither seeks nor exacts the dowry which I promised him," the husband could declare to his co-heir that he is ready to regard the dowry as satisfied or give security to that effect and so could enter upon the inheritance. But should the husband be instituted sole heir under such condition, he will not be prevented from entering upon the inheritance because there is no one to whom he may give security; for the condition is regarded as satisfied by the very fact that there is no one whom the husband could sue for the dowry, once he has entered upon the inheritance.

8 POMPONIUS, *Sabinus, book 5:* Suppose that a husband make the following legacy: "While my wife is with my son, let my heir give her so much"; should the woman, going into hiding, abandon her patron but have the intention of keeping her children with her, Trebatius and Labeo say that the legacy is due to her; for it is not requisite that she should be with her children at each and every moment; what is necessary is that she should have the intention and resolve of not dismissing her child from herself and that it is not her fault that the child does not go with her.

9 ULPIAN, *Sabinus, book 20:* It is our practice to hold that a husband who makes a legacy to his wife when she shall have children does not have in contemplation issue whom the wife has already borne.

10 ULPIAN, *Sabinus, book 23:* "To my daughter when she shall marry"; this condition is such that the testator will be satisfied by the mere fact of its being realized without stipulating when. It follows that even if she should marry in the testator's lifetime after the making of the will, the condition is regarded as satisfied; the more so since it is a condition which can be satisfied once and for all. Not all unions, however, will meet the terms of the condition; suppose, say, that a girl not yet of marriageable age be led to her husband's house; that does not meet the condition. Again, if she be joined with one to whom marriage for her is forbidden, we say the same. There is room for doubt whether she may satisfy the condition by a subsequent marriage as though not presently married. If, indeed, the testator had the first conjugal bond in mind, I think that the condition has failed; a liberal interpretation, however, suggests that a condition not yet satisfied has not failed. 1. Suppose a legacy "if the ship comes from Asia" and, unknown to the testator, the ship has already arrived at the time that the will is made; the condition should be held to be satisfied. One should hold likewise of a legacy "when he shall come of age."

11 PAUL, *Sabinus, book 4:* If what is specified by way of condition has already happened, to the testator's knowledge, one has to wait for it to happen again, if it can. Should the testator not know, the bequest is presently due. 1. Know also that common conditions, for example, "if he shall ascend the Capitol" and the like, should be satisfied after the testator's death, if they be there for the will to be complied with; conditions which are not common, for example, "if Titius shall have become consul," can be realized even in the testator's lifetime.

12 ULPIAN, *Sabinus, book 24:* Take this legacy: "Since my elder son removed ten from my chest, let my younger son and heir take ten therefrom"; the legacy is due because

it is left so that the positions of the sons may be equalized. This is certainly a motive; for a motive relates to the past, a penalty to the future.

13   PAUL, *Sabinus, book 5:* Where land is left to someone if he shall have given money to a *pupillus* or to a lunatic, he will be deemed to have satisfied the condition by giving to the tutor or curator.

14   POMPONIUS, *Sabinus, book 8:* A legacy provides: "Let Titius be heir, if he sets up statues in the town"; [Titius] is ready to erect them but the townsmen do not grant him a site; Sabinus and Proculus say that he will be heir and that the law is the same in the matter of legacies.

15   ULPIAN, *Sabinus, book 35:* Where a legacy is left to a woman under the condition, "if she marries within the family," the condition is treated as satisfied as soon as she is taken to wife, even though she has not yet entered her husband's bedchamber; for it is consent, not sleeping together, which makes a marriage.

16   GAIUS, *Praetor's Edict, Wills, book 1:* In respect of matters arising outside a will, a liberal interpretation is permissible; but that which springs from the will itself must be carried out in compliance with strict law.

17   GAIUS, *Praetor's Edict, Legacies, book 2:* It is a false particularization if, for instance, there be written "the slave Stichus whom I bought from Titius," "the Tusculan estate which was given to me by Titius." For, so long as it is clear which slave or estate the testator has in mind, it is irrelevant that he received as a gift what he says he bought or that he bought what he says was a gift. 1. Hence, even if a legacy be made in the terms, "I leave my cook, Stichus, or my cobbler, Stichus, to Titius," he will belong to the legatee, although not a cook or a cobbler, so long as it is established that this is the man whom the testator has in mind. Again, if there be some error in designating the person of the legatee but it is clear to whom the testator wishes to make his legacy, the legacy will be valid as though no error had occurred. 2. The law in respect of false particularization applies the more to a false explanation, for example, "I give the estate to Titius because he looked after my affairs" or "let my son Titius take the estate as a preferred gift because his brother abstracted so many gold pieces from the chest"; the legacy is valid, even though the brother did not take the money from the chest. 3. But suppose that the motive be framed conditionally, say, "I give the estate to Titius, if he has looked after my affairs" or "let my son Titius take the estate as a preferred gift, if his brother took one hundred from the chest," the legacy will be effective, only if the one did look after the affairs and the other's brother did remove one hundred from the chest. 4. But put the case that a legacy is left to a man for him to do something with it, for instance, to erect a monument to the testator, effect some work, provide a feast for the townsfolk, or give part of it to someone else; such legacy is regarded as subject to a modality.

18   GAIUS, *Provincial Edict, book 18:* One to whom anything is left, under a condition of not doing something, should give security, obviously under the Mucian undertaking, to the person to whom, in the event that the condition be not fulfilled, the legacy or inheritance would belong at civil law.

19   ULPIAN, *Disputations, book 5:* In the matter of conditions, the will of the deceased takes pride of place and determines the condition. Indeed, even with the condition, "if my daughter be married to Titius," it is settled that the time of the testator's death is not always that to which to be looked; for the paternal will may project to a later period. 1. The provision, "if Primus be heir, let him be under a charge to give," is not to be treated as a condition; the testator particularizes when the legacy will be due rather than lays down a condition, unless, perchance, the testator were of a mind to postulate a condition. Accordingly, the following would not create a condition: "I give and bequeath whatever should be given to me at Ephesus." Suppose, though, this legacy: "If Primus be not my heir, let Secundus be under a charge to give"; if Primus becomes heir, the legacy will not be due. Should Primus enter upon the inheritance together with Secundus, it would be fruitless to doubt that the condition has not been

satisfied. 2. If a patron, possession of the inheritance having been accepted despite the will, occupies his due share, his co-heir does not have to furnish to him legacies given under the provision, "if the patron be not heir." 3. Suppose a legacy to have been left away from Primus with the provision, "if Secundus be not heir, let him give twenty to Titius" and, in like manner, a legacy away from Secundus be made to the same Titius "if Primus be not heir"; should both become heirs, the condition of the legacy fails; if one does and the other does not become heir, the legacy will be due.

20 JULIAN, *Digest, book 27:* MARCELLUS notes: We do not doubt that base conditions are to be waived; among them are particularly conditions of oath-taking.

21 JULIAN, *Digest, book 31:* Whether a condition be one of fact or one of law is an issue of importance; for conditions such as "if the ship shall have come from Asia," "if Titius shall have been made consul" are a bar to the heir's entering upon the inheritance so long as he is unaware that they have been complied with. But with conditions of law, no more is necessary than that they have in fact been satisfied. For instance, one who thinks himself to be a son-in-power when in truth he is a head of household can acquire an inheritance. Hence, also one instituted heir in part can enter upon the inheritance, although unaware that the will has been opened.

22 JULIAN, *Digest, book 35:* Whenever a legacy is left to a woman under the condition "if she does not marry" and she is further charged on her honor to make it over to Titius if she does marry, the opportune rule is that even should she marry, she can claim the legacy and need not comply with the further charge.

23 JULIAN, *Digest, book 43:* The truer view is that where someone is directed to give ten to two heirs and to have an estate for himself, he cannot divide the condition lest the legacy itself be divided. Accordingly, although he give five to one heir, he can claim no part of the estate, unless he gives the remaining five to the other accepting the inheritance or, if the latter lets the inheritance pass him by, he gives all ten to the heir who alone accepts the inheritance.

24 JULIAN, *Digest, book 55:* It is accepted at civil law that whenever the fulfillment of a condition is prevented by one who has an interest in its nonfulfillment, the condition is to be treated as though it had been satisfied. Most jurists extend this to legacies and the institution of heirs. With these precedents, there are those who rightly think that a stipulation becomes enforceable when it is the fault of the promisor that the stipulator does not comply with a condition [of the stipulation].

25 JULIAN, *Digest, book 69:* Suppose a man to devise an estate to his wife when she shall have children and then they divorce and the woman has issue by another spouse and subsequently, her second marriage being dissolved, the woman returns to her first husband; the condition is not regarded as fulfilled; for it is unlikely that the testator contemplated issue sired by another during the testator's own lifetime.

26 JULIAN, *Digest, book 82:* The formulation "if he gives twenty or swears to do something" gives expression to a single condition having two parts to it. Accordingly, should someone be instituted heir "if he swear to give ten" or "to erect a monument," although the words of the edict admit him to the legacy or the inheritance, he nonetheless will be obliged to do what he was directed to swear to do, only the oath being waived. 1. When the same thing is left to one person unconditionally and to another subject to a condition or when one person is instituted heir unconditionally, another under a condition, then, if the condition fails, the part of the legacy or inheritance will go also to the heir of him to whom the legacy or inheritance was given unconditionally, assuming that his inheritance has been accepted.

27 ALFENUS VARUS, *Digest, book 5:* A man wrote in his will that he wished to be erected to himself a monument like that of Publius Septimius Demetrius in the via Salaria; should this not be done, he imposed a large fine on his heirs. When it was discovered that there was no monument of Publius Septimius Demetrius but that there was one of Publius Septimius Dama, which it was suspected that the testator intended as the model of his own memorial, the heirs asked what sort of monument

they should erect and, assuming that they erected none because they could not identify the intended model, whether they would incur the penalty. The reply was that if it
could be discerned which monument the testator sought to identify, even though he
misdescribed it, they should build on the model which he thought that he had identified; if, however, the testator's intention could not be ascertained, the penalty would
be ineffective because the model never existed which he bade them to copy; still they
would certainly have to erect a monument appropriate to the wealth and standing of
the deceased.

28   PAUL, *Epitome of the Digest of Alfenus, book 2:* Someone made the following legacy
to his daughter: "If my daughter, Attia, marries as directed by Lucius Titius, let my
heir give her so many [coins]." Titius having predeceased the testator, Attia married;
the question was whether the legacy was due to her; the reply was affirmative.
1. "Let my wife Attia select the slave, Philargyrus, and the slave-woman, Agathea,
who shall belong to me at my death." The testator sold the Agathea whom he owned
when making his will, subsequently bought other slave-women, and gave one of them
the name, Agathea. The question was: Did this one appear to be the object of the legacy? The answer was: Yes.

29   JULIAN, *Urseius Ferox, book 1:* The condition "if he shall go up the Capitol" is to be
taken in the sense: "if he goes up the Capitol when he is first able to do so."

30   JULIAN, *From Minicius, book 1:* A whole estate is left separately to me unconditionally and to you under a condition; you die before the condition is satisfied. I will be
in no way liable to satisfy the condition, seeing that even though the condition fails,
the part which you would have claimed inheres in my part.

31   AFRICANUS, *Questions, book 2:* A will contained the following provision: "Let
Stichus and Pamphila be free, and if they should marry each other, let my heir be
charged to give them a hundred"; Stichus died before the will was opened. [Julian]
replied that Stichus's share failed but that also Pamphila did not comply with the condition, and so her share would remain with the heir; moreover, even if both lived and
Stichus did not wish to marry the woman while she was agreeable to matrimony, her
legacy would indeed be due to her but the share of Stichus would lapse. For when a
legacy is made to someone in this way, "let my heir give one hundred to Titius if he
marries Seia," the condition is deemed to have failed, if Seia dies; moreover, if it were
Titius who died, nothing would pass to his heir because his death is treated as defeating the condition. Now, assuming that both survive but he does not wish to marry the
woman, he will acquire nothing from the legacy because it is his own act which defeats
the condition; should it, though, be the woman who refuses when he is ready for marriage, his legacy will be due to him.

32   AFRICANUS, *Questions, book 9:* Rendering accounts is nothing more than discharging balances; still if through the fault of both *statuliber* and heir, but without bad faith
on the slave's part, less be paid than is due and the accounts be deemed rendered
in good faith, the slave will be free. Did we observe differently, no one conditionally
manumitted would ever achieve liberty, if an underpayment were made through over-
sight. [Julian] says that this holds good if, when a slave is directed to render accounts,
he so renders accounts through error but without guile that the master is also in error
over the computation.

33   MARCIAN, *Institutes, book 6:* An erroneous particularization, for example, description as a brother, sister, grandson, or anything of the like, does not redound to the
disadvantage of a legatee, trust beneficiary, or instituted heir; this is observed by the
spirit of the civil law and in rulings of the deified Severus and Antoninus.   1. Again,
where several are in dispute over a name, he will prevail who establishes that the
deceased had him in mind.   2. Furthermore, should a legacy be made to someone as a
freedman, that is, among the freedmen, he will not lose his legacy on the ground that
he subsequently received the [gold] ring from the emperor; for that augments his
rank; it does not change his condition; so said the deified Severus and Caracalla in

rescripts.   3. Suppose someone to bequeath a thing if it be his at the time of his death and it be found no longer to be his at that time, not even its value is regarded as bequeathed.   4. What, then, of the provision, "I give and bequeath Stichus and Pamphilus, if they be mine when I die?" The testator alienates one of them; can the legatee, nonetheless, claim the other? It is settled that he can; for, despite the plural, such formulation is to be taken as though the testator had said disjunctively: "Stichus, if he be mine at the time of my death."

34   FLORENTINUS, *Institutes, book 11:* A legacy may be made to an individual by name, for example, "to Lucius Titius," or by identification of his person or of his calling or office, his proximity or affinity; it matters not at all for designation or description is often used in place of a name. Nor is it a matter of concern whether the particularization be correct or erroneous so long as it be clear whom the testator means.   1. Between particularization and condition, there is this distinction: Particularization generally relates to what has happened, condition to what is to happen.

35   POMPONIUS, *Rules, sole book:* In the matter of liberty, the most benevolent construction is to be placed upon a condition imposed thereon, however weighty or severe its content.

36   MARCELLUS, *Replies, sole book:* Publius Maevius made the following disposition in his will: "Whoever be my heir or heirs, I give and bequeath and charge to their honor that they give forty to Gaius Seius, my sister's son, on his attaining the honor of the consulate." Seius was designated consul during Maevius's lifetime and accepted his office; then he entered upon his consular rôle on January, and Maevius predeceased this. I ask: Are the forty due to Seius? Marcellus replies: They are.   1. In a codicil, Titia made the following provision concerning lands which she had devised to Septicia: "I ask you, Septicia, to return these lands to my son when he attains the age of sixteen; should he not reach sixteen, I ask you to restore and hand them over to Publius Maevius and Gaius Cornelius." Here is my query: Suppose that Septicia dies and then Titia's son dies in his fifteenth year, is the trust operative on completion of the fifteenth year, and do Septicia's heirs have to make it over to Publius Maevius and Gaius Cornelius? Marcellus replies that Septicia left to her heir the right which she had in the lands; it would further appear contrary to the wishes of the testatrix that fulfillment of the trust should be sought with the result that more would go to the substitutes than could come to the son from either Septicia or the heirs. The formulation does indeed suggest the trust, but it is improbable that the testatrix wished it to come more expeditiously to the substitutes. No new factor is introduced by the prior death of Septicia; for, even if the youth survived, Septicia's heirs could not be sued before she herself could be.

37   PAUL, *Lex Fufia Caninia, sole book:* Put the case that someone bequeathed a slave whom he could not himself manumit with a charge to the legatee that he manumit him. Although the legatee will not be denied the legacy, he will not be obliged to manumit, since the testator's wishes have to be complied with only when that does not involve an infraction of a statute; so wrote Neratius. He is, however, not to be denied the legacy because the testator clearly wished the legatee rather than his heir to derive some benefit from the slave.

38   PAUL, *Law of Codicils, sole book:* Suppose that I write: "what I shall leave to Titius in codicils"; although the legacy is set out in the codicils, it derives its efficacy from the will, only its quantification being deferred to the codicils. For there are to be found in the earlier jurists such legacies as "[let my heir give] the amount that I shall set out in a letter to him" or "the amount which I recover in such-and-such action."

39   JAVOLENUS, *Posthumous Works of Labeo, book 1:* A condition pertaining to a class of persons, not to specific, known persons, we treat as a condition of the will as a whole and as affecting all the instituted heirs. On the other hand, a condition adapted to specific persons we must relate only to that degree in which those persons are instituted.   1. Should a will contain the words "that something be done in the marketplace" and the marketplace be not specified, Labeo says that if the matter be in doubt, it is to be effected in the marketplace of the town in which the testator was domiciled.

I too endorse this view.

40   JAVOLENUS, *Posthumous Works of Labeo, book 2:* Those days will not be counted against you which, when you sought progress to comply with a condition, your neighbor barred your use of a public way, assuming that there was no deficiency on your part in subsequently bringing proceedings against him for his flouting of the law. 1. Posit the following legacy: "If Publius Cornelius gives to my heir the outlay which I expended on the Seian estate, let my heir give the Seian estate to Publius Cornelius." It was the view of Cascellius that the price of the estate was also included. Ofilius, however, was of opinion that the price was not included, only the expenses incurred after the purchase of the estate. Cinna was of the same view with the rider that the account of such expenses should not include [the value of] produce. I rather adhere to this opinion.   2. A man left one hundred to Titius, then ordained further: "Let my heir give what I have bequeathed to anyone, if my mother die." Titius survived the death of the head of household but died while the mother still lived; was the legacy due to the heirs of Titius? Ofilius said: "Yes," because the legacy was not made subject to a condition; it was first made unconditionally and then subjected to a qualification of time. Labeo, however, says: "Let us consider whether this is not false reasoning; for it matters nothing whether the formulation be, 'let my heir give the money which I have bequeathed, if my mother dies,' or 'let him give it if my mother has not died.'" In either case, consequently, the legacy is either granted or adeemed under a condition. I approve Labeo's reply.   3. A master left his slave five gold pieces thus: "Let my heir give to my slave, Stichus, whose freedom I have directed in my will, the five gold pieces which I owe him by our accounts." Namusa reports Servius to have been of opinion that there was no legacy to the slave, because a master could owe nothing to his slave. I think that we should take the natural, not the strict legal, implication of the testator's wishes; and that is the law which we observe.   4. Let us suppose that one who had no dotal land disposed as follows: "Let my heir give her the Cornelian land which she brought me as a dowry." The answer of Labeo, Ofilius, and Trebatius is that the legacy is due because, the Cornelian land existing, the erroneous attribution does not destroy the legacy.   5. Thermus Minor specified in his will those by whose judgment he wished a monument to be erected to himself and then made the following legacy: "Let my heir give one thousand to the Lucii, Publii, and Cornelii for the erection of my monument." Trebatius was of opinion that the provision was to be taken in the sense that these persons should give security that they would erect the monument out of the sum bequeathed. Labeo adhered to the view of Trebatius, because it was the testator's intention that the money should be expended upon the monument. Proculus and I endorse this opinion.

41   ULPIAN, *Edict, book 34:* Legacies left under a condition become due, not forthwith but when the condition is satisfied; it follows that they cannot be delegated in the interim.

42   AFRICANUS, *Questions, book 2:* A legacy was left to a son-in-power under the condition, "if he remains in the power of his head of household." [Julian] said that the legacy appears rather to have been made to the head of household who can claim it in his own name. The same rule would apply if the legacy were to a slave. One proof thereof is that even if a ration allowance were bequeathed to the slaves of Titius, it would indisputably be left to the master, not to the slaves.

43   PAUL, *Plautius, book 8:* PLAUTIUS: An heir was asked by his freedman testator to resell the whole inheritance, having taken ten for himself. Subsequently, the patron of the deceased claimed possession of the inheritance despite [the freedman's] will, taking also the part which was due [to the heir]. Proculus and Cassius say that the cestui que trust can recover, proportionately, his outlay. PAUL: We observe the following rule: Just as the praetor burdens the heir with trusts and legacies, so also the latter can recover his share.   1. The case is different if the *lex Falcidia* be applicable and reduce the legacy: In such cases, nothing is recoverable, because the condition must be complied with absolutely.   2. Again, the duty of giving is divided if the legatee cannot take the full share of the inheritance left to him: The truth is that he must make

good his share and those who take away from him make good a share, since more has been bequeathed than the statute permits.   3. Neratius, in the third book of his *Replies*, writes that where two heirs are instituted and one is asked to transfer the inheritance to you and you are asked to give a certain sum to Titius, in the event that an heir invokes the benefit of the *lex Falcidia* to reduce what he has to make over to you, it is not unfair that your liability to Titius be correspondingly reduced.

44   PAUL, *Plautius, book 9:* One charged to give to the heir is to give to the third party's slave who is instituted, not to his master. Even if he be directed to give to the slave of Titius, when someone else's slave is instituted, delivery is to be to the slave himself; for factual issues do not transfer to the master. In like manner, should I stipulate something for me or the slave of Titius, performance should be not to Titius, but to his slave. These statements are correct.   1. Now when the direction is to give to the heir, let us consider whether the delivery may be to his master; here too the delivery should be to the slave. 2. It is beyond doubt that a *statuliber* should make delivery to his master.   3. Conversely, one who should give to the master cannot satisfy the condition by giving to the slave, unless the master agree. For in such a case, no one can satisfy a condition, if the other party be in ignorance or unwilling.   4. When an inheritance is handed over under the *senatus consultum Trebellianum*, it is for the heir to satisfy any condition; nor is any restitution to be made by reason of a trust.   5. Now if the heir accepts a suspect inheritance and makes it over, a doubt arises whether the recipient is liable to deprivation. The benevolent interpretation is in the negative.   6. Now suppose that I am instituted heir and that a dispute is raised against me over the inheritance; should a legatee give security that he will restore the legacy if I be evicted from the inheritance? He must also be given security for the return of what he has given.   7. Should you be directed to give me ten and to accept the inheritance under the *senatus consultum*, I do not have to return the ten to you by reason of a trust.   8. When a legacy is left to the slave of two owners under a condition of giving, some say that he cannot satisfy the condition by giving parts; all the money must be given at one time. I think the opposite.   9. If part of a thing bequeathed has been usucapted, I have doubts whether the condition can be satisfied in full. It can, though, be said to be satisfied in part in accord with the testator's intentions.   10. PLAUTIUS: I left an estate to one of my heirs, if he gave one hundred to the heirs; he may deduct his hereditary share [of the money] and give the remainder to his co-heirs in their proportionate shares. But should an heir be instituted in part on the terms that he give one hundred to the heirs, he will become heir only if he gives the full sum to his co-heirs; he is not admitted to the inheritance until he has handed over the whole amount. For equally if a slave be freed by the will and instituted heir in part with the requirement that he should give ten to the heirs, it is settled that he becomes free and heir only if he has given the full ten to his co-heirs. PAUL: Such is the law which we apply.

45   PAUL, *Plautius, book 16:* Julian says that if a legatee to whom a bequest is made, "if he shall have given ten to the heir," gives the heir a formal release of what the latter owes him, he cannot indeed be regarded as honoring the condition, as having given; but since, in effect, it is the heir's fault that the legatee does not comply, the latter may claim his legacy, as if the condition were satisfied.

46   PAUL, *Vitellius, book 3:* Suppose that a *statuliber* is directed to pay money, say, within a hundred days and no date is specified for the commencement of the period, the period runs from the acceptance of the inheritance; it would be absurd that the period should expire before there was someone to accept within it. The same is to be said of all directed to give to an heir; hence, time for complying with a condition also runs for a legatee from the acceptance of the inheritance.

47   MARCELLUS, *Digest, book 14:* A slave was given his freedom in this form: "Let him be free, if he be mine"; a legacy or the inheritance was given to him unconditionally; then [the testator] alienated him. The legacy or inheritance will be due to his [new] master at whose direction he may accept. For the expression "if he be mine" in the grant of liberty admits the future possibility of an impediment to liberty, albeit unexpressed. Frequently, indeed, the effect of something is changed although the testator expresses what would be inherent, even if unmentioned.

48   MARCELLUS, *Digest, book 15:* I did not take the view that a trust had become due when the person to whom it was left when he reached sixteen had entered upon his sixteenth year; so, indeed, the Emperor Aurelius Antoninus adjudged on an appeal from Germany.

49   CELSUS, *Digest, book 22:* Where an heir is charged to give in ten years or someone be similarly bidden to be free, the legacy will become due or liberty result on the very last day of that period.

50   ULPIAN, *Duties of Consul, book 1:* Suppose that someone be given his freedom directly, subject, however, to the condition, "if he shall have rendered accounts"; the deified Antoninus authorized the granting of an arbitrator by the consuls in these words: "On your approach, the fully empowered consuls will grant an arbitrator who, having gone through the accounts, will not only resolve the balance due from Epaphroditus but also the accounts and documents which he should deliver or display to his owners. Once that arbitrator is satisfied, nothing will impede the freedom of Epaphroditus."

51   MODESTINUS, *Distinctions, book 5:* Where a slave is bidden to be free under separate, disjunctive conditions, he may select that condition which to him appears least onerous; where, on the other hand, a legacy is so bequeathed, the legatee must honor the condition last mentioned. 1. One directed to be free on giving to the heir may attain his liberty by giving to the heir's heir. Publicius says that the same does not hold good in respect of a legatee.

52   MODESTINUS, *Distinctions, book 7:* It can happen that things stated expressly may constitute an obstacle, although they could be tacitly understood and present no handicap. For instance, someone is given a legacy as follows: "I give and bequeath ten to Titius, if Maevius goes up the Capitol." For although it lies in Maevius's discretion whether he goes up the Capitol and so to wish the legacy to be given to Titius, the testator could not effectively have used the formulation: "If Maevius so wishes, I give ten to Titius"; for one cannot leave a legacy at another's pleasure. Hence, the expression "what is said, does harm; what is not, does not."

53   MODESTINUS, *Advice on Drafting, sole book:* Put the case that a man direct his slave to be free if he render accounts to [the master's] heir and subsequently veto the rendering of accounts; the slave will be a freedman under the will as though he had been manumitted unconditionally.

54   JAVOLENUS, *From Cassius, book 2:* Suppose that someone direct legacies, unqualified by modality, to be given on a date in the first, second, and third year and bequeath the money to someone when he shall have reached the age of puberty. In his *Commentaries*, Gaius [Cassius] writes that this legacy is due on the first, second, and third year after the attaining of puberty. I think not; the modality is interposed to delay a legacy which would else be presently due; the date of puberty, however, indicates a specification of time. 1. The same thing is left to two people, if they give the heir one hundred; if one of them gives fifty, he acquires his share of the legacy, and the share of the defaulter will accrue to him subject to its condition.

55   JAVOLENUS, *Letters, book 13:* Land is devised to Maevius, if he gives two hundred to Callimachus with whom the testator has no testamentary capacity; [Maevius] must comply with the condition and give the two hundred for the land to become his, even though he does not make the recipient owner of the coins. What difference can it make that he be told to give to "X" or to put it in some place or, indeed, to hurl it into the sea? No more will that which is due to come to a given person under a will come to him by reason of [the donor's] death.

56   JAVOLENUS, *Letters, book 14:* Where land is devised to someone, if he give ten, he can acquire no part of the land unless he pay the full sum. The case is different from that of the same thing being left to two people under a condition. In such case, the condition under the will can be regarded forthwith as divided between them. Hence, each individual can comply with the condition for his part and take what is left to him; for though the total is ascribed to the legacy as a whole, it can be regarded as divided, by a counting of heads. But in the case of a conditional legacy to an individual, there should be no adventitious division of the condition; the full number of those substituted in his place should, therefore, be taken into account.

57   POMPONIUS, *Quintus Mucius, book 9:* This question has been raised: Suppose that a slave be directed to be free if he give so many days' work to one outside the household, should such a condition be taken in the sense that we say about the performance of services what we say of the giving of money? The rule which we follow is that just as it is said that if a slave give from his *peculium* to an outsider, he will be admitted to freedom, so also, necessarily, if he perform services for him. In such circumstances, consequently, the heir would do wisely to prohibit performance of the services; in this way, the slave would indeed attain his liberty, but the outsider would not benefit from his services.

58   POMPONIUS, *Miscellaneous Readings, book 10:* A legacy is given to another's slave-woman, "when she marries." Proculus says that the legacy is valid because she could be manumitted and marry thereafter.

59   ULPIAN, *Lex Julia et Papia, book 13:* A legacy fails if the person to whom it was left under a condition dies.   1. What, then, if he does not die but ceases to be a citizen? Suppose a legacy to someone, "if he becomes consul," and he be deported to an island; is it to be said that the legacy is not destroyed in the interim, because he could be restored to citizenship? I think this the more acceptable view.   2. The same would not be said if he were subjected to a penalty entailing slavery; for slavery is equated with death.

60   PAUL, *Lex Julia et Papia, book 7:* Conditions consisting in a fact are varied and admit, really, of a triple classification: that something be given or done or happen; or their converse, that something be not given or done or happen. Of these, conditions of giving and doing pertain to the persons of those to whom something is left or to those of others.   1. The imperial treasury has to comply with the same conditions as does the person from whom some bequest comes to it; it thus claims the bequest subject to its burden.

61   ULPIAN, *Lex Julia et Papia, book 8:* When a man makes a bequest to his wife upon her having children, there is room for doubt whether the testator has in mind only those children who may be born after his death or also those conceived during his lifetime but after the making of the will, assuming that he dies while the marriage is still in existence. The equitable course, however, is to hold that the benefit accrues if any are born while the husband still lives or after his death.

62   TERENTIUS CLEMENS, *Lex Julia et Papia, book 4:* If, though, the testator should specifically state that even issue conceived of another after his own death are comprised, the woman should still be admitted to the legacy.   1. A person was left more than the statute allowed him, if he should give something to the heir; the question arises: Can he take by virtue of the legacy what he has to give to honor the condition (as not acquiring what he has to lose) or is that rather something extra so that he does not take more from the testator's substance than he would have done, had the legacy been unconditional? Julian most correctly writes that he can take as much more as is necessary for the implementing of the condition and that it matters not whether he be

directed to give to the heir or to a third person, for, the computation having been made which is always directed ad hominem leaves him no more than the amount permitted by the statute.   2. What is the legal position when a man makes a bequest to his wife over a period of years, "if she does not marry away from [their] children?" Julian's answer was that the woman could both marry and take the legacy. Had it run, however, "if she does not marry away from our children under puberty," the statute would not apply; for care of the children rather than widowhood would then be enjoined.

63   GAIUS, *Lex Julia et Papia, book 3:* In the event of a legacy, "if she does not marry Titius" or "Titius, Seius, or Maevius," and, generally, if several persons be included, the rule has rather become settled that should she marry any of them, she would lose the legacy; this is not regarded as imposing a condition of widowhood; for she could make a quite satisfactory marriage with someone else.   1. Now what of the legacy, "if she marry Titius?" There is, of course, no doubt that if she could respectably marry Titius, she would be barred from the legacy, unless she honored the condition. But if this Titius would, as a husband, demean her, it should be said that the statute allows her to make any marriage she likes. For one bidden to marry Titius is forbidden to marry anyone else. Hence, if Titius be unworthy, the situation will be as though it was said, generally, "if she does not marry." However, if we wish to stand on niceties, our present condition is more stringent than if it said, "if she does not marry"; for she is forbidden to marry anyone else at all and is directed to marry Titius, whom she cannot in honor marry.

64   TERENTIUS CLEMENS, *Lex Julia et Papia, book 5:* Julian says that the statute has no application to a legacy framed thus, "if she does not marry Lucius Titius."   1. However, a legacy, "if she does not marry at Aricia," raises the point whether a fraud on the statute is perpetrated; for if her case be such that she would not find marriage easy elsewhere, the provision is to be regarded as automatically rescinded as having been introduced to evade the statute; an enactment for the common good, namely, the procreation of issue, is to be furthered by its interpretation.

65   PAUL, *Edict, book 62:* When a legacy is bequeathed under a condition, should the heir, away from whom it has been so left, die while the condition is still pending, he leaves his own heir charged.

66   MODESTINUS, *Replies, book 10:* An heir manumitted a *statuliber* to whom he was requested to transfer a trust on the happening of a condition. The answer of Herennius Modestinus was that although he had manumitted the *statuliber*, he would be obliged to make over the trust bequeathed under the same conditions only when satisfied of their realization or if it were his own fault that they were not complied with.

67   JAVOLENUS, *Letters, book 11:* An estate was left to someone under this condition, "if he does not manumit the slave"; should he manumit him, the legacy of the estate was transferred to Maevius; the legatee gave security that he would not manumit and took the legacy, then subsequently freed the slave. I ask: Is anything given to Maevius? His reply was that if someone received a legacy, "if he did not manumit the slave," he could, having given security, take the legacy from the heir; should he later manumit the slave, then, becoming liable on his undertaking, he would restore to the heir the land or its value and, in such case, the heir would make it over to the person entitled under the second condition.

68   JAVOLENUS, *Cassius, book 2:* Suppose a legacy, "if she marry"; if the woman be, to the testator's knowledge, already married, a subsequent marriage is to be awaited for which it is irrelevant whether her second marriage comes during the testator's lifetime or after his death.

69   GAIUS, *Lex Julia et Papia, book 13:* In a note on Labeo, Proculus observes that a bequest, "I give and bequeath to Titius, if he want it," would go to the legatee's heir only if the legatee himself had wished to have it; for the condition is deemed to pertain to the legatee himself.

70   PAPINIAN, *Questions, book 16:* A mother instituted her two sons as heirs to specified parts on condition of their emancipation and gave them unqualified preferred legacies of several items. They accepted the inheritance. The father should be excluded from the benefit of the legacies by the consideration that in emancipating his sons, he voluntarily wished his wife's last wish to be observed.

71   PAPINIAN, *Questions, book 17:* One hundred are bequeathed to Titius to buy land; Sextus Caecilius is of opinion that Titius cannot be compelled to give an undertaking, because he may resort simply to the benefit of the legacy. But if [the testator] wished provision for a less industrious brother [of the legatee], one must hold that the heir has an interest and consequently that an undertaking should be given that the land will be purchased and not subsequently alienated.   1. One hundred were bequeathed to Titius to take to wife the widow Maevia; the condition will not be waived, nor accordingly will the undertaking. There is no conflict between this opinion and the fact that should someone promise money if there were no marriage to Maevia, the praetor would refuse an action. Depriving of free choice by fear of a penalty on one's option in marriage is one thing; to be invited into marriage by a will's provision is another.   2. One hundred are left to Titius not to abandon my monument or to establish his domicil in a given city. It can be said that there is no scope for an undertaking whereby the right of liberty is infringed; but our rule is different in respect of freedmen of the deceased.   3. "Let my heir give one hundred to my son-in-law, Titius, by way of dowry for my daughter, Seia." The benefit of the legacy indeed accrues to Seia who now has a dowry, but the interests of not only the woman but also the legatee, Titius, appear involved. Hence, the legatee himself is in mind and he should claim the legacy. Should the heir pay the money to the son-in-law subsequently to a divorce, he will equally be discharged from his duty; for the payment will be appropriated to the dowry. Moreover, even with the marriage subsisting and despite the woman's veto, payment is rightly made to Titius; for it is in the woman's interest that she should now find herself dowered. Again, even if one were to say that she herself could claim the money and she did not wish it to become a dowry, she would unquestionably be met by the defense of bad faith. Now should either Titius or Seia die before the nuptials, the legacy would remain with the heir. If, again, Titius should not wish to marry her, the ground of the legacy will be regarded as satisfied since it pertains to the woman herself, but a claim by Titius for the legacy would be foiled by the defense of bad faith. The view of Sabinus, however, was that once he married the woman, Titius could claim the legacy without any undertaking, since the money becomes dotal. Since, though, the legacy could be claimed even before the marriage, because it is unqualified, the undertaking "that the money will be rendered to the woman" would then become necessary. Now should the husband fail through his own fault and be insolvent, could not the innocent woman obtain relief against the heir in respect of the money destined for her dowry? Since both can claim the legacy, the wife will retain her action intact if the money is not paid to her husband.

72   PAPINIAN, *Questions, book 18:* Put the case of a legacy to Titia, "if she does not leave her children"; it has been denied that she validly gives an undertaking, since the condition of the legacy could eventuate after the death of the children. That view, however, did not commend itself; for so direful an interpretation of the nonrequirement of the undertaking was not to be set against a mother's aspiration.   1. Even when a patron bequeathed a sum of money to his freedman "if the latter did not desert [the patron's] children," the emperor allowed, in effect, a Mucian undertaking; it was, after all, both dangerous and grievous for a freedman, linked with the patron's children, to contemplate their demise.   2. Titius requested his instituted heir to restore the inheritance after his death, if the trust undertaking was not sought. He could not allow the precedent of the Mucian undertaking to take effect before the effecting of the remission of the other undertaking; for the condition could be satisfied within the lifespan of the intended beneficiary.   3. What say we then of the provision, "I ask you to make over the inheritance after your death," should no security of the trust be sought nor an account be required? Beyond any doubt, these words impose no condition of interposing an undertaking; the modality is restricted to the remission of negligence in the exacting of an account, not of bad faith. Such was the burden of a rescript in respect of one who conducted another's affairs and whose duty to account therefor was

waived by the will.   4. "If Seia marry to Titius's satisfaction, let my heir give her the land." Even should she marry during the life of Titius though without his approval, the answer should be that she gets the legacy; the provision is to bear the meaning that no absolute impediment to her marriage is involved. But, should Titius die during the testator's lifetime, then, though the condition fails, the woman is to be relieved; for what is in suspense should be treated as nonexistent.   5. "I give the estate, on my death, to Maevia, if she has not married." It can be said that even if she does marry, she will be admitted forthwith to the legacy. For it is not proved whether a specific or a nonspecific period has been written into the legacy.   6. The truer view is that an incorrect motivation is no impediment to a legacy because the reason for a bequest is no part of the bequest; still the defense of bad faith will generally be applicable if it be established that the testator would not otherwise have made the legacy.   7. Cassius and Caelius Sabinus describe as impossible this erroneous condition, "let Pamphilus be free if he pays Titius what I owe him," assuming that nothing is due to Titius; however, if there was a sum due which the testator paid after the making of the will, the condition would be regarded as failing.   8. Sabinus expressed the opinion that the false particularization of a legacy did not create a legacy. (A person, for instance, who had bequeathed nothing to Titius, might leave this provision: "Let my heir give to Seius fifty of the hundred which I have bequeathed to Titius.") This he deduced from the intention of the testator who so wrote with a view not to granting a legacy but to reducing one which he mistakenly thought himself to have left. Seius, however, could not, by reason of the false description, take more than if the legacy had been accurately described.

73   PAPINIAN, *Questions, book 19:* Land is left to Titius if he does not come into Asia; should he do so, the same land is left to Sempronius. Since, in the case of all conditions which will end with the demise of the legatee, it is accepted that the Mucian undertaking may be interposed, the heir accepts the undertaking from Titius and hands over the land to him. Should Titius later enter Asia, an *actio utilis* will oblige the heir to make over to Sempronius what the heir shall recover in proceedings on the stipulation of the undertaking. Should the undertaking lapse in the interim, however, not having been meticulously exacted, the heir will not be liable out of his own resources; since no reproach can be leveled against him, it will be enough that he make available [to Sempronius] the remedies which he has [against Titius]. Now suppose that on Titius's arriving in Asia Sempronius dies before receiving his legacy; there will be due to his heir what the deceased could have claimed.

74   PAPINIAN, *Questions, book 32:* A usufruct was left to a woman and Titius on condition that the woman did not marry. In the event of the woman's marrying, Titius, so long as he lives and his position is unchanged, will have his share of the usufruct. For the woman will be understood to receive, by the concession of the statute, only so much of the usufruct as she would have received if she had complied with the condition. And it would avail her nothing if Titius, not meeting the condition, repudiated the legacy.

75   PAPINIAN, *Questions, book 34:* A date uncertain of realization constitutes in a will a condition.

76   PAPINIAN, *Replies, book 6:* Resort to adoption does not exclude a trust left away from one's sons, "if any of them shall die without issue."

77   PAPINIAN, *Replies, book 7:* Having instituted her grandson part-heir on condition of his emancipation, a grandmother later wrote this codicil: "I further bequeath such-and-such fields to my grandson beyond his institution as my heir." One accepts that the condition of emancipation is repeated, although the grandmother may have made no such substitution in the legacy as in the institution to the inheritance. For also, in a case where a slave was made unconditionally free but conditionally instituted heir and further directed, if he did not become heir, to receive a legacy, the deified Pius ruled, in a rescript, that his freedom was repeated in the legacy.   1. The Mucian undertaking has no place if there be another condition which can delay an action for the legacy.   2. "Let the heir give one hundred to Titius if the woman marries"; Titius is charged to make over the same money to the same woman. If the woman marries

when the legacy has become operative, she can claim the trust; but if the trust were removed, the legatee could not invoke the precedent of the Mucian undertaking. 3. A head of household appointed tutors for his disinherited daughter and charged them that if the girl's mother died while the girl was still below puberty, they should take over the conduct of her affairs, since he had given his wife a mandate to make over, at her death, ten thousand to their joint daughter. The tutors are not regarded as appointed under a condition nor, if the girl require something in the meantime, are they inhibited from administering for her; an undertaking on the trust will, however, be waived for the mother. For an undertaking in respect of legacies or trusts can be waived by any indication of will. Accordingly, where no condition of exacting an undertaking is attached to a legacy or trust, the condition is not imposed *ipso facto*; nor is there any flaw in the matter, if someone did want an undertaking, but in fact it has not been forthcoming, since nowadays no public proceedings can be brought against an unwilling person, it having been settled that an undertaking can be dispensed with.

78   PAPINIAN, *Replies, book 9:* When either a *pupillus* or his tutor prevents the satisfaction of a condition inhering in the person of the *pupillus*, the condition is deemed to be fulfilled in the general law of both legacies and manumissions.   1. Where disjunctive conditions are prescribed, the failure of one does not prevent the realization, even at a later date, of the other; no more is it relevant whether conditions be within the power of the beneficiary to satisfy or fortuitous.

79   PAPINIAN, *Definitions, book 1:* "When Titius dies, let my heir give him one hundred." The legacy is direct, since it is suspended not by a condition but by a time lag; for the "condition" cannot fail to happen.   1. "Let my heir, when he himself dies, give one hundred to Titius"; this legacy *is* conditional because, though it is certain that my heir will die, it is not certain that he will do so in the legatee's lifetime. The legacy, consequently, does not become operative and it is uncertain that the legacy will come to the beneficiary.   2. One receiving a legacy on giving the Mucian undertaking has to restore also any produce from it to the heir if the stipulation becomes operative because he in some way breaches his undertaking; the legatee is constrained so to undertake from the very outset.   3. The legacy of a usufruct may be ineffective where the beneficiary dies; still the device of the Mucian undertaking has point where a usufruct is bequeathed with a condition that something be not done.   4. There is no validity in a provision written to impede marriage, contrary to the spirit of the statute, for instance, "let the heir give one hundred to the father, Titius, if the daughter in his power does not marry" or "let the heir give to a son-in-power if his father does not take a wife."

80   SCAEVOLA, *Questions, book 8:* Matters which forthwith preclude the doer should not be regarded in trusts as though they were conditions; on the other hand, we do, granted the undertaking, allow those with a time delay and expenditure; we do not treat *pari passu* one to whom something is given if he shall have erected a monument and the person to whom the gift is made to erect the monument.

81   PAUL, *Questions, book 21:* Julius Paul to Nymphidius: Your question is this: Suppose a provision of a will, "if Stichus renders accounts, let him be free together with the slave-woman with whom he lives and let the heir give them ten"; should Stichus die before rendering accounts, having an adjuster or balance, does the woman become free? And would we say the same of the legacy? Where freedom is granted on condition of rendering accounts, it is implicit therein that the person so charged be seen to render balances faithfully to his stewardship. If there be none, they will be held to have an unconditional grant of freedom; should the death occur after the heir's acceptance of the inheritance, the legacy, if freedom results, will be theirs also. But should Stichus die while still holding balances, the woman, being regarded as receiving freedom on the same terms, will be deemed not to have satisfied the condition. It is, though, not without a smack of elegance to say that Stichus indeed is conditionally manumitted but that his woman receives unqualified manumission, the linking of their names being, not to subject them to the same condition, but for the purpose of identification.   1. The condition will then be regarded as satisfied because its nonfulfillment is due to the one who would be liable if it had been satisfied.

82   CALLISTRATUS, *Questions, book 2:* A slave is directed to be free if he present his accounts, and the heir is charged to give him an estate; let us consider whether the condition be prepended to the freedom only or also to the legacy. Now if we were to accept that it concerns only the slave's liberty, further discussion would be unnecessary; the legacy being thus found unqualified would be ineffective. But if, as some justly think, the condition inheres also in the legacy, the legacy will become operative and effective once freedom ensues. What, then, is the import of the words: "if he present his accounts?" Some would say, "if he restore any balance," as though it mattered not whether the condition be rendering of accounts or restitution of any balance. For my own part, I do not consider the condition to be purely one of giving something or of doing something; rather it is a condition of mixed content. He will in no way become free if he hold a balance in some purse; the testator had not that in mind but rather that he should present accounts in the way in which a slave usually does present them; that is, he will present the accounts first for perusal and then for computation so that it can be established whether ascriptions have been properly or improperly made. Hence, in this way, the matter originates in activity but comes through to cash [settlement]. In the words, it is implicit that the heirs draw up advisement of the accounts so that they know what is written under which head of account. For the testator is understood to direct his heirs to effect what he would himself do, were he alive. And he certainly would not have merely signed the accounts of a slave showing cash in hand; he would want to read, check, and excerpt. All in all, then, when a slave is granted testamentary freedom subject to the condition, "if he render accounts," this means not merely that he produce to the heir all the records and documents of his stewardship but also discharge any balances.

83   PAUL, *Replies, book 12:* Lucius Titius made the following will: "If Aurelius Claudius, born of such-and-such woman, establish before a judge that he is my son, let him be my heir." Paul's opinion was that the supposititious son was instituted under a condition beyond his own power to realize and thus that the will was of no effect.

84   PAUL, *Replies, book 14:* "If they remain with my son, I want given to such-and-such freedmen by way of maintenance a hundred denarii each per month and a clothing allowance." The freedmen remained in obedience until the young man went onto military service, the effect of which was that leaving some of them at Rome, he set off to camp where he died. The question was whether the maintenance was due from his heirs. Paul replied that a condition pertaining to the persons of the freedmen who remained with the deceased's son, or who were not themselves at fault in failing to do so, was not taken to fail on the death of the testator's son. But if the testator's wish was that those with his son be given maintenance for the son's benefit, they should not be given a hearing on a claim contrary to the testator's intention.

85   SCAEVOLA, *Replies, book 3:* Titia charged it to the honor of her instituted heir, her son who had issue that he should "without any legal quibbling" restore her whole substance to his issue or to their children "when they should claim it." My query is whether the words "when they shall claim it from you" constitute a condition of the *fideicommissum*; the answer is: No.

86   MAECIAN, *Fideicommissa, book 3:* Our Julian was of the view that if a slave, directed to give ten and so become free, were manumitted by the testator during the latter's lifetime, he could not take a legacy which had been given to him with his freedom unless he complied with the [testamentary] condition; likewise, he would have to perform to his purchaser if he had been alienated. This, however, would hold good only in the case where the legacy could be acquired only with freedom, although the condition was not imposed on the legacy, that is, when the legacy was linked to the time of becoming free. 1. Now when freedom is granted subject to a condition but a legacy

as presently due, the question is whether the legacy is effective: the rationale of the *regula Catoniana* has no place here because even if the testator were to die forthwith, the legacy would not become wholly ineffective, since the condition of the slave's freedom could be realized before the heir's acceptance of the inheritance and the legacy so become due to the freedman, that is, of course, if there were no *heres necessarius*; in this latter case, the legacy would be quite invalid at civil law, since the gift of freedom was conditional.

87   VALENS, *Fideicommissa, book 1:* The rule is that in the case of legacies, one looks to the last stated condition but, in grants of liberty, to the most benign,

88   GAIUS, *Fideicommissa, book 1:* that is, to the one most to the slave's advantage.

89   VALENS, *Fideicommissa, book 1:* But this applies not only to those dispositions made commonly under diverse conditions but also to those which are made first without qualification and then subjected to a condition. Suppose, then, that the heir is directed to give or a legacy is made without qualification and then the same is subsequently left subject to a condition; the latter disposition prevails; but should the first disposition be conditional, the second unqualified, the latter takes effect. If, though, a conditional heir be charged or requested to make over a legacy forthwith, the case will be as if the same legacy were made with the previously inserted rider; the legacy [*per vindicationem*] can be claimed forthwith, if he so choose, by the legatee or he may seek it from the heir when the latter's condition has been satisfied, that is, unless, with a reference to the earlier bequest, a later one be framed thus: "Let my heir give to 'X,' if he shall have done this or that, the Stichus whom I bequeathed to 'Y'." In such case, the testator shows himself as revoking an existing bequest and making a conditional other one; then if [the new legatee] claim before the satisfaction of the condition, he may be met with the defense of bad faith.

90   GAIUS, *Fideicommissa, book 1:* When freedom is granted by *fideicommissum*, under a variety of provisos, one looks to not the most benevolent but the last, since the later wish prevails; a rescript of the deified Antoninus concurs.

91   MAECIAN, *Fideicommissa, book 2:* Conditions relating to the future are threefold in nature: Some look to the period of the testator's life; others, to the time after his death; and the others, to either period; the period comprised may be specific or indefinite. All this is applicable to *fideicommissa* no less than to the institution of heirs or to legacies. Take the condition: "to Titia if she becomes my wife"; this can obviously be satisfied only during the testator's life; now "if she attend my funeral"—clearly realizable only after the testator's death; but then, for example, "if she marry my son," this can be satisfied before or after the testator's death. Now the first and third of the above conditions are without limitation of time, since the condition is realized whenever she may marry; the second, on the other hand, pertains to a specific time.

92   ULPIAN, *Fideicommissa, book 5:* Suppose that a person to whom a legacy be left be asked to emancipate his children; will he be compellable to do so? I recall that I have held that the children have no claim for the *fideicommissum*; nor will the fideicommissary praetor come to their aid as he does to slaves. I also report that Papinian, in the ninth book of his *Replies*, writes that a man is not obliged to emancipate his issue. Still I am of opinion that, by extraordinary procedure, it should be established that he who accepts what was left to him in the expectation that he would emancipate his children, should be obliged to do so; for there should be no circumvention of the wishes of testators. The case should be treated as one of a legacy subject to the condition of manumitting his children or one for the purpose of so doing. With this there accords a rescript of the deified Severus. A certain woman instituted her grandsons as heirs with her son; their father, as co-heir, made each of them substitute heir in turn to the others and requested her son to emancipate his own issue; but she failed to ask him to make over the inheritance to them. On the authority of the deified Severus, the son was required to emancipate the grandchildren and make over the inheritance to them, with the further provision that in the event of his culpable delay, he would be charge-

able for interest; for one who appeared to delay over the emancipation should be taken to delay transfer of the *fideicommissum*.

93   PAPINIAN, *Replies, book 8:* A mother gave her son his own daughters as co-heirs without qualification and asked him to emancipate them, they to receive curators from the praetor. The son was held to have been charged to allow his daughters, become independent, entrance upon their grandmother's estate; that the father might seek a share equal to a daughter's by virtue of his institution (as heir) was not germane to the issue.

94   HERMOGENIAN, *Epitome of Law, book 1:* Liberty being granted in the form "if he give ten to Titius" (who is not the heir), a specific person is identified and, accordingly, only to that person can the condition be satisfied. Of course, if Titius dies and the slave has the money specified in the condition, he, as a *statuliber*, will, by settled law, acquire freedom without giving to anybody. The case would be different for a legatee; for him, there is no doubt, the condition fails, if Titius should die before the legatee gives the money.   1. Under the words "if he give ten to the heir or to the heir, Titius, let him be free," the slave can attain freedom by giving not only to the heir but to the heir's heir. Should the heir die without a successor, however, the law is settled that the slave becomes free without giving to anybody.

95   HERMOGENIAN, *Epitome of Law, book 4:* Where a legacy is left subject to a condition and is then transferred to someone else, the transfer is subject to the same condition unless its content be specific to a given individual.

96   PAUL, *Neratius, book 1:* A usufruct in a slave was bequeathed to Titius with the proviso that if the right should cease to be his, the slave received his freedom. Titius died during the testator's life. The grant of liberty has no effect for the condition never becomes operative. PAUL: It follows that the same be said, even if Titius survive but cannot take the usufruct.   1. A woman was left the legacy of a slave, so long as she was a widow. The same slave was directed to be free if the woman should marry. If the woman did marry, the slave would be free for freedom prevails over the legacy.

97   PAUL, *Neratius, book 2:* A legacy was left to townships, if they took an oath. The condition is not impossible of fulfillment. PAUL: But how can the towns comply with it? The oath will be sworn by those who conduct the town's affairs.

98   PAUL, *Neratius, book 3:* A conditional bequest can be made to me of something which is mine; for with this kind of legacy, one looks not to the time of the making of the will but to that of the realization of the condition.

99   PAPINIAN, *Questions, book 18:* Extrinsic conditions, not appearing in the will, that is, those tacitly inherent, do not make legacies conditional.

100   PAPINIAN, *Replies, book 7:* Titia was left two hundred if she did not marry; one hundred, if she did; she married. She may claim two hundred, but not also the further hundred; it would be absurd that the same woman should acquire both as spinster and as matron.

101   PAPINIAN, *Replies, book 8:* Her father by will designated Severiana Procula for marriage to her kinsman, Aelius Philippus; by fideicommissary words, he left this daughter a farm if she did marry Aelius Philippus, but if she did not so marry, he wished the same farm to go to Philippus. The girl died while still not of marriageable age. I gave the following opinion: where conditions in wills are concerned, we should look to the spirit rather than the words; the *fideicommissum* appears to be given to Aelius Philippus, if the deceased's daughter, Procula, declines to marry him; if, then, she dies before she becomes eligible for marriage, the condition does not seem to be realized.   1. Take this *fideicommissum*: "I want you to make over, if you die without issue"; the condition is not satisfied, if even one son be left surviving.   2. The words

of conditions laid down in wills are to be interpreted according to the testator's intention; hence, if tutors nominated in a will constitute themselves curators because the youth has meanwhile come of age, there will be deemed to be no failure of the condition, "if they administer the tutelage until he reaches eighteen," which is prefixed to a *fideicommissum*. 3. A mother-in-law left her daughter-in-law a *fideicommissum*, "if she continue to be my son's wife." A divorce being effected, without fault by the husband, after the mother-in-law's death, I gave the opinion that the condition had failed. The *fideicommissum* could not become operative without the prior death of husband or wife and the Mucian undertaking was inapplicable because the condition could have been satisfied by the husband's demise. 4. Monthly or annual *fideicommissa* were left to a freedman under the condition "so long as he conducts the affairs of the patron's daughter"; they have indeed to be paid, while the daughter forbids his administration of her affairs; but should the daughter change her mind, the condition revives; for the grants are individual.

102   PAPINIAN, *Replies, book 9:* A grandfather instituted as heirs his son and a grandson by another son; he then requested the grandson, should he die before the age of thirty, to make over the [whole] inheritance to his uncle. The grandson died leaving issue but before attaining thirty. My ruling was that considerations of duty meant that the condition of the *fideicommissum* failed, because less was expressed than was intended.

103   PAUL, *Questions, book 14:* Put this legacy: "Let him give to Titius after ten years, if he does not exact security from the heir"; Titius dies before the ten years are up. He [Titius] passes on the legacy to his own heir, because the condition is realized by his death.

104   PAUL, *Replies, book 14:* A person, deported after the opening of the will but then restored, can claim a *fideicommissum*, the condition of which is satisfied after his recovery of Roman citizenship.

105   POMPONIUS, *Letters, book 5:* Land was bequeathed by a testator subject to a condition; while the condition was pending, the heir left it to someone else; on the realization of the condition set out in the first will, ownership [of the land] will not be lost to the first legatee nor will the heir have been able to make any part of it religious or create a servitude over it: Indeed, any servitude already created will be ended by the satisfaction of the condition.

106   JULIAN, *Digest, book 25:* A legacy, "if she does not marry Titius", is to be treated as if the legacy were one after the death of Titius. There can thus be no taking of the legacy by reason of the interposition of the Mucian undertaking. But she will take the legacy by marrying someone else.

107   GAIUS, *Cases, sole book:* It sometimes happens that a seemingly conditional legacy is to be construed as without qualification; for example, it is left under the same condition as that under which the heir is instituted. So, also, if the legacy be, "if the heir accept the inheritance." Conversely, a legacy, apparently unconditional, becomes treated as conditional; put the case that there be a conditional ademption of a legacy bequeathed subject to the converse condition.

108   SCAEVOLA, *Digest, book 19:* A man left his house to all his freedmen, adding, "if they live in it, do not eschew [my] name and, reduced to one survivor, that survivor will get the house; it is my further wish that my said freedmen receive the Sosian estate." The question was: Does the condition of "not eschewing my name" apply to the further legacy? The answer was: Yes.

109   SCAEVOLA, *Digest, book 20:* An heir, requested by the testator to accept one hundred pieces of money and to make over the estate to his co-heiress, Titia, died after taking the inheritance; so did Titia, before giving the hundred. The issue was whether Titia's heir, by offering the hundred of the *fideicommissum*, could acquire the portion of the inheritance; the reply was that the heir could not fulfill the condition. CLAUDIUS: His answer, viewing the law generally, does not appear conspicuous for perspicacity; there is room for doubt whether the case raises an issue of a condition.

110   POMPONIUS, *Letters, book 9:* Suppose that a *statuliber* give money from his *peculium* to Titius, notwithstanding the protests of the heirs; the *statuliber* becomes a free man. But Titius, who takes the money, knowing of the heirs' disapproval, holds that money purely as possessor and it can be recovered from him by the reluctant heirs.

111   POMPONIUS, *Letters, book 11:* Someone is directed to be free on condition of presenting his accounts. He must establish general belief that in all that he performed, he concealed nothing of what he received, that he did not attribute to the accounts expenses which he did not incur; again, should there be any surplus, in the light of what he has written, he must pay it over; in no other way, can he attain the liberty accorded him, save as above set out. However, in the case of debtors whom he himself contracts, he does not have to show that they were solvent at the time of his master's death but only that advances were made to persons such as would have received credit from a diligent head of household.

112   POMPONIUS, *Letters, book 12:* Conditions imposed upon more than one, for example, "if they erect a monument," can be realized by all those persons together.   1. Again, "if Titius give one hundred to Symphorus and Januarius, I leave him the estate." Is the legacy lost if Symphorus be dead? Now, in this case too, I think that the interpretation should be on the following lines: While both were alive, Titius would have to comply; a liberal interpretation, however, suggests, assuming that there was no culpable default by Titius on Symphorus's death, that he can take half the legacy on giving fifty to Januarius.   2. This raises the further question whether an estate is devised to certain people if they bear the expense of the [deceased's] funeral and get him buried in another region. The condition can be satisfied only by both so that, unless both participate, there is a legacy to neither. Here again our more beneficent interpretation is that land being devised to two if they give ten, it is equally due to either who gives half that sum.   3. The declared view of Priscus was that a *statuliber* does not have to render accounts always in the place where the head of household died or where he himself is left or in any venue he personally choose; sometimes, he should go where the person is to whom he is to render his accounts, if the latter be away on state business. The best view is that the matter be determined in the light of all the circumstances.

113   PAUL, *Imperial Pronouncements in Judicial Proceedings, book 2 of 6:* A father asked of his son that, should he die before he was eligible to conduct his own affairs, he should make over the estate to Titius. The young man reached twenty and then died. A rescript held that the *fideicommissum* was to be honored.

2

THE *LEX FALCIDIA*

1   PAUL, *Lex Falcidia, sole book:* There was promulgated the *lex Falcidia* which, in its first chapter, granted free power of disposition by bequest up to "three quarters" of one's substance. The wording of that chapter is this: "Any Roman citizen who, after the promulgation of this statute, wishes to make a will, giving his money and possessions to whom he choose, shall have the right and power so to do, so far as this ensuing enactment permits." The second chapter imposes a limitation on legacies in the following terms: "Any Roman citizen who, after the promulgation of this statute, makes his will shall have the right and power, under the general law, to give and bequeath money to any Roman citizen so long as the legacy [or legacies] be such that the heirs take not less than a quarter of the estate under the will; those to whom anything be so given or bequeathed may lawfully take the money, and the heir charged to give that money will

have to give the sum with which he is charged." 1. The *lex Falcidia* is held applicable also to those who die in enemy hands by reason of the *lex Cornelia*; for this latter enactment confirms their testamentary dispositions as if they had died citizens. By virtue of this fiction, the *lex Falcidia* and all other testamentary enactments which may be relevant are applicable. 2. The *lex Falcidia* has no application to those who possess an inheritance in the absence of a will; but the import of the statute is introduced through the praetor's edict. 3. The same holds good whether a condition of an oath has been waived. 4. Even if a testator, having granted his slave his freedom, leave him a legacy, since that bequest is deferred until such time as he is free, as also if the bequest be to a prisoner of war or to a person yet unborn, this statute is operative. 5. So also with legacies to townships or even to the gods. 6. The statute governs legacies not only of the testator's own property but also of that of third parties. 7. Everything emanating from the deceased's estate is regulated by this enactment, be it corporeally specific or nonspecific, dependent upon weight, enumeration, or measurement or even a right (say, usufruct) or consisting in debts. 8. Again, suppose a legacy: "Let my heir provision Seius; if he does not do so, let him give him ten"; there are those who think that there is simply a legacy of ten, that the provisions are taken in contemplation of death, and thus that the heir cannot impute them to the statute. My teaching, however, has been that if the heir furnishes the provisions forthwith, they are to be regarded as bequeathed and so subject to the *lex Falcidia*; my saying "forthwith" must be taken to imply a certain time lapse. But if the heir, after culpable delay, make over the provisions, [Seius] does not accept them as a legacy and the *lex Falcidia* will not apply; for, in such a case, the legacy has been transformed, and the ten are due. So also if the legacy were from the outset: "If he does not provision him, let him give ten"; for such provisions do not constitute a legacy, and if the provisions are given, they are taken by reason of the death, the condition of the legacy having failed. 9. Suppose a legacy of a usufruct (which can even be divided; other servitudes are indivisible); the older jurists were of the view that the usufruct as a whole should be valued and the amount of the legacy thus determined. Aristo, however, diverged from the earlier opinion; he maintained that a quarter could be retained out of it as from corporeal things; and Julian correctly endorses this. But with a legacy of the services of a slave, neither use nor usufruct being comprised in such a legacy, the older view is essential for us to quantify the legacy; for a part can be removed from anything which is made up but one cannot envisage a part of a day's service. Indeed, even if the question arise over a usufruct how much the fructuary takes and how much is the valuation of the other legacies—and even of the usufruct itself so that the legacy does not exceed three quarters, one must necessarily have recourse to the opinion of the older jurists. 10. When a man bequeaths to his creditor what he owes him, either the legacy is pointless, if the creditor derives no benefit from it, or it may be beneficial (say, through the advantage of representation); in which case, that advantage will attract the *lex Falcidia*. 11. Should a legatee acquire possession and the thing cannot be taken away from him, he having acquired possession with the agreement of the heir who was in error, the heir will be given an action to recover the excess over three quarters. 12. Sometimes, it will perforce be necessary to make delivery in full to the legatee but with a stipulation that he will repay the excess which he takes beyond the *lex Falcidia*; let us take the case that legacies away from a *pupillus* do not exceed the Falcidian limit, but there is apprehension that should he die before puberty, there may be found other legacies which, when contribution is made, exceed three quarters. The same is to be said if, in the principal will, conditional legacies are made and it is uncertain whether they will be due. Accordingly, should the heir be willing to pay, without recourse to litigation, he should safeguard himself by this stipulation. 13. What comes to a co-heir through his substitution to his co-heir benefits the legatees; his case is akin to that of the heir instituted partly without qualification, partly with a conditionally appointed heir. Legacies bequeathed away from him, however, will not be increased, should he not take the inheritance, assuming that they are left away from him by name and not from "whoever shall be my heir." 14. Should the share of my co-heir be exhausted while mine remains intact and I claim mine, Cassius thinks that the shares are merged; but not so Proculus; in this case, Julian adheres to Proculus, and I too think his the more plausible view. But the deified Antoninus is reported to have ruled that the two shares are to be merged for the Falcidian computation. 15. Were I to adrogate my co-heir after the acceptance of the inheritance, there is no doubt that our shares are to be treated separately, just as would happen if I became heir to my co-heir. 16. Put the case of a legacy over several years to Titius; the legacies being both several and conditional, there will be scope for the edictal undertaking, "to restore the excess received." 17. What is due by reason of the nature of the inheritance and yet cannot, as such, be claimed is not recoverable if it has been made over, and so there are those who think that it is not to be counted in the inheritance. Julian, though, holds that such items do or do not increase the inheritance, according to the event, and so they are taken by right of inheritance and come into the restoration of the inheritance. 18. When a debtor becomes his creditor's heir, although the confusion of the claims releases him [as debtor], he still is held to take a more lucrative inheritance so that, despite the merging consequent upon his acceptance of the inheritance, the debt is to be taken into account. 19. The question has been posed whether the costs of erecting a monument can be deducted [for Falcidian purposes]. Sabinus holds them deductible if the erection had to be made. When consulted on the issue whether the costs of the funeral and of the monument, as directed by the testator, might be attributed to the debts [of the estate], Marcellus expressed the view that no more could be deducted than the funeral expenses; the case of the expenditure on the erection of the monument was different; for its erection was not essential for there to be a funeral and burial; it followed that a person to whom money was bequeathed to erect a monument would fall under the *Falcidia*.

2   MARCELLUS, *Digest, book 22:* No more is to be allowed than is adequate for a modest form of memorial.

3   PAUL, *Lex Falcidia, sole book:* An instituted heir sells the estate which was insolvent; can it be credited that an insolvent estate would find a purchaser? Right thinking directs that nothing is due to the legatees; for the instituted heir is to be held to have what he has through the purchaser's stupidity rather than from the substance of the deceased. Conversely, if the heir made an injudicious sale of hereditary assets, that would not detrimentally affect the legatees. In short, the heir derives the benefit of his prudent administration. 1. Again, if an insolvent bestowed legacies and his heir made a composition with his creditors to make less than payment in full, in consequence of which he salvaged something [from the estate], none of this would be due to legatees for the heir would have that money by reason of the composition, not by virtue of the inheritance. 2. Further, when Falcidian issues are raised in respect of a legacy from year to year to a community, Marcellus opines that the capital of the legacy is to be held to be the amount sufficient for the collection of interest amounting to one third of the sum bequeathed.

4   PAPINIAN, *Questions, book 16:* Land was bequeathed to me subject to a condition, and while the condition was pending, the heir instituted me as his heir; subsequently, the condition was realized. For Falcidian accounting, the land is attributed to my

legacy, not to the right of inheritance.

5 PAPINIAN, *Replies, book 8:* There is not necessarily left to a city, by words of legacy or of *fideicommissum*, what has to be performed by reason of a solemn promise. Hence, if the testator has exceeded in his will the amount due, the surplus alone will be diminished under the *Falcidia*; it cannot, therefore, be a charge on the honor of the legatee. But if a time clause or a condition will activate the legacy, the whole is claimable which has been given, not an assessment of its utility. Even if the day arrives or the condition is satisfied while the testator still lives, what has once become effective will not be nullified.

6 VENULEIUS, *Stipulations, book 13:* A husband who becomes his wife's heir and incurs expenses on her obsequies will not be seen to incur the whole outlay as heir; there will be a deduction of what he should contribute in respect of the dowry by which he profited.

7 PAPINIAN, *Questions, book 7:* Should the *lex Falcidia* come in the way, a servitude bequeathed, being indivisible, will be due in full, only if an assessment of the appropriate portion be tendered [by the beneficiary].

8 PAPINIAN, *Questions, book 14:* For Falcidian purposes, a debt left in the inheritance which one of the heirs is specifically charged to pay will be counted only in respect of that heir.

9 PAPINIAN, *Questions, book 19:* In respect of the *Falcidia*, the rule has commended itself that where crops are gathered subsequently which were mature at the deceased's death, they increase the valuation of the inheritance so far as concerns the land which appears to have been thereby the more valuable at the time of the death. 1. Where a slave-woman is *enceinte*, no distinctions of time are taken and rightly; issue yet unborn cannot be rightly said to be a slave.

10 PAPINIAN, *Questions, book 20:* What may come from other sources to the heir in excess of three quarters does not work to the heir's disadvantage where more than three quarters of the estate has been left in legacies; an example would be the inheritance of a *pupillus* who was substituted to a disinherited person who was the heir of the father of the *pupillus*.

11 PAPINIAN, *Questions, book 29:* For computations under the *lex Falcidia*, retentions of any period are attributed to the heir's quarter. 1. A slave, conditionally granted his liberty in the will, died; if, indeed, the condition were by then satisfied, the slave will not be held to have died to the heir's loss; should the condition have failed, however, reason points to the opposite conclusion, but he will be regarded as having died a *statuliber*. 2. The Emperor Marcus Aurelius ruled that heirs deprived of part of the estate will be chargeable for legacies only in respect of what they retain. 3. Someone was relegated with the loss of half his property; he appealed and, having made a will, died; after his death, his appeal was dismissed. The question was whether half had been removed as a debt so that only the residue constituted his estate or did it appear right to give relief to his heir. The latter course commends itself; for the aspirations of a litigant seeking a favorable decision authorize this view. 4. A slave manumitted by will who dies before the acceptance of the inheritance is certainly regarded as dying to the heir's loss. Should there not be, however, an assessment of his value as if he lived? For it has been held that those also who, at the master's death, are in such bad health that they surely cannot survive, subsequently die to the diminution of the inheritance. The case is no different from that of those who are under the same roof when a master is murdered by his household. 5. Let us examine the widespread dictum that where a father has made one will for himself and his son, a single Falcidian computation is to be made. For even though the substitute, if the son had become heir, owes what comes to him from the *pupillus* like any other debt, still, in respect of the second will [the substitute's own institution], there is scope for contribution. It can, in consequence, be the case that the substitute retains nothing or, conversely, that he has far more than a quarter of the father's substance. Now what if the son's inheritance does not meet the

legacies when the father's would have done so? The substitute will have to give out of his own purse because the father made the legacies out of his own wealth. It is irrelevant that under no will is performance due beyond the resources of the estate because in this branch of the law, legacies bequeathed under the second will are regarded as having been left conditionally in the first will.   6. It is a common topic of consideration whether, when a testator substitutes two [heirs] to his son and burdens the share of one of them, that substitute can invoke in his own right the *Falcidia* which would not avail the *pupillus* himself or the other substitute. It might glibly be said, following what appears above concerning the patrimony, that the *Falcidia* is not applicable and that the second substitute may be charged in excess of his share. The truer view, however, is the opposite one, that is, that of those who hold that a quarter must be left to this substitute just as if he had been heir to the father. For in the same way that the substance of the father and the contribution of the legacies take their form and origin from the father's will, so a plurality of substitutes, on the demise of the *pupillus*, are brought in as though instituted heirs. But what say we of the unburdened substitute? Suppose that the *pupillus* has not yet discharged the legacies bequeathed away from him, that, overall, more than three quarters of the estate has been disposed of, can he himself [the substitute] invoke the *Falcidia*? The fact is that he has his quarter, and a comparison with the instituted heir is not apposite. Indeed, were we to say otherwise, the reply would be manifestly at variance with the general view. There is thus scope for diversity; a person burdened in his own name may, like an instituted heir, claim a quarter; the other who is not burdened, will, as a substitute, not be liable in full, even though his share is enlarged, in consequence of the merger of the calculation. It follows that if security were given to the *pupillus* over the *Falcidia*, the stipulation is operative for both, obviously in respect of that share which each is entitled to retain for himself.   7. The following question has been put: If his co-heir be substituted to a *pupillus*, how is the spirit of the *lex Falcidia* to be interpreted and what of the common assertion of the separate accounting of legacies? My answer was that in respect of legacies bequeathed away from either the *pupillus* or the substitute by the testator father, no separation is to be made; they are subject to an overall calculation and import reciprocal contribution. Legacies bequeathed away from an instituted heir who is not one of the family, however, should not be mingled with other legacies; accordingly, a substitute will get a quarter of the share of the *pupillus*, even though he has his own quarter as though an instituted heir. The case is different from that of an heir appointed to differing shares; for then there is a general accounting of the legacies no less than if he had been named, once and for all, for the resultant total of the several shares left to him; and it is of no consequence whether he be instituted heir repeatedly or under a diversity of conditions.   8. Should someone substitute the instituted heir to his disinherited son and make legacies away from him also by the second will, the account will of necessity be merged; for Julian says that the legacies left away from the substitute are valid because he stands as heir to the father.

12   PAPINIAN, *Questions, book 30:* Suppose a debtor, having instituted his creditor as heir, request of him that for the purposes of the *lex Falcidia*, he should not account his debt against the legatees, there is no doubt that before the Falcidian arbitrator, the wishes of the deceased will be respected by virtue of the defense of bad faith.

13   PAPINIAN, *Questions, book 37:* It has been ruled that a slave, taking a tacit *fideicommissum* at his master's behest, will have the benefit of the *lex Falcidia*, since it was his duty to obey his master; the same was accepted in the case of a son in his father's power.

14   PAPINIAN, *Replies, book 9:* A head of household instituted as part-heiress his daughter who had divorced her husband and requested of her that she should make over her share to her brother and co-heir, having deducted one sixth in the Falcidian computation as compensation for her dowry. I gave the opinion that if, with the daughter's consent, the father had not claimed the dowry, the daughter would have her Falcidian entitlement by the law of succession and a claim to the dowry in her own right, since the dowry is not found among the assets of the father's inheritance.   1. Having instituted her grandsons as heirs, a grandmother charged them by *fideicommissum* that they should forego their Falcidian retention under another will and should pay their legacies in full to their brothers and coheirs. I said that the *fideicommissum* was valid, but its burden was one to be shared among them.   2. It is accepted that where a person substituted to two *impuberes* becomes

heir to each of them, he cannot invoke the *lex Falcidia* in respect of the estate of one, if he can, from the assets of the other, retain the quarter of the father's estate which should come to the sons. 3. But if one brother succeeds the other as heir at law and then the substitute succeeds the one dying later, the share of the father's assets which the intestate youth receives is not merged in the Falcidian account; the substitute will retain only that quarter received by the boy to whom he is in fact a substitute.

15 PAPINIAN, *Replies, book 13:* In the event that there should contribute to the estate under the *lex Falcidia* a debtor whose debt was waived by a pact in contemplation of death, what he should give will be retained through a replication framed on the facts of the case. 1. A brother, appointing as heiress his sister, provided that a third person should stipulate from his intended beneficiary that she would not invoke the *lex Falcidia* [against him] and that should she do so, she should pay a specified sum. It is established that statutes of general application cannot be flouted by private arrangements; the sister will thus have her right of retention under the general law, and no action on the stipulation will be granted. 2. Suppose that a legacy over a period of years had been paid, without deduction, to the legatee in the first and second years; the Falcidian reckoning is not deemed to be excluded thereby for the years still to pass. 3. The application of the Falcidian rationale will be that if his grandson be sole heir to his grandfather, anything that the latter owed the former as a result of his guardianship of him will, I gave as my opinion, be deducted as a debt from the [grandfather's] estate. It matters not that the grandfather-tutor asked his heir that should the latter die without issue before reaching a stated age, he should make over by *fideicommissum* both what he inherited and his own property; the inheritance is not thereby regarded as compensated for the debt, not least because it is expressly stated that there is no compensation or set-off, the deceased making clear that his heir has his own estate. Of course, where the condition of the *fideicommissum* was honored, fruits of the estate gathered after the grandfather's death would, no less than money, be a set-off to the guardianship debt. The grandson's heir, though, will still retain for himself a quarter of the assets which his grandfather left at his death. 4. A *fideicommissum* was due under the [deceased] mother's will on the death of the father; the father wished a set-off thereto to be made from his own inheritance which he left to his son; should Falcidian accounting be instituted, there will be a set-off against the debt to the son of a quarter of what he realizes from the father's estate and so only the balance of the debt, if any, will be deducted from the three quarters. 5. Whatever a woman's heir is obliged to give to her husband out of gifts made to her is not regarded as part of her assets. To the extent that he is enriched, she is deemed to have been the poorer. Any expenditure made by her heir, however, from her property will not be a detriment to the husband. 6. Where the produce of land, left conditionally by words of *fideicommissum*, is concerned, it is not brought within the concept of the *fideicommissum* in that for Falcidian purposes, the heir must be content to take a quarter of the estate at the time of the death and a quarter of the fruits as from then. This is inapplicable where the *lex Falcidia* is involved. For even granted its pertinence once the condition of the *fideicommissum* has been satisfied, the heir must still have his quarter of the produce as from the day of death. 7. A *fideicommissum*, granted to his mother to supplement the share to which her son has instituted her heiress, will go to the mother with the Falcidian reduction, and she will take it in addition to the quarter of her instituted share. 8. The quarter retainable under the *lex Falcidia* can be no more reduced than eliminated by the testator's assessment.

16 SCAEVOLA, *Questions, book 3:* Suppose that an heir duly hand over some of the numerous legacies; by the defense of the *lex Falcidia*, he can make retentions in respect of the remainder even on account of what he has already disposed of. 1. Again, should there be a single legacy, part of which has been discharged, full Falcidian retention may be made from the remainder.

17 SCAEVOLA, *Questions, book 6:* Let us imagine a soldier who makes codicils after his discharge from service and dies within the year; it is said that legacies in his will, made on service under military law, are to be paid in full, those in the codicils, subject to the Falcidian deduction. However, the matter works out as follows: Suppose that having four hundred, our soldier dispose of four hundred by will and then a further hundred in codicils;

from the codicilliary fifth, that is, eighty, which, but for the *lex Falcidia*, would go to
the legatee, the heir will retain twenty, that is, a quarter.

18 PAUL, *Questions, book 11:* A son-in-power on military service on his death charged
his head of household by codicil with a *fideicommissum* to make over to Titius his [the
son's] *peculium castrense*. The question was whether the heir could deduct a quarter.
My answer was that the deified Pius had extended the *lex Falcidia* on account of
fideicommissa even to the succession to intestates; in the present context, however,
there was no inheritance, although I would have agreed that had an heir outside the
family been instituted, his acceptance would have created an inheritance. Since,
though our deceased remained with his head of household, the erstwhile state continued and the property was *peculium*. This in no way conflicts with the fact that the
lex Falcidia regulates the will of one who dies a prisoner of war; for the fiction of the
lex Cornelia at once creates both inheritance and heir. I said further, however, that I
had no doubt that the spirit of the statute should [and would] be honored, if the father
were indeed required to transfer the assets as though they were those of a head of
household and he were sued in respect of legacies, on the pattern of the edict, as
though he were an instituted heir who did not make acceptance under the will.
1. Further to this, if the father in the interim had a quarter of the produce and the
produce of a quarter, we could also invoke the *senatus consultum Trebellianum*, and
actiones utiles would lie and the inheritance exist after its making over.

19 SCAEVOLA, *Questions, book 8:* Should an heir be charged to sell for five an estate
worth ten, he can certainly set five against the *lex Falcidia*.

20 SCAEVOLA, *Questions, book 9:* My slave having been instituted heir and a legacy
left to me, Maecian says that on my acquiring the inheritance, the legacy does not
come into the Falcidian computation because it is not a claimable debt.

21 PAUL, *Questions, book 12:* Suppose that a *pupillus* to whom ten were lent without
his tutor's authority be given a legacy by his creditor under the condition that he repay to the creditor's heir the ten which he received, the youth, by the single payment,
both satisfies the condition and discharges his natural obligation so that it is imputed
to the heir for Falcidian purposes. There would be no such imputation if the payment
were simply to discharge the condition. So far, indeed, is the youth regarded as having
paid his debt that even if he repudiate the legacy or if Stichus, its object, should die,
he can recover nothing.   1. My slave and I are instituted heirs to different shares;
three quarters are not charged on the slave; the legacies bequeathed away from me
will count against the *Falcidia* in respect of what comes to me from his share beyond
the Falcidian quota thereof. Conversely, if a slave were bequeathed to my slave and
ten to me, the slave's Falcidian assessment is not affected by my legacy of ten on the
very pattern of the Falcidian itself. For I retain a quarter through the person of my
slave although nothing be expended from my share.

22 PAUL, *Questions, book 17:* Nesennius Apollinaris to Julius Paul. Sir, this case actually happened. Titia instituted her three daughters as heiresses in equal shares and
appointed legacies from each to other; from one, however, she bequeathed away both
to her co-heiresses and to nonmembers of the family so that the *Falcidia* came into
play. My query is this: Can that daughter invoke against her co-heiresses, as against
whom she herself receives legacies, the *lex Falcidia*, and if she either cannot or can be
countered with the defense of bad faith, how will the Falcidian calculation be set in
process against the nonmember of the family? I replied as follows: What is acquired
from a co-heir by way of legacy does not avail the legatee for Falcidian relief in the
normal course of events; when the person to provide a legacy claims something from
the intended beneficiary under the will, he is certainly not to be heard in an attempt to
invoke the *Falcidia* against that beneficiary, if what he is to take by the testator's wish
makes up for what he seeks to offset. Naturally, he cannot set against the other
legatees the whole of what he has to give to his co-heir but only what he would have
had to give, if he received nothing from the latter.   1. Where a slave is instituted heir

and *fideicommissa* are bequeathed away from his master, legacies away from the slave, the legacies are first to be taken into reckoning and then, from the residue, the *fideicommissa*. For the master is liable in respect of what comes to him; but what comes to him is what is left after the legacies. Of course, he may exercise his Falcidian entitlement. 2. Even if the master, waiving acceptance of the inheritance for himself, bade the slave accept as his substitute, account would first be taken of what had been disposed of away from the master himself and then of what was left away from the slave, if the *Falcidia* applied. 3. Should a debtor receive a legacy of release from his debt, the whole legacy will come into account, even though he be insolvent, although the debt will not automatically increase the size of the inheritance. Hence, if the *Falcidia* be applicable, there will be deemed to be a legacy also of what is left to the debtor; the other legacies are reduced by it and it also by the others; for he is treated as receiving something by the fact of his release. 4. But were the debt bequeathed to someone else, there would be no legacy and no contribution to the others.

23 SCAEVOLA, *Questions, book 15:* Where land is left to me and also a right of way, then, in the Falcidian computation, if the right of way be worth as much as the excess over the Falcidian entitlement, the land will be taken in full and the right of way will not exist. Again, should a right of way be devised but the estate be insolvent, the servitude will not be due. Let us now consider the case when the land and the right of passage are left and less is required [by the *Falcidia*] from each devise than the value of the servitude. One may say by strained reasoning not only that the land is taken as a whole but also that the defense of bad faith exacts only any deficit so that [the heir] may not retain more than the *Falcidia* requires. Consequently, the servitude will fail only when more is demanded under the statute than the value of it.

24 PAUL, *Replies, book 14:* His answer was that if an account has to be taken under the *lex Falcidia*, it should be on the basis that the items taken away from the heir did not form part of the inheritance. 1. He gave the further opinion that the issue of slave-women born before the date of the *fideicommissum* belong to the heirs of the man charged with the trust and' that they are to be included in the quarter and the produce thereof if any question of the *lex Falcidia* should arise. 2. The same jurist replied that produce of something belonging to the heir himself, which is collected before the *fideicommissum* becomes operative, should not be included in the heir's quarter even though it does not have to be made over to the fideicommissary.

25 SCAEVOLA, *Replies, book 4:* A woman instituted her husband and their son as heirs in equal parts; the question was raised: In a Falcidian account, is there to be counted against the husband what he acquires also from the same inheritance through his son? The reply was that if the husband receives from the institution of the son as much as will satisfy the *lex Falcidia*, no deduction should be made in respect of the quarter. 1. A testator left away from his freedman to whom he had devised an estate a *fideicommissum* of ten per year to Seia; the problem: If the *lex Falcidia* reduces the freedman's legacy, is the annual *fideicommissum* of ten to Seia also held to be reduced since the income of the land would provide the payments? He replied that on the case as stated, there appeared no such reduction, unless it be shown that the testator was of a different mind.

26 SCAEVOLA, *Replies, book 5:* A testator bequeathed a string of thirty-five pearls which was, at the time of his death, in the hands of the legatee; my question is whether the *lex Falcidia* requires the return of the necklace to the heir. The reply was that the heir can achieve its return or, if he so prefer, vindicate the share of the necklace which should remain his by reason of accounting under the *lex Falcidia*. 1. Question: Does the *lex Falcidia* include the value of statues? Answer: It does.

27 SCAEVOLA, *Replies, book 6:* "If, within a month of my death, Seius and Agerius undertake to our state that, forgoing the protection of the *lex Falcidia*, they will be content with so many gold pieces, let them be my heirs. I substitute them, each to the other. If they do not comply with my wishes, be they disinherited." The issue was this: Can the instituted heirs accept the inheritance if they do not wish to honor the condition, since each has a substitute under the condition set out? The reply was that Seius and Agerius can accept, as instituted heirs of the first rank, as though the condition, added in circumvention of the statute did not exist.

28   MAECIAN, *Fideicommissa, book 1:* Where a son bequeaths legacies to his father, having instituted a different heir, the father is subject to a Falcidian account.

29   PAUL, *Fideicommissa, book 2:* If a *fideicommissum* or legacy be left away from me to you and you are charged to restore it to me after a certain time, I do not think this accountable under the *lex Falcidia*; for I subsequently begin to hold it as a fideicommissary.

30   MAECIAN, *Fideicommissa, book 8:* For the purposes of the *lex Falcidia*, the deaths of slaves or of animals, thefts, robberies, fires, collapse of buildings, shipwrecks, incursions of the enemy, brigands or footpads, bad debts, in short any loss, fall on the heir, if the legatee be without fault. By the same token, there accrue to the heir's benefit, fruits, the issue of slave-women, acquisitions through slaves such as stipulations, things delivered to them, legacies or inheritances which are given to them and other gifts, as also servitudes releasing, or enhancing the value of, land, and actions acquired through them, for example, for theft, damage wrongfully caused, and so forth—none of these calls for reckoning under the *lex Falcidia*.   1. Where someone is directed to sell or to buy at a stated price some land or any other item for the purposes of the *lex Falcidia*, when as much is obtained under that head as the legacy requires, any excess or deficiency in the thing in relation to the amount which the testator directed to be given or received is to be brought in; but so that a greater deduction be made in that share which will be created when the legacies have been excluded; for what we are deemed to take for ourselves is not that value as such but a legacy of the balance after it has been deducted.   2. It has further to be carefully observed that the dictum that losses occurring after the testator's death fall only on the heir is not to be accepted absolutely and without any qualification. What would be the full entitlement without the *lex Falcidia* will be the same entitlement in the share created by the *lex Falcidia*. This ensures that subsequent losses will not be taken into account, so that the portion lost will not diminish legacies or *fideicommissa*.   3. The truth is that a deduction is made only from those things which exist by weight, number, or measurement; subsequent incidental loss from the share established in the assessment of items existing at the testator's death produces no reduction.   4. In the case, however, of specified items and of those left in any of the following terms, "the money which I have in that chest," "the wine in those containers," "the weight of silver which I have in that warehouse," then, assuming that the items be lost or deteriorate without fault on the heir's part, it is beyond doubt either that nothing is due or that a share will be due of the items as they now stand, following the valuation of the items which existed at the time of the testator's death, in accordance with the *lex Falcidia*.   5. Nonspecific bequests, however, admit of distinctions; suppose that the testator leave something unidentified from his assets, for example, "the silver which he may choose," and all the testator's silver has been destroyed without fault on the heir's part, nothing will be due. Had a weight of silver, however, been unreservedly bequeathed, then, even though none of the testator's silver survived, a share thereof is, subject to the *lex Falcidia*, to be taken as it existed in the testator's possession at his death; subsequent causal losses do not avail to minimize the quantity in any way.   6. Where things have ceased to exist, neither they nor even their valuation will be due, any more than if each item had been bequeathed under a specific description.   7. Now, granted that items given to the heir for the fulfillment of a condition do not come into account under the *lex Falcidia*, nonetheless, anything that a person is charged to take, not by way of condition, from the person to whom he is directed to transfer the estate, it pleased the worthy Celsus and Julian to hold accountable; the case would be like that of the heir directed to sell those things at that figure, the situation being that no fulfillment of a condition is prescribed, but in a way, a price for the items is introduced. In this context, it has been further asked whether in these circumstances the fideicommissary would, even against his will, be compelled to give the sum and to accept the inheritance, as though the charge were to his honor. This is improbable since the formulation would appear intended to favor him rather than to redound to his disadvantage. 8. Where the *lex Falcidia* applies, legacies or *fideicommissa* left to the heir himself or to his slave, away from the heir, do not come into contribution. Different is the case of

benefactions granted with liberty for a specific date; once the date of freedom begins to run, such benefactions will be due to him and will come into reckoning. No more do ineffective bequests or *fideicommissa* to one's slave, but without his liberty, fall within the statute. 9. A thing which, beyond doubt, cannot be left, even by *fideicommissum*, to one's slaves, does not come within the assessment of the *lex Falcidia*.

31   POMPONIUS, *Fideicommissa, book 2:* The recipient of a *fideicommissum*, as also of a legacy, will have to give an undertaking to return anything which he receives in excess of what the *lex Falcidia* permits; such would be the case where the Falcidian problem is pending because of conditions attached to other legacies or *fideicommissa*. Indeed, according to Cassius and the earlier jurists, the recipient of *fideicommissa* from a *pupillus* will have to give security in respect of what may be left away from the youth's substitute. Even though there may be recovery of what is not due by way of *fideicommissum*, still, the person from whom the money comes, should have security that he will feel no loss through the failure of the payee.

32   MAECIAN, *Fideicommissa, book 9:* Penal actions, whether direct or praetorian, other than popular actions, are not the less to be included among the potential plaintiff's assets, because they may fall in through the death of the potential defendant. Conversely, these very actions in no way reduce the assets of the said defendant in the event of his death. But the action for affront cannot be included in the assets of even the plaintiff on his death; the action vanishes at the same time as his own demise, as would a usufruct or what is due to a person, daily, monthly, or yearly while he lives. Moreover, a possible defendant's assets will be reduced also by a right of action which passes to the plaintiff's heir. It in no way conflicts with this that, even in the defendant's life, the claim was not included in his estate; even had he stipulated that so long as he delayed the bringing of it, it should still be open to him, the estate [of the defendant] would be enlarged just as, if the latter himself had made a promise to the same effect, it would be diminished by his death. 1. Again, *actiones honorariae*, which the praetor propounds within a given period of time furnish with the plaintiff's assets an increase in the defendant's substance with the plaintiff's death, or a diminution, if the actions be such as are transmissible to heirs. 2. Julian writes that should the share of each heir be exhausted by legacies and one of them received a praetorian undertaking from the legatees, he will have a Falcidian account and action on the stipulation not on a basis of parity but in respect of his share. For all praetorian stipulations admit of the same interpretation; take the stipulation that a judgment will be honored; it is settled that be it the plaintiff or the defendant who leaves a plurality of heirs, the action is not to all and against all but only to those successfully suing against their defeated adversaries; equally, to those whose claim was undefended against those who made no defense. 3. Legacies are left annually, bienially, and trienially of a hundred gold pieces; it has been settled that a Falcidian deduction is to be made from the overall total, not that for the years to come. 4. Suppose that Titius's share is reduced in a legacy of twenty through the *lex Falcidia*, Titius himself being charged to give five to Seius; our friend Vindius says that a proportional reduction is to be made in Seius's five comparable to that in Titius's twenty. This view is both fair and logical; for the legatee is to be liable on *fideicommissa* on the pattern of the heir; he is to be allowed to offset the burden on himself even though, as legatee, he cannot invoke the *lex Falcidia* directly; this, unless the testator specifically make the *fideicommissum* one of "everything which [Titius] takes under the will." 5. If, however, a man be put under a *fideicommissum* to manumit a slave, whether his own or another's, he has an unqualified obligation to bring him to liberty. This does not conflict with what has just been said for the favoring of liberty often finds other benevolent expression.

33   PAUL, *Fideicommissa, book 3:* The senate has ruled that the *lex Falcidia* does not

apply where a slave has been bequeathed to you with a *fideicommissum* to manumit him and you receive nothing else under the will from which the Falcidian fourth could be retained.

34 MARCELLUS, *Digest, book 42:* JULIAN notes: The *lex Falcidia* does not apply to the testator's slave; it will, though, if the legacy be of money or something else and a *fideicommissum* be imposed upon the legatee to manumit his own slave or one of someone else.

35 ULPIAN, *Disputations, book 6:* Naturally, the *lex Falcidia* will be applicable to any legacy further left to the slave himself, the senate has ruled. In consequence, Scaevola says that deduction may be made from the additional legacy also in respect of the slave.

36 PAUL, *Fideicommissa, book 3:* If, however, it be not the slave himself who is bequeathed but money, the legatee then being charged to manumit his own slave, the *lex Falcidia* is operative and the legatee will be perforce obliged to effect the manumission, being treated as having assessed his slave at the relevant amount. 1. Suppose that the slave in issue belong to another; the legatee will be required to spend no more on his purchase than the amount of his legacy. 2. Should an heir, though, be charged with a *fideicommissum* to manumit his own slave, it is accepted that the slave's value is a chargeable debt. 3. If a single slave be bequeathed with a *fideicommissum* of his liberty, he can be claimed and sued for in full through the *lex Falcidia*; should the legatee receive anything else, however, the whole slave can be claimed, subject to that being off set; the reduction of a quarter in respect of each bequest, though, is to be made from the other legacy so that there may be no impediment to the slave's freedom. 4. Now it could be the case that doubt exists whether liberty will be due, the legacy is conditional, for instance, or to be implemented after some time; since the slave might die or the condition fail, should it not be during the period of uncertainty that the *Falcidia* be provisionally operative, and, then, when liberty become operative or due, that the legatee then recover what the *Falcidia* took from him? For Caecilius, anything which the heir acquired from the slave's services during the period of uncertainty should be attributable to his value in Falcidian reckoning.

37 VALENS, *Fideicommissa, book 6:* Such slave should be valued on the basis of being a *statuliber*. 1. Even if an heir were subject to a *fideicommissum* to manumit another's slave, the view prevailed that this slave's value should be deducted from the valuation of the inheritance.

38 HERMOGENIAN, *Epitome of Law, book 1:* 1. A *statuliber* is not an addition to the heir's servile household. Slaves owned in common count in the individual patrimony of each owner. 2. A slave in whom another has a usufruct is treated as part of his owner's property, one in pledge as the debtor's, one sold with a forfeiture clause or an *in diem addictio* as the vendor's.

39 PAUL, *Views, book 3:* There count as deductible debts not only the value of slaves given their freedom or under capital sentence but also that of one who has been granted his freedom by the praetor for exposing a murder plan or conspiracy.

40 HERMOGENIAN, *Epitome of Law, book 4:* The *lex Falcidia* applies to the will of an ex-soldier, be he head of household or son-in-power, even though he die within a year of his discharge. 1. An estate worth twenty has been devised to a legatee, if he give ten; he is considered legatee of the land in its fullness.

41 PAUL, *Edict, book 9:* A person cannot be regarded as lacking bad faith who, when a dispute has already arisen over the inheritance, pays legacies without taking any security.

42 ULPIAN, *Edict, book 14:* The Falcidian valuation of assets is to be made on their true worth.

43 ULPIAN, *Edict, book 19:* For Falcidian purposes, slaves returning from war captivity after the testator's death swell the value of the estate.

44 ULPIAN, *Edict, book 21:* There can be no place for the *lex Falcidia*, when a *statuliber* makes a payment from the funds of another, not of the deceased or again if a person already free satisfy the condition.

45 PAUL, *Edict, book 60:* Under the *lex Falcidia*, that which is bequeathed for a period is not regarded as unqualifiedly given; a computation is made of its interim benefit. 1. It was the view of Proculus that where the *lex Falcidia* comes up in relation to conditional legacies, their value is the price that they could fetch as such; this being so, a deduction is possible so that as much is due as the price for which the debt can be sold. That opinion has not found favor; it is preferable to resort to the giving and taking of security.

46 ULPIAN, *Edict, book 76:* A person who, honoring the testator's wishes, solemnly promises to give what the *lex Falcidia* would allow him to retain is bound to pay.

47 ULPIAN, *Edict, book 79:* Where it is operative, the *lex Falcidia* is applicable to all payments; circumstances will make this apparent. Let us take a legacy from year to year; so long as the *Falcidia* does not yet come into play, the annual payments will be given in full; should the year come, however, when anything be due in excess of the three quarters of the *lex Falcidia*, the result will be that, retrospectively, all the annual legacies will be reduced. 1. A legatee or fideicommissary never receives the benefit of the *lex Falcidia*, even though the inheritance be made over to him under the *senatus consultum Trebellianum*.

48 PAUL, *Curule Aediles' Edict, book 2:* When a purchaser becomes his vendor's heir or vice versa, is twofold or only the simple price to be deducted as a debt if the slave, the object of their contract, be evicted? It would be twofold, were the heir a third party. The more lenient view in our case is that the simple price be offset.

49 PAUL, *Plautius, book 12:* PLAUTIUS: I devised land to the slave whom I bequeathed to you. Atilicinus, Nerva, and Sabinus all say that first a Falcidian valuation is to be made in respect of the slave and the deduction in respect of him will be reflected in the legacy of the land; then, from the remainder of the land, a further Falcidian deduction will follow as with other legacies. Cassius says that since the slave loses part by the *lex Falcidia*, he becomes the joint slave of heir and legatee; but, when a legacy is made to a slave owned in common, the whole belongs to the [legatee] partner because only in that person can the legacy inhere. PAUL: We follow the view of Cassius; the deified Pius also, in a rescript, ruled that a *fideicommissum* bequeathed to a common slave went wholly to the co-owner. 1. It sometimes happens that by reason of the Falcidian account, a subsequent legacy is extinguished; for example, land is devised together with a right of passage to it through other land; if part of the land remain in the inheritance, the legacy of passage cannot be realized, since one cannot acquire a servitude as to part.

50 CELSUS, *Digest, book 14:* Without question, legacies from which the heir can bar the claimant by a defense are attributed to his quarter and do not affect the bequests of others.

51 JULIAN, *Digest, book 61:* It is of no consequence whether the legacy was inoperative from the outset or subsequent chance circumstances resulted in its nonactionability.

52 MARCELLUS, *Digest, book 9:* A freedman, having a total of two hundred and fifty, instituted his patron as sole heir, left one hundred and twenty to his son and the residue to a third party; the patron's making over to the outsider half of what was left to

him will avail the son for acquiring his whole bequest.   1. Whatever the reason for the nonpayment of legacies, those legacies will be reckoned in the quarter which should remain to the heir under the *lex Falcidia*.

53   CELSUS, *Digest, book 17:* If a Falcidian account be pending in respect of conditional legacies, they will not, being presently given, be claimable in full.

54   MARCELLUS, *Digest, book 15:* A father instituted as heir the son by whom he had three grandsons and charged him with a *fideicommissum* not to alienate the estate and himself to devise it within the family; the son, on his death, left his three sons as instituted heirs. We must investigate whether, in the manner of creditor, each can deduct something in a reckoning under the *lex Falcidia*, since it had been in the father's power to show to which among them he preferred to leave his substance. That reasoning would give none a deduction for Falcidian purposes. Let us consider whether this is not a harsh ruling; the father had the land like a debt since he was necessarily constrained to leave it to his sons.

55   MARCELLUS, *Digest, book 20:* Ten per annum are bequeathed to Titius and a judge is taking a Falcidian account between the heir and the other legacies; Titius being alive, he will have to make an assessment of what the legacy could amount to, granted that no one knows how long Titius will live; but, with Titius dead, the only consideration is the extent of the heir's obligation under that head.

56   MARCELLUS, *Digest, book 22:* A person against whom the *actio de peculio* was possible became heir to his creditor; your question is: As at what time is the *peculium* to be assessed for Falcidian purposes? Many hold that one should look to the state of the *peculium* when the inheritance is accepted. I have my reservations, since the time of death should be looked to in starting on an account under the *lex Falcidia*; what relevance, after all, can it have whether the slave's *peculium* be reduced after the creditor's death or the debtor suffer financial loss?   1. Someone may say: "Yes, but what if the slave acquire something before the inheritance is accepted?" My rejoinder: What if the finances have improved of a debtor who at that time, the death, was not solvent? And since, in that case, it be accepted that the inheritance has been subsequently enriched, as when a condition attached to the claim be realized after the death, so also an addition to the *peculium* increases the value of the inheritance.   2. SCAEVOLA notes: What, then, if the one slave owed ten each to the deceased and someone else and he had only the one ten? Clearly, the inheritance will be increased by the remaining part of the ten which were the object of the slave's natural obligation to the deceased. 3. The owner of a single slave bequeathed him to Titius on whom he laid a *fideicommissum* to manumit the slave after three years; a quarter of what Titius may obtain through the slave's services during that period will be due to remain the heir's, just as if the deceased had given the slave his freedom directly after a three years' delay and bequeathed the usufruct of him or left ownership of him to Titius by *fideicommissum*.   4. The testator left Stichus to you and ten to your slave or, conversely, ten to you and Stichus to your slave with a *fideicommissum* of his freedom. The *lex Falcidia* reduces the legacies; you will have to claim from the heir a share as though both legacies had been to yourself.   5. It is not uncommon for the heir to derive no benefit from the statute; suppose that their owner give one hundred and twenty-five gold pieces to someone, then institute that person as heir and make legacies of three quarters of his assets, nothing more will be forthcoming under the *lex Falcidia* because the

testator is seen to provide during his life for his prospective heir.

57   MARCELLUS, *Digest, book 26:* When a man bequeaths her dowry to someone to transfer on to his wife, it must be said that there is no place for the *lex Falcidia*. Indeed, there are many instances in which dispositions are observed without reference to the person of the intermediary.

58   MODESTINUS, *Rules, book 9:* Nothing hinders the heir's claiming his entitlement under the *lex Falcidia* long after the testator's death.

59   MODESTINUS, *Encyclopaedia, book 9:* He is unworthy of Falcidian relief whose invocation of it would destroy a *fideicommissum.*   1. Again, one charged to restore the inheritance to a nontaker is not granted retention of a quarter by the *senatus consultum Plancianum*; the quarter which he is not allowed to retain belongs to the imperial treasury under a rescript of the deified Pius.

60   JAVOLENUS, *From Cassius, book 14:* A father substituted an heir to his daughter, still below puberty; what he received by way of legacy from the father does not come into the computation of the *lex Falcidia*, when the substitution becomes operative. 1. Where a sworn valuation is made in a claim for a legacy, the *lex Falcidia* takes account not of the sum to which the legatee has sworn but of the true value of the thing claimed; accretions by way of penalty have no place in Falcidian reckoning.

61   JAVOLENUS, *Letters, book 4:* A testator made you a legacy of land belonging to someone else; the heir being unable to purchase the land save at an inflated price bought at such an overvaluation that the legatees were called to an account under the *lex Falcidia*. Here is my question: Since, if the land had been purchased at its true worth, the legacies would not have gone beyond the limit of the *lex Falcidia*, does the present position entitle the instituted heir to claim a share from the legatees on the ground that the deceased's wish caused him to pay more than the land was worth? Answer: The overpayment by the heir cannot be charged against the *lex Falcidia*; his remiss behavior should not constitute a detriment to the legatees, especially since, by revealing the position, he could have obtained a true valuation.

62   ULPIAN, *Lex Julia et Papia, book 1:* Julian says that in the matter of the *lex Falcidia*, this is the practice to follow: Where there are two persons liable on a promise or two creditors of a promise, assuming the obligation to be their joint venture, it is to be divided between them as though each had asked for or promised part of the money; if, though, they were not partners, there remains in suspense what is to be attributed to or deducted from the property of each.   1. Tangible property in the deceased's estate is to be valued at its true worth, that is, the price which it would presently command, be it known that no such item is to be given a nominal valuation.

63   PAUL, *Lex Julia et Papia, book 2:* Things acquire their value from their general usefulness not from the particular approach or utility of individuals. A man who possesses as a slave his own natural son is not thereby the richer because, did another hold the slave, he himself would pay a large ransom for him. Equally, a person who possesses the son of someone else does not have the value for which he can sell that son to his father nor the amount for which he might hope to sell him but his present value as a slave not as somebody's son. The case is the same with someone whose slave commits a delict; for no one becomes more valuable by wrongdoing. No more is the slave, instituted heir on the testator's death, worth any more than the higher price which he may realize, says Pedius; indeed, it would be absurd that being myself instituted heir, I should not be richer until I accepted the inheritance but that my wealth should be increased forthwith, were my slave instituted; many things could happen to prevent his accepting the estate at my behest. Of course, he acquires for me when he enters; but to say that I am richer before I have acquired would literally be preposterous.   1. One whose debtor is insolvent has as property what he can exact from him.   2. Sometimes place or time brings a variation in value; oil will not be equally

valued at Rome and in Spain nor given the same assessment in periods of lasting scarcity as when there are crops; in the latter case, prices are not determined by vicissitudes and chance events.

64   ULPIAN, *Lex Julia et Papia, book 13:* A will has the provision: "Let my heir be charged to give Lucius Titius ten and as much more as he would take less through the *lex Falcidia.*" The testator's view is to be upheld.

65   PAUL, *Lex Julia et Papia, book 6:* Suppose that land worth fifty be bequeathed subject to the condition that the legatee give fifty to the heir; there are many who think the legacy effective because the giving will be to realize the condition; for it is settled that the *lex Falcidia* is applicable. But if there be a legacy of fifty gold pieces, if the legatee give fifty, it must be said that the legacy is without point, indeed ridiculous.

66   ULPIAN, *Lex Julia et Papia, book 18:* There is this to be noted concerning the *lex Falcidia* where something is left under a condition or for a given period; should ten be left to someone under a condition which is realized after, say, ten years, it is not a sum of ten which is regarded as having been bequeathed but something less; for the time lapse and interest of the interval reduce the sum from ten.   1. Just as legacies are not due unless there be a surplus over the deceased's debts, gifts in contemplation of death are not due, being nullified by his liabilities. Hence, if the debts be excessive, a person will receive nothing of what is given to him in respect of death.

67   TERENTIUS CLEMENS, *Lex Julia et Papia, book 4:* Whenever someone is left more than he is entitled to take and the *lex Falcidia* comes into operation, the Falcidian account must first be taken, obviously so that only what remains after the Falcidian deduction will be due, assuming that it does not exceed statutory limits.

68   AEMILIUS MACER, *The Five Percent Succession Tax Statute, book 2:* For computation to be made in the matter of maintenance, Ulpian gives this formula: From birth to the twenty-fifth year, the amount of thirty years' maintenance will be assessed and the Falcidian quota thereof be due; between twenty and twenty-five, the amount up to twenty-eight; between twenty-five and thirty, the amount of twenty-five; between thirty and thirty-five, the amount of twenty-two; between thirty-five and forty, the amount of twenty; between forty and fifty there will be a computation of as many years as are lacking to sixty, with one year's remission; between fifty and fifty-five, the amount of nine years; between fifty-five and sixty, the amount of seven years; for any age over sixty, the amount of five years. Ulpian says that we observe this rule also for the computation of a usufruct. Still, it has been the practice for the computation from birth to thirty to be of thirty years but from thirty of as many years as are lacking to sixty. The computation never goes beyond thirty. So equally in the case of a legacy of a usufruct to the state, whether for the provision of games or without restriction, the valuation will be of thirty years.   1. If one of the heirs should claim a thing to be his own and then it be proved part of the estate, there are those who think that there cannot be a Falcidian retention in respect of it, since it makes no difference whether he

appropriated it or denied that it is part of the inheritance. Ulpian justly rejects this.

69 POMPONIUS, *Sabinus, book 5:* Where a usufruct of one's property is bequeathed, debts of the deceased are chargeable against all items because, after the *senatus consultum,* there is no item which does not fall within the legacy of the usufruct.

70 ULPIAN, *Sabinus, book 16:* A Falcidian stipulation becomes enforceable as soon as the condition of a legacy or debt is realized.

71 PAUL, *Edict, book 32:* In selling the inheritance, an heir may give security that even though the *lex Falcidia* intervene, legacies will be honored in full; the statute was enacted for the heir's benefit, and the latter is at no disadvantage, if he diminishes his own entitlement.

72 GAIUS, *Praetor's Edict, Legacies, book 3:* The extent of the patrimony is valued with the deduction of any expense incurred for the effecting of sales.

73 GAIUS, *Provincial Edict, book 18:* It became accepted that in ascertaining the extent of the estate, one looks to the time of death. Hence, suppose that someone, having one hundred, made bequests of the whole; it will not avail the legatees that before the inheritance is accepted, there be such accretion to the estate through slaves of the inheritance or the issue of slave-women thereof or the young of animals that after the removal of the hundred for legacies, the heir would have his quarter. It is requisite nonetheless that a reduction of a quarter be made in the legacies. Conversely, where a testator, having one hundred, made legacies of seventy-five and before acceptance the inheritance so diminished through fires, say, wrecks, or the death of slaves that no more than seventy-five—possibly, even less—remained, the legacies would be due in full. This occasions no harm to the heir who is free not to accept the inheritance; such latter course could achieve the result that the legatees, lest they get nothing through the nonoperation of the will, settle with the heir for a share of their legacies. 1. Great uncertainty existed in respect of debts the condition of which was pending at the deceased's death; is the conditional amount included in the creditor's assets and deducted from those of the debtor? Our rule is that the amount of the obligation in expectancy is deemed to accrue to the stipulator's wealth and to reduce the debtor's. Alternatively, the matter can be adjusted by the giving and taking of security so that one of two courses follows: An account is taken either as though the debt were unconditional or as if nothing were owing; then the heirs and legatees enter into mutual undertakings that if the condition should eventuate, the heir will make restoration of his underpayment or the legatees return the amount of their overpayment. 2. Again, if there be legacies, both unconditional and conditional, which have the result that if the condition be realized, the *lex Falcidia* will apply, the legacies are paid *simpliciter* but with security. In such a case, it is the usual practice to have payment of the direct legacies, as though there were no others which were conditional, but for the legatees to undertake to return the excess which they have received in the event of the condition's being satisfied. 3. An undertaking of this kind appears necessary also if the same will gives conditional freedom to certain slaves whose value will reduce the estate on the realization of the condition. 4. Obviously, legacies left as at a certain time come under a different regime; they are, from any point of view, due to the legatee or to his heirs; but the reduction to be made is that, corresponding to the deduction appropriate, until the day arrives, in the heir's benefit from the produce of and interest on the capital amount. 5. Overall, therefore, the most desirable course is that the heir from the outset should distribute legacies not exceeding three quarters of the estate. Should anyone exceed that limit, however, the statute makes an automatic, proportional reduction; thus, if the possessor of four hundred should leave the full amount in legacies, the legatees will be deprived of a quarter; should he bequeath three hundred and fifty, they lose an eighth. But what if one having four hundred should bequeath five hundred? A fifth is immediately deducted and then a further

quarter is to be written off; there is, after all, first to be deducted what does not form part of the estate and then the portion of the assets which should remain with the heir.

74 GAIUS, *Praetor's Edict, Legacies, book 3:* We take the proposition that if the heir receive a quarter of the estate by the wish of the deceased, he is liable for legacies in full in this way, if he receives the quarter by right of inheritance; anything, therefore, which he may receive from a co-heir by way of legacy, is not attributed to his quarter.

75 MARCELLUS, *Julian, Digest, book 40:* But should he be given a legacy to pay legacies and *fideicommissa* in full, he will be refused the action on legacy, if he prefer to invoke the *lex Falcidia*.

76 GAIUS, *Praetor's Edict, Legacies, book 3:* What is given by a co-heir, legatee, or *statuliber* for the implementation of a condition is not chargeable to the *lex Falcidia*, being received by reason of death. Of course, if an heir receive from a *statuliber* coins from the latter's *peculium*, they are to be attributed to his quarter because he does not take them in respect of death but is held to take them by his title as heir. 1. This reasoning brought acceptance that legacies which the legatees do not take, since they remain with the heir, are deemed so to remain by virtue of his title as heir and so count against his quarter; here it matters not whether the legacy never was or that the legacy remained with him.

77 GAIUS, *Provincial Edict, book 18:* There is no question but that the Falcidian account is to be taken in respect of each individual heir. In the case, therefore, where, Titius and Seius being instituted heirs, Titius's half of the estate being exhausted, Seius, having been left a quarter of the estate, Titius can invoke the concession of the *lex Falcidia*.

78 GAIUS, *Urban Praetor's Edict, Legacies, book 3:* Put the case that there being two heirs, one does not appear and the other is sole heir: Is the Falcidian account to be taken as though from the outset he were sole heir, or are the separate cases of their individual shares to be investigated? The view which has prevailed is that if the share of the one who does become heir be exhausted by legacies, the legatees can look for relief to the share which has fallen in; it is not laden with legacies; and legacies which remain with the heir produce the consequence that the remaining legatees incur no, or a modified, loss. Should the share fallen in, however, be defective, the Falcidian reckoning is to be made as though the share belonged to the heir from whom it has fallen in.

79 GAIUS, *Provincial Edict, book 18:* In the case of a twofold will, if our concern is the patrimony, we look only to what the head of household had when he died; subsequent acquisition or diminution by the son after that death is irrelevant. Should our query concern legacies, both those in the first and those in the second will go to make a single whole, just as if the testator left away from his own heir, under a different condition, what he bequeaths away from his son's heir.

80 GAIUS, *Praetor's Edict, Legacies, book 3:* A man, with a patrimony of four hundred, made his son, not yet of the age of puberty, heir, left two hundred, made Titius and Seius his substitute heirs, and made a legacy of one hundred away from Titius; what say we the law to be? Assuming the son to have died with the legacies still unpaid so that both are due, only the heir Titius can invoke the *lex Falcidia*; two hundred being due to him from the estate of the *pupillus*, he owes two hundred by way of legacy: one hundred from the two which the *pupillus* owes him [and Seius] and the hundred which he is bidden to give himself. Deducting a quarter from each, he will consequently have fifty. The *lex Falcidia* does not apply to Seius, however, since two hundred fall his way from the estate of the *pupillus* and he owes one hundred by way of legacy out of the two hundred left away from the *pupillus*. Should the *pupillus* pay the legacies, his tutors should ensure security from the legatees. 1. Some legacies, for example, the

various rights of passage, do not admit of division; for to no one can such a thing belong in part. But where an heir is directed to effect some work for the townspeople, the legacy is unitary. No one can be held to erect a bath, stadium, or theater, who does not determine the form which its completion will bring to reality. In respect of all such legacies, though there be a plurality of heirs, individuals are accountable in full. Legacies, then, which do not admit of division, belong exclusively to the legatee. The heir, though, can invoke the relief that having valued the legacy, he may give notice to the legatee that the latter bear his share of the valuation; should the latter not do so, the defense of bad faith will be applicable.

81   GAIUS, *Provincial Edict, book 18:* A usufruct comes into the Falcidian reckoning, admitting of division to the extent that if it be left to two, each automatically has his own share. 1. Dowry falls outside the *lex Falcidia,* obviously because the woman gets back her own property. 2. In like manner, the *lex* itself expressly states that things bought or provided for the woman's interests also lie outside the scope of the statute.

82   ULPIAN, *Disputations, book 8:* This question used to be put: A person who had assets consisting solely in a book-debt of four hundred bequeathed discharge from his obligation to the debtor himself and four hundred to Seius; if the debtor either was insolvent or could raise only one hundred, what would each get on the operation of the *lex Falcidia*? My reply was that out of what can be realized from the estate, the *lex Falcidia* gives a quarter to the heir, the remaining three quarters to be distributed among the legatees. Accordingly, if the hereditary debt does not meet all the provisions of the will, there will be a pro rata distribution of what can be realized and a sale of the residue, there being attributed to the inheritance the price for which the debt can be sold. Where, though, the will grants the debtor his discharge from his obligation, the debtor is regarded as solvent and, from his point of view, in funds; for if he be regarded as receiving his release as a liberality on death, he is deemed to have received four hundred even though he has no cash; he still receives full discharge, although penniless. Should he alone be granted release, then, by the *lex Falcidia,* he is remitted three hundred and the remaining hundred continue due and payable, and should the debtor acquire anything subsequently, it can be exacted from him up to the amount of one hundred. The same would hold if he received his discharge for four hundred as a gift in respect of death. In consequence, it is elegantly said that the formal release will be in a state of pendency; if, indeed, at the time of the testator's death, four hundred are found, the release will be effective for three hundred; should anything more be found in the estate for the heir to have his quarter, the release will be valid for the full four hundred. Now if the debtor of four hundred can raise only one hundred, he, being thus in funds, will have to make over that hundred. So if the debtor be in funds, the result will be that assuming that someone be instituted heir with legacies to the debtor of his release and to someone else of four hundred, assuming the debtor's solvency, he will keep one hundred and fifty out of three hundred, the other legatee will have one hundred and fifty due to him, and the heir will have a hundred. But if the debtor can raise only one hundred, the heir's quarter must be preserved out of that sum; the outcome will be that the hundred available for distribution will be divided into four parts, the legatee getting three quarters, the heir taking twenty-five, and the insolvent debtor settling with himself for one hundred and fifty. In respect of the outstanding one hundred and fifty which cannot be produced, the debt will be sold and that will be set up as the sole asset. In the event that the debtor can raise nothing, he will again be released in respect of one hundred and fifty and the remainder of the debt put up for sale; so says Neratius and we agree.

83   JULIAN, *Digest, book 12:* Should your son's creditor institute you as heir and you make a Falcidian reckoning, the value of the *peculium* as at the time of acceptance of the inheritance will be attributed to your quarter.

84   JULIAN, *Digest, book 13:* The case can be found in which the heir could sue though his testator could not; for instance, a tutor paying out legacies does not interpose a

stipulation for the repayment of what he disburses beyond what the *lex Falcidia* allows; the *pupillus* himself could not proceed by the action of guardianship against the tutor, but the latter would be liable on that count to the heir of the *pupillus*.

85   JULIAN, *Digest, book 18:* If dowry be given to a father-in-law and the son-husband become sole heir to his father, he will forthwith bring the dowry into the computation of the inheritance as a debt under the *lex Falcidia*; otherwise, he would appear to have an undowered wife. Now, should he have as co-heir someone from outside the family, he will himself still set off the dowry as a debt to the extent that he is his father's heir, the co-heir will deduct before the son-husband pre-empts the dowry.

86   JULIAN, *Digest, book 40:* In her will, Titia instituted her brother, Titius, heir to a third of her estate and charged him with a *fideicommissum* that keeping a quarter for himself, he should hand over the inheritance to Secunda and Procula; she also gave her brother certain lands as a preferred legacy. Question: Does Titius have to make over also these preferred legacies in the part of the inheritance affected by the *fideicommissum*, or does he retain them intact? My reply was that Titius should retain the legacies intact but that he should include in his quarter a twelfth of the value of the land. Had it not been particularized that he should keep a quarter, a full third of the value of the lands would be attributable to the *lex Falcidia*; for the *lex* would be invoked contrary to the testatrix's wishes.

87   JULIAN, *Digest, book 61:* A man, whose only asset was a plot worth one hundred, charged his heir to sell it for fifty to Titius; he is to be treated as having bequeathed a legacy of no more than fifty, so that the *lex Falcidia* is not in point.   1. Again, one having two plots worth in all one hundred made me and Titius his heirs; he charged me to sell Titius the Cornelian farm for fifty and conversely charged Titius to sell me the Seian estate for fifty; I do not advert to the question, how the *lex Falcidia* can operate, since each heir by hereditary title will have half of each estate, each having a half share of the inheritance; the one, charged to sell the Cornelian estate, has as heir his share of the Seian estate, just as the one charged to sell the Seian estate retains, as heir, his share of the Cornelian property.   2. Suppose someone to institute as heir one whom he puts under a *fideicommissum* to transfer one hundred on the latter's own death; one hundred comes into the Falcidian computation, because, had there been a different instituted heir, that hundred could be treated as a debt.   3. You have been instituted heir to a quarter, as also Titius, and then you are later made conditionally heir to a half, legacies, including some of liberty, also being granted. While the condition is pending, the gifts of freedom operate, and the legacies are to be paid in full; for either the condition will be satisfied, and, you being heir, both will be operative; or the condition will fail, and you and Titius will be heirs. Suppose that you ask, concerning the *lex Falcidia*, whether, on the realization of the condition, your quarter and the half are to be lumped together and that, on this basis, the account of the three quarters is to be made with those to whom legacies have been left away from you; our answer is that the two shares are to be merged.   4. A man instituted his underage son and Titius as heirs in equal shares, bequeathed away from his son the whole of the latter's share, left nothing away from Titius, and substituted Titius as heir to his son. The following question arose: Titius accepted as instituted heir, and, the youth dying, also became heir as substitute; how much had he to pay up in respect of legacies? The view adopted was that the legacies were payable in full. The two halves of the inheritance coming together mean that an account of the estate as a whole is taken for Falcidian purposes, and so legacies are payable in full. This, however, is true in the event that the son dies before becoming his father's heir. Should the youth be heir to his father, the substitute will be liable for no more in legacies than was the *pupillus*, being liable in the latter's name, not his own; and the *pupillus* was liable for no more than three quarters of a half.   5. If, though, the full half of a nonfamily heir were bequeathed away from him and he became substitute heir to the *pupillus* on whom no charge had been laid, it could be said that the legacies increase in value and that the course to

follow would be the same as that if he were substituted to any co-heir one please and, the latter not coming to the inheritance, he became sole heir; a substitute always makes his Falcidian account on the basis of what the head of household leaves. 6. This would also hold good if a father instituted as heirs two sons below puberty and made mutual substitutions between them and then, by right of substitution, the inheritance fell to one of them alone and a Falcidian account were taken. 7. A man had two sons under age; he instituted one as heir, disinherited the other, then substituted the disinherited one to the instituted heir, and subsequently Maevius to the disinherited one, leaving bequests away; the disinherited son became heir to his brother and then himself died under age. Since the paternal wealth came to him by way of inheritance, by virtue of his substitution, by the father's wish, it may be said that the legacies left away from him are to be set by reason of the *lex Falcidia* among the father's assets as at his time of death. It in no way conflicts with this that the father having given a legacy to the disinherited son, the substitute will not the more be burdened with the legacies because what came to him thereby was simply a legacy, not a share of his father's inheritance. I hear someone say: What, then, if the disinherited one became heir, not by substitution to his brother but by some statute or via an intervening person, and still died under age, is such a substitute to be held liable to legacies? Of course, not. The significance of the disinherited son's becoming heir by substitution to his brother or by some other route emerges from the fact that in the one case, the father could leave legacies away from him; in the other, not. It is, accordingly, consonant with reason that the father has no more jurisdiction over the person of his substitute heir than over the person to whom he makes him substitute. 8. Suppose that the co-heir appointed together with a *pupillus* discharge after a Falcidian account the legacies charged on his share and then, the youth dying, he became the latter's heir by substitution and the youth's half share be exhausted by legacies, a new Falcidian account is to be undertaken so that taking together the legacies left away from both himself and the *pupillus*, he still has a quarter of the estate. He may be the heir of the *pupillus*, but for the purposes of the *lex Falcidia*, the position is as though he were heir of the father. The legacies bequeathed away from himself beyond three quarters will not be augmented other than as they are augmented when a person, instituted heir in part and substituted to his co-heir, pay legacies, subject to Falcidian reckoning, while his co-heir still deliberates on acceptance or not, and then, by virtue of the substitution, he acquire also the other part of the inheritance.

88 AFRICANUS, *Questions, book 5:* A man with four hundred made legacies of three hundred; he then devised to you land worth one hundred gold pieces subject to the condition: "if the *lex Falcidia* has no application to [my] will." Question: What is the legal position? I replied that this is an impossible question, styled "a deception" by dialecticians. For whatever we assert to be true will be found to be false. Here is the proof: If we say that your legacy is valid, the *lex Falcidia* operates, and so, the condition failing, the legacy will not be due. Again, if the legacy be not valid because of the failure of the condition, there will be no place for the *lex Falcidia*. Furthermore, if the *lex* should not obtain, the condition will be realized, and the legacy will be due to you. Since, however, it would appear to have been the testator's intention that the legacies of others should not be abated by reason of that to you, our better course is to hold that the condition of your legacy is not complied with. 1. What, then, would we say if he made bequests of two hundred and the case be put that two hundred were likewise left to you under the same condition? That the condition of your legacy either is or is not met so that you get either all or nothing must be deemed unfair and contrary to the testator's intentions; yet it runs counter to common sense that a part should be due when it is of the essence that the condition of the *whole* legacy either be met or fail. The whole matter should then be regulated by the defense of bad faith. 2. Accordingly, when someone wish to effect such a legacy, he should do it in this form: "If I have or shall have left legacies beyond what the *lex Falcidia* permits, let my heir be

charged to take any deduction necessary to make up his quarter from my legacy to
Titius." 3. Someone with two hundred left me one hundred forthwith and you one
hundred under a condition; after some time, the condition was realized but in such
circumstances that from the return on what was left to you, the heir received no more
than twenty-five. The account under the *lex Falcidia* with the heir is to be taken in
such wise that we have to grant him twenty-five plus the retu.·n on fifty for the period
of pendency, say, five. Thirty thus being due to him, there are those who think that
each of us is to contribute fifteen apiece. Nothing of the sort! Although each of us receives a legacy of the same amount, it is obvious that mine is somewhat the more lucrative. Hence, we have to determine the reduction in your legacy through the heir's
interim enjoyment of the income. Consistently therewith, in the case envisaged, the
accounting should be set up on the footing that out of a sum divided into seven shares,
I contribute four sevenths and you three, there being in my legacy a quarter more
than in yours.

89   MARCIAN, *Institutes, book 7:* In a rescript, the deified Severus and Antoninus ruled
that money left for the maintenance of the young is subject to the *lex Falcidia* and
that in order that the money be allocated to the appropriate heads of account, the provincial governor should take it into his own charge.   1. By rescript, the deified Severus and Antoninus gave a general ruling to Bononius Maximus that interest was
payable by one who invoked the *lex Falcidia* as a delaying tactic.

90   FLORENTINUS, *Institutes, book 11:* An heir, charged with a *fideicommissum* that
accepting a specified sum, he make over the inheritance, departs from the testator's
wishes and seeks to invoke the *lex Falcidia*; even though he does not get what he
should when charged to make over the estate, he will still be obliged to honor the
fideicommissum because what the testator wished him to have meets the benefit of
the *lex Falcidia*.

91   MARCIAN, *Institutes, book 13:* The quarter of the inheritance to which the heir is
entitled under the *lex Falcidia* will comprise what he takes in his capacity as heir, not
what he may receive by way of legacy, *fideicommissum*, or for the fulfillment of a condition. Such items have no place in his quarter. Where an inheritance is to be made
over under a *fideicommissum*, there will be imputed to the heir's quarter any legacy
or *fideicommissum* to him as also any privileged claim which he is given or any deduction or retention which he is directed to make. Anything which he receives from a co-
heir is again outside his quarter. Should he, though, be charged to make over the inheritance accepting a sum of money, this last will count in his quarter as the deified
Pius ruled. Anything, though, which the heir receives from legatees for the satisfaction of conditions will not go toward the Falcidian computation. Suppose, then, that
the deceased left land valued at one hundred, if the legatee gave fifty to the heir; the
reckoning will be of a legacy of one hundred, and the fifty will lie outside the inheritance, not to be charged against the heir's quarter.

92   MACER, *Military Matters, bcok 2:* A soldier, having made his will, directed the
making over to you of half of his estate and then, after his discharge, drew codicils
requesting the transfer of the other half to Titius. In the event of his demise more than
a year after his discharge, the heir will keep a quarter against both you and Titius; for
the testator died at a time when his will had lost its principal advantage; were he to die

within a year of discharge, only Titius would suffer the loss of a quarter because the *fideicommissum* was made to him at a time when the testator had lost his capacity for testation under military law.

93   PAPINIAN, *Questions, book 20:* A man was charged with a *fideicommissum* to make over the inheritance to Maevius, on receiving one hundred from Maevius and then, on his own death, to give the money to Titius. Although the hundred may constitute a quarter of the estate, the second *fideicommissum* provides occasion for the retention of a quarter. A constitution of the deified Hadrian ordains that what meets the requirements of the *lex Falcidia* is that which remains with the heir; and only the person to whom the inheritance is left is the subject of the statute. The *Falcidia* has no application to the hundred taken by reason of the testator's death. Naturally, if a testator wrote thus, "I ask you to make over the inheritance on receiving one hundred," without indicating who should give the money, the money being held back [from the inheritance] as a preferred claim, the *Trebellianum* would operate.

94   SCAEVOLA, *Digest, book 21:* A testator, having instituted his son and daughter as heirs, left certain preferred legacies to each of them, the daughter, however, getting much the smaller amount; he also made her a preferred legacy of a mortgaged house with its effects and contents, adding: "This bequest is subject to the condition that Titius, my son's freedman, pay off any debt due on the house and the house become their common property." This question was posed: Should the daughter wish to invoke the *lex Falcidia* to keep a quarter of the inheritance, would she get her quarter out of the inheritance left her from what remained after discharge of the debt? The reply was that she had indeed a legal right to make such a claim but that she could receive what was left to her, assuming that thereby she got a quarter, only on complete compliance with the wishes of the deceased.

95   SCAEVOLA, *Digest, book 21:* A husband administered his wife's affairs additional to the dowry. The wife died before the husband had rendered an account of his administration, leaving him as sole heir with a *fideicommissum* that on his own death, he leave five sixths thereof to their son and one sixth to their grandson. The question was asked: "Does the husband have to include in the son's five sixths, proportionally with the other assets, what is found to remain with him from his administration of her affairs?" His reply was that what was due to the wife's inheritance should come into account.   1. A mother laid a *fideicommissum* on her daughter to make over the estate to Titius, if the girl herself died while still under age; the daughter's paternal uncle became her heir at law. In accounting under the *lex Falcidia*, this uncle wishes to deduct the capital from the interest on which the girl had been providing maintenance for a number of persons in her mother's name. The question was: If he should make such deduction, should he give security that he would himself make good the share of deceased dependents in proportion to the capital? Answer: Yes.   2. Three years having elapsed since acceptance of the inheritance, the heir seeks to set up the *lex Falcidia* against the legatees on the ground that the testator administered some guardianships, an account of which had not yet been rendered, and he himself denies that as much can be realized from debts due in that context as came into the security [given by the tutor]. Question: The legatees seeking the accounts of the deceased, should the heir be entitled to include an account of all documents, both those concerning the inheritance and those relating to the guardianships, since this might give him the opportunity to adduce what he please, thereby putting the legatees at a disadvantage? Answer: It will be the duty of the judge to ascertain how much is in the estate from the proofs submitted.

96   SCAEVOLA, *Questions Publicly Discussed, sole book:* While still a civilian, a soldier made a will, adding codicils after entering the army; his will comes within the *lex Falcidia*, not so the codicils.

3

ALLEGATION THAT A LEGACY EXCEEDS THE LIMITS OF THE *LEX FALCIDIA*

1 ULPIAN, *Edict, book 79:* If someone receive a legacy beyond the legal maximum and there be valid ground for doubt whether or not the *lex Falcidia* should come into account, the praetor affords the heir the relief that the legatee is to give him an undertaking that should it become apparent that he has taken by way of legacy more than is permitted to him by the *lex Falcidia*, he will give him the money value of the excess and that in the matter, there will be no bad faith on his part. 1. It matters not whether the issue arise on the primary will, the pupillary substitution, or both; the *lex Falcidia* comes in once and for all, even though the will be twofold, contribution being made both by legacies left away from the *pupillus* and by those left away from the substitute. 2. Let us suppose that a tutor was not subjected to a stipulation in the name of the ward himself; the action on guardianship will still lie to the heir of the *pupillus*. But, as Papinian says, the undertaking can become operative for both the heir and his substitute; for the heir himself, if the *lex Falcidia* become operative, while he still be alive. He says the same of the action on guardianship. 3. Marcellus says: A man, owning four hundred, instituted as heir his underage son and substituted to him Titius and Seius; the testator bequeathed nothing away from his heir but two hundred away from Titius; should two hundred be paid, it is said, or one hundred and fifty? For in no way can three hundred be taken from him. My view was that the truth is that he is obliged to put up no more from his share than the hundred lacking from that of Seius. From this, it emerges that the stipulation becomes enforceable not against one alone, but that it is applicable against all heirs naturally on an investing action of the issue. 4. Both the extent of legacies and the amount of debts bring the *lex Falcidia* into play. Of course, if the debts be obvious or ascertained, the computation is simple: Should there still, on the other hand, be uncertainty—a condition, for instance, is pending or a creditor has joined issue but the case is yet not decided— there may be hesitancy by reason of such uncertainty over what is due to the legatees. 5. Nowadays, though, *fideicommissa* are treated as an analogue. 6. Where the *lex Falcidia* is said to be operative, there is normally the appointment of an arbitrator for investigating the size of the estate, even though one person claim a modest amount in *fideicommissa*; such computation is not to embarrass the other beneficiaries who are not directed to the examination. Still the heir should give notice to the other recipients of *fideicommissa* that they should come before the arbitrator and there plead their causes; creditors also, especially, that they may establish the debts due to them. The account will be taken in such form in respect of both legacies and *fideicommissa* that if the heir, seeking to safeguard himself by such undertaking, offer payment in full of what was left, he is to have audience. 7. Where some legacies are left forthwith, others subject to a condition, the stipulation is to be introduced on account of the conditional legacies, provided that the others are discharged *instanter* in full. To sum up, Julian writes that should there be legacies, both unconditional and conditional, to guard against the *lex Falcidia's* becoming operative should the condition be realized, the unqualified legatees should be granted an action only on their undertaking to the heir in respect of "whatever they may take in excess of the limits of the *lex Falcidia*." 8. The pen of the same Julian informs us that one to whom a quarter is left conditionally, three quarters without reservation, should give the undertaking "to

restore anything which he receives beyond the limits of the *lex Falcidia*." 9. There is, then, scope for this stipulation; for even though overpayment may be reclaimed, it could happen that the payee is no longer solvent so that what was given is thereby no more.   10. It may be said that the stipulation pertains also to gifts made with a view to death.   11. The words of this stipulation "what you shall take by way of legacy beyond the limits of the *lex Falcidia*" embrace not only the person taking more than the statute allows him, so that he shall return, though also keeping, part but also one who may have to restore *in toto*. It follows that one should know that the *lex Falcidia* reclaims sometimes part, sometimes all, of the bequest. For when a Falcidian account of debts is launched, it often happens that, through the coming to light of some debt or condition, by reason of the liabilities the whole legacy is swallowed up. Again, the realization of the condition of grants of liberty may make a legacy wholly unpayable, since the valuation of legacies is consequent upon the account of the manumissions and the deduction of the value of the slaves.   12. There are, nonetheless, wills to which the *lex Falcidia* has no application; still it is to be noted that although the heir may not retain his quarter, the inheritance is such that it can bear the legacies, even with the deduction of debts and of the value of slaves freed in the will, whether directly or by *fideicommissum*.   13. Security is also to be given to a legatee by one from whom a *fideicommissum* is left away.   14. It may sometimes be that account is to be taken of not the *lex Falcidia* but some other statute; suppose that a patron be instituted sole heir and five twelfths be bequeathed unconditionally and a further amount conditionally, beyond the patron's entitlement; in such a case, we look not to the *lex Falcidia* but to that on the rights of patrons.   15. Should a thing bequeathed perish in the legatee's hands, the view to be adopted is that the promisor will be given a defense,

2   PAUL, *Edict, book 75:* to the value of his undertaking,

3   ULPIAN, *Edict, book 79:* unless anything occurred through his own bad faith; in such a case, he would be caught by the "bad faith" clause comprised in the stipulation under consideration and be open to a replication.   1. This undertaking, which is found in respect of the *lex Falcidia*, applies also to *fideicommissa*.   2. Money is bequeathed for a succession of days; once it is clear that the *lex Falcidia* applies, Pedius says that the case is one not for an undertaking, but for a computation to estimate the total of what is so bequeathed, and the legacy will be held to be what the valuation reveals so that, in its light, an account may be taken at once under the *lex Falcidia* of all the several legacies.   3. Whenever we have the situation that the *lex Falcidia* will obviously be operative, even in advance, a computation thereof is made. For where a condition is pending, we await its realization; but once the day arrives, taking an account and valuation under the *lex Falcidia* also of the intervening period, we deliberate on the statute and say that the stipulation becomes enforceable.   4. Although all legatees and beneficiaries of a *fideicommissum* are under obligation to give the stipulation, the deified brothers held in a rescript that in some cases, it may be dispensed with, for example, where modest maintenance is left. This was their rescript to Pompeia Faustina: "The case which you put forward of the ten gold pieces per annum left to you by your patroness, Pompeia Crispiana, is not in the same category as the maintenance and clothing allowance left to her freedmen; we think, therefore, that these latter should be spared the burden of an undertaking."   5. Know also that the undertaking is not exacted from the imperial treasury, although the treasury can be sued as though it had given one. But in a rescript, the deified Pius ruled that all others, whatever their rank and dignity, will be compelled to give the undertaking, even though they have already received their legacies; this rescript reveals to us that the emperor wished the stipulation to be given, even after the legacies have been discharged.   6. A legatee gives security for the return of the legacy he has received to the heir who is already involved in or anticipates a dispute over the inheritance; the inheritance is

evicted—but through the negligence or even bad faith of the heir who paid the legacy. In such a case, our rule is that the stipulation is not enforceable by reason of the criterion of the "judgment of a good man" which is inherent in such stipulation.   7. Again, if the person who paid the legacy should find himself evicted on some other ground, say that he is found to be instituted in a later will in which no legacy is made to that legatee, we hold the stipulation enforceable on the criterion mentioned.   8. All in all, wherever the inheritance, a sum, or benefit is made over by one who has covered himself by extracting this undertaking, it is to be said that the stipulation becomes enforceable, provided that there has been no fault on the part of the stipulator.   9. It has been asked whether the stipulation can become repeatedly enforceable; it can if the inheritance be taken away gradually.   10. A legacy was paid over before this stipulation was taken; can a *condictio* be brought for the legacy to enforce the giving of the undertaking? The question is prompted by the fact that anything left out or paid up by mistake can be recovered by *condictio*; in our case, more would appear to be given by reason of the absence of the stipulation. Pomponius says that the *condictio* may be invoked for the purpose of exacting security, and I think that policy considerations dictate endorsement of his opinion.

4   PAUL, *Edict, book 75:* There is scope for this form of security if there appear good ground for it. It would be unfair that it be taken in all cases, no dispute having yet arisen; for threats may be illusory. The praetor, accordingly, reserves the matter for his own consideration.   1. Suppose that two persons separately claim the whole estate under a will; they have, for instance, the same name, actions will lie to creditors and legatees against both the possessor of the estate and his adversary.   2. This undertaking is particularly necessary when a man pays his own money or delivers his property. But if he pays money or delivers something from the inheritance, there are those who think that security is unnecessary since, if he should lose his title to the inheritance, he cannot be liable on that score since he neither possessed nor ceased to possess in bad faith. This holds good if he pays before any dispute arises; in other circumstances, he will be liable for fault.   3. Where the claimants' name is the issue between them, need there be security given to the one who delivers the hereditary property, since one of them, anyhow, will be discharged of liability? What, say, if he pay a debt of the inheritance? Where a claimant pays his own money or gives his own thing, however, he will have nothing from which he can make a retention, and thus the undertaking will be needed.

5   MARCELLUS, *Digest, book 21:* Let us consider this point: Should the stipulation "whereby you received more than the *lex Falcidia* allows" be available against one charged with a *fideicommissum* to transfer his legacy to someone else; it may suffice to say that no *fideicommissum* is laid upon him; the fideicommissary, of course, will also give an undertaking to the legatee, unless the latter, to avoid circuity of process, prefer that he do so to the heir. Still the legatee is also to be secured, if (as is usually fair) he be allowed to make a proportional retention from the *fideicommissum*, even though sufficient of the legacy will remain with him to allow the meeting of the *fideicommissum*.

6   CALLISTRATUS, *Judicial Examinations, book 4:* Since a legatee or fideicommissary may have difficulty in providing security and, on that account, be excluded from claiming his testamentary liberality, should he not be relieved of the burden of an undertaking? This view would derive support from the following words of a rescript of the deified Commodus: "The official charged with the case will, if he find that security is being demanded of you to prevent your claim for the *fideicommissum*, ensure that you are relieved of the burden."

7   PAUL, *Lex Julia et Papia, book 7:* The deified Pius ruled that an undertaking in respect of the shares of those who left this life should not be required of one directed to make a preferred claim for yearly legacies to be distributed, unless his instruction so to give security were express.

8   MAECIAN, *Fideicommissa, book 10:* An heir asserts that part, or indeed all, of the inheritance is the object of an information to the imperial treasury; he also states the existence of a *fideicommissum.* The decision is that performance be made to a claimant giving an undertaking that "restitution will be made, if there be eviction from the inheritance."

9   MAECIAN, *Fideicommissa, book 12:* Let us suppose that the dispute be not one over title but one on usufruct (it can well be that Titius is given ownership of a thing while a usufruct in it is given to someone else); in such a case, security for its return should be given, not to the heir but to Titius. Titius is the person to be secured, even if, in the interim, the usufruct be not bequeathed away from the heir; suppose that ownership were left to him, subject to a devised usufruct, the latter going to Seius. In such a case, what would be the point of security to the heir, who would receive no benefit, were the usufruct to fall in? Put, though, the case that, a usufruct being left to Seius, the full title be left to Titius in the terms that Seius ceasing to have a right, the property shall be his; in such a case, security to the heir would be requisite from the fructuary but also from the latter to Titius; for there is no guarantee that the usufruct lapsing, ownership would revert to Titius.

BOOK THIRTY-SIX

1

THE *SENATUS CONSULTUM TREBELLIANUM*

1 ULPIAN, *Fideicommissa, book 3:* Now that we have finished our account of *fidei-commissa* of individual things, let us pass to the interpretation of the *senatus consultum Trebellianum.* 1. This *senatus consultum* was made in the time of Nero, on the eighth day before the Kalends of September, in the consulate of Annaeus Seneca and Trebellius Maximus, and its words are as follows: 2. "Whereas in all fideicommissary inheritances it would be most equitable, should any actions be pending concerning those goods, that those actions should lie against those to whom the right and the fruits are transferred rather than that any man should be endangered by keeping faith, it is resolved that those actions which are commonly granted against the heir or to the heirs shall be granted neither against nor to those who have restored that which was committed to their faith as they were asked to do, but to and against those to whom the *fideicommissum* was restored under the testament, that the last wills of persons deceased may be better confirmed for the future." 3. By this *senatus consultum*, an end is put to the doubts of those who resolved to refuse inheritances either from fear of lawsuits or under pretext of such fear. 4. Although the intention of the senate was to relieve heirs, it has also relieved the fideicommissary. The heirs are relieved, because they have a defense if they be sued. That the heirs may be met by a defense if they sue and that the fideicommissaries are entitled to bring actions are obviously for the advantage of the fideicommissaries. 5. Moreover, this *senatus consultum* applies whether the heir be instituted by testament or whether he be an heir on intestacy who is asked to restore the inheritance. 6. The *senatus consultum* also applies to the dispositions of a son-in-power who is a soldier, who may dispose by will of his *peculium castrense* and *quasi-castrense.* 7. Those who have been granted *bonorum possessio* or other successors may restore the inheritance under the *Trebellianum.* 8. It is a question whether one to whom an inheritance has been restored

by a *fideicommissum* under the *senatus consultum Trebellianum* can pass rights of actions if he in his turn restore it under the same *senatus consultum*, and Julian writes that he also passes rights of action, an opinion which Maecianus approves and with which we agree.   9. But in case an heir be asked to restore the inheritance to two, to one unconditionally or upon a future day, and to the other upon condition, and he says that the inheritance is suspect, the senate has decided that the whole inheritance is to be restored in the meantime to him to whom he was asked to restore it unconditionally or upon a future day, but that when the condition happens, should the other fideicommissary wish to receive his part, the actions pass to him by operation of law.   10. If a son or slave be instituted heir and asked to restore the inheritance, and the father or the master restore it, the actions pass under the *Trebellianum*. The law is the same should they be asked to restore in their own names.   11. So it is if the father be asked to restore the inheritance to the son himself.   12. But also if a tutor, or the curator of a *minor* or of a lunatic be asked to restore the inheritance, there is no doubt that the *Trebellianum* will apply.   13. It was questioned whether, if a *pupillus* be asked to restore to his own tutor, he may make restitution with his [tutor's] authority, and the deified Severus adjudged that he cannot restore the inheritance to his tutor with his tutor's own authority, for he cannot give authority in his own case. 14. On the other hand, an inheritance may be restored to the curator of a *minor* by the *minor*; for no authority is necessary for the restitution.   15. Should it be a *collegium* or body corporate which is asked to restore by resolution to one of those who are of the *collegium* or the corporation, this restitution is good to individuals in view of their collective personality, for no one of them is deemed to restore to himself.   16. If the heir be asked to take a farm for himself and restore the inheritance, he restores the inheritance under the *senatus consultum Trebellianum*; nor is it of much consequence if the farm has been pledged; for the personal action for the debt does not follow the farm, but him to whom the inheritance has been restored under the *senatus consultum Trebellianum*. The fideicommissary, however, should give a *cautio* to the heir, so that should the farm happen to be evicted by the creditor, the heir may be secured. Julian, however, thinks that no *cautio* should be given, but that the farm should be valued at what it is worth without this *cautio*, that is, at the sum for which it might be sold without a *cautio*, and if without any *cautio* it may be sold for a sum which is equal to the value of the fourth part of the estate, the actions will pass under the *Trebellianum*. If for less, restitution should still be made under the *Trebellianum* with a deduction for the deficiency. This opinion resolves many questions.   17. If a testator whose estate is worth four hundred leave legacies of three hundred and ask his heir to deduct two hundred and to restore the inheritance to Seius, is the fideicommissary charged with three hundred or only to the value of what he has received from the inheritance? Julian says that three hundred may indeed be demanded from him, but that no action will be granted against the fideicommissary for more than two hundred and for one hundred against the heir; and Julian's opinion seems to me the true one, or the fideicommissary might suffer a loss which exceeded the value of what came to his hands from the inheritance; for no one is bound to pay more as a legacy than has come to his hands from the inheritance, even if the *lex Falcidia* do not apply, as is stated in a rescript of the deified Pius.   18. Indeed, even under a soldier's testament no more is due in legacies than the value of the inheritance after deduction of the debts. And yet the fideicommissary is not permitted to retain the fourth part.   19. Hence, Neratius writes, if an heir be asked to restore, and he restore the entire inheritance without deducting the Falcidian portion to one who is himself asked to restore to another, the latter should not deduct the fourth part against the second fideicommissary, unless the heir intended his bounty for the first fideicommissary alone.   20. But if a testator who is worth four hundred leave a legacy of two hundred to Titius and ask that one half of his inheritance be restored to Sempronius, Julian says that restitution should be made under the *Trebellianum* and that the actions for the legacies should be divided, so that one hundred is demanded of the heir, and the legatee demands the other hundred of the fideicommissary. Julian so holds because upon this view the heir has a clear fourth part, that is, one hundred clear.   21. Julian also writes that if a testator whose estate is worth four hundred have left three hundred in legacies and asked his heir to deduct one hundred and restore the inheritance to Sempronius, we should hold that when the hundred has been deducted and the inheritance restored, the action for the legacies should be granted against the fideicommissary.

2   CELSUS, *Digest, book 21:* A testator who left four hundred left a legacy of three hundred to Titius and imposed a *fideicommissum* on his heir that he should restore the inheritance to you. He alleged that the inheritance was suspect and accepted and restored it by command of the praetor. The question was: What should you give to the legatee? We should hold that the testator is to be presumed to have wished the *fideicommissum* to be restored subject to the burden of the legacies and that you should, therefore, pay Titius the whole three hundred; for we should take it that what was asked of the heir was that he should put you in his place and that he should restore you that balance which, had he restored the inheritance unasked, would have remained in his hands after the discharge of all his obligations as heir, that is, after payment of the legacies. What, then, would he have? One hundred, and this is what he is asked to restore to you. Thus, the Falcidian fourth is to be reckoned in the same manner as if the heir were condemned to give three hundred to Titius and one hundred to you, whence it follows that had he accepted the inheritance of his own accord, he would have paid Titius two hundred twenty-five, and seventy-five to you. No more, therefore, is due to Titius than if the inheritance had been accepted without the praetor's command.

3   ULPIAN, *Fideicommissa, book 3:* Marcellus, however, in his notes to Julian, deals with this case as follows. If the testator has stated that the legacies are to be charged upon the heir and the heir has accepted the inheritance of his own accord, the Falcidian fourth should be reckoned in the same manner as if four hundred had been left by *fideicommissum* and three hundred by legacy, so that the three hundred should be divided into seven parts, of which the fideicommissary should take four and the legatee three. If, on the other hand, the inheritance be said to be suspect and the heir do not enter and restore of his own accord, that hundred out of the four hundred which the heir would have had remains in the hands of the fideicommissary, but the remaining three hundred is to be divided in the same manner, so that the fideicommissary will have four parts of it and the legatee the remaining three; for it would be most inequitable that the legatee should take more because the inheritance was alleged to be suspect than he would have taken if it had been accepted voluntarily. 1. What we have said of a suspect inheritance may equally well be said of those testaments to which the *lex Falcidia* does not apply—I mean to the testament of a soldier or of any other such person there may be.   2. Pomponius also writes that if the heir be asked to restore the inheritance after deducting the legacies, it is a question whether the legacies are to be discharged in full and the fourth may be deducted from the *fideicommissum* alone or whether the fourth be deductible both from the legacies and from the *fideicommissum*; and he reports that Aristo held in a consultation that it is to be deducted from all, that is, from the legacies and the *fideicommissum*.   3. Things which have been disposed of by the heir are set off against the heir's fourth.   4. A testator instituted his children in unequal shares, also leaving them legacies to be received before division, and divided much the greater part of his patrimony between his children in this latter fashion. He asked any child who should die without children to retore his portion to his brothers. Our emperor held in a rescript that the legacies also were subject to the *fideicommissum*; for the testator did not speak of his portion of the inheritance, but simply of his portion, and the legacies were to be deemed to be included in his portion.   5. If before the testator's household slaves have been put to the torture an heir who has been asked to restore the inheritance should open the testament or accept the inheritance or do any other of those things which are prohibited by the *senatus consultum* [*Silanianum*], and the' inheritance, therefore, be confiscated,

the imperial treasury acquires the inheritance subject to the charges upon it. Thus, the benefit of the fourth which the instituted heir would have had belongs to the imperial treasury, and the actions pass under the *Trebellianum.* But if the heir prevented his testator from fetching a scribe to write his testament or from bringing the witnesses together or failed to avert his death or if for any other cause the inheritance is claimed by the imperial treasury, here also the benefit of the fourth belongs to the imperial treasury, but three quarters are to be restored to the fideicommissary.

4   ULPIAN, *Fideicommissa, book 4:* Because it might happen that the instituted heir would not accept the inheritance, fearing that he might suffer loss by doing so, it was provided that if the fideicommissary should say that he wishes the inheritance to be accepted and restored to him at his risk, the instituted heir is to be compelled by the praetor to accept and to restore the inheritance. If this be done, the actions pass under the *Trebellianum,* and the heir is not entitled to the benefit of his fourth when he makes restitution; for since he accepted the inheritance at another's risk, he will be very properly excluded from all benefit. Nor is it material whether the inheritance be solvent or not. It is enough that it has been refused by the instituted heir. Nor is any inquiry made to determine whether the inheritance be solvent or not solvent; for it is the opinion or the fear, or the pretext of him who will not accept the inheritance that is considered, not the substance of the inheritance, and this is not unreasonable; for we should not prescribe to the instituted heir why he should fear or should not wish to accept the inheritance, since men vary in their wishes; some fear business, some trouble, some the amount of the debts, though the inheritance may seem wealthy; some fear to give offense to others or to provoke their envy; some wish to do a favor to those to whom the inheritance is left, but without charge to themselves.

5   MAECIANUS, *Fideicommissa, book 6:* But even a man of distinguished station or of great note may be compelled to restore the inheritance of a gladiator or of such a woman as sold her body for money.

6   ULPIAN, *Fideicommissa, book 4:* The heirs may refuse to accept the inheritance not only if they be present but also if they be absent or by letter; for a decree may also be prayed against the heirs in their absence, whether their intention to refuse to accept and restore the inheritance be certainly established or not, so little is their presence necessary.   1. It should be borne in mind that the senate speaks of the instituted heir. Whether the *senatus consultum* applies on intestacy is therefore discussed in Julian's works, but the better opinion and the one which we apply as law is that this *senatus consultum* also applies to intestates, whether their successors take by civil or by praetorian title.   2. But this *senatus consultum* also applies to the son who is under parental power and to other *heredes necessarii,* so that they are compelled by the praetor to intermeddle with the inheritance and then to restore it; and when they have done so, they are deemed to have transferred the actions.   3. If ownerless goods devolve upon the imperial treasury, which will not acknowledge its title to the goods and restore them to the fideicommissary, it will be very just for the imperial treasury to make restitution in the same manner as if it had claimed them.   4. So if the townsmen of a municipality be instituted heirs and allege that the inheritance is suspect, we should hold that they may be compelled to accept the inheritance and to restore it, and the same should be said of a *collegium.*   5. Titius was instituted heir. Sempronius was substituted to him, and he [Titius] was asked to restore the inheritance to Sempronius [himself]. The instituted heir said that the inheritance was suspect. The question is whether he should be compelled to accept and to restore the inheritance. The point is debatable, but the better view is that he should be compelled; for it may be in the interest of Sempronius to take the inheritance under the institution rather than under the substitution, if the substitution be charged with legacies or with manumissions; for the law is also so taken if he to whom the inheritance is left by *fideicommissum* be heir upon intestacy.   6. If the heir be commanded to restore the inheritance at another place and allege it to be suspect, Julian writes that he is compellable in the same manner as one who is asked to restore upon a day to come.

7   MAECIANUS, *Fideicommissa, book 4:* But it must be noted that the expenses which would be necessary to perform the journey are also to be taken into account; for were he instituted thus, "if he have given ten to Titius," he would be compelled only if the money

were tendered him. His health and his social position are also to be considered; for what if one afflicted with disease were commanded to accept at Alexandria, or to bear the name of a testator who was a grave robber?

8   PAUL, *Fideicommissa, book 2:* His age and the law, that is, whether it be lawful for him to go there or not, are also to be considered.

9   ULPIAN, *Fideicommissa, book 4:* But if he be commanded to accept at another place and be absent upon public duty, Julian says that he is likewise to be compelled to accept the inheritance and to restore it at the place where he is. 1. Clearly, if the heir demand time for consideration and it is granted, and then after the time allowed him for consideration he accept and restore the inheritance, he is not deemed to have done this under compulsion; for he did not accept a suspect inheritance under compulsion, but of his own accord after consideration. 2. But if he allege it to be suspect, he should declare that it is not in his interest to accept the inheritance; for he need not say that it is insolvent, but he must declare that he does not think it in his interest to accept the inheritance. 3. If one were named heir upon a condition, no act of his is valid pending the condition, though he be ready to restore the inheritance.

10 GAIUS, *Fideicommissa, book 2:* But even if the inheritance be restored before the date or before, the condition happens, the actions do not pass; for the inheritance is not restored as the testator asked that it should be. However, if he ratify the restitution of the inheritance after the condition has happened or the date has come, it is more benevolent to take it that the actions are then to be deemed to have passed.

11 ULPIAN, *Fideicommissa, book 4:* In the works of Julian this case is put: If a legacy be left to the instituted heir "if he be not heir," and he allege the inheritance to be suspect in order that he may not lose his legacy, the amount of the legacy must be tendered to him by the fideicommissary, and then he is to be compelled. Nor will Julian allow that he may demand the legacy from his co-heir in the same manner as if he had not accepted the inheritance; for he did accept, but he thinks that it is rather to be paid him by the fideicommissary. But if he claim any other interest, he is not compelled to accept unless the loss or gain be made good to him by the fideicommissary, or unless the burden which he refuses be remitted by the praetor. 1. Julian also says that if two were instituted by the father, together with his son, who was below the age of puberty, and these two were substituted to the son, it is enough for him who has received a *fideicommissum* in the second instrument to compel one of the instituted heirs to accept the father's inheritance; for once this is done and the father's testament confirmed, both may be compelled to accept under the substitution and to restore the inheritance. 2. We must consider whether an inheritance may be restored only to one who is present or also to one who is absent on his procurator's application to the praetor. I think that an instituted heir may be compelled to accept and to restore even in the absence of the fideicommissary, and that the heir should not fear that the loss may be left to fall upon him; for the praetor may grant him relief, whether a *cautio* be given him or not, and the fideicommissary dies before the inheritance is restored to him. There is a precedent which we may take to govern this case in a rescript of the deified Pius upon the following facts. Antistia at her death instituted Titius her heir, left Albina her liberty directly, left her daughter to her by *fideicommissum*, and asked her to manumit her daughter, but she also asked Titius to restore the inheritance to Albina's daughter after she had been manumitted. Therefore, when Titius alleged that the inheritance was suspect, the deified Pius decided by his rescript that he was to be compelled to accept the inheritance. Upon his acceptance, Albina would be entitled to her liberty. Her daughter was to be conveyed to her and to be manumitted by her. A tutor was to be appointed to the manumitted daughter by whose authority the inheritance was to be restored to the daughter immediately, though the heir had been asked to restore it to her only when she should attain marriageable age; for since, as he said, it might happen that she who had been left her liberty and the inheritance by *fideicommissum* died in the meantime, and he who accepted an inheritance under compulsion ought not to suffer loss, he provided a remedy; should any of these events happen, it was to be allowable to sell the estate of Antistia in the same manner as if she had left

no heir. Since, therefore, the deified Pius has shown that an instituted heir who has accepted under compulsion is relievable, we may say that this precedent is to be followed in other cases also, whenever it may happen that the fideicommissary inheritance is not restored to him who has obtained an order that the heir accept and restore the inheritance to himself.

12   PAPINIAN, *Questions, book 20:* But when an heir was instituted to part and a *fideicommissum* of the inheritance was charged upon him conditionally, the Emperor Titus Antoninus held in a rescript that his constitution did not apply; nor should the *pupillus* be granted extraordinary relief, especially if what was prayed were a new benefit which would cause wrong to another.

13   ULPIAN, *Fideicommissa, book 4:* One on whom a *fideicommissum* has been charged upon condition has no reason to object that the condition may fail and leave him liable to the actions; for he will suffer no loss.   1. It follows, therefore, from what we have said that the presence of the heir is now unnecessary.   2. If the testament be called in question for any reason, an heir who alleges that he deems the inheritance suspect ought not to be heard; for no matter what he may allege against the testator's right to make a will or the validity of the will or upon his own status, he is not to be heard. 3. What, therefore, if it be the effect of the *fideicommissum* that is under discussion? This is not a question which should be passed over. But what if a fideicommissary should say: "Let him accept first, and then let us discuss this question"? I think that sometimes the fideicommissary should be heard, if the cause be likely to depend for some considerable time; for suppose that the text of the *fideicommissum* has to be brought from a distance to settle a reasonable doubt upon the amount of the *fideicommissum*, we should hold that the heir is to be compelled to accept, or he might disappoint the fideicommissary by dying before acceptance.   4. It is now time to ask who may compel an heir to accept and restore the inheritance; for instance, if a praetor or consul have been instituted heir and allege the inheritance to be suspect, may he be compelled to accept and restore? And we must hold that a praetor has no power of command over a praetor, nor a consul over a consul, though the praetor grants actions against them if they submit themselves to his jurisdiction. But should the praetor himself be instituted heir and allege the inheritance to be suspect, he cannot compel himself; for he cannot act in three capacities, as the party who alleges the inheritance to be suspect, the party who is compelled, and the party who compels him; but in all these and in like cases the emperor is to be petitioned for his aid.   5. If a son-in-power hold a magistracy, he may compel his father, in whose power he is, to enter and restore if he allege an inheritance to be suspect.

14   HERMOGENIAN, *Epitome of Law, book 4:* For so far as public law is concerned, the right of paternal power is not regarded.

15   ULPIAN, *Fideicommissa, book 4:* But even an heir who has repudiated an inheritance will be compelled to accept and to restore that same inheritance, if just grounds for it be alleged.   2. However, if the estate have been sold, the praetor should not grant restitution even to a *pupillus* except for good cause, as the deified Pius stated in a rescript.   3. If an heir accept under compulsion an inheritance given him by a testament under which a pupillary substitution has been made by a second instrument, it has been questioned whether his acceptance serves also to confirm the second instrument, which was deemed to have failed when no one accepted the father's inheritance.

Julian, in his fifteenth book, writes that the second instrument is also confirmed, which is a very true opinion; for no one doubts that legacies are payable and gifts of liberty take effect and that the other provisions of the testament, whatever they may be, are valid to precisely the same extent as if the heir had accepted the inheritance of his own accord.   4. As the heir who accepts under compulsion loses other advantages, so he should lose them in this case, or he would be entitled to change his mind and retain his fourth, and I find that our emperor and his deified father have so ruled in a rescript.   5. It is not everyone, however, who can compel an heir to accept a suspect inheritance lost by repudiation and to restore it to himself, but only a party to whom the actions may pass; for it is not equitable to compel an heir to accept an inheritance in order that he may pay over the assets of the inheritance and himself remain charged with the liabilities.   6. Thus, if a *fideicommissum* of money be left to anyone, the heir cannot be compelled, though he be offered a *cautio* for his indemnity.   7. So also, it is only he who is asked to restore an inheritance who is compelled to restore.   8. But if he should be asked to restore the testator's "goods" or his "family fortune" or his "money" or "all my property"

16   (15)   PAUL, *Fideicommissa, book 2:* or "all that is his,"

17   (16)   ULPIAN, *Fideicommissa, book 4:* the heir may be compelled. So also should he be asked to restore the testator's "patrimony" or his "resources" or "whatever I have" or "my wealth" or "my fortune" or "my substance," and should the testator have said "my *peculium*," since most people use the word *peculium* as a diminutive for their patrimony, the heir is compellable; for this testator also was speaking of his succession. I am not unaware that in some of these cases Maecianus doubts and holds it a question of intention whether the testator were thinking merely of his money or of his succession also. If the words be ambiguous, however, I hold that we should take it that it is rather his succession that is meant to save the *fideicommissum*.   1. But even if the testator have asked thus of his heir, "whatever have come to you from my inheritance, I ask that you restore," he may be compelled to accept and to restore the inheritance under the *senatus consultum Trebellianum*, although properly speaking all that can be said to come to someone is what comes to him after deduction of the debts.   2. And, thus, we may say that, generally speaking, it is only in case the heir have been asked to restore a particular thing or quantity that he cannot be compelled to accept and restore the inheritance. If, on the other hand, it appear that the testator was thinking of his whole estate, it is beyond question that if he allege the inheritance to be suspect, he may be compelled, or if he accept of his own accord, the actions pass under the *Trebellianum*.   3. Thus, it is a question whether he may be compelled to accept and restore the inheritance if he were asked to restore it after deduction of debts or of legacies; for if we take the words literally he is asked to restore the residue of the inheritance rather than the inheritance. There are those, Maecianus among them, who hold that this deduction is void; for a quantity cannot be deducted from a right, any more than if the heir were asked to restore a landed estate after deduction of debts or legacies; for a landed estate cannot be reduced by the amount of debts or of a legacy. But he reports that Julian thinks that the *senatus consultum Trebellianum* applies, and in order that the fideicommissary may not be doubly charged, first when the heir deducts the debts or the legacy and a second time when he is sued by the creditors and legatees when the inheritance has been restored to him under the *Trebellianum*, he should either not suffer this deduction by the heir, or the heir should give a *cautio* that he will be defended against the legatees and others.   4. If one be instituted heir and asked to restore not the whole, but a part of the inheritance, or if he be asked to restore to two, and one of them wish the inheritance to be restored to him and the other refuse, the senate has resolved that if he allege the inheritance to be suspect he is discharged in both these cases and that the whole inheritance passes to him who compels him to accept.   5. But also should the testator have asked his heir to restore not the half of his inheritance, but either the whole or a part of the inheritance of Seia, which has come to his hands, and the instituted heir allege that the inheritance is

suspect, since the view of Papinian, that the actions pass under the *Trebellianum*, has been accepted, it may be said that if the inheritance be alleged to be suspect, the instituted heir is to be compelled to accept and restore the inheritance, and the whole inheritance belongs to him to whom it is restored.   6. But also if a soldier have asked his heir to restore his property in Italy or his property in the provinces, we should hold that if he allege the inheritance to be suspect, he is compelled to accept and to restore; for as Maecianus elegantly puts it in the sixth book of his *Fideicommissa*, since a soldier may institute an heir to particular property and actions will be granted to him, by a parity of reason actions will pass under the *Trebellianum*, and though it be settled that if a testator ask his heir to restore the inheritance and the goods which have come to him from someone or which he has in some part of the world the actions do not pass under the *Trebellianum*, yet he says that we should hold the contrary in the case of a soldier's testament; for, says he, as soldiers are allowed to dispose separately of different kinds of goods in instituting their heirs, so if a soldier take the same course in a *fideicommissum* charged upon the instituted heirs, the *senatus consultum Trebellianum* should be applied.   7. A testator instituted two heirs, substituted them to one another, and demanded of them that whether both or either of them should be heir, his inheritance as to one moiety thereof should be restored to another after five years. The heirs named alleged that they held the inheritance suspect. The fideicommissary desired that the inheritance be accepted at his risk. The senate resolved that both heirs or either one was to be compelled to accept the inheritance and to restore it to the fideicommissary and that actions should lie at the suit of the fideicommissary and against him as if the inheritance had been restored under the *Trebellianum*.   8. Maecianus writes: When one of the fideicommissaries was absent and those who were present desired to accept the inheritance at their own risk, once the actions have been transferred outright to him who compelled the heir, those who were absent, if they wish to accept the *fideicommissum*, should claim from him who was present. It follows, says he, that he will not be able to retain the fourth part against his fideicommissaries; for the heir could not have done so.   9. Maecianus also asks whether he who is asked to restore the inheritance to two or more may accept under compulsion from one of them and take the benefit of the *lex Falcidia* against the shares of those who did not join in the application, whether they also prayed that restitution be made to them or whether another have succeeded to their rights. And since, as the law is applied nowadays, the whole passes to him who compelled the heir, it follows logically that the heir who was compelled has lost the right to retain the fourth; for the actions passed outright to the party who compelled him. If, however, we suppose that the fideicommissary did not compel the heir to accept in order to transfer the whole inheritance to himself, then when the others pray in their turn that the inheritance be restored to them, we should hold that he may rely upon the *lex Falcidia*. Maecianus, therefore, is right in saying that it makes a great difference whether the fideicommissary prayed that the whole inheritance should be restored to himself or only his share of it; for if only a share be transferred the *Falcidia* will apply to the residue; if the whole inheritance be transferred, the benefit of this statute is lost. 10. If an heir be asked to restore an inheritance to a slave who has two masters, he alleges that it is suspect; one master wishes to compel him, and the other refuses to receive restitution; we should adopt the same solution as in the case of two fideicommissaries of whom one wishes to receive the inheritance and the other does not. 11. If a father be asked to restore an inheritance to his son, who is under his parental power, can the son compel his father, if he say that the inheritance is suspect? And there is no doubt that the son may compel the father by the aid of the praetor. 12. But also if that *fideicommissum* will fall into the *peculium castrense*, and the son-in-power was a person who discharged a military duty or were in charge of some other office, it is far clearer that he may apply for his father to be compelled to accept and restore the inheritance, though such a prayer may seem contrary to the *obsequium* due to his father.   13. But if an heir be asked to free his slave and restore him the inheritance, we may say that whether the slave receive his liberty directly or by *fideicommissum,* he cannot be compelled by his slave to accept the inheritance, although, should he have accepted of his own accord, he would be compellable to manumit him according to the *fideicommissum* and to restore the inheritance, and so Maecianus writes in the seventh book of his *Fideicommissa.* 14. He also asks, if there be someone willing to give the master a *cautio* for his indemnity, can he be compelled to accept the inheritance, especially also if he be tendered the price of the slave? And he rightly says that he is not bound to commit himself to the acceptance of an inheritance under the doubtful protection of a *cautio.* 15. If those who are not entitled to take the full amount left to them be instituted heirs to the whole estate and asked to restore it in full, they will be compelled to accept the inheritance and restore it; for they will not remain liable to any charge. 16. I am instituted heir, and I, or another legatee, am asked to manumit Stichus. A *fideicommissum* is imposed on me to restore the inheritance to Titius. The testator then imposed a *fideicommissum* on Titius to render it to Stichus. Stichus may compel me to accept the inheritance and restore it. 17. The deified Pius also decided the following case. A slave was left by legacy to one of the heirs, who was required by *fideicommissum* to manumit him, and the other was required to restore him the inheritance. The deified Pius answered the consultation of Cassius Dextrus in these words: "If Hermias was left by legacy to Moscus Theodotus by Pamphilus the testator, who instituted him heir to part of his estate, and if Theodotus after he had accepted the inheritance and before the inheritance was accepted by the co-heir of the same Pamphilus lawfully freed him, and, therefore, the case has reached the stage at which the legator cannot be intestate, Metitius Evarestus is to be compelled upon the application of Hermias to accept the inheritance at his risk and to restore it under the *fideicommissum.*"

18   (17) ULPIAN, *Fideicommissa, book 2:* In one case, the question arose whether a man may be asked by *fideicommissum* to institute someone his heir. The senate resolved that no one may be asked to make someone his heir, but that by this form of words the testator is to be taken to have asked his heir to restore his own inheritance to him, that is, that he should restore him whatever he had acquired from the inheritance. 1. Julian, in the fortieth book of his *Digest,* also says that a *fideicommissum* will be good in this form: "I commit it to your faith that you restore the inheritance of Titius," if he to whom it is addressed have been instituted heir by Titius. 2. I may ask a man to make someone his heir not only if I have named him my own heir but even if I have left him a legacy or anything else; for they will be bound to the extent of what has come to their hands. 3. If a testator should use these words, "I ask that you give to such a one" or "that you leave a *fideicommissum* to such a one" or "that you leave such a slave his liberty," they are allowable; for since the senate resolved that an heir may be effectively instituted in these terms, we should hold the same in other cases. 4. If one be asked to restore the inheritance should he die without children, Papinian, in the eighth book of his *Replies,* writes that even a natural son will defeat the condition, and in the case of a freedman, a son born in slavery and manumitted with his father. This is his opinion. To me, however, it would seem that where natural children are concerned, it is a question of intention what kind of children the testator had in mind; but this is to be judged according to the station in life and the intention and the situation of the creator of the *fideicommissum.* 5. I remember that this problem arose in an actual case. A woman had asked her son that if he died without children he should restore the inheritance to his brother. He was subsequently deported to an island, and there had issue. Thus, the question was whether the condition of the *fideicommissum* had failed. Our view is this. Issue conceived before deportation, though they be born afterward, defeat the condition. Issue had after deportation do not avail, since they are treated as if they were issue of another person, especially since the goods are also forfeited to the imperial treasury, subject to charges, in a manner of speaking. 6. If one be prayed to restore the inheritance to his sons or to

such of them as he shall choose, Papinian holds that even if he be deported, he is entitled to choose to whom he wishes to restore the *fideicommissum* after he is made free. But should he have been reduced to penal slavery and have no issue conceived before, he cannot now perform the condition and is deemed to have died without issue. But when he dies that right of choice which Papinian allows to one deported should not be allowed to him.   7. On the other hand, one who has had a son but has lost him during his own life is deemed to die without issue. However, we must consider whether the condition has failed if he has perished at the same time as his father in a shipwreck or the collapse of a building or a hostile attack or in any other manner. And I think the preferable view is that the condition has not failed, because it cannot truly be said that his son has survived. Either, therefore, the son survived the father and extinguished the condition of the *fideicommissum*, or he did not survive him and the condition has happened; but if it do not appear who died first and who subsequently, we should rather hold the condition of the *fideicommissum* to have happened.   8. If a testator should leave a *fideicommissum* in these terms, "I commit it to your faith, my son, that should you die leaving a stranger your heir, you restore the inheritance to Seius," the deified Pius held in a rescript that he is to be deemed to have had children in mind. When, therefore, upon a death without children the maternal uncle had obtained *bonorum possessio* on intestacy, he ruled that the condition of the *fideicommissum* had happened.

19   (18)   ULPIAN, *Sabinus, book 15:* It is settled that the fruits are not to be included in the restitution of a fideicommissary inheritance unless the heir have delayed restitution, or he were especially asked to restore the fruits also.   1. The fruits are set off against his fourth, however; and it has been so ruled in a rescript.   2. Whenever anyone is asked to restore an inheritance, he is deemed to be asked to restore that which belongs to the inheritance, but the fruits are not derived from the inheritance, but from the things themselves.   3. If a legacy be left to an heir and he be asked to restore his portion of the inheritance, he may retain only so much as he received from his co-heir. What is charged upon his own portion is subject to the *fideicommissum*. This the deified Marcus decreed.

20   (19)   PAUL, *Sabinus, book 3:* When a *fideicommissum* has been given without condition, if the testator add, "I ask that you give it your son and cause it to come to his hands," it has been decided by rescript that it is to be deemed to be given at such time as he may take it, that is, when he attains his independence.   1. "I ask you, Lucius Titius, that you share my inheritance with Attius." Aristo says that actions will lie under the *senatus consultum Trebellianum* against him to whom the inheritance has been restored; for it is to be understood as "I ask that you restore that inheritance," and the words of the *senatus consultum* are not considered, but the sense, whatever the words, if the testator meant that his inheritance was to be restored.   2. The expense which is incurred in disposing of or in preserving the goods which form part of the inheritance should be charged to the heir.

21   (20)   ULPIAN, *Sabinus, book 19:* But also if a legacy were made payable when the legatee should have children and he has died leaving his wife pregnant, he transmits the legacy to his heir.

22   (21)   POMPONIUS, *Sabinus book 22:* An heir who should have retained his fourth restored the whole inheritance and did not secure himself by the stipulation provided in the Edict. Aristo says that he is in like case with those who fail to use rights of retention when that is all they have, but he may sue for or take possession of the goods of the inheritance and use the defense of fraud to bar any action brought against him and warn the debtors to prevent the debts being paid.

23   (22)   ULPIAN, *Disputations, book 5:* A woman who had left two sons in the power of their father and married another man instituted her second husband her heir and asked him to restore her inheritance to her children or to the survivor of them after the death of their father. The case was: The step father had restored the inheritance to

them after their father had emancipated them, and one of the sons had died in the life of the father. It was asked whether the survivor of the two sons could demand the share restored to his brother on the ground that it had been given him too soon. Scaevola reports that the deified Marcus decided a like case in the imperial auditory. A *fideicommissum* was left to the sons of one Brasidas, a Spartan and a man of praetorian rank, by his wife, who had been separated from him by divorce, if they became independent by the death of their father. He had emancipated them. After emancipation, they claimed the *fideicommissum*. He reports, therefore, that the deified Marcus held that the *fideicommissum* was to be paid to them forthwith upon consideration of the mother's intention. It was because she had not believed that the father would emancipate them that she had postponed the *fideicommissum* to his death, and she would not have postponed it to the end of a life if she had hoped that he would emancipate. I should accordingly hold that the judgment of the deified Marcus is to be extended to the case put, and that the *fideicommissum* was properly paid to both.   1. There is no doubt that the instituted heir may be compelled to accept and to restore the inheritance to slaves, whether they be given their liberty directly or by *fideicommissum*; for the status of the person who compels him does not entitle the heir to disregard him. Even he may have access to the magistrate, so that one who could as yet neither demand the liberty left to him by *fideicommissum* nor sue for that left to him directly may yet appear before the praetor even in his own person because of the possibility that he may become entitled to his freedom and the inheritance.   2. If the heir should restore after a long interval when the *fideicommissum* is presently due, he may deduct the fourth when he makes restitution; for the fruits which have been taken are deemed to have been taken by the negligence of the claimant rather than by the will of the deceased. The case is different if he be asked to restore upon a condition or on a date to come; for then what he receives excludes the *Falcidia*, if it be so much as amounts to a fourth of the inheritance and a fourth of the fruits; for the fruits which are received in the meantime are deemed to be received under the will of the testator.   3. But if an heir be asked to restore an inheritance and slaves have died or other goods have perished, it is settled that he is not compelled to restore what he does not have, though he must, on the other hand, render account of his fault, but of such fault as is close to fraud, and so Neratius writes in the first book of his *Replies*. But also if, when he should have sold the goods, he failed to do so by grave fault, not by slight negligence and such as he was accustomed to show in his own affairs, he must render account of such a matter. But also if a house have been burned by his fault, he must render account. Moreover, if there be any offspring of slaves, and offspring of those offspring, for they are not classed as fruits. But if he himself have expended money on the goods of the inheritance, it is deductible. But if by lapse of time without any act of his a house have been acquired by usucapion, it will be most equitable for him to pay nothing, since he is not at fault.   4. The case put was this. A testator had instituted his daughter his heir and had asked her to restore the inheritance to Titius if she should die without children. She had given her husband a dowry of a certain sum and then, dying without children, had instituted her husband her heir. The question was whether the dowry were deductible. I said that an act which accorded with the modesty of the woman and with her father's wish could not be said an act which defeated the *fideicommissum*. We, therefore, should hold that the dowry is to be deducted in the same manner as if the woman had been asked to restore the residue of the inheritance, but if the woman received in fruits from the inheritance a sum so large that the dowry may be satisfied out of it, we should hold that the dowry is to be charged against the fruits rather than against the *fideicommissum*.   5. If the *Trebellianum* is to apply, it is not enough that I have been asked to restore the inheritance, but I must be asked as heir. Thus, if a legatee have been left a portion of the inheritance (for we hold that even a portion of the inheritance may be left by legacy) and he be asked to restore this part, there is no question that restitution cannot be made under the *senatus consultum* and therefore the fourth is not deductible either.

24   (23)   JULIAN, *Digest, book 39:* The head of a household who commands one or two of his heirs to restore to their co-heirs is to be taken to give them the same shares in the *fideicommissa* as he did in the distribution of the inheritance, but if those to whom the *fideicommissum* is given be commanded to pay money and to receive their *fideicommissa* upon that condition, his intention is to be inferred from the amount of money which they are

commanded to give; for if they be named heirs in unequal shares and commanded to give in equal shares, it is more probable that they are to receive back equal shares; if, on the other hand, the sum of money to be given correspond to their portions, they should receive the same portions as they have in the inheritance.

25 (24) PAPINIAN, *Questions, book 15:* The contrary view has sometimes been taken, however, both in rescripts and by judges from deference to the intention of the testator, that is, if the *fideicommissum* be not left them under the name of heirs, but their own names be expressed.

26 (25) JULIAN, *Digest, book 39:* A testator had written thus: "I demand of you, my heir, and I commit it to your faith that you give and restore whatever shall come to you from my inheritance as and when you receive it to my son or, should anything first befall him, to his mother." The boy had died before the inheritance had been accepted, and the question was whether the *fideicommissum* were due to the mother. I replied that if the boy had died before the *fideicommissum* vested, the *fideicommissum* was transferred to the mother; if, on the other hand, he died after the *fideicommissum* vested, the *fideicommissum* belongs to the heir of the boy. The praetor will decide, however, upon consideration of what manner of woman the mother is and what manner of person is the heir of the boy, whether it were the intention of the head of the household that if the son should die before the *fideicommissum* had been restored, it should go to his mother rather than to his heir. MARCELLUS: But it accords with the testator's intention that the *fideicommissum* should pass to the mother whenever the boy may have died, whether before the *fideicommissum* vested or afterward, if the boy have not received it already, and this is the law we apply in practice. 1. If a slave be named as heir and his master is asked to restore the inheritance to the same slave when he becomes free, the *fideicommissum* is valid. 2. If a testator instituted his son heir to his whole estate and by codicils, which he ordered to be opened after the death of the son, imposed a *fideicommissum* on him that he restore the inheritance to his sister should he die without children, and if the son, knowing what was written in the codicils, commanded by his testament that Stichus, a slave of the inheritance, should be free, the heirs of the son should pay the value of that slave to the sister of the deceased, since liberty is preserved by the favor due to it. Furthermore, although the son had not known of the codicils which his father had made, his heirs, nonetheless, ought to pay the value, lest the act of one man should cause loss to another. 3. But also if this slave were instituted heir by Sempronius and accepted that inheritance after he had been freed by the brother's testament, the heirs of the brother should also pay the value of the inheritance to his sister; for had he not been manumitted, he might have accepted it by command of the woman. If, however, Sempronius had died in the lifetime of the son, the inheritance would not be subject to the *fideicommissum*; for had he been commanded to accept by the son himself, he would have acquired the inheritance for him.

27 (26) PAUL, *Senatus Consulta, sole book:* The *senatus consultum Apronianum* commands that fideicommissary inheritances should and may be restored to all *civitates* which are under the rule of the Roman people. It is also settled that actions will pass against them under the *Trebellianum* and that the citizens of these municipalities are admitted to sue.

28 (27) JULIAN, *Digest, book 40:* But those to whom the inheritance is restored are to choose an *actor*, both to sue and to answer actions. 1. An heir who had accepted under compulsion commanded a slave of the inheritance to accept an inheritance left to that same slave by another and then restored the inheritance which he had said that he held suspect. The question was whether he should also have restored that inheritance which was acquired through the slave. I said that this inheritance should no more be included in the restitution than should anything which a slave of the inheritance had stipulated for after the inheritance was accepted or had acquired by delivery or the fruits gathered from the property of the inheritance, that is, provided that performance of the *fideicommissum* had not been wrongfully delayed; but if a slave had stipulated for anything before the inheritance was accepted or received it by delivery,

that should be restored, just as fruits taken before the inheritance is accepted are included in the restitution.   2. The heir who states that he holds the inheritance suspect receives no advantage under the testament which he would not have had though he had not been instituted or had not accepted the inheritance. Hence, if he were substituted to a *pupillus* thus, "whoever shall be my heir, let him also be heir to my son," he will be compellable to restore the inheritance which has come to him under the substitution. If, on the other hand, he were substituted without the phrase, "whoever shall be my heir," thus, "let Titius be heir to my son," then, if he alone be heir to the father, he will still be compellable to restore the inheritance of the *pupillus*, but if he had a co-heir, he may retain the inheritance of the *pupillus*; for since the co-heir has accepted, he might himself have accepted under the substitution though he had refused the father's inheritance.   3. If the father appointed as heir a son whom he had under his parental power and demanded of him that he restore the inheritance to Sempronius and the son say that he holds the inheritance suspect, the inheritance may be restored under the *senatus consultum Trebellianum*. Hence though he have not intermeddled with the inheritance, yet the actions which lay for and against him are nonetheless transferred to Sempronius.   4. If one who is appointed heir by the father and substituted to a disinherited son be asked to restore the inheritance which may come to him under the substitution to Titius, he is not compellable to accept the father's inheritance during the lifetime of the *pupillus*, first, because the *fideicommissum* is given upon condition and second, because it is not proper to litigate about the inheritance of a living child, but when the *pupillus* is dead, he should be compelled to accept the father's inheritance.   5. But if there were two heirs instituted by the father and a *fideicommissum* was imposed on both that they should restore the inheritance of a disinherited son, it will be sufficient to compel only one to accept; for once this is done, the heir who did not accept the father's inheritance may also be compelled to accept and restore the inheritance of the son.   6. In any case in which an emancipated son receives *bonorum possessio contra tabulas*, there is no reason to compel the heir to restore the inheritance, and as he is not compelled to pay either legacies or other *fideicommissa*, so he should not be compelled even to make restitution of the inheritance. MARCELLUS: Clearly, he is not compellable to accept if the son [have] already [received] *bonorum possessio*, [but he may be compelled if the son have not applied for it], in case the *fideicommissum* should fail by the death of the instituted heir and the renunciation of *bonorum possessio* by the son.   7. Should one who has restored an inheritance under the *senatus consultum Trebellianium* sue the debtors or should he be sued, he may be aided or defeated by the defense of restitution of the inheritance. Those actions will lie for the fideicommissary which the heir had at the time when he restored the *fideicommissum*. MARCELLUS: But it is settled that those actions which were subject to a condition and had not vested at that time will also lie for the fideicommissary. Before the inheritance has been restored, on the other hand, the heir is not to be aided by any defense; for he will restore that much the less under the *fideicommissum*.   8. The *senatus consultum Trebellianum* applies whenever a testator imposes a *fideicommissum* of the whole or a part of his inheritance on his heir.   9. Hence, if Maevius has instituted you heir and has asked that you accept and restore the inheritance of Titius and you have accepted the inheritance of Maevius, the *fideicommissum* is demandable from you in precisely the same manner as if you had been asked to restore a landed estate which was left to you by Titius as a legacy. Even if, therefore, you allege that the inheritance of Maevius is suspect, you ought not to be compelled to accept it.   10. But if Maevius has asked you to restore both his inheritance and that of Titius and you have accepted the inheritance of your own accord, you will take the benefit of the *lex Falcidia*, retain one quarter of Maevius's inheritance, and restore three quarters under the *fideicommissum*; nor will it be material whether you were asked to restore both inheritances to the same person or the inheritance of

Maevius to one and the inheritance of Titius to another. But should you have alleged that the inheritance of Maevius is suspect, you will be compelled to accept and restore it to him to whom you were asked to restore it, but he to whom you were asked to restore the inheritance of Titius will not be able to compel you to accept.   11. If the heir have restored the inheritance under the *Trebellianum* and retain the fruits of the landed estates, or the landed estates themselves, or if he were in debt to the testator, the fideicommissary has to be given an action against him. MARCELLUS: The same course must necessarily be taken when a share of the inheritance has been restored, and proceedings for the division of the inheritance are taken between him who restored the inheritance and him who received it.   12. He who is asked to restore an inheritance to an emancipated son [of the testator] may be compelled to accept and to restore, though the son might be granted *bonorum possessio contra tabulas*.   13. If a patron be instituted heir for the share due to him and asked to restore the inheritance and he say that he holds the inheritance suspect, I think it the more correct course for the praetor that he should compel him to accept and to restore, though he might upon changing his mind be entitled to retain that share of the inheritance.   14. If the heir has been asked to restore the inheritance after he has taken certain things for himself and he has accepted under compulsion, may he take them? I replied: He who accepts an inheritance by the command of the praetor should be deprived of all advantage.   15. But if a legacy were left him under this condition, "if he be not heir," and he allege that he holds the inheritance suspect, he is not to be compelled to accept, unless the legacies which were given upon condition that he be not heir be restored to him, not indeed by his co-heirs; for they should not be burdened, but by him to whom the inheritance was restored; for if he be compellable to accept the inheritance that he may do what faith requires, yet he ought not to suffer loss upon that account.   16. My cousin was instituted heir to the whole estate, and a *fideicommissum* was imposed on her that she should restore one moiety of the inheritance to Publius Maevius immediately and the other moiety to the same Publius Maevius when she should die. In addition, other legacies were given to others. Publius Maevius received a moiety of the inheritance at once, and gave a *cautio* that anything which he had received in excess of the amount permitted by the *lex Falcidia* should be restored. The other legatees also received the full amount, and gave similar *cautiones* for the restitution of any excess which they had received. My cousin has died, and Publius Maevius requires that the other part of the inheritance be restored to him with its fruits. Therefore, I ask how much I ought to restore to him. Is it the amount which had remained in the hands of my cousin over and above the fourth part of the goods and no more? Should I demand repayment of anything from the others to whom legacies have been paid and of how much? I ask further: Should the amount which I receive from them under the stipulation and the amount which had remained in the hands of my cousin over and above her fourth not make up a moiety of the inheritance, ought I to supply it from the increase and the fruits of that sum which remained in the hands of my cousin over and above her fourth, provided that the amount to be restored do not exceed the moiety of the inheritance? Should, on the other hand, the whole of what has been received, save for a fourth part of the goods and the fruits of that fourth, be restored to Publius Maevius as he requires? I replied: If the surplus above the fourth which remained in the hands of your cousin amount, with the addition of the fruits, to no less than the value of a moiety of the inheritance as at the time of death, the whole is to be restored to Publius Maevius, and nothing can be reclaimed under the stipulation from those to whom the legacies have been paid. If, however, the value of the fruits be greater than the moiety, the surplus will accede to your fourth and its fruits. If, on the other hand, the fruits of that part which had remained in the hands of your cousin over and above her fourth do not make up the value of a moiety of the goods, an action will lie on the stipulation. In short, the account is to be taken upon the principle that since the fruits exceed the fourth in any event, if they have grown to an amount which exceeds the value of the moiety of the goods, you may also retain the surplus.   17. If an heir have been asked to manumit his own slaves and to restore the inheritance to them, he should deduct the price of the slaves from the inheritance before restoring.

29   (28) AFRICANUS, *Questions, book 6:* An heir was instituted to the whole estate and asked to restore one part of the inheritance to me unconditionally and another to you upon condition. He alleged the inheritance to be suspect, accepted upon my application, and restored the whole to me under the *senatus consultum.* It was doubted, not without reason, whether I must restore you the fruits of your part whenever the condition may happen. The majority opinion is that they are not due, since they would not have been due from the heir had he accepted of his own accord, and it is enough for you that your rights are preserved for you unimpaired without your receiving any new advantage.   1. The same jurists, however, held that if an heir instituted to the whole be asked to restore a fourth to me unconditionally and also a fourth to you upon condition and he allege the inheritance to be suspect and I compel him to accept, if the condition should happen, a half is to be restored to you.   2. I do not think that in the case put I may take advantage of the *lex Falcidia,* though the heir appointed in the testament might have done so, had he accepted of his own accord.

30   (29) MARCIAN, *Institutes, book 4:* If a testator who made a previous testament have made a subsequent testament, though in the later document he instituted heirs to specific property, the former testament is still avoided, and so the deified Severus and Antoninus held in a rescript, and I have given the text of this constitution, since there are other points mentioned in it. "The Emperors Severus and Antoninus to Cocceius Campanus. There is no question that the testament made in second place, though an heir of specific property be named in it, takes effect in law as if that property had not been mentioned, but that the heir named is bound either to rest content with the property given him or to make up his fourth under the *lex Falcidia* and to restore the inheritance to those who were named heirs in the former testament, because of the words of *fideicommissum* which the testator inserted, which stated that the previous testament was to remain in force." This rule is to be taken to apply if the contrary be not explicitly stated in the second testament.

31   (30) MARCIAN, *Institutes, book 8:* If an envoy allege an inheritance to be suspect, he is compellable to answer the proceedings even during his mission, for he is not much occupied with his duties. Though he allege that he is considering whether to accept, he should be compelled to accept, though not to restore immediately, but so that after his return home he may take the benefit given him by the *lex Falcidia* or the testament if he think it to his advantage, and if he do not think it to his advantage, he may restore the whole inheritance and escape the liabilities.   1. If a testator have asked his heir to restore "his goods" or "all that is his," we should take him to mean a fideicommissary restitution [of the inheritance]; for the terms "mine" and "yours" are to be taken to include actions.   2. If an inheritance be restored to a son-in-power or a slave and afterward the father or master ratify, the actions pass under the *senatus consultum Trebellianum.*   3. It makes a great difference whether the heir retain a part as a share of the inheritance or in goods or money; for in the former case, the actions are divided between the heir and the fideicommissary, but in the latter, it is the fideicommissary who has the actions.   4. And if [the emperor] be instituted heir and be asked to take a certain sum or thing and to restore the inheritance, though what he

is to take be less in value than the fourth part, the emperor does not [ordinarily] allow that more be claimed.   5. Even should he have been asked to restore the inheritance without taking anything, our emperors have usually made a gift of the fourth part, and so the deified Trajan and Hadrian and Antoninus have decided by rescript.

32   (31)   MARCIAN, *Institutes, book 9:* If a slave be left his liberty unconditionally and the inheritance by *fideicommissum* upon condition, the heir is compelled to accept the inheritance, if he allege it to be suspect, and to restore it, and if the condition fail, he [the slave] cannot be deprived of his liberty.   1. But if the inheritance have been left by *fideicommissum* to a slave who has been given his liberty at a time to come, the deified Pius held in a rescript to Cassius Hadrianus that it cannot be accepted as suspect in the meantime; for the inheritance cannot be restored to one who is not yet free, nor, on the other hand, should the slave be given his freedom contrary to the intention of the deceased.   2. If an heir who has been instituted upon a condition and asked to restore the inheritance do not wish to perform the condition and to accept the inheritance, if the condition be to do an act, he should do it and accept and restore, or if it be to give, upon tender by the fideicommissary. If, however, the heir should refuse to perform the act, the fideicommissary will be given permission to perform the act in the same manner as if the condition were to give, and then the heir is compelled to accept the inheritance. Other conditions, which are not within the power of the heir, do not concern the duties of the praetor.

33   (32)   CELSUS, *Digest, book 20:* Baelista thus instituted a son-in-power his heir: "If Rebellanius shall give a *cautio* to the colony of Philippi that, should he die without children, then whatsoever sum or sums of money have come to him from my inheritance or from my goods, the same shall wholly come to the colony of Philippi." I replied, upon the words which you quote, that is, "money," I think that he should also restore the fruits which he has taken from the inheritance in the same manner as if the testator had specially expressed that he should.

34   (33)   MARCIAN, *Institutes, book 8:* Celsus writes in the twentieth book of his *Digest* that if one who had goods worth four hundred demand of his heir that should he die without children, as much money as has come to him from the testator's inheritance may be restored to Maevius, and he receive four hundred from the fruits pending the condition and then die without children, his heir will owe four hundred to Maevius. And after discussing at length and in detail whether because the heir receives the increase he should bear the risk, or whether the law be contrary, he finally says that it is unjust that the fideicommissary should bear the loss, when the increase does not belong to him, and whether, says he, the increase also will belong to him so far as may be necessary to supply any deficiency in the four hundred, that is, that up to the sum of four hundred both the losses and the fruits are to be taken into the account, which I think the better view.

35   (34)   MARCIAN, *Rules, book 2:* If the father wished that the share of the inheritance given to such son of his as should die last should be restored to a kinsman and the brothers died together, it is clear that if the kinsman do not show which died last, he cannot be admitted to the inheritance, but the mother will be admitted to the inheritance of both under the *senatus consultum Tertullianum.*

36   (35)   ULPIAN, *Duties of Proconsul, book 6:* When a lunatic who was instituted heir had been asked to restore the inheritance, the deified Pius decreed that her curator might transfer the actions after receiving *bonorum possessio secundum tabulas.*

37   (36)   PAUL, *Edict, book 13:* Where an inheritance has been restored under a *fideicommissum*, I think that if the heir has previously been a party to an arbitration, the fideicommissary should give a *cautio* to the heir, as he should where the heir has

administered extensively before restoring; for though it is said that he should retain, this is not a universal rule. What if there be nothing for him to retain, as if the inheritance be all in debts or in physical things which are not in his possession? Clearly, he to whom restitution has been made may claim all, and yet the heir will remain bound by the actions which have been brought against him or by the stipulations which he has been obliged to give. Therefore, he will not be compelled to restore unless a *cautio* be given him.

38   (37)   ULPIAN, *Edict, book 16:* An inheritance is deemed to be restored either in deed, if, say, the heir have allowed possession to be taken of all or of some of the goods of the inheritance with the intention that he should restore them and you should receive them, not if he thought you to possess for some other reason. But also if he ratified afterward, the same view will have to be taken. But also if he state by word that he restores, or if he restore by letter or by messenger, he is to be heard. But also if by your wish he restore to another, the actions will pass against you. Again, if another have restored by my command or if I have ratified the restitution, the actions are deemed to have passed.   1. A *pupillus*, however, should restore himself with the authority of his tutor. The tutor should not restore without the *pupillus* unless the *pupillus* be an *infans*; for the tutor has no power to assign the actions of his *pupillus*. In the case of Arrius Honoratus, a *pupillus* who had restored to his paternal uncle and tutor, Arrius Antoninus, the deified Severus held that a *pupillus* could not restore to his tutor himself even with his authority.   2. But also if it be to the *pupillus* that restitution is to be made, it is clear that an inheritance cannot be restored to a *pupillus* without his tutor's authority.

39   (38)   PAUL, *Edict, book 20:* For the restitution of an inheritance is not a payment, but a succession; for he is bound.

40   (39)   ULPIAN, *Edict, book 16:* But nor can restitution be made to the tutor himself in all cases.

40   (41)   PAUL, *Edict, book 20:* Although the senate speak of the transferring of those actions which lie for and against the heir at civil law, yet praetorian actions pass; for there is no distinction. Indeed, the right or duty under a natural obligation passes.   1. The *Trebellianum* mentions the instituted heir, but as the law now stands the heir's successor may properly restore under the *Trebellianum*: for example, the heir or the *bonorum possessor* or the father or the master for whom the inheritance has been acquired; for they should all restore, under the *senatus consultum Trebellianum*, such right as they have, nor is it material whether it be he who is instituted who is asked to restore or his father or master.   1. It is immaterial to whom restitution is made in our name, whether he be head of a household or one under the power of another,

42   (41)   PAUL, *Fideicommissa, book 2:* woman or man, and thus restitution is well made to a slave with our consent, or if we have ratified.

43   (42)   PAUL, *Edict, book 20:* For it is precisely as if the inheritance had been restored to me.   1. Rights of sepulcher remain with the heir after restitution of the inheritance.

44   (43)   ULPIAN, *Edict, book 22:* Papinian discusses this case. An heir has been instituted to a half of the estate and asked to restore the inheritance. He says that it is suspect and accepts under compulsion. Subsequently, the fideicommissary learns that since the restitution a further portion has accrued to the heir named in the testament. Does he require another action? And he says that he has no reason to worry about that. He holds that the only question is whether he requires a new restitution after the

portion has accrued, but not even this is necessary.

45   * * * He who is asked to restore what has come to his hands from the goods of a testator restores what he has from the inheritance and not what he has personally acquired.

46   (44)   MARCELLUS, *Digest, book 15:* The heir accepted a suspect inheritance at the suit of Stichus, who had received his liberty and a *fideicommissum* of the inheritance under the same testament. Stichus then died before he had been guilty of [culpable] delay in receiving the inheritance, leaving Titius his heir. I ask whether actions will lie under the *senatus consultum* against Titius if he will not receive the fideicommissary inheritance. I replied: Since he who is compelled to accept an inheritance ordinarily restores it forthwith, the *senatus consultum* speaks only of the freedman, and no mention is made of his heir. It may happen, however, that the heir has postponed restitution, as if the deceased owed him money, which he would rather retain than sue for. For the rest, I think we should lay down the same rule in the case of the freedman's heir as is laid down in the case of the freedman; for why should he refuse what he whose inheritance he has taken could not have refused? But if the freedman should happen to die without heir before the restitution of the inheritance, the creditors of the inheritance are to be allowed to sell his goods in precisely the same manner as if he had died after the inheritance had been restored.   1. But I pray that you will tell me whether I have taken the right view upon this question. A daughter, and sole heir, has been asked to restore a moiety of the inheritance, deducting some very small legacies and debts of no great amount, so that the *lex Falcidia* does not apply. The restitution of the *fideicommissum* has not been delayed. I require that the inheritance, in the literal sense of that term, should be restored to me, so that by the *senatus consultum Trebellianum* and by the actions which lie under it I may also sue for the interest falling due between the date of the death and the time of restitution. I ask the same question of the rents; for the inheritance included the benefit of certain leases. I demand no fruits from the heir, but she requires me either to repay her the interest and the rents or to assign her my actions for them. I cannot persuade her that by the name of "the inheritance," which she was asked to restore to me, this stipulation for interest also belongs to me. I replied: these are all included in the term "inheritance"; for so far as concerns this question there is no difference between these and other sums promised upon condition or yearly or monthly. Certainly, these are treated as fruits of the thing which is included in the inheritance, and fruits do not go to the fideicommissary, if there have been no delay, but since he does not demand that the heir should make up the *fideicommissum*, if that be the right way to put it, but requires that the inheritance be restored to him in the state in which it now is, the heir has no ground to refuse this; for it was the intention of the senate that the fideicommissary in a sense should be admitted to share the inheritance and should stand in the place of an heir for that part for which the inheritance had been restored to him. But if the heir have placed money of the inheritance out at interest or have taken fruits from the farms,

there is nothing due on that ground to him to whom the inheritance has been restored by *fideicommissum*, if there have been no delay; this, because the heir lent the money or bestowed his labor in cultivating the farm or in gathering the fruits at his own risk, and it would not be just to make him a sort of procurator for another. When the inheritance has been increased in any of the ways about which I am asked, however, this has involved no expenditure or labor on the part of the heir.

47   (45) MODESTINUS, *Advice on Drafting, sole book:* If an heir who is asked to restore the whole inheritance do not wish to retain the fourth part, but to render faithful obedience to the desires of the deceased, he will have to accept the inheritance of his own accord as one who proposes to restore it under the *Trebellianum*. I should rather persuade him, however, to say that the inheritance is suspect and restore under compulsion by the praetor; for in this case, he is deemed to restore under the letter of the *Trebellianum*, and since he has claimed to fear to accept the inheritance, he transfers all the actions to him who has received it.

48   (46) JAVOLENUS, *Letters, book 11:* Seius Saturninus, a chief pilot of the British fleet, by his testament left Valerius Maximus, a captain, his fiduciary heir and demanded of him that he restore the inheritance to Seius Oceanus, the testator's son, on his attaining the age of sixteen. Seius Oceanus died before he had attained that age. Now Mallius Seneca, who claims to be the maternal uncle of Seius Oceanus, demands these goods by right of relationship, but Maximus, the captain, claims them for himself on the ground that he to whom he was to restore them is dead. I am asking, therefore, whether these goods belong to Valerius Maximus, the fiduciary heir, or to Mallius Seneca, who claims to be the maternal uncle of the dead boy. I replied: If Seius Oceanus to whom the fideicommissary inheritance should have been restored under the testament of Seius Saturninus at his age of sixteen by Valerius Maximus, the fiduciary heir, has died before he attained the prescribed age, the fiduciary inheritance belongs to him who was entitled to the other goods of Oceanus; for the *fideicommissum* vested in the life of Oceanus, that is, if he be deemed by deferring the time of payment to have allowed the fiduciary heir the guardianship of the goods, rather than to have made the *fideicommissum* payable upon an uncertain day.

49   (47) POMPONIUS, *Readings, book 1:* If what was due to the testator under a natural obligation be paid to his heir, it is to be restored to him to whom the inheritance has been left by *fideicommissum*.

50   (48) PAUL, *Replies, book 14:* Paul replied: If the case be put that a certain portion of an inheritance has been left to one and he has stolen certain things belonging to the inheritance, it is rightly held that he should be denied any claim for those things which he has taken.

51   (49) PAPINIAN, *Questions, book 3:* When an inheritance is being restored under the *senatus consultum Trebellianum*, if the matter be urgent and there be reason to fear that an action may be time-barred, through the absence of the fideicommissary, for instance, the heir is compelled to answer the suit. 1. In the same manner, if a son be deliberating whether to apply for *bonorum possessio contra tabulas*, the heir appointed in the testament may be sued by the creditors of the inheritance.

52   (50) PAPINIAN, *Questions, book 11:* Vivius Cerealis had been asked to restore an inheritance to his son Vivius Simonides, if he should cease to be subject to his paternal power, and was proved to have done many acts in fraud of the *fideicommissum*. The Emperor Hadrian commanded that the inheritance be restored to the son in such manner that he [the father] should have no right in that money so long as his son should live; for since no *cautio* could be given while he retained his paternal power, he deprived him of the benefit of the condition because of his fraud. By force of this judgment the son, so far as that inheritance was concerned, was to be treated in the same manner as a son who was a soldier, if goods were to be demanded of those in

possession of them or debtors were to be sued. But it accords with the reverence due a parent that a father who is perhaps in want should receive benefit from the increase of the inheritance by the discretion of the judge.

53 (51) PAPINIAN, *Questions, book 17:* Should the heir be asked by *fideicommissum* to restore the inheritance after deduction of legacies, it is settled that those legacies which are not demandable are not deductible. If, however, a wife who is named heir to a share of the estate have her dowry left to her by *praelegatum*, and she be asked to restore the inheritance after deduction of legacies, then although the quarter which she retains under the *lex Falcidia* amount to as much as she has in her dowry, she may yet deduct a part of the dowry left to her proportionate to her share; for since she may claim both, there is no difference between this woman and any other creditor who is instituted heir and asked to restore the inheritance. The law is the same, though the *fideicommissum* be charged upon her without deduction of legacies.

54 (52) PAPINIAN, *Questions, book 19:* If another's thing were left by legacy to Titius, who instituted the owner heir and requested that he restore the inheritance to Maevius, Maevius will claim the legacy in vain; for he cannot recover what could not pass to the instituted heir, that is, the owner. 1. A slave was to receive his liberty from one of the heirs and a *fideicommissum* of the inheritance from the other. Should neither wish to accept, there will be no action which the praetor can take; for acceptance cannot be compelled because of the gift of liberty alone, and the heir from whom the slave is not to receive his liberty cannot be compelled to accept for the benefit of one not yet free, and the *senatus consultum* applies when the slave is to receive his liberty, whether directly or by *fideicommissum*, from all the persons from whom he is also to receive the inheritance. Should it happen, however, that the heir from whom the slave is to receive his liberty has repudiated his share or been excluded by a condition, since his share has passed to the other, it is arguable that the other may be compelled to accept; for what difference does it make by what right the liberty and the inheritance have come to be due from the same person?

55 (53) PAPINIAN, *Questions, book 20:* An heir is not to be compelled to accept a suspect inheritance by one who has been left his liberty from a legatee and the inheritance from the heir; for the status of the man depends upon the legacy, and for the sake of a legacy no one is compelled to subject himself to the actions which lie against an heir; for what if the legatee should delay manumission and the slave die in the meantime? Should, however, the legatee die in the life of the testator, it is benevolently held that he is to be compelled to accept, since it is in his own power to manumit the slave and restore him the inheritance.

56 (54) PAPINIAN, *Questions, book 19:* Titius was asked to restore the residue of an inheritance to Maevius. What has been alienated or spent in the meantime will not be demandable thereafter, provided that it be not proved that any such act was done with the intention of defeating the *fideicommissum*; for it is clear that words of *fideicommissum* imply good faith. Hence, the deified Marcus, hearing a case of a fideicommissary inheritance, took the view that the words "whatever shall remain of my inheritance I ask that you restore" imply that what is to be restored is to be determined as an upright man would determine it; for he decided that those amounts which were alleged to have been spent from the inheritance did not go merely in reduction of the *fideicommissum*, but were to be ratably apportioned according to the value of the patrimony which the heir had of his own. His decision, as it seems to me, was influenced not merely by motives of equity, but by precedent; for when it was the extent of the obligation of the emancipated son to collate his goods in favor of his brothers that was in question and it was accepted that what a soldier had acquired upon service should be left to him alone, the emperor ruled in answer to a consultation that the expenses which the soldier had incurred were not to be deducted merely from that property which was subject to collation, but ratably, taking his military funds also into the account. Since this is the position, Maevius should require a *cautio* for the

fideicommissum, which he should do not because he may demand anything under the stipulation which he could not demand under the *fideicommissum*, but so that he may have verbal sureties for the sum which he could demand under the *fideicommissum*.

57 (55) PAPINIAN, *Questions, book 20:* If the son of a patron have restored the inheritance to a stranger under the *Trebellianum*, the action for the freedman's services, which could not be transferred, will remain with the heir, nor will he be barred by any defense; for it could have been of no profit to him who received the *fideicommissum*, and we should hold it for a general principle that the heir will be neither barred from nor discharged of those claims which are not included in the restitution. 1. The Emperor Titus Antoninus decided in a rescript that if the fideicommissary have been given his liberty directly after the lapse of a certain time, the inheritance is not to be restored forthwith, when there is no person to whom restitution may be made. 2. He who has received the whole of a fideicommissary inheritance under the *Trebellianum*, because it was alleged to be suspect is compelled to restore the whole, if he himself be asked in his turn to restore it to another, and the *Trebellianum* applies to this restitution also; for the *lex Falcidia* does not entitle the fideicommissary to retain the fourth, and it is not material that the second *fideicommissum* would have failed had the first fideicommissary not demanded that the inheritance be accepted; for once the inheritance has been accepted, all the dispositions of the deceased are confirmed. It is no argument to the contrary that he is not required to pay out more than three fourths of the estate in other legacies; for it is one thing to be chargeable with the liabilities of the heir, another to be bound in one's own name by the requests of the deceased. Hence, it may be said that the instituted heir should not be compelled to accept at the suit of the first fideicommissary alone in any case in which no part of the estate will be left in his hands; if, that is, he be asked to restore immediately or after an interval with the fruits, but even should he have been asked to restore without the fruits, the amount will not be sufficient to entitle him to force acceptance upon another. It will be immaterial that the first fideicommissary has also been given his liberty; for like a gift of money, a gift of liberty is not sufficient to entitle him to compel the instituted heir. Should the first fideicommissary have refused, however, it is settled that the second may demand in his own name that the heir should enter and restore to him. 3. What, then, if he were asked to restore not to another, but to the heir himself? Since the fourth which the heir has lost is not to be restored to him in any case, his right to retain this portion entitles him to be heard. But we should not constantly overlook that the instituted heir who has accepted under compulsion is to be refused any remedy for the *fideicommissum*; for why should it not be deemed an unworthy thing that he who has repudiated the last requests of the deceased should obtain anything under his dispositions? This argument is more forcible if he have been compelled to accept after a condition has been performed. For if the condition were still pending, it would be harsh to take the same view; for he might invoke the *lex Falcidia* if he changed his mind. I am not unaware that it may be said that the right to proceed for enforcement of a *fideicommissum* is by no means to be denied to him who is striving to acquire rights of sepulcher; yet the senate was so firmly of the opinion that nothing of the share which he abandoned should be left to him that he can neither invoke the *lex Falcidia* nor keep any specific legacy which was left to him nor take under a substitution made by a second instrument in these terms: "Whoever shall be heir to me, let him be heir to my son." 4. One to whom the inheritance of Titius has been restored under the *senatus consultum Trebellianum* may himself restore the inheritance of Maevius, which Titius, the deceased, should have restored under the *Trebellianum* to Sempronius, as any other successor may. 5. The actions under the *Trebellianum* cease to lie if the inheritance be evicted from an heir against whom judgment is given after he has restored the fideicommissary inheritance, if, that is, the suit against him have reached joinder of issue before restitution; for by force of the eviction the restitution is deprived of its effect, since it has been determined that the *fideicommissum* was not due. If, however, the *fideicommissum* be also charged upon the plaintiff who succeeded in the subsequent action, it is arguable that the actions under the *Trebellianum* lie still; for when the possessor accounts for the inheritance, he may debit the heir with the share which he has restored to the fideicommissary.

58 (56) PAPINIAN, *Replies, book 7:* A father willed that his daughter should take certain things for herself and restore the inheritance to her brothers. It was ruled that before the

inheritance was restored the daughter also was to be sent into possession of the inheritance. In the interval, however, the sons had sold the whole interest in certain of the testator's goods and had also pledged others. When the inheritance was subsequently restored, it was clear that by that act the sales of the other portions also and the pledges were confirmed.

59 (57) PAPINIAN, *Replies, book 8:* "Whatever shall come to the hands of my heirs from my inheritance or my goods, let them restore it all after their deaths to my native place, the colony of Beneventum." It was agreed that the testator was not to be held to have included the fruits taken pending the condition.   1. The words were: "I commit to the faith of my sons that should either of them die without leaving children before the other he restore his share to his surviving brother, but should both die without children, I wish my inheritance to pass to my granddaughter Claudia." One died leaving a son, and the second died without children. The granddaughter seemed prima facie to be excluded because of the wording of the condition, but since it is agreed that in *fideicommissa* the intention is to be considered, I answered that it would be absurd to refuse any share to the granddaughter if the first substitution failed, when the grandfather had wished that she should have the whole had the surviving brother taken his brother's share also.   2. "I request of you, my dearest wife, that when you die you restore my inheritance to my sons or to one of them or to my grandsons or to such of them as you wish or to my kinsmen, should you wish to choose any from among my whole kindred." I answered that the sons were to be taken to be substituted for one another by *fideicommissum*, but that as to the grandchildren and other kindred the testator had given a power of choice. If any grandchildren survived, however, the woman was not entitled to choose from among the other kindred because of the degrees prescribed in the *fideicommissum*, but should there be none in the degree of grandchildren, she might choose any individual she wished from among the kindred.

60 (58) PAPINIAN, *Replies, book 9:* An heir was asked to deduct the fourth part and to restore the inheritance. Before he had restored, he became heir to a debtor of the inheritance. Since the action thus extinguished cannot be revived by the *Trebellianum*, three fourths of the sum due is also demandable as a *fideicommissum*. This will include interest, whether due by contract or by the discretion of the judge, for the time before the date upon which the action is extinguished, but not for the subsequent period, unless performance of the *fideicommissum* be delayed.   1. If by a *fideicommissum* an inheritance is to be restored on a date to come, the debts will not be at the risk of the heir merely because the heir has got in the money from some of the debtors.   2. An heir who is asked to restore an inheritance after an interval is not bound to restore the interest which he has received from debtors of the inheritance if it fell due after the creditor's death. Should he fail to exact it, the action for the whole arrears of interest passes under the *Trebellianum*; for the stipulation was part of the inheritance. Hence, the heir has no claim to recover back anything on the ground that he has paid what was not due. Similarly, if the interest falling due in the meantime be not paid to a creditor of the inheritance, the fideicommissary will be liable for this also under the *Trebellianum*, and it is no ground of complaint that the heir did not pay the interest out of the fruits, which he took in his own right; but should the heir have paid the interest in the meantime, he will not be entitled to retain for it, since he was acting for himself. If he has been compelled to pay the principal to a creditor, he cannot charge the fideicommissary with anything for interest in the meantime.   3. An heir who has been asked to take a hundred for himself and to restore the inheritance is to be deemed, under the *lex Falcidia*, to receive the whole sum, as if he were directed to retain the money out of the goods, and so the rescript of the deified Hadrian has been taken. So we should also hold, if he be asked to restore a part of his share to his coheir. The case is different, where landed property is retained for a share of the inheritance, since the whole of a sum of money may be retained from his portion, but he cannot receive the other portion of the land except from his co-heir, who has the ownership. When, however, the land was of greater value than the portion of the inheritance, it was held that the *lex Falcidia* was applicable to the excess at the suit of

the fideicommissary; for it has been settled that a competing money claim is set off.   4. One who has been asked to restore the inheritance at his death, the profits excepted, will not be entitled to keep the children of slave-women, or such young of animals as have been added to the flock to keep up the numbers.   5. Before the *fideicommissum* vests, fruits and interest, though the debtors of the inheritance have paid it after the date of vesting, and also rents which the heir has received from the landed property, are to be counted as part of his fourth share.   6. Since, on the other hand, an heir who is asked to restore an inheritance after his death is not obliged to sell goods of the inheritance, he will not be deemed to have received the interest of the capital sum which might have been raised from their price because he has had the use of them in the meantime, and indeed slaves and buildings are not at his risk, though, should they suffer wear and tear or accident, the value of his fourth is also reduced. 7. If the heir be asked to restore what shall remain of the inheritance at his death, he is not deemed to be asked to restore the surplus of the fruits; for these words permit diminution of the inheritance, but cannot be construed as requiring that the fruits be added to it.   8. The heir of one who was asked to restore the surplus of the goods after his death is not bound to redeem goods of the inheritance which have been pledged, if this were not done fraudulently.

61   (59)   PAUL, *Questions, book 4:* One who owed money on *pignus* instituted his creditor and asked him to restore the inheritance to his daughter, that is, to the daughter of the testator. Since he was unwilling to accept, deeming the inheritance suspect, he accepted under compulsion by command of the praetor and restored. Having failed to find a buyer for the *pignus*, he prayed that he might be allowed to keep it as his own property. I replied: The obligation is certainly extinguished by acceptance of the inheritance. What we have to consider is whether the natural obligation is also extinguished and the *pignus* released. Let us then consider the substance of the matter, whether the creditor, plaintiff, and heir be in or out of possession. And should he be in possession, no action will lie against him at the suit of the fideicommissary. He cannot sue on the *pignus*; for that action belongs to the inheritance. He cannot demand his *fideicommissum*, upon the ground that too little has been restored, as he might have done had there been no *pignus*; for the defendant is in possession of the thing as creditor. But also if it be the fideicommissary who possesses, the Servian action will lie even here; for it may be truly alleged that the money is unpaid, just as it may be where the action is barred by some defense. Thus, the *pignus* may not merely be retained, it may be demanded, and the money, if paid, cannot be recovered back. Because of the *pignus*, therefore, the natural obligation continues. Had nothing been done, however, I should have thought him not compellable to accept unless a *cautio* were first given him for his indemnity, or the money were paid; for also when the heir appointed in the testament loses a benefit, because, for instance, he has received a legacy should he not be heir, it has been held that he is not to be compelled to accept unless the legacy be paid him. In this case, it could indeed be argued that the heir is not to be compelled to accept in a sense against the wish of the deceased, who, by giving a legacy to the heir should he not accept, referred the acceptance to his choice; but though the testator gave him one or the other, we allow him both.   1. Upon giving a dowry, a woman agreed with her husband that should she die during the marriage, a part of the dowry should be restored to her mother, but the mother took no stipulation for it. Then the wife, on her death, made her mother and her husband her heirs and requested of her mother that she should restore the inheritance to Titius. The judge who heard the cause for division of the inheritance had adjudged that part to the mother, as if it had been due under a valid agreement. The question was whether that portion also should be handed over under the *fideicommissum*, and I do not think that it is to be restored; for she did not take it as heir, but as mother under the agreement, nor did she have it by reason of the inheritance but, erroneously, under the agreement.

62   (60)   PAUL, *Questions, book 11:* A patron who was instituted heir for the portion due him and asked to restore the sixth part restored it. The actions do not pass under the *Trebellianum*; for what he restored was his due, and hence it may even be recovered back, if he acted under a mistake.

63   (61)   PAUL, *Replies, book 14:* Paul replied in these terms: "Sempronius, I have not named you heir because I am weak and writing in haste, and therefore I wish him to be given so much as he would receive for a twelfth of the inheritance." It would indeed appear that this is a disposition of an amount rather than a portion of the inheritance, but the words are to be so taken that he is to be deemed to have been thinking of a restitution of the twelfth part.

64   (62)   SCAEVOLA, *Replies, book 4:* A testator asked of his daughter that should she die leaving children, she should restore a part of what had come to her from her father's goods to her brother, and if without children, that she should restore the whole. She has died married, survived by a daughter, and the question is whether her heir, together with the part of the inheritance, should also restore a part of what was given in dowry. He replied that that which formed part of the dowry was not included in the part of the inheritance which was to be restored, but that even if anything were due under a promise of dowry, it was to be treated as a debt.   1. A testator left a pecuniary legacy to his foster son and directed that Sempronius should receive it and should pay interest at a certain rate to the foster son until he attained his twentieth year. He then committed it to the faith of his foster son that should he die without children, he should restore part to Sempronius and part to Septicia. The foster son died before his twentieth year. The question was whether the substitutes might demand the *fideicommissum* or should wait until that time when the foster son, had he lived, would have attained his twentieth year. I replied that upon the case as stated they might.

65   (63)   GAIUS, *Fideicommissa, book 2:* When restitution is made to the fideicommissary, he to whom the inheritance is restored holds as part of his estate all the goods at once, though he has not yet taken possession of them.   1. If the fideicommissary has taken a stipulation for the restitution of the inheritance from the heir and the inheritance were restored to him when he sued on the stipulation, it is clear that the actions pass nonetheless, that is, if the defendant restore the inheritance. If, on the other hand, he were condemned to pay the value of the inheritance because he did not restore, the actions belonging to the inheritance remain with the defendant, who was condemned, and the plaintiff recovers a sum of money.   2. If the heir appointed in the will have restored the inheritance and afterward his title be challenged and he be defeated or do not contest the suit, it has been settled that the actions which have been once transferred to the fideicommissary still lie. 3. If the heir restore a greater part than he was asked to do, the actions are not transferred in respect of the additional part, but when the heir is asked to take some thing or sum of money for himself and then to restore, if he take nothing and restore the whole inheritance, the actions are rightly held to pass.   4. If the heir, before he has restored the inheritance, has commanded a slave of the inheritance instituted heir by a stranger to accept his inheritance, Julian holds that this inheritance need not be restored, because he was not asked to restore it, and this we must admit. There is, however, a further question to be asked: Was the heir asked to restore the inheritance with its increase? For if this were the case, he is compelled to restore that inheritance also, unless the heir should prove by the clearest of evidence that the slave was instituted heir with the intention of benefiting him.   5. It is provided by a rescript of the deified Antoninus that if an heir be asked to restore the inheritance to Titius on receiving from him a sum equal to the value of the fourth of the inheritance, the money is to be paid without interest though it be paid late; for the longer a fideicommissary delays payment, the longer it will be before he receives the *fideicommissum*, and he loses the fruits taken in the meantime. Hence, if he were in possession of the inheritance before payment of the money, he must restore to the heir the fruits which he has taken.   6. The law is the same, if a *fideicommissum* be charged on the heir in these terms: "I ask that if Titius give you a hundred, you restore my inheritance to him."   7. If an heir be instituted upon condition and state that he deems the inheritance suspect, should the condition involve no difficulty, no immorality of any description, and no expense whatever he is to be commanded to fulfill the condition, to accept, and so to restore. If, on the other hand, the condition be immoral or difficult, it is manifestly unjust to compel him to fulfill it on another's account. But it has also been held unjust for the praetor to remit it, since it is absurd that one who demands a *fideicommissum* should be given more by the

praetor than the testator intended; for it is clear that unless the condition were performed, the testator neither offered the inheritance to the heir whom he appointed nor
intended that he should restore the inheritance to the claimant.   8. If a condition to
pay money be imposed upon the heir, he who claims the *fideicommissum* should offer
him the money, so that he may accept and restore the inheritance after performing the
condition.   9. But if a condition be imposed, and it is such as the praetor remits,
the Edict meets the case, as Julian says. He is to be commanded merely to accept the
benefit of the praetorian actions or to demand *bonorum possessio secundum tabulas*,
so that when he has thus acquired the actions he may transfer them under the *senatus
consultum* when he restores the inheritance.   10. If the condition be to bear a certain
name, which the praetor insists upon, it is indeed considered that he would be acting
properly if he were to fulfill it, since there is no harm in taking the name of a respectable man; for the praetor does not insist upon this condition in case of infamous or
shameful names. Nevertheless, if he refuse to bear the name, the condition is to be
remitted him, as Julian says, and *actiones utiles* are to be allowed or *bonorum possessio secundum tabulas* granted, so that when he has acquired the actions he may
transfer them under the *senatus consultum*.   11. If upon my application and by the
command of the praetor you have accepted an inheritance which was thought suspect
and have restored it to me, I shall be entitled to take the benefit of the *lex Falcidia*
against the legatees if you might have taken advantage of the statute and to the same
extent that you might; for if, in addition, there be anything left by *fideicommissum*
from me to someone, this is treated as though it were left from a legatee and does not
come into the account under that statute, but is reckoned separately.   12. If Titius be
asked to restore the inheritance to Maevius and Maevius to restore a sum certain in
money to Seius and Titius has taken advantage of his right to retain the fourth against
Maevius, Neratius writes that it is equitable that Maevius should pay that much the
less to Seius, lest he should have to bear the loss from his own property.   13. Julian
says that if the instituted heir be asked to restore to Titius and the substitute to
Maevius and the instituted heir say that he holds the inheritance suspect, he is to be
commanded to accept and to restore upon the application of Titius.   14. If a *fideicommissum* be imposed on a *bonorum possessor* that he restore the inheritance and he
have allowed the time for claiming *bonorum possessio* to pass, and for some reason he
to whom the inheritance should be restored was unable to appear during that time
before the praetor and to pray that *bonorum possessio* should be demanded and the
inheritance restored, he should be relieved, that is, restitution should be granted
against the lapse of the time for receiving *bonorum possessio*, so that the *fideicommissum* may be performed.   15. It is to be noted, however, that if an insolvent have
instituted Titius his heir, commanded that a slave be free, and asked Titius to restore
the inheritance to him, it is hardly possible to compel Titius to accept the inheritance if
he refuse to do so; for though Titius should have accepted the inheritance on the application of the slave, the slave would be disentitled to claim his liberty, as being given
him in fraud of creditors, though Titius be wealthy; and, therefore, the inheritance
cannot be restored to him either. But we should hold that by the intention of the statute the case is to be treated as if the slave had been freed and made sole heir, and
Titius were not heir.

66   (64)   MAECIANUS, *Fideicommissa, book 4:* If the inheritance of a *pupillus* to whom
money has been lent without the *auctoritas* of his tutor have been restored to me under the *senatus consultum* and I pay the creditor, I cannot recover back the money.
Granted, if the heir pay after restitution he may recover it back, but for no other reason than that the natural obligation is deemed to have been transferred from him to
me. So, if the inheritance of one who had lent to a *pupillus* without the *auctoritas* of
his tutor were restored to me, should the *pupillus* pay me, he cannot recover it back,
but should he pay the heir, he may recover, though he could not recover if he had paid
before restitution.   1. If *heredes necessarii* be instituted upon a condition, which,
though it be a very easy one, they are not prepared to perform, we should hold that
they may be compelled to restore the inheritance upon the application of those to
whom they were asked to restore it; for *heredes necessarii* also are to be compelled to

perform a condition in order to restore a fideicommissary inheritance. 2. If an heir be asked to restore an inheritance and die before he restore it, his heir may restore the inheritance, and the actions pass under the *senatus consultum Trebellianum*, but should he have left two heirs, upon restitution by each the actions will pass for that part; for had he himself restored a part, it is the better view that the actions would pass in part for the time. So if there be several heirs to one who was asked to restore an inheritance, and at the moment some only have restored, or there are several heirs to him to whom restitution should have been made, each will have the actions under this *senatus consultum* for that part for which the inheritance has been restored to him. 3. If a patron instituted heir for the part due to him have been asked to restore it to the disinherited children of the deceased freedman, and he have accepted of his own accord, the *lex Falcidia* will apply. If he accepted under compulsion, the actions will pass in their entirety under this *senatus consultum*.

67 (65) MAECIANUS, *Fideicommissa, book 5:* An inheritance cannot be effectively restored to a slave against the will or without the knowledge of his master, but should he afterward ratify, the restitution will be confirmed; obviously, it is to the master himself that the actions pass. Although this restitution resemble the acquisition of an inheritance, it does not follow that the master's command must precede the act, but, as has been said, it is enough if his ratification follow it by analogy with *bonorum possessio*, and so far as the present question is concerned, it is immaterial whether the heir be asked to restore the inheritance to the master himself or to the slave; nor is the consent or the act of the slave required for this purpose, whereas for *bonorum possessio* or for the acceptance of an inheritance his consent is necessary. Hence, if the heirs allege the inheritance to be suspect, they are to be compelled to accept and restore the inheritance at the suit of the master. 1. If the testator have asked his heir to restore the inheritance to a woman, should she not have married, we should hold that if the heir allege the inheritance to be suspect, he is to be compelled to accept it and to restore it to the woman, although she be married, and our Julian also holds the same in the case of other conditions which likewise cannot be performed until the end of the party's life. Upon this view, he should restore the inheritance only after a *cautio* has been given to those interested by those to whom he was asked to restore upon these conditions. 2. When after a hearing the praetor has erroneously or even corruptly commanded that the inheritance be restored as under a *fideicommissum*, it is also in the public interest that it should be restored; for judgments should be conclusive. 3. If an heir have been asked to restore the inheritance to a *pupillus* who is *infans* and he accept of his own accord, the inheritance may be restored either to his slave or to the *pupillus* himself with the *auctoritas* of his tutor; for the fact that he cannot speak will be no more of an impediment in this case than it would be in the case of a dumb man over the age of puberty who wished the inheritance to be restored to himself. If, however, the heir refuse to accept the inheritance, it is difficult to find a solution; for the *senatus consultum Trebellianum* will not apply if the tutor pray that the inheritance be accepted at the risk of the *pupillus*, and the *pupillus* cannot so pray himself; for he cannot speak. Where the dumb are concerned, this difficulty may be met to some extent, if they be able to hear or, when asked, can indicate by a nod that they wish the inheritance to be accepted at their risk, as the absent may do by messenger. But I have no doubt that the *infans* also is to be aided in all cases, and we should so hold by analogy both with the civil and with the praetorian law; for had he been instituted heir, he is undoubtedly deemed capable of acting as heir with his tutor's *auctoritas*, and if it were a question of *bonorum possessio*, it might be claimed for him by his tutor. Consequently, the heir may also be compelled by the tutor to accept and restore the inheritance. Upon the same principle, a dumb man who can understand nothing is aided by his curator. 4. If the heir deliver particular articles by my order to one to whom I have sold them, there is no doubt that restitution is to be taken to have been made to me. The law is the same if they be delivered by my order to one to whom I was bound to give them under a *fideicommissum* or upon any other ground or to whom I wished to make a loan or a gift.

68   (66) PAUL, *Fideicommissa, book 2:* An heir instituted "if his co-heir have accepted" may rely on the *lex Falcidia* though his co-heir accepted under compulsion, provided that he accepted the inheritance without compulsion himself.   1. Julian held that an inheritance might be restored under this *senatus consultum* even to the procurator of one who was absent, if he applied, provided that he gave a *cautio* that his act would be ratified, if the intention of the absent party were not clear, but we should hold that an heir who alleges the inheritance suspect is not to be compelled to accept if it be doubtful whether any mandate were given, even if a *cautio* be given him; for the *cautio* may prove insufficient. Should he accept of his own accord, however, he suffers no great hardship, but if there were no mandate, the actions will pass at the moment of ratification.   2. Should a slave of the inheritance be injured, though the heir has become entitled to an action through a slave of the inheritance, yet the action under the *lex Aquilia* does not pass to the fideicommissary; for those actions pass which form part of the estate of the deceased.   3. If an envoy accept the inheritance under compulsion and restore it at Rome, the fideicommissary is compelled to answer actions at Rome, though the heir is not compelled.   4. Ought the fideicommissary to be sued where the deceased should have been sued? If the heir accepted of his own accord and restored the inheritance, it is arguable that the fideicommissary is bound to defend in three places: in the domicile of the deceased, in the domicile of the heir, and in his own. Hence, the fideicommissary should be sued either where he has his domicile or at the place where the greater part of the inheritance which has been restored is.

69   (67) VALENS, *Fideicommissa, book 3:* If you have accepted a suspect inheritance at my suit by the decree of the praetor, and I then do not wish it to be restored to me, nor to intermeddle with the goods, the course to be taken (as Octavenus not inelegantly held) is for the praetor to grant actions against me in the same manner as if I had received the inheritance, which is the juster solution.   1. Even after you have resolved to defraud your creditors, you may accept a suspect inheritance and restore it to me without danger of the *interdictum fraudatorium*; for though there had been no *fideicommissum* in the case, you would have been free to defraud your creditors of such an advantage as this if you did not wish to accept the inheritance, and I do nothing improper in receiving that inheritance which your creditors could not have compelled you to accept without my suit.   1. But even if a son who is *suus heres* to his father be asked by his father to restore the inheritance to me, and restore it to me as suspect by the decree of the praetor after resolving to defraud his creditors, the *interdictum fraudatorium* can hardly apply; for if the goods of his father were sold, his creditors could take nothing for themselves from that inheritance, unless perhaps the son's own creditors are entitled to be heard, if they ask that they may be permitted to sell the goods themselves on paying off the creditors of the father.   3. If the heir have said that he holds the inheritance suspect and have restored it to one who was not entitled to take the whole with the intention of giving it to him, that part which he was not entitled to receive will be taken from him. We should hold the same if the fiduciary heir took this course without any intention of making a gift.

70   (68) VALENS, *Fideicommissa, book 4:* If an heir have been asked to restore the inheritance by a testator who died insolvent and he say that he holds the inheritance suspect, there is no doubt that nowadays he may restore it under compulsion under the *senatus consultum Trebellianum*; but even if he have accepted of his own accord, he will restore under the same *senatus consultum*, although, if an insolvent have given a sum of money or an individual thing by *fideicommissum*, it is no more due than a legacy would be; for he to whom the *fideicommissum* has been left stands in place of a legatee in this case and of an heir in the former case.   1. If you were asked to restore the whole inheritance and have accepted of your own accord and restored it without deducting the fourth part, it will be difficult to believe that you did this from ignorance rather than in performance of the *fideicommissum*, but should you prove that you have failed to retain the fourth by mistake, you may recover it back.

71   (69) MAECIANUS, *Fideicommissa, book 8:* When the heir restores the inheritance, he need give no *cautio* against eviction of the land or the slaves or any other goods of

the inheritance. Indeed, upon the contrary, the heir is entitled to a *cautio* in case any of them which have been sold by the heir himself should be evicted.

72 (70) POMPONIUS, *Fideicommissa, book 2:* If the instituted heir have been asked to restore the inheritance to Titius and Titius to restore it to the heir after an interval, the direct actions will serve the heir well enough. 1. If before the heir restored the fideicommissary inheritance he has alienated anything from the inheritance, or manumitted a slave of the inheritance or broken anything or shattered or burned it, no civil action lies against him after the inheritance has subsequently been restored under the *senatus consultum Trebellianum,* but this loss should be claimed for in proceedings on the *fideicommissum.* Should the heir, on the other hand, have done any of these things after restoring the inheritance, we should hold that he may be sued under the *lex Aquilia,* if, for instance, he have wounded or killed a slave of the inheritance. 1. If the inheritance include an action which must be brought within a limited time, the time before restitution during which the heir might have sued will be taken to have run against the party to whom it has been restored.

73 (71) MAECIANUS, *Fideicommissa, book 10:* Anyone who is considering whether to accept an inheritance may be compelled to accept upon the application of one who wishes the inheritance to be accepted at his risk, not to restore immediately, but upon the terms that he may take the benefit of the testament in the same manner as if he had accepted of his own accord if, after lapse of the time allowed for consideration, he find the inheritance to be beneficial, but if, on the contrary, he think it burdensome, he may be discharged of the liabilities of the inheritance on restitution.

74 (72) POMPONIUS, *Fideicommissa, book 4:* The heir was asked to take a farm for himself and to restore the inheritance. The farm did not belong to the testator. Aristo said that we must consider whether the testator wished the heir to have the farm in all events or only if it were his own, but that he preferred the former view; and, therefore, the value of it is to be retained.

75 (73) MAECIANUS, *Fideicommissa, book 13:* If the heir have lent money of the inheritance and taken *pignora* for the debt, no actions will lie against the *pignora* themselves at the suit of him to whom the inheritance has been restored, but there will be some room for doubt if the heir have become entitled under a contract of the deceased, and have taken a *pignus* for it before he restored the inheritance. However, the fideicommissary would not be allowed to sue even in this case, but he may have an action under the *fideicommissum* against the heir, that he cede him his action for the benefit of the pledge. 1. When an inheritance is restored under the *senatus consultum Trebellianum,* the servitudes to which the lands of the heir and of the testator were entitled one against the other are not affected.

76 (74) PAUL, *Imperial Judgments, book 2:* The father of a son and a daughter had addressed these words to his daughter in his testament: "I command that you make no testament until children are born to you." The emperor decided that a *fideicommissum* was due under this clause on the ground that by prohibiting her to make a testament he had requested that she make her brother her heir; for the clause was to be so taken as if he had asked her to restore his inheritance. 1. Fabius Antoninus left a son, Antoninus, who was *impubes,* and a daughter, Honorata. He disinherited them, instituted their mother Junia Valeriana his heir, charged her with a bequest of three hundred and of certain articles to the daughter, and willed that the whole residue of the inheritance should be restored to his son Antoninus when he had attained his twentieth year; but should his son die before his twentieth year, he commanded that the inheritance be restored to Honorata. The mother died intestate, leaving both the children as her *legitimi heredes.* Then the son, at his full age of nineteen, having begun but not completed his twentieth year, died leaving his daughter, Fabia Valeriana, his heir. Her aunt demanded from her the *fideicommissum* and a share of the inheritance under the testament of her father, and had succeeded before the governor of the province. The tutors of Antoninus's daughter Valeriana pleaded her poverty and cited

a constitution of the deified Hadrian in which he commanded that where *munera* were in question, the current year of a man's age was to be reckoned as complete. Our emperor pronounced against the plaintiff both upon the equity of the case and upon the words of the will, "if he [attain] his twentieth year," though he remarked that he knew that the deified Marcus had declined to excuse one who had begun his seventieth year from tutelage. We offered arguments from the *lex Aelia Sentia* among others.

77   (75)   SCAEVOLA, *Digest, book 18:* A testator wrote a letter to his heir in these words: "Titius to his heir Cornelius, greeting. I request of you, Cornelius, since my mother's share has devolved upon you, as also the share of the unfortunate Sempronius lately my curator, and thus my whole estate is likely to come to you, that you render and restore one third to Gaius Seius." Sempronius had been granted *restitutio in integrum* by the emperor, who had deported him, and had accepted the inheritance. The question was whether he were also asked to restore the inheritance from his portion. He replied that it was not stated that Sempronius had been asked, but that the heir Cornelius should make restitution to Seius in proportion to the value of the maternal goods of the deceased. 1. A woman imposed a *fideicommissum* on her instituted heir that he should retain the fourth part and restore the residue to her former daughter-in-law upon whom she imposed a *fideicommissum* in these words: "I ask that you cause what shall come to you from my goods to come to your son." The question was when this *fideicommissum* should be restored, after her death or at once. He answered that the *fideicommissum* was to be referred to the time when the daughter-in-law should die.

78   (76)   SCAEVOLA, *Digest, book 19:* Scaevola replied: If a father have named his son, an *impubes*, as heir to his whole estate and have substituted to him by codicil and the son have then died, although the substitution be invalid, since an inheritance may be neither given nor adeemed by codicil, yet it is settled that by a benevolent interpretation the mother, who succeeded to the *pupillus* on intestacy, takes subject to a *fideicommissum* in favor of the substitutes. So if they be substituted to one another, the substitution also takes effect in relation to the *fideicommissum*, and if one of them be dead, the survivors take the whole.

79   (77)   SCAEVOLA, *Digest, book 20:* A testator instituted his children of both sexes his heirs, asked each of them that any of them who should die without children should restore his share of the inheritance to his brother or sister, or should there be no brother or sister, to his mother, and added these words: "And it is my wish, my dearest children, that you should be bound to one another by this *fideicommissum* until each of you has brought up two children." The question was: If one of the children have begotten two sons, though they did not survive him, is the *fideicommissum* due from his heirs? He answered that, upon the case as put, it would seem that they are released from the burden of the *fideicommissum*. 1. Titius instituted his grandchildren by a daughter and his lunatic daughter his heirs, and imposed a *fideicommissum* on his daughter that should she die without children, the share given to her should go to her co-heirs. Titius himself gave the lunatic in marriage, and she bore a daughter after the death of her father. The question was: If the lunatic be dead, leaving a daughter born of such a union as this, is the *fideicommissum* due to the co-heirs? He answered that since she was stated to have left a daughter, the *fideicommissum* was not due. CLAUDIUS: For though there could be no marriage with a lunatic, yet a condition such as this is satisfied.

80   (78)   SCAEVOLA, *Digest, book 21:* Lucius Titius had a wife and an emancipated daughter by her. Dying intestate, he inserted these words in his codicils: "The following codicils concern my wife and daughter. I ask, therefore, that whatever I shall leave

or you yourselves have may be common between you, which you would have done from family affection had I not asked it." The daughter received *bonorum possessio* of the estate of her intestate father. The question was whether any part of the inheritance of Lucius Titius were due by *fideicommissum* from the daughter to the mother. He replied that upon the case as put, a part was due, if the wife also were prepared to put her property in common.　1. Maevia left her two sons as her heirs, and in the same testament provided thus: "But I commit it to the faith of my heirs that my whole substance be left upon deposit without interest in the hands of Gaius Seius and Lucius Titius, whom I should also have appointed curators of my substance to the exclusion of all others, had it been lawful, so that they may restore it to my grandchildren, to be divided equally between those who shall attain the age of twenty-five years, or should one alone attain that age, the whole to him." The question was whether the heirs appointed in the testament were bound to perform the *fideicommissum* in favor of Gaius Seius and Lucius Titius. He replied that upon the case as put, neither Lucius Titius nor Gaius Seius could demand the *fideicommissum*.　2. A testatrix named three heirs: her brother Maevius for three fourths, Seius for one sixth, and Stichus, who was the slave of the said Seius but the natural son of Maevius, for one twelfth, and she imposed a *fideicommissum* on Seius that he should manumit Stichus in these words: "I request of you, Seius, that you manumit Stichus; I have given you the wherewithal." By codicils, however, she also provided as follows: "I wish the twelfth for which I have made Stichus my heir to revert to my brother Maevius, should Seius raise any dispute. Do you, brother, according to your good faith and family duty, restore whatever shall come to you from my inheritance to your son Stichus, and I commit it to your faith that you do so." The question was: Seius had accepted the inheritance and had in consequence been compelled to manumit Stichus; ought he to restore the twelfth of the inheritance for which Stichus was instituted heir to Stichus after manumission? He replied that it was not stated that Seius had been asked to restore the twelfth to him.　3. The same client asked: If Seius should wish to raise some dispute about the twelfth for which Stichus was instituted and Maevius should recover the twelfth from Seius under the *fideicommissum*, should he restore to the said Stichus only the twelfth for which Stichus was instituted or also the three fourths for which Maevius himself was instituted? He replied that the testatrix had meant that everything should be restored which had come to Maevius in what manner soever.　4. A father instituted a boy and a girl his heirs, substituted them to one another, and, should neither be heir, substituted several to them, and he substituted the substitutes to one another in these words: "I substitute my substituted heirs to one another." He imposed a *fideicommissum* on his said children that should either of them survive the other and die without children before the age of thirty, he should restore the inheritance to those who were substituted as heirs. The son outlived his sister and died without children before the age of thirty. The question was: One of the substitutes had died before the heir; did his portion, which belonged to the other substitutes who had survived, belong to them in equal shares or in the shares for which they had been substituted in the inheritance? He replied that it was logical that the *fideicommissum* should belong to them in those shares for which they were substituted.　5. Maevia instituted her son her heir for five twelfths, her daughter Titia for a quarter, and her son Septicius for one third, upon whom she imposed a *fideicommissum* in these words: "I ask you, Septicius my son, that should you die without children before the age of twenty, you restore whatever shall come to you from my inheritance to your brother and sister." The question was: Her son Septicius being dead without children before the age of twenty, did this *fideicommissum* belong to his brother and sister in proportion to their shares in the inheritance or equally? He replied: in proportion to their shares in the inheritance.　6. Titia, who was named heir to the whole of the testator's estate, had restored a moiety of the inheritance to Maevia as she was asked to do. She refused to redeem a property which the testator had charged, but when the creditor sold it, she gave Seia a mandate to purchase it. The question was whether Titia were liable to Maevia under the *fideicommissum*. He replied that since it was stated that she was asked to restore the inheritance, no reason had been stated why she should not be liable. CLAUDIUS: For he implies that as much is due as the property is worth, above the amount which should have gone to the creditor. 7. A testator instituted Gaius Seius for one half, Titia for a quarter, and others for the remaining portions, and provided as follows: "But I commit it to your faith, Gaius Seius and Lucia Titia, that after your deaths you render and restore to Titius and Sempronius the half of that patrimony and portion which I have given you." The question was: Both had accepted the inheritance; Gaius Seius had subsequently died and had instituted Lucia Titia his heir; was that moiety of the half which Gaius Seius had been asked to restore due from Lucia Titia forthwith, or should she restore the entire *fideicommissum*, as well that charged upon herself as that charged upon Gaius Seius, only after her own death? He answered that Lucia Titia was at once bound to restore the moiety of the half on behalf of Seius. 8. A testator named his daughter his heir, substituted to her the grandson whom he had by her, and provided thus: "To Lucius Titius, my brother's son and my son-in-law, I leave two hundred aurei, with which legacy I know him to be content; for he also is to share in all that I have, since I have appointed as heirs to my whole estate my daughter and grandson, and I commend them to one another." The daughter accepted the father's inheritance and then divorced her husband. The question was whether Titius, her former husband, could claim either in his own name or in the name of his son that the goods should be put in common, either in the life of his former wife or after her death. He replied that it was not stated that the son-in-law had been given any other *fideicommissum* than that for two hundred aurei. 9. The same client stated that the same wife had named her husband her heir, subject to a *fideicommissum* that when, he should die, he should restore all that had come to him from her inheritance to their common son. He asked whether those things and possessions which had been given in dowry and restored to the woman after the divorce were also included in the *fideicommissum*. He replied that what the woman had left in her estate was what was included in the *fideicommissum*. CLAUDIUS: On another occasion, when he was consulted in the same case, he replied thus: If the things had been restored, they were to be reckoned part of the estate of the woman according to his answer above; if they had not been restored, then, since they were to be restored under the stipulation which had been taken for the return of the dowry, the inheritance was to be reckoned larger by that much. 10. A woman who had a son and a grandson by him, both of whom were under the power of her husband, named her husband heir to her whole estate and charged him with a *fideicommissum* in these words: "Should Titius my husband be heir to me, I request and commit to his faith that whatever shall come to him from my inheritance he render and restore when he shall come to die to Gaius, our son, upon condition, however, that Gaius is to have five sixths, but our grandson Seius is to have one sixth, and I commit it to the faith of Titius my heir that this be done." The father emancipated his son, lost his grandson, and died, leaving his son surviving. The question was whether by the first clause the whole of the mother's inheritance were due by *fideicommissum* to the son and the following words "upon condition, however, that the son is to have five sixths but the grandson is to have one sixth" were intended by the deceased to take effect only if their son and grandson were in being when the *fideicommissum* vested; hence, since the grandson had not survived to the date of vesting, the latter clause was ineffective. He replied that the facts stated showed that five sixths only were given to the son. 11. An instituted heir who was asked to restore the whole inheritance to his wife deducted the fourth and restored it. The question was: Since the testator had asked the wife to restore the fourth part of the inheritance to another immediately and the residue after an interval, was she entitled, in restoring the *fideicommissum*, to take the amount of which the heir had deprived her for his fourth into the account? He replied that she was bound by the *fideicommissum* to the extent of what she had received.   12. A testator imposed a *fideicommissum* on his heirs, that they should restore whatever should come to them from a third part of his inheritance to Gaius Seius, the testator's foster son, when he should attain the age of fifteen, and he added these words: "In the meantime, from that support for his poverty which shall come to you, maintain him from the interest received according to the amount of the money. In addition, [I leave] to my same foster son the slave Caletanus, the shoemaker of my own breeding, who will be able to maintain him with the wages received in his trade." The question was: Since the heirs appointed in the testament had provided much less in maintenance than the interest of the sum realized amounted to, should they be compelled to pay the residue for the whole period or from the day on which he completed his fifteenth year? Also since the slaves which had been specially left to him in order that he might be maintained from their wages had been immediately sold, ought he to claim their wages or interest? He replied that upon the case as stated the testator was to be taken to have intended that the whole profits and the wages of the slaves were to be restored. 13. A testator instituted several heirs, among them three freedmen, for three fourths of the estate. He left them a legacy *per praeceptionem* of certain farms, and requested of them that they should not alienate them and that the last survivor should receive those farms in their entirety; then he imposed a *fideicommissum* on Otalicius, one of the freedmen, that he should restore whatever had come to him from the inheritance or the estate to Titius, deducting the debts and legacies for that portion, and twenty aurei for himself. The question was whether he should deduct the third parts of the farms which had been left to him and his fellow freedmen as a *praelegatum*. He replied that upon the case as put, he was not bound to restore the *praelegatum*; for the testator himself had wished that legacies should also be excepted.   14. A husband instituted his wife heir for the third part, gave her a number of *fideicommissa*, and left her a *praelegatum* of her dowry in these words: "I wish that my wife Seia be given by my sons the amount of the dowry which I received on her account," and he imposed a *fideicommissum* on his wife that after her death she should restore her share of the inheritance and whatever legacies he had left her to Titius, their common son. The question was whether she ought also to restore the amount of her dowry to her son under the *fideicommissum* together with the other legacies. He replied that she should not, unless it were clear that the testator was thinking also of restitution of the dowry, and though this were his intention and it were proved, the dowry would be demandable in addition only if the amount which remained in her hands under the *lex Falcidia* were no less than the amount of the dowry. 15. An heir was asked to restore the inheritance to Septicius at his age of twenty. In the interval, he sold certain farms which had been pledged to the deceased; the debtor, therefore, brought an action upon the pledge against him; he died, leaving Sempronius his heir, and he restored the inheritance to Septicius while the action was still pending. The question was whether he nonetheless should be condemned in the suit; for he might have retained or taken a *cautio* for what he would have to pay under the judgment. He replied that the judgment nonetheless might still be executed against the heir, even after the inheritance had been restored.   16. The heir of one who had been asked to restore the entire inheritance after his death restored a very small amount to those to whom the *fideicommissum* was due, and alleged that there was no more in the estate. Documents were subsequently discovered from which it appeared that the inheritance amounted to four times as much. The question was whether he might be sued for the residue under the *fideicommissum*. He replied that upon the case as put, if there had been no *transactio* on the claim, he might.

81   (79) SCAEVOLA, *Questions Publicly Discussed, sole book:* If a *pupillus* have become heir to his parent, have restored a part of the inheritance which was subject to a *fideicommissum*, and be then abstained from his father's inheritance, the fideicommissary is to be required to elect whether he will accept the portion of the *pupillus* as well or renounce the whole; or the estate is to be sold in all events, that the surplus may be kept for the *pupillus*, and if the estate cannot be sold in its entirety, the

fideicommissary is to be granted no actions on any terms; for it was in his power to take the whole and, should there be any surplus, to save it for the *pupillus*.

82   (80)   SCAEVOLA, *Digest, book 5:* Lucius Titius named as his heirs his mother and his maternal uncle, who were also his creditors, and imposed a *fideicommissum* on them that after their deaths they should restore what remained of the testator's estate to Septicius. The heirs consumed a considerable part of the testator's goods and left numerous heirs with whose knowledge Septicius took possession of numerous articles which remained from the estate of Lucius Titius. The question was whether what Lucius Titius owed to his mother and his uncle might be claimed by their heirs from Septicius. He replied that it might not. CLAUDIUS: For by the acceptance of the inheritance the obligation was merged and destroyed, but the *fideicommissum* might be recovered back, and the equity upon which this latter remedy is grounded failed in the case of those who are stated to have consumed a great deal from the inheritance.

83   (81)   PAUL, *Imperial Decisions Pronounced in Judicial Examinations, book 1 of 6 books, or Judgments, book 2:* Julius Foebus, when he made his testament, had instituted as his heirs his three children, Foebus and Heraclia, who were born of the same mother, and Polycrates, who was born of a different mother. He gave them equal shares and requested of Polycrates, the younger brother, that he should take a certain estate for himself and grant the inheritance to his brother and sister, and he substituted the two born of the same mother to one another, should either of them not be heir. He made a second testament for Polycrates, should he die under the age of puberty, and entrusted it to his mother, to be opened should he die under that age. Finally, he requested of his elder children that should either of them die without children, he should restore his portion, except for those goods which had come to him from his mother and from his grandparents, to him or them who should survive. Heraclia, the sister, died without children and instituted her brother Foebus, her heir. Polycrates had claimed the *fideicommissum* and succeeded before Aurelius Proculus, proconsul of Achaia. There was an appeal, and though Foebus alone appeared to prosecute it, he failed; for the words "to him or them" included both the brothers. Though it was true that he had substituted only the first two to one another; yet this also appeared to be the intention of the father; for he had excepted the goods which they had from their mother because Polycrates had a different mother, who was indeed still living, and on whom he had imposed a *fideicommissum* that on her death she should restore to her son Polycrates the legacies which he had given her in his testament.

84   * * * : If a testator appoint as his heir one whom he alleges to be his debtor, and who denies the debt, and ask him to restore the inheritance to another, he is not accountable for the debt in the suit for the *fideicommissum* if he is prepared to defend the action for the debt.

85   * * * : If an inheritance be restored to a son-in-power, we must consider how far those actions which follow the inheritance are rightly granted to him and against him after emancipation.

2

WHEN A LEGACY OR A *FIDEICOMMISSUM* VESTS

1 PAUL, *Sabinus, book 2:* On the death of his father, though a *pupillus* be living, legacies charged on the substitute vest.

2 ULPIAN, *Sabinus, book 15:* If a usufruct or a right of use or of habitation be left unconditionally, they do not vest before the inheritance is accepted, nor does the right to demand them pass to the heir. The law is the same if a usufruct be left from a future date.

3 ULPIAN, *Disputations, book 5:* For since it does not pass to the heir, it would be in vain to say that it vested before.

4 ULPIAN, *Sabinus, book 19:* If a legacy be given "when the heir shall die," this is a conditional legacy; hence, if the legatee die in the lifetime of the heir he does not transmit it to his heir. If, on the other hand, the legatee be given a legacy when he himself shall die, there is no question but that the legacy will pass to his heir.

5 ULPIAN, *Sabinus, book 20:* If the legatee should die after the legacy vests, he passes the legacy to his heir. 1. Hence, if a legacy be unconditional, it vests on the date of death, but if legacies be left payable at a future date, they vest in the same manner as unconditional legacies, unless the legacy happen to be of something which does not pass to the heir; for such a legacy cannot vest before the date, as if a usufruct be left to commence after a year; for this is the opinion which we approve. 2. But if a legacy be left upon condition, it does not vest before the condition is performed, not even if it be such a condition as is in the power of the legatee. 3. But if it be such a condition as the praetor remits, the legacy vests at once. 4. The law is the same in case of an impossible condition; for the legacy is treated as unconditional. 5. Also if the condition be such, that it is not by the act of the legatee that it is unperformed, but by the act of the heir, or of that person to whom he has been commanded to perform the condition, the legacy vests; for the condition is treated as performed; if, for example, I have been commanded to give ten to the heir and he will not receive it. But if a legacy be left to me on condition that I marry Seia and she will not marry me, the legacy is to be held to vest; for it is not by my act that I have not performed the condition, but it is by the act of another that the condition is unperformed. 6. A legacy is payable to the heir at the same times, that is, by the same payments, as it was payable to the legatee himself. 7. If when the legacy first vests the legatee be dependent, the legacy is due to those upon whom he was dependent, and thus if the legacy were unconditional and he became free after the legacy vested, he will leave the legacy with his master, but if the legacy were of a usufruct and he become independent before the inheritance is accepted, though after the death of the testator, he acquires the legacy for himself.

6 PAUL, *Sabinus, book 3:* An unconditional gift which is ademed upon condition is treated as a conditional legacy. 1. But if the effect of the legacy be suspended by some external circumstance, not by the terms of the testament itself, though the legatee first die, we hold that he has transmitted the legacy to his heir; if, for example, a husband have left something from the dowry to a stranger and a sum of money to his wife for the thing from her dowry, and then, while the wife was considering whether to choose her dowry, the legatee has died, and the wife has chosen the legacy, it has been held that the legacy passes to the heir, and so Julian advised; for the legacy is to be taken to be deferred rather than to be left upon condition. 2. Those legacies which are left in codicils vest in the same manner as those which are left by testament.

7   ULPIAN, *Sabinus, book 20:* Though a legacy cannot be demanded until the heir has accepted, its vesting is not postponed.   1. Hence, whether an heir unconditionally instituted be late in accepting or an heir conditionally instituted be prevented from accepting by the condition, the legatee is secure.   2. But though the instituted heir be not yet born, or be in the hands of the enemy, this likewise will not harm the legatee; for the legacy has vested.   3. Thus, we also hold that if a legacy be charged upon a substitute, any time which the instituted heir takes for consideration will not harm a legatee who has died, if the instituted heir subsequently repudiated; for he has transmitted his claim to his heir.   4. The law is the same if a legacy be charged on the substitute of an *impubes*; for he passes the legacy to his heir.   5. However, if one who has been substituted to an *impubes* be charged with a legacy *per damnationem* to give a hundred to Seius, if the testator's son die under puberty and Seius die in the life of the *pupillus*, it is arguable that the legacy will not pass to his heir on the ground that the implied condition has been expressly stated—and it is the better view that it passes to the heir of the legatee.   6. A legacy is sometimes in suspense until acceptance of the inheritance, as if it be left to a slave who is manumitted, or if a slave be left by legacy, and a legacy given to the slave; for the legacy left to the slave does not vest before acceptance of the inheritance.

8   ULPIAN, *Sabinus, book 24:* For since he is not entitled to his liberty until the inheritance is accepted, it has been held to be most equitable that the legacy should not vest before; otherwise the legacy would be void, if it were to vest before he could claim his liberty, as happens if a slave be given an unconditional legacy and is commanded to be free upon condition, and the condition is still pending when the inheritance is subsequently accepted.

9   ULPIAN, *Sabinus, book 21:* If a right of habitation be left to a son-in-power or to a slave, I think that the legacy is not acquired for the master or the father if the son or slave should die before the inheritance is accepted; for since it is inseparable from the person, it is rightly held not to vest before the inheritance is accepted.

10   ULPIAN, *Sabinus, book 23:* It is settled that if a legacy be payable "in every year," this is not one legacy, but several.

11   JULIAN, *Digest, book 37:* Nor is it material whether every aureus be payable every year or a thousand aurei in the first year, a slave in the second, and corn in the third.

12   ULPIAN, *Sabinus, book 23:* And it does not vest once and for all, but year by year.   1. But whether it vest at the beginning or at the end of each year was a question, and Labeo, Sabinus, Celsus, Cassius, and Julian supported the opinion that if anything be left payable in every year, this legacy vests at the beginning of each year.   2. Hence, Julian says that if this legacy be left to a slave and he then become free after the first or second year, he acquires for himself.   3. Celsus also writes and Julian agrees with him that this legacy vests when the testator dies, not when his heir accepts the inheritance, and should it happen that the inheritance is accepted after many years, the legacies for all these years are due to the legatee.   4. But if a legacy be left "annually," it seems to me that in this case also it is the beginning of each year that is to be considered, unless perhaps it should be clear that the intention of the testator in thus dividing it into annual payments was not to provide for the legatee, but to spare the heir, so that he should not be pressed for payment.   5. If anything be left "by the year" or "annually" to provide the legatee with a home, or for his education, the legacy is taken to be payable upon the same days upon which the rent of his home or the fees for his instruction are due, since this is conjectured to be the testator's intention.   6. Finally, Pomponius writes that it is not material whether a legacy be given "every year," or "annually," or "every month," or "monthly," or "every day," or "daily." I am also a supporter of this opinion, just as we should hold the same if so

many aurei be left "by the year."   7. If a general legacy of "a slave" be left to one who has died before bringing a *vindicatio*, he passes the legacy to his heir.   8. If Titius be left the slave "whom Seius shall choose" and Seius have died after choosing, the *vindicatio*, once acquired, still lies.

13   POMPONIUS, *Sabinus, book 6:* A legacy in these terms "whether such a thing be done or be not done, I give and bequeath" does not pass to the heir unless one or other event have happened in the life of the legatee; for nothing can be due before there is some ground upon which it is due, nor will the legacy be due in all events merely because one or other must happen; for a legacy such as "let my heir give when he shall die" is certain to be due; yet it does not pass to the heir of the legatee if he die in the life of the heir.

14   ULPIAN, *Sabinus, book 24:* If the testator leave a usufruct or ten, as the legatee shall choose, the date of the testator's death and the date of the acceptance of his inheritance are both material: of his death, because of the ten, and of the acceptance, because of the usufruct; for although the choice be the legatee's, he cannot yet make his choice if we take it either that the testator is not yet dead or that though he be dead, his inheritance has not yet been accepted.   1. Hence, Julian asks whether if the legatee die after the testator, he passes the ten which has been left him to his heir, and in the thirty-seventh book of his *Digest*, he writes that we may hold that the ten have passed; for the legacy vests on the death of the legatee. He uses this case as an argument for his opinion: "Let my heir give Seia ten, or if she bear a child, a farm"; for, says he, if she should die before bearing a child, she will transmit the ten to her heir.   2. If a legacy be left to a son-in-power upon condition that it be paid to him personally, the legacy is allowable, and the heir is not responsible because he has paid to the son rather than to the father; for suppose it to be expressly stated, "so that he pay to the son," clearly if the father sue, he should be barred by a special defense.   3. If the legacy has vested and the legatee has then become subject to the power of another, the legacy is rather due to him under whose power he has come, for the debts due to him pass with him; but if the legacy were left upon condition it does not pass, but will wait upon the condition and be acquired to him in whose power he is at the time when the condition happens, but if at that time he be independent, he will acquire instead for himself.

15   ULPIAN, *Disputations, book 5:* If a *fideicommissum* were left to the children, if they should become independent by the death of their father, and they have become heads of households not by the demise of their father but by emancipation, no one would doubt that the gift which would have vested on the death of the father has also vested on emancipation.

16   JULIAN, *Digest, book 35:* If a legacy be left thus, "let my heir give Stichus or the child that shall be born of Pamphila," this legacy does not vest until a child has been born of Pamphila, or it has become certain that none can be born.   1. A slave was left by legacy. Before the inheritance of the legator was accepted, he was left a legacy of a usufruct by another. The inheritance of the testator who left him the usufruct was first accepted. There is no reason why we should hold that the legacy vests before that inheritance from which the slave has been left by legacy is also accepted; for no benefit can be acquired for the inheritance at the moment, and if the slave should have died in the meantime, the legacy is extinguished. Therefore, we should hold that when the inheritance is accepted, the usufruct goes to him to whom the slave who has been left by legacy belongs.   2. But if the slave to whom the legacy of the usufruct was left were not himself left by legacy, we should hold the usufruct to belong to the inheritance, since it did not vest before the inheritance was accepted.

17   JULIAN, *Digest, book 36:* If a slave be left by legacy, and a legacy be left to him, the legacy given to the slave vests not at the time of the death, but when the inheritance is accepted, and thus the rule [*regula catoniana*] is no reason why the legacy should not

be due to him after manumission; for though the head of the household had died forthwith, the same person would not have been at once entitled to the benefit and subject to the burden of the legacy. The case in question, therefore, is the same as if a son were instituted heir and a legacy left to the father, which is taken to be valid because, though the testator should die forthwith, the son may accept the inheritance after emancipation, and thus owe the legacy to his father.

18   JULIAN, *Digest, book 37:* If one to whom a legacy has been left "when he shall have issue" should die leaving his wife pregnant, it is deemed that he has died after the condition was performed and that the legacy is valid, provided that a posthumous child have been born.

19   JULIAN, *Digest, book 70:* If a legacy were given thus without any limitation of time, "let my heir give my wife my household stock; if he do not give it, let him give one hundred," this is taken as a single legacy of a hundred and is demandable at once. The effect of the condition to give the household stock is merely that the heir is discharged if he has handed over the household stock before joinder of issue.   1. But if the testator have written thus, "if he have not given my household stock before the Kalends, let him give one hundred," the result is not to make two legacies, but the hundred is taken to have been left upon condition, and thus if the wife have died before the Kalends, she will leave to her heir neither the household stock, for it was not left to her, nor the hundred, for the legacy has to vest in the lifetime of the legatee.   2. My interest vests at once, if a *fideicommissum* in my favor be charged upon one to whom a legacy was left on condition, as it does if an heir be instituted upon condition and a legacy left to me unconditionally.   3. If a debtor be left what is due from him on condition, this is an immediate legacy, he may at once sue upon the testament to obtain his release, and if he have died after the death of the testator, he passes the action to his heir.   4. We should hold the same though the legacy be not left to the debtor himself, but to anyone else.

20   MARCIAN, *Institutes, book 6:* If a legacy be left for a limited number of years, as "ten to Titius for each of the next ten years," Julian writes in the thirtieth book of his *Digest* that we must distinguish. If the legacy were left for the maintenance of the legatee, there are several legacies, and should the legatee die, he does not pass the legacy for the years yet to come to his heir, but if the testator did not leave it for maintenance, but divided it into a number of installments to relieve the heir, in this case, says he, there is a single legacy of all the annual sums, and if the legatee die within ten years, he transmits to his heir the legacy for the years yet to come as well, and this is the true opinion.

21   PAUL, *Vitellius, book 2:* If a legacy be not made payable at a future date, it is due at once or at once belongs to him to whom it was given. If a date be named, though a distant one, if it be certain, as upon the Kalends of January a hundred years hence, the legacy vests at once, though it cannot be demanded before the date; but if it be uncertain, as "when he shall attain puberty" or "when he shall marry one of my family" or "when he shall become a magistrate" or indeed "when he shall do anything which the writer of the testament sees fit to express," the thing cannot belong to him nor can the legacy vest unless the date come or the condition happen.   1. If a legacy be left to Titius upon the same condition upon which I have instituted you my heir, Pomponius thinks that this legacy vests in the same manner as if it were left unconditionally; for it was certain to be due if the heir took the inheritance; for legacies do not become uncertain if the heirs be conditionally instituted, and that legacy does not much differ from this: "If he be heir, let him give."

22   POMPONIUS, *Quintus Mucius, book 5:* If a legacy have been left to Titius "when he should have reached the age of fourteen," and he has died before his fourteenth year, the true view is that the legacy does not pass to his heir, because this legacy is not merely payable at a future date but contains in it the condition: "if he has reached the age of fourteen"; for one not in being could not be deemed to be fourteen years of age. And it is not material whether the testator write: "if he shall attain the age of fourteen" or "when"; for in the first case the condition states the date of payment, and in the second the date of payment states the condition, but it is the same condition in either case.   1. There are also certain conditions, however, which are surplusage, as if a testator write thus: "Let Titius be my heir; if Titius accept my inheritance, let him give ten to Maevius"; for this condition will be treated as if it were not stated, so that the legacy will pass to the heir of Maevius in any event, though Maevius have died before the inheritance was accepted. So also, should the testator write thus: "If Titius accept my inheritance, let him give ten to Maevius within a hundred days"; for this legacy is payable at a future date, not upon a condition, since the true definition is that of Labeo, who holds that a legacy which is certain to be due if the inheritance be accepted is a legacy which passes to the heir of the legatee.   2. If, on the other hand, I institute two heirs and leave a third party a legacy charged upon all my heirs if one of them accept the inheritance, this condition will not be treated as surplusage, but it will be valid for the portion of his co-heir, though it will be surplusage for the portion of the heir named in the condition, just as if he alone had been instituted heir and a legacy were left in this manner.

23   ULPIAN, *Lex Julia et Papia, book 4:* If a legacy be left payable in every year, it is unquestionable that we should hold that whether the legatee will be entitled to take or not will depend upon his position in each year, and if he be the slave of several masters, it is the individual masters who must be considered.

24   PAUL, *Lex Julia et Papia, book 6:* If the heir have been charged with a legacy *per damnationem* to give the testator's household stock or a farm, and to give ten if he do not, I have been taught that this is a legacy of the household stock, which is converted into a legacy of ten if the heir will not give the stock, that the money is due when he has refused to convey the farm upon demand, and that should the legatee have died in the meantime the farm alone will be due to his heir; for by the words "but let Publicius give a farm," the legacy is complete, and when the testator then says, "if he do not give it, let him give a hundred," this is taken as a conditional ademption of the legacy upon the same event upon which the hundred is to become due. Since this condition did not happen in the lifetime of the legatee, perhaps because no demand was made upon the heir, it follows that the ademption did not take effect, and the legacy of the farm has remained in force.   1. If, however, the legacy be "if he do not give my household stock, let him give ten," we hold this no legacy of the household stock.

25   PAPINIAN, *Questions, book 18:* If a legacy be of this thing or of that, the inclusion of an enumeration of several things in the disjunctive does not make several legacies, and no other view is possible of a legacy of one farm unconditionally or of another upon condition; for there will be no right of election pending the condition, and should the legatee die, the legacy will not be held to have passed to his heir.   1. "Let my heir give to Titius what Seius owes me." If Seius be a *pupillus* who received money without the *auctoritas* of his tutor and has not been enriched and if the creditor were speaking of a present debt, then, since Seius owes nothing, the legacy will be ineffective. If by the word "debt" he were thinking of the natural obligation and the future payment, Titius can demand nothing in the meantime, as if the legacy were subject to a tacit condition, just as if the testator had said, "let him give to Titius what the *pupillus* shall pay," or if he had left a legacy of "the child that shall be born of Arethusa" or "the crop which shall grow upon such a farm." There is no inconsistency

in holding that if the legatee die in the meantime, and then the child be born, the crop be grown, or the *pupillus* pay the money, the heir of the legatee may demand the legacy; for a legacy which is not expressed to be subject to any condition vests although it must wait upon an external event.

26 PAPINIAN, *Replies, book 9:* "I wish that my brother Firmius Heliodorus be given fifty from the profits of my estates in the year next following." I replied that it appeared that the testator had not added a condition to the legacy, but had deferred the time for payment of the money. If fruits to the amount of the money left were not gathered, the abundance of the second year would be necessary. 1. A testator had wished that his heirs should give one hundred to his foster son and that the money should be transferred to a third party upon the terms that the foster son was to receive interest on that sum at the rate of four percent until his twenty-fifth year, and the capital itself after that age. I replied that upon his death within his twenty-fifth year the *fideicommissum* had passed to the boy's heir; for it appeared that the testator had fixed a particular age for the payment of the capital—he had not inserted a condition into an unconditional *fideicommissum*. Since, however, the *fideicommissum* could not be demanded of the party in whose hands the testator wished the money to be placed, it should be demanded of the heirs by force of the words "and you will take care to restore it to my foster son after his above-written age." For the heirs should have taken a stipulation for repayment of the money, but verbal guarantors were not to be demanded of one to whose good faith the testator had preferred to trust. 2. A father wished that his wife should pay so much a year from the fruits of the property which he had left to her as an addition to the patrimony of his son until he attained his twenty-fifth year, over and above the son's maintenance, which he also entrusted to his mother. It was clear that this was not several *fideicommissa*, but a single *fideicommissum* payable by installments. Thus, on the death of the son within the above-written age, the *fideicommissum* for the remaining time passed to his heir, but the money was not demandable at the beginning of each year; for the father wished the son to be provided for from the fruits which he had given to the wife. If, on the other hand, the father had appointed an annual sum for his son's maintenance, there would be no doubt that the ground of the obligation would be extinguished when the person failed.

27 SCAEVOLA, *Replies, book 3:* A testator unconditionally instituted a son-in-power his heir to part of his estate, gave him a *fideicommissum*, and by the same testament provided thus: "Whereas I have instituted Lucius Titius heir, I wish him to accept the inheritance only if he shall be freed from parental power." The question was whether a legacy given to the son-in-power had vested when his co-heirs accepted the inheritance. He replied that if it were given unconditionally, a share of the *fideicommissum* proportionate to his share in the inheritance might be demanded of the co-heir of the son. 1. The testator left ten denarii monthly to each of his slaves who was to be manumitted. The question was: Since they had obtained their liberty under the *senatus consultum* in the absence of the heirs, from what time was their maintenance due to them? He replied that, upon the case as put, their maintenance was due to them from the time that they first became free.

28 SCAEVOLA, *Replies, book 4:* If a farm be left with fixtures, fittings, and live and dead stock, the question is whether it should be conveyed stocked and equipped as it was at the date of the death or at the date when the codicils were executed or at the date of proceedings. He replied that the stock and equipment with which the farm was provided when the legacy vested were due.

29 VALENS, *Fideicommissa, book 1:* "I ask that my heir give ten to Titius at some time." Clearly, the heir will owe ten, but there is room for doubt when, whether it vests and is demandable from him when he is first able to pay. . . .

30 LABEO, *Posthumous Works Epitomized by Javolenus, book 3:* If a legacy have been left to a *pupilla* "when she marries" and she has married before reaching marriageable age, the legacy will not be due to her until she become marriageable; for one who is too young for a husband cannot be deemed married.

31 SCAEVOLA, *Digest, book 14:* A testator instituted his wife heir to one half of his estate, gave her a substitute, and imposed a *fideicommissum* upon his heir, that if his
wife should not be heir, he should give her her dowry and certain other things. After
the death of the husband, the wife died before the condition happened and before she
had accepted the inheritance. The question was whether the *fideicommissum* was to
be deemed to have vested when she died and was therefore due to her heirs. I replied
that if the wife died before she accepted the inheritance, the *fideicommissum* is to be
held to have vested.

3

THAT A *CAUTIO* BE GIVEN FOR THE SECURITY
OF LEGACIES OR *FIDEICOMMISSA*

1 ULPIAN, *Edict, book 79:* The praetor has thought it good that security be given for
legacies and that those to or for whom the testator wished that anything should be
given or done should stipulate that it be given or done upon the dates appointed and
that no fraud should be committed.   1. The heir is always compelled to give security
whatever his rank and whatever his wealth.   2. It was not unreasonable of the praetor to take the view that as the heir has the possession of the goods, so the legatees
ought not to be deprived of the goods of the deceased, but either security will be given
them, or if security be not given, it is the will of the praetor that they go into possession.   3. Not only should security be given to all the legatees, but it is now settled
that security should be given to the successors of the legatees, though they be admitted to claim like creditors by right of succession and not by the intention of the
deceased.   4. But security should also be given to the procurators of the legatees, and
this is the practice.   5. Obviously, if a legacy be left to one who is under the power of
another, the *cautio* will be given to him to whom he is subject.   6. It is not only heirs
who give a *cautio* for legacies but also their successors.   7. So also he to whom the
inheritance has been restored under the *senatus consultum* is no less bound to give a
cautio.   8. And those who have become heirs through others or are praetorian successors are compelled to give security.   9. However, if the legatee have joined issue
in a suit for the legacy without taking the stipulation, it is the better view that the
stipulation should not be required.   10. We should also hold the same view where
fideicommissa are concerned.   11. If a legacy or *fideicommissum* be left upon condition that should the beneficiary lose it, it is again left him, we must consider whether
he may demand a *cautio* for the subsequent legacy or *fideicommissum*. The questions
are whether this legacy or *fideicommissum* be due and how often it is due and
whether the legatee himself should give a *cautio* that he will not lose it. Upon all these
matters, there is a rescript of the deified Pius to Junius Mauricus in these terms:
"Upon the facts stated in the letter, the legacies or *fideicommissa* should be paid under the testament of Clodius Felix to Clodius Fructulus without any obligation to give
a *cautio* that he will not dissipate any part of them; for the effect of the *fideicommissum* imposed upon the heir by the same testator, that so often as Fructulus shall
have lost what is left to him in the testament the heir shall restore it to him again, is
neither that Fructulus should be required to give security for the legacies first left
him, nor that the heir is to be charged without limit, and obliged to restore him the
same amount upon every loss, but his legacies are to be taken to be left him once again
by *fideicommissum*, so that should he consume anything after this latter *fideicommissum* has been paid to him, the heir is at no further risk." Hence, this rescript
shows that the legatee should not give a *cautio* to the heir that he will not lose his
legacy. Conversely, whether the heir should give a *cautio* for the second legacy or
fideicommissum is questionable, and I should think that no *cautio* ought to be given
him; for it is in his own power not to lose what has been left to him, although if we
were to consider it merely as a disposition on condition, we should hold that security
ought to be required.   12. The *cautio* is clearly due from one who owes either the

whole or a part of the legacy, whether he be instituted or substituted heir.   13. It is an excellent question whether the amount due under this stipulation be increased by the value of the fruits or the interest of the money, and it has been rightly held that the amount due under the stipulation is increased by delay on the part of the heir, so that it includes all that will be due from him.   14. If a legatee who has stipulated for a legacy upon condition have died while the condition is pending, the stipulation fails; for the legacy does not pass either. It is to be known that the same grounds of claim, subject to the same conditions, are implied in this stipulation as in an action for the legacies. Hence, it is held that if there be any defense which may be opposed to the plaintiff if he demands the legacy, it may also be opposed to him if he sues upon the stipulation.   15. If the heir give a stipulation for a legacy to the procurator of a legatee who is alleged to be absent, Ofilius says that the promise should be on the condition that he in whose name the *cautio* is taken still live, so that the heir may not be liable if he be already dead.   16. It is also a question whether this stipulation be for the things themselves which have been left by legacy, or for their value, and it is the better view that this stipulation comprehends either the things or their value.   17. If I have been left a legacy of the ten which were in the testator's strongbox, and the usufruct of them have been left to you, if both our legacies were unconditional, the legatee of the property may bring a *vindicatio* for the ten at civil law, while it is clear that the fructuary must sue under the *senatus consultum* and demand the usufruct of five, but when the owner brings the *vindicatio* for the ten, he may be barred by the defense of fraud, if the heir be willing to pay him five and to assign him the stipulation, by which the fructuary guarantees that the five shall be restored to the heir. If, however, a legatee have possession of the ten aurei, Marcellus says that either the heir or the fructuary should be given an *actio utilis* against the legatee, provided that a *cautio* be given him. But if the ten be left to him upon condition, the ten will be given in the meantime to the fructuary upon tender of a *cautio*, and in the meantime, the legatee to whom the property has been left is to receive the stipulation for payment of legacies. But if he do not take the stipulation, Marcellus says that when the condition happens, he may have an action for production. But if the heir unwittingly gave the ten to the fructuary, it is obvious that no action for production will lie against him. Marcellus, however, says that the legatee is to be relieved against the fructuary.   18. If a portion of the inheritance have come to the imperial treasury, this stipulation will not be given; for it is not the practice for the imperial treasury to give security.   19. If one who is heir for a greater part be in possession of a smaller part of the inheritance, it will be safer for the heir if his portion of the inheritance have been reduced by operation of law; for he is not liable under the stipulation to the legatees for a greater share than that for which he is heir. If, on the other hand, they remain wholly heirs in name, though they have less of the inheritance in effect, and they have given a *cautio* for legacies, it would seem that they will be charged; for by operation of law the legacies are due from them in the same shares for which they are heirs. It is nonetheless most equitable that they should pay to the legatees a share no greater than that of which they have the benefit. This is what happens when a part of the inheritance is restored under the *Trebellianum*; for the heirs are to be proportionately discharged for that share, the benefit of which has been taken from them.   20. If a legacy be left payable at an uncertain date to one who is under the power of another, the *cautio* is to be given to him who has him in his power, not in unqualified terms, but upon condition, "if, when that legacy vests, he shall be in his power," but if he should then be independent, it was felt that it would be unjust if the payment were secured to the father, when the legacy is due to another, although even if the *cautio* were to be given without this addition, we should bar the father or master by a special defense, should they not have them in their power when the condition happens. The consequence of this, however, is that there is a case in which the legacy is unsecured; for if they be independent when the condition happens, it is unsecured.

2   PAPINIAN, *Questions, book 28:* Even if perhaps the father be willing to give a *cautio* that there will be no further claim, the heir is not to be compelled to pay a legacy, which the son may now demand, to anyone other than to him to whom it is due.

3 ULPIAN, *Edict, book 79:* But a *cautio* should also be given to those who are under another's power in the same manner as a *cautio* is commonly given if the same thing have been left to two upon different or contrary conditions; for security is given to both, but the same verbal guarantors are liable in either case.

4 ULPIAN, *Edict, book 15:* If the inheritance be in the hands of the party under a *fideicommissum* and he do not give security for legacies, the legatee will be sent into possession against him.

5 PAPINIAN, *Questions, book 28:* The heir had been captured by the enemy, and subsequently the condition of a legacy which had been secured by the edictal stipulation happened. I held that the verbal guarantors were not liable in the meantime; for there was neither any right nor any person to which the words of the stipulation might be taken to refer. 1. In a rescript to Julius Balbus, the Emperor Marcus Antoninus stated that a defendant from whom goods were being demanded under a *fideicommissum* and who had appealed, should either give a *cautio*, or, if his opponent gave a *cautio*, possession should be transferred to his opponent. It rightly pleased the emperor that a *cautio* should be given for the *fideicommissum* even after appeal; for the benefit of what should have been done before sentence, if the date upon which the *fideicommissum* was to be demanded had been delayed, should not be lost after victory in the cause when the demand has been deferred.[1] But why did he state that if the appellant did not give a *cautio* for the *fideicommissum*, and his opponent gave a *cautio*, possession was to be transferred to him, when the Edict provides otherwise? For the legatee is not required to give a *cautio* in his turn, and in place of security he is given possession to enable him to take custody of the goods, and the successful party is put into possession by the praetor or the governor. Moreover, the praetor, for his part, allows possession to be taken of everything which still belongs in any manner to the inheritance in order to preserve the *fideicommissum*, whereas the emperor allowed mutual *cautiones* for those things for which judgment had been given, just as, if a son who has received *bonorum possessio* cannot give a *cautio* that he will collate his property, since he is then allowed no actions, his brothers according to the regular course are offered the opportunity of giving a *cautio* that they will restore what they have received from their brother's portion as soon as he collates his own property, but if they also cannot give a *cautio*, it is accepted for reasons of policy that both parties should choose an upright man with whom as stakeholder the fruits are to be deposited, and who may bring *actiones utiles* which the praetor gives him. Under the rescript recited above, however, possession is not to be transferred to the party who demands the *fideicommissum* unless he gives a *cautio*, and it is quite immaterial that his opponent has refused to give a *cautio* not from poverty, but from contumacy; but if the successful party cannot give a *cautio*, either the thing is to be deposited, or he is to be sent into possession under the Edict. 2. If it be alleged that the right to claim or to sue for a legacy or a *fideicommissum* is postponed by a condition or until a future date, and security has been prayed for that reason, but the heir contends that the demand is vexatious, and denies that it was left, the party who demands a *cautio* is not to be heard unless he produce a writing by which he can support his allegation that it was left to him. 3. When it was asked in what place a *cautio* should be given to secure a *fideicommissum*, the Emperor Titus Antoninus answered in a rescript that if the heir had no domicile at Rome and all the inheritance were in a province, the fideicommissary should be sent into the province to receive security for the *fideicommissum*. Hence, if the heir pray that he may be remitted to the place of his domicile to give a *cautio*, but the legatee demand that a *cautio* be given in the place where the inheritance is, the heir is not to be remitted, and so the Emperor Titus Antoninus provided in his rescript. 4. He added in this letter that if the goods have already been sold, either by the permission of the testator or with the consent of the legatee, the price should be placed upon deposit to secure the *fideicommissum*.

---

1. A particularly obscure text. The translation follows Cujas, Observationes et Emendationes Lib. 15, c. 10, in assuming the point of the text to be that since caution should have been given if the right to claim the legacy were suspended by condition or *dies*, it should also be given if the right to enforce the judgment be suspended by appeal.

6   ULPIAN, *Fideicommissa, book 6:* If the amount of a *fideicommissum* be uncertain, the magistrate will estimate the sum, and verbal guarantors may be demanded for this amount.   1. It, however, should be noted that it is the practice to remit security for *fideicommissa* to *res publicae,* even when they are compellable to pay, but they should be required to promise that they will carry out the intention of the deceased.

7   PAUL, *Handbook, book 2:* A legacy has been left upon condition to a son or a slave, charged upon his father or master, who has been instituted heir. They cannot demand security for this legacy, but should they be emancipated or manumitted pending the condition and then demand security the question may be raised whether they should be granted a hearing, lest the benefit conferred on the father or master should be a burden to them or whether they should blame themselves for giving them the opportunity to proceed against them. But the best solution is to adopt a middle course and to be satisfied with a bare personal *cautio* and a hypothec of their goods.

8   ULPIAN, *Sabinus, book 48:* When security has been given for legacies, they fall due immediately under the stipulation upon the same dates upon which they vest.

9   PAUL, *Sabinus, book 12:* But it does not follow that they are immediately demandable; for what is payable to a legatee at a certain date is said to be due, though the date have not yet come.

10   POMPONIUS, *Sabinus, book 26:* If I have been left a conditional legacy which has been charged upon you as heir, you have given security for legacies after accepting the inheritance, and the condition of the legacy has happened after your death and before your inheritance has been accepted, Sabinus says that the verbal guarantors are liable to me; for the legacy is payable in any event, and the stipulation was that it should be paid, not that any particular person should pay it.

11   GAIUS, *Provincial Edict, book 13:* If a procurator or anyone else give a *cautio* in my name to the legatees who have been sent into possession against me to secure their legacies, the praetor grants me an interdict commanding the legatees to leave possession exactly as though I had given a *cautio* myself.

12   MARCIAN, *Institutes, book 7:* Though a condition that no *cautio* be demanded be expressed in the testament, it is not taken as a condition, and, hence, although the legatee have prayed that a *cautio* be given him, his interest is not held to be defeated by the condition; for since it has been settled that this *cautio* is remitted as a matter of public law, the heir is not charged with finding a *cautio,* and this clause is not even understood as a condition.

13   NERATIUS, *Parchments, book 7:* The legatee who is given the action for legacies against one who has refrained from taking under the institution and who is in possession of the inheritance on intestacy is also entitled to security for legacies, and if no security be given, he will be sent into possession to secure the legacies; for it is the intention of the praetor that these legacies should be as well protected as those which are due at civil law. Aristo is of the same opinion.

14   ULPIAN, *Edict, book 79:* This stipulation is also applicable to *fideicommissa,* whether the *fideicommissum* be left unconditionally or payable upon a date certain or uncertain or upon condition, and whether it be a thing or an inheritance or a right that is left.   1. The deified Pius has also stated in a rescript that when the case is clear and it is certain that there is no way in which the *fideicommissum* can take effect, it is extremely inequitable to burden the heir with a superfluous *cautio.*

15   PAUL, *Edict, book 75:* This security is to be given even for a legacy which is immediately payable; for legal proceedings entail some delays.   1. If the legatee have received security for legacies both from the instituted heir and from the Trebellian fideicommissary, both are indeed chargeable under the stipulation, but the heir may

protect himself by a special defense, since he should not have given a *cautio*; but if a part of the inheritance have been restored, both should give a *cautio*.   2. This stipulation is also to be given if a *fideicommissum* is due upon intestacy.

16   GAIUS, *Provincial Edict, book 27:* If two persons of the same name are in dispute over a legacy, security is to be given to both, and this is no hardship to the heir, since he may join the same verbal guarantors in both stipulations, nor is it any hardship to them, since in the event they will be liable only to one of the parties.

17   PAUL, *Edict, book 48:* If we have received security for legacies from one of the heirs, when our legacy was charged upon all the heirs, if the share of a co-heir accrues to the promisor, the verbal guarantors are liable for the whole, if the whole legacy has become due from him.

18   SCAEVOLA, *Digest, book 29:* A testatrix who left a legitimate son named as heir to her whole estate her father, who had been manumitted by the same master as herself, and imposed a *fideicommissum* on him that when he should die, he should restore to the son of the testatrix, his grandson, whatever he had received from her inheritance, and she added these words: "I forbid a *cautio* to be exacted from my father Seius." The question is: this Seius is dissipating his property, and the fideicommissary's father fears that the *fideicommissum* will be defeated; can the father of the deceased be compelled to give security for the *fideicommissum*? He replied that, upon the case as put, he was not to be compelled to give a *cautio*.   1. The same client put this question: The testatrix had deposited goods with the husband by whom she had left a son, and had taken no *cautio* for the deposit; should the thing be restored to her father and heir, or, since the benefit of the whole inheritance was to revert to the son of the deceased, should it remain in the hands of the husband as the dowry had done? He replied that whatever had remained the property of the woman and had formed no part of dowry was to be restored to the heir.   2. Upon notice from the legatees a tutor, who was also co-heir with his *pupillus*, himself gave a *cautio* for the full amount of a *fideicommissum*. The question was whether an *actio utilis* should be granted against the *pupillus* after his full age. He replied that it should be granted.

4

THAT IT BE LAWFUL TO BE IN POSSESSION FOR THE SECURITY OF LEGACIES AND *FIDEICOMMISSA*

1   ULPIAN, *Edict, book 52:* If a legatee were forbidden to receive security and has received it, can the heir demand back the security by bringing a *condictio* for his release? If the heir knowingly gave a *cautio* for a sum not due, he cannot demand it back, but what if he did not know that the obligation to give security had been remitted him? The *condictio* lies. If, on the other hand, he thought that this duty could not be remitted, can a plaintiff who has mistaken the law maintain a *condictio*? Yet it may still be benevolently held that a *condictio* lies for the security. Finally, if the stipulation have become payable, should we take it that the verbal guarantors may plead a defense or not? And the better view is that they may plead a defense; for the security was given for a demand which ought not to have been secured.   1. The praetor does not require that it should be by his own default that the heir has not given a

cautio, but has deemed it sufficient that it be not by his own default that the legatee or fideicommissary has not received it. Thus, if there be no one on whom demand may be made for a *cautio*, that is, if he upon whom the legacy or *fideicommissum* is charged be absent, the legatee and fideicommissary may clearly be sent into possession under this edict, since on these facts it is not by the default of the party who should have received the *cautio* that no *cautio* has been given. It is not also necessary, however, that security should be offered to the legatee, but it is enough that he has made a demand and a *cautio* has not been given him or that he has no one from whom he may demand security.   2. If a debtor be left his release, he cannot require a *cautio*; for he has the legacy in his own hands, since he may plead the defense of fraud if he be sued, and is thus in the same position as one to whom a legacy has been paid.   3. In a rescript to Aemilius Equester, the deified Pius ruled that the praetor should not allow security when it is clear that the legacy is not due.   4. Security is to be given for legacies before acceptance of the inheritance only when it is still uncertain whether the inheritance have been accepted or not. If, on the other hand, it be certain that the inheritance has been repudiated or has not been taken up or that the *necessarii heredes* have been granted leave to abstain, it is vain to seek the benefit of this edict, when it is certain that the legacy or *fideicommissum* is not due.

2   ULPIAN, *Edict, book 79:* If, however, it be certain that the inheritance has not yet been accepted, neither security nor possession is grantable.

3   ULPIAN, *Edict, book 52:* If the party from whom the legatee demands security should offer a *cognitio* and say, "let the *fideicommissum* be proved today; let us litigate today," we should hold that no security ought to be granted; for the claim to the *fideicommissum* can be determined before the application for security.   1. The heir ought also to ask for a *cognitio* if he allege that the demand of security is vexatious. This is true of all cases in which security may be ordered; for the deified Pius held in a rescript that the magistrate before whom security is demanded should investigate whether the security be demanded vexatiously and should determine the question summarily.   2. If a procurator have demanded security for legacies, and he has a mandate to do so, he will not have to give a *cautio* that his act will be ratified, but security is to be given him. If, on the other hand, it be doubtful whether he have a mandate or not, a *cautio* for ratification should be required.   3. It has been questioned whether, if security have been once given, a *cautio* ought to be again given should it be alleged that the verbal guarantors are men of straw, and it is the better view that a *cautio* should not be given; for the deified Pius so ruled in a rescript to Pacuvia Liciniana: She who has accepted insufficient verbal guarantors should blame her own carelessness; for the party from whom security is demanded is not required to renew it from time to time.

4   PAPINIAN, *Questions, book 28:* However, should there be some new matter alleged, as that a verbal guarantor has died or even that he has lost his property by some unexpected stroke of fortune, it will be equitable that a *cautio* should be given.

5   ULPIAN, *Edict, book 52:* He who has not been given a *cautio* for legacies or for *fideicommissa* will never become entitled to possess as owner; for it is not so much the possession as the custody of the goods that is granted him, and he cannot evict the heir, but is ordered to possess together with him, so that he may extort a *cautio* from the heir if only by the annoyance of perpetual custody.   1. If one party have been sent into possession on account of threatened damage and another to secure legacies, he who has been sent into possession to secure legacies may also give security against the threatened damage. Should he have given security, he should not give up possession unless a *cautio* be also given him for the obligation which he has assumed for threatened damage.   2. If several legatees have demanded to be sent into possession, all should go into possession; for he who is in possession as legatee possesses on his own account and not on account of any other. The case is different when creditors are sent into possession to secure the property; for he who possesses does not possess on his

own account, but on behalf of them all.   3. The legatee who is first sent into possession is not preferred to the legatee who is sent into possession subsequently; for there are no priorities between legatees, but all are simultaneously and equally protected. 4. After the creditors have taken possession to secure the property, one who has previously been sent into possession to secure legacies will not be preferred to the creditors.   5. One who is sent into possession to secure legacies goes into possession of the goods of the inheritance, that is, of those which still form part of the inheritance, in all events, but he is sent into possession of such goods as are not part of the inheritance only if they have ceased to be so in consequence of a fraud and not then in all cases, but after investigation.   6. Under the term "goods" will be taken to be included those things the property in which belongs to the heir.   7. But should there be public lands held under long lease or goods placed in the testator's hands as *pignus*, the legatee is sent into possession of them also.   8. Moreover, in all events the legatee and the fideicommissary are sent into possession of the offspring of slave women and of the young of cattle, as also of fruits.   9. But should the deceased have bought another's thing in good faith, the legatee should clearly be sent into possession of it; for this thing also passes with the inheritance.   10. If a thing were deposited with the deceased or lent to him for his use, the *missio* will not include it; for these things are no part of the inheritance.   11. If one of two heirs be willing to give security and the other not, indeed, *missio in possessionem* should be granted of his share, but the consequence will be that when the legatees have been sent into possession, they will also prevent the heir who has given security from administering the property. The heir, therefore, should be persuaded to give security for the whole, so that his administration may not be impeded.   12. If a legacy be charged upon one who has been substituted to an *impubes* and the *impubes* have died, the *missio in possessionem* will extend not only to those goods which were the testator's but also to those which the *impubes* has acquired; for they too belong to the inheritance. In the lifetime of the *impubes*, neither *missio* nor security is grantable.   13. If there be no heir upon whom the *fideicommissum* is charged, but there be a successor under some other name, we should hold that the edict applies, and that his fraud should be taken into account.   14. But even should it be the heir of the heir who acted fraudulently, it should be equally prejudicial to him.   15. We should also take gross neglect to be fraud, but not all fraud, but such as is committed to defeat the claims of legatees and fideicommissaries.   16. For certain reasons, the Emperor Antoninus Augustus provided in a rescript that the legatees and fideicommissaries are also to be sent into possession of the heir's own goods, if default be made in giving security for more than six months after suit has been commenced before the tribunal of the magistrate who has jurisdiction of the cause, and they are to take the fruits of them until the wishes of the deceased be satisfied. This remedy was also to be used against those who delay the performance of a *fideicommissum* for any reason.   17. Though the word "satisfaction" have a wider meaning, it is taken to refer to payment of the legacy.   18. Hence, though the security be remitted, yet the rescript will apply on the ground that the payment is delayed.   19. I think that the period of six months should be taken to run continuously, not reckoned by sessions of the magistrate.   20. We do not hold there to have been a default if a *pupillus* have no tutor or a lunatic or a *minor* no curator; for such persons should not be prejudiced by their failure to take those steps which they should, since they have no one to act for them. Clearly, if the inheritance have been vacant for any period, this period is to be deducted.   21. It may be asked whether these fruits be taken in lieu of the interest which is due upon *fideicommissa*, and since we follow the analogy of *pignus*, the sums received from the fruits should be applied first to the payment of the interest and then, if there be any surplus, of the capital. Indeed, should the legatee have received more than is due to him, an *actio utilis* should be granted for repayment, by analogy with the action on *pignus*. One who has a *pignus*, however, may sell it, but in this case, the constitution merely allows him the enjoyment to hasten satisfaction.   22. He who is sent into possession to secure legacies should take custody of the fruits and other goods. Indeed, he should permit the heir to till the fields and reap the fruits, but the legatee should keep the fruits, so that the heir cannot consume them, but if the heir will not gather the fruits, the legatee should be allowed to gather the fruits and to conserve them when he has gathered them. Indeed, should the fruits be such as are best sold as soon as may be, the legatee is to be allowed to sell them and to put by the price. Where other goods of the inheritance are concerned, the duty of the legatee sent into possession is to collect the entire property of the inheritance and to keep it in the place where the deceased had his domicile, and if there be no house, he is to rent a lodging or a warehouse where the goods which he has collected may be kept, and in my opinion, the legatee ought so to keep the goods of the inheritance that the heir may not be deprived of them, and they may neither perish nor deteriorate.   23. But where *missio in possessionem* has been granted under the constitution, steps must be taken to ensure that the legatee is not forcibly prevented from using and enjoying.   24. The wishes of the deceased are taken to be satisfied, if they be satisfied insofar as it is possible to satisfy them, whether from the fruits or from any other source.   25. Moreover, the constitution of the deified Antoninus applies to those upon whom a *fideicommissum* has been effectually charged, though they be not heirs; for the same policy extends to both cases.   26. If a legatee sent into possession to secure legacies have joined issue in an action for his legacy, he should not leave possession until he has received a *cautio* for the amount of the suit.   27. If one who is sent into possession be not admitted, there is an interdict provided for him, or he is to be introduced into possession by the apparitor or by the prefect's officer or by the magistrate.   28. *Missio* is grantable not only if the party be asked to restore the legacy left him but also if he have been asked to restore something from it or something else in return for it.   29. If a legacy have been left to Titius unconditionally, subject to a *fideicommissum* that he restore it to Sempronius on condition, Julian wrote that if the legatee did not give security for the conditional *fideicommissum* before he received his legacy, the praetor would do no injustice if he allowed Sempronius to sue for the legacy in his stead, upon his giving security for the restitution of ten to the legatee upon failure of the condition; but also, if Titius have received the ten from the heir, Julian says that it is equitable that he should be compelled either to give security in his turn or to deliver up the ten and for Sempronius to give a *cautio* to Titius, and this is the present practice; for Marcellus also takes the same view.   30. What, then, if both the legacy and the *fideicommissum* be left upon condition and security be not given for the *fideicommissum*? The most equitable solution will be for the fideicommissary to take security for the legacy from the heir, if the legatee do not give him a *cautio*, that is, provided that he himself give a *cautio* to the legatee. If, however, the legatee have already received security from the heir, it should be ordered that the action upon the security be granted to the fideicommissary rather than to the legatee, in case, that is, that the condition of his *fideicommissum* have happened. The action for the legacy itself is also to be given to the fideicommissary, if it be not yet paid and the condition upon which it is payable have happened, provided, that is, that the fideicommissary be willing to give a *cautio* to the legatee.

6   JULIAN, *Digest, book 38:* If a legacy of the usufruct of coined money be left and it be provided in the testament that security be not given for it, this is not a legacy of the ownership, but the legatee is to be allowed to give security and to have the usufruct of

the money, and there is little need for the praetor to intervene in such a case as this; for unless security be given, he will not be able to sue the heir.   1. He who has been sent into possession to secure a *fideicommissum* should not give up possession until the *fideicommissum* be paid to him or security given for it; for he should give up possession when the heir offers to do what, had it been done before any steps were taken, would have prevented him from being sent into possession.

7   MARCIAN, *Rules, book 3:* When the widow is in possession on behalf of her unborn child, no one is entitled to be in possession to secure legacies.

8   PAPINIAN, *Questions, book 6:* If security be not given for legacies and the inheritance have been restored, the legatee is also to be put into possession of those things which have ceased to be part of the inheritance by the fraud of him to whom restitution has been made.

9   PAPINIAN, *Questions, book 19:* Even if judgment have been given against the heir and he do not pay the money, the legatee may demand to be sent into possession. 1. When the same thing is left to two upon contrary conditions, if a *cautio* be not given, both are sent into possession.

10   PAUL, *Views, book 3:* If there be no goods of the inheritance of which the legatees or fideicommissaries may be given possession, they cannot be sent into possession of the goods of the heir, but they may bring the heir's actions by the aid of the praetor, who will refuse them to the heir.

11   HERMOGENIAN, *Epitome of Law, book 4:* If you have been sent into possession to secure *fideicommissa* or legacies and you have a thing which has been left by *fideicommissum* to me, it is more equitable that I to whom it has been left should have it than that it should remain in your hands, when you have taken possession of it in right of another *fideicommissum*; for if a legacy be left to me upon condition and in the meantime you are put into possession of it to secure legacies and then the condition be performed, my right to sue for the thing will not be affected. So also, should you have taken possession of a *statuliber* upon the same ground, when the condition has been performed, you cannot prevent him having the liberty to which he is lawfully entitled.   1. If one of the heir's own creditors have been sent into possession to secure the property and have taken possession of a thing which was left to me by *fideicommissum*, it is settled that his act should not prejudice me in any respect, any more than if he had received the thing as a *pignus* from the heir himself.

12   MAECIANUS, *Fideicommissa, book 12:* There is no doubt that a *fideicommissum* may be left to municipalities, but should a *cautio* be not given, we have never questioned that it is possible to go into possession against the citizens of the municipality under this edict, but that the citizens themselves, if a *cautio* be not given to them, will not obtain the same advantage, but an extraordinary remedy will be required, that is, that their *actor* be sent into possession by the decree of the praetor.

13   CALLISTRATUS, *Monitory Edict, book 3:* However small the value of the thing which is left by legacy or by *fideicommissum*, yet unless it be paid by the heir or a *cautio* be given for it when a *cautio* is due, the praetor sends the legatee or fideicommissary into possession of all the goods which belong to that inheritance to secure the legacies.

14   LABEO, *Posthumous Works, Epitomized by Javolenus, book 2:* A woman in possession to secure legacies is entitled to her aliment at the cost of the estate if she were the daughter, granddaughter, great-granddaughter, or wife of the deceased, and be not married and have nothing of her own.

15   VALENS, *Actions, book 7:* There are cases in which, though property has ceased to be part of the inheritance by the fraudulent act of the heir, the legatee cannot be sent into possession of it, as if he have made ground *religiosus* or have publicly consecrated

something, that is, by permission of the emperor, or have manumitted a slave without fraud upon his creditors.

16   * * * : If Titius leave Maevius a legacy of a slave upon condition, and Sempronius leave the same slave a legacy upon condition, pending both conditions, both Maevius and the heir of Titius are entitled to demand security from the heir of Sempronius.

17   * * * : If legacies to a son-in-power be charged upon his father, who has been instituted heir, the father cannot be compelled to give security by his son, but if he maladministers the estate, a curator is to be appointed of those things which have been left to the son, who is to pay the income to both, or if it be a sum of money that is left, application must be made to the emperor.

BOOK THIRTY-SEVEN

1

BONORUM POSSESSIONES

1 ULPIAN, *Edict, book 39: Bonorum possessio*, once granted, confers both the advantages and disadvantages relating to an inheritance as well as ownership of the things comprised among such *bona*; for all these are contingent on the grant of the *bona*.

2 ULPIAN, *Edict, book 14:* For *bonorum possessores* are considered in all respects to stand in place of heirs.

3 ULPIAN, *Edict, book 39:* But *bona* (property) in this sense, as we are commonly accustomed to state, are to be interpreted [as indicating] succession to the whole position of each man, whereby a person succeeds to the legal position of the deceased and assumes the advantages and disadvantages attaching to his property; for, whether the *bona* pass solvent or not, whether they entail loss or gain, whether they exist in substance or lie in action, in this context they are properly termed *bona*. 1. But possession of an inheritance, or *bonorum possessio*, is, as Labeo observes, not to be construed as the possession of property; for it is a legal, rather than actual, possession. Accordingly, even though there is nothing corporeal in an inheritance, Labeo says that *bonorum possessio*, nevertheless, has properly been granted in respect of it. 2. And so we shall correctly define *bonorum possessio* as the right of following and preserving the estate or property owned by each man when he dies. 3. No one, however, obtains *bonorum possessio* against his will. 4. *Bonorum possessio* can be claimed by municipalities and partnerships and decuries and corporations. Accordingly, whether an agent or someone else receives it in his name, *bonorum possessio* is the appropriate legal remedy; but even if no one should sue for or have claimed *bonorum possessio* in the name of a municipality, the municipality will receive *bonorum possessio* in virtue of the praetor's edict. 5. *Bonorum possessio* may be awarded in respect of property of the head of a household as well as that of a son-in-power, provided that the latter had the right of testamentary disposition over his *peculium castrense* or *quasi-castrense*. 6. There is no doubt that *bonorum possessio* can also be granted in respect of the property of a man who has died in captivity, albeit he died in slavery. 7. A person can obtain *bonorum possessio* either at his own suit or through that of another. But if *bonorum possessio* is sought on my behalf without my instructions, it will be legally effective only when I have confirmed what has been done. Accordingly, if I should die before such confirmation, clearly I cannot validly be granted *bonorum possessio*, because I have not ratified the application myself, nor can my heir do so, since the right to *bonorum possessio* does not pass to him. 8. If, after the case has been investigated, *bonorum possessio* is granted, it will be awarded only by the court, because a decree cannot issue extrajudicially; nor, when the case has been heard, can *bonorum possessio* be awarded anywhere except before the court. 9. It is to be understood that there is a right of accrual in relation to *bonorum possessio*. Accordingly, if several persons have a right to *bonorum possessio*, one of whom has received *bonorum possessio* and the others have not,

4 GAIUS, *Lex Julia et Papia, book 8:* for instance, because they have rejected their right or have been excluded from application for *bonorum possessio* by lapse of time or have died before they brought suit for *bonorum possessio,*

5 ULPIAN, *Edict, book 39:* the one who has been granted it receives additionally by way of accrual those portions which would have belonged to the others if they had sought *bonorum possessio.*

6 PAUL, *Edict, book 41:* But in the case where the praetor promises a patron *bonorum possessio* of a fixed part [of an estate] contrary to the terms of a will, but awards possession of the other part to the instituted heir in accordance with the will, it is established that the right of accrual is not involved. Therefore, if the heir named in the will does not make application, [the praetor] expressly promises *possessio* of the other part too to the patron, while others, who enjoy the right of accrual, need apply only once for *bonorum possessio.* 1. The uses of *bonorum possessio* are several; for in some cases it is effective contrary to the wishes of the deceased, in others in accordance with them, and, yet again, in cases of intestacy, where claimants have a legal right or are without such right on grounds of their change of civil status. For even if children who have ceased to be *sui heredes* on account of their change of civil status have a defective claim at civil law, the praetor, nevertheless, revokes such change of civil status in the interests of equity. He also awards *bonorum possessio* to promote the observance of laws. 2. Wills written in shorthand are not covered by the edict, because Pedius observes in the twenty-fifth book of his *Edict* that shorthand does not constitute writing.

7 ULPIAN, *Sabinus, book 1:* A slave may properly be granted *bonorum possessio,* provided that the praetor is certain of his status; for *bonorum possessio* may be awarded both in absence of and without suit on the part of the claimant, if the praetor is not unaware of this one fact. 1. Therefore, a woman, too, will be able to claim *bonorum possessio* of another's property. An *impubes* can neither receive *bonorum possessio* nor engage in legal proceedings without sanction of his tutor. 2. Because a tutor and a father can respectively enter suit for *bonorum possessio* on behalf of a *pupillus* or son who is an *infans,* it is resolved that time begins to run from the day on which the tutor or father is aware of the entitlement of the *minor* [for the limitation period within which suit for *bonorum possessio* must be brought].

8 PAUL, *Plautius, book 8:* But a tutor may not renounce *bonorum possessio* to which his *pupillus* has a legal right, because a tutor is allowed to make application for it, but may not also renounce it.

9 POMPONIUS, *Sabinus, book 3:* If several degrees of *possessio* are to be awarded, as long as it remains uncertain whether the first entitled has made application or not, it is established that time does not begin to run against him whose entitlement is subsequent.

10 PAUL, *Sabinus, book 2:* Ignorance of the law is of no advantage in the matter of *bonorum possessio* in that it will not defer the date from which time runs; for this reason time runs against an instituted heir even before the will is opened. For it is enough to know that the testator has died and that one was the nearest cognate relative, and to have had a number of persons from whom to seek advice; for the knowledge demanded is not to be thought of as the specialist kind possessed by lawyers, but that which every man inherently possesses or may acquire by consulting those wiser than himself.

11 GAIUS, *Provincial Edict, book 14:* If a tutor seeks *bonorum possessio* on behalf of his *pupillus,* and in this instance *bonorum possessio* entails more disadvantage than advantage, the tutor is liable in the action on tutelage.

12 ULPIAN, *Edict, book 48:* It is not disputed that certain persons, for example, the unborn, the insane, and likewise those who seek *bonorum possessio* on behalf of a person in captivity, should often be granted it both against the imperial treasury and against the state. 1. Wherever a law or *senatus consultum* or constitution forbids

the taking of an inheritance, the right to *bonorum possessio* also lapses.

13 AFRICANUS, *Questions, book 5:* By the praetor's edict *bonorum possessio* is denied to those condemned on a capital charge, who have not been completely reinstated. A capital charge is one where the prescribed sentence is death or interdiction from fire and water. But if anyone has been sentenced to relegation, he is admitted to *bonorum possessio*.

14 PAPINIAN, *Questions, book 13:* When some relative lays an accusation to the effect that a will has been forged and after a long period of time has proved his case, although the time for suit for *possessio*, which he should perhaps have claimed as soon as he was sure of his charge, seems to have lapsed, nevertheless, because he drew up his accusation with the object of preserving his own right, he will, not without reason, appear to have laid claim to the succession.

15 PAUL, *Replies, book 11:* Paul gave the opinion that application by a mother alone has not been successful in obtaining *bonorum possessio* for a daughter who is an *impubes*, except where the grantor manifestly intended to award it to an *impubes*.

16 PAUL, *Views, book 3:* Whenever a man for whom *bonorum possessio* has been demanded by another becomes insane, the more widely approved view is that he appears to have ratified the proceedings; for formal ratification merely goes to confirm a prior demand.

2

IF A WILL EXISTS

1 PAUL, *Sabinus, book 3:* An heir whose name has been unintentionally deleted, in such a way that it practically, cannot be read at all, can scarcely be awarded *bonorum possessio*, because he would not seem to have been properly named as heir on the basis of mere inference, although, if the will has been defaced after it has been made public, *bonorum possessio* issues. For if there was a will at the time of death, *bonorum possessio* may be granted despite its subsequent destruction, because the will in fact existed.

3

BONORUM POSSESSIO IN THE CASE OF AN INSANE PERSON, AN INFANT, OR ONE WHO IS DUMB, DEAF, OR BLIND

1 PAPINIAN, *Questions, book 15:* Titius has been substituted as heir in place of an insane person; as long as the latter remains insane, time does not begin to run against either the instituted or the substitute heir. Nor if his *curator* is able to receive *possessio* on his behalf, will the passage of the time, which is prescribed in the case of those who are aware of the position, on this ground appear to run against one who is insane; for a father, too, receives *possessio* on behalf of an infant son, but if he is remiss in doing so, the *infans* is not thereby excluded. What, then, is the position,

should the *curator* be unwilling to accept *possessio*? Will it not be fairer and more expedient to award *possessio* in the same way to the next in line, lest the *bona* remain unpossessed? If this proposition is accepted, the substitute heir is obliged to execute a *cautio* in favor of all those to whom the *bona* must be delivered up, if, for instance, the instituted heir should happen to die while insane or if, when he has recovered his senses, death should supervene before he claims his inheritance. For it can happen that the substitute heir dies in the lifetime of the insane one and that the latter, nevertheless, does not impede the claims of others, if he too dies before taking the inheritance.
2   ULPIAN, *Edict, book 39:* Dumb, deaf, or blind persons can receive *bonorum possessio* if they understand the transaction.

4

BONORUM POSSESSIO CONTRARY TO THE TERMS OF A WILL

1   ULPIAN, *Edict, book 39:* In *bonorum possessio* contrary to the terms of a will, we should include children whether natural or adopted, provided that they have been neither instituted nor disinherited.   1. But children are called to *bonorum possessio* contrary to the terms of a will by the same right and in the same order as they are called to succession at civil law.   2. But this section appears to apply also to *postumi*.   3. But Pomponius submits that sons who have returned from captivity with *postliminium* are also admitted to *bonorum possessio* contrary to the terms of a will.   4. If one of three sons has been captured by the enemy, *bonorum possessio* in respect of two thirds [of the estate] belongs to the two sons who are in the *civitas*.   5. The same holds good in the case of a *postumus*; for, so long as there is prospect of a *postumus*, he is in the position of parcener.   6. And the praetor admits children who have become *sui juris* to *bonorum possessio*. (They are admitted, therefore, to *bonorum possessio*, whether they have been emancipated or have passed out of parental power in some other way). But the [emancipated child] of an adoptive father cannot be admitted to [*bonorum possessio* of his property]; for to be capable of admission one must rank as a child.   7. A man who had a son and had a grandson of whom that son was the father emancipated the son and adopted him as a grandson and then emancipated him; the question is whether he impedes the grandson's claim. I prefer the view that the grandson in question is not excluded, whether his father had remained as an adoptive grandson or whether he was emancipated. For I submit that even if his father had been emancipated, the grandson, too, is admitted together with his father in accordance with the edict.   8. A man had a son and a grandson of whom that son was the father; the son was emancipated or, still being in parental power, was deported; the question is whether he impedes the grandson's claim. The better view is that in either case the grandson should be admitted; for those who have been deported should be treated as if they were dead.   9. If both father and son have been deported and both have been reinstated, we shall hold that the son is admitted to *bonorum possessio*. But even if the son has been condemned to the mines or to some other penalty that has the effect of making him a slave, and has been reinstated, he nonetheless will be admitted; otherwise not.
2   HERMOGENIAN, *Epitome of Law, book 3:* The same holds true if the father, being [condemned] to punishment, also becomes a slave and is later restored to his former status.
3   ULPIAN, *Edict, book 39:* But not only are those who have been emancipated themselves admitted to *bonorum possessio* but also their descendants too.   1. If a man with two grandsons has emancipated one of them and adopted him in place of a son, we must see whether he alone may be admitted in the quality of son; and this indeed is the result if he has been adopted as the father of the grandson who had been kept in power; but the better view is that he alone can come into *bonorum possessio*.   2. But if the grandson in question has been emancipated, it is true to say that he cannot be

admitted in the quality of son; for this quasi-son does not rank as a child, since the rights acquired by adoption are canceled by emancipation.   3. If I have a son and a grandson of whom that son is the father and I have adopted the grandson as my son, both will be admitted; but, clearly, if the grandson has been emancipated, he will not be admitted, because his father takes precedence.   4. If a man after emancipation has acquired a son, and has permitted his father to adopt him as his son, it is most equitable that the rights pertaining to any son adopted by *adrogatio* should be observed in his case, and for that reason he is to be joined with his father. But if it is supposed that the grandson in question has been emancipated after his adoption, it will be most equitable for him to withdraw (for he recovers his own position), and he should not be joined with his father.   5. If an emancipated son should obtain a son by a wife married in contravention of his father's wishes and then the grandson, after the death of his father, wishes to obtain *bonorum possessio* in respect of his grandfather's property, he is to be admitted to it; for a legitimate son's rights will not be lost if his emancipation is rescinded, since rescission is employed to increase the number of those admitted, and not to diminish it. For even if the son has married such a low-born wife that he has brought degradation on himself as well as his father through such a marriage, we shall hold that even this woman's son is to be admitted to *bonorum possessio* of his grandfather's property, since it is open to the grandfather to make use of his own rights and disinherit the child. For the judge before whom a complaint concerning an undutiful will is to be heard will, in the case of the grandson in question, weigh up the wrongs committed by his father as well as the deserts of the son.   6. If an emancipated son has been passed over in the terms of a will and, before seeking *bonorum possessio*, has allowed himself to be adopted by *adrogatio*, he loses his right to *bonorum possessio* contrary to the terms of a will.   7. If a man has emancipated his son while keeping in his power the grandson of whom that son is the father and then has given the grandson in adoption to the son, that grandson is admitted to *bonorum possessio* contrary to the terms of a will in respect of his grandfather's property, if his father has predeceased him, because he is part of the family of one who could himself have been admitted to *bonorum possessio* contrary to the terms of a will.   8. And, moreover, the same is true, if the emancipated son has given in adoption the son he had acquired after his emancipation to his father and has then died; for this grandson, too, should be admitted to *bonorum possessio* in respect of his father's property, as if he were not part of another family.   9. If a father, but not his son, has entered an adoptive family, can the son receive *bonorum possessio* in respect of his father's property, if the latter dies in his adoptive family? And I submit that the following opinion is the less harsh, that the son in question, despite the fact that he is not part of the same family as his father, nevertheless, should be admitted to *bonorum possessio* in respect of his property.   10. Children who cannot be instituted heirs by law cannot apply for *bonorum possessio* contrary to the terms of a will. But these words "cannot be instituted" are referable to the time of death.   11. If one of the children has been appointed heir, he must not be called to *bonorum possessio* contrary to the terms of a will; for when he can have *possessio* in accordance with the will, what advantage is there to him in being granted it contrary to the terms of a will? Obviously, if another initiates the edictal procedure, he too will be admitted to *bonorum possessio* contrary to the will.   12. But if he has been appointed under a condition, he cannot receive *bonorum possessio* contrary to the will, and Julian, too, has observed likewise in the twenty-third book of his *Digest*. What is the position, then, if the condition has failed? He can indeed receive *bonorum possessio* contrary to the terms of a will.   13. If an emancipated son has been instituted heir under a condition which it is not within his power [to fulfill], inasmuch as he is appointed heir, he can, and should, receive *bonorum possessio* in accordance with the will and cannot receive it contrary to the will; and if the condition happens to have failed, he will have to be protected by the praetor to the amount that he would take, if he had received *bonorum possessio* contrary to the terms of a will.   14. But, likewise, if a grandson has been appointed heir under a condition of this kind, the same ruling will have to be made.   15. If any one of the children has not been appointed heir, but his slave has been named, and he has ordered him to accept the inheritance, he should be denied *bonorum possessio* contrary to the terms of a will.   16. The same holds good, too, if he has elected to take a legacy which was left to him or to his slave; for we hold that in this case too, *bonorum possessio* should be denied.

4   PAUL, *Edict, book 41:* It is to be noted that *bonorum possessio* contrary to the terms of a will, which is promised to children, is available whether an heir shall have existed or not; and this is what we mean [when we say] that children have a right to *bonorum possessio* contrary to the will itself; the opposite is true in the case of a patron.   1. If a man has instituted his son-in-power heir or has disinherited him and has passed over a grandson of whom that son is the father, there is no place for *bonorum possessio*, because the grandson would not have been *suus heres*. The same principles also apply in the subsequent degrees.   2. The edict dealing with *bonorum possessio* contrary to the terms of a will does not apply to women's wills, because they do not have *sui heredes*.   3. If someone passes over an unborn child, the person instituted as heir can receive *bonorum possessio* contrary to the terms of a will even if the child has not yet been born, because it is inequitable that he cannot apply for *bonorum possessio* in his capacity as appointed heir so long as it can be sought contrary to the terms of a will, nor contrary to the terms of a will as long as the child who has been passed over remains unborn, so that even if he dies beforehand, the right to *bonorum possessio* passes to his heir. This provision is of the greatest importance in the case of an emancipated son who is appointed heir; for he cannot meantime enter on the inheritance.

5   JULIAN, *Digest, book 24:* But likewise, if they have died before making application for *bonorum possessio*, it is not inequitable for the praetor to resolve in favor of their heirs that the benefit of *bonorum possessio* in accordance with, or contrary to, the will, will be preserved.

6   PAUL, *Edict, book 41:* If an emancipated son has produced a son and has subsequently died and the child's grandfather also dies, then the grandson can obtain *bonorum possessio* in respect of his grandfather's property.   1. But if [the testator] has emancipated both son and grandson, the grandson will not obtain *possessio* so long as his father is alive, but after his death will obtain *bonorum possessio* in respect of his grandfather's property.   2. Also in the case where only the grandson has been emancipated and his grandfather has died, followed by his father, a grandson who has been passed over will receive *bonorum possessio* in respect of his father's property, because he would have been *suus heres* to his father, had he not left his grandfather's power. 3. Where a son has been emancipated, if a grandson is kept in power, and both are passed over, both will receive *bonorum possessio*.   4. If an emancipated son should produce a son while in an adoptive family, not even the grandchild will obtain *bonorum possessio* in respect of his natural grandfather's property. But, likewise, if an emancipated son, having produced grandchildren, allows himself to be adopted in such a fashion that his sons follow him [into adoption], the same rule will apply. Obviously, if a grandson begotten in his adoptive grandfather's family has been emancipated, he will be able to claim *bonorum possessio* in respect of his natural grandfather's property. Adoption impedes rights only so long as a man may be a member of another family. However, once emancipated, he obtains *bonorum possessio* in respect of his natural parents' property, but he must have been emancipated in their lifetime, not after their death; for the more correct view is that a man emancipated after their death is not admitted.

7   GAIUS, *Provincial Edict, book 14:* If a grandson has been retained in power when a son was emancipated, the grandson is admitted to *bonorum possessio* in respect of his father's estate in his grandfather's lifetime.

8   ULPIAN, *Edict, book 40:* The praetor did not believe that those singled out for disherison and removed [from succession] should be admitted to *bonorum possessio* contrary to the terms of a will, just as they do not upset their parents' wills at civil law; clearly, if they wish to lodge a complaint concerning an undutiful will, it is in their discretion to do so.   1. It is not sufficient for the disinherited person to be mentioned in any part of a will; he must be referred to in that degree against which *bonorum possessio* is claimed. Wherefore, if a son has been disinherited in the first degree and passed over in the second and those appointed in the first degree have not applied for *bonorum possessio*, he will be able to receive *bonorum possessio* contrary to the terms of a will.   2. Disherison expressed in any fashion does not serve to exclude a son from *bonorum possessio* contrary to the terms of a will, but only that duly effected in the proper manner.   3. If a son has been disinherited in relation to one of the heirs, Marcellus observes in the ninth book of his *Digest* that he is not regarded as having been disinherited, and that, as a result, *bonorum possessio* contrary to the terms of a will can be sought against each heir.   4. Where a son has been disinherited and then instituted [heir], provided that the degree in which he has been instituted comes into effect, I submit that if another son invokes the edict, he too can seek *bonorum*

possessio contrary to the will.   5. A son has been passed over in the first degree and disinherited in the second. If none of those appointed in the first degree are alive at the time of the testator's death, it is to be held that [the son] who has been passed over cannot seek *bonorum possessio* contrary to the terms of a will. For the inheritance is bound up in the second degree, not in the first in respect of which neither the inheritance can be taken nor *bonorum possessio* be claimed. But if the appointed heirs have died after the testator, the same Marcellus submits that *bonorum possessio* contrary to the terms of a will, once there is a basis for it, continues to be available. But even if the condition on which the heirs were instituted has failed, he holds that the son who has been passed over in that degree would still have the same justification in applying for *bonorum possessio* contrary to the terms of a will. His view is the same, too, where a *postumus* who has not been instituted has not been born; for Marcellus says that the son still has a right to *bonorum possessio* contrary to the terms of a will.   6. If a man has written in his disherison in his own hand, let us see whether he can receive *bonorum possessio*. And Marcellus, in the ninth book of his *Digest*, says that this disherison does take effect against him, since, because it is against him, the senate does not treat the provision as if it had not been written.   7. If a man has disinherited his emancipated son and subsequently adopted him by *adrogatio*, Papinian, in the twelfth book of his *Questions*, says that his natural rights are paramount, and for that reason disherison prejudices his position.   8. But in the case of one who is not a member of the family, he approves the opinion of Marcellus, that the disherison has no adverse effects on the rights of a subsequent adoptee by *adrogatio*.   9. But it is to be observed that a disherison previously executed takes effect against a son who returns [from captivity] with *postliminium*.   10. If his natural father has disinherited a son who has been adopted and the son subsequently has been emancipated, the disherison will take effect against him.   11. The praetor did not intend sons given in adoption to be excluded, provided that they have been instituted heirs, and Labeo says that his observance of this practice was most just; for they are not entirely strangers to the family. Therefore, if there have been appointed heirs, they will receive *bonorum possessio* contrary to the terms of a will, but they themselves will not initiate the edictal procedure on their own unless another of the children that normally do so has been passed over. But if [an adopted son] has not himself been appointed heir, but another, who can obtain the inheritance for him, has been, he is not in a position to be admitted to *bonorum possessio* contrary to the terms of a will.   12. To be admitted to *bonorum possessio* they must rank as children. However, if I have given my adoptive son in adoption and have appointed him heir and others initiate the edictal procedure, he will not be given *bonorum possessio* contrary to will.   13. But *possessio* contrary to the terms of a will is given to one who is in an adoptive family, if he has been appointed heir in that degree against which *bonorum possessio* may be sought.   14. It is not a novelty that an emancipated son who has been passed over should confer greater rights on his brothers who have been appointed heirs than they would have had, if only they themselves had been involved; for, if a son-in-power is appointed heir to a twelfth part, while an emancipated son has been passed over, he attains a half share thanks to his emancipated brother, whereas if he did not have an emancipated brother, he would have received a twelfth. But if he has been instituted heir to a very small portion, he is to be protected, once the edictal procedure has been started, not in respect of the portion to which he was appointed, but can receive a greater share through *bonorum possessio*. For the principle on which the praetor works when he awards *bonorum possessio* contrary to the terms of a will is to assign to each of the children that portion of the estate he would have received, had his father died intestate, if he had remained in power; and for that reason, if an emancipated son or one who has remained in power or has been adopted, has been appointed heir to a very small portion, he is not restricted to the portion in respect of which he was appointed, but receives his due share.

9   GAIUS, *Provincial Edict, book 14:* It is of no import, however, whether the adoptive father is alive or dead; for inquiry is made only upon this point, namely, whether [the son] is part of an adoptive family.

10   ULPIAN, *Edict, book 40:* If, after the testator's death, a son instituted heir allows himself to be adopted, he can receive *bonorum possessio* contrary to the terms of a will, because the adoption of the instituted heir does not normally prejudice those named as heirs.   1. If a son given in adoption to his maternal grandfather has been instituted heir by his natural father and a third party initiates the edictal procedure, there is greater reason for him to be capable of receiving *bonorum possessio*; for we do not demand that he accepts the inheritance, but it is sufficient that it has been offered to him and that it is capable of acquisition.   2. If an adoptee, after accepting the inheritance at the bidding of his adoptive father, has been emancipated, he can receive *bonorum possessio* contrary to the terms of a will, and will himself take the inheritance rather than his adoptive father.   3. It is to be observed that, likewise, if an adoptee has accepted the inheritance, [*bonorum possessio*] contrary to the terms of a will is awarded him; but otherwise, if one claims a legacy or portion left to him, he is barred from *possessio* contrary to the will.   4. Children who cannot take contrary to the will do not count in calculating the shares, if the edictal procedure is initiated by another; for what point is there in admitting them in counting the shares, when they will take nothing?   5. Disinherited children, insofar as they do not set in motion the edictal procedure, in the same way, if others initiate it, will not come into *bonorum possessio* with those others; and their only remedy is the complaint, if they enter suit concerning an undutiful will.   6. Those who sue for *bonorum possessio* contrary to the terms of a will because of others do not need to wait for those who have been passed over to receive *possessio*, but they too can also seek *bonorum possessio* contrary to the terms of a will; for when they have once been admitted to that benefit taking benefit from others, it is no longer their concern whether others seek *bonorum possessio* or not.

11   PAUL, *Edict, book 41:* Where an adopted person is appointed heir by his natural father under a condition, if the edictal procedure contrary to the terms of a will is initiated by another, he too will be admitted; but if the condition has failed, he is barred from this [kind of] *possessio*. I submit that the same obtains in the case of one who has been appointed heir unconditionally, but not in due legal form.   1. *Bonorum possessio* contrary to the terms of a will also follows the regular law in the matter of distribution. Thus, grandchildren born to one son will take one share [of the grandfather's estate].

12   GAIUS, *Provincial Edict, book 14:* If two sons and two grandchildren of which a third son is the father have a right to *bonorum possessio* and one of the two grandchildren does not make application for it, his share accrues to his brother. But if one of the two sons does not apply, his omission to do so benefits his brother as well as the grandchildren; for in that case, the estate falls into two halves, of which the son obtains one and the grandchildren the other.   1. If an earlier will exists, made in due legal form, whereby a son was disinherited, and a second will which is not in proper order, where the son has been passed over in silence, the son can properly sue for *bonorum possessio*, if the heirs appointed in the later will, in the event of the son's exclusion in this instance too, are in a stronger position with regard to the inheritance in question [than those named in the earlier will]. And thus, the law has it that when a person against whom a son seeks *bonorum possessio* can obtain the estate in the event of the son being altogether barred, the son too is regarded as being within his rights in applying for *bonorum possessio*; but if the heir against whom he claims could not obtain the inheritance, the son too is excluded.

13   JULIAN, *Digest, book 23:* When an emancipated son receives *bonorum possessio* contrary to the terms of a will, the appointed heir is to be compelled to yield up to the claimant both the lands and the slaves that form part of the estate; for it is equitable that the whole legal position, obtained by the appointed heir in virtue of the fact that it devolves on him by will, should be transferred to him whom the praetor has appointed

in place of the heir. 1. A man having two sons and a grandson of whom one was the father had the grandson adopted and instituted him heir, while passing over the other son; the question is what rule should be observed in these circumstances, whether he may be admitted to his father's share or should take an equal portion. I have given it as my opinion that the grandchild, who has been given in adoption and appointed as heir, cannot receive *bonorum possessio* contrary to the terms of a will, so long as his father remains in power, or has been emancipated; but even if his father has died before receiving *bonorum possessio*, the grandson is not admitted to *bonorum possessio*. 2. Where a father, passing over his emancipated son, has appointed two heirs, the son he had in power and a second son whom he had given in adoption, and he has two grandchildren through this son, whom he had kept in the family, and who themselves have likewise been passed over in the will, the emancipated son and the son-in-power will receive *bonorum possessio* in respect of one third each, while the son who has been adopted and his sons will together receive *possessio* in respect of a third in such a way that a sixth falls to the grandchildren and a sixth to their father. 3. Where a father of two sons has emancipated one son who himself is the father of sons, and adopted as a son one of his grandchildren whom he had pi eviously emancipated, and, after passing over his emancipated son in his will, dies, it will be more just to aid the grandson who has acquired the status of son and to divide the estate into three parts, so that the son who has remained in power takes one, the grandson adopted as a son another, and the emancipated son together with his son, who has retained the place of grandson, the third. But even if, in the event of the son's death, one of the two grandsons has been adopted as a son, the estate will fall into three parts, since it is fairer for the grandson adopted as son not to have less than if he had not been one of the grandchildren, but had been a stranger to the family who had been adopted.

14 AFRICANUS, *Questions, book 4:* Where one of two emancipated sons has been instituted heir and the other has been passed over, if the instituted heir has accepted the inheritance, although the edict does not cover the point explicitly, [Julian] has given it as his opinion that he nevertheless cannot seek *bonorum possessio*, because he has accepted the disposition made by his father; nor can an emancipated son be admitted to *bonorum possessio* if he has accepted a legacy, whether he has received it from the instituted heirs or from those who have applied for *possessio* contrary to the terms of a will. But it is to be noted that the praetor should protect the instituted heir who has accepted the inheritance to the extent of the portion to which he has been appointed, so long as it is not more than he would have taken if he had received *bonorum possessio* with the result that he may have prejudiced his situation, because, if he has been instituted in respect of a smaller share, he can retain only that share, and because he is compelled to pay legacies to strangers to the family too. But if one in power has been instituted heir, since he becomes a *necessarius heres*, it cannot be denied that he too can seek *bonorum possessio*, provided that he has not meddled with the estate; for in that case, because he seems to have approved the disposition made by his father, he should be considered in the same position as an emancipated son. 1. A son in an adoptive family has married and produced a son whom he has emancipated after his adoptive father's death; this grandson in [Julian's] opinion can seek *bonorum possessio* contrary to the terms of a will by decree in respect of his natural grandfather's property. Likewise, if an emancipated son, having produced a son and emancipated him, has allowed himself to be adopted by *adrogatio* and dies after the death of his adoptive father, there is little room for doubt that the son can be admitted to *possessio* in virtue of a decree, contrary to both his father's and grandfather's wills, lest he should otherwise be excluded from the property of everyone.

15 MARCIAN, *Rules, book 5:* If an emancipated son who has been passed over has pleaded the defense of fraud against the heir suing in the matter of a debt owed by the son to his father, in my opinion he cannot sue for *bonorum possessio* contrary to the terms of a will; for by his very action he has, as it were, renounced *bonorum possessio*.

But this is to be understood as applying if the son has refused to rebut the heir's claim for the debt by using the defense, "if *bonorum possessio* contrary to the terms of a will cannot be awarded to a son," but rather has used the defense of fraud.

16   POMPONIUS, *Sabinus, book 4:* Suppose that an emancipated son by *fideicommissum* imposed on an heir who is stranger to the family had left an inheritance for a grandson who remained in his grandfather's power [when the father was emancipated], provided that he had been freed from his grandfather's power; if the grandfather should be suspected of intending to spend his grandson's inheritance, *bonorum possessio* is not to be awarded to him.

17   ULPIAN, *Sabinus, book 35:* If a father has allowed himself to be adopted and his emancipated son, whom he has freed beforehand, does not follow him [into adoption], because the father is in one family and the son is in another, his son cannot take *bonorum possessio* contrary to the terms of a will; and Julian has observed that such is the case. But Marcellus says that it seems inequitable to him that [emancipated sons] should be excluded from *bonorum possessio* when a father has allowed himself to be adopted; for when a son is not given in adoption, but a father allows himself to be adopted, he does not give his son a father; and this opinion is not without merit.

18   HERMOGENIAN, *Epitome of Law, book 3:* A son disinherited under a condition will seek *bonorum possessio* contrary to the terms of a will, although, where he has been instituted heir under a condition, he is barred from *bonorum possessio* contrary to the terms of a will; for a definite decision must be given if children are to be excluded from succession to their parents. 1. One who has received *bonorum possessio* contrary to the terms of a will may not claim a legacy or *fideicommissum*; moreover, he is denied the right to keep a gift made in contemplation of death, and it makes no difference whether the gift is acquired by the [beneficiaries] themselves or through the agency of another.

19   TRYPHONINUS, *Disputations, book 15:* When it is commonly said that *bonorum possessio* awarded to children is against the will, it is to be understood in the sense that it is sufficient that a will existed at the time of their father's death, as a result of which the inheritance could be accepted or *bonorum possessio* in accordance with the will could be sought, even if neither course has been followed or could have been followed. For if all the instituted or substitute heirs have predeceased the testator, or the person named as heir did not have *testamenti factio*, it is useless to apply for [*bonorum possessio*] contrary to a will, which would be without effect.

20   TRYPHONINUS, *Disputations, book 19:* A man has disinherited the son he had in power and passed over his emancipated son; the question is to what extent the emancipated son may take *bonorum possessio.* I have held that if the appointed heirs, being strangers to the family, have accepted the inheritance, the son who remained in power is to be excluded. But if they have renounced the inheritance (which they are quite likely to do, since they will take nothing from it on account of him who has received *bonorum possessio* contrary to the terms of a will), the son will be discovered to be *suus heres,* his father being intestate. If the emancipated son, however, applies for *bonorum possessio* contrary to the terms of a will, he alone will obtain *bonorum possessio.* But since the disherison is of no effect if the inheritance is not taken up in accordance with the will's provisions (and Julian, therefore, has correctly given it as his opinion that it presents no obstacle to [the son's] receiving *bonorum possessio* contrary to the wills of his father's freedmen, lest the will, being in all other respects void, should seem to have taken effect only in respect of the slur of disherison), the matter is now resolved by the intestacy procedure, with the result that the praetor protects the emancipated son in respect of one half of the estate against the son who is sole *suus heres* on his father's intestacy. The appointed heir who is a stranger to the family, therefore, will be in a position to sell the benefit given to him with the result that although he himself will obtain nothing by right of inheritance, by accepting the inheritance, he bars the son who remained in power and offers the entire estate to the emancipated son in virtue of his right to *bonorum possessio* contrary to the terms of a will; but if he has failed to take the estate, he will effectually admit the disinherited son to his portion of the property, since the latter thereby legally becomes sole *suus heres.* But just as the praetor may protect the emancipated son if the inheritance has not been accepted, so the son who has remained in power will not be totally barred if it has been accepted, but is to be allowed to sue for the estate by reason of his entering the complaint concerning an undutiful will against the emancipated son.   1. Let us see, however, in the case where both are admitted to their father's property, whether the emancipated son is obliged to collate in favor of [the son-in-power]; for he is not compelled to do so expressly according to that section of the edict, whereby he has received *bonorum possessio* contrary to the terms of a will, which provides that security should be given by the emancipated son in respect of collation between those to whom *bonorum possessio* contrary to the terms of a will shall be given

in this way; for because the son-in-power has been explicitly disinherited, he has not been called to *bonorum possessio* contrary to the terms of a will. Nor [is the emancipated son obliged to collate] in virtue of that section of the edict, whereby an emancipated son, admitted to *bonorum possessio* on his father's intestacy, is compelled to bring [his property] into hotchpot, because, although his brother is heir on intestacy, it is not on these grounds that the emancipated son has received *bonorum possessio*. And I fear that the appointed heir's failure to take up his inheritance has advantaged the son-in-power insofar as to admit him to part of his father's property, but not also to the property which the emancipated son held as his own; and that this is a consequence of the fact that where a son-in-power has been appointed heir to a lesser portion and his emancipated brother by being admitted to *bonorum possessio* contrary to the terms of a will renders him the service of increasing his share, although it is introduced in the wording of the edict, the view must be taken that in accordance with the praetor's intention, hotchpot should be denied. But the benefit of hotchpot should far rather be denied the son-in-power in the instant case, because, since he has been disinherited by his father and not been called to *bonorum possessio* contrary to the terms of a will by the praetor, he has obtained the title of *suus heres* in virtue of the appointed heir's failure to take up his inheritance (in circumstances where he would receive nothing on account of the praetor's offer of *bonorum possessio* contrary to the terms of a will to the emancipated son).   2. The emancipated son in this case will not be compelled to pay from his portion legacies to children and parents in their entirety, but is obliged to pay only half, because the son who remains in power bears the rest. But there is no reason for bringing an action for legacies against him who has become heir solely by right of intestacy.   3. But he who has received *bonorum possessio* contrary to the terms of a will, even though the inheritance has not been taken up by the appointed heir, pays the legacies donated in that part of the will against which he has received *bonorum possessio*. In this case, therefore, the situation of the son who remained in the family will be better than it would have been if he had not been disinherited.

21   MODESTINUS, *Encyclopaedia, book 6:* If a man who had in power a son and a grandson of which that son was the father has given the son in adoption while keeping the grandson in power and the son, after being emancipated by his adoptive father, dies, having instituted as his heirs strangers to the family, the son of such a man, who remained in his grandfather's power, will be able to sue for *bonorum possessio* contrary to the terms of a will in respect of his father's property, although he has never been in his power. On this basis, it does not seem necessary to have been in power. For if any other rule is observed, where a son has been emancipated, the grandson of whom he was the father and who has remained in his grandfather's power will not be able to seek *bonorum possessio* contrary to the terms of a will.   1. And there is the same principle of law where the emancipated son's son has remained in his grandfather's power and has subsequently been given in adoption to his father; that is, he will be able to seek *bonorum possessio* contrary to his grandfather's will, because he has not been in another family as a result of adoption.   2. But if my emancipated son has adopted a son who is a stranger to the family, the son who has been adopted will not be able to seek *bonorum possessio* contrary to my will because he has never been in the relationship of grandson to me.

5

PAYMENT OF LEGACIES WHERE APPLICATION FOR *BONORUM POSSESSIO* CONTRARY TO WILL HAS BEEN MADE

1   ULPIAN, *Edict, book 40:* This section [of the Edict] has a certain natural equity and is to some extent innovatory in order that those who nullify their father's dispositions by obtaining *bonorum possessio* should pay legacies and *fideicommissa* in accordance with his wishes to certain persons, that is, to children and parents, and a legacy to a wife and daughter-in-law as dowry.   1. The praetor, in general, has made particular mention of parents and

children and has not enumerated degrees of descent or ascent; therefore, [legacies] will be paid to them as far as the line stretches. But he has not described the persons in detail, whether they are descended from the male or female line. Therefore, whoever shall have stood in the relation of descendant or ascendant will be allowed to sue for a legacy, but only in the event that they are linked by ties of cognate relationship. 2. But we admit children to suit for legacies, even those who have been adopted or are adoptive children, provided that they retain the status of children. 3. Legacies left to *postumi* will in any case be paid.

2   JULIAN, *Digest, book 23:* And, for that reason, if a son with a pregnant wife has been emancipated and has received *bonorum possessio* contrary to the terms of a will, he will be obliged to pay a legacy to the grandson.

3   ULPIAN, *Edict, book 40:* But also if gifts made in contemplation of death have been conferred on specifically excepted persons, I believe they are to be safeguarded; but if the persons are not those excepted, I submit that gifts made in contemplation of death are to be taken away from them. 1. But the praetor has had regard only to children and parents and has not preserved a legacy even to a brother or sister. 2. But that alone is due which has been left to the parents themselves and the children; but if it has been given to one of their slaves or to a person legally subject to them, it is not due; for we do not inquire for whose benefit it is acquired but whom it was intended to favor. 3. But if a legacy has been left to a man jointly with a person to whom it is not payable, only his portion will be preserved to him. 4. Likewise, if any of these persons has been asked to pay a legacy left to him to an outsider, it is to be held that the legacy is not to be paid, because the benefit does not accrue to him. 5. But if one supposes a legacy to have been left to an outsider and that he has been asked to pay it to someone who has the status of child or parent, we shall hold that it follows that it should be paid. 6. Moreover, even if it has been left to a stranger to the family with the qualification that he pays it to one of the children, it will be equitable to hold that the praetor should not deny him an action. 7. Those who receive *bonorum possessio* contrary to the terms of a will pay only those legacies which have been effecively donated; but they are not payable merely because a son receives *bonorum possessio* contrary to the terms of a will,

4   JULIAN, *Digest, book 23:* since for this reason those appointed as heirs frequently refrain from accepting the inheritance, as they know that the emancipated son has sought or will seek *bonorum possessio* contrary to the terms of a will.

5   ULPIAN, *Edict, book 40:* A man named as heir his son who was an *impubes* and appointed a substitute heir in his stead but passed over the son he had emancipated; subsequently, both sons received *bonorum possessio*; legacies charged on the substitute heir were also left, not only to children and parents, but to strangers to the family too. The question is whether, in the event of the death of the *impubes*, the substitute heir should be compelled to pay them. If they were left charged on the *impubes*, they are to be paid only to children and parents, but if they were charged upon the heir substituted to the *impubes*, he should pay them all, taking account of the *lex Falcidia*, so that, namely, out of the half of the father's property that comes to him he retains a quarter, that is to say, an eighth of the whole estate. 1. But if the *impubes* was instituted heir merely to one twelfth, there is more reason for him to pay the legacies to the extent of one half, taking account of the *lex Falcidia*; for although the *impubes* has been instituted in respect of one twelfth, nevertheless, his coming into shares will increase the legacies left payable by the substitute heir. 2. But the praetor intended that legacies were to be paid to all the children with the exception of those to whom he awarded *bonorum possessio* for the reasons given above; for if he

has awarded *bonorum possessio*, he does not consider that they have [the right] to claim legacies. A child claimant, therefore, must decide for himself whether to sue for *bonorum possessio* contrary to the terms of a will or, in fact, to claim a legacy; if he has elected in favor of the former, he will not take the legacy; if he has elected in favor of the legacy, the law is that he may not enter suit for *bonorum possessio* contrary to the terms of a will.   3. Suppose someone has received *bonorum possessio* contrary to the terms of a will, then it has subsequently become clear that he was not one of the children capable of receiving that [type of] *bonorum possessio*, but was one of those to whom legacies are to be paid; [the praetor] held that he should not be denied the right to petition for legacies, whether he has sought *bonorum possessio* in the ordinary way or in accordance with the Carbonian Edict.   4. But not only is a legacy denied him who has received *bonorum possessio* but also anything else he has accepted in accordance with the testator's wishes. Julian's observation is consonant with this rule in the case where a man has been named as substitute heir to his brother who is an *impubes* and has received *bonorum possessio* contrary to the terms of a will; in these circumstances he is denied the right to sue for the inheritance left to the dead brother who was an *impubes* and in whose place he was appointed substitute heir by his father.   5. If legacies have been left to children and strangers to the family, although the paying out of both sets of legacies would bring the *lex Falcidia* into play and reduce the children's legacies, nevertheless, now on account of the fact that legacies are not paid to strangers to the family, those of the children are increased.   6. But if part of the estate has been granted to one who is a descendant or ascendant should it be preserved to him, as is usually the case with legacies? And Julian has very frequently observed that with regard to a part of the estate the same procedure is to be recommended as in the case of a legacy, an opinion confirmed by a rescript of the divine Pius, since the gift of an estate brings in its train not only a more honorable title but also a greater burden.   7. But such persons are to be aided to the extent that if they have been given a greater portion of the estate than their equal share, they are protected to the extent of an equal share, but if they have been given a lesser share, they are permitted actions up to the share to which they have been appointed. The same procedure is observed with regard to legacies and *fideicommissa*, which have been left to them, and in the case of gifts made in contemplation of death.   8. But is one whose share of the estate is preserved to him compelled to pay legacies to everybody or only to the persons specifically excepted? The better view is that they are to be paid only to the excepted persons; nevertheless, this procedure is not solely to his advantage. For if his share has been burdened by legacies to descendants or ascendants, as well as to strangers to the family, we do not doubt that the sum withheld from the strangers to the family will go to the benefit of the ascendants or descendants. Therefore, what is not paid to the strangers is shared with the applicant for *bonorum possessio* contrary to the terms of a will, only if it has not been payable to legatees who are descendants or ascendants.

6   JULIAN, *Digest, book 23:* Salvius Aristo to Julian, greetings. A man who had an emancipated son passed him over in his will, and instituted his father heir, together with a stranger to the family and gave a legacy to his father; the son applies for *bonorum possessio* contrary to the terms of a will. I ask if both, or either, or neither, of them had accepted the inheritance, whether, and how much of, the legacy is to be due to the father. [Julian] stated his opinion: I have often observed that this part of the Edict, whereby an emancipated son, who has received *bonorum possessio* contrary to the terms of a will, is bidden to pay legacies to ascendants and descendants, has some defects; for if three quarters of the estate has been left as a legacy, the legatee is in a position to receive more than the emancipated son. And so the position will have to be modified by decree, so that both the emancipated son pays out a share of the inheritance in such a way that the appointed heir does not receive more than the emancipated son, and the amount of the legacies is modified, so that no one receives more from the legacies than will remain with the emancipated son in virtue of *bonorum possessio*.

7   TRYPHONINUS, *Disputations, book 16:* For, according to the constitution of the divine
Pius [addressed] to Tuscius Fuscianus, legate of Numidia, it was resolved that parents and
children who are also instituted heirs should be protected to the extent of an equal share on
the model of legacies, lest such persons should take more as a result of their institution than
would come to him who received *bonorum possessio* contrary to the terms of a will.

8   ULPIAN, *Edict, book 40:* Let us see how "equal shares" is to be interpreted. Suppose
there are two persons who receive *bonorum possessio* contrary to the terms of a will, one
of whom is an ascendant or descendant [of the testator], the equal share will be one third
[of the estate]; but if there are three who have received *bonorum possessio* contrary to the
terms of a will, the equal share will be one quarter; the same rule will also be observed in
the case of legacies. But if there is one person who is a descendant and has received
bonorum possessio contrary to the terms of a will, and several being descendants or ascendants, who have received legacies, the rule is to be interpreted thus, that a son who has
been passed over takes a half and all others, being descendants or ascendants, a half.   1. If
a descendant or ascendant has both been instituted heir and has received a legacy, do we
preserve to him only the portion [of the estate in respect of which he was instituted] or, in
fact, the legacy too or whichever of the two he has elected to take? It is more reasonable
that both be preserved, but in such a fashion that he takes no more than an equal share in
either case.   2. If a person whose equal share is preserved to him has accepted an inheritance, the freedom [granted to his slaves by the testator] will necessarily take effect
through his acceptance of the estate. But, nevertheless, we must see whether he who accepts the estate is liable to an action for fraud. And it is more likely that where he is
warned by the person who has been passed over in the will and who has received *bonorum
possessio* contrary to the terms of a will, and accepts the inheritance despite the latter's
promise of an equal share, the facts may tell against him, and he may be liable to an action for
fraud; for he incurs loss to the estate, since the [grants of] freedom [made to the slaves by
will] take effect.   3. If anything has been left to a wife or daughter-in-law apart from a
dowry, it will not be paid if *bonorum possessio* contrary to the terms of a will has been received.
4. There is, however, no doubt that the expression "daughter-in-law" includes a grandson's
wife and other such female relatives.   5. But when a legacy is left in lieu of dowry, I submit that the wife or daughter-in-law should not have it reduced to an equal portion, since
the woman in question is merely coming into the sum owed to her.   6. The praetor's [edict]
comprehends not only a dowry bequeathed before the property is to be divided but also
anything that has been left in lieu of dowry, for instance, where the dowry consists of property, and an amount of money is left to her in lieu of the property, or the other way round,
provided, nevertheless, that it is described as left in lieu of dowry.

9   PAUL, *Edict, book 41:* But even if the legacy consists of more than the dowry, an action
will lie [to claim the legacy].

10   ULPIAN, *Edict, book 40:* But if the testator has appointed such a woman as heir to any share
in lieu of dowry, I submit that she should be protected.   1. But we shall require that she is
a wife at the time of death. If the testator has left a dowry to his son's wife to be paid out
before the estate is divided and she is married at the time of death, the legacy is void,
because the dowry is not yet owed; but since, even when the marriage subsists, an action
will be granted against the heirs of the father-in-law, it is to be held that the right to sue
should be granted even in the case of a dowry left as a legacy to be paid out before the
estate is divided.   2. Not all legacies which have been charged upon all degrees are to be
paid by the applicant for *bonorum possessio* contrary to the terms of a will, but only those
which have been given in that degree against which he has received *bonorum possessio*.
But sometimes *bonorum possessio* has been sought against one degree but the legacies are
charged on another, for example, when the testator has appointed heirs in two degrees and
has passed over his emancipated son, but has left legacies in both degrees to descendants
and ascendants. Julian states: If, in fact, any one [of the heirs] in the first degree is still
alive, [the grantee of *bonorum possessio*] will pay those legacies which have been given to
descendants and ascendants in the first degree; but if none of them is alive, he will pay the
legacies left in the following degree. But if none of the heirs either of the first or of the
second degree remains alive at the time of the testator's death, then *bonorum possessio*
falls to the son rather who has been passed over on intestacy, and no legacies are to be paid

to anyone; but if the instituted heirs have died after the testator's death before accepting the estate, [although it may be said that *bonorum*] *possessio* appears in fact to have been sought against them, nevertheless, the legacies left charged on them are not to be paid out, but those which have been left charged on the substitute heirs.

11   PAUL, *Edict, book 41:* But where both the instituted and the substitute heirs are alive, even if no one takes up the inheritance, we hold that those legacies which have been charged on the instituted heir ought to be paid.

12   ULPIAN, *Edict, book 40:* But whether the instituted heirs have failed to take up the estate or not, it is to be held that the legacies left charged on them are to be paid, even if the heirs instituted in the second degree have, on their refusal, accepted the inheritance.

13   TRYPHONINUS, *Disputations, book 2:* Likewise, we hold that legacies charged on the substitute heir are payable, if the instituted heir had failed to satisfy a condition that it was not in his power to fulfill. For if he has not fulfilled a condition that was in his power, he is to be treated as one who has refused the estate, when, being in a position to receive no benefit, he quite reasonably has not obeyed the terms of the condition.

14   ULPIAN, *Edict, book 40:* Sometimes a man takes *bonorum possessio* contrary to the terms of a will and in the same legal position as if he had *bonorum possessio* according to will. For example, an emancipated son was instituted heir, another emancipated son passed over, the instituted heir took *bonorum possessio* contrary to the terms of a will, the son passed over neglected to do so; it is quite apparent that he is compelled to pay legacies to everyone just as if recourse had not been had to the edictal procedure; for the existence of an emancipated son who has been passed over should not be a source of gain to the instituted heir, when the one passed over neglects to avail himself of his rights.   1. If a legacy has been given expressly to one of the descendants or ascendants payable by one of the sons instituted as heir and he has received *bonorum possessio* contrary to the terms of a will together with the others, it is better to approve the view that all those who have received *bonorum possessio* contrary to the terms of a will should be compelled to pay that legacy.

15   PAUL, *Edict, book 41:* A [son]-in-power who has been passed over will not be obliged to pay legacies, in spite of the fact that he has applied for *bonorum possessio* contrary to the terms of a will, because even if he had not sought *bonorum possessio*, he would obtain the estate on an intestacy; for the defense of fraud presents no obstacle to him, and it is ridiculous for him to be compelled to pay out legacies on the ground that he has applied for *bonorum possessio*, since, even without it, he will take the estate in his own right. Wherefore, if two sons have been passed over, an emancipated son and one in power, some authorities hold the view that the emancipated son is not obliged to pay the legacies either, because, as a result of his brother's [application], he takes a half share, since his brother, even if he were not claiming [*bonorum possessio*], would, as sole *suus*, take the [whole] estate. What, then, is the position? Where the son who has been passed over is *suus [heres]*, the view given [above] is the better one, but where he has been appointed [as heir], and enjoys the favor of his father, he should be liable to the legatees, although he has not applied for *bonorum possessio*.   1. But if one emancipated son has been appointed as heir and the other has been passed over and both have received *bonorum possessio* contrary to the terms of a will, the instituted heir, too, pays out the same legacies as [the son] who has been passed over. But if the [son] instituted as sole heir has received *bonorum possessio* contrary to the terms of a will, he will be obliged to pay legacies to everyone, just as if he had accepted the inheritance. But if the [son] appointed heir has actually accepted the estate, but the one who has been passed over has applied for *bonorum possessio* contrary to the terms of a will, the latter, in that he has received *bonorum possessio*, will be obliged to pay legacies to specific persons, but the position with regard to the one appointed heir is questionable. And several authorities submit that he, too, should pay [legacies] to the specified persons, which I submit to be the more correct view. For the praetor, too, protects him on the basis that he is one of the children who could have sought *bonorum possessio* contrary to the terms of a will.   2. But he is to be protected in this way to the extent of a half share, if he has either been instituted heir to more than a half or to a half share; but if he has been instituted heir to less than a half share, we hold that he is not to be protected in relation to a greater share than that for which he has been instituted; for by what reasoning can he take a larger share

when he has not received *bonorum possessio* and has not been instituted for a greater share? 3. No legacy will be payable to her who has no dowry, even though it is left to her in the guise of dowry. 4. If a stranger to the family has been instituted heir and a legacy has been left to a specifically excepted on condition that the beneficiary gives ten to the heir, he will have an action for the legacies if he has handed over the sum to the person who has received *bonorum possessio* contrary to the terms of a will, and not to the instituted heir, because it is irrational that the latter should reap the advantage of the inheritance, while another bears the burden of paying out the legacy. But even if he has been instructed to give the sum to Titius, he should give it not to him but to the son [who has received *bonorum possessio* contrary to the terms of a will].

16   ULPIAN, *Disputations, book 4:* If it is imagined that there are two sons, one in power who has been passed over, the other emancipated, who has been instituted heir, it is clear that the edictal procedure has been brought into play by the son-in-power; and if both had sought *bonorum possessio* contrary to the terms of a will, the [son] in power will not, in fact, pay legacies to descendants and ascendants, since he takes the property on intestacy. But does the emancipated son not pay them either, because he takes a share of the property from his brother, who would not have had to pay them if he were alone? But it is more reasonable that he too should be liable at least for legacies to descendants and ascendants. Accordingly, if [the emancipated heir] has not received *bonorum possessio* contrary to the terms of a will, it is to be held that he is to be protected to the extent of his share and that he will certainly pay legacies to descendants and ascendants. But I doubt whether he must pay everyone; nevertheless, because he enjoys a full measure of the testator's goodwill, for his part he should also show a full measure of obedience to his wishes.

17   JULIAN, *Digest, book 36:* If, while passing over his emancipated son, a father had instituted as heir a stranger to the family and had left a legacy of a specific thing charged on him and, after the inheritance had been accepted, the property had been destroyed as a result of fraud on the part of the appointed heir, an *actio utilis* will have to be granted against the emancipated son, namely, to the person to whom the son is compelled to pay the legacy, because the praetor acts on the principle that *bonorum possessio* contrary to the terms of a will is not awarded to the detriment of other persons.

18   AFRICANUS, *Questions, book 4:* A grandson who remained in power and a son, also in power, were instituted heirs; the [testator] gave a legacy to the grandson; his father, being emancipated, applies for *bonorum possessio*; the grandson is satisfied with the legacy. Certain authorities have given it as their opinion that an action for the legacy should be granted to the grandson only against the [son] who was in power, because nothing is taken away from him, and the emancipated son obtains his son's share to which the burden of the legacies would not be attached. But the better view will be that the grandson should be given an action only against the emancipated son, and, in fact, not beyond one fourth of the estate,

19   AFRICANUS, *Questions, book 5:* because, even if all parties had sought *bonorum possessio*, the grandson's half would be divided between him and his father.

20   MARCIAN, *Rules, book 4:* If an emancipated son has sought *bonorum possessio* contrary to the terms of a will, it is established that descendants and ascendants are to be protected. But if the testator has given gifts of a miscellaneous nature to the persons specifically excepted in contemplation of his death, they will proportionately contribute them to make up a full portion for the emancipated son, just as happens in the case of shares of an inheritance and legacies. 1. But if his father dies intestate, a son will not be able to enter a complaint in relation to gifts made in contemplation of death, since no comparison with legacies occurs.

21   PAPINIAN, *Questions, book 13:* If a share of the estate, which a specifically excepted could have taken thanks to a statute, is refused in relation to that share too, the son who has received *bonorum possessio* shall pay legacies only to specifically excepted persons.

22   PAPINIAN, *Replies, book 5:* When *bonorum possessio* contrary to the terms of a will has been given to an emancipated son who has been passed over in the will, a second son appointed as heir, who has received *possessio*, or, being satisfied with his position at civil law, has not done so, will not take [any] legacies payable before division of the property.

23   HERMOGENIAN, *Epitome of Law, book 3:* Those to whom the constitution of the divine

Pius has preserved a legacy or an equal portion will take none of the slaves that have been unable to obtain their freedom in consequence of a grant of *bonorum possessio* contrary to the terms of a will.

24 TRYPHONINUS, *Disputations, book 16:* There arises the question at what point must a legatee count as a descendant in order that he can take a legacy from the son who receives *bonorum possessio*? And it is agreed that it is necessary to be in that relationship at the point when the right to the legacy vests.

25 MARCELLUS, *Digest, book 9:* A man who had emancipated his son and had kept a grandson of whom his son was the father, in power disinherited the son by will, instituted the grandson heir to a certain share, and passed over another son, who had been emancipated. It is possible to maintain that the grandson, too, can apply for *bonorum possessio* contrary to the terms of a will; for *bonorum possessio* is conferred on each in respect of the share to which he would be *suus heres* on intestacy, if his father were not *suus heres*. 1. A man whose son had been adopted appointed as his heir the grandson whom the son had subsequently fathered, but passed over his emancipated son; surely the grandson does not take *bonorum possessio* in accordance with the edict? Nevertheless, he is to be protected on the pattern of the ascendants and descendants to whom those who have received *bonorum possessio* are compelled to pay legacies. 2. If the testator happened to have kept in power one or more grandchildren of whom the same son was the father, without doubt [the grandson] is to be protected in respect of the share for which he would be protected, if a grandson born of a daughter or the mother of the deceased had been instituted heirs; for he is on a par with them.

6

HOTCHPOT

1 ULPIAN, *Edict, book 40:* The equitable nature of this section is plain; for when the praetor admits emancipated children to *bonorum possessio* contrary to the terms of a will and gives them a share in their father's goods along with those who are in power, he believes it to be fitting that those who apply for their father's property should bring their own goods, too, into hotchpot. 1. Hotchpot will be provided for among those to whom *bonorum possessio* has been granted. 2. Obviously, if the praetor has restored a *minor* or another whom it is his habit to restore to his former position for the purpose of seeking *bonorum possessio* contrary to the terms of a will, where he had neglected to do so, he likewise restores to him also the advantage of hotchpot. 3. If a son-in-power has been instituted heir to a twelfth and a stranger to the family heir to a quarter, Julian says that an emancipated son, on receipt of [*bonorum possessio*] contrary to the terms of a will, would bring into hotchpot his own property only in respect of one fourth, because he has taken only a fourth from his brother. Pomponius adduces an argument for this view, namely, that an emancipated son is compelled to make a contribution only to [those of the testator's] grandchildren of whom he is the father. 4. A father appointed as his heir the son he had in power and a stranger to the family, and passed over his emancipated son. Both sons received *bonorum possessio* contrary to the terms of a will. A convenient view is that the emancipated son should make a contribution to his brother only in the case where he has taken something from him by way of inheritance; for if the son-in-power has been instituted heir to less than a half share, it will seem inequitable to demand a contribution from one on whose account he is about to take more from his father's estate. 5. Therefore, there is a place for hotchpot whenever the son-in-power suffers some disadvantage by the intervention of an emancipated son. If this is not the position, however, hotchpot will not take place. 6. But it must certainly be most strongly stressed that the emancipated son should not contribute if he was entitled under a disposition made by his father and obtains no more than his father has given him. 7. But even if he has received by way of legacy half [of the estate] or as much as he obtains by way of *bonorum possessio*, it is to be held that he is not to be obliged to bring his own property into hotchpot. 8. In the same place, Julian says that if a son-in-power should die after *bonorum possessio* has been received, the emancipated son

is to be compelled to bring his property into hotchpot, so that he confers on his brother's heir what he would confer on his brother himself if he were alive. But if the *suus* [*heres*] has died before *bonorum possessio* has been granted, the praetor will be obliged to protect his heir, he says, to the extent of the share to which the son-in-power was named heir, but not beyond an equal share; but he does not permit him a right to hotchpot in this case, since there has been no grant of *bonorum possessio*.   9. But the praetor rules that hotchpot must take place in such a manner that the proper *cautio* is given; but Pomponius says that the *cautio* should be made with security. Let us see whether it is possible for a *cautio* to be given by way of pledges. And Pomponius has observed in the seventy-ninth book of his *Edict* that a *cautio* for hotchpot may properly be given both by personal promises and by pledges, and I too hold this view.   10. If the brother is unable to give a *cautio*, a curator of his share is appointed with whom the converted proceeds [of the goods] are to be deposited, so that he may finally receive the converted estate at the time when he has brought his own property into hotchpot. But if actions have been denied [him] on the ground of his recalcitrance and he subsequently offers a *cautio*, he recovers his former right [to them].   11. But although the praetor's edict speaks of a *cautio*, nevertheless, in the thirty-ninth book of his *Edict*, Pomponius has observed that hotchpot can also be effected in terms of property. For he says that hotchpot is either to be effected in terms of property or by means of a *cautio*. Therefore, he says, let him divide his property with his brothers, and even if he does not give a *cautio*, he complies with the edict. But even if he shares out certain property, and, in respect of other property, gives a *cautio*, we equally hold that he has complied with the edict. But since it is possible for property to be concealed, the person who has not given a *cautio* does not properly bring his property into hotchpot, even if he shares it out. If, therefore, the parties agree on an inventory of the emancipated son's property, division of the property constitutes effective hotchpot; if there is no agreement, but certain property is alleged not to have been brought together into the common pool, then, on the grounds of uncertainty, a *cautio* will have to be interposed.   12. But it is also to be held that the emancipated son appears to have made sufficient contribution where he perhaps merely remits in relation to his father's property as much as the *suus* [*heres*] ought to take from hotchpot. The same is true in the case where he has assigned a debt due to the estate, or has surrendered a farm or other property in respect of the share of goods which he should have contributed.   13. If, in the case where he was obliged to contribute in favor of two persons, he has made a contribution to the one but not to the other, whether he gives a *cautio* or shares out his property, we must see if only the benefit of a sixth of the estate should be taken from him or whether he should be deprived of a whole third. And I submit that if, in fact, he does not give an undertaking through recalcitrance, actions for recovery of the whole third should be denied him (for he does not appear to have given an undertaking in that he has not given it to all parties); but if he has failed to give a *cautio* through indigence, actions for recovery only of the sixth should be denied him, in such a way, however, that he may supply the lack of a *cautio* by way of hotchpot, or the other means to which we have referred above, or a *curator* may be appointed to ensure that the property is secured to him. For where mere recalcitrance is not the cause, the reasons of one who fails to bring his property into hotchpot should be taken into consideration.   14. A person who is in an adoptive family is also compelled to make contribution, that is to say, he does not do it himself, but his adoptive father does it, if he has chosen to take *bonorum possessio* contrary to the terms of a will. Obviously, if the adoptive father in question has emancipated him before application for *bonorum possessio* has been made, he will not be compelled to enter into hotchpot, and so it is stated in a rescript of the divine brothers; but an adoptive son who has been emancipated will deprive his brothers of hotchpot only in the case where he has acted in good faith.   15. Neither *peculium castrense* nor *quasi-castrense* is contributed to brothers; for it is stated in many constitutions that this should be treated as particular property.   16. But let us see whether anyone is compelled to bring into the common reckoning sums given or owed by a father on account of an office. And Papinian says in the thirteenth book of his *Questions* that he is not to be compelled to do so; for money paid on account of the burdens of office should be held particular. But if the money is still owing, this statement is to be interpreted as follows, namely, that he who has obtained office does not alone bear the burden, but the burden of the sum due falls on all heirs in common.   17. A man who returns from captivity after his father's death, although he had nothing at his father's death, since he was in captivity, nevertheless both will be admitted to *bonorum possessio* and will certainly contribute those things which he would have had at his father's death, if he had not been captured by the enemy. But, likewise, where he is found to have been ransomed from the enemy and this is discovered at the time of his father's death, he will equally have to bring his property into hotchpot. 18. If an emancipated son has been left a legacy, "when his father shall die," he must also bring this into contribution. 19. If a *fideicommissum* has been left for a son, charged on his father himself, the instituted heir, and due when he dies, should it be brought into hotchpot, as this *fideicommissum* is effective? And it will turn out to be considered as if it had been left after the death of the father, and the [son] in question will not be compelled to bring it into hotchpot, because it would not have existed at his father's death. 20. If an emancipated son has a dowry received from his wife, he does not bring it into hotchpot at all, even if his wife has died previously. 21. If, in accordance with the rescript of the deified Pius, a fourth is owed to an *impubes* who has been adopted by *adrogatio*, we must see whether, in the event that he makes application for *bonorum possessio* in respect of his natural father's property, he must bring the fourth into account. The question turns on whether he is leaving his action for the fourth to his *suus heres* or not. It is more reasonable that he should transfer it to his heir, since it is a personal action; therefore, he will also be obliged to give an undertaking with regard to bringing the fourth into hotchpot. But this occurs only in the case where a claim for the fourth already exists. However, if the adoptive father who emancipated him is still alive, it is to be held that the *cautio* lapses too; for the hope of bringing the fourth into hotchpot is untimely, since he from whose property it is due is still alive. 22. If a man who is about to bring his goods into hotchpot has a son with *peculium castrense*, he will not in any case be compelled to bring the son's *peculium* into account. But if the son was already dead at that time and he will have the *peculium castrense* when the person in respect of whose property *bonorum possessio* is to be sought shall die, is he to be compelled to bring it into account? But since it is unnecessary for the father to claim it, it will have to be held that it should be brought into account by way of hotchpot; for it is not being acquired at this stage, but it is not being taken away. I further hold that even if he has been instituted heir by the son and has not yet accepted the inheritance and has a substitute heir, because the *peculium* is not being acquired at this point rather than not being alienated, it should be brought into hotchpot. 23. But property not belonging to him, which he has fraudulently seen to it that he does not have, is also subject to hotchpot. But this rule is to be interpreted in such a way that only what has ceased to be his by an act of fraud is subject to contribution; however, if he performed such an act in order to avoid acquiring it, it does not fall into hotchpot; for he has thereby prejudiced himself too. 24. Shares of the proceeds of hotchpot will have to be worked out as follows; for example, there are two sons-in-power, an emancipated son with three hundred; he distributes two hundred to his brothers, one hundred to himself; for he makes a share with them, although he does not belong to the class of persons to whom contribution is normally offered. But if there are two emancipated sons with three hundred and two in power, it is equally to be held that each one contributes a hundred to each of the ones in power and keeps a hundred, but that they contribute nothing to each other. Contribution of a dowry, too, will be effected in the same manner, so that whoever makes the contribution also counts himself when it comes to working out shares.

2   PAUL, *Edict, book 41:* When we hold that a *postumus* grandson born after his grandfather's death should receive *bonorum possessio* in the name of an emancipated son, it will be necessary to hold that he brings his own property into hotchpot, although it cannot be held that he had property at the time of his grandfather's death, since he had not yet come into the world. Therefore, whether he has received an inheritance from his father or a legacy, he will be obliged to bring it into hotchpot. 1. It is to be understood, however, that the son has as his property what remains after the payment of debts. But if a debt is owed under a condition, he will not have to subtract the sum immediately, but will be obliged to bring it too into hotchpot; on the other hand, however, he will have to take an undertaking from a son-in-power, so that if the condition is fulfilled, he is protected in respect of the portion which he has contributed. 2. Concerning those things which have perished after his father's death without fault on the part of an emancipated son, the question is to whose detriment such loss should fall. Most authorities submit that those things which have perished without the intervention of fraud or fault are not included in the mass of property brought into hotchpot; and this is to be understood from the words in which the praetor orders property to be brought into hotchpot in accordance with the decision of a man of probity. Such a man, however, is not likely to judge that that should be contributed which the contributor does not have or has ceased to have without the intervention of fraud or fault. 3. Anything owed to an emancipated by stipulation under a condition, must also be brought into hotchpot. The situation is different in the case of a conditional legacy, because even if [the beneficiary] had been in power and the condition had been fulfilled after his father's death, he himself would have an action. 4. If the emancipated son has an action for insult, he should contribute

nothing; for he has a claim for redress rather than money; but if he has an action for theft, he will be obliged to make contribution.   5. If there are three emancipated sons and two in power, Gaius Cassius, in the seventh book of his *Civil Law*, submits that they should contribute thirds, with the result that the emancipated sons, because they do not make contributions to each other, are regarded as one person; and they should not make objection if they contribute more and receive less because it was in their power not to apply for *bonorum possessio*. Julian, too, follows Cassius's opinion. 6. If a grandson, child of an emancipated son, also being emancipated, where his father and grandfather have died at the same time, has received *bonorum possessio* [in respect of] both [estates], when each has left a *suus heres*, contribution can be settled in the following manner, so that if, for example, he had one hundred in property, he should contribute fifty to his uncle and fifty to his brother; for reckoning produces this result, whether we count in terms of persons or shares.   7. If two grandsons, children of a son, now dead, being emancipated, apply for *bonorum possessio* in respect of their grandfather's estate, the question is whether they should [each] contribute a half or a quarter of their property to their uncle. And it is more reasonable that [each] should contribute a half, because even if they had acquired, say, two hundred in the lifetime of their grandfather, when they were in his power, the son [the uncle] would take one hundred and the two brothers [the grandsons] one hundred through the disposal of the grandfather's estate.   8. If two emancipated sons have applied for *bonorum possessio*, and one has made contribution and the other has not, the latter's share should benefit only the son-in-power, not his emancipated brother too, since it is for the advantage of the son-in-power that he [the noncontributor] is denied the right to actions.   9. If, through indigence, the emancipated son is unable to give an undertaking, *bonorum possessio* is not to be transferred from him right away, but is to stay with him until he can find verbal guarantors, nevertheless, [in such a way] that an action is given to those in power with regard to property which is liable to deteriorate with delay and they themselves give a *cautio* that they will bring it into hotchpot if they have been given an undertaking.

3   JULIAN, *Digest, book 23:* The praetor does not promise *bonorum possessio* contrary to the terms of a will on condition that property is brought into hotchpot, but indicates what should occur, once *bonorum possessio* has been granted. Otherwise, the emancipated son will be at a great disadvantage if he were understood to receive *bonorum possessio* only where he had given an undertaking with regard to hotchpot; for if he himself had died in the meantime, he would leave nothing to his heir. Likewise, if his brother had died, he would not be admitted to *bonorum possessio*. What, then, is the position? It is to be understood that he takes *bonorum possessio*, and first he gives an undertaking; but if he has not given a *cautio*, the rule will be that the whole estate remains with the son-in-power.   1. An emancipated son takes issue with an *impubes* who declares himself to be a son and to have been in parental power; I ask whether the emancipated son should bring his own property into hotchpot in his favor. PAUL remarks: I submit that contribution should be made, a *cautio* having been demanded to the effect that should he fail in his claim, just as he yields up the estate, so he surrenders the property which has been brought into hotchpot.   2. JULIAN: Whenever *bonorum possessio* contrary to the terms of a will is granted, emancipated children should contribute their own property only to those who have been in parental power. It is often asked how this should be carried out; for if the property left by the father and that of the emancipated children is brought together into a common pool and equal portions are then taken from it, it will turn out that the emancipated children, too, benefit by the contribution that they themselves have made. Let us, therefore, see whether it is not most convenient for the emancipated children to take a quarter of their father's goods and a third of their own. Illustration will clarify my argument. Let us imagine that a father has left four hundred and two sons-in-power, two who are emancipated, one of which has one hundred, the other sixty, in property; the one who will have one hundred will take one hundred thirty-three and one third; the one who has contributed sixty, one hundred twenty, and thus, it will turn out that the advantage of hotchpot is reaped only by those who have remained in power.   3. Emancipated

children are required to unite their property with those who have been in power.
4. Wherefore just as a son-in-power receives his wife's dowry in advance, so an emancipated son, too, should keep it as if he were receiving it in advance. 5. If an emancipated son who has been passed over has given an undertaking with regard to
hotchpot, while he is considering his position, and has not applied for *bonorum possessio*, should his brother bring an action on the stipulation itself, he will be protected
by operation of law. But even if he has contributed money, he recovers it by *condictio*;
for if he neglects to apply for *bonorum possessio*, the heir will have no ground for
retaining the money. 6. A man who had two sons-in-power and a grandson of which
one was the father emancipated the son who was the father of the grandson; then the
son who had been emancipated produced a son, whom his grandfather adopted as a
son, and then died, either intestate or having passed over his emancipated son in his
will; it was asked what was the law concerning *bonorum possessio* and what concerning hotchpot respectively. I gave it as my opinion that three shares should be made of
the property in question, one of which belongs to the son who remained in power, the
second to the grandson adopted in place of a son, the third to the emancipated son and
grandson who has remained in power in such a way that his father should make contribution to him alone along with whom he receives *bonorum possessio*.

4 AFRICANUS, *Questions, book 4:* That an emancipated son is not obliged to bring into
hotchpot a dowry which he has provided in the name of his daughter, because a dowry
is not, as it is in the case of a mother's property, understood to form part of the property of the father from whom it has come.

5 ULPIAN, *Edict, book 79:* If a man has a son who is *sui juris* and a grandson in his
power of whom that son is the father, where the grandson receives *bonorum possessio*
in respect of his emancipated father's goods, it will accordingly have to be held that the
[grandfather] should give an undertaking with regard to bringing his own property
too into hotchpot and that he is in a similar position to an adoptive father; for the deified brothers have issued a rescript to the effect that a grandfather is compelled to
bring his property into hotchpot. In the same rescript, the following words have
clearly been added: "unless it happens that the grandfather has no wish to acquire any
benefit from this property and is prepared to release the grandson from power, so that
the full advantage of *bonorum possessio* may accrue to the emancipated [grandson].
For that reason a daughter born after her father's emancipation, who has become his
heir, will not be able to complain with justification," it says, "that she is thereby excluded from the advantage of hotchpot, since, whenever her grandfather dies, she is
capable of taking his property together with her brother." This reasoning cannot be
given in the case of an adoptive father, and yet, in that case, too, we shall give the
same ruling if he has emancipated the son in good faith. 1. But the stipulation for
contribution comes into operation when, being called upon to collate within some time
in which he could have made contribution, the emancipated son does not do so, especially in view of the fact that there is contained in the praetor's edict the provision that
contribution takes place in accordance with the decision of a man of probity. 2. Therefore, whether contribution has failed to take place at all or has been only partially
effected, this stipulation will take effect. 3. And whether a man fails to contribute in
conformity with this stipulation, or has acted fraudulently so as to avoid contributing,
whatever the value of the matter in question may be, judgment will be awarded
against him for an equivalent amount.

6 CELSUS, *Digest, book 10:* It is inquired whether a dowry provided by a paternal
grandfather should be restored after his death to the father of a daughter that has died
while married. The equity of the situation suggests that what my father has given on
my account for the sake of my daughter is in the same case as if I have given it myself, because the duty of a grandfather toward his granddaughter depends on the
duty of a father toward his son and because a father should give his daughter a dowry
for the same reason that a grandfather should give one to his granddaughter on
his son's behalf. What if the son has been disinherited by his father? In my view,

the same can be sensibly maintained in the case of a son who has been disinherited, nor is it an opinion unfavorable [to the son] that he takes from his father's property at least what was donated on his behalf.

7   CELSUS, *Digest, book 13:* If grandsons have succeeded to the position of a son, one share [of their grandfather's property] should be contributed in their favor, as they take one share in *bonorum possessio;* but they, too, must make their contributions as if all of them constituted one person.

8   PAPINIAN, *Questions, book 3:* Sometimes the praetor does not turn away one who changes his views and respects the deliberations of the man who changes his mind. As a result of which, some authorities have submitted that an emancipated son, who was unwilling to give an undertaking to his brothers in the matter of bringing his property into hotchpot, should later be given a hearing, if, after offering a *cautio*, he wished to exercise his right to *bonorum possessio*. Though it may be answered that one who has been unwilling to observe the procedure of *possessio* appears to have renounced *possessio;* but the opposite view is less harsh, especially when there is a dispute between brothers over a father's property. However, in my opinion, it should be made easier for him to gain admission, if he offers a *cautio* within the period for granting *possessio;* for a year after *bonorum possessio* has been granted, it is more difficult to excuse his voluntary delay in executing a *cautio*.

9   PAPINIAN, *Replies, book 5:* The emancipated son of a father who died intestate has received *bonorum possessio*. A grandson of whom this son is the father and who has been kept in the family will take half the estate with the addition of what he acquires from hotchpot. If the same grandson later receives *possessio* in respect of his father's goods, the latter dying intestate, he will be compelled to bring into hotchpot his own property in favor of a brother born after his father's emancipation and kept in the family.

10   SCAEVOLA, *Questions, book 5:* If a son-in-power, being instituted heir, accepts the inheritance, and, on his emancipated [brother's] petition for *bonorum possessio* contrary to the terms of a will, does not himself enter a claim, no contribution is to be made to him [by his brother], and so the edict runs. SCAEVOLA: But I prefer the view that just as he retains part of the estate in virtue of the fact that he was in a position to apply for *bonorum possessio*, so he should receive a contribution, seeing that he is in any case injured through the grant of *bonorum possessio*.

11   PAUL, *Replies, book 11:* Paul has given it as his opinion that an emancipated son is not required to contribute to a brother left in parental power property which ought to have been given to the [emancipated] son after his father's death, although he obtained it before it was due to him, since, after his father's death, he appears to hold it not by way of gift, but rather as a debt due to him.

12   PAUL, *Edict, book 41:* If a man has left a pregnant wife, and she has been put in possession in the name of her unborn child, the matter of hotchpot is meantime suspended. For before he is born, the child cannot be said to have been in the power of the deceased; but contribution will be made to him when he is born.

7

COLLATION OF A DOWRY

1   ULPIAN, *Edict, book 40:* Although the praetor compels a daughter to bring into hotchpot a dowry only in the case where she applies for *bonorum possessio*, nevertheless, even if she makes no application, she will be obliged to bring it into account, if at any point she meddles with her father's property. And the deified Pius has stated this in a rescript [addressed] to Ulpius Adrianus that even the [daughter] who has not applied for *bonorum possessio* may be compelled to bring her dowry into hotchpot by the arbitrator in an action for the division of the inheritance. 1. Where the dowry has been made the subject of a stipulation, whether the woman herself has in fact stipulated for it or the transaction has been made for her benefit, she will in both cases be obliged to bring it into hotchpot; but if the [benefit of the] stipulation has been

acquired by another, it is to be held that hotchpot does not take place. Even if the dowry has merely been promised, it will be subject to contribution.   2. If there are a grandson and granddaughter, being the children of the same son, and the granddaughter has been given a dowry, and there is another son who is not their father, the granddaughter is in a position of having to bring the whole dowry into hotchpot, but only to the advantage of her brother. But an emancipated granddaughter will bring into hotchpot her dowry and her property to the advantage of the grandson alone and not also for her uncle's benefit. 3. But if there is only a granddaughter and no grandson born to the same father, then contribution is made to the uncle and likewise to a grandson or granddaughter, being the child of another son.   4. Also in the case where there are two granddaughters, being the daughters of different sons, they will make contribution both to each other and to their uncle. If they have the same father, they will contribute only to each other.   5. When a dowry is brought into hotchpot, expenses necessarily incurred are subtracted, but others are not.   6. But if the marriage has already been dissolved and the husband is insolvent, the whole dowry will not have to be reckoned to the woman's account, but only what she can obtain, that is, the amount her husband is capable of paying.   7. If a father or stranger to the family has promised to provide a dowry on a condition, a *cautio* will be required to the effect that the woman will bring into hotchpot her dowry the moment she has received it.   8. A daughter who is heir to her father on intestacy should, in fact, bring her dowry into hotchpot, but she should in consequence free her brother from a promise of the dowry, to the extent of one half of the sum promised; for it is fairer for her to have received her whole dowry from her own property.   9. If an emancipated son who has received *bonorum possessio* contrary to the terms of a will has a daughter who already has a dowry, he should not bring her dowry into hotchpot, because it is not part of his property.

2   GAIUS, *Provincial Edict, book 14:* A daughter who has been given in adoption and instituted heir should thus, like an emancipated daughter, bring into hotchpot not only her own property but also the dowry which she will be able to hold as her own. If her adoptive father is still alive, he will have to make the contribution.

3   ULPIAN, *Disputations, book 4:* If a daughter has been instituted heir, she will not contribute by bringing her dowry into hotchpot. Wherefore, if the edictal procedure has been initiated by another and she has had to take *bonorum possessio* contrary to the terms of a will, it is to be held that since she is not prejudicing her brother, she is not obliged to bring her dowry into hotchpot; for what she had as a result of the disposition in her favor is converted into *bonorum possessio* contrary to the terms of a will. Obviously, if she had been instituted heir to a lesser share, and *bonorum possessio* contrary to the terms of a will conferred on her certain other things with the effect of increasing her portion, it will have to be held that she fulfills the requirements of hotchpot, unless possibly she has been satisfied with the portion left to her; for, in that case, it is to be held that entering, as she does, on her inheritance, in accordance with the disposition made by her parent, she should not have to bear the burden of contribution.

4   POMPONIUS, *Quintus Mucius, book 3:* If a father has promised a dowry for his daughter, and has subsequently left her a legacy, having disinherited her or even emancipated her and passed her over in his will, the daughter will take both the dowry as her own special property and the legacy.

5   PAPINIAN, *Replies, book 5:* An emancipated son who could have taken *bonorum possessio* contrary to the terms of a will, received *possessio* on his father's intestacy; and thus a daughter who remained in power and who had been instituted heir together with her [other] brother, who was member of the same family, repeating the mistake of her emancipated brother, received *possessio* on her father's intestacy. She will not be compelled to bring her dowry into hotchpot in favor of the brother appointed heir, since the claim for *possessio* in this case has been fruitless, and she retains the disposition made to her by her father of an equal share in the estate, that is, they all take thirds, and, by a fiction, the application for *bonorum possessio unde liberi* is assumed to have been one for *bonorum possessio* contrary to the terms of a will.   1. A daughter who, on the dissolution of her marriage, should have brought her dowry into hotchpot delayed doing so; the ruling of a man of probity will compel her to contribute interest on the dowry as well, since her emancipated brother contributes profits too, and the daughter is receiving profits on her part.

6 PAPINIAN, *Replies, book 6:* A father instituted his emancipated son as heir and disinherited his daughter, who, by bringing suit alleging an undutiful will, took away half the estate. I gave it as my opinion that the brother should not be compelled to bring his own property into hotchpot; for it was resolved that freedom [conferred on slaves] also took effect.

7 PAUL, *Replies, book 11:* And she will not bring her dowry into hotchpot in favor of her brothers when their claim as heirs is on a different legal basis.

8 PAPINIAN, *Replies, book 11:* A father gave his daughter on marriage certain property apart from her dowry and kept her in the family and appointed her co-heir with her brothers on condition that she should have brought into hotchpot the dowry and other gifts he gave her on marriage. When the daughter renounced her part in the estate and her brothers brought a *vindicatio* for the property which was not given as dowry, it was resolved that the defense of fraud obtained, since the father intended the daughter to take one or the other.

9 TRYPHONINUS, *Disputations, book 6:* It was a matter of debate whether, if a daughter, being *sua heres* to her father together with her brothers, refrains from meddling with the inheritance, being satisfied with her dowry, she is bound to bring the dowry into hotchpot. And the deified Marcus ruled in a rescript that she is not bound to do so when she renounces her share of her father's estate. Therefore, not only will a dowry already handed over remain with the husband but also one that has been promised will be exacted from the brothers, and is treated as a debt; for she has taken no part of her father's estate.

8

THE JOINING OF HIS CHILDREN
WITH AN EMANCIPATED SON

1 ULPIAN, *Edict, book 40:* If any of those to whom the praetor promises *bonorum possessio* was not in parental power at the time of the testator's death, if the estate shall belong to them in their own name and they have not been deservedly disinherited, *bonorum possessio* is given to [an emancipated son] and the children he had in his family of that share which would belong to him if he had remained in power throughout in such a way that [he takes] half that share and his children the other half, provided that he brings his own property into hotchpot in their favor. 1. This edict is indeed most equitable in that the emancipated son alone does not come into the estate and exclude grandsons in power, nor can the grandsons, in virtue of being in power, hinder their father's claim. 2. And a son given in adoption and instituted heir falls within this edict, so that a grandson in the power of his natural grandfather is joined with him. But a grandson is also joined with his emancipated father, whether his father has been passed over in the will or instituted heir. And there will be this difference between an adopted and an emancipated son, that [the grandson] is not joined with a son given in adoption unless the latter has been instituted heir, and the edictal procedure has been initiated by a third party, but he is joined with an emancipated son, whether the latter has been instituted heir or passed over. 3. In the case where a son-in-power has been instituted heir in respect of two thirds and an emancipated son in respect of one third, Julian states that a grandson who has been passed over, and has sought *bonorum possessio* contrary to the terms of a will, will take a sixth from his uncle and a twelfth from his father. 4. If a father who has been emancipated has been disinherited and the grandsons of whom he is the father had been kept in power and have been passed over, the grandsons are admitted; for it is illogical, when they are joined with a father who has been passed over, for them to be excluded if he has been instituted heir or disinherited. 5. But if their uncle, who was in power, has been passed over, and their father disinherited, the grandsons should be admitted; for their father, being disinherited, is treated as if he were dead. 6. If a father who has stayed in

power has been disinherited or instituted heir, Scaevola states that the grandson of whom he is the father, whether he stays in power or has been emancipated, is not called to succession to his grandfather's property, nor should he be so called; for the interests of a grandson are to be considered whenever he has been kept in power after his father's emancipation. Children, therefore, should be in the family in order for this section to come into operation, that is to say, the family of the man in respect of whose estate *bonorum possessio* is being sought. But if a *postumus* has been born to an emancipated son and the child was conceived before the emancipation took place, the same ruling will apply. 7. For the praetor does not call all children together, but by degrees, that is, those who are *sui*, namely grandchildren, if there are any, if not, those who occupy a lower degree; and we shall not mingle the degrees. Obviously, if there is a grandson, who is the child of an emancipated son, and a great-grandson, the child of another grandson of the testator, it will have to be held that both are to be joined with [the emancipated son]; for both have succeeded in place of *sui* [*heredes*]. 8. If a grandson has returned [from captivity] by the right of *postliminium*, it is to be held that he is joined with his emancipated father. 9. A father had two sons in power; he emancipated one and adopted the grandson, of whom the latter was the father, as a son and died, having passed over his emancipated son in his will. Julian says that aid should be given to the grandson adopted as a son, so that as a son he may take the share which he would have had even if he had been adopted as a stranger to the family. Thus, it will come about, he says, that the son who was in power [takes] a third, the grandson adopted as a son a second third, while the emancipated son shares the final third with the other grandson who had been kept in power. For the grandson adopted as a son should not take less than if he had been adopted by a stranger to the family. 10. It is of no importance how great a share of the estate belongs to the grandson or whether [he takes] only a very modest share; for even if it is a modest one, nevertheless, we shall hold that this part of the edict comes into play. 11. The estate is divided between the son himself and his children in such a fashion that he himself takes a half and his children take a half. Accordingly, imagine that there is only one emancipated son and two grandchildren in power, and no one else who is numbered among the children. The emancipated son will take a half share of the estate and the two grandchildren the other half, namely a quarter each. But if there is another son besides, it will come about that the son who is not the father of the grandchildren will take one half share in the estate, the other son a half together with his sons in such a manner that he himself takes a quarter and a quarter is divided between his children. But if both sons have been emancipated and each has descendants, it will come about that each shares a half with his descendants in such a fashion that the sons themselves take quarters and the grandchildren the residuary quarters; and if one son has two sons, the other three, one quarter is split into two parts, the other into three. 12. If any of the grandchildren has neglected to take his share, it will turn out that it belongs not to his father, but rather to his brother. But if all the grandchildren forgo their shares, nothing will fall to their uncle by way of accrual but only to their father; but if the father, too, has renounced his share, then it will fall to the uncle by way of accrual. 13. If the emancipated son has none of his descendants in their grandfather's power, he will make contribution to his brothers; but if there are grandchildren, the praetor intended him to contribute only to his sons who are in power, and rightly so, because, in entering into *bonorum possessio*, he prejudices them alone. 14. Now let us see how much he contributes to them. When the emancipated son makes contribution to his brothers, he in fact always deducts an equal share for himself. Does he deduct an equal portion in this case too, or in fact because he has a half share in *bonorum possessio* does he contribute a half share too of his own property? And I submit that he contributes only a half share of his goods to them; for if one son has been emancipated and another kept in power, the emancipated son will contribute only one share to the two grandchildren in question and will give one share to their uncle who remained in power and will take a third share for himself. What is contributed to grandchildren by an emancipated uncle will not be contributed by them to their father; for it comes to them not from their grandfather's property, but is an accession to them on account of the property. 15. Therefore, it will come about that if an emancipated father has one hundred in his property, he deducts fifty for himself and contributes the remaining fifty to all the grandchildren, that is, to his own sons, or if the emancipated son has only one child who is a grandson and two great-grandsons descended from another grandson, he divides the fifty so that the grandson takes twenty-five and the great-grandsons descended from another grandson twenty-five together; for both have one share in *bonorum possessio*. 16. Where there is a son-in-power and another son has been emancipated, there is one grandson in power, child of a deceased son, and another grandchild who has been emancipated, Scaevola nicely considers the question of how much the emancipated uncle brings into hotchpot in favor of the grandchildren and how much in favor of his brother. And he says it can be held that he divides his property into three parts: one for himself, one to be contributed to his brother, and one to the grandchildren, although they are in a position to take less than their uncle from their grandfather's estate, since their father takes with them; and this is a valid opinion. 17. But even if there are two grandchildren descended from the same son and they have been emancipated, and a great-grandson, of whom one is the father, who remained in the power of the testator, one grandchild will take one share, the other a second together with his son. But even if there are a grandchild and two great-grandchildren descended from another grandchild now deceased, one of the great-grandchildren, being emancipated, makes a contribution only to his brother, or, if his brother is dead, only to his uncle, but not to his great-uncle as well.

2 PAUL, *Edict, book 41:* The praetor has made no provision in this part of the edict for the grandchild to pay legacies to the persons specifically excepted. But an earlier dictum can be applied to this case too; for it is absurd for his father in fact to pay his legacies, while he himself takes more, since they are called to the same share on the same condition.

3 MARCELLUS, *Digest, book 9:* A man had two sons and emancipated one, but kept a grandson, of whom the latter was the father in power; the emancipated son acquired [another] son, and was disinherited by his father; I ask: Since the emancipated son's brother, himself likewise emancipated, has been passed over and the grandchildren descended from the emancipated son have been instituted heirs by their grandfather, what is the law concerning *bonorum possessio*? And what difference does it make, if we suppose that the emancipated son, too, who was father of the grandchildren, was passed over? I have given it as my opinion that if the testator has emancipated his son, while keeping in his power the grandson of whom that son is the father, and the emancipated son has produced a son and both grandchildren have been instituted heirs, while their father has been disinherited, and another son has been passed over, only the son that has been passed over will be able to apply for *bonorum possessio* contrary to the terms of a will; for a son that has been disinherited impedes the claims of his sons begotten after emancipation. But *bonorum possessio* ought to be given to the grandson kept in power since, if his emancipated father had been passed over, he could take *bonorum possessio* together with him under this head of the edict, which was introduced by Julian, that is, in accordance with the new section; and he should be in no worse position because his father has been disinherited. And the benefit of the section will have to be accorded him in the case where he, too, has been passed over. But the position of his brother, who was born after his father's emancipation, is different; nevertheless, an equal share in the estate is to be preserved to him too, just as the Emperor Antoninus has also ruled in a rescript respecting a grandson born of a daughter.

4 MODESTINUS, *Encyclopaedia, book 6:* A father emancipated his son while keeping in power the grandchildren of whom that son was the father; the emancipated son had other children and later died. It was resolved that those who stayed in their grandfather's power took *bonorum possessio* [of their father's property] by decree along with those born after the emancipation, always providing that if the grandfather wishes to acquire [part of the estate] for himself, he is to bring his own property into hotchpot or emancipate the grandchildren, so that they obtain the advantage from their father's estate for themselves; and the divine Marcus has so ruled in a rescript.

5 MODESTINUS, *Distinctions, book 6:* If a grandson has been disinherited but has been appointed heir to his grandfather's heir, then his father who has been emancipated, being passed over the will, takes *bonorum possessio* contrary to the terms of a will in respect of

his father's estate, the grandson will not be able to be joined with his father, but will be excluded as a stranger, because he was not heir to his grandfather in his own name.

6 SCAEVOLA, *Questions, book 5:* If a man with a son-in-power adopts a stranger to the family as a grandson, as if his son were the latter's father and later emancipates the son, this grandson will not be joined with the emancipated son, because he has ceased to rank as one of the children of the emancipated son.

7 TRYPHONINUS, *Disputations, book 16:* If, after a son's emancipation, a grandson were born to him, a share will have to be preserved to him, but let us see how great a share. For imagine that this grandson has been made co-heir along with his uncle who was appointed heir, but that his father, who has been passed over in the will, has received *bonorum possessio* contrary to the terms of a will. Insofar as the praetor's edict is concerned, the property will be divided into halves; but now, after the constitution of the divine Pius, if a share is preserved to the grandson, should an equal portion or a fourth be reserved to him? For if he had been born in his grandfather's power, he used to be joined with his father to the extent of a single share. And let us suppose that there is another grandson, of whom the same son is the father, in his grandfather's family; two [grandchildren] would have been in a position to take a quarter, on their father's acquiring *bonorum possessio* contrary to the terms of a will, if they had been in their grandfather's power; is the one who was not kept in the family now to be protected, therefore, to the extent of one eighth? And from whom will the share which is to pass to the grandson in question be taken, from his father alone or also from his uncle? I submit that it is to be taken from his uncle too; for had a legacy been left to the same grandson, he would pay it.

9

PLACING AN UNBORN CHILD IN POSSESSION AND HIS CURATOR

1 ULPIAN, *Edict, book 41:* Just as the praetor has taken care of those children who are among the living, so, in view of the prospect of their birth, he has not neglected those yet unborn. For he has protected them under this section of the edict also, whereby he places an unborn child in possession instead of granting him *bonorum possessio* contrary to the terms of a will.   1. It is necessary that the woman be actually pregnant; her word to that effect is not enough. Therefore, a grant of *bonorum possessio* does not obtain, unless she was genuinely pregnant, both at the time of death and at the time when she seeks to be placed in possession.   2. In these circumstances, the unborn child is always placed in possession, if he has not been disinherited and if the child that will be born will rank among the *sui heredes*. But even if it is uncertain, but may by some event come about that the child who is born will be *suus*, we shall put the unborn child into possession. For it is more just that expense should even sometimes be incurred in vain than that maintenance should ever be refused him that is in a position to be owner of the property in some event.   3. Wherefore, even if he has been disinherited in the following manner, "if one son shall be born to me, let him be disinherited," because a daughter can be born or several sons or boy and girl twins, the unborn child will be placed in possession. For in view of the uncertainty of the child to be born, it is preferable to maintain even a child who has been disinherited than to allow one who has not been [disinherited] to starve, and the withdrawal [of funds from the estate] should be ratified, even though a child is born who is rejected.   4. The same will have to be held in the case where a woman who was in possession had miscarried.   5. But, likewise, if a *postumus* has been disinherited under a condition, while the condition is in suspense, we allow the view of Pedius who submits that the unborn child should be put in possession, because, where there is uncertainty, it is more expedient for the unborn child to be maintained.   6. If the unborn child has been disinherited in respect of the instituted heirs and passed over in that of the substitute heirs, Marcellus holds that he cannot be placed in possession as long as the instituted heirs are alive, because he has

been disinherited, which is true. 7. But, on the other hand, if the unborn child has been passed over in respect of the instituted heirs and disinherited in respect of the substitute heirs, he is to be placed in possession if the instituted heirs are living; but if they are not alive, he holds that he is not to be put in possession, because the estate has devolved on the degree in respect of which he was disinherited. 8. If a son has been made prisoner by the enemy, his pregnant wife is to be put in possession of her father-in-law's property; for, in some event, there is a prospect of her child being among the *sui heredes*, for example, if his father dies while in enemy hands. 9. But even if a man had disinherited an unborn child, "let the child born to me within three months of my death be disinherited" or "the child born to me after three months," the unborn child will in any case be put in possession, because in some event he is in a position to be *suus heres*, and, clearly, it will be the praetor's duty to be more favorably disposed in this direction, lest the child in prospect should perish before birth. 10. But the praetor most properly has nowhere referred to a wife, because it is possible that the woman who declares herself pregnant by him was not a wife at the time of death. 11. An unborn child of an emancipated son is also admitted to possession. Whence the question is raised by Julian in the twenty-seventh book of his *Digest*, if a man, whose wife is already pregnant, has been emancipated and if he had subsequently died and his father has also died, whether the unborn child can be put in possession of the estate of his emancipated father. And he has most correctly written that there is no reason why an unborn child whom the edict admits should be turned away. For it is most just that the interests of the offspring be consulted, who, when born, is in a position to receive *bonorum possessio*. But even if his grandfather were alive, we shall admit the unborn child in the same manner. 12. If a son, who had been given in adoption, has died leaving a pregnant wife, then subsequently, his adoptive father has died, the unborn child will be put in possession of the estate of his adoptive grandfather. But let us see whether he will also be put in possession of the property of [his natural grandfather], who had given his son in adoption. And if the *postumus* grandson in question has been instituted heir by his natural grandfather, he will be put in possession, because, if no one else is numbered among the children, *bonorum possessio* according to will can be given to him when he is born, or if there are children who have been passed over, he can also obtain *bonorum possessio* contrary to will along with them. 13. If a father has emancipated his son while his daughter-in-law is pregnant, the unborn child should not be totally excluded; for, when born, he is normally joined with his father in accordance with the new edict. And in those cases where a child is joined with his father, an unborn child is usually to be admitted to possession. 14. If a woman that wishes to go into possession is alleged not to be, or have been, a wife or daughter-in-law, or not to be pregnant by the testator [or his son as the case may be], the praetor issues a decree on the pattern of the Carbonian Edict. And the deified Hadrian addressed a rescript to Claudius Proculus, the praetor, couched in the following terms: namely, that he should hear the case according to summary procedure, and if there shall appear to be clear proof of litigation in bad faith on the part of the woman who desires to be put in possession in the name of her unborn child, he should make no new decree; if there shall be room for doubt in the matter, he should take care not to prejudice the claims of the child she is carrying, but the unborn child ought to be put in possession. And so it is clear that unless the woman is plainly litigating in bad faith, she should elect [to obtain] a decree; and where there shall quite justifiably be room for doubt whether she is pregnant by the testator [or his son as the case may be], she is to be protected by a decree, lest her offspring's claims be prejudiced. The same ruling applies if there is dispute about the woman's status. 15. And, in general, for the reasons for which the praetor has been accustomed to award Carbonian *bonorum possessio* to a child already born, we have no doubt that he ought to aid an unborn child too, and the more readily, because the latter has a better case than the child already born. For the unborn child is favored so that he shall see the light of day, the boy already born so that he may be introduced into the family; for the unborn child of which we are speaking is to be maintained, who is born if not for the advantage of the parent alone, whose child he is said to be, yet also for that of the state. 16. If a man whose first wife is pregnant later marries another and has rendered her pregnant and has died, the edict will cover both wives, providing, of course, no one disputes the facts or accuses the woman of litigation in bad faith. 17. But whenever an unborn child is put in posses-

instituted as heir, the unborn child is only put in possession, if his mother cannot be maintained from any other source, in case we may perhaps appear to have denied aliment to the child who, when born, is in a position to be *bonorum possessor*.

7 ULPIAN, *Edict, book 47:* Whenever someone is admitted [to *bonorum possessio*] on intestacy, the unborn child is also admitted, if, of course, the unborn child has been in such a relationship that if he were of the living, he could apply for *bonorum possessio*; the effect is that the unborn child is treated as if already born in all parts of the edict. 1. Sometimes the unborn child should not be put in possession indiscriminately, but only after examination of his case, if there is anyone who disputes his claim. But this will apply only where the unborn child is being admitted along with [the testator's other] children. However, if he is put into possession *unde legitimi*, or under some other section of the edict, it is to be held that investigation of his case is unnecessary, for it is not equitable for an unborn child to be maintained by another up to the age of puberty, because the dispute regarding his claim has been deferred to this time. But certainly it is settled that all disputes involving a dispute of status, as it were, should be deferred to the time of puberty, but not [in such a way] that the dispute regarding status is deferred with the child in possession, but without [concurrent] possession. 2. But although the praetor puts the unborn child into possession with those to whom he has awarded possession, yet, even if he is alone, the unborn child will be admitted to *bonorum possessio*.

8 PAUL, *Adultery, book 1:* If a woman has been put in possession in the name of an unborn child, the deified Hadrian has ruled in a rescript to Calpurnius Flaccus that accusation of adultery should be postponed, lest the child born be prejudiced.

9 ULPIAN, *Sabinus, book 15:* When an unborn child is put in possession, what has been spent from the estate on its maintenance is subtracted as a debt.

10 PAUL, *Questions, book 7:* A *postumus* born at any time, provided he shall have been conceived by the time of the testator's death, can claim *bonorum possessio*; for the praetor also puts an unborn child into possession of the estate in accordance with all sections of the edict, though naturally he would not do so, if he were not intending to award *bonorum possessio* to him once born.

10

THE CARBONIAN EDICT

1 ULPIAN, *Edict, book 41:* Where there is a dispute with anyone as to whether he is one of the children, and he is an *impubes*, when the case has been investigated [by the praetor], *bonorum possessio* is given, just as if there were no dispute about the matter, and once the case has been so investigated, the hearing by the judge is deferred until the time of puberty. 1. If security has not been given to the person who raises the dispute in respect of the *pupillus*, the praetor orders him to be put into possession of the property in question at the same time. 2. Not only males, but females too, provided that they are descendants through the male line, will have the advantage of the Carbonian Edict. 3. And, in general, we hold that the Carbonian Edict applies precisely to those to whom *bonorum possessio* contrary to the terms of a will applies, but not to those who are barred from *bonorum possessio* contrary to the terms of a will. 4. If a child sustains an objection, not from a third party, but from his father himself, to the effect that he is not one of the children, for instance, a grandson, who says that he was kept in his grandfather's power, [is challenged] by his emancipated father with whom he wishes to be joined, should the matter be deferred? It is more reasonable that the matter be deferred; for it makes little difference who raises the objection against him, since, even if the testator has asserted that he is not one of the children, but has not disinherited him by will, the Carbonian Edict may issue. 5. But even where someone is said not only not to be of the children but also is alleged to be a slave, born, perhaps, of a female slave, Julian has observed that the Carbonian Edict can still issue; the deified Pius has also made this ruling in a rescript; for even greater attention must be paid to the interests of those who are threatened with greater risk. For, if some other rule is observed, a method will have been discovered whereby every

instituted as heir, the unborn child is only put in possession, if his mother cannot be maintained from any other source, in case we may perhaps appear to have denied aliment to the child who, when born, is in a position to be *bonorum possessor*.

7   ULPIAN, *Edict, book 47:* Whenever someone is admitted [to *bonorum possessio*] on intestacy, the unborn child is also admitted, if, of course, the unborn child has been in such a relationship that if he were of the living, he could apply for *bonorum possessio*; the effect is that the unborn child is treated as if already born in all parts of the edict.   1. Sometimes the unborn child should not be put in possession indiscriminately, but only after examination of his case, if there is anyone who disputes his claim. But this will apply only where the unborn child is being admitted along with [the testator's other] children. However, if he is put into possession *unde legitimi*, or under some other section of the edict, it is to be held that investigation of his case is unnecessary, for it is not equitable for an unborn child to be maintained by another up to the age of puberty, because the dispute regarding his claim has been deferred to this time. But certainly it is settled that all disputes involving a dispute of status, as it were, should be deferred to the time of puberty, but not [in such a way] that the dispute regarding status is deferred with the child in possession, but without [concurrent] possession.   2. But although the praetor puts the unborn child into possession with those to whom he has awarded possession, yet, even if he is alone, the unborn child will be admitted to *bonorum possessio*.

8   PAUL, *Adultery, book 1:* If a woman has been put in possession in the name of an unborn child, the deified Hadrian has ruled in a rescript to Calpurnius Flaccus that accusation of adultery should be postponed, lest the child born be prejudiced.

9   ULPIAN, *Sabinus, book 15:* When an unborn child is put in possession, what has been spent from the estate on its maintenance is subtracted as a debt.

10   PAUL, *Questions, book 7:* A *postumus* born at any time, provided he shall have been conceived by the time of the testator's death, can claim *bonorum possessio*; for the praetor also puts an unborn child into possession of the estate in accordance with all sections of the edict, though naturally he would not do so, if he were not intending to award *bonorum possessio* to him once born.

10

THE CARBONIAN EDICT

1   ULPIAN, *Edict, book 41:* Where there is a dispute with anyone as to whether he is one of the children, and he is an *impubes*, when the case has been investigated [by the praetor], *bonorum possessio* is given, just as if there were no dispute about the matter, and once the case has been so investigated, the hearing by the judge is deferred until the time of puberty.   1. If security has not been given to the person who raises the dispute in respect of the *pupillus*, the praetor orders him to be put into possession of the property in question at the same time.   2. Not only males, but females too, provided that they are descendants through the male line, will have the advantage of the Carbonian Edict.   3. And, in general, we hold that the Carbonian Edict applies precisely to those to whom *bonorum possessio* contrary to the terms of a will applies, but not to those who are barred from *bonorum possessio* contrary to the terms of a will.   4. If a child sustains an objection, not from a third party, but from his father himself, to the effect that he is not one of the children, for instance, a grandson, who says that he was kept in his grandfather's power, [is challenged] by his emancipated father with whom he wishes to be joined, should the matter be deferred? It is more reasonable that the matter be deferred; for it makes little difference who raises the objection against him, since, even if the testator has asserted that he is not one of the children, but has not disinherited him by will, the Carbonian Edict may issue.   5. But even where someone is said not only not to be of the children but also is alleged to be a slave, born, perhaps, of a female slave, Julian has observed that the Carbonian Edict can still issue; the deified Pius has also made this ruling in a rescript; for even greater attention must be paid to the interests of those who are threatened with greater risk. For, if some other rule is observed, a method will have been discovered whereby every

presumptuous rogue may inflict substantial damage on an *impubes*, insofar as he compounds both more and more serious falsities about him. 6. But even if the deceased himself is alleged to be a slave, the same will have to be maintained. 7. But even if the imperial treasury raises an objection to the *impubes*, the Carbonian Edict can issue. 8. Pomponius, in the seventy-ninth book of his *Edict*, has observed that when a son has been appointed heir or disinherited, the Carbonian Edict does not apply, even if he is alleged not to be a son, because either he has *bonorum possessio* as heir, even if he is not a son, or he is barred as having been disinherited, even though he appears to be a son, unless, he says, a *postumus* happens to have been instituted heir, and, when born, is alleged not to be a son, but is said to be supposititious, in which case he is to be awarded *bonorum possessio* of that share only in respect of which he has been instituted. 9. The same authority remarks that when a certain man disinherited his son on the ground of his allegation that the child was conceived in adultery, because this objection was raised against him as to whether he was one of the children, *bonorum possessio* was open to him in accordance with this section of the Edict, whereas, if he had been disinherited without explanation, he would not have *bonorum possessio*. And the same is true also if the following has been written: "Let whoever he is who says he is my son be disinherited" because he has not disinherited a son. 10. If someone has instituted his son in respect of a very small share as follows, "let him who has been born of her be heir," not as if he were talking about his own son, then the man in question argues that his father has died intestate and that he is *suus heres*, it makes a difference whether the co-heirs deny that he is a son or whether they in fact argue that the will is valid. If they argue that the will is valid, the dispute is not to be deferred, and the Carbonian Edict does not apply; but if they deny that he is a son and allege that the estate belongs to them rather as being brothers and sisters, *bonorum possessio* is to be given to the *impubes*, and the dispute is deferred until he reaches puberty. 11. If the mother is accused of introducing a supposititious child, the question is whether the inquiry should be deferred on account of the status of the child. And if the status of the *pupillus* is called into doubt, the inquiry should be deferred until time of puberty for fear that he may not be properly represented; but when the mother is accused and will at any rate defend the case with her credibility unimpaired, and the more vigorously if no long time has elapsed, there is no doubt that the investigation should proceed, and after it has been concluded, if it has appeared that the child is supposititious, actions in respect of the estate are to be denied him, and the whole matter is to be treated just as if he had not been appointed heir.

2 MARCIAN, *Institutes, book 14:* Even though the woman who is alleged to have faked the birth has died, nevertheless, if there are accomplices to the crime, the matter is to be heard at once. But if there is no one who can be punished, because all accessories to the deed have perhaps died, investigation is to be deferred until the time of puberty according to the Carbonian Edict.

3 ULPIAN, *Edict, book 41:* The Carbonian Edict has been adapted to *bonorum possessio* contrary to the terms of a will and on intestacy, although it may in certain instances appear to be the requisite Edict in possession according to the terms of a will, for example, if the head of a household has instituted his heir as follows: "Let my *postumus* be heir" or "let my *postuma* be heir," and the truth of what has been written in the will is denied. 1. And when a question of *fideicommissa* or legacies is involved, the case may be postponed until the time of puberty; for this ruling has been given by the deified Pius to Claudius Hadrianus in a rescript. 2. Although it is certain that *bonorum possessio* is not promised to the appointed heir in accordance with the Carbonian Edict, nevertheless, it is far from doubt that the investigation of status should be deferred until the time of puberty. Therefore, if, in fact, a dispute arises concerning the father's property and at the same time questions of status are also involved, this Edict will apply; but if the dispute concerns status alone, the investigation will be put off until the time of puberty, but not as a result of the Carbonian Edict, but in accordance with constitutions [on the subject]. 3. The Carbonian Edict is of no help to anyone over the age of puberty, even though he is less than twenty-five years old. But even if, being beyond puberty, he has insinuated himself as though he were still an

impubes and has received *bonorum possessio*, it will have to be held that he has effected nothing; for even if he were an *impubes*, the benefit of *bonorum possessio* would terminate as soon as he became adult. 4. The investigation of the case [by the praetor] is directed to the point that if those who were applying for *bonorum possessio* for those [who are still] infants, should clearly appear to be litigating in bad faith, *bonorum possessio* would not be granted. Therefore, when *bonorum possessio* is sought in accordance with the Carbonian Edict, the praetor ought summarily to investigate the case, and if, in fact, he has found an open and shut case and it is clearly proved that the child is not a son, he should deny him *bonorum possessio* of the Carbonian variety. But where he has found the case ambiguous, that is, even moderately inclined in the child's favor, so that it is not clear that he is plainly not a son, he will award him *bonorum possessio* of the Carbonian type. 5. But there are two investigations of the case, one for the award of Carbonian *possessio*, which has the advantage that the *impubes* receives *possessio*, just as if he were not the object of any dispute, the other involving the question whether the case should be postponed until the time of puberty or whether it should be dealt with immediately. But the praetor must investigate most carefully whether it is to the advantage of the *pupillus* that the case should be dealt with immediately or rather deferred until the time of puberty, and he should principally examine the cognate relations, the mother, and tutors of the *pupillus* upon the point. Suppose that there are certain witnesses, who, in the event that the dispute is deferred, shall either change their view or die, or who will not carry the same conviction on account of lapse of time; or suppose that the midwife or the female slaves who can make known the truth in respect of the birth are elderly; or suppose that there are documents sufficiently adequate for a favorable verdict or certain other proofs, so that the *pupillus* will rather suffer loss from the fact that the hearing is postponed rather than gain from the fact that it is not immediately discharged; suppose that the *pupillus* cannot give security and that if those who are raising the dispute about the estate have been admitted to possession, they can effect a multitude of withdrawals, institute many changes, and engage in numerous machinations; [in these circumstances], it will be the act of a stupid or unjust praetor to postpone the matter until puberty, thus inflicting the greatest disadvantage on the party whose interests it is his intention to consult. The deified Hadrian has also given the following ruling in a rescript: "As to the fact that the matter is usually postponed until the time of puberty, such postponement is made in the interests of *pupilli*, lest they are at risk in the matter of status, before they can protect themselves. However, if they have suitable persons to defend them and such a clear-cut case that it is in their interests for it to be heard promptly and their tutors wish to go to trial, a procedure devised in their favor should not be observed to the disadvantage of the *pupilli*, and their status should not be left in uncertainty when it can be free from doubt." 6. If the mother of an *impubes*, being accused of procuring a supposititious birth, has won her case, it may be that the question of status will still remain unresolved; for instance, if it is said that the child was not the deceased's child or that, in fact, he was, but was born out of wedlock. 7. If the person who raised the issue of status against the son and declared that he alone was a son [of the testator] has died and his mother has been appointed his heir, if she raises the same issue as her son did against the *impubes*, who declares that he was a child by another woman, namely that she denies that he is a son [and argues] for that reason that the whole estate should belong to her in the name of her deceased son, Julian says that the case is deferred until the time of puberty, because it is of no importance whether the person raising the issue does so in his own name or as heir to another. Obviously, if the mother agrees that [the *impubes*] too is a son of the deceased, and for that reason is claiming only a half share of the inheritance from the father's estate for herself, the hearing will not have to be deferred until the time of puberty; for the issue with the *impubes* does not concern his father's, but his brother's, property. 8. In the same place, Julian raises the question: If two *impuberes* are the subject of a dispute concerning their status, and one has reached puberty, should one wait for the other, too, to arrive at puberty, namely, so that thus in fact the question concerning the status of both may be dealt with in such a way that the *impubes* is not in any way prejudiced through the one who has reached puberty? 9. It makes little difference whether the *impubes* whose status is at issue is petitioner or *possessor*; for whether he is in possession or entering suit, the matter is deferred until the time of puberty. 10. If two *impuberes* each dispute the status of the other, it makes a difference whether each says that he is the only son or [if one maintains so and the other declares that] he too is a son. For if [one] says that he is the only son, it is to be held that the issue is to be postponed until such time as both reach puberty, whether he is petitioner or *possessor*. But if one says that he is the only son and the other likewise maintains that he too is a son, if the one that says that he is the only son has reached maturity, the dispute should still be deferred on account of the fact that the other, who also claims to be a son, is still a child, but only with reference to part [of the estate] and not to the whole. For in any case, there is no dispute concerning part of it. But if the one that alleges that he too is a son has reached maturity, and the one that says he is the only son is an *impubes*, the issue is not postponed; for the *impubes* is not the subject of the dispute but the cause of it, since, when the adult declares that he too is a son, he does not deny that the other is a son.   11. If a man is manumitted and bidden to be heir and raises the issue of status against an *impubes*, who is said to be a son and to have broken his father's will, Julian says that both the hearing respecting the estate and that concerning the issue of free- dom are to be postponed until the time of puberty; for neither can be resolved in such a manner that the question of the status of the one that argues that he is a son is not prejudged. Other questions too concerning freedom that depend on the will are post- poned until the time of puberty.   12. Whenever an *impubes* claiming to be a son of the deceased appears and debtors deny that he is a son of the deceased and allege that the estate belongs to an agnate who will perhaps be abroad, the child will need to avail himself of the Carbonian Edict. But the interests of the absentee will have to be pro- tected, so that a *cautio* is executed.   13. But the praetors are eager to establish as possessor him who has been put in possession in accordance with the Carbonian Edict. But if he has begun to sue for the estate or for individual objects, as being *bonorum possessor* in virtue of the Carbonian Edict, Julian most properly observes in the twenty-fourth book of his *Digest* that he is to be rebutted by the defense [of fraud]; for he should be satisfied with the privilege that the praetor has bestowed in temporarily establishing him as *possessor*. If, therefore, he wants to sue for the estate or for indi- vidual objects, let him do so, he says, by a straightforward action in the quality of heir, so that it may be decided on the basis of that action whether he is heir *qua* one of the children, lest the presumption in his favor conferred by Carbonian *bonorum possessio* should be a source of prejudice to his opponents; and this view is both reasonable and equitable.   14. However, this form of *possessio* is awarded within a year, just as are the usual kinds, too, which are awarded to children within a year.   15. But one who claims to be a son will not only have to take Carbonian *possessio* but also claim the usual sort.   16. But each type of *bonorum possessio* has a separate limitation period. In the case of the usual sort, [time runs] from the point when [the claimant] knows his father has died and has had the opportunity of seeking *bonorum possessio*, but in the case of Carbonian [*possessio*] from the time when he realized that an issue was being raised against him.

4   JULIAN, *Digest, book 24:* For that reason, if he has not sought *bonorum possessio* in accordance with the first part of the Edict, he will sometimes be able to receive *bonorum possessio* in accordance with the following part of the Edict on the pattern of the Carbonian Edict, at others he will not be able to. For if an issue has been raised against him immediately after his father's death on the question of whether he can receive *bonorum possessio* along with the children, the year will appear to have elapsed at the same time with reference to a case involving either Edict; but if he has become aware that an issue is being set in motion against him after an interval of time, he will be able, even if the time within which he had accepted *bonorum possessio* in accordance with the first part has elapsed, to apply for *bonorum possessio* in accor- dance with the second part. When he has received it, he will always use possessory actions; but if judgment has been awarded against him after puberty, such actions will be denied him.

5   ULPIAN, *Edict, book 41:* But if the person raising the issue against the *impubes* is one of the children, it will come about that whether the one whose status is in dispute gives security or not, nevertheless, he will be admitted to possession together with the other.   1. If the *impubes* offers no defense and his opponent has thereby also been put in possession, who will engage in actions connected with the management of the estate? And Julian says in the twenty-fourth book of his *Digest* that a *curator* should be appointed to take care of everything and engage in [such] actions. Finally, he ob- serves that he who has been put in possession together with the *impubes* may also bring actions against the *curator* and is not to be prevented from so doing; for no

prejudice attaches to the estate thereby; for if he had given security, he would properly bring a case against the *pupillus* himself.   2. Whenever the *impubes* does not
offer security, his opponent is put into possession, whether he gives security or not. If
the opponent wants the administration to be entrusted to him, he should give security
to the *pupillus*; however, if he does not, a *curator* ought to be appointed to administer
the estate. But if the opponent has given security, he should sell off perishable or
wasting assets; likewise, he should recover money owed by debtors that will be freed
from their obligation after the expiry of the limitation period; the rest of the estate he
will hold together with the *pupillus*.   3. Let us see whether one who has been put in
possession in accordance with the Carbonian Edict can draw maintenance from the
estate. And if, in fact, an *impubes* has given security, whether the presiding officer of
the court has so ordered or not, he draws maintenance and makes restitution less this
amount to the heir suing for the estate. But if he has not been in a position to give
security and does not appear to be able to maintain himself in any other way, he is to
be put in possession to the extent required for the purpose of withdrawing an amount
necessary for his food. And it should not appear to be a matter of surprise for an estate
to be reduced on account of the provision of food for one whom it will perhaps be decided is not a son, since by the Edicts of all authorities an unborn child is put in possession and food is provided for the mother on account of a child who may not be born, and
greater care should be employed lest a son starve than lest a smaller estate come to
the heir suing for it, if it has appeared that he is not a son.   4. But I emphatically
submit that if the opponent has been put in possession, it is to be required from the
praetor not to submit the documents to his possession; otherwise, the *pupillus* will be
defrauded while his opponent is either being furnished with information [from them]
or is in a position to abstract them.   5. But when both the *pupillus* and his opponent
are remiss in offering security, a curator is to be appointed to administer the estate
and to hand it over at the appropriate time to the party who has prevailed in an action.
What is the position, however, if the tutors of the *pupillus* wish to assume the administration? They will not gain a hearing unless they have given security in the name of
the *pupillus* or have themselves also been appointed *curatores*.

6   PAUL, *Edict, book 41:* The question is whether a decree is to be issued concerning
the mother's property. And a decree in fact is not to be issued, but a very long deferment is to be granted, which will draw out the business until the time of puberty.
1. Obviously, if a dispute simultaneously involves the father's and the mother's property or even that of a brother, Julian has given the opinion that these issues too should
be postponed until the time of puberty.   2. But this Edict applies even if children are
coming to *bonorum possessio* on intestacy, although they sue in accordance with the
later sections [of the Edict], whereby *legitimi* are called, since they are *sui*, or under
the section that gives possession to cognate relations.   3. But this Edict applies only
in the case where the dispute involves questions of status and of the estate; for if the
dispute is only one of status (for instance, [the *impubes*] is alleged to be a slave), and
there is no dispute respecting the property, in this case an action on the question of
freedom will have to be heard right away.   4. If the author of the dispute with the
pupillus has been put into possession along with him at the same time, it will not be
the case that he has to be maintained from the deceased's property nor cause it to be
reduced in any way; for this type of possession is given as a form of security.   5. Not
only should food be provided for the *pupillus*, but payment is to be made for education
and other necessaries in proportion to the resources available.   6. After puberty, it is
inquired whether one who has been put in possession in accordance with the Carbonian Edict should take the part of plaintiff. And the opinion has been given that he
should take the part of defendant, particularly if he has given security. But even if he
had not given security, if he is now prepared to do so, he is to be sued as *possessor*; but
if he does not give security now, possession is transferred on his opponent's offer of
surety, just as if the estate were now being sued for by him for the first time.

7   JULIAN, *Digest, book 24:* If it is argued that an *impubes* has not been legally
adopted, and for that reason a dispute arises with him over his [adoptive] father's estate, it will not be unjust for a decree similar to the Carbonian to be issued.   1. Like-

wise, if an *impubes* is said to have been given in adoption and it is therefore alleged that his natural father's estate does not belong to him, because in this case too, the question is whether he can obtain the estate in the quality of son, the Carbonian Edict will issue.   2. But when it is alleged that the son has been disinherited, it is not necessary to postpone the issue until the time of puberty, because it is not the legal position of the son, but the validity of the will, that is in question.   3. If the mother of one against whom an issue is raised involving both his freedom and his father's estate is called to the investigation on the question of freedom, a hearing concerning the mother will not always have to be postponed until the time of puberty; for a decision is commonly also given immediately in the case of him who is said to be a supposititious child if there be good cause.   4. Whenever the Carbonian Decree issues, the matter should be dealt with in the same place, as it would be if there were no issue with him who has received *bonorum possessio*.   5. But when one of two brothers, who have been put in possession in accordance with this Edict, does not defend his father's estate on his own behalf, the other is obliged to defend the whole or yield it in its entirety to the creditors.   6. Sometimes even a disinherited son will receive *bonorum possessio* in accordance with the Carbonian Decree, if he is not applying for *bonorum possessio* contrary to the terms of a will, but on intestacy *unde liberi* (because his case is that his father's will is not such that *bonorum possessio* can be granted him in accordance with it), and is alleged not to be a son.   7. If a *pupillus* seeks *bonorum possessio* in respect of the estate of a freedman of his father but is alleged not to be the son of the patron, the case is not to be deferred because there was no dispute with him over his father's estate. But if, after the Carbonian Decree has issued, this dispute too should arise, this case should be deferred until that time [puberty].   8. It has been asked whether both a *pupillus* under the Carbonian [Edict] and the appointed heirs according to the terms of a will should take *bonorum possessio* at the same time. I have given it as my opinion that if he were not a son and had not taken *bonorum possessio* contrary to the terms of a will or on intestacy, both he, under the Carbonian [Edict], and the heirs, in accordance with the terms of a will, according to the terms of a will, would take *bonorum possessio* at the same time.

8   AFRICANUS, *Questions, book 4:* The man I declare to be my son and in my power has died. There is an *impubes* who says that he was head of a household and that the estate belongs to him; [Julian] has given it as his opinion that a decree is necessary.   1. Likewise, my emancipated son has died intestate, leaving a son who is an *impubes*, who declares that he is *suus* [*heres*] to him; I argue that he was conceived before the emancipation and, therefore, is in my power and that the property of my emancipated son belongs to me. And, in fact, it is established that the man in question is a son, but there is this query about his status insofar as the question whether he has been in parental power or not is concerned; from the tenor of the Edict, however, it is quite clear that he is admitted in accordance with the Carbonian [Edict].

9   NERATIUS, *Parchments, book 6:* As to Labeo's comment that whenever a *pupillus* is alleged to be a supposititious child with whom there is an issue concerning the father's estate, the praetor ought to see to it that he is put in possession, I submit that he intends [his words] to be understood with reference to him who, after the death of the head of the household, who believed that he was dying without issue, began to be referred to as his son; for the case of one who has been acknowledged by him whose property is in question is stronger in this instance than that of a *postumus*.

10   MARCELLUS, *Digest, book 7:* When a woman to whom the heir tenders an oath has sworn that she is pregnant, *bonorum possessio* should be awarded her in accordance with the Carbonian Edict, or denied, if she has tendered the oath to the heir, since

bonorum possessio is granted after an investigation of the case [by the praetor], lest an award of *bonorum possessio* to the heir should prejudice the *pupillus* or its denial deprive him of his normal legal rights.

11   PAPINIAN, *Questions, book 13:* When a son who is the subject of dispute is capable of being heir without the intervention of the praetor, perhaps because he has been named [as such], the Carbonian Edict does not apply; and, likewise, when it is certain that although he is a son, nevertheless, he will not be heir, for example, in the case where Titius has been instituted heir and a *postumus* or *impubes* who has been disinherited is alleged not to be a son. The fact that his paternity makes a difference in certain cases, for instance, where the property of a brother born of a different mother is involved, or rights affecting freedmen or tombs, is irrelevant; for it is established that matters of that kind do not fall within the Carbonian [Edict].

12   PAPINIAN, *Questions, book 14:* An appointed heir against whom a son who is an *impubes*, and who is alleged to be a supposititious child, seeks *bonorum possessio* in accordance with the first edict, cannot meanwhile receive possession in accordance with the terms of a will, after the manner of a *legitimus.* But if, in the meantime, the appointed heir, or he who has been able to take possession on intestacy, dies, their heirs will have to be aided; for what is the situation if they have not been able to accept the inheritance because their rights have lapsed, or they are in a dubious position on account of the [projected] lawsuit [with the *impubes*]?

13   PAUL, *Replies, book 11:* Titia has given birth to a *postuma* after the death of her husband. Sempronius has alleged before the governor of the province that the same Titia is guilty of adultery; I ask whether the inquiry concerning the adultery should be postponed until the time of puberty, for fear of prejudging the case of the *postuma.* Paul has given it as his opinion that if no suit concerning the father's property is being brought against the *pupilla* in question, it is pointless for the tutors to require that investigation of the adultery, too, should be postponed until the *pupilla* reaches puberty.

14   SCAEVOLA, *Replies, book 2:* The question is asked whether an *impubes* who has received possession in accordance with the Carbonian Edict and who has attained puberty before possession has been transferred to him ought to appear in the role of petitioner. [Scaevola] has given it as his opinion that the burden of proof lies on him in that he will be suing the possessor.

15   HERMOGENIAN, *Epitome of Law, book 3:* This type of *bonorum possessio*, if security has been given, is of advantage not only for obtaining possession but also for suing to recover the property and for exacting a debt [owed to the estate], and for enforcing hotchpot, both of dowry and of all the other things which we have held are to be contributed.

16   PAUL, *Edict, book 41:* But just as security is given to an emancipated son in respect of his father's property, so security is to be taken in respect of those things which he contributes to [the *impubes*].

11

BONORUM POSSESSIO ACCORDING TO WILL

1   ULPIAN, *Edict, book 39:* By "will" we should understand the whole form of the material [on which a will is written]; therefore, whether a will is written on wood, or on any other material, whether it is of papyrus, parchment, or if it is [written] on the skin of some animal, it will properly be termed a will.   1. But the praetor does not follow all wills in this section of the Edict, but the last, that is, the one which has been made most recently, after which no other has been made; for the last will is not one made at the very time of death but the one after which no other has been made, although it may be an old will.   2. But it is sufficient that a will exists, even if it is not made public, if it is certain that it exists. Therefore, even if the will is in the hands of a thief or with the person with whom it has been lodged, it should not be doubted that *bonorum possessio* can be permitted, and there is no need to open the will in order that *bonorum possessio* according to the terms of a will may be claimed.   3. But it is required that a will was at one time in existence after the testator's

death, although it has ceased to exist. Therefore, even if it has been lost afterward, it will be possible to apply for *bonorum possessio.* 4. However, we shall require knowledge that the heir knows of the existence of the will and is certain that *bonorum possessio* is open to him. 5. If a man has made two copies of his will, and one exists and the other does not, a will is regarded as existing, and application can be made for *bonorum possessio.* 6. But likewise, if on two sets of pages, sealed at the same time, he has named two sets of heirs, and both sets of pages are in existence, *bonorum possessio* takes effect in accordance with both as if [they were] one, because it is to be treated as one will, and we shall accept both [sets of papers] as the last [will and testament]. 7. But if the testator has made one as being his will and the other by way of a copy, where the one he intended as a will in fact exists, application will be made for *bonorum possessio*; but if only the copy exists, it will not be possible to apply for *bonorum possessio,* as Pomponius has observed. 8. The praetor requires that the person in respect of whose property *bonorum possessio* is being awarded has had the legal capacity to make a will at two periods, both when he makes it and when he dies. Accordingly, if an *impubes* or an insane person or any other of those persons who cannot make a will has done so and then has died at a time when he has the capacity to make a will, it will not be possible to apply for *bonorum possessio.* But also where a son-in-power, believing himself to be head of a household, has made a will and is found to be head of the household at the time of his death, there can be no application for *bonorum possessio* according to the terms of a will. But if the son of a household, being a veteran, makes [a will] in respect of his *peculium castrense* and then, through emancipation or by some other means, has become head of a household and dies, *bonorum possessio* can be sought in respect of his property. But if a person has had the capacity to make a will at both [pertinent] times and did not have it in the interim, it will be possible to apply for *bonorum possessio* according to the terms of a will. 9. But if a man has made a will and then has lost the capacity to make a will through insanity or because he has been interdicted from his goods, *bonorum possessio* may be sought in respect of his property, because his will is good at law. And in general this may be held of all those in this sort of position who have lost the capacity to make a will at the time of death, but a will made by them previously is good. 10. If the thread by which the will is tied up has been cut, where someone else has done this against the wish of the testator, *bonorum possessio* can be sought; but if the testator himself has done it, the will does not qualify as sealed, and for that reason, no application can be made for *bonorum possessio.* 11. If the will has been nibbled by mice or the thread has otherwise been broken or has decayed through age, either because of the place where the will has been kept or [some] accident, even so the will is regarded as having been sealed, especially if you imagine that even one thread binds it. If the thread were perhaps wound round three or four times, it is to be held that the will was sealed, although part of one has been cut or nibbled.

2 ULPIAN, *Edict, book 41:* The praetor has observed a very fair order of claims; for he intended that first *bonorum possessio* contrary to the terms of a will should devolve on children; then, if that has not already been taken up, that the wishes of the deceased should be observed. Therefore, one will have to wait for children as long as they can seek *bonorum possessio*; but if the limitation period has run its course or they have died before it has done so or have renounced or lost the right to seek *bonorum possessio, bonorum possessio* reverts to the named heirs. 1. If a son has been instituted heir under a condition, Julian has consistently submitted that *bonorum possessio* according to the terms of a will belongs to him as if to the named heir, of whatever nature the condition may be, even if it is as follows: "if a ship arrives from Asia," and although the condition has failed, the praetor, in that he has admitted him to *bonorum possessio* according to the terms of a will, nevertheless, will have to protect the son, as if he has received *bonorum possessio* contrary to the terms of a will; and such protection is necessary for one who has been emancipated. 2. Each heir will receive *bonorum possessio* in respect of the share for which he has been named, in such a manner, however, that if there is no one who is making the same claim as he, he alone takes *bonorum possessio*; nevertheless, so long as one of the heirs is deliberating whether to accept *bonorum possessio* or not, a share in *bonorum possessio* is not offered to his co-heir. 3. Where Primus, in fact, has been appointed substitute heir, [should the heir die] within ten years, and Secundus [if he dies] after ten but within fourteen years; if he has, indeed

died within ten years, Primus will be sole heir, and will receive *bonorum possessio*; but if he has died after ten years, but within fourteen, Secundus will be sole heir and will receive *bonorum possessio*; and they are not joined with each other since each has been substituted in his own particular circumstances. 4. *Bonorum possessio* according to the terms of a will is offered to the heirs named in the first degree, then, if they do not claim it, to those in the following, not only to the substitute heirs but also to the substitutes of the substitute [heir], and we admit the substitutes in order. But we should understand by those named in the first degree all who have been named in first place; for just as they have the first claim to enter on the inheritance, so, too, are they to be admitted to *bonorum possessio*. 5. If a man has written as follows, "let Primus be heir in part; if Primus shall not be heir, let Secundus be heir; let Tertius be heir to the other half; if he shall not, let Quartus be heir," Primus and Tertius are called to *bonorum possessio* in the first place. 6. Where a man has instituted heirs as follows, "let whichever of my brothers has married Seia be heir to three quarters, and whichever has not married [her] heir to one quarter"; if Seia has in fact died, it is established that the heirs will take equal shares; but if she has been married by one of them, three quarters and one quarter [respectively] belong to them. But neither can seek *bonorum possessio* before the condition is fulfilled. 7. If the name of the heir has been deliberately crossed out, undoubtedly the approved view is that he cannot seek *bonorum possessio*, just as he who has been written in as heir without the testator's consent cannot; for a name he did not intend to be written is treated as if it were not written. 8. Where two heirs, Primus and Secundus, have been instituted, and Tertius has been made substitute to Secundus, if Secundus neglects to apply for *bonorum possessio*, Tertius succeeds. But if Tertius has refused to accept the inheritance or to take *bonorum possessio*, *bonorum possessio* reverts to Primus. And it will not be necessary for him to sue for *bonorum possessio*, but it will accrue to him as of right; for just as his share of the inheritance accrues to the appointed heir, so too does *bonorum possessio*. 9. If a slave has been appointed heir, *bonorum possessio* is offered to the master to whom the inheritance will belong; for *bonorum possessio* moves with ownership. Wherefore, if at the time of [the testator's] death Stichus, the instituted heir, was the slave of Sempronius and Sempronius did not instruct him to accept the inheritance but died or even transferred his property in the slave and he came into the ownership of Septicius, it turns out that if Septicius has given him the instruction, *bonorum possessio* is offered to Septicius; for the inheritance belongs to him. Whence, if the slave has passed through the hands of many masters, three or more, we shall grant *bonorum possessio* to the most recent.

3   PAUL, *Edict, book 41:* It is true that every *postumus* that was unborn at the time of the testator's death can seek *bonorum possessio*, if he has been born.

4   ULPIAN, *Edict, book 42:* The word papyrus refers both to new and to used papyrus; accordingly, even if someone has written his will on the back of a papyrus, *bonorum possessio* may be sought on this basis.

5   ULPIAN, *Disputations, book 4:* If someone has been instituted heir under a condition and when he has received *bonorum possessio* according to the terms of a will, the condition has failed, it sometimes happens that the property is to be surrendered to the *possessor*, for instance, if an emancipated son has been instituted heir under a condition; for if the condition has failed, Julian observes that he nevertheless takes *bonorum possessio* according to the terms of a will. But, likewise, if he was a person who would be *bonorum possessor* on intestacy, he has observed that he is to be protected, and we observe this rule. 1. It is to be considered whether legacies are payable by them. And a son, by his acceptance of *bonorum possessio*, in fact appears to take the property, as it were, contrary to the terms of a will; but the others take as if on intestacy; and for that reason the son will be obliged to pay the legacies that have been left only to ascendants and descendants, and not to others. Obviously, payment will have to be made to him to whom a *fideicommissum* has been left payable by

intestacy, as if he appears to have been cheated of this very thing, because *bonorum possessio* has been sought in accordance with the terms of a will.

6 ULPIAN, *Disputations, book 8:* Lastly, those heirs conditionally instituted, who have been effectively instituted, can apply for *bonorum possessio* while the condition is still open and not yet fulfilled; but, if someone has not been effectively instituted, an ineffectual institution is of no avail for the purpose of seeking *bonorum possessio.*

7 JULIAN, *Digest, book 23:* When the will has been sealed with the seals of several persons and some of the seals are not visible, but seven seals remain, it is sufficient for the granting of *bonorum possessio* that the seals of seven witnesses are evident, even though the seals of all those who attached their seals are no longer in evidence.

8 JULIAN, *Digest, book 24:* Suppose a will runs as follows: "Let Sempronius be heir to a half share. Let Titius, if a ship arrives from Asia, be heir to a third. Let the same Titius, if the ship does not arrive from Asia, be heir to a sixth." Titius is to be understood not as having been appointed heir to two shares, but as having been made substitute heir in his own stead, and for that reason does not appear to have been appointed heir to a share greater than one third. According to this reasoning, since a sixth is left unattributed, Titius will take *bonorum possessio,* not only of his third but also of the share that accrues to him from the sixth. 1. Just as the man substituted to an *impubes* son in the following words, "if my son dies before reaching full age, then let Titius be heir to me," claims the estate, just as if the words "to me" had not been added, so he can also gain *bonorum possessio* of it. 2. But even when there has been an error in the *praenomen* [or] *cognomen*, the person to whom the inheritance belongs also takes *bonorum possessio.* 3. But a person whose name has been erased from the will by the testator's wish is understood not to have been named, both for the purpose of accepting the inheritance and for seeking *bonorum possessio,* even though his name is legible. 4. A man made his own will in writing but appointed a substitute heir to his son, an *impubes,* by oral declaration. I gave it as my opinion that the praetor's view in granting *bonorum possessio* is such that the heirs of the father and of the son should be separately determined; for just as *bonorum possessio* can be given separately to the son's heir and the father's heirs where the son's heir is appointed in writing, so it can be regarded as given separately to an heir of the son appointed orally and to the heirs of the father appointed in writing.

9 POMPONIUS, *Sabinus, book 2:* In order that *bonorum possessio* according to the terms of a will naming a substitute in the event of the death of the *pupillus* may be granted, it is asked whether the father's will has been sealed, even though the second portion of the will [containing the substitution] is produced unsealed.

10 PAUL, *Plautius, book 8:* If a slave has been instituted heir under a condition, it is doubtful whether he can receive *bonorum possessio.* And our own Scaevola approves the view that he can.

11 PAPINIAN, *Questions, book 13:* "Let Titius be heir to whichever of my children shall die last before attaining puberty." If two [children] have died abroad and the substitute heir does not know which of the two has died last, Julian's view is to be adopted, namely that in view of the uncertainty of the condition, *bonorum possessio* may be sought even in respect of the one who died first. 1. A son who had been instituted heir returned from captivity after his father's death; he will receive *bonorum possessio,* and the period of a year [which he has in which to apply for *bonorum possessio*] will be reckoned from the time of his return. 2. After making a will, Titius has allowed himself to be adopted by *adrogatio,* and later, having become *sui juris,* has died. If the heir appointed in his will seeks possession, he will be rebutted by means of the defense of fraud, because, by giving himself in adoption by *adrogatio,* the testator

transfers together with his person his fortune, too, to another family and household. Obviously, if having become *sui juris*, he has declared in a codicil or other written document that it is his intention to die [possessed of] the same will, his intention, which had lapsed, will be deemed to have been restored by his new statement of decision in the same way as if a man had made a second will and had torn up the last will, so as to leave the former will as his last. No one should think that a will is [here] being constructed on a bare statement of intention; the validity of the will is not being raised as a principle, but by the pleading of a defense. And although [the defense] is set up against the plaintiff in these proceedings, its value depends on the character of him who sets it up.

12   PAUL, *Questions, book 7:* In order that the appointed heir can claim *bonorum possessio,* I submit that it is to be required that he has both been indicated by proper indication and that the portion assigned to him can be discovered, even if he has been instituted without [reference to] a [specified] share; for an heir instituted without reference to a [specified] share takes the residue or some other unit [of division]. But if he has been instituted heir in such a way that he is in some circumstances excluded from the will for the reason that the share in respect of which he was instituted is not discoverable, he cannot apply for *bonorum possessio* either. This happens if someone has instituted his heir in the following way: "Let Titius be heir to the share to which I have appointed him heir in my previous will" or "let him be heir to the share to which I have appointed him in a codicil," he is not found to have been appointed [at all] in this way. But if I have written as follows, "Titius, if I have appointed him heir to a half [share] in my previous will" or "if I have appointed him heir to a half [share] in a codicil, let him be heir to a half," then he will take *bonorum possessio* as being appointed heir under a condition.

12

IF SOMEONE IS MANUMITTED BY A PARENT

1   ULPIAN, *Edict, book 45:* A son emancipated by his parent is in the position that in *bonorum possessio* contrary to the terms of a will he suffers the fate of a freedman. And this appeared most just to the praetor, because he has received from the parent the facility of acquiring property in that if he were the son of the household, he would be acquiring for his father the benefit of whatever he were to obtain for himself. And for that reason we have reached the position that a parent is admitted to *bonorum possessio* contrary to the terms of a will on the model of a patron. 1. The names of those manumitting, therefore, are listed in the edict as follows: "in the case of him who [has been emancipated] by his father or paternal grandfather or great-grandfather on his father's side, his father's grandfather." 2. A grandson manumitted by his grandfather gave himself in adoption by *adrogatio* to his own father; whether he has died while in his father's power or departed this life after being manumitted, only his grandfather will be admitted to succeed to his property by the interpretation of the Edict, because the praetor offers *bonorum possessio* just as if he had been manumitted from slavery. Moreover, if this had happened, then either he would not have been adopted by *adrogatio*, because adoption by *adrogatio* of a freedman is not permitted, or if he has cheated [his way into adoption], the patron's rights, nonetheless, would remain intact. 3. If a parent has either accepted money to perform the emancipation or if the son, in his lifetime, has given at a later date his father sufficient to insure that he does not contest his dispositions by will, he will be rebutted by a defense of fraud.   4. There is another situation where a parent does not receive *bonorum possessio* contrary to the terms of a will, [namely] if it happens that the son has engaged on military service; for the deified Pius has ruled in a rescript that the father may not claim *bonorum possessio* contrary to the terms of a will. 5. But it is established that children of the manumitter do not have a claim to *bonorum possessio* contrary to the terms of a will in respect of the property of the son, although those of the patron do so.   6. But Julian has observed that a father, having received *bonorum possessio* contrary to the terms of a will, can claim for himself the former right which he had even without the manumission; for the fact that he had a patron's rights should not prejudice him, since he is also the man's father.

2   GAIUS, *Provincial Edict, book 15:* A parent is not to be so far equated with a patron that he is also given a Fabian or Calvisian action, because it is inequitable that freemen should not have full power to alienate their own property.

3   PAUL, *Plautius, book 8:* Paconius says that if a son, emancipated and manumitted
     by his father, had appointed as his heirs base persons, such as a prostitute, *bonorum
     possessio* contrary to the terms of a will in respect of the whole property is given to
     the parent; or [he receives possession] of the designated share if the person instituted
     heir were not of the baser sort.   1. If an emancipated son has passed over his father
     in his will, or has instituted him heir, the father will not be compelled to execute
     fideicommissa from the share which is owed to him, even if he has accepted the inheri-
     tance. But also if a daughter or granddaughter has been manumitted and a father or
     grandfather who has been passed over applies for *bonorum possessio*, the same is to
     be held as in the case of the son.
4   MARCELLUS, *Digest, book 9:* The praetor gives no ruling about obligations imposed
     in return for freedom by a father who has emancipated his son, and for that reason a
     father will not stipulate effectively for services from his son.
5   PAPINIAN, *Questions, book 11:* The divine Trajan compelled a father who was mal-
     treating his son contrary to a father's duty to emancipate him. After the son's death
     the father claimed that *bonorum possessio* belonged to him in the quality of manu-
     mitter; but, on the advice of Neratius Priscus and Aristo, it was denied him on the
     grounds that he must pay the price for abusing a father's duty.

13

BONORUM POSSESSIO ARISING OUT OF A SOLDIER'S WILL

1   ULPIAN, *Edict, book 45:* There is no doubt that the intentions of those who in any
     way had made their final dispositions [while serving] in enemy territory and had there
     met their end should be confirmed. For although the condition of soldiers is very dif-
     ferent from those persons the main constitutions except, nevertheless, since those en-
     gaged in battle experience the same risks, they deserve to claim the same rights for
     themselves. Therefore, all those, generally, who are not in a position to make a will
     according to military law, if they are cut off in enemy territory and die there, will
     make a will as they wish and as they are able, whether such a person be governor of
     a province or legate or anyone else who cannot make a will according to military
     law.   1. Likewise, there is no doubt that ships' masters and captains of the triremes
     of the fleets can make a will according to military law. In the fleets, all the rowers and
     sailors count as soldiers. Likewise, watchmen are soldiers, and there is no doubt that
     they can make a will in accordance with military law.   2. If a soldier has been trans-
     ferred from one company to another, although he has been taken out of the one and has
     not yet arrived in the other, nevertheless, he will be able to make a will according to
     military law; for he is a soldier, although he is not in the ranks.

14

THE RIGHTS OF A PATRON

1   ULPIAN, *Duties of Proconsul, book 9:* Governors should hear complaints by patrons
     against freedmen and not deal with such cases in a routine manner, since if a freedman
     is ungrateful, the patron should not have to see his behavior go unpunished. But if,
     in fact, he is undutiful to his patron, male or female, or their children, he should
     merely be reprimanded with a threat that strong action will not be lacking if he again
     offers cause for complaint, and he should be dismissed. Certainly, if he has insulted or
     uttered abuse against them, he will have to be sent into exile for a time; but, if he has
     used force, he will have to be condemned to the mines, likewise, if he has drawn up a

false accusation against them or suborned an informer or started some case against them.

2   ULPIAN, *Opinions, book 1:* Freedmen should not be prevented from engaging in lawful business by their patrons.

3   MARCIAN, *Institutes, book 2:* If a man has been appointed as a tutor where a female slave had been left to him with a request that he manumit her and he has claimed the legacy and manumitted her and has excused himself from tutelage of the *pupillus*, the deified Severus and Antoninus have ruled in a rescript that such a man is indeed a patron but is deprived of all the benefits which a patron enjoys.

4   MARCELLUS, *Institutes, book 5:* The deified Severus and Antoninus have set forth in a rescript a most indulgent rule that the rights over freedmen are preserved to the children of patrons, where their father has been condemned on a charge of treason, just as rights over freedmen are preserved to the children of those punished for any other reason.

5   MARCELLUS, *Institutes, book 13:* The deified Claudius ordained that a freedman, who has been proved to have suborned informers against his patron to give rise to an investigation about his status, is to be a slave of his patron.   1. By a rescript of our emperor it is provided that if a patron has not maintained his freedman, he loses the right of patron.

6   PAUL, *Lex Aelia Sentia, book 2:* [Even a patron] who allows his freedman to take an oath [not to have issue] is understood [as being in breach of the statute forbidding a patron to] compel a freedwoman to swear not to marry or [a freedman] not to have children. But if, without his knowledge, his son has demanded the oath, or has demanded a promise, it will in no way be prejudicial to him. Clearly, if one in power has done so on the orders of the patron, it is to be held that he is liable under this law.   1. A patron has stipulated that a hundred days labor be given or five gold aurei to be paid in respect of each day; he does not appear to have stipulated contrary to the law, because it is in the freedman's power to provide services.   2. Although no person is excepted from the law, nevertheless, it is to be understood that the law concerns those who can have children. And so, if a patron forced a freedman that has been castrated to take the oath, it is to be held that he is not to be punished under this law.   3. If a patron has forced a freedwoman to swear to marry him, if he did so with the intention of marrying her, he will appear to have done nothing contrary to law, but if he did so with no intention of marrying her, but solely on the ground that she should not marry another, Julian says that the patron has committed a fraud on the law, and is liable, just as if he had compelled the freedwoman to swear not to marry.   4. By the *Lex Julia de maritandis ordinibus* regulating marriage between different classes, an oath imposed on a freedman to prevent his taking a wife or on a freedwoman not to marry is relaxed, provided that they wish to contract a proper marriage.

7   MODESTINUS, *Manumissions, sole book:* The deified Vespasian decreed that if a female slave has been sold under this law [on condition] that she should not be prostituted and if she should have been used for that purpose that she should be free, where she has subsequently been sold by the buyer to a third party without condition, she is to be free by virtue of the condition of sale, and is the freedwoman of the initial vendor.   1. It is provided by mandates of the emperors that in the provinces, too, governors hearing complaints of patrons are to exact penalties from freedmen according to the tort that has been committed. Sometimes the following penalties are imposed on an ungrateful freedman: either part of his property is confiscated and handed over to the patron, or he is beaten with sticks and set free.

8   MODESTINUS, *Rules, book 6:* When a slave is manumitted by a son-in-power on military service, the divine Hadrian ruled in a rescript that the soldier makes him his own freedman and not his father's.   1. A slave sold under the law that he is to be manumitted within a [certain] period obtains his freedom without manumission; and on the expiry of the period he will become a freedman of the buyer, even though he is not manumitted.

9   MODESTINUS, *Rules, book 9:* Sons who refuse an inheritance from their fathers do not lose their right over their father's freedmen; the same is true in the case of an emancipated son.   1. Some persons are excluded by law from having any standing in the matter of their freedmen's property; a person condemned on a capital charge, if he has not been reinstated, if he is or has been informer of a crime on the part of his freedman, or, being over twenty-five years of age, has accused his father's freedman on a capital charge.

10   TERENTIUS CLEMENS, *Lex Julia et Papia, book 9:* It is settled that a patron who
has accused his freedman on a capital charge is excluded from *bonorum possessio* contrary to the terms of a will. Labeo was of the opinion that an accusation on a capital
charge is one where the penalty involved is death or exile. He who has impeached another is to be understood to have accused him, unless he seeks to have the case withdrawn; Servilius reports that this definition found favor even with Proculus.

11   ULPIAN, *Lex Julia et Papia, book 10:* But he is not admitted to his legal claim to the
inheritance [of his freedman], which is offered to him in accordance with the *Twelve
Tables* either.

12   MODESTINUS, *Replies, book 1:* Gaius Seius dies having made a will naming as part-
heir, together with his sons, his freedman Julius, as if he were himself a son; I question
whether he can change his freedman's condition of status by a disposition of this kind.
Modestinus has given it as his opinion that he cannot change his status.

13   MODESTINUS, *Encyclopaedia, book 1:* A son-in-power cannot manumit a slave that
is part of his *peculium.* But he can do so on his father's orders, and the manumitted
slave becomes the freedman of the father.

14   ULPIAN, *Lex Julia et Papia, book 5:* If I have sworn that I am a patron, it is to be
held that I am not a patron insofar as succession is concerned, because an oath does
not make a patron. It is otherwise if it has been judicially determined that I am a patron;
for the judgment will stand.

15   PAUL, *Lex Julia et Papia, book 8:* A man who has compelled a freedman to take an
oath in contravention of the *lex Aelia Sentia* neither has any right [over the freedman]
himself nor do his children.

16   ULPIAN, *Lex Julia et Papia, book 10:* If a freedman commits a fraud on the law by
reducing his worth to less than one hundred thousand sesterces, his act will have no
validity in law, and for that reason his patron's standing with regard to his property
will be as if in relation to the property of a freedman worth one hundred thousand.
Therefore, the alienation of whatever he has alienated by whatever means is of no
effect. Obviously, if he has alienated property to defraud his patron, and, nevertheless, still remains worth more than one hundred thousand after such alienation, the
alienation will in fact take effect, but the objects alienated by fraud will be recoverable
by the Fabian and Calvisian action; and Julian frequently makes remarks to this
effect, and we observe this rule. But there is a reason for the distinction. Whenever
alienation takes place with the object of effecting a fraud on the law, the act is void; but
it is done with the object of fraud when someone reduces his worth to less than one
hundred thousand for the purpose of evading this provision of the law. But when, having effected the alienation, nonetheless, he is worth one hundred thousand, the act is
not regarded as a fraud on the law, but only as a fraud on his patron; therefore, the
alienated property will be recoverable by the Fabian or Calvisian action.   1. If a man,
by alienating several items of property at the same time, has reduced his worth to less
than one hundred thousand and, by the recovery of one or by portions of all, becomes
worth more than one hundred thousand, do we recover them all or effect recovery proportionately from individual items to bring him up to one hundred thousand? And the
more reasonable interpretation is that the alienations are void in toto.   2. Obviously,
if he has not alienated the property at one and the same time, but some items at an
earlier date, and some subsequently, the property subsequently alienated will

not be recoverable by operation of law, but only that previously alienated; the Fabian action will issue with regard to the later alienations.

17   ULPIAN, *Lex Julia et Papia, book 11:* The deified brothers issued the following ruling in a rescript: "We have learned from those skilled in giving legal opinions that it has sometimes been doubted whether a grandson can seek *bonorum possessio* in respect of the property of a grandfather's freedman, if the grandson's father, being twenty-five years old, had accused the freedman of the grandfather on a capital charge and that Proculus, clearly no light-weight authority in the matter of law, had been inclined to think that the grandson should not be granted *bonorum possessio* in this kind of case. We, too, followed this opinion when we dispatched a rescript in answer to the petition of Caesidia Longina; but likewise, our friend Volusius Maecianus, as well as being carefully attentive of the civil law, apart from his ancient and well-established skill in it, was induced by respect for our rescript to declare in our presence that in his opinion no other reply should be given. But when we discussed the matter more fully with Maecianus himself and other legal experts of our acquaintance, who had been summoned to a meeting, the better view appeared to be that neither in the words nor by the spirit of the law nor of the praetor's Edict is the grandson excluded from the property of his grandfather's freedman as a result of his father's character, or any stain upon it; and that such was the view of several legal authorities too, but that it had also been the opinion of our acquaintance, the most honorable Salvius Julianus." 1. Likewise, the question was posed, if the patron's son has accused a freedman of a capital crime, whether it should prejudice the son's children. And Proculus, in fact, was of the opinion that the stain thereby inflicted on the [character of the] patron's son was prejudicial to his children, but Julian denied that this was the case; but in this instance we shall have to agree with Julian's ruling.

18   SCAEVOLA, *Replies, book 4:* I ask whether a freedman can be prevented by his patron from engaging in the same kind of trade in the same colony in which the patron himself is in business. Scaevola has given it as his opinion that he cannot be restrained from so doing.

19   PAUL, *Views, book 1:* An ungrateful freedman is one who refuses obedience to his patron or refuses to administer his affairs or undertake the tutelage of his son.

20   PAUL, *Views, book 3:* Just as, when a freedman dies leaving a will, his patron is entitled either to claim payments in respect of his freedom or *bonorum possessio* of a share [of his estate], so, where he has died intestate, he still has the choice as to which course of action he takes.

21   HERMOGENIAN, *Epitome of Law, book 3:* If a patron or his freedman suffers deportation, and is subsequently reinstated, his rights at patron and of making application for *bonorum possessio* that have been lost are recovered; and this right is preserved also in the case where the patron or freedman has been condemned to the mines and is subsequently reinstated. 1. A patron is likewise excluded from *bonorum possessio* where he is instituted heir to a twelfth, and the money lacking to make up the share owed to him can be acquired for him without condition or delay, through a slave by a disposition made by the freedman from the estate or a legacy or *fideicommissum.* 2. One of two patrons, having been instituted heir to the portion due to him without condition or delay, will not be able to sue for *bonorum possessio*, although, if a lesser portion had been left to him, and he had sought *bonorum possessio*, the second portion [belonging to the other patron] could have accrued to him. 3. Natural children of a freedman, who have been disinherited when another person has been instituted heir to a share, where they have obtained succession to their father in respect of a share acquired through a slave, are a source of prejudice to the patron. 4. If a freedman's son has been instituted heir and has refused the property, the patron is not excluded.

22   GAIUS, *Cases, sole book:* It is sufficiently established that even if the son of a patroness is in parental power, nonetheless, he has a legal right to the estate.

23 TRYPHONINUS, *Disputations, book 15:* If a son has left his father's murder un-avenged, where his slave has disclosed the crime and thereby gained his freedom, I have held that he is not to be treated as son of the patron, because he is unworthy. 1. When an heir, as a result of a forged codicil, which was believed genuine at some point, in ignorance of the fact, offered slaves their freedom, as if in accordance with a *fideicommissum,* it was ruled by the deified Hadrian in a rescript that they are in fact free but must pay their value; and it is rightly approved that they rank as freedmen of the manumitter, because the right of the patron is preserved even in the case of these freedmen.

24 PAUL, *Imperial Decisions Pronounced in Judicial Examinations or Decrees, Books 1–6, book 1:* Camelia Pia had appealed from Hermogenes on the grounds that the judge, in a matter concerning division of an estate between herself and her co-heir, had divided not only the property but also the freedmen and alleged that he had had no right to do so. It was resolved that the freedmen should not be divided, but the division of the obligation of aliment made by the judge between the co-heirs on the same principle be allowed to stand.

15

THE OBEDIENCE TO BE OFFERED
TO PARENTS AND PATRONS

1 ULPIAN, *Opinions, book 1:* The principle of duty toward parents should hold good even for soldiers; wherefore, if a son who is a soldier has committed some offense against his father, he should be punished according to the offense. 1. And between a mother and a son who have become free together the principle of duty should be pre-served according to nature. 2. If a son abuses the mother or father he should re-spect, or offers violence to them, the prefect of the city punishes an offense in respect of public duty in accordance with its enormity. 3. A man who has alleged that the father and mother whom he claims have brought him up are evil-doers is to be ad-judged unworthy of military service.

2 JULIAN, *Digest, book 14:* It is to be attributed to the respect accorded parents and patrons that although they are sued through a procurator, an action for fraud or *injuria* is not given against them; for although by the words of the edict they are not branded with infamy, if condemned in such an action, they do not escape its mark in fact or in respect of public opinion. 1. The *interdictum unde vi* is also not to be granted against them.

3 MARCELLUS, *Replies, sole book:* Titius bought a slave whom he commanded to be sold many years later; subsequently, in response to a plea, having accepted the price of his manumission, he set him free. I ask whether the son and heir of the manumitter can accuse him of ingratitude. [Marcellus] gave it as his opinion that he could, if there were nothing else to prevent him; for it is most important to distinguish whether a man has granted freedom in respect of payment taken from his own slave or a friend of the slave or from a slave who, being the property of another, has fallen under his pro-tection. For the former, although not without remuneration, nevertheless, has pro-vided him with a benefit, while the latter can be regarded as doing no more than doing him a service.

4 MARCIAN, *Public Trials, book 2:* The deified Severus and Antoninus have ruled in a rescript that a freedman can be accused of ingratitude through an agent.

5 ULPIAN, *Edict, book 10:* A parent, patron, male or female, or children or parents of

the patron, male or female, are not liable to an *actio in factum*, whether they were said to have taken money in return for doing some business, or for not doing it. 1. But neither are actions involving *infamia* given against them, nor those which involve fraud or deceit.

6 PAUL, *Edict, book 11:* Nor will the action for corruption of a slave be brought [against them],

7 ULPIAN, *Edict, book 10:* although [these actions] do not lead to *infamia*. 1. And judgment is given against them [only] to the extent of a sum which they can pay. 2. Nor are the defenses of fraud or violence or duress admitted against them, nor the *interdictum unde vi* or *quod vi*. 3. Nor when they tender an oath do they swear in respect of their own bad faith. 4. And if a patroness is said to have been put in possession in the name of an unborn child in bad faith, a freedman who makes such allegation will not be heard, because the question of a patron's bad faith is not to be entertained. For respect will be accorded to those persons also in other sections of the Edict. 5. But respect will be accorded to these persons themselves and not to their representatives; and if they should intervene on behalf of others, they will be respected.

8 PAUL, *Edict, book 10:* The heir of a freedman has all the rights of a stranger so far as the patron of the deceased is concerned.

9 ULPIAN, *Edict, book 66:* A freedman and a son should always consider the person of a father and patron honorable and inviolable.

10 TRYPHONINUS, *Disputations, book 17:* [A father] has no right to payment for manumission over an emancipated son because no charge is normally imposed on children. And no one has [ever] held that a son is bound by an oath to his father *qua* manumitter, as is a freedman to his patron; for children owe duty to their parents, not services.

11 PAPINIAN, *Replies, book 3:* A freedwoman is not ungrateful if she practices her profession against the wishes of her patroness.

BOOK THIRTY-EIGHT

1

THE SERVICES OF FREEDMEN

1 PAUL, *Readings, sole book:* Services are days of work.
2 ULPIAN, *Edict, book 38:* The praetor sets up this edict to restrain actions for payments on account of [a grant] of freedom; for he observed the fact that the practice of offering payment in return for freedom had grown beyond all bounds, so as to oppress and burden persons of the freedman class. 1. At the beginning, therefore, the praetor promises to give judgment for services against freedmen and freedwomen.
3 POMPONIUS, *Sabinus, book 6:* The patron who has stipulated for services cannot sue for a day's work before the day is over. 1. Nor can part of the day's work be discharged [by working] on an hourly basis, because it is the nature of a day's work [that it demands a day]. And so the freedman who has merely been on hand during the six hours before noon does not acquit himself of his obligation for that day.
4 POMPONIUS, *Sabinus, book 4:* A man manumitted by two [patrons] had promised services to each of them; if one has died, there is no reason why his son should not sue for the services, even though the other [patron] is still alive. And this has nothing to do with inheritance or *bonorum possessio*; for services are sued for from freedmen in the same way as a loan. Aristo, whose view, I submit, is correct, has observed this to be the case; for it is resolved that an action be granted to an heir who is a stranger to the family even in respect of past services without fear of the defense [of fraud being pleaded against him]. Therefore, [an action] will be granted even if the other patron is alive.
5 ULPIAN, *Sabinus, book 15:* If a patron has stipulated for services for himself and his children, the stipulation extends even to *postumi*.
6 ULPIAN, *Sabinus, book 26:* Services of skilled workers and other types of services that consist, as it were, in the payment of money pass to the heir, but those that constitute a duty do not.
7 ULPIAN, *Sabinus, book 28:* For an oath to be binding, he who swears it must be a freedman, and he must swear in return for his freedom. 1. Obviously, where someone has left a legacy to his freedman on condition that he swears to pay his son ten in lieu of services, there is a question whether he is bound by the oath. And Celsus Juventius says that he is and that it makes little difference why the freedman has sworn the oath in respect of services; I concur with Celsus's view. 2. But to be bound, he must swear after manumission; and whether he has done so immediately or after an interval, he is bound. 3. But he should swear to furnish days of work or a gift or service, any kind of work, providing that it is honestly, justly, and legally imposed. 4. It has been ruled by the deified Hadrian and his successors that the right to services ceases where a slave has gained his freedom by reason of a *fideicommissum*. 5. An action for services will be awarded against an *impubes* when he has

grown up, but sometimes even while he is still an *impubes*; for an *impubes*, too, may perform a service, if he happens to be a scribe or *nomenclator* or accountant or an actor or entertains his master in some other fashion.   6. If the patron's children have been instituted heirs to unequal shares, should they have an action for services in relation to a half or in relation to the size of their individual portions of the estate? And I submit that the more correct view is that the children will have an action in respect of equal shares.   7. But it makes little difference whether the children have been in power or have in fact been emancipated.   8. But if the patron has appointed as heir [a child] who has been given in adoption, there is more reason for services to be owed to him.   9. Nor are the children of a patroness debarred from suit for services.

8   POMPONIUS, *Sabinus, book 8:* Whenever a freedman has sworn to render services to two patrons, Labeo rules that part of the services can be owed and can be claimed, since services due in the past that cannot now be rendered can always be claimed. And this happens if [the freedman] swears or makes a promise to the patrons themselves, or to a slave jointly owned by them, or where there are several heirs to one patron.   1. It is resolved that anyone can go surety in respect of a freedman's oath.

9   ULPIAN, *Sabinus, book 34:*   1. Services have no existence in nature. But those which are in the nature of a duty are in the future and can be owed only to a patron, since the property in them resides in the person who performs them, and in him for whom they are performed. But skilled services or others are of the kind that can be discharged by anyone for anyone. But obviously if [the services] consist of skilled work, they can, on the patron's orders, be performed for another.

10   POMPONIUS, *Sabinus, book 15:* The following stipulation taken by the slave of a patron from a freedman is bad: "Do you promise to render me services?" And so it is to be stipulated that the services be rendered to the patron.   1. When a freedman takes an oath in respect of services, to perform them for "my patron or Lucius Titius," he cannot discharge them in favor of Lucius Titius, in order to release himself from his obligations to his patron,

11   JULIAN, *Digest, book 22:* (it makes no difference, however, whether Lucius Titius is a stranger to the family or the [patron's] son),

12   POMPONIUS, *Sabinus, book 15:* because the services given to Lucius Titius will be different services. But if, in return for his freedom, the freedman promises money to his needy patron or to Titius, the addition of Titius is quite valid.

13   ULPIAN, *Edict, book 38:* If anyone has been bought on condition that he be manumitted and has become free in accordance with the constitution of the deified Marcus, the services imposed upon him will be of no effect.   1. But the person to whom the property has been adjudged, in accordance with the constitution of the deified Marcus; for the purpose of preserving the gift of freedom [made to the slaves] will not be able to claim services from those who have received a direct grant, nor from those who have received it by way of *fideicommissum*, although those who have received the latter type of grant become his freedmen. For they do not become freedmen in the same way as are our own [freedmen] whom we have manumitted without any compulsion.   2. The action for services issues only when the services are overdue. But they cannot be overdue before they become due, and they become due when they have been specified.   3. Even if a freedman has a wife, his patron is not prevented from demanding services.   4. If the patron is an *impubes*, a freedwoman does not appear to have contracted a valid marriage by his consent unless such consent has been ratified by his tutor's sanction.   5. Ratification is an obstacle to a patron in the matter of the marriage of his freedwoman.

14   TERENTIUS CLEMENS, *Lex Julia et Papia, book 8:* Obviously, when she has ceased to be married, almost all agree that services can be claimed.

15   ULPIAN, *Edict, book 38:* A freedman, who, after the requirement of his services has
      been announced, is impeded by his health from performing them, is not bound to do so; for
      the failure to perform them cannot appear to rest with him. It will not be possible for
      services to be promised, discharged, owed, or claimed in part. For that reason Papi-
      nian submits that if there are not one but several services and there are several heirs
      to the patron who has stipulated for the services, it is proper that the obligation should
      be divided by the number of heirs. Finally, Celsus observes in his twelfth book that if a
      freedman shared by two patrons in common has sworn to perform a thousand days'
      services or has made such promises to a slave they jointly own, five hundred are owed
      rather than half of each of the individual services.

16   PAUL, *Edict, book 40:* The freedman will have to offer services in the skill that he
      has learned after manumission if they are of a kind which, at whatever point they are
      provided, [are provided] honorably and without risk to his life, and not necessarily
      those which should have been rendered at the time of his manumission. But if [the
      freedman] has later engaged in dishonorable work, he will have to offer those which he
      offered at the time of his manumission.   1. The type of services offered to the patron
      should be assessed in accordance with the age, status, health, need, way of life, and
      other such considerations in respect of either party.

17   PAUL, *Right of a Patron, sole book:* A patron is not to be heard if he demands ser-
      vices, the performance of which the age and state of health of his freedman does not
      tolerate, or those alien to the mode and tenor of his life.

18   PAUL, *Edict, book 40:* Sabinus, in the fifth book of the *Urban Praetor's Edict,* ob-
      serves that the freedman should provide services, while being himself responsible for
      his food and clothing; but if he cannot maintain himself, the patron is to provide his food.

19   GAIUS, *Provincial Edict, book 14:* Or clearly services are to be required from [the
      freedman] in such a way that on those days on which he is performing them, he is
      given enough time to earn sufficient for his food.

20   PAUL, *Edict, book 40:* And if this is not the case [Paul maintains] that the praetor
      will deny such provision of services to the patron; and this is true, because everyone
      should provide what he has promised at his own expense, so long as what he owes
      exists in nature.   1. Proculus says that a freedman should come from the province to
      Rome for the purpose of rendering services, but the patron loses those days which
      have passed while he is on his way to Rome, so long as the patron was residing at
      Rome as a man of good character and careful head of the household or is setting out for
      his province; however, if he wishes to roam the world, his freedman is not to be obliged
      to follow him everywhere.

21   JAVOLENUS, *Cassius, book 6:* Services should be performed in the place where the
      patron resides, naturally at the latter's expense and provision of transport.

22   GAIUS, *Provincial Edict, book 14:* When a patron has stipulated for services, the
      stipulation comes into effect at the point when he has demanded them and the freed-
      man has not complied with the demand. It makes no difference whether the words
      "when I have demanded them" have been added or not; for services are one thing,
      and other matters another. For since the provision of services is nothing other than
      the fulfillment of a duty, it is ridiculous to believe that a duty is due on a day other than
      that on which the person to whom it is to be discharged wanted it.   1. When a freed-
      man has promised that he will render services to his patron and has not added, "and to
      his children," it is established that they are due to the children only in the case where
      they have fallen to be heirs to their father; in Julian's view the fact that they have
      fallen to be heirs to their father advantages them for the purposes of claiming services
      only in the case where they [are heirs in their own right and] have not become heirs
      through another. And so if a man has disinherited his emancipated son and appointed
      his slave heir and the son has fallen to be heir through that slave, he should be barred
      from claiming services, just as would a patron who had not imposed the services or
      who had sold back to his [freedmen] the services he had imposed.   2. In the case of all

services, it is particularly to be observed that sufficient time is allowed the freedman to care for his bodily needs.

23   JULIAN, *Digest, book 22:* These services which are promised by the freedman are quite different from those of a craftsman or services which are of an artistic nature. Another thing: If a freedman has been a craftsman or an artist, so long as he shall practice his craft, he is compelled to render these services to his patron. Wherefore, just as anyone can stipulate for services requiring the skill of a craftsman for himself or for Titius, so a patron properly stipulates for services from his freedman for himself or Sempronius. And the freedman will be released from his obligation if he has rendered to a stranger such services as would by their performance free him from his obligation to his patron.   1. If several patrons have deliberately gone to different areas and have at the same time prescribed services from a freedman, it can be held that the time for services [begins to] run, but that the freedman is not bound, because the failure to render the services would not be his fault, but that of the patrons, as happens when services are prescribed from a freedman who is ill. But if the patrons come from different communities and each stays in his own, they should agree on the services they are to receive from him; otherwise, when the services are simultaneously prescribed, if there is no agreement about who is to receive what, it is hard for one who can gain his freedom within ten days by the performance of services to be compelled to pay five days' worth of services to the other [patron].

24   JULIAN, *Digest, book 52:* Whenever a certain type of services is made a matter of stipulation, for instance, those of an artistic or skilled nature, they in fact cannot be sued for except when overdue, because a period of time is inherent in the obligation, not in the words [in which it is framed], but in the execution of the service itself, just as when we stipulate that "x" is to be provided at Ephesus, the day [for its performance] is contained [within the stipulation]. For that reason, the following stipulation is ineffective: "Do you promise to provide one hundred of your artistic services today?" However, the services become due from the day when the stipulation was framed. But services which a patron demands from a freedman are not due immediately, because the transaction between them appears to provide that they were not due before they had been called for; naturally, since the freedman should provide services according to the convenience of the patron; and this cannot properly be said in the case of a craftsman or painter.

25   JULIAN, *Digest, book 65:* The patron who hires out the services of his freedman is not immediately to be perceived to be making a profit out of him; but this can be inferred from the kind of services and from the character of the patron and his freedman.   1. For if someone has as a freedman a ballet dancer or mimic and is of such limited fortune that he cannot otherwise use his services than by hiring them out, he is to be considered as demanding services rather than as engaged in business.   2. Likewise, doctors have often produced as freedmen slaves [who are skilled] in the same art, whose services they cannot otherwise continually use except by hiring them out. And the same can be said in the case of other skilled work.   3. But a [patron] who can use the services of his freedman and prefers to get a price for them by hiring him out is to be considered as making a profit from the freedman's services.   4. But sometimes patrons provide services on hire at the request of the freedmen themselves; and if they do, they are to be considered as taking a price for the services rather than making a profit from them.

26   ALFENUS VARUS, *Digest, book 7:* A freedman who was a doctor, because he thought that if his freedmen were not to practice medicine, he would have far more patients, demanded that they accompanied him but did no work. Does he have a right to do so or not? [Alfenus Varus] gave it as his opinion that he has, provided that he required nonservile services from them, that is, so as to let them rest at noon and pay attention to their health and hygiene.   1. Likewise, I asked: If freedmen were unwilling to provide these services, what value should be put on them? He gave it as his opinion that they should be assessed in accordance with the profit from their services, not from the advantage the patron would obtain as a result of the inconvenience afforded them if he were to prevent them from practicing medicine.

27   JULIAN, *Minicius, book 1:* If a freedman practices the profession of a ballet dancer, it is true that he should provide his services free, not only for his patron himself but also for the latter's friends' entertainments; just as it is true that a freedman too who practices

medicine will attend, if his patron wishes it, the latter's friends without payment. For the patron, in order to use his freedman's services, is not obliged to be forever giving entertainments or being ill.

28   PAUL, *Right of a Patron, sole book:* If a freedwoman shared between two or more patrons has married with the consent of one of them, the other patron retains the right to her services.

29   ULPIAN, *Edict, book 64:* If there has been an action in a suit for services with a freedman and the patron has died, it is agreed that it is not to be transferred to an heir who is a stranger; but a son, even in the case where he is not heir, and even if issue had not been joined, nevertheless has every right to it, provided that he has not been disinherited.

30   CELSUS, *Digest, book 12:* If a freedman has sworn to render as many services as his patron has judged fit, the judgment of the patron will be ratified only where it is a fair one. And the intention of [freedmen] who nominate a person instead of a fixed limit is roughly that they do it because they hope his judgment will be proper, not that they wish to be immoderately bound.   1. An action in respect of services due before her marriage is given against a freedwoman who has married with her patron's consent.

31   MODESTINUS, *Rules, book 1:* Where no services have been imposed, a slave who has been manumitted cannot be compelled to perform services which he has not promised, even if he has performed them of his own free will at some time or another.

32   MODESTINUS, *Encyclopaedia, book 6:* A freedman who has bound himself to pay money to his patron [which the patron has requested merely] to increase the price of his liberty is not bound. Alternatively, if the patron has exacted the money, he cannot seek *bonorum possessio* in respect of the freedman's estate.

33   JAVOLENUS, *Cassius, book 6:* Services cannot be imposed in such a manner as to make the freedman furnish his own food.

34   POMPONIUS, *Quintus Mucius, book 22:* It must be understood that obligations to perform services are sometimes decreased or increased or changed. For while a freedman is ill, his patron loses days of work which have begun to be reckoned. But if a freedwoman who has promised services attains such social position that it is not fitting for her to render them to her patron, these obligations will be extinguished *ipso jure.*

35   PAUL, *Lex Julia et Papia, book 2:* A freedwoman over the age of fifty is not compelled to perform services for her patron.

36   ULPIAN, *Lex Julia et Papia, book 11:* Labeo says that it is clear that a partnership contracted between a freedman and his patron in consideration for freedom has no validity in law.

37   PAUL, *Lex Julia et Papia, book 2:* "The freedman who shall have two or more male or female children in his power apart from one who has engaged in acting or has hired out his services to fight with wild beasts; none such is to give, do, or perform any work by way of gift or service or anything else which he has sworn, promised, or bound himself to do for his patron, male or female, or their children in return for his freedom."   1. And if he has not two [children] in power at the same time, but one of five years in age, he will be freed from the obligation of performing services.   1a. Children who are dead benefit a freedman in respect of services subsequently imposed, as Julian says.   2. But if, after the loss of one child, he binds himself and then another is born, Pomponius says that it is more reasonable for the dead child to be associated with the second one so as to free him [from the obligation of services].   3. But it is of no importance whether he makes a promise to the patron himself or those in his power.   4. But if a patron has assigned a freedman to his creditor, the same cannot be maintained; for this assignment represents consideration in lieu of payment. Nevertheless, it is possible to hold that if, in respect of a service promised to his patron, he has subsequently been assigned to another, he is freed [from his obligation] in accordance with this law; for it is true that he expressed the promise to his patron, although it is not now due to the patron; but if the freedman initially made his promise on being assigned by the patron, he is not freed from it.   5. Release is effective not only insofar as future services are concerned but also with regard to those that are past.   6. Julian [maintains that] even if the services have already been claimed, release is to be

granted him if he has produced children. But if he has been condemned for failure to render services, he cannot be released, since money has already become payable.   7. A *postumus* born to a freedman does not release his father's heirs, because release should proceed from the freedman himself, and it is incomprehensible that anyone can be released after death. But children already born procure [for their father] an advantage in accordance with the law.   8. Even if release has been conferred on the person of the freedman, his guarantors will also be released in accordance with the view expressed by the law; but if the freedman has offered an *expromissor*, this section will be of no advantage to the latter.

38   CALLISTRATUS, *Monitory Edict, book 3:* Only those services are understood to have been imposed that can be performed without endangering reputation or life. For if a prostitute has been manumitted, she should not perform the same services for her patron, although she still earns her living by prostitution; nor should a gladiator offer such services after manumission, because they cannot be performed without endangering life.   1. If, however, a freedman practices a craft, he will have to offer services of this kind to his patron, even if he has learned his craft after manumission. But if he has ceased to practice it, he will have to perform services of a kind that are not detrimental to his status, for instance, to reside with his patron, go abroad, and execute his business.

39   PAUL, *Plautius, book 7:* If a stipulation has been made by a patron in the following terms, "if you have not provided ten days' work, do you promise to give twenty sesterces," it is to be seen whether an action for twenty [sesterces] is to be refused on the ground that they have been promised with the object of restricting the [freedman's] freedom, as well as [an action] for services, which have not been promised. Or are the services to [be treated] by a fiction as though they had been promised, to the extent that the patron is not totally barred [from his rights]? And the praetor, too, is of the opinion that the services have to this extent been promised.   1. The next question is whether the freedman should secure that judgment is not passed against him for a sum greater than twenty, because the patron seems in some wise to have set this valuation on the services, and therefore should not [be allowed] to exceed his estimate of twenty. But it is inequitable, and the freedman should not be allowed to take advantage of this loophole, because, on the one hand, he cannot approve [the terms of] the obligation and, on the other, complain that it is unjust.

40   PAPINIAN, *Questions, book 20:* If a patron's property has been sold, he will be granted an action for services due after the sale, even though he can maintain himself. But an action for services due before the sale will not be granted, because he is pleading [an action] on the basis of what has gone before [the sale].

41   PAPINIAN, *Replies, book 5:* A freedman who has been released from his obligation to provide services and has thereby attained an unfettered right to make a will is nonetheless obliged to hold his patron in respect. The matter of the provision of food is a different one, when it is agreed that a freedman supplies a patron in need.

42   PAPINIAN, *Replies, book 9:* I want my slave Cerdo to be manumitted in such a way that he "promises" services to my heir. The manumitted slave is not compelled to promise, but even if he has promised, an action will not be awarded against him. For a person who has granted freedom by way of *fideicommissum* has not been in a position to derogate from public law.

43   PAPINIAN, *Replies, book 19:* A freedman who is bound to perform services shall not enlist in the army without incurring wrong to his patron.

44   SCAEVOLA, *Questions, book 4:* If a freedman has been tardy in performing his services, his guarantor is liable; there can be no delay on the part of the guarantor [in this sense]. But in the case of a slave due, a guarantor is personally liable also as a result of his own delay.

45   SCAEVOLA, *Replies, book 2:* Can the freedman of a clothing merchant engage in the same business in the same community and the same area without the permission of his patron? [Scaevola] has given it as his opinion that there is no rule to prevent him, if his patron will not suffer as a result.

46   VALENS, *Fideicommissa, book 5:* It is established that a claim for services should not be awarded against a freedwoman in concubinage with her patron, any more than if she were married to him.

47   VALENS, *Fideicommissa, book 6:* Campanus observes that the praetor should not allow a gift, duty, or services to be imposed on one who is manumitted as a result of a *fideicommissum*. But if, knowing that he could refuse, [a freedman] has allowed himself to be bound, a claim for services

should not be frustrated because he appears to have given them [voluntarily].

48 HERMOGENIAN, *Epitome of Law, book 2:* Just as a patron, so too his son, grandson, and great grandson, if they have consented to the marriage of a freedwoman, lose the right to demand services. For the woman to whose marriage a patron has agreed should be in the service of her husband. 1. But if the marriage to which the patron has consented is void, the patron is not prevented from demanding services. 2. The right to services is not denied a patroness or likewise the daughter, granddaughter, or great-granddaughter of a patron who has consented to the marriage of a freedwoman, because their performance incurs no slight on them nor on the married freedwoman who performs them.

49 GAIUS, *Cases, sole book:* A freedman of two patrons can, on occasion, perform in full different services for each of them at one and the same time, for instance, where he is a scribe, and renders services to one patron by copying books, but the other [patron], while traveling abroad with his household, has prescribed as [the freedman's] services the caretakership of his house; for nothing prevents him from copying out books while looking after the house. And Neratius has made this point in his work, *Parchments.*

50 NERATIUS, *Replies, book 1:* [Neratius says that] the performance of services depends on the character of the person performing them; for those services are to be performed which befit his station, abilities, habits, and occupation. 1. But not only the freedman, but anyone else engaged in performing services, is to be provided with food, or to be allowed sufficient time to earn the price of his food, and all are to be left time to take necessary care of themselves.

51 PAUL, *Handbooks, book 2:* Sometimes a claim for services survives, even though there is no right as patron, as happens in the case of brothers of the assignee of a freedman, or where the grandson of one patron survives and the son of the other.

2

FREEDMEN'S PROPERTY

1 ULPIAN, *Edict, book 42:* This edict has been put forward by the praetor for the purpose of regulating the respect which freedmen are to show to their patrons. For, as Servius observes, in former times [patrons] were accustomed to make the most severe demands on their freedmen, that is, to repay the enormous privilege conferred on freedmen when they are brought out of slavery to Roman *civitas.* 1. And indeed Rutilius was the first praetor to proclaim that he would not allow a patron more than an action for services and partnership, namely, where a pledge has been made, so that where a freedman did not show due obedience to his patron, the latter would be admitted to partnership [in his goods]. 2. Later praetors promised patrons *bonorum possessio* of a fixed part [of the freedman's property]; for evidently the idea of partnership had led to an offer of the same share with the result that what the freedman in his lifetime used to offer in the name of partnership he gave after his death.

2 POMPONIUS, *Sabinus, book 4:* Where a patron who has been passed over in a freedman's will will has been in a position to seek *bonorum possessio* contrary to the terms of a will and has died before doing so, or the time within which he may claim *bonorum possessio* [in respect of the freeman's estate] has passed, his children, or those of the freedman's other patron, will be able [to claim it] in accordance with that part of the edict whereby, in the event of the first claimant's failing to enter a claim, or even not wishing the property to fall to him, [*possessio*] is given to those next entitled, as if the former were not members of that category. 1. But if a patron who had been instituted heir had died in the lifetime of the freedman leaving children, it has been asked whether [the children] can seek *bonorum possessio* contrary to the terms of a will; and the argument has reached the point that the time of death in respect of which *bonorum possessio* is offered is to be examined, to see whether the patron is already

dead at that time with the result that if he is not, his children cannot seek *bonorum possessio* in accordance with the first part of the edict. 2. If an emancipated son had left a grandson in the power of his grandfather, that son is to be given *bonorum possessio* of a half share where a freedman dies intestate, although at law the estate actually belongs to the grandson on an intestacy, because *bonorum possessio* of his due share would rather be given to the son, even contrary to the terms of a will of that freedman.

3   ULPIAN, *Edict, book 41:* Although the freedman has obtained the right to a ring from the emperor, the patron succeeds in contravention of his will, as is prescribed in many rescripts; for he lives as a freeborn man but dies as a freedman. 1. Obviously, where he has been restored to his birthright, *bonorum possessio* contrary to the terms of a will does not issue. 2. Likewise, if he has obtained from the emperor an unfettered capacity to make a will. 3. But if someone has bought him with the proviso that he manumit, he will fall under this part of the edict. 4. If someone has accepted a cash payment to manumit him, he does not take *bonorum possessio* contrary to the terms of a will. 5. For a patron to receive *bonorum possessio* contrary to the terms of a will, the estate must have been accepted or *bonorum possessio* claimed; but it is enough if one of the heirs has accepted the estate or claimed *bonorum possessio*. 6. On the other hand, the patron is totally excluded from property acquired by a freedman during military service. 7. If a patron has been deported and reinstated, he can receive *bonorum possessio* contrary to the terms of a will in respect of his freedman's property. The same is to be held in the case of a freedman who has been deported and has been reinstated. 8. If a son-in-power has manumitted a slave forming part of his *peculium castrense*, he is under the constitution of the deified Hadrian a patron and will be admitted to *bonorum possessio* contrary to the terms of a will as a patron. 9. If the person to whom a freedman has been assigned has accused him on a capital charge, he cannot seek *bonorum possessio* contrary to the terms of a will and will not impede his brothers' claims; but they will apply for *bonorum possessio* as they would if they were grandchildren through a second son; for a freedman assigned to one of two sons does not cease to be a freedman of the other; and there is more to be said; although a brother has neglected to apply for *bonorum possessio*, the other brother to whom the freedman was not assigned can succeed and apply for *bonorum possessio* contrary to the terms of a will. 10. A patron is called to *bonorum possessio* contrary to the terms of a will whenever he has not been instituted heir to the portion owed him. 11. If a patron has been instituted under a condition and that condition has been fulfilled in the lifetime of the testator, he cannot receive *bonorum possessio* contrary to the terms of a will. 12. What, therefore, is the position, if the condition is in suspense at the time of death but has been fulfilled before *bonorum possessio* is offered to the *patronus*, that is, before he has accepted the inheritance? Is he to be called in accordance with this part of the edict? And it is more reasonable to look at the time when the inheritance is accepted; and we observe this rule. 13. But, nevertheless, if the condition was imposed with reference to past time or to the present, the patron does not appear to have been instituted under a condition; for either it has been fulfilled in which case he has been unconditionally instituted or else it is nonexistent in which case he has not been instituted heir. 14. If a freedman has appointed his patron heir in the following words, "if my son dies in my lifetime, let my patron be heir," the appointment does not appear to be bad; for if the son has died, he will be able, as the condition is fulfilled, to take *bonorum possessio*. 15. If his due portion has been left to the patron as a legacy, even though he has not been appointed heir, he has received satisfaction. 16. But even if he has been instituted in respect of a smaller portion than that owed him, but the remaining portion owed him has been supplied to him from legacies or *fideicommissa*, he also appears to have received satisfaction. 17. But the patron may also be able to be provided with his due portion from gifts made in contemplation of death; for such gifts take the place

of legacies. 18. But even if the freedman has not made gifts in contemplation of death to his patron, but gifts, nevertheless, have been made to him in contemplation of his due portion, the same will have to be held; for in that case they either will be thought of as if made in contemplation of death, or will, as though claimed, serve to prevent the patron [from claiming] *bonorum possessio* contrary to the terms of a will. 19. If something has been given to the patron for the purpose of fulfilling a condition, it will have to be reckoned toward the portion due to him, provided that it has had its origin in the property of the freedman. 20. For we give the patron the portion due to him of those goods the freedman had at the time he died; for we look to the time of death. But if he has rid himself of property by fraud, the praetor intended such property to be considered as if it were part of his estate.

4   PAUL, *Edict, book 42:* If a slave has detected the murder of his master, the praetor normally rules that he is free; and it is established that he obtains his freedom as if in virtue of a *senatus consultum*, and is no one's freedman. 1. If a freedman has been captured by the enemy and has died in captivity, although the name of freedman does not apply to him, nevertheless, by provision of the *lex Cornelia*, which validates his will just as if he has died in the community, *bonorum possessio* will also have to be given to his patron. 2. If the patron has suffered deportation, his son has a right to *bonorum possessio* in respect of the freedman's property, and the condition of the patron, who is considered as one dead, is no obstacle to him. And the case is different if the patron is in captivity; for he impedes his children's claim on the ground of the prospect of reinstatement by *postliminium*. 3. If a stranger has been instituted heir by the freedman and has been requested to hand back the estate to the son, the patron is to be barred [from succession], since, in accordance with the *senatus consultum Trebellianum*, when the estate is handed back, the son is considered to take the place of the heir.

5   GAIUS, *Provincial Edict, book 15:* If a freedman who has a patron with children has instituted the patron heir to the share due to him, he should appoint his [patron's] children as substitute heirs to the same portion, so that even if the patron has died in the lifetime of his freedman, satisfaction appears to have been given to his children. 1. If a freedman has a patron with an emancipated son who is father of a grandchild who has remained in his grandfather's family, the freedman will have to give satisfaction only to the son, and not to the grandson as well; for the fact that both are called together to succession to the [emancipated son's] father is irrelevant.

6   ULPIAN, *Edict, book 43:* Even if the freedman's children have been instituted in respect of a modest portion, [the patron] cannot seek *bonorum possessio* contrary to will; for Marcellus has also observed in the ninth book of his *Digest* that a freedman's son, whatever the size of the share he be appointed heir, displaces the patron. When a patron's daughter had been instituted heir by a freedman and the will in which the appointment had been made had been alleged a forgery and the daughter died after an appeal had been entered and was pending, the deified Marcus came to the aid of the daughter's heirs with the result that they took what she would have taken had she lived. 2. If a freedman's son who had been instituted heir by him, has refrained from taking the estate, although he is nominally heir, the patron is admitted [to succession]. 3. But also in the case where a man has meddled in his father's estate or who has accepted the estate and through *restitutio in integrum* has refrained from [taking] it, a patron will be capable of admission. 4. If a patron and his children have accepted an estate in accordance with the disposition of a deceased freedman or have chosen instead to claim a legacy or *fideicommissum*, they are not admitted to *bonorum possessio* contrary to the terms of a will.

7   GAIUS, *Provincial Edict, book 15:* For it is ridiculous to permit the same man partly to comply with, and partly to set aside, the disposition of the deceased.

8   ULPIAN, *Edict, book 43:* If his application has in fact been unsuccessful, I hold that he is not prevented from receiving assistance. Further, even if he accepted, as if instituted in respect of the share owed to him, and it later appeared that he had accepted a lesser portion than he hoped for, it is equitable that he should be allowed the assistance due to him. Even if the heir agreed before witnesses to pay his legacy and later regretted it, I submit that he can be granted assistance. 1. If a patron has claimed a legacy left him and it has been recovered by a judgment, he is entitled to the assistance prescribed by law, because he does not take what he hoped to take. But even if it has not been recovered in full, but he takes somewhat less than he thought, assistance will have to be granted him. 2. If a patron has claimed a legacy left to his slave or his son, he will be barred from suit for *bonorum possessio* contrary to the terms of a will, just as if he had claimed a legacy left to himself. 3. But if he has claimed a gift made in contemplation of death, it is to be held that he is barred from *bonorum possessio* contrary to the terms of a will, provided he has claimed it after the freedman's death. But if the freedman has made the gift in his lifetime,

and he has accepted it, he will not thereby be excluded from *bonorum possessio* contrary to the terms of a will, because he can say that he hoped his freedman would show gratitude to him in his will as well; and he should be allowed to give up what he has received or make it up to his portion proportionately.   4. Wherefore it is held that even if a gift has been made to the patron after the death of the freedman for the purpose of fulfilling a condition, he is excluded from *bonorum possessio* contrary to the terms of a will, as if he had recognized the disposition.   5. If a patron, being under twenty-five years old, has recognized a disposition made by a freedman, we are of the opinion that he should be restored to his previous position so that he may receive [*bonorum possessio*] contrary to the terms of a will.

9   PAUL, *Edict, book 42:* A person who has sought to reduce his father's freedman to slavery cannot receive *bonorum possessio* as a child [of the patron].

10   ULPIAN, *Edict, book 44:* If one of the patrons has not received satisfaction, so that the other is left more than his share of a freedman's property, the one who has not received satisfaction shall be granted an action to supplement his portion from what has been left to an heir who is a stranger and to the [other] patron above and beyond his share. The same rule will apply where there are several patrons.   1. Julian says that a person who has been disinherited by his grandfather is excluded from the property of the latter's freedmen, but is not debarred from the property of his own father's freedmen; but if he has been disinherited by his father, but not his grandfather, he not only is debarred from the property of his father's freedmen but also should be excluded from the property of those of his grandfather, because he acquires his grandfather's freedmen through his father; but if his father has been disinherited by his grandfather, but not he himself, the grandson can seek *bonorum possessio* contrary to the terms of a will in respect of the property of his grandfather's freedmen. Julian also says that where my father has disinherited me and my grandfather has disinherited my father and my grandfather has died first, I am excluded from the property of the freedmen of both; but if my father had predeceased my grandfather, it will have to be held that disherison by my father in no way prejudices me in respect of the property of my grandfather's freedmen.

11   JULIAN, *Digest, book 26:* But if my father has been disinherited by his father and I have been disinherited neither by my father nor by my grandfather, in the event of my father's death I shall have rights in respect of my grandfather's and my father's freedmen; so long as my father is alive, as long as I am in his power, I shall not seek *bonorum possessio* in respect of the property of my grandfather's freedmen, and if emancipated, I shall not be barred.

12   ULPIAN, *Edict, book 44:* If a patron, having made his will under military law, has disinherited his son by omitting to mention him, the disherison will necessarily be prejudicial to him; for it is a fact that he has been disinherited.   1. If a man has assigned his freedman to his son and has disinherited him, [the son] can be admitted to *bonorum possessio* in respect of the freedman's property.   2. If someone has been disinherited by his father without malice, but for some other reason, the disherison does not prejudice him; suppose, for instance, he has been disinherited by reason of insanity or because he was an *impubes* and the instituted heir has been requested to restore the estate to him.   3. If someone, being disinherited, has been adjudged, even wrongly, not to have been disinherited, he is not debarred; for, once given, such judgment is to stand.   4. If a patron's son, being disinherited, has succeeded in a complaint against an undutiful will in respect of part of the estate and has failed with regard to part of it, let us see whether the disherison is prejudicial to him. And I judge that it is, because the will in which he was disinherited is valid.   5. But in the case of a will where the inheritance has not been accepted and *bonorum possessio* has not been sought, disherison does not prejudice the children; for it is ridiculous for the will to be valid only insofar as to render the disherison effective, when it is not valid in other respects.   6. If the patron's son has been named heir in the first degree and disinherited in the second, the disherison does not prejudice him, since either he has fallen to be heir by his father's wish or could have been heir; for the father should not appear to have thought the son whom he has called to his own property in the first place unworthy of the property of his freedmen. And it is not to be supposed that even a person who has been disinherited in the first degree and then appointed substitute heir is debarred from a freedman's property. Therefore, a person who has been instituted heir in the first or subsequent degree or any other, even though he has been disinherited in the same will, is not to be excluded from a freedman's property.   7. If a patron's son, being emancipated, has refused to accept the estate or a son-in-power has refused to keep it,

nevertheless, he will take *bonorum possessio* in respect of a freedman's property.

13 JULIAN, *Digest, book 26:* The son of a patron who has been disinherited cannot receive *bonorum possessio* contrary to the terms of a will in respect of the property of his father's freedmen, even if his own son has been appointed heir; for although he is *necessarius* [*heres*] to his father, he is admitted to the estate, not in his own right, but through another. And it is clearly established that if an emancipated son has been disinherited and his slave appointed heir, even if he has ordered his slave to accept the inheritance and has thus fallen to be his father's heir, he will not take *bonorum possessio* contrary to the terms of a will in respect of the property of his father's freedmen.

14 ULPIAN, *Edict, book 45:* A man who, being over twenty-five years of age, has accused a freedman of a capital crime or has sought to reduce him to slavery is barred from *bonorum possessio* contrary to the terms of a will. 1. But if a *minor* has accused him, it is to be held that he is not excluded, whether [the *minor*] himself has framed the accusation or whether it has been made by his tutor or curator. 2. But if a *minor*, in fact, has instituted the prosecution, but has received judgment on attaining his majority, the indulgent view will have to be taken that he should be pardoned, because he started [the accusation] as a *minor.* For the fact that he did not drop the accusation or seek to have the case withdrawn cannot be raised as an objection against him; for in the one case, he would come up against the [*senatus consultum*] *Turpillianum,* and the other is not easy of achievement. Obviously, if the case had been publicly withdrawn and, on attaining majority, he reopens proceedings at this very time, it is to be held that he is to be barred from [*bonorum possessio*]. For on majority, he could have dropped the accusation which had been withdrawn without fear [of any repercussions]. 3. He particularly appears to have instituted an accusation for a capital crime who prosecutes it in proceedings where the punishment is the supreme penalty or exile, an alternative to deportation, where *civitas* is lost. 4. But if someone has accused a freedman on a charge where the penalty is not capital, but the judge was however resolved to increase the penalty, the patron's son is not thereby impeded; for the judge's lack of skill or severity should not present an obstacle to the patron's son who has brought a charge of a lighter nature. 5. But if he has not accused him, but has given evidence against the freedman on a capital charge or has provided an accuser, I submit that he is excluded from [*bonorum possessio*] contrary to the terms of a will. 6. If the freedman accused the patron's son of *maiestas* and the patron's son has demanded that he receive capital punishment for calumny, he should not be barred by this edict. I submit that the same is true where he has been impeached by [the freedman] and has laid countercharges against him; for he is to be pardoned if he wanted to punish him in the face of provocation. 7. If the son considered it necessary to avenge his father's death, is it to be held that he is to be assisted in this instance too, where he has accused his father's freedman on the ground that he happened to be his father's doctor, or attendant, or had another such occupation that had given him access to the father? And I submit that he is to be assisted, if, influenced by affection for his father and the risk to his father's estate, he felt it necessary to bring an accusation, albeit one of no real substance. 8. But we hold that a person who has preferred charges and who has wound up his case, bringing it to the point of obtaining a verdict, has brought an accusation. But if he has stopped at an earlier stage, he has not made an accusation, and we observe this rule. But if he has given up when an appeal has been lodged, he will be indulgently regarded as not having carried through his accusation. If, therefore, the freedman has died pending appeal, the patron's son will be admitted to *bonorum possessio,* because the freedman by his death is freed from sentence. 9. If a patron's son has supplied the role of advocate to the freedman's accuser, he is not to be barred [from *bonorum possessio*]; for the advocate is not the accuser. 10. If the father in his will has made provision for the freedman to be impeached on the ground that he had procured poison [to use] against him or had committed some other crime against his person, it is more reasonable that the children who have not of their own accord assumed the prosecution should be pardoned. 11. But even if the patron's son has brought an accusation and proved the charge and the freedman in question has subsequently been reinstated, he will not have to be barred [from *bonorum possessio*]; for he carried through to its conclusion the charge that he brought.

15 TRYPHONINUS, *Disputations, book 17:* The same is true in the case of a charge proved against a freedman, whereby he had deserved capital punishment, but was punished more leniently, for instance, by *relegatio*; for the praetor has passed judgment on a vexatious accuser.

16 ULPIAN, *Edict, book 45:* A person who has opposed the demand for liberty of a man who was in a state of slavery does not appear to have demanded [the reduction of a freedman] to slavery, but one who has sought to reduce to slavery a man who was free. 1. But should a person be debarred as if he has sought to reduce to slavery a man he claims was not entirely his own property, but of whom he had partial ownership or usufruct, or on whom he had some other claim that he cannot have on him unless he is a slave? And this seems to be the proper view. 2. If he has claimed him as a slave and won his case and, when the truth subsequently became known, has allowed him to remain free, he should not be prejudiced, especially if he had good reason for the mistake. 3. A person does not appear to have claimed another as a slave if he has dropped his claim before joinder of issue; but even if issue has been joined, it is to be held that he is not prejudiced since he has not persisted to gain a verdict. 4. If a patron's son has been disinherited or has sought to reduce his father's freedman to slavery or has accused him of a capital crime, his children who are not in power are not thereby prejudiced. And the deified brothers have made this ruling in a rescript addressed to the Quintilii. 5. If someone has received *bonorum possessio* contrary to the terms of a will in respect of a freedman's property, he is barred from any disposition made by the freedman, not merely if he has been appointed heir by the freedman but also in the case where he has been substituted to his son who is an *impubes*. For Julian has also observed, if a patron, after claiming *bonorum possessio*, has accepted a freedman's estate belonging to his son who is an *impubes*, he should be refused actions [in respect of it]. 6. But if something has been left to a patron in a codicil or a gift has been made to him in contemplation of death, he will likewise be denied the right to recover them. 7. Sometimes, obviously, a patron will be granted the right to recover a legacy after he has claimed *bonorum possessio* where he will gain nothing from it, because he has perhaps been asked to hand it over to another. 8. Furthermore, the praetor declares that he will refuse them not only what has been expressly given to them but also where, suppose, something is to come to them through others, for instance, through persons in power, which, in fact, they are in a position to take and not to hand over to others. 9. We shall grant a patron the right to sue for a legacy if the freedman of the patron has given his freedom to a slave, having left the price of the slave to the patron to be taken before division of the property. 10. The person who has been appointed substitute to the patron who has sought *possessio* contrary to the terms of a will is not given an action for that portion, possession of which has been awarded to the patron. 11. If the patron has been made substitute heir and has died in the lifetime of the testator, it is established that the son of the patron who seeks *bonorum possessio* contrary to the terms of a will obtains the share, not of the substitute heir alone, but takes something from all the heirs in respect of his portion.

17 ULPIAN, *Edict, book 47:* Where a freedman dies without children, his patrons, male and female, are among the first to take *bonorum possessio* and, indeed, do so together. But if there are persons next in line to the patrons, male and female, they too are admitted together.

18 PAUL, *Edict, book 43:* Children of a patroness, even if born out of wedlock, will take *bonorum possessio* of the property of their mother's freedman, but those of a patron take only if they are legitimate.

19 ULPIAN, *Disputations, book 4:* If a patron who had been instituted heir to a share less than that to which he was entitled at law had alleged that the will was a forgery and had not taken under it, it is clear that *bonorum possessio* contrary to the terms of a will is not offered to him from the fact that he has lost his inheritance by his own act when he rashly declared that [the will] was a forgery. 1. But if he has been instituted in respect of the share due to him, whether he has accepted it or not, he is barred from *bonorum possessio* contrary to the terms of a will, as if he has taken the portion due to him. And he will not be able to seek *bonorum possessio* contrary to the terms of a will.

20   JULIAN, *Digest, book 25:* A freedman under a condition of having to swear an oath, which the praetor normally relaxes, has instituted his patron heir; I submit that it should not be doubted that he is to be excluded from *bonorum possessio*; for the fact is that he has been appointed heir.   1. If Titius had been left a legacy as the subject of a *fideicommissum* to be handed over to the patron, Titius is denied an action for legacies, if satisfaction in respect of the portion due to him has been given to the patron by the appointed heir.   2. A freedman appointed as heir his patron together with a stranger in respect of a half share; the whole fourth in respect of which the patron had been instituted will have to be assigned to him; he takes the residue of the share due to him from all the heirs in proportion to their respective shares.   3. It will be suitable to preserve the same rule in respect of a legacy left jointly to the patron and Titius, so that part of the legacy is assigned to the patron to make up the portion due to him, and of the remaining part, as much is taken from Titius as from the heir according to the size of his share.   4. If a freedman has conditionally instituted his emancipated son heir and, on the failure of the condition, the substitute heir has accepted the inheritance, I ask whether the praetor should assist the patron against the substitute heir in respect of the portion due to him or against the emancipated son with regard to the whole estate. I have given it as my opinion that when a father has conditionally instituted his son heir in the first degree, if the condition under which the son has been instituted fails, the estate devolves on the second degree; or if the son has died while the condition is still in suspense, the patron has the right to *bonorum possessio* in respect of the share due to him against the substitute heir. And the position is the same too, if the son, being barred by lapse of time, has failed to seek *bonorum possessio* or has renounced it. But if, on the failure of the condition, the inheritance belongs to the son, the praetor will rather protect the emancipated son against the substitute heir. For in my opinion, whenever a son is conditionally appointed heir, sometimes his disherison in the substitute degree is necessary, at other times it is superfluous; for if the condition is of a kind to be within the son's power, for instance, "when he has made a will," I submit that even where the condition has not arisen, the son gives place to the substitutes; but if the condition were not in the son's power, for instance, "if Titius has become consul," then the substitute heir is not admitted unless the son has been expressly disinherited in that degree.   5. If a freedman has instituted his emancipated son heir and has given him a *fideicommissum* to hand over the whole estate to Sempronius, and the son, when he said the inheritance was onerous, has accepted it on the praetor's orders and has handed it over to Sempronius, the patron will not unjustly be granted *bonorum possessio* of the share due to him, just as if, not the son, but the person to whom the inheritance has been handed over had been heir to the freedman. 6. Likewise, when the son of a freedman has failed to claim his father's estate and the co-heir has assumed the whole burden of it, the patron will have to be given *bonorum possessio*. For in either case, the share is taken not from the son, but from the stranger.

21   JULIAN, *Digest, book 26:* If one of three patrons gives up his suit for *bonorum possessio,* the [remaining] two will take equal shares.

22   MARCIAN, *Institutes, book 1:* If the son-in-power, being engaged in military service, manumits [a slave], according to the view of which Julian in fact approves in the twenty-seventh book of his *Digest,* he will make him a freedman of his father; but as long as he is alive, he says, the son takes precedence over the father so far as the freedman's property is concerned. But the deified Hadrian in a rescript to Flavius Aper has ruled that he makes him his own freedman, not his father's.

23   JULIAN, *Digest, book 27:* If a freedman has passed over his patron and has instituted a stranger as his heir and the patron has allowed himself to be adopted before seeking *bonorum possessio* and the appointed heir has failed to take the inheritance, the patron can seek *bonorum possessio* in respect of the freedman's entire estate as heir at law.   1. If a freedman has died intestate where there are left a patron's son and two grandchildren, being the children of a second son, the grandchildren will not be admitted as long as there was a son, because it is plain that the next in line are called [in turn] to the inheritance of a freedman.   2. But if one of two patrons had left one son and the other two, I have held that each takes a proportionate share.

24   JULIAN, *Digest, book 65:* If one of two patrons has exacted from a freedman shared by

them in common an oath not to marry or has predeceased the freedman, the one who had no part in this blameworthy conduct or has survived will alone take *bonorum possessio* of the share due to each of them.

25   JULIAN, *Urseius Ferox, book 1:* As long as *bonorum possessio* of the portion due to him can be given to a patron a defense is granted to debtors against an heir who brings a claim: "if the patron is not in a position where he can claim *bonorum possessio* contrary to the terms of a will in respect of the portion due to him."

26   AFRICANUS, *Questions, book 2:* A farm worth forty had been left to a freedman who has eighty. He died on the day when the time for claiming the legacy began to run, leaving a stranger as his heir. [Julian] gave it as his opinion that the patron can claim the share due to him; for it appears that the deceased had at the time of his death property worth more than one hundred, since his estate can amount to more on account of reckoning in the legacy. And it makes no difference whether the instituted heir renounces the legacy left to the freedman or not; for if the *lex Falcidia* comes into question, a legacy of this kind, even though it has been refused, is reckoned toward the fourth of the estate for the legatees.

27   AFRICANUS, *Questions, book 4:* If a grandson is disinherited in the lifetime of a son, the disherison will prejudice him in respect of the property of his grandfather's freedmen.

28   FLORENTINUS, *Institutes, book 10:* If a freedman has been sentenced to capital punishment, the right his patrons would have to his property, if he on whom sentence had been passed had died a natural death, is not to be taken from them. But it is resolved that the remainder of the property which does not belong to the manumitter at civil law is to be claimed for the imperial treasury.   1. The same rules are observed in the case of property of persons who from fear of accusation have committed suicide or escaped, as have been established in the case of the property of those persons who have been condemned.

29   MARCIAN, *Institutes, book 9:* A person manumitted in accordance with a *fideicommissum* is in fact the freedman of the manumitter, and the latter can come into his property as if patron, both contrary to the terms of a will and in the case of intestacy. But he is not able to impose services on him, nor sue for services he has imposed on him.   1. But if the deceased has left a slave to his son with a request to manumit him, with the intention that he should have the full right of patron, it is to be argued that he can legally impose services on him.

30   GAIUS, *Urban Praetor's Edict, Chapter on Suit concerning a Person's Freedom, book 2:* If someone has sought to reduce to slavery his father's freedman with the intention of preserving his action for recovery of property, he does not lose the benefit of *bonorum possessio.*

31   MARCELLUS, *Digest, book 9:* A freedman left to his patron a farm which he had bought from him, although it belonged to a third party, and the patron agreed that the legacy belonged to him; he cannot take *bonorum possessio* contrary to the terms of a will, although the legacy has brought him no advantage, because the freedman has left him another's property, since the patron himself had sold it to the freedman.

32   MARCELLUS, *Digest, book 10:* If my freedman has been reduced to slavery and has later been set free by another and has become his freedman, his manumitter takes precedence over me in *bonorum possessio* contrary to the terms of a will.

33   MODESTINUS, *Manumissions, sole book:* If a patron has not maintained his freedman, the *lex Aelia Sentia* takes away impositions levied in return for his freedom, both from the patron and from another interested party, likewise the inheritance from him and his children, unless he has been appointed heir, and *bonorum possessio,* except where it is according to will.

34   JAVOLENUS, *Cassius, book 3:* If a freedman with two patrons has passed over one, made the other heir to half his estate, and left half to a second person who is a stranger, the patron appointed heir takes the share due to him without diminution, but the other patron must be satisfied from the other part of the first patron's share, left to him over and above what was due to him and from the half left to the stranger proportionately.

35   JAVOLENUS, *Letters, book 3:* Seius left the usufruct of a farm to be given to Maevius by his freedman who was his heir; the freedman died leaving Maevius as his heir; I ask, since Seius's son has sought [*bonorum possessio*] contrary to the terms of a will against Maevius, whether the share due to him in the farm is to be handed over to him less the usufruct or in its entirety, because he has received *bonorum possessio* of the property which the freedman had when he died. [Javolenus] gave as his opinion: I submit that the usufruct should be restored to its former condition. And so it will be best to request an arbitrator so that, as a result of his decision, there may be *restitutio in integrum* in respect of the usufruct.

36   JAVOLENUS, *Letters, book 8:* A freedman who was insolvent, having passed over his patron, left as his heirs strangers; I ask whether the patron can seek *bonorum possessio* contrary to the terms of a will. [Javolenus] gave as his opinion: Since the inheritance has been accepted by the appointed heirs, the patron can seek *bonorum possessio*, because the estate which finds an heir is in a state of solvency. And clearly, it is ridiculous to weigh up the right of a patron to apply for *bonorum possessio* contrary to the terms of a will by the reckoning of others and not by his own judgment and for there to be taken from the patron the modest amount he is in a position to claim. For there can be many reasons why it is expedient for a patron to seek *bonorum possessio*, even if the extent of the debt which the freedman has left exceeds the resources of his property, for instance, if there are estates among the freedman's property in which a patron's ancestors have been buried, and the patron considers it worth a great deal that the rights to *bonorum possessio* should belong to him in respect of that part [of the estate] or where there is some slave who is to be assessed not in accordance with the price he would fetch but his sentimental value. Therefore, the right to claim *bonorum possessio* should not be curtailed in the case of one who assesses his freedman's property by his own feelings rather than the arithmetic of others, since the property appears to be adequate from the fact that it has both an heir and a *bonorum possessor.*

37   ULPIAN, *Lex Julia et Papia, book 11:* Julian says, if a patron has sold back services imposed in return for freedom to a freedwoman, his son is barred from *bonorum possessio* for the reason that he does not receive *bonorum possessio* contrary to the terms of a will of a freedman whenever his father has sold back a gift, benefit, or services to the freedman. Obviously, if the son of the patron has sold back the impositions made on account of the grant of freedom, [he says that] the family, nonetheless, takes *bonorum possessio* contrary to the terms of a will of the freedman's property, because a son, by selling back services imposed in return for freedom, does not debar his brother.   1. If a freedman has appointed an heir and he has accepted the inheritance before holding an inquiry of the household slaves, Julian says that the patron is not admitted to *bonorum possessio*; for the patron, too, should have avenged the freedman's death. And the same will have to be held in the case of a patroness.

38   TERENTIUS CLEMENS, *Lex Julia et Papia, book 9:* It is asked whether, when a son has been disinherited, his children are also excluded from *bonorum possessio* in respect of a freedman's estate. And the question undoubtedly has to be decided along the following lines, so that, while the son is alive, so long as his children remain in his power, they are not admitted to *bonorum possessio*, lest those who are barred from *bonorum possessio* in their own name may acquire it through another; but if they have been emancipated by their father or have become *sui juris* in some other way, they are admitted to *bonorum possessio* without any obstacle.   1. If a freedman's son has failed to take his father's estate, his neglect to do so benefits the patron.

39   TERENTIUS CLEMENS, *Lex Julia et Papia, book 10:* If a patron's daughter is in an adoptive family, she is admitted to the property of her father's freedman.

40   TERENTIUS CLEMENS, *Lex Julia et Papia, book 12:* If a father, while disinheriting his son, has provided that he should keep his right over a freedman, the disherison is not prejudicial to him in this respect.

41   PAPINIAN, *Questions, book 12:* If a freedman gives satisfaction to his patron in respect of the portion due to him, but tries to exact something from him against his will, it is asked what ruling we should adopt. For what if ten are left as an additional legacy to the patron instituted heir in respect of the portion due to him, and he is asked to manumit his own slave who is worth ten or less? It is inequitable for him to be willing to take the legacy and

unwilling to free the slave; but, providing he has received his due portion, [it is fair] that he should abstain from taking the legacy and not be forced to liberate the slave, lest he may be compelled to manumit a slave who may be far from deserving manumission. What if the freedman in question has made the same request of a patron instituted sole heir? If there is a substitute heir, it will be possible for the remedy of a decree to issue with justice, so that, on the patron's acceptance of the portion due to him, the remainder comes to the substitute heir in such a fashion that if the slave had perhaps been capable of being purchased, his freedom would be offered him. But if there is no substitution, the praetor who hears cases concerning *fideicommissum* compels the patron who accepts the inheritance of the freedman to grant the slave his freedom.

42 PAPINIAN, *Questions, book 13:* A son appointed heir to his father has adopted by *adrogatio* his brother who has been disinherited and has died leaving him as his heir. The disinherited [son] will not take *bonorum possessio* in respect of the property of his natural father's freedmen; for where adoption of this kind would prejudice a person who has not been disinherited, it should prejudice a person who has been disinherited; for the penalty exacted by law or edict would not be circumvented by adoption. PAUL remarks: He who comes to succession by a right different from the one he has lost is not prejudiced by what he has lost, but is benefited by what he has; so it has been held that a patron, being the son of a patroness, is not impeded by a transgression as patron if he may be admitted as son of the patroness. 1. PAPINIAN. A freedman made Titius heir to property that was *castrensis* and appointed another as heir to the rest. Titius accepted the inheritance. We preferred the view that the patron is not yet in a position to apply for *bonorum possessio*. But the question arose, if the one who received the remaining property fails to take it, whether it accrues to Titius just as if they had received shares of the same inheritance. It is more fitting in my opinion for the remaining property to be offered according to the law on intestacy. Titius, therefore, as heir, will not be able to summon the manumitter, since nothing is being taken from him or from the remaining property that is not yet the subject matter of a case concerning the will. 2. When the son of a freedman, being an *impubes* who is alleged to be a supposititious child, takes *bonorum possessio* in accordance with the first part [of the edict], it has been asked whether the patron of the deceased can take possession. And there is no doubt that those in the succeeding degree are meanwhile debarred; for when one *possessio* takes precedence, the next [person] in line cannot take [possession]. Obviously, if judgment has been given against the allegedly supposititious child, [*possessio*] is not interpreted as having been awarded. But the same will have to be held too in the case of the patron so long as the matter is in dispute. Obviously, insofar as the character of the patron is concerned, the dispute will have to be deferred. 3. If a freedman's will had been alleged a forgery by others in the province and the matter had thus been prolonged by appeal and the patron's daughter whom the freedman had instituted as his heir had died in the meantime, the deified Marcus has preserved to the woman's son that share of the property which the patron's daughter could have taken even on an intestacy had she lived.

43 PAPINIAN, *Questions, book 14:* Julian submits that the patron who, having been substituted to Titius, the instituted heir, in respect of a half share, has accepted *bonorum possessio* while Titius was debating [whether to take the property or not], has taken nothing from the person who has accepted the estate in the event of Titius's subsequent refusal, any more than if he had been instituted under a condition. Therefore, so long as Titius is debating the matter, it will be uncertain whether his half share is converted into possession as a result of substitution, or, in the event of Titius's acceptance, whether the shares due to individual heirs are taken away from them.

44 PAUL, *Questions, book 5:* If you institute a patron heir to the portion owed to him and simply ask him to give [up] a farm and conditionally leave him a sum in compensation, this *fideicommissum* is subjected to a condition. He will be stimulated to action by the following circumstance; for the patron will be burdened by [the necessity of] giving security in respect of the *fideicommissum*. But it is to be held that security is to be given by the *fideicommissarius* through whom the legacy has been made payable to the patron, so that the patron's right is preserved from every point of view. 1. A patron who has been instituted heir with a legacy of a slave, by means of whom the portion due to him would be

supplied, will not seek *bonorum possessio* contrary to the terms of a will, even though the slave has died before the will has been opened.   2. Where a freedman has handed over the due portion from property in existence at the time of his death [by instituting the patron heir to] the estate, or by a legacy, a slave of the freedman, on his return from captivity, nevertheless, increases the estate; the patron cannot complain on the grounds that he has less property in the slave than he would have had if he had been instituted in respect of the portion due to him. The same is also true in the case of alluvium when satisfaction has been given from the property in existence at the time of death. The same is also true where part of a legacy left to a freedman accrues from him who had simultaneously received a gift or [part] of an inheritance on the refusal of his co-heirs to take their inheritance.

45   PAUL, *Questions, book 9:* If a patron has been instituted heir to a sixth and his slave to the remaining share, a *fideicommissum* is not payable from the slave's portion; but if only the slave has been instituted heir, I submit that in this case, too, it is not to be paid from the share due [to the patron].

46   PAUL, *Replies, book 3:* Paul gave it as his opinion that a patron, who, being under a mis-apprehension, has acceded to a spurious disposition of the testator, is not precluded from obtaining *bonorum possessio* contrary to the terms of a will of his freedman.

47   PAUL, *Replies, book 11:* Paul gave it as his opinion that the disherison of a grandson which has been effected not with the intention of dishonoring him, but from some other motive should not prejudice him so as to preclude the possibility of application for *possessio* of property contrary to the terms of a will of his grandfather's freedman.   1. I ask whether, if Titia, daughter of the patron, alleges that her father Titius before his death had written to her a letter, intimating that criminal attempts had been made on his life by his freedmen, and that she, in accordance with the letter, after her father's death, had laid charges against the freedmen, whether this explanation can assist her in any way. Paul gave it as his opinion that inasmuch as she has laid charges in accordance with her father's wishes, she should not be restrained [from seeking] *bonorum possessio* contrary to the terms of a will, since she acted in accordance with not her own, but another's judg-ment.   2. A patron's son sent a letter of a type such as the following to a freedman: "Sem-pronius to his freedman Zoilus, greeting. By reason of your services and on account of the loyalty you have always shown me, I grant you an unfettered power of testamentary dis-position." I ask whether he could leave nothing to his patron's son. Paul gave it as his opin-ion that the freedman in question does not appear to have obtained an unfettered power to dispose of his property by will.   3. Paul gave it as his opinion that a grandson, even if con-ceived after his grandfather's death, can apply for *bonorum possessio* contrary to the terms of a will of his grandfather's freedman, provided that the freedman survived his grandfather, and may be admitted in the case of his intestacy; for Julian's opinion relates only to the question of intestacy, [and] likewise to application for *bonorum possessio* of the grandfather's property.   4. Paul gave it as his opinion that although sons who have been passed over by a father engaged in military service are considered disinherited, never-theless, their father's silence should not prejudice them to the point that they are also to be prevented from obtaining the property of their grandfather's freedmen. The same opinion has been given in respect of the property of their father's freedmen too.

48   SCAEVOLA, *Replies, book 2:* My question concerns one who has indicted a freedman on a charge of burglary. [Scaevola] has given it as his opinion that if he has been indicted on a charge of burglary of the kind that, were it proved, would lead to punishment by condemna-tion to the mines, he should be denied *bonorum possessio*.

49   PAUL, *Views, book 3:* A patron does not lose his rights in the case of a freedman who has been secretly adopted by *adrogatio*.

50   TRYPHONINUS, *Disputations, book 17:* It makes no difference whether a patron, being appointed heir to a lesser portion [than his due], has himself taken the inheritance or whether he has instructed his slave, being the appointed heir, to take the inheritance which he retains; for in either case he will effectively be barred from *bonorum possessio* contrary to the terms of a will.   1. However, if, before ordering his slave to take the inheritance, he has sold or manumitted the slave and thus the new freedman himself or the buyer have fallen to be heirs, the patron is not prevented by the drafting of the edict from acquiring *bono-*

rum possessio contrary to the terms of a will. 2. But should the praetor deny him possessory actions where he intended to use his edict as an instrument of fraud with the object that, being in receipt of a higher price or in virtue of a silent bargain, he would take advantage both of the inheritance offered to him in accordance with his institution and of *bonorum possessio* contrary to the terms of a will? And a patron is more susceptible to the suspicion of getting his hands on the freedman's estate when it is his son who has been appointed heir, albeit that he takes after emancipation, since, in accordance with a [natural] inclination, we hand over to our children all that we possess. 3. But if, before the freedman's will was opened, when the patron was in ignorance of the disposition he had made, he did any of the acts mentioned above in relation to the instituted heir while subject to his power, he will employ his right in the matter of *bonorum possessio* contrary to the terms of a will without suspicion of fraud. 4. If a patron, being appointed heir to his due portion by his freedman and being requested to transmit the inheritance, declared it was onerous and on being compelled to take it has handed it back, although he could have kept it, he will not be able to take *bonorum possessio* contrary to the terms of a will, both because he recognized the disposition made by his freedman and because he spurned and, as it were, rejected, *possessio* in respect of it. 5. Far removed from this is the case of the son of the patron whom the freedman has adopted by *adrogatio* and appointed heir to a lesser portion [than his due] since there was no other member of the patron's family living; for although he is perceived as heir in his own right, inasmuch as he is *suus*, provided that he has not meddled with the inheritance as pertaining to his father, but has held aloof from it, nevertheless, he is to be admitted to *bonorum possessio* contrary to the terms of a will in his capacity as son of the patron. 6. If a freedman had left [as a legacy] to his patron, who was indebted to him for a sum certain, release [from the debt] and the patron had pleaded the defense of fraud against the heir claiming to recover the debt or has been freed from the debt by formal release on account of the legacy, it is to be held that he cannot take *bonorum possessio* contrary to the terms of a will.

51 LABEO, *Plausible Views, Epitomized by Paul, book 1:* If you have accused of a capital crime one and the same freedman as your father manumitted, it will not be possible for *bonorum possessio* of that freedman's property to be awarded to you in accordance with the edict. PAUL: The contrary will rather be the case if you have accused a slave who has subsequently become the property of your father, and he has later manumitted him.

3

FREEDMEN BELONGING TO COMMUNITIES

1 ULPIAN, *Edict, book 49:* Municipalities have full rights over the property of their freedmen and freedwomen, that is to say, the same rights as pertain to the patron. 1. But it is questionable whether they can make application for *bonorum possessio* at all; for the fact that they cannot reach a consensus affects the issue, but they may themselves obtain *bonorum possessio* through the agency of another, once application has been made for it. But as the senate has ordained that an inheritance may be restored to them in accordance with the [*senatus consultum*] *Trebellianum*, so, by the same reasoning, they have been allowed by another *senatus consultum* to take the inheritance when instituted heirs by a freedman; thus, it is to be held that [they can] also apply for *bonorum possessio*. 2. Time for making application for *bonorum possessio* in the case of municipalities runs from the point at which they could have taken a decision about making the application. And this is also the opinion given by Papinian.

4

THE ASSIGNMENT OF FREEDMEN

1 ULPIAN, *Sabinus, book 14:* In the *senatus consultum* which was made in the time of Claudius [Nero] in the consulship of Suillius Rufus and Ostorius Scapula, provision is made for the assignment of freedmen as follows: "If a man, having in his power two or more children begotten in lawful wedlock, had made known with regard to his freedman or freedwoman to which of his children he intended that freedman or that freedwoman to belong, he or she, whenever the party who has manumitted him or her, whether in his lifetime or by will, had ceased to be a member of the community, would be his sole patron or patroness, just as if he or she obtained his freedom from him or her. And that if one of the children had ceased to be a member of the community

and had no children, all rights are to be preserved to the manumitter's other children, just as if that father had not made known his intentions concerning that freedman or freedwoman." 1. Although the *senatus consultum* was expressed in the singular, it is clear that both more than one freedman or freedwoman may be assigned and to more than one child. 2. A freedman who has fallen into enemy hands may be assigned. 3. A man may make an assignment in any words he pleases or by conduct, by will, by a codicil, or in his lifetime. 4. He will be able to invalidate the assignment merely by a bare indication of his wish. 5. But even if a man has assigned a freedman to a son he has disinherited, the assignment is valid, and the dishonor incurred by disherison is not prejudicial to him insofar as the rights of patron are concerned. 6. But if he has been disinherited after the assignment, disherison will not invariably invalidate the assignment unless it has been done with this intention. 7. But if the assignee has repudiated the transaction, I submit that the position is rather as Marcellus, too, has observed, [namely] that [the assignee's] brothers may be admitted [to the rights of patron]. 8. If one patron has one son and the other two and the freedman has been assigned to one of them, it is to be seen how the freedman's estate is to be divided, whether into three parts, so that the assignee takes two, that is, his own and that of his brother, or whether it is to fall into [two] equal shares, since the brother is excluded by reason of the assignment. And Julian has observed in his seventy-fifth book that it is more reasonable that the assignee who excludes his brother takes two thirds; and this holds good so long as the brother is alive or could have been admitted in the case of intestacy. However, if he has suffered loss of civil status, they will take in equal shares.

2   POMPONIUS, *Senatus Consulta, book 4:* But if my assignee had died, being survived by a son and a brother and the son of the other patron, [Pomponius states that] my grandson will take the half share which my surviving son would take, had I not made assignment of the freedman.

3   ULPIAN, *Sabinus, book 14:* The same will have to be held in the case where a [patron] with a son and grandson has assigned the freedman to his grandson; the grandson will be admitted in the case of intestacy, even though the other son of the patron survives, and the uncle's survival affects the question; however, if the latter were not longer alive, the assignment would be of no advantage to him in restricting the rights of the other son of the patron. 1. But it is certain that assignment can also be made to a grandson, and it is established that the grandson of the assignor is preferred to his son. 2. As a result, will it be possible to inquire whether, in the case where he has a son and a grandson of whom that son is the father, he can plead the rule of the *senatus consultum* in that he has two in power? Why do we not admit it in this case too, since it is resolved that assignment [can] also be made to him who is about to fall back into power; for we cannot deny that both are in power? 3. But it will be possible to consider whether the one who is in power can be admitted on an intestacy. And, since there are many cases in which a person in power may also have a freedman, why should this too not be allowed and his father be admitted through him and profit from the intestacy? And this view also appears correct to Pomponius. But even sons-in-power have freedmen, for instance, where someone has manumitted a slave forming part of their *peculium castrense.* 4. I submit that the emancipated sons of the assignee of a freedman also have the benefit of the *senatus consultum,* not for the purpose of gaining admission on an intestacy, but for the purpose of taking what they are capable of taking. 5. According to this doctrine, if a freedman dies intestate, since they cannot be admitted on an intestacy, it is to be seen whether the son of the assignor who has remained in the family is to be admitted or not. And I would submit that the emancipated sons are to be preferred by the praetor. 6. But we should understand as children of the assignee not only sons but also grandsons and granddaughters and further [lineal] descendants. 7. If a man has assigned a freedman to two [sons] and one has died as a member of the community without issue and the other has not,

4   POMPONIUS, *Senatus Consulta, book 4:* or, being alive, has refused to accept the freedman's estate,

5   ULPIAN, *Sabinus, book 14:* should the portion of the one who has died or has renounced [his share] be restored to his family? Or should it rather accrue to the one in whose person the assignment subsists? And Julian has observed in his seventy-fifth book that it belongs solely to the person of the latter alone and that he alone should be admitted, which is correct. 1. But if he has not died without issue, are his children to be admitted along with the [brother] who is still alive? And [Julian] submits that the latter alone should be admitted at this point, but that after his death, his brother's children succeed and that the freedman does not return to the family. 2. But if, of the two sons, one has left sons and the other grandsons, are they to be admitted together on an intestacy? I submit that they are to succeed in due order.

6   MARCIAN, *Institutes, book 7:* If a slave has been bidden to be free and bequeathed to a son and subsequently the testator has manumitted him in his lifetime, the freedman belongs to the son as if he had been assigned to him. And this is the case whether the direction is express or he has clearly understood that he did not bequeath him as a slave but made assignment of him as a freedman.

7   SCAEVOLA, *Rules, book 2:* Assignment may be both simple and conditional and can be effected by letter or declaration or under one's own hand, because assignment of a freedman does not operate as a legacy or *fideicommissum;* finally, assignment cannot be loaded with a *fideicommissum.*

8   MODESTINUS, *Distinctions, book 7:* The children of the patron, although in several cases they themselves are gauged by the rights arising from the manumitter, nevertheless, will be unable to assign their father's freedman to their own children, even if [the freedman] has been assigned to them by their father. And both Julian and Marcellus approve this view.

9   MODESTINUS, *Encyclopaedia, book 9:* It is often doubted whether a patron, where he has no fewer than two further sons-in-power, can assign a freedman only to a son he has in power or to an emancipated son as well; the more reasonable view is that he can.

10   TERENTIUS CLEMENS, *Lex Julia et Papia, book 12.* Where a freedman has been assigned conditionally or where the assignment is not to take effect before a certain date, then, until the date occurs or the condition is fulfilled, all matters will be regulated just as if he had not been assigned; and so, should he die in the interim, his estate and *bonorum possessio* will belong to all the children. 1. If a freedman has been assigned to one absolutely and to another conditionally, it is to be held that pending fulfillment of the condition, the absolute assignee alone has the right of patron.

11   PAPINIAN, *Replies, book 14:* I have given it as my opinion that freedmen who have been handed over to sons for the provision of their food do not appear to have been assigned to the sons, since the patron's intention has been to consult the interest of the freedmen, so that they may more easily obtain profit from his good will without resort to public law.

12   POMPONIUS, *Letters, book 12:* If one of two patrons has assigned a freedman to his son, the transaction does not in any way infringe the other patron's own right.

13   POMPONIUS, *Senatus Consulta, book 4:* It is possible both to manumit a slave by will and to make assignment of the same slave as a freedman. 1. The senate has given a ruling concerning children in power; therefore, no provision is made in this *senatus consultum* in respect of *postumi;* nevertheless, for my part, I submit that *postumi,* too, are embraced within it. 2. As to the senate's statement "if any of the children had ceased to be a member of the community," it means one who had ceased to be a member of the community for good and does not include the case of a man captured by the enemy who may be returned. 3. It is also possible to assign from a specific date, but it is hardly possible to do so up to a certain date; for the senate itself has set a limit to this transaction.

5

IF A FRAUD HAS BEEN COMMITTED ON A PATRON

1   ULPIAN, *Edict, book 44:* If something is alleged to have been done by fraud on the part of a
freedman, whether the latter has died leaving a will or intestate, to prevent the due portion of
the property falling to any of those who can apply for *bonorum possessio,* the praetor takes notice of the fact and takes care that no fraud ensues.   1. If the property has been alienated
by fraud, we do not inquire whether [the alienation] was effected in contemplation of death or
not; for it is recoverable in any event. But if it has not been effected by fraud, but in some other
way, then the burden of proof that it was alienated in contemplation of death will be on the plaintiff. For if you suppose that alienation has been effected in contemplation of death, we do not ask
whether it has been effected by fraud or not; for it is enough to make known that it was effected
in contemplation of death and not wilfully. For gifts in contemplation of death are equated with
legacies and, just as in the case of legacies we do not inquire whether a legacy has been made
with the object of fraud or not, so it is with gifts made in contemplation of death.   2. But a gift to
a son in contemplation of death is not recoverable; for where a man had full power to leave a son
whatever he wished, he does not appear to have defrauded his patron by making a gift of it.
3. But every transaction carried out with a view to defrauding a patron is voidable.   4. The act
of fraud should be interpreted as that of the person who effected the alienation, not that of the
person in whose favor the property was alienated; and so it comes about that a person who was
not privy to the fraud or bad faith must be deprived of property that has been alienated by a
fraud on a patron, even though he considered that the party in question was a freeborn person
and did not believe him to be a freedman.   5. A Fabian action is not effective against a co-patron
who has neglected to apply for *bonorum possessio,* if the property given away does not exceed
the portion owed to the patron. Therefore, if it has been the subject of a gift made to him in
contemplation of death, he will share it with his co-patron in the same way as a patron taking as
legatee shares it [with his co-patron].   6. But we must see whether a Fabian action applies solely
to the recovery of property, by the removal of which a freedman has diminished his estate, or also
to property which [he has not troubled to] acquire. And Julian says in the twenty-sixth book of
his *Digest* that if a freedman has refused to accept an estate with the object of defrauding his
patron or has rejected a legacy, a Fabian action has no application; and in my opinion, this appears to be the correct view. For although a legacy, unless it is refused, belongs to us retrospectively [from the date of death], yet, when it is refused, it is clear that it has not been ours
retrospectively. In the case of other gifts, too, which a freedman donee has failed to accept, the
view that a Fabian action fails will likewise have to be approved; for it assists the patron where
his freedman has not alienated any of his own property to the [patron's] detriment, but not where
he has failed to acquire property. Accordingly, where property had been conditionally left to him
and he took steps to see that the condition should not be fulfilled or where he has stipulated under
a condition and preferred to allow it to lapse, it is likewise to be held that a Fabian action
fails.   7. What is the position if he wished to be defeated in a lawsuit? If, in fact, he has had
judgment go against him or has made a damaging admission, it will have to be held that a Fabian
action is appropriate. But if he engaged on his suit with no intention of succeeding, we must
consider the position at this point. And I submit that he has reduced the size of his estate; for he
has reduced his chances in a property action, just as much as if he had allowed the [limitation]
period for the action to expire.   8. But suppose that he refrained from bringing a complaint
which he could have brought concerning an undutiful will or some other action, for insult, perhaps, or the like, the patron cannot on that account attempt a Fabian action.   9. But if he compromised the suit so as to defraud his patron, the patron will be able to employ a Fabian action.
10. But if the freedman has given his daughter a dowry, he does not appear to have defrauded his
patron in respect of the amount of the dowry, because [the exercise of] a father's duty is not to be
the object of censure.   11. If a freedman has given gifts to several persons with the object of
fraud or has made gifts in contemplation of death to several persons, the patron will have a joint
action against all of them, whether Fabian or Calvisian, for the portion owed to him.   12. If
a man has sold, hired out, or converted property with the object of defrauding his patrons, let
us examine the likely nature of the judgment. Where property has in fact been alienated,
the buyer must be given the option of keeping the property and paying a fair price or of yield-
ing it up and recovering the price paid; the sale should by no means be rescinded so as to imply
that the freedman has not had the right of disposing [of the property] by sale, nor shall we

cheat the buyer of the price he has paid, especially as it is not a question of his bad faith, but of the freedman's. 13. But if the freedman has made a purchase with the object of defrauding the patron, it is likewise to be held that the patron is to have relief in respect of the price if he bought at over value, although he has not been offered the option of resiling from his purchase, but the seller [is put to his election] whether he prefers to adjust the price or to take back the article he sold on repayment of the purchase price. And we shall likewise observe the same practice where property has been exchanged or hired out or leased. 14. But if a freedman has sold an article in good faith and without obtaining any benefit but has given the price he was paid to a third party, we shall have to see whether it is the purchaser or donee of the price who will be liable to a Fabian action. And Pomponius has rightly observed in his eighty-third book that the buyer is not to be liable; for the fraud has been committed on the patron in respect of the price, and it, therefore, is the donee of the price who is sued in the Fabian action. 15. And in other cases, where the patron says that the property was in fact sold at a fair price, but his concern is not that it was put up for sale, and the fraud lies in this, that a possession in which the patron had an interest, whether because of its location or neighborhood or climate, or because he was brought up there or his parents were buried there, has been sold, let us see whether he ought to be heard if he wishes to recover the property. But he will in no wise have to be heard; for fraud is understood in the sense of pecuniary loss. 16. But perhaps in a case where both the article has been sold at an undervalue and the price has been given to a third party, both the purchaser at undervalue and the donee of the proceeds will be sued in the Fabian action. Nevertheless, if the purchaser opts to restore the property, he will hand it back only on receipt of the price he paid. But what if the purchaser has been charged to pay the person intended as donee by the freedman, would he nonetheless recover the price? And it is more reasonable that he should recover it, even though the price has fallen into the hands of a third party who is insolvent; for even if the freedman had spent the price he obtained, we would hold that the payer should nonetheless recover it, if he is willing to resile from his purchase. 17. Let us see whether a Fabian action issues if a freedman has accepted a loan with the intention of defrauding his patron. What is the remedy in this case? He has accepted a loan; if he has given away what he received, the patron sues the donee of the freedman, but where he has received it and squandered it, the person who made the loan should not finish up the loser, nor should his reason for making it be held against him. 18. Obviously, if he did not take it, but promised it to a third party by way of stipulation, a Fabian action will issue. 19. Let us see whether a Fabian action issues where a freedman has lodged security for bail with me or has given his own property as a pledge on behalf of a third party to the detriment of his patron, and whether the patron should not be given any relief to my detriment; for he has not given anything to me, if he has interposed himself on behalf of a third party who was insolvent; and we observe this rule. Therefore, it will not be possible to sue the creditor in the Fabian action; it will be possible to sue the debtor, but he can also be sued in an action on mandate. Clearly, if an action on mandate does not lie because he has intervened as donor, a Fabian action will lie. 20. But in a case where a freedman has stood as mandator in relation to a third party, the same argument will have to be approved. 21. But although a Fabian action applies only in part, yet, in the case of property that is indivisible, it applies to the entirety, for instance, in the case of a servitude. 22. If a freedman has given something to my slave or a son-in-power, so as to defraud his patron, let us see whether the Fabian process issues against me. And in my opinion, it avails against me and the father, and the judgment concerns what has been turned into property [for my benefit or the father's benefit] as well as what remains in [the slave's or the son's] *peculium*. 23. But if the agreement with the son was made on the father's orders, the father will equally be liable. 24. If a freedman has committed a fraud on his patron by contracting with a slave and he has been manumitted, it is questionable whether he is liable to a Fabian action. And since we have held that it is only the fraud on the part of the freedman that is to be taken into account and not that of the other party to the contract, it is possible that the manumitted slave in this case is not liable to a Fabian action. 25. And a further possible question is whether, in the case of a slave's death or alienation, an action must be brought within the year. And Pomponius says that it must. 26. This is an action *in personam* and not *in rem*, and lies against the heirs and other successors, and is for the benefit of the heir and other successors to the patron, and is not an hereditary action in relation to the freedman's property, but is proper to the patron. 27. If a freedman has made a gift so as to defraud his patron and, where the latter has predeceased the freedman, his son has subsequently obtained *bonorum possessio* contrary to the terms of the will of the freedman, may a Fabian action be employed to recover the alienated property? And it is right that he has the advantage of a Fabian action, a view approved by Pomponius in his eighty-third book and likewise by Papinian in the fourteenth book of his *Questions*; for it is sufficient that the alienation was effected with the object of defrauding the patron of his rights; for we understand it as a fraud on a thing rather than on the person. 28. This action also takes into account interest accruing after joinder of issue.

2 MARCIAN, *Rules, book 3:* In a Fabian or Calvisian action, it will rightly be held that past interest also accrues in that the praetor intends to deprive the entire fraud committed by the freedman of effect.

3 ULPIAN, *Edict, book 44:* If a patron has been instituted heir in respect of his due portion, and has accepted his inheritance while in ignorance of the fact that his freedman has alienated certain property with the object of defrauding him, let us see whether his ignorance should occasion relief to prevent him being cheated by the deception of his freedman. And Papinian, in the fourteenth book of his *Questions*, has given it as his opinion that the property that has been alienated remains in the same condition, and, therefore, the patron must account it his own fault in that when he could have received *bonorum possessio* contrary to the terms of a will on account of the alienation or gifts made in contemplation of death, he did not do so. 1. This action is a perpetual one, since he has the right to follow the property. Where a patron has been instituted sole heir and wishes to avail himself of a Fabian action, the praetor allows him to do so, because it was unjust for a person to be excluded from a Fabian action who did not accept the inheritance of his own free will, but because he could not apply for *bonorum possessio* contrary to the terms of a will. 3. If a freedman has died intestate, by taking the estate, a patron recovers by a Calvisian action property alienated by fraud so as to prevent the due testamentary portion of the freedman's property coming into the hands of the patron or his children; and this is so, whether the patron has made application for *bonorum possessio* on an intestacy or not. 4. If there are several patrons and patronesses, individually they will recover only their per capita shares, even if they employ a Calvisian action. 5. If a freedman has died intestate leaving his patron his due portion or a little more but has alienated some property, Papinian observes in the fourteenth book of his *Questions*, that nothing is recoverable; for a freedman with the capacity to make a bequest by will, providing that he additionally leaves the proper portion to his patron, appears to have effected no fraud in disposing of his property by way of gift.

4 ULPIAN, *Edict, book 43:* Whatever has been alienated by fraud is recoverable by a Fabian action. 1. Although there are several patrons, all will take one portion; but if they do not apply for their per capita shares, the others gain such share by accrual. What I have said respecting patrons applies equally in the case of their children; but they will not take together, but only where there are no patrons.

5 PAUL, *Edict, book 42:* He who accepts in person will be just as liable to a Fabian action as one who directs that his gift be handed over to a third party. 1. In a Fabian action, where there is no specific restitution, the defendant will be condemned in the amount assessed by the plaintiff under oath.

6 JULIAN, *Digest, book 26:* If a freedman with the intention of defrauding his patron has lent money to a son-in-power contrary to the *senatus consultum*, a Fabian action

will not have to be refused, because the freedman is to be understood in this case as having given [the money] with the object of defrauding his patron rather than as having lent it contrary to *senatus consultum.*

7   SCAEVOLA, *Questions, book 5:* Therefore, if the *senatus consultum* does not apply, a Fabian action does not issue since it is possible to sue for restitution.

8   JULIAN, *Digest, book 26:* But if he has made a loan to a son-in-power under twenty-five years of age, the [patron] should be assisted after the examination of the facts.

9   JULIAN, *Digest, book 64:* A freedman may make gifts in his lifetime to deserving friends of his, but he cannot bequeath property even to deserving friends so as to reduce his patron's portion.

10   AFRICANUS, *Questions, book 1:* If property alienated by a freedman with the object of fraud no longer exists, the patron's action fails, just as if the freedman had thrown away his money to effect a fraud, or likewise if the donee of a gift made by the freedman in contemplation of death had sold the object concerned and a purchaser in good faith had usucapted it.

11   PAUL, *Lex Aelia Sentia, book 3:* A patron does not appear to be defrauded in a transaction to which he has given consent, just as, too, a gift made by a freedman at his patron's instigation will not be recoverable by Fabian action.

12   JAVOLENUS, *Letters, book 3:* A freedman intended to transfer a farm to Seius with the object of defrauding his patron; Seius gave Titius a mandate to accept it so as to contract a mandate between Seius and Titius. I ask whether the patron, after the death of his freedman, has an action against Seius insofar as he gave the mandate, or against Titius who holds the farm; or can he institute proceedings against whom he pleases? [Javolenus] has given it as his opinion: An action is granted against him for whose benefit a gift has been obtained, always provided that the property has come into his possession, since every transaction carried out with his compliance contributes to his culpability. Nor does it appear that he should give up what a third party has in his possession, since he can obtain the property by an action of mandate, so as to make restitution himself to the patron, or compel the party with whom he contracted the mandate to make restitution. For what shall we say if one who has been introduced as third party in the transaction has acted in good faith? We shall not doubt that there can be no possible suit against him. For how can one who has compromised his good faith for a friend, thereby acquiring for a third party rather than for himself the spoils of a freedman's fraud, appear to have acted from motives of fraud?

13   PAUL, *Lex Julia et Papia, book 10:* By a constitution of the deified Pius, provision is made concerning the adoption of an *impubes* with the result that of the property pertaining to his adoptive father at his death, a quarter falls to the adoptee; but it also directs that property acquired by him for his father be restored to him; if he has been emancipated after judicial inquiry, he loses his fourth. If, therefore, property has been alienated so as to defraud him, it is recoverable as if by a Calvisian or Fabian action.

6

IF THERE SHALL BE NO WILL, *UNDE LIBERI*

1   ULPIAN, *Edict, book 44:* After the praetor discussed *bonorum possessio* where there is a will, he turned to those who die intestate, following the same order as the *Law of the Twelve Tables* followed. For in former times it was the normal practice to discuss first in cases where there is a will and then to treat succession on intestacy in the same fashion. 1. But he divided succession on intestacy into several parts; for he made different degrees, the first of children, the second of heirs at law, the third of cognate relations, and then of husband and wife. 2. But *bonorum possessio* on an intestacy can thus apply where *bonorum possessio* according to the

terms of a will or contrary to the terms of a will has not been claimed.   3. Obviously, if there was ample time in which to make an application for *bonorum possessio* in accordance with the will, but *bonorum possessio* has nevertheless been renounced, it will have to be held that *bonorum possessio* on intestacy starts to issue; for since a person who has refused to apply for *bonorum possessio* cannot do so after refusal, it will follow that the way is open for application for *bonorum possessio* on intestacy. 4. But even if *bonorum possessio* has been granted in accordance with the Carbonian Edict, it is more reasonable for us to hold that application can nonetheless be made on intestacy; for as we have indicated in the proper context, Carbonian *bonorum possessio* is no impediment to *bonorum possessio* granted in accordance with the edict. 5. But the praetor, when dealing with intestate succession, has properly begun with children, so that just as he offers them *bonorum possessio* contrary to the terms of a will, so he also calls them on intestacy.   6. But we should understand as children those whom we have held to be admissible to *bonorum possessio* contrary to the terms of a will, that is, adoptive children as well as natural children; but we admit adoptive children only insofar as they have been in power; but if they have become *sui juris*, *bonorum possessio* is not open to them, because the rights of adoption have been lost by emancipation.   7. In a case where a man has adopted his emancipated son as a grandson and has emancipated him, having another grandson of whom that son is the father, the question has been raised in Marcellus whether the fact that the adoption has been rescinded bars the grandson. Now, although it is customary for a grandson to be joined with his emancipated father, is there any authority which will not hold that although he has been adopted, even where the adoption is as a son, nonetheless, he does not impede the claims of his own son, because he is in power as an adoptive son and not as a natural son?   8. If the instituted heir does not have the testator's goodwill, either because the will has been opened or has been canceled or because for some reason the testator has changed his wishes and has preferred to die intestate, it is to be held that those who have been granted *bonorum possessio* will take the property on intestacy.   9. If an emancipated son has been disinherited but one who had been in power has been passed over, the praetor should protect the emancipated son to the extent of one half [of the estate] where he applies for *bonorum possessio unde liberi* on intestacy, just as if his father had died intestate.

2   JULIAN, *Digest, book 27:* If an emancipated son who has been passed over has not received *bonorum possessio* contrary to the terms of a will and the appointed heirs have taken the estate, he has lost his inheritance from his father through his own fault; for although no application has been made for *bonorum possessio* according to the terms of a will, nevertheless, the praetor will not protect him to the extent of granting him *bonorum possessio unde liberi*; for the praetor does not normally protect a patron who has been passed over either, if he does not apply for *bonorum possessio* contrary to the terms of a will, vis-à-vis the appointed heirs under that head of the edict whereby heirs at law are called.

3   ULPIAN, *Sabinus, book 8:* It is possible to make application for *bonorum possessio* on an intestacy, if it is clear that there is not a will sealed with the seals of seven witnesses.

4   PAUL, *Sabinus, book 2:* Children who have suffered a change of civil status are also called to *bonorum possessio* of their parents' property by the praetor's Edict, unless they have been adopted; for these last also lose the title of children after emancipation. But if natural children have been emancipated and [subsequently] adopted and have [then] been emancipated a second time, they keep the natural right of children.

5   POMPONIUS, *Sabinus, book 4:* If any of those to whom the praetor promises *bonorum possessio* has not been in the power of the father whose property is in question

at the time of his death, *bonorum possessio* is granted to him and any children he shall have in the family of the deceased, provided that the estate shall belong to them in his name and they have not been expressly disinherited of the portion which would belong to him had he remained in power; and so he takes half that portion, and his children, the remainder, and he brings his own property into contribution with them.   1. But if a father has emancipated his son and the grandson of whom that son is the father, only the son will come into *bonorum possessio*, although change of civil status is no ground of objection so far as the edict is concerned. Indeed, even those who have never been in power or held the rank of *sui heredes* are called to *bonorum possessio* of their parents' property. For if an emancipated son has left a son in the power of his grandfather, the latter will be granted *bonorum possessio* of his emancipated father's property; and if [the son] has fathered a child after his emancipation, *bonorum possessio* of his grandfather's property will be granted to that child, his father clearly constituting no bar to him.   2. If an emancipated son has not applied for *bonorum possessio*, the grandsons' rights all remain intact, just as if the son had not been alive, so that what the son would have taken, had he applied for *bonorum possessio*, falls only to those grandsons of whom he is the father and does not also accrue to the others.

6   ULPIAN, *Edict, book 39:* If a father has emancipated his son and kept the grandson [of whom that son is the father] and the son has subsequently died, both equity and the edict that provides for the grant of *bonorum possessio* to children bring it about that his interest is considered, and *bonorum possessio* is granted to him on his father's intestacy, with the result, however, that the grandfather who stands to profit by the grant of *bonorum possessio* through the grandson is compelled to make contribution to the sister who has fallen to be *necessaria heres* to her father, unless the grandfather intends to take no interest in the property and is prepared to release the grandson from power, so that the entire profit of *bonorum possessio* falls to [the grandson he has] emancipated. And the sister who fell to be heir to her father will have no reasonable cause for complaint on the ground that she is thereby excluded from the benefit of contribution, since she can come into her grandfather's property together with her brother when, at any point, he has died intestate.

7   PAPINIAN, *Questions, book 29:* While the appointed heir was considering whether to take the estate or not, the son who had been disinherited died, and in these circumstances, the appointed heir failed to take the estate. The grandson, being the son of the disinherited son and subject to his grandfather's power, will fall to be heir, and his father will not appear to have prejudiced his claim, since the estate is offered to him by way of intestacy after his father's death. And it cannot be held that the grandson will be heir but that he will not be *suus* on the ground that he has never been in the first degree, since he, too, has been in power and his father has not taken precedence over him in respect of succession at law. Otherwise, if he is not *suus heres*, by what right will he be heir? For without doubt he is not an agnate. However, even if the grandson has not been disinherited, it will be possible for the appointed heir to take the estate in accordance with the will on the death of the son; therefore, [the father], who does not bar his claims on the law of intestacy, will appear to have done so by the law relating to testate succession.   1. The estates of children are not due to their parents in the same way as [an estate] of parents is to their children; for parents are admitted to their children's property by reason of compassion, whereas children are admitted to their parents' estates by the [expectation afforded them by] nature in conjunction with the common prayer of their parents.

8   PAPINIAN, *Replies, book 6:* A son-in-power has claimed *possessio* with his father's consent as nearest cognate relative; although he has been barred from inheriting by a condition stated in the will, because he has remained in power, nevertheless, he will effectively appear to have claimed *possessio* and will not fall within the wording of the edict; for he has not claimed *possessio* according to will, since he has not been able to take the estate under this head, and it has not been in the son's power to fulfill the condition, and it will not readily be possible to compel the father to emancipate his son.

9   PAUL, *Replies, book 11:* If an emancipated son, after applying for *bonorum possessio* to his father's estate, has changed his status, [Paul observes that] there is no objection to his keeping what he has obtained; but if he has changed his status prior to application, he cannot seek *bonorum possessio*.

7

UNDE LEGITIMI

1   JULIAN, *Digest, book 27:* The following words of the edict, "then the person who ought to be

heir to him if he had died intestate," are understood in an extended meaning, allowing for a certain passage of time; for they are not referred to the time of the testator's death, but to the point at which application would be made for *bonorum possessio*. For that reason, it is obvious that the heir at law is excluded from this [kind of] *bonorum possessio* where he had suffered a change of civil status.

2   ULPIAN, *Edict, book 46:* If the *sui* have renounced *bonorum possessio* on an intestacy, we shall still hold that they bar the heirs at law, that is, those to whom the estate could have been offered on intestacy; the reason is that because of their refusal of *bonorum possessio* qua children, they begin to take it qua heirs at law.   1. But this [type of] *bonorum possessio* is offered not only in the case of males but also in that of females, and not only in the case of freeborn persons but also where freedmen are involved. Therefore, it is common to many different types of person. For females, too, can have cognate relations and agnates, and freedmen can likewise possess patrons and patronesses.   2. And not only males can receive this [type of] *bonorum possessio* but also females.   3. If someone has died and it is doubtful whether he is head of a household or a son-in-power, because his father has been captured by the enemy and is still alive, or his status was in suspense for some other reason, the more reasonable view is that application for *bonorum possessio* of his estate is not possible, because it is not yet clear that he has died intestate, since it is uncertain whether he has the capacity to make a will. Therefore, application for *bonorum possessio* is to be made only when his status has been clarified, not when it has begun to be clear that he died intestate, but when it has begun to be clear that he is head of a household.   4. But this type of *bonorum possessio* embraces everyone who could have been heir on an intestacy, whether the *Law of the Twelve Tables* makes him heir at law or some other law or *senatus consultum*. Finally, a mother who comes [into an estate] in virtue of the *senatus consultum Tertullianum*, likewise those who are admitted as heirs at law on an intestacy in accordance with the *senatus consultum Orphitianum* can claim this [type of] *bonorum possessio*.

3   PAUL, *Edict, book 43:* Therefore, it is to be generally known that whenever a law or *senatus* [*consultum*] offers an estate without reference to *bonorum possessio*, it should be applied for in accordance with this part [of the edict]; but when it directs that *bonorum possessio* is also to be granted, then application should be made in accordance with that part in virtue of which [persons are called] in accordance with [particular] laws; but [application] will also be possible under this head [of the edict].

4   JULIAN, *Digest, book 27:* If one of two brothers has died leaving a legally valid will, then, while the heir is considering whether to take the estate, the second brother, too, has died intestate, and the appointed heir has failed to take the estate, the brother's uncle on their father's side will take the estate on an intestacy; for this [type of] *bonorum possessio*, "then the person who ought to be heir," is referred to the earliest moment at which *bonorum possessio* on intestacy could have been sought.

5   MODESTINUS, *Encyclopaedia, book 3:* This is the difference between agnate and cognate relatives, namely, cognate relatives are subsumed under agnates, but agnates are not likewise subsumed under cognate relatives. For instance, a father's brother, that is, an uncle on the father's side, is both an agnate and a cognate relative, but a mother's brother, that is, a maternal uncle, is a cognate relative but not an agnate. 1. As long as there is a prospect that some *suus heres* exists to the deceased, there is no place for blood relatives, for example, where the deceased's wife is pregnant or his son is in captivity.

6   HERMOGENIAN, *Epitome of Law, book 3:* Those born after their father's death or captivity or deportation but also those who were in power at the time of his captivity or deportation share the right conferred by their blood relationship, although they have not fallen to be their father's heirs, just as [do] disinherited children.

8

WHENCE COGNATE RELATIVES

1 ULPIAN, *Edict, book 46:* This type of *bonorum possessio* has its origin simply in the generosity of the praetor and does not spring from civil law. For he calls to *bonorum possessio* those who cannot be admitted to succession at civil law, that is to say, cognate relatives. 1. But they have been called cognates as if they were all sprung from the same person, or, as Labeo says, as if they have had a common origin. 2. But this law does not apply to servile relationships. For it is not easy to define any servile tie as a cognate relationship. 3. But the following [type of] *bonorum possessio* granted in accordance with this part of the edict, embraces six degrees of cognate relations, and in the seventh two persons, son and daughter of a male or female cousin on a sister's side. 4. Adoption also creates a cognate relationship; for an adopted person becomes a cognate relation to those to whom he becomes an agnate; for whenever cognate relatives are under discussion, we shall likewise understand [the term] to embrace cognate relatives by adoption in such contexts. It comes about, therefore, that a person given in adoption retains the rights of cognate relationship in the family of his natural father, as much as he acquires them in his adoptive family, but he only acquires such relationship in his adoptive family with those to whom he becomes an agnate, but in his natural family, he will retain his relationship with all members. 5. But a person who is alone [in his class] will also be understood as next in line, although "next" strictly suggests the existence of several. 6. We should understand him to be next in line at the time when *bonorum possessio* is offered. 7. If the cognate relative next in line has died while the appointed heirs are deliberating [whether to accept the estate], the person following will be admitted as the next in line, that is, whoever was then perceived to hold the next place. 8. If there is a prospect of a nearer cognate relative being born, the case is that he should be held to bar [the claims of] relatives following [him]; but where he has not survived birth, we shall admit the one who appeared to be next in line after the expected child. This will be the position only in the case where the child said to be expected was conceived in the lifetime of the person of whose property *bonorum possessio* is in question; for if he was conceived after his death, he will not prejudice [the claims of] another, nor will he be admitted himself, because he was not the nearest cognate relative to a person in whose lifetime he has not yet been alive. 9. If a pregnant woman has died and the child has been born by Caesarian section, that child is in a position of being capable of receiving *bonorum possessio* of his mother's property *unde proximi cognati.* But after the *senatus consultum Orphitianum* he will also be able to apply for it *unde legitimi,* because he was in the womb at the time of her death. 10. But cognate relatives are admitted by degrees to *bonorum possessio;* those who are in the first degree are all admitted together. 11. If someone has been in captivity at the time of the death of the person of whose property *bonorum possessio* is in question, it is to be held that he can apply for *bonorum possessio.*

2 GAIUS, *Provincial Edict, book 16:* Under this head [of the edict] the proconsul, urged by natural equity, promises *bonorum possessio* to all cognate relatives called by reason of ties of blood to an estate, even though they fail at civil law. And so even illegitimate children can apply for *bonorum possessio* of their mother's property, and the mother can apply for *bonorum possessio* of the property of such children; and brothers, too, can likewise apply for *bonorum possessio* of each other's property in accordance with this head [of the edict]; because they are cognate relatives in respect of one another. And this principle extends to the case of a freedwoman who has given birth to a child, so that the child is a cognate relative of the mother, and the mother of the child, and her children, too, are related to one another.

3   JULIAN, *Digest, book 27:* Cognate ties acquired by adoption are destroyed through a change of civil status. Therefore, if within one hundred days after the death of, say, an adoptive brother, his adoptive brother has suffered a change of civil status, he will not be able to receive *bonorum possessio* of his brother's property open to him as next of kin; for it is clear that the praetor has regard not only to the time of death but also to the point at which application is made for *bonorum possessio.*

4   ULPIAN, *Rules, book 6:* If a bastard has died intestate, his estate falls to no one on grounds of consanguinity or agnation, because rights of consanguinity and agnation spring from a father; but his mother or brother born of the same mother can apply for *bonorum possessio* of his property as next of kin in accordance with the edict.

5   POMPONIUS, *Sabinus, book 4:* Heirs at law who have suffered a change of civil status are not granted *bonorum possessio* qua heirs at law, because they are not in the same situation as children, but they are again called in the degree of cognate relationship.

6   ULPIAN, *Edict, book 45:* The fact that they have laid an accusation does not prejudice cognate relatives, if they have laid it against their own cognate relations.

7   MODESTINUS, *Rules, book 6:* A man who has become a slave for some reason does not in any way recover his cognate relationship by manumission.

8   MODESTINUS, *Replies, book 14:* Modestinus gave it as his opinion that grandchildren are not prevented from being allowed their maternal grandmother's property on an intestacy, merely because they are alleged to be illegitimate.

9   PAPINIAN, *Replies, book 6: Possessio* is offered to an agnate of the eighth degree in virtue of his right as heir at law, even though he has not fallen to be heir, but it is not offered to him as nearest cognate relative, although he has fallen to be heir.   1. When a nephew, being instituted part-heir, alleged that his uncle was deaf and for that reason could not have made a will and received *possessio* as next of kin, it was resolved that time should be reckoned from the date of death, because it did not seem probable that so close a relative should have been in ignorance of the deceased's state of health.

10   SCAEVOLA, *Replies, book 2:* A woman died intestate, leaving a sister Septicia, who had been born by a different father, and a mother, who was pregnant by a different husband. I ask, if the mother has refused the estate while still pregnant and has subsequently given birth to a daughter Sempronia, whether Sempronia, too, can receive *bonorum possessio* of Titia's estate. [Scaevola] gave it as his opinion that if the mother has been barred from the estate, the daughter who, as was supposed, has been subsequently born, can receive it.

9

THE EDICT REGULATING SUCCESSION

1   ULPIAN, *Edict, book 49:* An edict regulating succession has been promulgated to prevent inheritable property from remaining without an owner for any length of time and imposing excessive delay on creditors. As a result of which the praetor has thought to prescribe a time for those to whom he has offered *bonorum possessio* and to settle [an order of] succession among them, so that the creditors may know in good time whether they have a party to sue or whether *bona vacantia* have been offered to the imperial treasury or, on the other hand, whether they should proceed to *bonorum possessio,* as if the deceased had no successor.   1. For each can refuse *bonorum possessio* for his own part but not on behalf of another.   2. Accordingly, my agent cannot renounce my interest in *bonorum possessio* without my consent.   3. A master can renounce *bonorum possessio* offered through a slave.   4. Let us see whether the tutor of an *impubes* can renounce *bonorum possessio.* And the more reasonable view is that he cannot; but the *impubes* can do it with his tutor's sanction.   5. The curator of an insane person will by no means be able to renounce *bonorum possessio,* because it has not yet been offered.   6. A person who once decided not to make application for *bonorum possessio* has lost his right to do so, although there time still runs. For

when he has signified his refusal, the right to *bonorum possessio* begins already to belong to others, or to allow in the imperial treasury.   7. Let us see whether *bonorum possessio* awarded pursuant to decree may be renounced. And indeed it can be barred by time, but it is truer to say that it cannot be renounced, because it has not yet been offered, when it was decreed; again after it has been decreed, renunciation is too late, because what has been obtained cannot be renounced.   8. If the first [claimant] has died within one hundred days, the next can straightway be admitted.   9. When we say, "*bonorum possessio* can be applied for within one hundred days," it is to be understood in the sense that *bonorum possessio* can be applied for on the hundredth day itself too, just as within the period up to the first of the month includes the first of the month. The same is true of the expression "within one hundred days."   10. If any of those to whom *bonorum possessio* can be granted in accordance with the edict has signified his refusal to accept a grant or has not obtained it within the statutory period, *bonorum possessio* is then open to the others, just as if no member of the group has had a previous claim.   11. But we must see whether a person barred is also to be admitted along with others. For instance, a son is in power; *bonorum possessio* has been offered to him in accordance with the first part of the edict, whereby it is offered to children; he has been barred by lapse of time or by his refusal; it is offered to the others, but is he to succeed to his own claim [under the first head] in virtue of this part of the edict regulating succession? The more reasonable view is that he does, so that he can make application *unde legitimi* and after the heirs at law in his own place in accordance with that part whereby the nearest relatives are called. And we observe this rule with the result that he is admitted; therefore, he will be able to succeed to his own place in accordance with the ensuing section. It will be possible to hold this, too, in the case of *bonorum possessio* according to will, so that where a person who could also have taken on intestacy has not applied for *bonorum possessio* according to will, he succeeds to his own place. 12. A more generous period of time is granted to parents and children to make application for *bonorum possessio*, ostensibly by way of respect to their ties of blood, since those who are practically coming into their own property should not be pressed. And so it was resolved that a year be prescribed for them, evidently thus allowing them a reasonable but not excessive period, so that they themselves should not be forced to apply quickly for *bonorum possessio*, and the property should not remain untenanted for too long. Obviously, sometimes, if creditors are pressing, such persons are to be asked in court whether they are claiming *bonorum possessio* for themselves, so that if they say that they are renouncing it, the creditors may know what steps they should take; if they say they are still thinking about it, they are not to be hurried.   13. If a man has been made substitute heir by his father to a son who is an *impubes*, he will be able to seek *bonorum possessio* within one hundred days, not a year.   14. But this period of time is allowed parents and children, not only when they come in their own right, but there is also a year in which to seek *bonorum possessio* where a slave of one who is numbered among the parents or children has been instituted heir. For that person who is entitled to the advantage of *bonorum possessio* applies for it.   15. But even if a father is willing to take *bonorum possessio* of the property of his emancipated son contrary to the terms of a will, it is established that he has a year in which to do so.   16. And, in general, Julian says that parents and children in all cases have a year in which to apply for *bonorum possessio*.

2   PAPINIAN, *Replies, book 6:* A cognate relative of a lower degree did not have the benefit of the edict regulating succession when a previous claimant had received *bonorum possessio* in accordance with the appropriate part of the edict. And it was irrelevant that the prior claimant had had the opportunity of refusing on account of his age. Therefore, it was resolved that the *bona* were properly offered to the imperial treasury as *vacantia*.

10

THE DEGREES OF RELATIVES AND THEIR NAMES

1   GAIUS, *Provincial Edict, book 8:* Some degrees of cognate relationship are in the ascendant, and some in the descendant, while others are oblique or collateral. Parents are in the ascendant, and children in the descendant. Brothers, sisters, and their children are

obliquely or collaterally [related].   1. But an ascendant or descendant cognate relationship begins in the first degree, while in the case of an oblique or collateral relationship there is no first degree, and for that reason [such relationships] begin in the second degree. And so cognate relatives in the first degree, whether in the ascendant or descendant, can run together, but no one in an oblique relationship can ever run with that degree. But in the second and third and subsequent degrees, certain persons, even where they are in an oblique relationship, can run together with cognate relatives in the ascendant.   2. But whenever we are dealing with a question of inheritance or *bonorum possessio*, we should be advised of the fact that those who are of the same degree do not always run together. 3. In the first degree, a father and mother are in the ascendant, and a son and daughter in the descendant.   4. In the second degree, a grandfather and grandmother are in the ascendant, and a grandson and granddaughter in the descendant. A brother and sister are in a collateral relation.   5. In the third degree, a great-grandfather and great-grandmother are in the ascendant, and a great-grandson and great-granddaughter are in the descendant; consequently, the son and daughter of a brother or sister are in the oblique relation, as [are] an uncle and aunt on the male side and on the female side.   6. In the fourth degree, a great-great-grandfather and a great-great-grandmother are in the ascendant, and a great-great-grandson and a great-great-granddaughter are in the descendant. The grandson and granddaughter of a brother and sister are in an oblique relation, as consequently [are] a great-uncle and great-aunt on the male side (that is, the brother and sister of a grandfather) a great-uncle and aunt on the female side (that is, the brother and sister of a grandmother), likewise, brothers and sisters descended from a father's brother (that is, the male and female offspring of two brothers), likewise, male and female cousins (that is, the offspring of two sisters as if co-sisters' offspring), likewise, male and female cousins on the male side (that is, male and female children of [a father's] brother or sister). But almost everyone generally refers to them by the common name [of cousin].   7. In the fifth degree, a great-great-great-grandfather and a great-great-great-grandmother are in the ascendant, and a great-great-great-grandson and a great-great-great-granddaughter are in the descendant. In an oblique relation are the great-grandson and great-granddaughter of a brother and sister, and consequently a grand-uncle and grand-aunt on the male side (that is, a great-grandfather's brother and sister), a grand-uncle and grand-aunt on the female side (that is, the brother and sister of a great-grandmother), daughter or son of a male or female cousin on the father's side, and likewise of a male or female cousin on the mother's side; likewise, the son or daughter of the male or female offspring of a father's sister; male or female second cousin (they are son or daughter of a great-uncle or great-aunt on the male or female side),

2   ULPIAN, *Edict, book 46:* that is, male or female cousin or father's brother's son of the father of the person whose ties of relationship are in question.

3   GAIUS, *Provincial Edict, book 8:* In the sixth degree, the great-great-great-great-grandfather and great-great-great-great-grandmother are in the ascendant, and great-great-great-great-grandson and great-great-great-great-granddaughter in the descendant. In an oblique relation are the great-great-grandson and great-great-granddaughter of a brother or sister, and consequently the great-grand-uncle and great-grand-aunt on the male side (that is, brother and sister of a great-great-grandfather); likewise, the grandson and granddaughter of a great-uncle and great-aunt on the male or female side; a grandson or granddaughter of a father's brother's son or daughter or of a mother's sister's son or daughter or a father's sister's son or daughter; the son or daughter of a great-grandfather's brother or sister or of a great-grandmother's brother or sister, likewise, the issue of a father's brother's children or a mother's sister's children or a father's sister's children, who are properly called cousins.   1. It is obvious from what we have said above how many persons can be embraced within the seventh degree.   2. Nevertheless, we must bear in mind that the persons of parents and children are always doubled; for we shall understand grandfather and grandmother to include maternal, as well as paternal, grandparents; likewise, grandsons and granddaughters may be children of a son as well as of a daughter; and we shall obviously follow this scheme in all subsequent degrees, whether dealing with persons in the ascendant or descendant.

4   MODESTINUS, *Encyclopaedia, book 12:* But, so far as our law is concerned, when a natu-

ral cognate relationship is in question, it is not easy for anyone to fall outside the seventh degree, inasmuch as nature does not permit the lifetime of cognate relations to extend virtually beyond that degree. 1. Cognate relatives are thought to be so called on the ground that they have been, as it were, born together at one and the same time, or have their origins in, and spring from, the same person. 2. The substance of *cognatio* is understood in a dual sense by the Romans; for some cognate relationships are bound together by civil law, and some by natural law, and sometimes, when both laws coincide, the relationship is cemented by both natural and civil law. And, indeed, the cognate relationship which descends through the female line which has produced illegitimate children is understood purely as a natural relation without civil ties. But a purely civil relationship, which is also called a legal relationship apart from natural law, exists through adoption. A cognate relationship reflecting both types of law exists when forged by a legally contracted marriage. But a natural tie of *cognatio* is known as such. But civil *cognatio*, although it, too, may of itself in the fullest sense be called by this term, is nevertheless properly termed *agnatio*, because it takes effect through males. 3. But since some rights between relations by marriage are also involved, it is not out of place briefly to discuss in this context relations by marriage too. Relations by marriage are the cognate relatives of husband and wife, so called from the fact that two sets of relationships which are individually different are wedded as a result of marriage, and the one set of relationships abuts onto the other. For the reason for joining relationships by marriage arises from the marriage. 4. And these are the names of such relations: father-in-law, mother-in-law, son-in-law, daughter-in-law, stepmother, stepfather, stepson, stepdaughter. 5. But there are no degrees of relation by marriage. 6. The father of the husband and of the wife is called father-in-law [of the other], and the mother of either party mother-in-law [of the other], although the Greeks commonly call the husband's father by the particular name of *hekyros*, but his mother *hekyra*, while the wife's father is called *pentheros*, and her mother *penthera*. But a son's wife is called daughter-in-law, and a daughter's husband, son-in-law. A wife is known as stepmother to children by another wife, and a mother's husband is called stepfather in relation to children fathered by another husband; each of them calls children born to a different parent stepsons and stepdaughters. The [position] can also be defined as follows: My father-in-law is my wife's father, and I am his son-in-law. My wife's grandfather is called my grandfather-in-law, and I am his grandson-in-law; and, working the other way, my father is my wife's father-in-law, and she is his daughter-in-law; and my grandfather is my wife's grandfather-in-law, and she is his granddaughter-in-law. Likewise, my grandmother-in-law is my wife's grandmother, and I am her grandson-in-law; and, working the other way, my mother is my wife's mother-in-law, and she is her daughter-in-law; and my grandmother is my wife's grandmother-in-law, and my wife is her granddaughter-in-law. My stepson is my wife's son by another husband, and I am his stepfather; and, on the other hand, my wife is said to be stepmother to my children born of another wife, and my children are her stepsons. A husband's brother is a brother-in-law. He is called *daer* in Greek, as Homer relates, for Helen addresses Hector as follows:

> O brother-in-law of mine, what a horrible scheming
> bitch I am!

A husband's sister is called a sister-in-law, *galōs* in Greek. The wives of two brothers are called *janitrices*, in Greek *einateres*, which the same poet, Homer, demonstrates in one line:

> Or some of the sisters-in-law or well-garbed brothers' wives.

7. And so it is unlawful for those who, on account of their relation by marriage, are considered to hold the place of parents or children to be joined in marriage.   8. It is to be known that there can be no cognate relationship or relationship by marriage, unless the marriage whereby such relation is forged has not been forbidden.   9. Freedmen and freedwomen may be related to each other by marriage.   10. Where a person has been given in adoption or emancipated, he retains whatever cognate relationships and relationships by marriage he had, but loses his rights of agnation. But he has no cognate relative in the family to which he comes by adoption, except his father and those to whom he is bound by agnation. But he has no relation by marriage at all in that family.   11. A person who has been banished by interdict from fire and water, or who has changed his civil status in some way so as to lose his freedom and his citizenship loses both all the cognate relationships and relationships by marriage which he formerly had.

5   PAUL, *Plautius, book 6:* If I have emancipated my natural son and adopted another, [Paul says that] they are not brothers. If I have adopted Titius on the death of my son, Arrian says he appears to have been a brother of the deceased.

6   ULPIAN, *Lex Julia et Papia, book 5:* Labeo observes that the wife of the grandson of whom my daughter is the mother appears to be my daughter-in-law.   1. A man or woman who is betrothed is also included in the term son-in-law or daughter-in-law; likewise, the parents of the betrothed appear to be included in the term father-in-law and mother-in-law.

7   SCAEVOLA, *Rules, book 4:* The illegitimate son of a woman who has subsequently become my wife is also a stepson, just as, too, is the child born in the concubinage of a mother who has later married another.

8   POMPONIUS, *Manual, book 1:* Servius rightly held that the names of father-in-law, mother-in-law, son-in-law, and daughter-in-law are acquired also from the time of the betrothal.

9   PAUL, *Views, book 4:* The *stemmata* of cognate relationships are separated by a straight line into two lines, one of which represents the ascendant and one the descendant. But from the ascendant there are also horizontal lines starting in the second degree all of which we have incorporated into a sole book with rather broader treatment.

10   PAUL, *On Degrees and Relationships by Marriage and their Names, sole book:* The jurisconsult should know the degrees of relations and relations by marriage, since inheritance and tutelages have normally been referred to the nearest agnate; but the praetor also gives *bonorum possessio* to the nearest cognate relative in accordance with the edict; moreover, by the law relating to public trials, we are not compellable witnesses against relations and relations by marriage.   1. The name *cognatio* appears to be derived from Greek; for [the Greeks] call persons whom we call *cognati syngenneis*.   2. Those whom the *Law of the Twelve Tables* calls agnates are also cognate relatives, but these are cognate relatives of the same family through a father, but those who are related through women are only called cognate relatives.   3. The nearest of the agnates are called *sui*.   4. There is therefore the same difference between agnates and cognate relatives as there is between a genus and its species; for a person who is an agnate is also a cognate, but a cognate is not also an agnate in the same way; for the one expression [derives from] civil law and the other from natural law.   5. We do not refrain from using these names, that is, the names of cognate relatives, even in the case of slaves; and so we talk about the parents and sons and brothers of slaves too, but servile relationships do not belong to [the realm of] the laws.   6. *Cognatio* has its origin in and takes effect through women alone; for a brother includes a person who has merely been born of the same mother; for those who have the same father, albeit different mothers, are also agnates.   7. For ascendants are called by a particular term by the Romans back to the great-great-great-great-grandfather; persons farther

back who have no special name are called ancestors; likewise, descendants [have particular names] down to the great-great-great-great-grandson; persons more remote are called descendants. 8. There are also collateral relatives, such as brothers and sisters and their offspring, likewise, uncles and aunts on the male or female side. 9. For whenever it is asked in what degree each person is, we must begin with him whose relationship is in question, and if it is in the descendant or ascendant, we shall easily find the degrees by a straight line of those going upward or downward, if we count the nearest [person] in each case throughout the individual degrees; for the person next nearest to him who stands in the next degree to me is in the second degree to me. For the number [of degrees] similarly grows as the individual persons are reckoned up. The same process will have to take place in the case of the horizontal degrees; thus, a brother is in the second degree, since the father or mother through whom he is connected is counted first. 10. But they are called degrees from their resemblance to steps or steep places which we approach in such a way that we pass from the nearest to the next, that is, to the person who is, as it were, born of the other. 11. Now we count up the individual degrees. 12. In the first degree of relationship, there are two [persons] in the ascendant, a father and a mother. In the descendant, there are two, a son and a daughter, although there can be more of them. 13. The second degree embraces the following twelve persons: a grandfather, that is, a father of a father and a mother, likewise, a grandmother, paternal as well as maternal, in the same fashion. A brother, too, of either party is included, that is, either on the mother's side only or on the father's or on both sides, that is, of either parent. But he does not increase the number, because he is no different from one who merely has the same father, except that he has the same cognate relations both on his father's and on his mother's side; and so, in cases where persons are born of different parents, it usually comes about that my brother's brother is not my cognate relative. Imagine that I have a brother, and that we share only the same father, and that he has [a brother] with whom he shares the same mother; they are related as brothers, but the second one is not a cognate relative of mine. A sister is counted in the same way as a brother. A grandson is also understood in two senses, as the son of a son or daughter; the same is also true of a granddaughter. 14. There are thirty-two persons in the third degree: a great-grandfather, who is understood in four ways; for he is the father of a paternal or maternal grandfather, likewise, of a paternal or maternal grandmother. A great-grandmother also denotes four persons; for she is the mother of a paternal grandfather or grandmother, likewise, of a maternal grandfather, and, similarly, of a maternal grandmother. An uncle on the male side, however, is a father's brother and is himself to be understood in two senses, as having the same father or mother [as the father]. My paternal grandmother has married your father and has given birth to you, or your paternal grandmother has married my father and given birth to me; I am your uncle on the male side and you are mine. This happens if two women have married each other's sons; for sons born of these unions are paternal uncles one to another, and daughters are paternal aunts to each other; likewise, the sons will similarly be uncles on the male side to the daughters, and the daughters will be aunts on the male side to them. If a man has married a woman's daughter, and she has married his son, the issue of the father of the son will call the children born of the mother of the girl their brother's sons, and they [will call them] their uncles and aunts. An uncle on the female side is the mother's brother, who is of the same significance as explained in the case of a paternal uncle. If two men have each married the other's daughter, any sons born of these unions will be maternal uncles one to another, and any daughters will be maternal aunts to each other, and, by the same token, the males will be maternal uncles of the females, and they will be their maternal aunts. An aunt is a father's sister in the sense to be understood above. An aunt on the female side is a mother's sister in the same way as explained above. It is to be noted that the sons and daughters of a brother and sister do not have a special name for their relationship in the same way as brothers and sisters of a father and mother are called paternal or maternal uncles and aunts, but they are indicated as sons and daughters of a brother or sister; and it will be clear from later examples that the same thing happens in other cases too. A great-grandson and great-granddaughter are also understood in four senses; for they descend, either from a grandson fathered by a son, or from a grandson born of a daughter, or they are issue of a granddaughter fathered by a son, or a granddaughter born of a daughter.   15. In the fourth degree, there are eighty persons. A great-great-grandfather, whose connotation extends to eight persons; for he is the father of a paternal or maternal great-grandfather, each of whom we have said is to be understood in a dual sense, or the father of a paternal or maternal great-grandmother, and they, too, are understood in a dual sense; great-great-grandmother; she is also counted eight times over; for she is the mother of a paternal or maternal great-grandfather, likewise, of a paternal or maternal great-grandmother. A great-uncle on the male side is a grandfather's brother; when a person who is a grandfather and likewise his brother is understood in two ways, this term embraces four persons, so that he who is the child of the same father, that is, a great-grandfather, or merely of the same mother, that is, a great-grandmother, is brother of a paternal or maternal grandfather; but my great-uncle on the male side is my father's or my mother's uncle. My great-aunt is my grandfather's sister; but my grandfather, and likewise his sister, as we have observed above, are understood in two senses, and for that reason here, too, we understand four persons; likewise, my father's or my mother's aunt on the male side will be my great-aunt. My great-uncle is my grandmother's brother; four persons are subsumed under this name in the same manner, and my mother's and father's uncle on the female side is my great-uncle. My great-aunt on the female side is my grandmother's sister; and she, too, is understood in four senses for the same reason. My father's or mother's aunt on the female side is called my great-aunt. Father's brother's sons are in the same degree, likewise father's brother's daughters, father's sister's sons and daughters and mother's sister's sons and daughters; but these are the children of brothers and sisters. Some authorities have distinguished them as follows, so that male children of brothers are father's brother's sons, and female children of brothers are father's brother's daughters; but the third class may contain male or female children of a brother or sister; but male and female children of sisters are known as male or female cousins on the female side as children of sisters. But the majority refers to them all as cousins, as does Trebatius. The following sixteen persons are embraced by this term. A paternal uncle's son and likewise his daughter are counted in two different ways as [explained] above; for the uncle can be my father's brother where he merely shares the same father or the same mother; son or daughter of a paternal aunt, son or daughter of a maternal uncle; son or daughter of a maternal aunt, the paternal aunt and maternal uncle and aunt being understood in a double sense according to the same principle. The grandson and granddaughter of a brother or sister are in the same degree; but the brother and sister and grandson and granddaughter, each being understood in two senses, will include the following sixteen persons:

The grandson of a brother born of the same father being the child of his son	A grandson born of a daughter
A grandson of a brother born of the same mother but of a different father being the child of a son	A grandson born of a daughter
A granddaughter of a brother born of the same father being the child of a son	A granddaughter born of a daughter
A granddaughter of a brother born of a different father but the same mother being the child of a son	A granddaughter born of a daughter

For the same reason, they will make up eight persons, so that the grandsons and granddaughters descended from the children of a sister form another eight, and are counted by us in the same fashion. But my brother's grandson and granddaughter call me great-uncle on the male side, and my brother's and sister's grandsons and granddaughters and mine too are each others' cousins. Great-great-grandson and great-great-granddaughter: These are the son and daughter of a great-grandson and great-granddaughter, or the grandson and granddaughter of a grandson and granddaughter, or the great-grandson and great-granddaughter of a son or daughter, the grandson being understood to be descended from a son or daughter, and the granddaughter likewise being descended from a son or daughter, so that we thus come down to individual persons by degree:

Son	Grandson	Great-Grandson	Great-Great-Grandson
Son	Grandson	Great-Grandson	Great-Great-Granddaughter
Son	Grandson	Great-Granddaughter	Great-Great-Grandson
Son	Grandson	Great-Granddaughter	Great-Great-Granddaughter
Son	Granddaughter	Great-Grandson	Great-Great-Grandson
Son	Granddaughter	Great-Grandson	Great-Great-Granddaughter
Son	Granddaughter	Great-Granddaughter	Great-Great-Grandson
Son	Granddaughter	Great-Granddaughter	Great-Great-Granddaughter

These persons will be counted out in the same way, where descended from a daughter, and thus will number sixteen.   16. In the fifth degree, one hundred and eighty-four persons are included, that is to say, a great-great-great-grandfather and great-great-great-grandmother; a great-great-great-grandfather is the father of a great-great-grandfather or great-great-grandmother, the grandfather of a great-grandfather or great-grandmother, the great-grandfather of a grand-father or grandmother, the great-great-grandfather of a father or mother. This name embraces sixteen persons, who are counted through the male as well as the female line, so that we arrive at individuals in the following way:

Father	Grandfather	Great-grandfather	Great-great-grandfather	Great-great-great-grandfather
Father	Grandfather	Great-grandfather	Great-great-grandmother	Great-great-great-grandfather
Father	Grandfather	Great-grandmother	Great-great-grandfather	Great-great-great-grandfather
Father	Grandfather	Great-grandmother	Great-great-grandmother	Great-great-great-grandfather
Father	Grandmother	Great-grandfather	Great-great-grandfather	Great-great-great-grandfather
Father	Grandmother	Great-grandfather	Great-great-grandmother	Great-great-great-grandfather
Father	Grandmother	Great-grandmother	Great-great-grandfather	Great-great-great-grandfather
Father	Grandmother	Great-grandmother	Great-great-grandmother	Great-great-great-grandfather

They will be counted in the same way if the person of the mother is substituted [for that of a father]. A great-great-grandmother includes the same number of persons counted in the same way, that is, sixteen. A great-uncle on the male side is the brother of a great-grandfather, the great-uncle of a father or mother; there will be eight persons of this name, and they will be counted as follows:

Father	Grandfather	Great-grandfather	Great-great-grandfather	Brother of great-grandfather
Father	Grandfather	Great-grandfather	Great-great-grandmother	Brother of great-grandfather
Father	Grandfather	Great-grandfather	Great-great-grandfather	Brother of great-grandfather
Father	Grandfather	Great-grandfather	Great-great-grandmother	Brother of great-grandfather

There will be the same number if the person is the mother and her great-grandfather is sub-stituted, but in counting the brother of a great-grandfather, we put in before him a great-great-grandfather, for the reason that, as indicated above, we shall not arrive at the person in question in any other way unless we have first gone through those from whom he is descended. Grand-uncle on the female side, that is, brother of a great-grandmother, great-uncle of a mother or fa-ther; counting them off in the same way we shall reckon eight persons here too, leaving only unchanged the fact that he is supposed to be brother of a great-grandmother. Grand-aunt on the male side, that is, sister of a great-grandfather, great-aunt of a father or mother. The same will apply in respect of the count and explanation of persons, leaving only unchanged the fact that the sister of the great-grandfather is placed in the last column. Grand-aunt on the female side, that is, the sister of a great-grandmother, the great-aunt of a father or mother; the number of persons is the same with the result that the sister of the great-grandmother is put in the last column. Some authorities refer to all those whom we trace back to a grand-uncle as follows: grand-uncle on the male side, grand-uncle on the female side, grand-aunt on the male side, grand-aunt on the female side; however, the relations I call by these names refer to me, on the other hand, as great-grandson of a brother or sister. Son or daughter of a great-uncle: These are son or daughter of a grandfather's brother, grandson or granddaughter of a great-grandfather or great-grandmother, being fathered by a son, and male or female cousin of a mother or father; we shall also count eight persons here, because a grandfather and his brother, as already stated, are understood in a dual sense; and for that reason the son or daughter of a great-uncle represents four persons. Son or daughter of a great-aunt on the female side: These are the son or daughter of a grandfather's sister, the grandson and granddaughter of a great-grandfather and great-grandmother being children of a daughter, and male and female cousin of a father or mother; the number of persons is the same as above. Son or daughter of a great-uncle on the female side: These are the son and daughter of a grandmother's brother, grandson and granddaughter of a great-grandfather or great-grandmother, being offspring of a son, male or female cousin of a father or mother; the number is the same. Son or daughter of a great-aunt on the female side: These are the son or daughter of a grandmother's sister, grandson or granddaughter of a great-grandfather or great-grandmother, being offspring of a daughter, male or female cousin of a father or mother; they are counted in the same way. The persons which we have counted out from the son of the great-uncle on the male side are called second cousins of the person whose relationship is under discussion; for, as Massurius says, the person who refers to his father's or mother's male or female cousin as his second cousin is called by the latter son or daughter of a male or female cousin. Grandson or granddaughter of an uncle on the male side; these are the great-grandson or granddaughter of a paternal grandfather or grandmother, being the offspring of a grandson or granddaughter who is the child of a son, the son or daughter of a male or female cousin. They will include eight persons: the grandson representing four, the granddaughter representing four, because the uncle on the male side, too, is understood in two senses, and the grandson or granddaughter constitutes a double entity under the individual persons of the uncles. The grandson or granddaughter of an aunt on the male side: These are the great-grandson or great-granddaughter of a paternal grandfather or grandmother, being the offspring of a grandson or granddaughter born of a daughter, and the son or daughter of a male or female cousin; their number is the same. The grandson or granddaughter of an uncle on the female side: These are the great-grandson or great-granddaughter of a maternal grandfather or maternal grandmother; in other respects the same applies as in the case of a grandson or granddaughter of an uncle on the male side. The person whose relationship is in question is second cousin to all of the supposed descendants of the grandson of the uncle on the male side; for he is their father's or mother's cousin. The great-grandson or great-granddaughter of a brother: These will include sixteen persons, the brother being understood in two senses, and the great-grandson and great-granddaughter respectively in four senses, as we have indicated above. The great-grandson and great-granddaughter of a sister likewise comprehends sixteen persons. A great-great-great-grandson or great-great-great-granddaughter: These are the son or daughter of a great-great-grandson or great-great-granddaughter, the grandson or granddaughter of a great-grandson or great-granddaughter, the great-grandson or great-granddaughter of a grandson or granddaughter, the great-great-grandson or great-great-granddaughter of a son or daughter. Thirty-two persons will be counted under this name, because the term great-great-grandson includes sixteen, and great-great-granddaughter comprehends the same number. 17. In the sixth degree, the following four hundred and forty-eight persons are contained. Great-great-great-great-grandfather: He is the great-great-great-grandfather of a father of a father or mother, the great-great-grandfather of a grandfather or grandmother, the great-grandfather of a great-grandfather or great-grandmother, the grandfather of a great-great-grandfather or great-great-grandmother, the father of a great-great-great-grandfather or great-great-great-grandmother, called, as it were, grandfather three times removed; but [great-great-great-great-grandfather] embraces thirty-two persons; for the number in the case of the great-great-great-grandfather without making changes throughout the individual persons on account of the great-great-great-grandmother is necessarily doubled, so that the great-great-great-great-grandfather is understood to be the great-great-great-grandfather's father in sixteen ways, and similarly the great-great-great-grandmother's. A great-great-great-great-grandmother, being counted in the same way, will make thirty-two persons. A great-grand-uncle: He is the brother of a great-great-grandfather, the son of a great-great-great-grandfather and great-great-great-grandmother, the grand-uncle of a father or mother. He will include sixteen persons as follows:

Father	Grandfather	Great-grandfather	Great-great-grandfather	Great-great-great-grandfather	Brother of great-great-grandfather
Father	Grandfather	Great-grandfather	Great-great-grandfather	Great-great-great-grandmother	Brother of great-great-grandfather
Father	Grandfather	Great-grandmother	Great-great-grandfather	Great-great-great-grandfather	Brother of great-great-grandfather
Father	Grandfather	Great-grandmother	Great-great-grandfather	Great-great-great-grandmother	Brother of great-great-grandfather
Father	Grandmother	Great-grandfather	Great-great-grandfather	Great-great-great-grandfather	Brother of great-great-grandfather
Father	Grandmother	Great-grandfather	Great-great-grandfather	Great-great-great-grandmother	Brother of great-great-grandfather
Father	Grandmother	Great-grandmother	Great-great-grandfather	Great-great-great-grandfather	Brother of great-great-grandfather
Father	Grandmother	Great-grandmother	Great-great-grandfather	Great-great-great-grandmother	Brother of great-great-grandfather

There will be the same number of persons if we substitute the mother. Great-grand-uncle on the female side: he is the brother of a great-great-grandmother or the grand-uncle of a father or mother. And there will be the same number and explanation of persons as above with this change only: that the brother of a great-great-grandmother is substituted for the brother of a great-great-grandfather. Great-grand-aunt on the male side: She is the sister of a great-great-grandfather, the grand-aunt of a father or mother; the other relationships are as in the case of a grand uncle with this change only: that where a brother of a great-great-grandfather stands, sister of a great-great-grandfather is to be read. Great-grand-aunt on the female side: She is sister of a great-great-grandmother, grand-aunt of a father or mother. The other relationships are as above with the substitution only of sister of a great-great-grandmother in the last column instead of brother of a great-great-grandmother. Some people call all those whom we have indicated from the great-grand-uncle on the male side by the following names: great-great-great-uncle on the male side and great-great-great-uncle on the female side; great-great-great-aunt on the male side and great-great-great-aunt on the female side. And so we, too, shall use these names without distinction. But those whom I call great-grand-uncles on the male and female side and great-grand-aunts on the male and female side indicate me as great-great-grandson of a brother or sister. Son or daughter of a grand uncle: These are son or daughter of the brother of a great-grandfather, grandson or granddaughter of a great-great-grandfather or great-great-grandmother through a great-grandfather, being the offspring of a son; there will be sixteen persons under this [heading], counted as in the fifth degree when we were dealing with the grand-uncle, adding only the son or daughter, since it is inevitable that the grand-uncle's son embraces as many persons as the grand uncle, that is, eight. The number stated above will be made up by counting the same number from the person of the daughter. Son or daughter of a grand aunt on the male side: These are son or daughter of a great-grandfather's sister, grandson or granddaughter of a great-great-grandfather or great-great-grandmother through a great-grandfather, being born of a daughter; and here we shall count up the same number of persons by the same calculation. Son or daughter of a great-uncle on the female side: These are son or daughter of a great-grandmother's brother, grandson, or granddaughter of a great-great-grandfather or great-great-grandmother, through a great-grandmother being fathered by a son. The same method of counting is to be adopted here as in the case of a son or daughter of a grand uncle. Son or daughter of a grand-aunt on the female side: These are son or daughter of a great-grandmother's sister, grandson or granddaughter of a great-great-grandfather or great-great-grandmother through a great-grandmother, being the child of a daughter; the number of persons and their explanation is as above. All of those whom we have set out from the son of the grand-uncle are cousins of the great-great-grandfather and great-great-grandmother of the person whose relationship is in question and of their brothers and sisters, but second cousin of his father and mother and their brothers and sisters. The grandson or granddaughter of a grand-uncle on the male side, grandson or granddaughter of a grand-aunt on the female side and grandson or granddaughter of a grand-aunt on the female side; each of these terms includes sixty-four persons. For since the person of a great-uncle, for instance, is understood in four senses, and his grandson in two senses, the number is doubled, if only the grandson is counted, and the number that had been doubled is quadrupled. And it is doubled also where a granddaughter is counted, and we set out the breakdown of one instance alone by way of example:

Father	Grandfather	Great-grandfather	Grandfather's brother who is great-uncle	His son	His grandson being offspring of that son	Likewise his granddaughter
Father	Grandfather	Great-grandmother	Grandfather's brother who is great-uncle	His son	His grandson being offspring of that son	Likewise his granddaughter
Father	Grandfather	Great-grandfather	Grandfather's brother who is great-uncle	His daughter	His grandson being offspring of that daughter	Likewise his granddaughter
Father	Grandfather	Great-grandmother	Grandfather's brother who is great-uncle	His daughter	His grandson being offspring of that daughter	Likewise his granddaughter

The same number is arrived at in the same way if a mother's name is substituted, that is, so as to count grandsons and granddaughters of the brother of a maternal grandfather. We shall also count out the grandsons and granddaughters of a great-aunt on the male side in the same fashion, that is, the sister of a grandfather; and the same holds good in the case of a great-uncle on the female side, that is, the brother of a grandmother. [We proceed] by the same method in the case of a great-aunt on the female side, that is, sister of a grandmother, and the whole number derived from these persons adds up to sixty-four. These are all great-grandsons or great-granddaughters of the great-grandfather or great-grandmother of the person whose relationship is in question, or grandsons and granddaughters of the brother or sister of his grandfather or grandmother; on the other hand, his grandfather and grandmother is their great-uncle or great-aunt on the male side or on the female side; for his father and mother and their brothers and sisters will be second cousins of theirs, and he himself is their cousin and they are his cousins. Great-grandson or great-granddaughter of an uncle on the male side: They will represent eight persons; for there are sixteen of them of either sex as follows:

Father	Grandfather	Uncle on male side	Son of uncle on male side	Uncle's grandson being offspring of his son	Uncle's great-grandson being offspring of a grandson fathered by a son	Likewise a great-granddaughter
Father	Grandmother	Uncle on male side	Son of uncle on male side	Uncle's grandson being offspring of his son	Uncle's great-grandson being offspring of a grandson fathered by a son	Likewise a great-granddaughter
Father	Grandfather	Uncle on male side	Daughter of uncle on male side	Uncle's grandson being offspring of his daughter	Uncle's great-grandson being offspring of a grandson born to a daughter	Likewise a great-granddaughter
Father	Grandmother	Uncle on male side	Daughter of uncle on male side	Uncle's grandson being offspring of his daughter	Uncle's great-grandson being offspring of a grandson born to a daughter	Likewise a great-granddaughter
Father	Grandfather	Uncle on male side	Son of uncle on male side	Uncle's grandson being offspring of his son	Uncle's great-grandson being child of a granddaughter fathered by a son	Likewise a great-granddaughter
Father	Grandmother	Uncle on male side	Son of uncle on male side	Uncle's grandson being offspring of his son	Uncle's great-grandson being child of a granddaughter fathered by a son	Likewise a great-granddaughter
Father	Grandfather	Uncle on male side	Daughter of uncle on male side	Uncle's grandson being offspring of his daughter	Uncle's great-grandson being child of a granddaughter born to a daughter	Likewise a great-granddaughter
Father	Grandmother	Uncle on male side	Daughter of uncle on male side	Uncle's grandson being offspring of his daughter	Uncle's great-grandson being child of a granddaughter born to a daughter	Likewise a great-granddaughter

Great-grandson or great-granddaughter of an aunt on the male side. He accounts for the same number of persons by the same reckoning, an aunt on the male side being substituted for an uncle on the male side; likewise, the great-grandson and great-granddaughter of an uncle on the female side, the uncle on the female side being substituted for the uncle on the male side. Great-grandson and great-granddaughter of an aunt on the female side; and if the aunt is counted here in place of the uncle we shall find the same number of persons. All of these are grandsons or granddaughters of the cousins of the person whose relationship is in question. Great-great-grandson or great-great-granddaughter of a brother and sister: They constitute sixty-four persons, as can be gathered from what has been said above. Grandson and granddaughter in the fifth degree: These are the great-great-great-grandson or great-great-great-granddaughter of a son or daughter, the great-great-grandson or great-great-granddaughter of a grandson or granddaughter, the great-grandson or great-granddaughter of a great-great-grandson or great-great-granddaughter, the grandson or granddaughter of a great-grandson or great-granddaughter, the son or daughter of a great-great-great-grandson or great-great-great-granddaughter. These names denote sixty-four persons; for a great-great-great-great-grandson embraces thirty-two [persons], and likewise a great-great-great-granddaughter. For from the grandson onward the number, being quadrupled on itself makes thirty-two, the grandson representing two persons, the great-grandson four, the great-great-grandson eight, the great-great-great-grandson sixteen. To these are added the great-great-great-great-grandson and great-great-great-great-granddaughter, one being the child of the great-great-great-grandson, the other the child of the great-great-great-granddaughter. But through the individual degrees a doubling takes place for the reason that the females from which the next in line is born are added to the males, and they are counted as follows:

		Great-	Great-great	Great-great-great-	Great-great-great-great-	Also great-great-great-great-
Son	Grandson	grandson	grandson	grandson	grandson	granddaughter
Daughter	Grandson	grandson	grandson	grandson	grandson	granddaughter
Son	Granddaughter	grandson	grandson	grandson	grandson	granddaughter
Daughter	Granddaughter	grandson	grandson	grandson	grandson	granddaughter
Son	Grandson	granddaughter	grandson	grandson	grandson	granddaughter
Daughter	Grandson	granddaughter	grandson	grandson	grandson	granddaughter
Son	Granddaughter	granddaughter	grandson	grandson	grandson	granddaughter
Daughter	Granddaughter	granddaughter	grandson	grandson	grandson	granddaughter
Son	Grandson	grandson	granddaughter	grandson	grandson	granddaughter
Daughter	Grandson	grandson	granddaughter	grandson	grandson	granddaughter
Son	Grandson	granddaughter	granddaughter	grandson	grandson	granddaughter
Daughter	Grandson	granddaughter	granddaughter	grandson	grandson	granddaughter
Son	Granddaughter	grandson	granddaughter	grandson	grandson	granddaughter
Daughter	Granddaughter	grandson	granddaughter	grandson	grandson	granddaughter
Son	Granddaughter	granddaughter	granddaughter	grandson	grandson	granddaughter
Daughter	Granddaughter	granddaughter	granddaughter	grandson	grandson	granddaughter
Son	Grandson	grandson	grandson	granddaughter	grandson	granddaughter
Daughter	Grandson	grandson	grandson	granddaughter	grandson	granddaughter
Son	Granddaughter	grandson	grandson	granddaughter	grandson	granddaughter
Daughter	Granddaughter	grandson	grandson	granddaughter	grandson	granddaughter
Son	Grandson	granddaughter	grandson	granddaughter	grandson	granddaughter
Daughter	Grandson	granddaughter	grandson	granddaughter	grandson	granddaughter
Son	Granddaughter	granddaughter	grandson	granddaughter	grandson	granddaughter
Daughter	Granddaughter	granddaughter	grandson	granddaughter	grandson	granddaughter
Son	Grandson	grandson	granddaughter	granddaughter	grandson	granddaughter
Daughter	Grandson	grandson	granddaughter	granddaughter	grandson	granddaughter
Son	Grandson	granddaughter	granddaughter	granddaughter	grandson	granddaughter
Daughter	Grandson	granddaughter	granddaughter	granddaughter	grandson	granddaughter
Son	Granddaughter	grandson	granddaughter	granddaughter	grandson	granddaughter
Daughter	Granddaughter	grandson	granddaughter	granddaughter	grandson	granddaughter
Son	Granddaughter	granddaughter	granddaughter	granddaughter	grandson	granddaughter
Daughter	Granddaughter	granddaughter	granddaughter	granddaughter	grandson	granddaughter

18. The seventh degree embraces the following one thousand and twenty-four persons: father and mother of the great-great-great-great-grandfather or grandmother, who will account for one hundred and twenty-eight persons; for as many persons can be fathers of a great-great-great-great-grandfather as can be great-great-great-grandfathers of the person in question; likewise the same number of persons can be mothers [of a great-great-great-great-grandfather]; these account for sixty-four, and the same number represents the parents of a great-great-great-great-grandmother. Brother or sister of a great-great-great-grandfather or great-great-great-grandmother: These are the son and daughter of the great-great-great-great-grandfather, the uncle and aunt on the male and female sides of a great-great-grandfather or great-great-grandmother, the great-uncle and great-aunt on the male and female sides of a great-grandfather and great-grandmother, the grand-uncle and grand-aunt on the male and female sides of a grandfather and grandmother, the great-grand-uncle and great-grand-aunt on the male or female side of a father or mother. The persons of the great-great-great-grandfather's brother number thirty-two; for to the sixteen represented by the great-great-great-grandfather are added a further sixteen on account of the dual person of his brother; for it is necessary to count sixteen brothers of a great-great-great-grandfather reckoning from the father, and sixteen reckoning from the mother. In the same way, there are thirty-two sisters of a great-great-great-grandfather; these amount to sixty-four persons, and the same number will be represented by the brother of a great-great-great-grandmother and also by her sister. Son and daughter of a great-grand-uncle on the male side: These are grandson and granddaughter of a great-great-great-grandfather, being the offspring of a son, the son or daughter of the brother of a great-great-grandfather. Son or daughter of a great-grand-aunt on the male side: These are the grandson or granddaughter of a great-great-great-grandfather, being the offspring of a daughter, the son or daughter of a sister of a great-great-grandfather. Son and daughter of a great-grand-uncle on the female side: These are grandson and granddaughter of a great-great-great-grandfather being the offspring of a son, son or daughter of the brother of a great-great-grandmother. Son or daughter of a great-grand-aunt on the mother's side: These are the grandson and granddaughter of a great-great-great-grandfather, being offspring of a daughter, the son or daughter of a sister of a great-great-grandmother. All these persons, whom we have counted out from the son of the great-grand-uncle on the male side, are cousins of the great-grandfather and great-grandmother of the person whose relationship is in question, and second cousins of his grandfather and grandmother. The individual names account for sixteen persons, because, since the great-grand-uncle represents sixteen, his son accounts for the same number, as also his daughter, and all of these which we have included from the son of the great-grand-uncle amount to one hundred and twenty-eight, multiplying sixteen by eight. The grandson of a grand-uncle on the male side accounts for sixteen (for he is the great-grandson of a great-great-grandfather or great-great-grandmother), and, since the great-great-grandfather is counted eight times, the grandsons being reckoned as sixteen make up the aforesaid number. The granddaughter of a grand-uncle on the male side likewise [accounts for the same number]. The grandson and granddaughter of a grand-uncle on the female side will number thirty-two persons on the same reckoning. The grandson and granddaughter of a grand-aunt on the male side will produce the same number by the same reckoning, as will the grandson and granddaughter of a grand-aunt on the female side. Thus, the whole yields one hundred and twenty-eight. The grandfather and grandmother of the person whose relationship is in question are second cousins to these persons while his father and mother are cousins. The person whose relationship is in question is son of a cousin; the other is defined in relation to him by a circumlocution as cousin of his parent, as Trebatius says, and he gives as the reason for the name the fact that the final degrees of relationships are those of cousins, and so son of a cousin is rightly the nearest way of describing him. He will be called son of this cousin by the cousin himself, and for that reason the children of cousins call each other by the approximate term; for they have no proper name by which to refer to each other. The great-grandson or great-granddaughter of a great-uncle on the male side; the great-grandson or great-granddaughter of a great-uncle on the female side; the great-grandson or great-granddaughter of a great-aunt on the male side; the great-grandson or great-granddaughter of a great-aunt on the female side. All

of these make up one hundred and twenty-eight persons, because each name accounts for sixteen; for when, for example, the great-uncle is understood in four senses, the great-grandson, being quadrupled in respect of the persons of each of the great uncles, and likewise the great granddaughter, will give thirty-two persons, and these, multiplied by four, will make up the above-mentioned sum. Their fathers and mothers are male and female cousins of the person whose relationship is in question, but he himself in relation to them is the son of a male or female cousin. Great-great-grandson and great-great-granddaughter of an uncle on the male side; great-great-grandson and great-great-granddaughter of an uncle on the female side; great-great-grandson and great-great-granddaughter of an aunt on the male side; great-great-grandson and great-great-granddaughter of an aunt on the female side. Each of these names embraces sixteen persons; for the great-great-grandson of an uncle on the male side, for instance, will be counted in the following way with the result that, the uncle being understood in two senses, the great-grandson in four, the great-granddaughter represents the same number, and thus we arrive at their sons, who are counted as sixteen; the same reckoning applies to the daughter and likewise to the others; and as a result, all these will make up a number of one hundred and twenty-eight persons. These are the grandsons and granddaughters of the cousins of the person whose relationship is in question, and they are the son and daughter of the great-grand-uncle on the male and female sides and great-grand-aunt on the male and female sides of [the person] whose relationship is in question, likewise cousins of a great-grandfather or great-grandmother. Great-great-great-grandson and great-great-great-granddaughter of a brother or sister: They number one hundred and twenty-eight persons. Son of a great-great-great-great-grandson, likewise daughter [of the same]. They number one hundred and twenty-eight persons because, since the great-great-great-great-grandson and granddaughter, as we have shown above, account for sixty-four, their son or daughter will be counted by the same reckoning.

11

WHENCE HUSBAND AND WIFE

1   ULPIAN, *Edict, book 47:* To enable application for *bonorum possessio unde vir et uxor* there must be a valid marriage. However, if a marriage has not been according to law, it will by no means be possible to seek *bonorum possessio*, just as it is not possible to take an inheritance in accordance with a will or to apply for *bonorum possessio* according to will; for nothing can be taken on account of the fact that the marriage was invalid.   1. For this [type of] *bonorum possessio* to issue there must be a wife at the time of death. But if divorce has ensued, notwithstanding the fact that the marriage subsists at law, there is no room for this [type of] succession, but this occurs in cases of the following kind. A freedwoman has gained a divorce against the will of her patron: The *lex Julia* regulating marriage between the orders keeps her in the married state so long as it would prevent her marrying another against her patron's will. Likewise, the [*lex*] *Julia* on adultery, unless divorce has been effected by regular procedure, holds it to be invalid.

12

SUCCESSION TO VETERANS AND SOLDIERS

1   MACER, *Military Law, book 2:* Paul and Menander observe that a soldier who has merited capital punishment should be allowed to make a will, and on his intestacy his property, if he has been punished, belongs to his relations, provided, however, that he has been punished for a military offense and not a general offense.

2   PAPINIAN, *Replies, book 16:* The *bona castrensia* of a soldier who has died intestate are not claimed for the imperial treasury when an heir at law exists up to the fifth degree, or the nearest cognate relative of the same degree has received *possessio* within the permitted time.

13

THOSE IN WHOSE FAVOR *BONORUM POSSESSIO* DOES NOT ISSUE

1 JULIAN, *Digest, book 28:* Suppose my slave has been instituted heir and I have procured by fraud that the testator should not change his will and have subsequently manumitted the slave. It has been asked whether he should be deprived of the right of action. I gave it as my opinion: This case does not fall within the words of the edict. But if the master has procured by fraud that no change should be made in the will in which his slave has been appointed heir, even though he has taken his inheritance after manumission, it is equitable for [an action] to be denied him, since it is denied to an emancipated son, too, where his father has procured by fraud that there should be no change in a will.

14

THAT *BONORUM POSSESSIO* MAY BE GRANTED IN ACCORDANCE WITH STATUTES OR *SENATUS CONSULTA*

1 ULPIAN, *Edict, book 49:* The praetor says: "I will grant *bonorum possessio* in such manner as any law or *senatus consultum* shall oblige me to grant it." 1. *Bonorum possessio* which has been claimed in accordance with a part of the edict never prejudices this [kind of] *bonorum possessio.* 2. When someone takes an inheritance in accordance with the *Law of the Twelve Tables*, he does not apply under this section, but under the head, "then the person who ought to be his heir," in that *bonorum possessio* issues in this case just as if a law specifically offers it to him.

15

THE ORDER TO BE PRESERVED IN [GRANTS OF *BONORUM*] *POSSESSIO*

1 MODESTINUS, *Encyclopaedia, book 6:* The following degrees are called on an intestacy: first, the *sui heredes*; second, the heirs at law; third, the nearest cognate relatives; lastly, husband and wife. 1. Whether a will exists or not, if no one has taken *bonorum possessio* in accordance with, or contrary to, it, *bonorum possessio* is to be awarded on intestacy. 2. On a father's intestacy, *bonorum possessio* is given not only to those children who have been in power up to the time of his death but to emancipated children.
2 ULPIAN, *Edict, book 49:* There is an effective time for obtaining *bonorum possessio*, but time is effective in such a fashion that individual days of a period are effective, that is to say, the days on which the [claimant] has been aware [of his rights] and has been able to obtain it. However, there is no doubt that on a day on which he was unaware [of his rights] or has not been able [to obtain it] time does not run against him. But it can come about that a person, who has been initially aware [of his claim] or has been capable of obtaining *bonorum possessio* begins to be uncertain [of it], or not to be capable of obtaining it, that is to say, in a case where, although he knew initially that a certain party had died intestate, subsequently, as if receiving better information on the point, he had begun to doubt whether he had died leaving a will or whether he is still alive, because this rumor had later become current. The principle can also be

understood in the opposite sense, so that a person who has initially been unaware of the position later begins to be aware of it.   1. It is clear that the days for applying for *bonorum possessio* are effective days, but the days when the court sits will not be counted provided that *bonorum possessio* is of the type which could be sought extrajudicially. But if it is of the kind which requires a hearing before the court or demands a decree, we shall have to count the days on which [the praetor sits] and those on which no action has been taken by the praetor to prevent a grant of *bonorum possessio*.   2. In the case of *bonorum possessio*, which is granted before the court, it is asked whether in fact the praetor is sitting in court but has not acceded to the demand; it is possible to hold that the time [for seeking] *bonorum possessio* does not run, since the presiding officer has been engaged with other matters of a military or custodial nature or of an inquisitional nature.   3. If the governor of the province has been in a neighboring city the length of the journey should be accounted for and added to the time available, that is to say, reckoning twenty miles [to the day], for we should not expect the governor of the province to come to the prospective applicant for *bonorum possessio*.   4. If an unborn child has been put in possession, it is quite clear that time [for seeking] *bonorum possessio* does not run against those who are next in line, and this is not confined merely to the hundred days, but applies to the whole period of time in which the child may be born; for even where the child has been born, it is to be known that *bonorum possessio* is first offered to him.   5. The knowledge required, Pomponius says, is not that which is expected of those skilled in law, but that which everyone was capable of acquiring either independently or through others, that is to say, by consulting those wiser than himself in the way in which it is right and proper for a careful head of a household to take advice.

3   PAUL, *Edict, book 44:* A father's knowledge about the time for seeking *bonorum possessio* does not prejudice a son who is in ignorance of the fact.

4   JULIAN, *Digest, book 28:* If you had been substituted to your co-heir and have taken *bonorum possessio* whenever your co-heir has decided against seeking *bonorum possessio*, the whole [estate] is understood as having been granted to you; your co-heir will have no further opportunity to apply for *bonorum possessio*.   1. Where a son is called to *bonorum possessio* not only qua son but also in the case where he is called as agnate or cognate relative, he has one year in which to apply, just as a father who had manumitted his son, although he takes *bonorum possessio* as manumitter, nevertheless has a year in which to be granted *bonorum possessio*.

5   MARCELLUS, *Digest, book 9:* When *bonorum possessio* has been offered to a son-in-power, the days on which he is unable to inform his father, so that he may direct him to claim *bonorum possessio* or may ratify a claim for *bonorum possessio*, do not run [against him]. Let us imagine that on the very first day on which it has been offered [to him], he has immediately claimed *bonorum possessio* [but] cannot inform his father to gain his approval. The hundred days do not run against him, but they start to run when [his father] could have been informed. But ratification will be useless once the hundred days have passed.   1. It may be asked if, when a son could apply for *bonorum possessio*, his father being absent, so that he cannot inform him, or even insane, he has neglected to make application, whether he is precluded from further application. But how can lack of application for *bonorum possessio*, which, if it had been applied for, would not be obtainable without the father's prior approval, be prejudicial [to him]?   2. If a slave belonging to another had been sold after being instituted heir, it is questionable whether the time for suit for *bonorum possessio* should run against the later master. And it is resolved that whatever time has been available to the later master is reckoned against him.

16

HEIRS WHO ARE *SUI* AND HEIRS AT LAW

1 ULPIAN, *Sabinus, book 12:* They are properly termed intestate who have failed to make a will when it was in their power to do so. But a man who has made a will, where his estate has not been accepted or his will has been ruptured or is invalid may properly be said to have died intestate. Obviously, a person who has not had the capacity to make a will is not properly intestate, for instance, an *impubes*, an insane person, or one interdicted from his property; but we should understand these persons too as intestates, and likewise also a person in captivity, since under the *lex Cornelia* succession is offered to those persons to whom it would be offered if he had died as a member of the community; for the estate is considered to have belonged to him too.   1. It will be possible to ask if a child conceived and born of a slave-woman who has suffered a delay in [the matter of obtaining the] freedom left to her by way of *fideicommissum* is [effectively] *suus* to his father. And since it is resolved that he is born free, as has been laid down in a rescript by the deified Marcus and Verus and our Emperor Antoninus Augustus, why should his mother not be considered as completely manumitted so that after marriage she may produce a *suus*? It should not be remarkable for a freeman to be born of a slave when it has been laid down in a rescript that a man born of a woman in captivity is born free. Wherefore I would dare to hold that although the father of the child may have been in the same condition, where his mother has suffered a delay in the matter of granting her freedom by way of *fideicommissum* and he himself has suffered a delay, he is born *suus* to his father on the precedent of parents in captivity with whom he has returned. Therefore, whether his father is later manumitted after a delay, he will take him in his power or whether he has died before [doing so], it will have to be resolved that a *suus* exists.   2. We should understand as *sui heredes* sons and daughters whether natural or adopted.   3. Sometimes even a son who is *suus* is barred by a preference for the imperial treasury, for instance, where his father has been posthumously condemned for *perduellio*, to the end that the son in question does not even have rights in respect of tombs.   4. If a son has ceased to be *suus heres*, all the grandsons and granddaughters of whom that son is the father and who are in power succeed to his share, which is consonant with natural equity. But a son ceases to be *suus heres*, if, by a great or lesser change of civil status, he has fallen out of power. But if a son is in captivity, the grandchildren do not succeed so long as he is alive. Accordingly, even if he has been ransomed, they do not succeed before payment, but if he had died meantime, although it is resolved that he has died after recovery of his status, he will bar the grandchildren.   5. But if a person has not ceased to be in power, but has never been in power, for instance, where my son has been taken captive by the enemy in my father's lifetime, and he has died there after I have become head of the household, my grandchildren will succeed to his place.   6. But granddaughters will succeed no less than grandsons to the places of their parents.   7. Sometimes, although a man's parent has not ceased to be in power, but has never been in power, nevertheless, we hold that the children who succeed to him are *sui*; for instance, I have adopted by *adrogatio* a man whose son has been captured by the enemy, but who had a grandson in the community. If the son adopted by *adrogatio* dies and the one in captivity dies among the enemy, that great-grandson will be *suus heres* to me.   8. But it is to be known that grandsons and sometimes their descendants can nevertheless be *sui heredes* even though their parents have taken precedence to them at the time of [their grandfather's] death, although there is no succession among *sui heredes*. And this happens as follows: If the head of a household has died leaving a will and has disinherited his son, and later, while the instituted heir is deliberating [whether to take the estate or not], the son has died and the instituted heir has then subsequently renounced the estate, it will be possible for the grandson to be *suus heres*, as Marcellus, too, has observed in his tenth book, since the estate has not been offered to the son. The same will have to be held also in the case where the son has been [appointed heir] to the whole under a condition with which it was in his power to comply, or a grandson instituted under a general condition, and they have died before its fulfillment. For it will have to be held that their *sui* can succeed, provided that

they have been alive at the time of the testator's death, or at least have been conceived. Both Julian and Marcellus accept this view.   9. Blood relatives are called immediately after the *sui*.   10. Cassius defines blood relatives as persons connected with one another by blood. And it is true that they are blood relatives, even though they have not fallen to be *sui heredes* to their father, as, for instance, where they have been disinherited; but even if their father has been deported, nonetheless, they are blood relatives one with another, even though they had not been *sui heredes* to their father; and those who have never been in power will be blood relatives of each other, for instance, those born after the captivity or death of their father.   11. But not only natural but also adopted children will share the rights of consanguinity with those who are members of the family or who are unborn or born after their father's death.

2   ULPIAN, *Sabinus, book 13:* After blood relatives agnates are admitted, if they are not blood relatives, and rightly so. For if there are blood relatives, even if they have not accepted the estate, it is not offered to the heirs at law. But this will have to be understood in the sense that [it applies] where there is no expectation of there being blood relatives; however, if there is a possibility of a blood relative being born or returning from captivity, agnates are barred.   1. But agnates are cognate relatives of the male sex sprung from the same person. For after *sui* and blood relatives my immediate next of kin is the son of my blood relative, and I am [next of kin] to him; my father's brother, too, who is called uncle on the male side, and then the rest, if there are any who trace their origins from him, and so on.   2. The inheritance in question is offered to the nearest agnate, that is, the person over whom no one takes precedence. And if there are several of the same degree [it is offered] to all of them, that is to say, in per capita shares. Suppose I had two brothers or two uncles. One of them has left one son, the other two. My estate will be divided into three shares.   3. But it makes little difference whether the agnate in question is such by virtue of birth or adoption; for a person who is adopted becomes an agnate to those same persons to whom his father was agnate, and he will take their estate in the case of an intestacy, and they his.   4. In the case of an intestacy, the estate is offered only to the closest person. It does not matter whether he is one person on his own or the nearer of two or more of the same degree who either take precedence over the others or stand alone, because he is the next in line over whom no one takes precedence, and he is the last [in line] who is followed by no one, and sometimes the same person can be first and last where he stands alone.   5. Sometimes we admit an agnate who is further removed. Suppose a man has made a will, having an uncle or nephew. While the appointed heir was deliberating [whether or not to take the estate], the uncle has died; subsequently, the instituted heir has renounced the estate; the uncle's son will be admitted. Therefore, he can also apply for *bonorum possessio*.   6. We do not look for the person who was nearest at the time the head of the household died, but the nearest at the point when it is established that he died intestate. According to these principles, even if there was a *suus* who took precedence or a blood relative, if neither is alive at the point when the estate is renounced, we accept as nearest the person who has first [claim] when the estate is renounced.   7. Hence, it is a nice question whether we are still to award succession after such renunciation. Suppose that an appointed heir has been asked to hand over an estate and has renounced it when he could nonetheless have been compelled to take it and hand it over as the deified Pius has ruled in a rescript. Imagine, for the sake of argument, that he has survived one hundred days and that the next in line has meantime died and that the person who has been asked to hand over the estate has also later died; it is to be held that the person subsequently entitled is to be admitted [to the estate] with the burden of the *fideicommissum*.

3   ULPIAN, *Sabinus, book 14:* It is true that when a freedman has died intestate, the estate is first to be offered to his *sui*; if he has none, then to his patron.   1. We should understand as a freedman a person whom someone has brought out of slavery to Roman *civitas*, whether on his own initiative or by compulsion, in that he has been asked to manumit him; for he is also admitted to the estate on his [freedman's] intestacy.   2. If a person has manumitted a slave who came to him as part of a dowry, he himself is accorded the rights of patron, and will be admitted in the case of intestacy.   3. A person whom I have bought on condition that I manumit him, although he has obtained his freedom

in accordance with a constitution of the deified Marcus, nevertheless, as is made clear by the same constitution, is clearly my freedman, and his estate will be offered to me on his intestacy. 4. What if he has uncovered his master's murder and has been adjudged worthy of his freedom by *senatus consultum*? If the praetor has assigned him to the man whose freedman he is, he will doubtless belong to him, and the latter will be offered his estate on an intestacy; but if the praetor made no such assignment, he will certainly become a Roman citizen but will be the freedman of the person whose slave he most recently was, and the latter will be admitted on the freedman's intestacy, unless at any point it has been necessary to deny him the estate on the grounds of his unworthiness. 5. If anyone has bound his freedwoman by oath not to marry illegally, he should not be liable under the *lex Aelia Sentia*. But if the oath runs, "that he is not to marry within a certain time," or "not to marry any other woman without his patron's consent," or "to marry only a fellow freedwoman" or "a relation of his patron," it is to be held that he falls under the *lex Aelia Sentia* and is not admitted on an intestacy. 6. If the townspeople have manumitted a slave, they will be admitted in the case of an intestacy to the property of an intestate freedman or freedwoman. 7. A soldier who manumits a slave, part of his private property, will make him a freedman and is admitted to the latter's estate in the case of intestacy. 8. It is patently clear that the emperor is admitted to the property of his freedmen. 9. Likewise, it is also clear from the *Law of the Twelve Tables* that an unborn person is admitted in the case of intestacy, providing that he has been duly brought to birth. Hence, he usually stays the claims of the agnates who follow him to whom he is preferred, if he has been born; hence, he also shares with those who are of the same degree, as in the case where there is one brother and one unborn brother, or one nephew and one who is not yet born. 10. The question of the proportion in which the share is to be divided has also been treated, because a pregnant woman may give birth to more than one child. And it has been resolved, if it is humanly ascertainable that the woman who declares she is pregnant is not pregnant, the person already born is already heir to the whole, since he becomes heir without being aware of the fact. Therefore, if he has died before the woman has run her time, he hands on the estate intact to his own heir. 11. A person born more than ten months after the death will not be admitted in the case of an intestacy. 12. But in the case of a person born on the hundredth and eighty-second day, Hippocrates has observed, and the deified Pius has stated in a rescript to the priests, that he appears to have been born at the proper time and does not appear to have been conceived for slavery, when his mother had been manumitted before the hundredth and eighty-second day.

4 POMPONIUS, *Sabinus, book 4:* Persons whose parent has suffered a change of civil status retain their rights on an intestacy both over other persons and among themselves, and, conversely, the others preserve their position with regard to them.

5 ULPIAN, *Edict, book 46:* If a man with a brother and uncle on the male side has died leaving a will and the brother has died intestate, while a condition pertaining to the appointed heirs is in suspense, and that condition has later failed, it is settled that the uncle may be admitted to the estate of either by way of intestacy.

6 JULIAN, *Digest, book 59:* Titius, having disinherited his son, conditionally appointed a stranger as heir. It has been asked, if, after the death of the father, while the condition was still in suspense, the son had married and fathered a son, and had then died, and the condition imposed upon the instituted heir had subsequently failed, whether the estate of his grandfather would devolve by way of intestacy on this posthumous grandson. [Julian] gave it as his opinion: a person conceived after his grandfather's death can neither take the estate on the latter's intestacy as *suus heres* nor receive *bonorum possessio* as cognate relative, because the *Law of the Twelve Tables* calls to the inheritance a person who has been alive at the time of the death of the man whose property is in question.

7 CELSUS, *Digest, book 28:* Or if he has been conceived in the latter's lifetime, because he has been conceived, he is regarded in some sense as being alive.

8 JULIAN, *Digest, book 59:* The praetor in his edict likewise promises *bonorum possessio* to those who have been cognate relatives of the deceased at the time of his death in virtue of their relationship. For although their grandsons are commonly called the cognate relatives even of those after whose death they have been conceived, such usage is not proper

and occurs through misuse or rather by analogy. 1. Where a man had left a pregnant wife and a mother and sister, if the mother had died in the wife's lifetime and if the wife's child had been stillborn, the estate falls to the sister alone by way of intestacy, because it is clear that the mother had died at a point at which the estate did not belong to her by way of intestacy.

9   MARCIAN, *Institutes, book 5:* If, out of several heirs on an intestacy, some have neglected to take their inheritance or have been prevented from doing so by death or some other reason, their share accrues to the remainder who have accepted, and even if [the latter] have died before such accrual, this right belongs to their heirs. The case of the instituted heir and the substitute co-heir is different; for the estate is offered to the latter by way of substitution in his lifetime, but it does not also follow his heir if he has died.

10   MODESTINUS, *Distinctions, book 6:* If the estate of an intestate son devolves by way of intestacy on the father who was his manumitter, or *bonorum possessio* is available to [a father who] is not a manumitter, the mother of the deceased is barred [from succession].

11   POMPONIUS, *Quintus Mucius, book 10:* Succession on an intestacy arising out of the *Law of the Twelve Tables* is extinguished by change of civil status, whether such change of civil status intervenes during the [testator's] lifetime, or before the estate is accepted, since [the person who would otherwise take] ceases to be properly called *suus heres* or agnate, but the provisions of recent laws and *senatus consulta* are by no means similar.

12   POMPONIUS, *Quintus Mucius, book 30:* A son is the nearest agnate to his father.

13   GAIUS, *Lex Julia et Papia, book 10:* No woman can either have *sui heredes* or cease to have them by reason of loss of civil status.

14   GAIUS, *Lex Julia et Papia, book 13:* In the case of *sui heredes*, formal acceptance is not a requisite because they immediately fall to be heirs by operation of law.

15   PAPINIAN, *Questions, book 29:* If a father dies in captivity, we believe that the son who had already predeceased him as a member of the community died as head of a household, although he has not been fully freed from his father's power in his lifetime; and so he will have an heir if his father has not returned. But if the father has returned by right of *postliminium* after the son's death, he will take whatever the latter has acquired in the meantime; and it is not surprising if the *peculium*, too, of a son since dead is offered to his father, since he becomes a son in his power through the constitution pertaining to the suspension of rights.

16   PAPINIAN, *Replies, book 12:* A father included in the instrument relating to the dowry a clause to the effect that his daughter had received a dowry without any other expectations from her father's estate; it is certain that this clause has not ousted the rights of succession; for the provisions of individuals do not derogate from the authority of the law.

17

SENATUS CONSULTUM TERTULLIANUM AND *ORPHITIANUM*

1   ULPIAN, *Sabinus, book 12:* Whether a mother is freeborn or a freedwoman, her children can be admitted to her estate in accordance with the *senatus consultum Orphitianum*. 1. If the mother is a person about whose status there is doubt whether she is mother of a household or a daughter-in-power as, for instance, in the case where her father has been captured by the enemy, should it become evident that she is the mother of a household, her children will be admitted. Therefore, the question may be considered whether, in the intervening period while her status is in doubt, her children should be assisted by the praetor, lest, as a result of their death in the intermediate period, they fail to hand on anything to an heir; and the more reasonable view is

that they are assisted, as has been resolved in many cases.   2. But illegitimate children, too, are admitted in the case of their mother's intestacy.   3. Sometimes, too, succession on an intestacy will have to be permitted to a child born in slavery, as where a child has been born after there has been a delay in granting his mother's freedom which had been made the object of a *fideicommissum*. Obviously, if he has been born after his mother's manumission, even though he was conceived in slavery, he will be admitted on an intestacy. But also where he has been conceived in captivity and born of a woman taken prisoner and has returned together with her, according to the rescript of our emperor and his deified father addressed to Ovinius Tertullus, he will be able to be admitted in accordance with this *senatus consultum*, as if he were illegitimate.   4. Where a son, who, at the time of his mother's death, was a Roman citizen, is taken into slavery before accepting the estate, he is not offered it by way of intestacy, even if he has later become free, unless perhaps in the case where he has been made a *servus poenae* and been restored to his former status by the emperor's prerogative.   5. But if a child has been born by Caesarian section, it is rather to be held that he, too, is admitted on his mother's intestacy; for he could have applied for *bonorum possessio*, both as instituted heir according to will, and, in the case of intestacy, *unde cognati*, and, even more so, *unde legitimi*; and there is proof of this in the fact that an unborn child is put in possession under every head of the edict.   6. A man who has hired out his services, for instance, by fighting wild beasts, or who has been condemned on a capital charge and never restored to his former status, was not admitted to his mother's estate by virtue of the *senatus consultum Orphitianum*, but by a generous interpretation it was resolved to admit him. The same will have to be held where the son in question is in the power of one who is in the aforementioned case, namely, that he can be admitted in accordance with the *Orphitianum*.   7. But where a mother has made a will and appointed one of several sons heir conditionally, if he has sought possession while the condition is in suspense and the condition has subsequently failed, it is equitable that intestate succession should not be denied the remaining sons, as Papinian also has observed in the sixteenth book of his *Questions*.   8. A change of civil status that impinges on children without affecting their position is not prejudicial so far as intestate succession is concerned; for only the old [type of] inheritance offered by the *Law of the Twelve Tables* is extinguished by a change of civil status, but new [types of intestate succession] offered, either in accordance with a law, or in accordance with *senatus consulta*, are not extinguished by a change of civil status. Accordingly, if someone undergoes a change of civil status before it is offered, he will be admitted to the estate on an intestacy, unless a great change of civil status supervenes, such as to remove his citizenship, for instance, if he is deported.   9. "If none of the sons or those to whom succession on an intestacy is offered at the same time should be willing to take that estate to himself, let the old law be observed." This ruling is stated for the reason that, so long as even one son wishes to take on an intestacy, the old law does not apply; and so, if one of two sons has accepted and one renounced an estate, the former's share is increased by accrual. And if there are perhaps a son and a patron, on the son's refusal, the estate is offered to the patron.   10. If a man, having accepted his mother's estate, has refrained from taking it through *restitutio in integrum*, can the old law have a place? The wording permits it to do so: "should he be willing," it says, "to take that estate to himself"; for the man in question is also unwilling, although he was once willing; and I hold that the old law can apply.   11. But is succession offered to him who is then discovered to be heir at law, or to him who was heir at law at the time it was offered to the son? Let us imagine, for instance, that the deceased woman had a blood relation and a son, and that while the son was deliberating whether to accept the estate or not, her blood relation died and the son later renounced his mother's estate; can the son of the blood relation be admitted? And Julian rightly submits that so far as the *Tertullianum* is concerned, there is place for the agnate who succeeds [to another].   12. And the senate's saying "let those matters which have been adjudicated, transacted, or concluded, remain ratified" is to be understood in the sense that "adjudicated" should be understood to mean by him who had the right of judging them; "transacted," that is to say in good faith, so that the

transaction is valid, "concluded," either by agreement or gone to sleep as a result of long silence.
2   ULPIAN, *Sabinus, book 13:* Whether a mother is freeborn or a freedwoman she will have the
benefit of the *Tertullianum.*   1. But we should understand son or daughter to mean those legally begotten or illegitimately conceived. And Julian has made this observation in the case of
illegitimate children in the fifty-ninth book of his *Digest.*   2. But if a son or daughter will have
become freedman or freedwoman, their mother will not be able to claim their estates on an intestacy, since she has ceased to be the mother of sons of this kind. And Julian, too, has observed
this, and it has been the subject of a constitution of our emperor.   3. But if she has conceived a
son while a slave and has given birth to him after manumission, she will be admitted to his estate
on an intestacy; and likewise, if she has conceived while a *serva poenae* and has given birth to the
child after restoration to her former status; the same applies if she conceived as a freewoman and
gave birth as a *serva poenae* and has later been restored; but also if she has conceived as a freewoman and has given birth to the child after being reduced to slavery and has subsequently been
manumitted, she will be admitted on his intestacy. Likewise, if she has been manumitted when
still pregnant, it will have to be held that she reaps the advantage [of the *Tertullianum*]. And a
mother will be admitted on the intestacy of the son born to her in slavery, for instance, where she
has given birth after there has been a delay in granting her freedom which is the object of a
fideicommissum, or if he was born while she was in captivity and she has returned with him, or if
she gave birth after being ransomed.   4. A woman who has incurred infamy will be admitted on
the intestacy of her children.   5. It is certain that an *impubes* to whom his father has made a
pupillary substitution has died intestate at the point when the substitute heirs have failed to take
the estate. Therefore, even if the *impubes* has been adopted by *adrogatio,* it is to be held that in
a case where he had died intestate, his mother is admitted to any property he had.   6. Children
of the deceased who are in fact *sui* will bar his mother whether they are male or female, and,
whether natural or adopted, exclude a mother, but *bonorum possessores* [have this effect] even if
they are not *sui* and indeed where they are only natural children. But adoptive children are admitted after emancipation in this way, provided that they have been of the number of natural
children, for instance, a natural grandson who has been adopted by his grandfather; for although
he has been emancipated, once he has received *bonorum possessio,* he will bar his mother.   7. But
if a son is in captivity or is expected to be born, the rights of his mother are in suspense until he
has returned or is born [as the case may be].   8. But if there are heirs who are *sui,* but the
estate does not belong to them, let us see whether a mother is admitted, for example, where [the
sui] have refrained from taking the estate. Africanus and Publicius urge holding that in the
case where the *sui* refrained [from taking the estate] the mother's claims come into question, and
that they only bar her whenever they actually take the property, so that the mere term *suus
heres* does not prejudice a mother; and this is the more equitable view.   9. But if a man had died
leaving a daughter whom he had allowed to be legally adopted and her mother also survives her
husband, the deified Pius has decreed that the *senatus consultum Tertullianum* falls into abeyance, and both mother and daughter are to be admitted together to *bonorum possessio unde
proximi cognati.* But the same Julian's observation to the effect that the mother cannot be admitted in accordance with the *senatus consultum* if the daughter has given up her suit for *bonorum
possessio* will not be true; for she succeeds to her daughter. And so it will have to be held that a
mother cannot take *bonorum possessio* as long as her daughter is in a position to sue for it, since
she could hope to succeed as heir at law.   10. If, having accepted *bonorum possessio,* an emancipated son has refrained from taking an estate through *restitution in integrum,* it is true that the
senatus consultum can operate; but if he has involved himself with the estate a second time, the
mother must again refrain from it.   11. If an unborn child has been put in possession and has
later been born, and, before taking *bonorum possessio,* has died, we must see whether he prejudices his mother in virtue of his position as *bonorum possessor.* And I submit that he does
not prejudice her, if he was not born *suus* to his father after the latter has made his will; for it
is not enough for him to be put in possession, unless he has also been born and has accepted
bonorum possessio. Therefore, in this case too, where *possessio* has been applied for on behalf of
an insane person by decree, and, before he has been restored to sanity and applied for *bonorum
possessio* in his own person, he has died, he will not prejudice his mother.   12. But if someone
who was involved in a dispute about his status has merely accepted Carbonian possession, it has
indeed been asked whether *bonorum possessio* is prejudicial to his mother; but since this [type of
bonorum possessio] is determined by time, it is to be held that he does not prejudice his mother
after lapse of time, or, in the case where he has died an *impubes,* that she can be admitted.
13. But if application for *possessio* has been made for an *infans* by his tutor, even though he has
died immediately, it will have to be held that he has barred his mother; for [such *possessio*] is not
on a par with that awarded to an insane person.   14. But a mother will be deprived of the advan-

tage of the *senatus consultum* only in the case where her son has accepted intestate succession; however, where he has neglected to do so, the mother will be admitted in accordance with the *senatus consultum Tertullianum*. But if that son is not the only heir at law, but there are others who are admissible together with him, the mother is not to be called to a share in their part in virtue of the *senatus consultum*. 15. A father, whether he fall to be heir or *bonorum possessor*, precludes a mother in the case of property of either a son or daughter. But neither a grandfather nor great-grandfather prejudices a mother under the *Tertullianum*, even if they have contracted a fiduciary relationship. But only a natural father and not an adoptive father prejudices a mother; for it is true that when he has ceased to be father [of the deceased], he is barred by the mother, but that he is not admitted to *bonorum possessio* contrary to the terms of a will either, since he has ceased to be his father. 16. But under whatever head a natural father has taken *bonorum possessio*, whether as heir at law or contrary to the terms of a will, he bars the mother under every section. 17. If an agnate of the deceased survives him and his natural father is in an adoptive family and he has a mother too, we admit the mother, since the agnate has barred the father. 18. Where the deceased is survived by a sister of the blood, and his mother also survives him, while his father has been adopted or emancipated, if his [sister] of the blood wishes to take the estate, it is resolved that her mother takes with her in virtue of the *senatus consultum* and the father is barred; but if the [sister] of the blood refuses the estate, the mother is not admitted in virtue of the *senatus consultum* on account of the father; and although in other cases a mother does not normally await the reaction of a female blood relative to see whether she is prepared to take the estate or not, in the present instance, she will nevertheless wait; for she is a female blood relative who excludes the father. Therefore, if the [sister] of the blood renounces *bonorum possessio*, the mother will take with the father as cognate relative, but in this case too she will experience delay and will not receive *bonorum possessio* before the father has made application for it, since, if he neglects to do so, she can succeed in virtue of the *senatus consultum*. 19. But where the mother herself embraces the relation of sister of the blood, for instance, because the mother's father has adopted the grandson born of his daughter, and the deceased's natural father additionally survives him, if the mother in question is admitted as blood relation she will bar the father; if she has renounced the blood relationship or has lost it through a change of civil status, she cannot be admitted in virtue of the *senatus consultum* on account of the father; but if he refuses [the estate], she can again be admitted in virtue of the *senatus consultum*. 20. If a mother has not accepted her son's or daughter's estate in virtue of the *senatus consultum Tertullianum*, the old law is to be preserved in the matter of *bonorum possessio*; for, although there was a preference, on the mother's failure to take the advantage afforded by the *senatus consultum*, the old law takes its place. 21. But if the mother has renounced *bonorum possessio*, but is debating whether to accept the estate, it will have to be held that an agnate does not succeed, because it is not yet true to say that the mother has not accepted. 22. But as to our pronouncement that the old law is preserved on the mother's failure to accept, we must see to which person the estate is offered, whether it be the one who is now discovered to be next in line on the mother's refusal, or the one who was next in line at the point when it is established that there had been an intestacy. For instance, at the point when the deceased died intestate, there was an uncle on the male side and the uncle's son; on the mother's refusal, the estate had not yet been offered to the uncle, and for that reason, on the latter's death during the period in which the mother was debating [whether to take the estate], the uncle's son is called [to inherit]. 23. If a mother has not made application for suitable tutors for her sons or has relieved former tutors of their duties or discharged them without immediately pronouncing the names of new ones, she does not have the right of claiming her sons' property in the case of their intestacies. And, indeed, if she does not make application, she falls under [the penalty imposed by the *senatus consultum*]; for it says, "or does not apply." But not to make application to whom? The constitution in fact talks about the praetor; but I submit that it has a validity in the provinces too, even if she does not apply to the municipal magistrates, since the obligation of appointing [tutors] is enjoined on municipal magistrates too. 24. What is the position if she has made application but on the advice of her freedmen or relations, does she fall under [the penalty imposed by] the *senatus consultum*? And I submit that she does, if she has done so under compulsion, but not in the case where, on making her application without delay, she has received advice. 25. What if the children's father had prevented her from making application for a tutor, since it was his wish that their mother should have the administration of their property? If she does not make application or administer the tutelage legally, she will fall [under the penalty].

26. But if she makes no application where her sons are in abject poverty, she is to be pardoned. 27. But if she has perhaps been anticipated in her absence by her freedmen or others, it is to be held she is not barred unless [such anticipation] perhaps occurred at a point when she was deceiving them. 28. She is penalized by not making application on behalf of her sons and undoubtedly in the case of her daughters too. What if [the application is] on behalf of grandsons? She is likewise punished for failure to make application. 29. What if she has failed to apply for curators? There is no reference to this case in the rescript, but it is to be held that if in fact she has not applied for curators for *impuberes*, the same reasoning applies but that if the children are already adult, it should not do so. 30. What if while pregnant she made no application for a curator for the property? I hold that she falls under the stricture [of the *senatus consultum*]; for even if she had an *impubes* in captivity, the same will have to be held. 31. What if she has not applied for a tutor or curator for an insane child? The more reasonable view is that she incurs [the penalty of the *senatus consultum*]. 32. But it does not bind only the woman who has failed to make application but one who has done so in a cursory manner, as the rescript makes plain, for instance, [by requesting] a man who is exempt by virtue of privilege or already burdened with three tutelages, but only in the case where she had acted advisedly. 33. What if she has made application for such persons who have nonetheless assumed the office or have been held back from so doing? The mother will be excused. 34. What if she has made application for unworthy persons, that is, those of a character unsuitable for tutelage, since she knew that the praetor would not appoint them? What if the praetor did appoint them in accordance with the mother's application? The offense in this case is, in fact, on the part of the praetor, but we also penalize the mother's strategem. 35. Therefore, if it happens that they have been excused [from the office] or have been disapproved of, the mother must make application for others without delay. 36. Therefore, whether she has failed to make application, or has made application for unsuitable persons, she will be penalized even if the praetor erred in appointing unsuitable persons. 37. But it can be a matter for doubt whether she should apply for persons who are suitable as regards their means or character. But I submit that she is readily pardoned if the persons for whom she has made application are wealthy. 38. But where former tutors have been excused or discharged and she has not immediately supplied the names of others, she is penalized. 39. What if they have not all been excused or discharged? It is to be seen whether the fact that she has not made application for a tutor in place of one who has been excused is to be held against her. And I submit that it should be. 40. What if some of the tutors have died? I submit, although there is no specific reference to the fact, that the tenor of the constitution applies. 41. But where we have used the word "discharged," do we understand this in the sense "not appointed by the praetor," or does it apply too in the case where the tutors have fallen under suspicion, and have been removed, or have been rejected for carelessness or indolence? One will rightly hold that these too have been discharged. What if they attempt to evade the court? But this is a tedious question; for not even the fact that she has not brought them under suspicion is to be reckoned against her; otherwise, even if they were evading proceedings, under the edict she could have requested the praetor to summon them to appear and discharge them as suspect persons, if they did not appear. 42. What if she has not obliged them to involve themselves in tutelage? And since we should demand total duty from a mother, she must attend to these matters too, lest they prejudice her in the matter of the estate. 43. But "immediately" will have to be understood in the sense "at her earliest opportunity," that is to say, she took into consideration the amount of business before the praetor sitting in this cause, unless she happened to be prevented by the state of her health, or for some other good reason, such as to prevent her from mandating her petition for tutors; nevertheless, such considerations should apply only to the extent that she has not exceeded the year allowed her. If the death of her son has intervened, nothing is to be held against the mother. 44. It can be a nice question for consideration whether the constitution falls into abeyance where a large legacy has been left to a *pupillus* under the condition that "he has had no tutors," and for that reason his mother has made no application on his behalf, lest he should fail to fulfill the condition. And I submit that it lapses if the loss is less than the amount of the legacy. And this question is treated by Tertullian in the case of municipal magistrates. And he submits that an action should be granted against them insofar as more was entailed in the loss than in the legacy. Unless, perhaps, one submits that a condition of this nature should be struck out as contrary to public policy as many others have been, or, by quibbling over the wording, one has reckoned against the mother the fact that she failed to make application for curators. But imagine that the condition has been expressed in full; will the mother not be pardoned? Or is it to be held against her that she did not petition the emperor to have the condition struck out? And I

submit that it should not be held against her.   45. Even in the case where a mother has failed to make application for a tutor for an *infans* who is insolvent, I submit that she should be pardoned; for she consulted his interests, in that, as one without support, he would be less troubled by creditors.   46. And where a man has appointed his wife and the mother of their son heir, and has requested her to refrain from seeking security and to hand back the estate to her son when he is of age, and she failed to apply for tutors for him, it should be held that the constitution ceases to apply, since she has followed his father's wish and has not applied for tutors for a son who takes nothing. But if she has not released her claim for security, the contrary will apply, since on this ground alone he should have had tutors. But if the *impubes*, after the time in which his mother had available to seek tutors, has been adopted by *adrogatio*, and has died an *impubes*, it will have to be held that no action is available to the mother against the *adrogator* as a result of the stipulation.   47. We shall have to see whether, where a mother is prevented from claiming her rights, we are to admit others, as if there were no mother, or do we hold that she becomes heir or succeeds in some other guise while denying her the [right of] action? And we have found a rescript from our Emperor Antoninus Augustus and his deified father to Mammia Maxima dated to the twelfth of April in the second consulship of Plautianus, that when the mother has been set aside, those are admitted who would be so admitted if there had been no mother; therefore, agnates, too, and others will succeed, or if there is no one, the property will be treated as *bona vacantia*.

3   MODESTINUS, *Rules, book 8:* Most authorities approve of the view that an adoptive father does not bar a mother.

4   MODESTINUS, *Rules, book 9:* It is a rule of law that where a mother has died intestate, her estate belongs to all her children, even if they have been offspring of different marriages.

5   PAUL, *Senatus Consultum Tertullianum, sole book:* It has appeared most equitable for all sons to be preferred to a mother, even though they had been left in the family through adoption.   1. But a grandson, too, who has been fathered by an adoptive son, will also bar a mother in accordance with the words of the *senatus consultum.*   2. If a grandfather has manumitted a grandson of whom his son is the father and he has died with his father and grandfather and mother surviving him, it can be asked whose claims should rank first. For if the mother has barred the grandfather who was his manumitter and who is preferred to his father, the father of the deceased will be let in by the praetor's Edict, and, if he is admitted, the *senatus consultum* fails to take effect, and the grandfather will again be called [to succeed]. And so the proper view is that the grandfather preserves his right, because he normally takes *bonorum possessio* against the appointed heirs too.

6   PAUL, *Senatus Consultum Orphitianum, sole book:* A son's mother is admitted to his estate in accordance with this *senatus consultum* even if he is in another's power.   1. It is to be seen whether a son who has declared he does not wish to accept his mother's estate can change his mind and accept before a blood relative or agnate has accepted on account of the words, "if none of the sons were willing to take the estate," because they are of wide interpretation. And when words are [capable] of wide interpretation, his change of mind is to be allowed up to the space of one year, since a mother, too, is allowed a year in which to apply for *bonorum possessio* of her son's estate.

7   PAUL, *Senatus Consultum Tertullianum et Orphitianum, sole book:* If a man has died survived by his mother and blood brother or sister, even though they have been adopted by *adrogatio*, the same rights are preserved in the person of his mother as where natural children exist.

8   GAIUS, *Senatus Consultum Tertullianum, sole book:* A mother's rights are suspended where the emancipated son of the deceased is debating whether to apply for *bonorum possessio.*

9   GAIUS, *Senatus Consultum Orphitianum, sole book:* The speech of our most reverend emperor provides that the estate of a mother who dies intestate belongs to her children even though they are in another's power.

10   POMPONIUS, *Senatus Consulta, book 2:* If a son-in-power who is on military service has made no provision in his will about property he acquired in the course of military service, it is to be seen whether it falls to his mother. But I submit that this is not the case; for it is rather that a benefit conferred on the discretion of soldiers, not that [they] are in all respects in the same position as heads of households.   1. When the question is in suspense whether certain persons can bar a mother and fate has procured that they were not admitted, the mother's right will remain intact, because it has been in suspense in the meantime. For instance, if, where a son died intestate, a *postumus* could have been born to him and he has not been born or has been stillborn, or the fact, too, that a son who was in the enemy's power has not returned by way of *postliminium*.

BOOK THIRTY-NINE

1

NOTICE OF NEW WORK

1 ULPIAN, *Edict, book 52:* This edict offers the assurance that if a piece of work, whether or not it is being carried out legally, is restrained by a notice of new work, the prohibition will be relaxed insofar as the person who served the notice has no right to prevent the work being done. 1. This edict, and the remedy consisting in notice of new work, is introduced against future works, not against past ones, that is, against pieces of work not yet carried out and with the purpose of preventing their being carried out. For if work has been carried out which ought not to have been, the edict of notice of new work is inapplicable and recourse must be had instead to the interdict "for restoration of something done by force or stealth" or "for restoration of something done in a consecrated or religious place" or "for restoration of something done on a public river or public river bank," since it is by application of these interdicts that any illegal construction will be restored to its original condition. 2. The serving of notice under this edict does not necessitate application to the praetor, since one can serve a notice even without making such an application. 3. Again we can serve a notice both in our own name and in somebody else's. 4. Again a notice can be served on any day. 5. A notice of new work is effectual even against persons who are absent or who have acted under constraint or in ignorance. 6. By serving a notice of new work we make the person in possession our adversary. 7. But if somebody on whom a notice of new work has been served carries out building-work before the withdrawal of the notice and then starts an action to establish his right to keep what has been thus built, the praetor must deny him the action and grant an interdict against him for the restoration of the construction to its former condition. 8. One can serve a notice, even if one does not know what work is being carried out. 9. After a notice of new work the litigants subject themselves to the praetor's jurisdiction. 10. Hence, the following question is raised by Celsus in the twelfth book of his *Digest:* If, after the serving of a notice of new work, you reach an agreement with your adversary for you to carry out the work, should a defense of agreement be allowed? Celsus says that it should and that there is no danger of a bargain between private individuals appearing to be preferred to the praetor's direction, since what else, after all, was the praetor attempting to do but to put an end to the parties' disagreements; if they abandon them of their own accord, the praetor will have to ratify that state of affairs. 11. Anyone who alters the original appearance of a construction, by either building or removing something, is held to be carrying out new work. 12. This edict does not embrace all kinds of work; rather, it is only constructions which are attached to the soil whose construction or demolition is held to contain an element of new work. For this reason it is agreed that if somebody gathers a harvest, cuts down a tree, or prunes a vine, although he is carrying out work, it has nothing to do with the present edict, because the latter applies to such pieces of work as are carried out on the soil. 13. Let us consider whether we can serve a notice of new work on someone who props up an old building. The preferable view is that we cannot; for such a person is not carrying out new work, but repairing an existing construction by strengthening it. 14. The serving of a notice of new work is appropriate to new work carried out both inside towns

and outside towns, whether in country houses or on open fields, and both on private and on public property. 15. Now let us consider for what reasons, by whom, to whom, where, and with what effect notices are served. 16. Notice is given either in order to preserve our own rights or to prevent the occurrence of injury or to protect public rights. 17. We serve a notice either because we have some right of prevention, for example, in order to receive a *cautio* against anticipated injury from someone who happens to be engaged in some work on public or on private property, or if work of some sort is being carried out contrary to the laws or to imperial edicts issued in reference to limitations on buildings, on consecrated or religious property, or in a public river or on a public river bank. Interdicts are also issued for such reasons. 18. Where, however, somebody is building on the sea or on the seashore, although he is not doing so on his own property, nonetheless, he makes it his under the law of nations. Hence, if somebody wishes to prevent him building there, he has no right to do so, and he cannot serve a notice of new work except for the sole reason that he wishes to receive a *cautio* against anticipated injury. 19. Where the purpose is preservation of our own rights or prevention of injury, a notice of new work can be served by the person affected. 20. A usufructuary, however, cannot serve a notice of new work in his own name. But he will be able to serve a notice as a procurator or bring a *vindicatio* of the usufruct against the person who is carrying out the work. Such a *vindicatio* will provide him with an amount equal to his interest in the new work not being carried out.

2 JULIAN, *Digest, book 49:* But if he serves a notice on the owner of the property, that notice will be invalid. For he cannot bring an action against the owner, as he can against a neighbor, to deny the former's right to increase the height of the building against his wishes. Instead, if this increase of height prejudices the usufruct, he will have to sue for the usufruct.

3 ULPIAN, *Edict, book 52:* A notice of new work will also be appropriate to work done on provincial land. 1. If work of some sort is being carried out on jointly owned property, a notice will be appropriate against either owner. Of course, if one of us carries out work on a property that we own in common, I cannot, as a co-owner, serve a notice of new work on the other owner; but I will be able to restrain him through an action for dividing common property or by application to the praetor. 2. But, can I serve a notice of new work on my co-owner if he carries out new work in a tenement which we own in common and I possess a tenement of my own which is thereby damaged? Labeo thinks that I cannot, because there are other means by which I can prevent him building, that is, either by application to the praetor or to the judge in an action for dividing common property. This view is correct. 3. If I hold a right of *superficies* and a new work is carried out by my neighbor, can I serve a notice? An influential consideration is that I am a sort of urban tenant. But the praetor grants me an *actio utilis in rem*, and, therefore, an action in respect of servitudes will be granted to me and I must also be allowed to serve a notice of new work. 4. If work is being carried out on public property, any citizen can serve a notice of new work,

4 PAUL, *Edict, book 48:* since it is in the state's interests to allow as many people as possible to defend it at law.

5 ULPIAN, *Edict, book 52:* The question of a *pupillus* arises; Julian, in the twelfth book of his *Digest*, wrote that the execution of a notice of new work should not be granted to a *pupillus* unless the issue affects his individual convenience, for example, if the new work in question blocks his light or obstructs his view. A notice served by a *pupillus* will only be ratified if it was served with the participation and *auctoritas* of his tutor. 1. A notice of new work can be served on a slave, but a slave cannot himself serve such a notice, and a notice served by a slave will have no effect. 2. It will have to be remembered that a notice must be served at the site in issue, that is, in the place where the work is being carried out, whether building is already going on or is only just being started. 3. It is by no means necessary for a notice to be served on the owner. It is sufficient for it to be served at the site in issue to someone who is there—so much so that a notice of new work can be served on builders or craftsmen who are at work there. Indeed, as a general rule, a notice of new work can be served

on anyone who is at the site in issue in the name of the owner or for the purpose of carrying out the work, and neither the identity nor the status of this person is of importance, since, even if the notice is served on a slave or a woman or a boy or a girl, it holds good. For it is enough for the notice of new work to be served at the site in issue and in such a way that it can be passed on to the owner.   4. It is very well established that if someone serves a notice of new work on the owner in the forum that notice is of no significance, since a notice must be served at the site in issue and, I would almost say, in the midst of the work. The reason for this being accepted practice is to ensure that the notice secures an immediate cessation of work. Otherwise, if the notice is served elsewhere, there is the inconvenient consequence that any work done in ignorance of the notice while the parties were coming to the site of the work turns out to have been done in contravention of the praetor's edict.   5. If the property on which new work is being carried out belongs to several persons and a notice is served on one of them, that notice has been correctly served and is regarded as having been served on all the owners. However, if one of them carries out building-work after the serving of the notice of new work, the rest, who have not done so, will not be liable, since the action of one person ought not to harm another who has done nothing.   6. If work causes harm to a property belonging to several owners is a notice served by one of them sufficient, or must they all serve a notice? The more correct view is that a notice served by one of them does not suffice for all and that they must each individually serve a notice, because it can happen that one of those serving a notice has the right of prevention and the other does not.   7. If somebody wishes to serve a notice of new work on the praetor himself, he must do so at the end of the latter's term of office, having ensured that, in the meantime, he calls witnesses to the fact that he was not able to serve the notice; and if he serves a notice at this subsequent time, anything built in the interim will have to be destroyed, the serving of the notice being in effect backdated.   8. But even if somebody inserts something into our house or builds on our property, it is fair for us to preserve our rights by means of a notice of new work. 9. Sextus Pedius neatly defined the reasons for a notice of new work as threefold: deriving from nature, public interest, and imposition. A natural reason exists when something is inserted into our house or built on our property; a public reason exists whenever it is laws, *senatus consulta* or imperial *constitutiones* that we are protecting by means of a notice of new work; a reason of imposition exists when someone diminishes his own rights and increases somebody else's, that is, imposes a servitude on his house, and subsequently infringes that servitude.   10. It will be necessary to remember that whenever somebody builds on our property or tries to insert something into or make something project over our property, it is better to restrain him by application to the praetor or by our own hand, that is, by throwing a pebble, than by means of a notice of new work; otherwise, by serving a notice of new work we will make the recipient of that notice the possessor of the property in question. But if it is on his own property that somebody is carrying out work which causes us harm, a notice of new work is the obligatory procedure. And if someone should persist in building on our property, it will be quite fair to use against him the interdict against force or stealth or the interdict for possession of land.   11. Where someone wishes to repair or clean watercourses or sewers, the serving of a notice of new work is quite properly forbidden, since it is in the interests of public health and safety for watercourses or sewers to be cleaned.   12. In addition, as a general rule the praetor has excepted from liability to notice of new work other types of work delay in the carrying out of which would occasion some danger, since he considered that in these cases also a notice of new work should be defied. For who can doubt that it is much better for the notice of new work to be excluded than for the urgent construction of some necessary work to be hindered? However, this part of the edict is relevant only when delay will occasion some danger.   13. Accordingly, if somebody has served a notice of new work, where the work is such as to occasion danger if there is delay or where it is a case of repair of sewers or watercourses, we will say that the question should be raised before a judge of whether the work is of such a sort that the notice ought to be defied; for if it appears that the work is being carried out on a sewer or a watercourse or in a context in which delay will occasion danger, it must be held that there should be no fear of the notice in question causing harm.   14. Anyone who serves a notice of new work must swear that he is not doing so maliciously. This oath is tendered on the praetor's authority; consequently, it is not required that the person who demands the oath should be the first to swear.   15. Anyone who serves a notice of new work must indicate with reference to what place he is doing so, so that the recipient of the notice knows where he can build and where for the moment he must desist. However, this indication is to be made only in cases where the notice refers to a part of a work. If, on the other hand, it refers to the whole, it is not necessary to make an indication of this sort, but merely to say that this is the case.   16. If work is being carried out in several places, is one notice sufficient or are several required? Julian, in the forty-ninth book of his *Digest*, says that because a notice is served at the site in issue several notices are required and, in consequence, several relaxations.   17. If somebody on whom a notice has been served gives security or makes an undertaking as a result of the notice of new work, or if it is not his fault that he has not given security or made an undertaking in accordance with the judgment of a sound citizen, the position is just as if the notice of new work has not been served at all. This remedy has some utility, since it removes the inconvenience of coming before the praetor and requesting relaxation of the notice.   18. If somebody who has served a notice in the capacity of procurator does not give security for his principal's ratification of his action, the notice is abrogated without question, even if the procurator is genuine.   19. Anyone who requests a relaxation in the name of an absent party, whether in reference to private or public rights, is compelled to give security, since he is acting as defender [of another's rights]. This security, however, relates not to the question of ratification but to the serving of the notice of new work.   20. If a procurator serves a notice of new work against me and receives security and I then employ an interdict against him to prevent him from using force to stop me building, he must, under the interdict, give security for the payment of the fine, since he is acting as defender [of another's rights].

6   JULIAN, *Digest, book 41:* And for that reason defenses of procuratory must not be used against him, and he is not to be compelled to give security for his principal's ratification of his action.

7   ULPIAN, *Edict, book 52:* If he fails to give security, he must be debarred from execution of the notice of new work, and any actions that he lays in the name of his principal must be denied him.   1. Both a tutor and a curator can properly serve a notice of new work.

8   PAUL, *Edict, book 48:* I will be able to serve a notice of new work not only on my immediate neighbor but on a more distant one, given that some servitudes can exist even where other land, public or private, intervenes.   1. Anyone who serves a notice of new work must give in evidence a report on any work that has already been carried out so that it will be clear what has been carried out subsequently.   2. If I serve a notice of new work on you in a case in which I can, on the basis of my own rights, prohibit you carrying out work, you will have no right to build unless you give security.   3. But if it is to stop you illegally carrying out work on public property that I serve a notice on you, you will have to make an undertaking since I am disputing about the work in question in defense of someone else's rights not my own, and as a petitioner on behalf of someone else's rights, I must be content with an undertaking.   4. It must be understood that once a notice of new work has been served, the recipient must desist until either he gives a *cautio* or a relaxation of the notice is issued. At that stage, if he has the right to build, he will properly be able to do so.   5. To ensure that it can be proved what was built after the serving of the notice the person who serves it must take measurements. The praetor normally decrees the taking and presentation of such measurements.   6. The death of the person who has served a notice extinguishes that notice, just as does his alienation of the property, since in these ways the right of prevention lapses.   7. But if the recipient of a notice of new work dies or alienates his house, the notice of new work is not extinguished. This is evident from the fact that in the stipulation which is used in such cases there is mention of the heir.

9   GAIUS, *Urban Praetor's Edict, Chapter on Notice of New Work:* A creditor to whom

an estate is obligated by way of pledge is allowed by right, that is, in virtue of a servitude, to serve a notice of new work, since a *vindicatio* of a servitude is granted to him.

10   ULPIAN, *Sabinus, book 45:* A notice of new work is served *in rem* and not *in personam.* Therefore, it can be served on a lunatic or on a child, and the tutor's *auctoritas* is not required in the case of such a notice.

11   PAUL, *Sabinus, book 11:* For a notice served on anyone capable of understanding it, for example, on a workman, is binding on a child or lunatic.

12   PAUL, *Sabinus, book 13:* Where a *cautio* has been given arising out of a notice of new work, the stipulation takes effect for the sum for which a decree has been given.

13   JULIAN, *Digest, book 41:* When a procurator serves a notice and gives security for his principal's ratification of his action, any relaxation is also granted with reference to the person of the principal.   1. If the principal serves a notice of new work within the period covered by a stipulation made under a notice of new work, the stipulation comes into operation. If he serves the notice after the period has expired, the stipulation does not come into operation. For even the principal himself, once he has served a notice, is not permitted to serve a second one as long as the stipulation arising from the first notice of new work holds.   2. If a procurator acts in a matter of relaxation on behalf of the person who served the notice of new work, the praetor must deal with the matter to ensure that a false procurator does not cause harm to the absent party, since it is unacceptable for a benefit conferred by the praetor to be lost through the intervention of any person whatsoever.

14   JULIAN, *Digest, book 49:* If somebody who has a right of way serves a notice of new work against a person who is building on that right of way, his action is invalid; but he is not prohibited from bringing a *vindicatio* of the servitude.

15   AFRICANUS, *Questions, book 9:* He says that if an action is brought against a neighbor before any building has been done to deny him the right of increasing the height of his house and the case is not defended by the said neighbor, the function of the judge will be simply to order the party against whom the action is being brought to give a *cautio* that he carries out no building-work until he has, on his own initiative, established his right to increase the height of his house. The same applies in the contrary case: When somebody wishes to bring an action to establish his right to increase the height of his house without his adversary's consent and the latter does not defend the case, in this case too, he says, the judge's duty will consist in ordering the adversary to give a *cautio* that he will neither serve a notice of new work nor employ force against the person who is carrying out building-work. This procedure ensures that a person who fails to defend his case is punished to the extent of having to prove his own rights; for to do that is to play the part of plaintiff.

16   ULPIAN, *Edict, book 13:* If the praetor orders the serving of a notice of new work and then forbids it, no action can be brought under the erstwhile notice on grounds of contravention of his edict.

17   PAUL, *Edict, book 57:* If a procurator restrains someone who is carrying out new work, an interdict against force or stealth is available to the principal.

18   PAPINIAN, *Questions, book 3:* In the case of a jointly owned house, if a notice is served on one of the owners because of new work, it will be binding on all the owners, provided that the work is being carried out at the wish of all of them. But if some of them are unaware that it is going on, the person who has acted in contravention of the praetor's edict will be liable for the whole sum.   1. Nor is it relevant who is the owner of the soil on which the work is being carried out. All that matters is who is discovered to be in possession of that soil, provided that it is in his name that the work is being done.

19 PAUL, *Questions, book [12]:* It must be understood that when the execution of a notice of
new work is denied actions at civil law remain nonetheless unimpaired, just as they also do
in those cases in which from the outset the praetor refuses to allow a notice of new work.
20 ULPIAN, *Edict, book 71:* The praetor says: "Where notice to prevent the carrying out of
new work is served in respect of a site which is the matter in question, any work done on that
site before the notice was relaxed or a stage was reached at which it ought to be relaxed
must be restored to its original condition." 1. This interdict is introduced for the following
reasons, as is stated in the edict: to prevent the carrying out of any work after the serving
of a notice of new work until either the notice is relaxed or, in place of such a relaxation,
security for the restoration of the construction to its former condition has been given.
Therefore, anyone who carries out work, even if he has the right to do so, nonetheless, is
held to be acting in contravention of the praetor's edict and is compelled to demolish the
said work. 2. This interdict will be equally appropriate whether the site at which the notice was served is vacant or built on. 3. The praetor says: "Any work that has been done
must be restored to its former condition." He orders the restoration of anything that has
been done, and it makes no difference whether it was done legally or not. The interdict will
be appropriate whether the work was done legally or illegally. 4. Any work that is carried
out before the relaxation of the notice or before anything tnat is considered to take the
place of a relaxation is to be regarded in the same light as if it had been done illegally.
5. If someone is prepared to give security but the person bringing the action is unwilling to
make a stipulation, the position is that the notice must be relaxed. For since it is the person
bringing the action who is responsible, it is evident that the position is that the notice must
be relaxed. 6. This interdict is granted in perpetuity and is available to the heir and other
successors. 7. The interdict will be appropriate both against the person who has carried
out the work and against the person who has ratified it. 8. Of course, if the question
arises of whether this interdict is available against the heir of the person who carried out
the work, it must be understood that Labeo thought that it ought to be granted only in
reference to that which has passed to him or that which would have passed to him had he
not engaged in fraud to prevent it doing so. Some think that an action *in factum* should be
granted to him rather than an interdict and this is the correct view. 9. Next the praetor
says: "When a notice to prevent the carrying out of a new work has been served in respect
of a site, which is the matter at issue, if security has been given in respect of a *cautio* given
or it is your fault that it has not been given, I forbid the use of force to prevent the other
party from being able to carry out new work at the site in question." 10. This interdict is
prohibitory and is to stop anyone preventing the carrying out of work by somebody who
has given security; for the nonabandonment of buildings is something that affects the embellishment of cities. 11. It makes no difference whether the person who is building is
doing so legally or illegally, since the person who served the notice of new work is safe once
he has received a *cautio.* 12. This interdict is available to the person who has given security; and there is an additional clause, "or it is your fault that security has not been
given." 13. By the same token, if no security but only an undertaking is given, this interdict will not be appropriate, since building should not have been allowed on public land until
it was clearly established by what right it was being carried out. 14. If security has been
given but the *cautio* does not continue, this interdict is not available. 15. If at one stage it
was the fault of the person serving the notice that security was not given, but later this
ceases to be so, the interdict is not available. 16. This interdict is available even after a
year and to the heir and other successors.
21 ULPIAN, *Edict, book 80:* A stipulation is normally made in reference to a notice of new
work where somebody claims the right to prevent his neighbor carrying out new work
without his consent. 1. If someone wishes to build with impunity after the serving of a
notice of new work, he must offer security to the person serving the notice. It is to the
advantage of both parties for him to do this, to the person who served the notice because he
has a *cautio* for the restoration of the work to original conditions and to the recipient of the
notice because his construction work is not impeded; for he is compelled by means of a res-
titutory interdict to demolish any work carried out before the giving of a *cautio.* 2. However, this stipulation contains the condition that it becomes operative only if a judgment

has been given or if something occurs before the matter comes to judgment to prevent a defense being offered. A clause about fraud is also subjoined. 3. We consider work to have been carried out not if one or two stones have been put down, but if something has been laid out which has the shape and, so to speak, the completed appearance of a piece of work. 4. Whether judgment has been given or the case was not defended, the stipulation is operative to the end of securing restoration to the original condition in accordance with the judgment of a sound citizen. If such restoration does not occur the defendant will, if the plaintiff agrees, pay a sum of money equivalent to the value of the matter at issue. 5. If several owners are engaged in building-work, do they all have to give a *cautio*? Labeo says that one of them must do so, because there cannot be a partial restoration of the construction to its original condition. 6. Labeo says that even if several persons serve a notice, one should see to it that security is given to one of them, if this is agreeable to them all. Clearly, if it is not, then a *cautio* will have to be given to them individually. 7. Labeo says that it must be additionally stated in the stipulation that as much be paid as corresponds to the value of each party's interest, if this is what they prefer. Otherwise, he says, if the *cautio* is for "the value of the matter at issue," there will be doubt as to whether these words refer to the valuation of the whole property or to that of the interest of the person who is making the stipulation. I think that even if a *cautio* is given to one of the owners "for the value of the matter at issue," the view can be defended that the stipulation is adequate, since it relates to the extent of the work.

22   MARCELLUS, *Digest, book 15:* A person on whom a notice of new work had been served died after carrying out work before the relaxation of the notice. His heir must give his adversary permission to demolish the construction, since in respect of restoration of a construction of this kind it is the person who acted in contravention of the praetor's edict who is subject to a penalty. But the heir certainly does not succeed to the penalty.

23   JAVOLENUS, *Letters, book 7:* A person on whom a notice of new work had been served sold the property. The purchaser carried out some building-work. Do you think that it is the purchaser or the vendor who is liable as having acted in contravention of the edict? He replied: Where a notice of new work has been served, if any building-work is carried out the purchaser, that is, the owner of the estate, is liable, because a notice is served in relation to a piece of work not a person, and it is the person who is in possession of the site which has been the subject of a notice of new work who is bound by it.

2

ANTICIPATED INJURY AND HOUSE-EAVES AND PROJECTIONS

1   ULPIAN, *Edict, book 1:* Since anticipated injury is a matter that requires speedy handling and the praetor views as dangerous the delay that would arise if he reserved jurisdiction in such a case to himself, he rightly thought that the matter should be delegated to municipal magistrates.

2   GAIUS, *Provincial Edict, book 28:* Anticipated injury is injury that has not yet occurred but which we fear may occur in the future.

3   PAUL, *Edict, book 47:* Injury (*damnum*) and injuring (*damnatio*) are derived from the taking away from (*ademptio*) and the diminution (*deminutio*), so to speak, of an estate.

4   ULPIAN, *Edict, book 1:* If the period allowed for giving a *cautio* has expired, it will be the duty of the praetor or the governor, depending on the case, either to censure the defendant or to defer him and, if this requires an investigation on the spot, to pass

the matter on to the municipal magistrates.   1. If a *cautio* is not given within the period laid down by the praetor, the plaintiff must be granted *missio in possessionem* of the property in question. "The property in question" is understood to mean either the whole property or a part thereof.   2. Can a party who does not admit the plaintiff be constrained by the magistrates even by means of pledges? I think not; but he will be liable to an action *in factum*, since that is the action that we must employ in the event of the plaintiff not being admitted despite a grant of *missio in possessionem* from the praetor.   3. There are, therefore, two matters that the praetor or governor enjoins upon municipal magistrates, that is to say, the giving of a *cautio* and the granting of possession. The rest he keeps in his own jurisdiction.   4. If failure to give a *cautio* should persist, permission to take possession (which normally comes after the case has been investigated) will be given not by the *duumviri* but by the praetor or governor; similarly, when possession is to be abandoned on cause shown.   5. The praetor says: "While I order that in the case of someone who is absent, a notice should first be served on him at home." Anybody who does not appear in court is also held to be absent, an opinion which Pomponius approves. However, the praetor orders the notice to be served politely and that the recipient is not to be removed from his home. We interpret "be served on him at home where he resides" in such a way that if the defendant is living in someone else's house the notice will be served there. But if he has no residence, the notice will have to be served at the property in question either to a procurator or, at least, to the tenants.   6. It is to be understood, however, that the praetor only demands the serving of a notice if there exists somebody on whom it can be served. If, on the other hand, such a person does not exist, for example, if a tenement is part of an inheritance which has not yet been accepted or if there is no heir and the tenement is uninhabited, this part of the edict is not applicable. However, the safer course is to affix a written notice to the house itself, since it can happen that when alerted in this way, a defendant may emerge.   7. Anyone who fails to see to any of the provisions stated above has a *judicium* established against him to the value of the matter in relation to which a *cautio* against anticipated injury has not been given. This does not refer to the whole sum but to the extent of the party's interest and is a matter of his advantage not of penalty.   8. However, such a *judicium* is subject to the condition that it was requested. If, on the other hand, it was not requested, no legal proceedings can be brought. We use "request" in the strict sense of seeking before a tribunal and not elsewhere.   9. If a municipality is so close to the city that, should the magistrate fail to intervene, the praetor or governor could have been consulted, it can be said that this action against the magistrates lapses on the grounds that their inaction makes no difference when it was within your power to request a grant of *missio in possessionem* from the praetor or governor.   10. This action is granted to and against an heir and in perpetuity, since it involves suit for recovery of property.

5   PAUL, *Edict, book 1:* It is the praetor's duty to see to it that somebody who has been granted *missio in possessionem* can even take the property into his own ownership by reason of the lapse of a long period of time.   1. If there are several owners who ought to give *cautiones* and one of them fails to do so, the plaintiff is granted *missio in possessionem* of that owner's share. In the contrary case, where there are several persons who request the receipt of *cautiones* and some have more, some less valuable houses, or they all have unequal shares of one house, nonetheless, they will be granted *missio in possessionem* not in accordance with the extent of their individual ownership, but all on an equal footing.   2. If both the owner of a property and its usufructuary request the receipt of a *cautio* against anticipated injury, they must each be given a hearing. The person making an undertaking will not thereby suffer any loss since he will not have to offer either of them more than corresponds to the extent of his interest.

6   GAIUS, *Provincial Edict, book 1:* It turns out that sometimes when injury has been caused no action is available because no *cautio* has previously been taken, as, for example, if my neighbor's house, being in a ruinous condition, falls onto my house. So much so, that several authorities hold that the neighbor cannot even be compelled to remove the rubble provided that he treats everything lying on the ground as abandoned.

7   ULPIAN, *Edict, book 53:* The praetor says: "In the matter of anticipated injury, I will order an undertaking to be given in a party's own name and security in anyone else's name to a person who has sworn that he does not, or that the person in whose name he is acting,

will not, make this request maliciously. This undertaking or security is to last until a time I shall appoint after investigating the case. If there is any disagreement as to whether the person who will be giving security is the owner, I shall order the security to be given subject to a proviso. In the case of work which is being carried out on a public river or its bank, I shall order security to be given for a period of ten years. I shall order *missio in possessionem* of that property in respect of which security is demanded in favor of the party who does not accordingly receive security; and where the case seems just, I shall order the latter to take full possession as well. I shall grant a *judicium* against the party who neither gives a *cautio* nor allows a grant of *missio in possessionem* or of full possession to take effect, requiring him to pay as much as he ought to have paid if he had given a *cautio* about the property in question in accordance with my decree or that of any person to whom my jurisdiction with respect to that property had been transferred. If I have granted *missio in possessionem* of a certain property and if no security against anticipated injury is given by the person who is in possession of the property, I shall at the same time order the person who has not received security to be in full possession." 1. The present edict has regard to injury not yet done, whereas other actions relate to reparation for injuries which have occurred, as in the action under the *lex Aquilia* and in other cases. No provision is made in the edict about injury actually done. For granted that animate objects which have caused damage do not normally expose us to a greater burden than the surrender of the said animate objects as recompense, it is even more clear that inanimate objects ought not to expose us to a burden beyond a similar degree especially in view of the fact that whereas animate objects that have caused injury themselves continue to exist, a house which causes injury by falling down has ceased to exist. 2. Therefore, there arises the question whether, if a house falls down before a *cautio* is given and the owner does not wish to remove the rubble, but abandons it, there is any action that can be brought against him. The case in which a ruinous house collapsed before a stipulation against anticipated injury had been introduced was put to Julian, and he was asked what the person onto whose house the rubble had fallen ought to do to secure reparation. He replied that if the owner of the house that had collapsed wished to take away the rubble, this should be permitted only if he took away everything, that is, including the useless material, and that he should give a *cautio* about not only future but also past injury; but that if the owner of the house which had fallen down did nothing, an interdict should be granted to the person onto whose house the rubble had fallen by means of which his neighbor would be compelled either to remove the rubble or to regard the whole house as abandoned.

8   GAIUS, *Urban Praetor's Edict, Chapter on Anticipated Injury:* This will perhaps be the correct view to take when it was not as a result of his negligence, but of some impediment that he failed to make provision for himself.

9   ULPIAN, *Edict, book 53:* Furthermore, Julian says that it can be held that he must be compelled to give a *cautio* about the past injury as well since it is not unfair for the protection which is provided while the property is intact to be provided also after the collapse of the house. However, while the property is intact, each party is compelled either to give a *cautio* in respect of anticipated injury or to lose the house which he fails to repair. Finally, he says that if somebody has been unable to make a stipulation against anticipated injury because of lack of time or because he was absent on public business, it is not unfair for the praetor to see to it that the owner of the defective house either makes good the injury or loses the house. Expediency supports Julian's opinion. 1. The question arises of whether an interdict can be granted relating to things carried onto one's property by the force of a river. Trebatius reports that on an occasion when the Tiber flooded and carried a great deal of property belonging to many people into other people's houses, an interdict was granted by the praetor to prevent force being used against the owners to stop them taking away their possessions, provided that they made undertakings in return against anticipated injury. 2. Alfenus also writes that if marble work falls off your property on to mine and you seek to get it back, a *judicium* relating to the injury already done must be granted against you. Labeo approves this view. For the injury that I have already suffered is not covered by the decision of the judge before whom the claim is made for the material that has fallen off and an action is to be granted only for the removal of everything that fell off. The same Alfenus says, however, that a *vindicatio* of the marble can be made only if it has not coalesced with or become part of my land. A tree which has been carried into a field

of mine and has coalesced with my land cannot be made the object of a *vindicatio* by you. But I will not be able to bring an action against you to deny your right to have the marble if it has not already coalesced with my land.   3. Neratius writes that if a boat has been carried onto my land by the force of a river, you should not be enabled to take it away unless you have given me assurances about the past injury as well.   4. If the soil belongs to one person and the *superficies* to another, the question arises of whether the holder of the *superficies* should give an undertaking or a *cautio* against anticipated injury. Julian writes that when a superficiary tenement is defective the owner must make an undertaking about defect of the soil and of the building or the person to whom the *superficies* belongs must give security about both, and that if either of them fails to do so, the neighbor must be granted *missio in possessionem*.   5. Celsus certainly writes that if the usufruct of your house belongs to Titia, then either the owner must make an undertaking against anticipated injury, or Titia must give security against the same. But if the person who ought to have received a *cautio* is granted *missio in possessionem*, he will prevent Titia from enjoying her usufruct. Celsus also says that a usufructuary who fails to make repairs is to be prevented by the owner from enjoying his usufruct. Therefore, if the usufructuary fails to give a *cautio* about anticipated injury and the owner is compelled to make an undertaking, the former must be prevented from enjoying his usufruct.

10   PAUL, *Edict, book 48:* Cassius says that although the usufruct may belong to someone else, the owner must make an undertaking. If the proprietor fails to give an undertaking in full or if the usufructuary fails to give security, the person who has not received a *cautio* must be granted *missio in possessionem*. But Julian writes that if a usufructuary does not give a *cautio* to a proprietor who is making an undertaking, the actions for the enjoyment of his usufruct should be denied to him. But if the usufructuary has paid anything as a result of a defect in the soil, the right of the owner should be transferred to him.

11   ULPIAN, *Edict, book 53:* What are we going to say about a creditor who has received a building as a pledge? Will he have to give an undertaking on the grounds that it is his own rights that he is protecting or security on the grounds that he is not the owner? This type of case is treated by Marcellus from the opposite point of view, that is, whether a *cautio* against anticipated injury should be given to a creditor who holds a building as a pledge. Marcellus says that a *cautio* given to him has no effect and that the same is to be laid down in the case of somebody who did not purchase the property in question from the owner, since a stipulation cannot become operative in relation to his person either. However, I think that it is quite fair for provision to be made for such a person, and for the creditor as well, by means of a stipulation.

12   PAUL, *Edict, book 48:* The person who has not received a *cautio* against anticipated injury is in a stronger position than those who have received property as a pledge if he has been permitted to have full possession and acquire the property by reason of the lapse of a long period of time.

13   ULPIAN, *Edict, book 53:* Consideration must be given to whether someone who has in good faith purchased a property from a person who was not its owner should make an undertaking rather than give security. The latter is the opinion of some authorities; however, it is reasonable that he should make an undertaking rather than provide security since he is acting in his own name.   1. Whether it is the owner of a piece of property or somebody who has rights in it, for example, a servitude, giving a *cautio* about anticipated injury, I think that he must make an undertaking and not give security because it is in his own name and not somebody else's that he is acting.   2. When there is between your house and my house another house that is not defective, consideration must be given to whether it is only you who must give me a *cautio* or whether the owner of the nondefective house must do so as well or whether it is only the latter who must do so or whether you must both do so. The better view is that you must both give a *cautio* because it can happen that the collapse of the defective house onto the nondefective one causes me injury. Someone might say that it was not through any defect in the house which was in good condition that the collapse onto it of another house caused injury; but granted that the owner of the nondefective house could have taken the precaution of securing a *cautio* against anticipated injury and failed to do so he deserves to be made the object of legal proceedings.   3. The person who requests the provision of a *cautio* must first swear an oath on the subject of malice. Anyone who has sworn such an oath is then allowed to make a stipulation and the question whether or not he has an interest or of whether or not he has a neighboring house is not raised. However, the whole question of who should and should not receive a *cautio* is to be submitted to the praetor's jurisdiction.   4. On the other hand, a *cautio* does not have to be given to anyone who walks on my land

or washes thereon or stays in an inn belonging to me. 5. Labeo says that a *cautio* must obviously be given to neighbors, their tenants, and their tenants' wives as well as to those who reside with them. 6. The question arises of whether the owner of a house can give a *cautio* to his own tenants. Sabinus says that a *cautio* is not to be given to tenants since either they rented a house that was defective from the outset and they have only themselves to blame or the house has fallen into disrepair subsequently and they can institute legal proceedings under the lease. This view is the more correct one. 7. Anyone who has built something next to a monument or has allowed a monument to be constructed next to his own house does not subsequently have to receive a *cautio* about anticipated injury since he has permitted an illegal action. In other cases, however, where a building causes damage to a monument and no blame attaches to the person to whom rights over the monument belong, the latter must receive assurances. 8. Nowadays it is agreed that a holder of the right of *superficies* and a usufructuary can validly make a stipulation against anticipated injury. 9. But Marcellus says that a stipulation against anticipated injury is not available to a person who in good faith purchases a property from someone who is not its owner. 10. Julian deals with the question of whether somebody who has served a notice of new work must nonetheless receive a *cautio* against anticipated injury. He prefers the view that he ought to receive a *cautio* on the grounds that a *cautio* must be given even to the person who brings an action to deny his adversary the right to increase the height of his building. Again, Julian says that a person against whom the interdict against force or stealth is available must give a *cautio*, since no *cautio* has been given about either defect in the building or injury caused by the work. 11. Suppose that somebody has been granted *missio in possessionem* because he has not received a *cautio* and then the person whose house it was, having another house, requests from the recipient of *missio in possessionem* a *cautio* against anticipated injury in relation to the house to which the *missio* applies; let us consider whether he should be given a hearing. Julian writes: Where a person who has ceded a defective house retains one which is in good condition, is there not something improper in his demanding a *cautio* from the person who has just got possession of the defective house, given that it was precisely because he did not himself give security against anticipated injury that he lost possession? In fact, it is surely barely proper for him to request a *cautio* in relation to a house for which he himself disdained to give a *cautio*. This view is correct. 12. If somebody swears an oath preparatory to making a stipulation but then does not make the stipulation, let us consider whether he has to swear an oath if he subsequently wishes to make a stipulation. I consider that he must swear again because it may be the case that either on the first or the second occasion he is behaving maliciously. 13. If I request the provision of a *cautio* against anticipated injury in someone else's name, I must swear that the person in whose name I am requesting the *cautio* will not turn out to have been requesting it maliciously. 14. But if the person in whose name I am making the request is someone who would not be compelled to swear an oath if he were making the request himself, for example, a patron or a parent, it must be held that an oath is not appropriate, since in a case in which the principal does not have to swear an oath the person who makes a request on his behalf does not have to do so either in the present stipulation. 15. A time limit must be inserted in this stipulation within which the *cautio* becomes applicable if some injury occurs, since a person must not be bound by a stipulation in perpetuity. The praetor, therefore, will prescribe a time limit for the stipulation, the calculation of the period being dependent on the nature of the case and the extent of the injury which it is expected may occur.

14   PAUL, *Edict, book 48:* In the investigation of the case the remoteness of the site and the size of the work involved must also be examined.

15   ULPIAN, *Edict, book 53:* If the time limit set down in the *cautio* has expired, a completely new *cautio* must be given in accordance with the decision of the praetor. 1. Where, however, the stipulation was made without the addition of a time limit, if this was because there was an agreement that action under the stipulation could be brought whenever the condition was fulfilled, there will be an action on the stipulation; but if it was because the time limit was omitted through error, the preferable view is that a request for release should be made to the praetor on the expiry of the period for which a *cautio* is normally given. 2. Next the praetor says: "In the case of work which is being carried out on a public river or its bank, I shall order security to be given for a period of ten years." Here security is required, and it is because the work is being carried out on public property that the praetor attaches the time limit to the stipulation. And because work is being carried out on someone else's property, the praetor enjoins provision of security. 3. It should be noted that a *cautio* is given only with reference to defect in the work and not with reference to defect in the site as well, although, if the work is being carried out on private land, the *cautio* is given with reference to defect in both the work and the site. But when the site is public, the

person carrying out work there does not have to give a *cautio* against anticipated injury respecting any defect other than that of the work in question.   4. Any injury that occurs within ten years is, therefore, covered by the stipulation.   5. As for the praetor's words "in the case of work," take these to refer to such injury as results from the work in question.   6. If work is being carried out on a public road, security must be given since it is being done on someone else's property.   7. But the praetor will, after investigating the case, determine the time limit on the basis of the nature of the work involved.   8. However, if someone is strengthening the road or carrying out work of some other sort on a public road, a *cautio* will have to be applicable in case private individuals sustain injury as a result.   9. With reference to other types of public site no special rule is laid down about the *cautio*, but by application of the general rule, it is security against anticipated injury that will have to be given on the grounds that the work is being done on someone else's property.   10. Where a public site is being repaired at public expense, Labeo quite correctly writes, and we follow this rule, that no *cautio* has to be given against anticipated injury caused by defect in the site or the work, but that certainly the conditions under which the work is carried out should be to the effect that no damage or injury be caused to the neighbors. 11. Under this edict, if no *cautio* is given, the complainant is granted *missio in possessionem* in respect of that part of the building which appears to be in a ruinous condition.   12. Let us see whether *missio in possessionem* in respect of the whole of the house can be appropriate. There exists a view of Sabinus that *missio* can be granted in respect of the whole of a house. Otherwise, he says, if it is from the superstructure that injury is apprehended, the matter will have no solution, and it will be of no use to the complainant to be granted *missio in possessionem* of a property which he cannot possess or which it is of no value to him to possess. Sabinus's view is the more correct one.   13. But if a house is divided into several parts, let us consider whether one is to be granted *missio in possessionem* of a part or of the whole of the house. If the house is so big that there is space between the defective and the nondefective parts, it is to be held that *missio* should be granted only in respect of the former. But if the defective part is closely joined to the nondefective by the construction of the building, then *missio* is to be granted in respect of the whole of the house. Consequently, even in houses of great extent, it is better to hold that *missio* should be granted in respect of that part of the house which is closely joined to the defective part. Still if it is but a modest portion of a very large house that is defective, how can it be held that somebody who has not received a *cautio* against anticipated injury should be directed to take possession of the whole of the house, given that it is so very large?   14. Again, where it is a tenement adjacent to a house that is defective, are we going to say that *missio in possessionem* is to be granted of the tenement or of the whole of the house? The preferable view is that it should be granted of the tenement not the house.   15. If there are several people who request a *cautio*, they are usually all granted *missio in possessionem*. Labeo approves this view, even where one person has already been granted *missio in possessionem* and another requests the same, since we take no account of order, but allow that both persons will have possession. But where one person has already been directed to take possession and another requests a *cautio* against anticipated injury then, if that *cautio* is not given, the second person is granted *missio in possessionem*.   16. Julian writes that someone who is granted *missio in possessionem* on grounds of anticipated injury can only start to take ownership by reason of the lapse of a long period of time after he has been appointed owner by a second decree of the praetor.   17. If, before this decree, someone else has also been granted *missio in possessionem*, they both become equally owners of the house, that is, when they have been directed to take possession. But if, after the first recipient of *missio in possessionem* has already been appointed owner, Titius requests receipt of a *cautio* against anticipated injury and the other person declines to give it, Titius will be in sole possession.   18. When several people are granted *missio in possessionem*, the grant is made equally to all of them and not in proportion to the several injuries which might occur to them. And it is right that it should be so, since, when a single individual is granted *missio in possessionem*, this grant is not made in proportion to the injury but in full; therefore, when several people are granted *missio in possessionem*, they are all together made a grant in full and will consequently obtain shares by the concurrence of their rights.   19. But if one of them, having been granted *missio in possessionem*, incurs some expense and they are then directed to take full possession, can the one who incurred expense recover it and, if so, by what sort of *judicium*? It is agreed that he can recover it by a *judicium* for dividing common property.   20. Where somebody has been granted *missio in possessionem* but has not yet been directed to take possession, let us consider whether the owner has to abandon possession. Labeo says that he does not just as he does not when creditors or legatees are granted *missio in possessionem*, and this is the more correct view.   21. When the praetor makes a grant of *missio in possessionem*, he does not direct the taking of possession immediately but only when just cause is shown (hence, some interval of time will have to elapse), for example, when prolonged silence shows that the owner regards the house as abandoned or when no *cautio* is given to the person who has been granted *missio in possessionem* and has remained in that position for some time.   22. Where it happens that the owner is absent on public business or for some other good reason or is of an age which normally commands protection, the view is to be approved that the praetor ought not to proceed hastily to a decree directing the taking of possession. Indeed, even if he has issued a decree nobody doubts that he would concede *restitutio in integrum*.   23. Where, however, someone has been directed to take possession the owner will have to be dispossessed.   24. Where any rights are owed to those who were in a position to give security about anticipated injury, assertion of them against the recipient of *missio in possessionem* will have to be denied. Labeo approves this.   25. Again, in the case of a creditor holding a pledge, the question is raised of whether assertion of that pledge against someone who has been directed to take possession will be denied. The preferable view is that it will be denied if the debtor has made no undertaking and the creditor has given no security. Celsus correctly writes that this applies also in the case of a usufructuary.   26. Where a *cautio* is not given in relation to a house liable to *vectigal*, we will hold that the complainant must be granted *missio in possessionem* and not directed to take possession (since he cannot obtain ownership by possession), but that a decree must be issued to the effect that he is in the same legal position as the person who gave no *cautio*. After this decree, he will be able to employ an action for property subject to *vectigal*.   27. But in the case of an estate liable to *vectigal*, if the members of a municipality fail to give a *cautio*, it is to be held that ownership can be acquired by the lapse of a long period of time.   28. If injury occurs while the praetor is deliberating about the granting of a stipulation, a pretty question arises as to whether that injury can be made good. A grant of *missio* will in any event be irrelevant; but the praetor must issue a decree to the effect that a *cautio* should also be given in relation to the injury that has occurred, or, if he considers that the granting of an action would be valid, he may issue a decree to that effect.   29. If a *pupillus* has no tutor with whose *auctoritas* to give an undertaking against anticipated injury, *missio in possessionem* will be appropriate, the matter being in effect undefended.   30. There are those who think that if someone has been granted *missio in possessionem* against anticipated injury, he must prop up and repair the tenement and that he is liable for fault if he fails to do so. This is based on the analogy of the person who receives property as a pledge. However, we adopt a different rule, that is to say, that since the sole reason for the grant of *missio in possessionem* was to put him in possession in lieu of receipt of *cautio*, no blame can attach to him for not carrying out repairs.   31. Again, suppose a *cautio* to be offered to him after he has been granted *missio in possessionem*; let us consider whether he should only withdraw when he has also received a *cautio* about any injury which occurred after the grant of *missio in possessionem*. In fact, such a view is the one more strongly supported. Consequently, a back-dated undertaking will have to be made. Furthermore, he will also have to receive a *cautio* in relation to any expenses he may have incurred.   32. The following question is raised: From what moment should the reckoning of injury be made? Is it from the time at which entry into possession occurred or from that at which the praetor issued the decree authorizing entry into possession? Labeo says the latter; Sabinus, the former. I think that when the case is investigated, sometimes one view and sometimes the other is to be approved, since it is usual for assistance to be given even to a person who is granted *missio in possessionem* but who for some reason either does not enter into possession or does so belatedly.   33. However, once one has been directed by the praetor to take possession in right of ownership, there will be no place for the offering of a *cautio*. This is Labeo's view. Otherwise, he says, there will be no end to the case; and this is the most correct view, leaving aside the cases in which people should get assistance because of age or other just cause.   34. Suppose that a house has already collapsed; let us consider whether the person who has not received a *cautio* should nonetheless be granted *missio in possessionem* of the ruins or the site. The preferable view is that he should, and Labeo holds this view. But he adds the proviso that the house should have fallen down after the praetor decreed that the complainànt be granted *missio in possessionem*. I think that Labeo's view is correct. Consequently, even if he carries out some repairs one will have to approve the view that he should not withdraw until the damage is made good and a *cautio* is given about the past injury. He can, however, also recover what he has spent by means of an action *in factum*; but he cannot get more than the cost as adjudged by a sound citizen. The same applies if someone else acting on my order or request has done any of these things in good faith and I am condemned on that account or have paid in good faith.   35. Labeo writes that where somebody has abandoned possession through fear of collapse, provided that he does so because he is unable to protect the property, he retains his full rights just as if he had continued in possession; but that if he chose to leave when he could have remedied matters, he has lost the praetor's benefit and must not be granted a hearing, should he subsequently want them to be remedied for him. But Cassius says that if it was through fear of collapse and not with the intention of abandoning the building that he withdrew, he should be restored to possession. However, he writes that someone who is granted *missio in possessionem* and does not take it up has lost the praetor's benefit, should the building collapse. This should be interpreted as referring to the case where he neglected to enter into possession not where the house collapsed while he was doing so. 36. If someone who has been granted *missio in possessionem* by the praetor under the present edict is not permitted to enter into possession, he will be able to employ an action *in factum* to secure payment to him of as much as he should have been paid if a *cautio* had been given about the matter in question, since the action extends to the time at which the injury is done.

16   PAUL, *Edict, book 48:* Before injury is done, the action of a person who neither makes an undertaking nor permits the plaintiff to enter into possession remains unpunished, provided that the former either gave a *cautio* or withdrew from possession before the occurrence of injury.

17   ULPIAN, *Edict, book 53:* Where someone does not permit a person who has been granted *missio in possessionem* to enter into possession because he is in someone else's power, most authorities think that a noxal action is available on that account. 1. What, then, happens if it is a procurator who prevents entry into possession? Do we grant an action against him or against his principal? The more correct view is that one should be granted against the procurator. 2. The same will have to be said in the case of someone acting on behalf of members of a municipality, of a tutor, and of others who are involved on behalf of someone else. 3. This action, which is one *in factum*, will be granted in perpetuity and to and against an heir and against and to other persons. 4. A judge who hears a case relating to anticipated injury normally makes an estimate of the whole of the injury which occurred before the *judicium*, even where the estate been alienated by the person against whom the action has been brought.

18   PAUL, *Edict, book 48:* A stipulation against anticipated injury is available not only to a person of whose goods the property is part but also to one who is responsible for it. 1. Where a person making an undertaking has acquired property by usucapion after the carrying out of work of some sort, Pomponius says that he is not liable on that account since it was not because of defect in the site or the work that he made the acquisition but on the basis of public law. 2. It is not necessary for a *cautio* about a defect in a house to be given to the usufructuary of the house, even if he owns another neighboring house, since he has the opportunity of making repairs; for, given that he should exercise his usufruct as befits a sound citizen, he acquires also the ability to make repairs. By the same token, the proprietor should not be given a hearing either if he wishes to receive a *cautio* from the usufructuary in respect of a house belonging to him and neighboring on the usufructuary, since he can bring an action against the latter to make him enjoy his usufruct as befits a sound citizen. 3. But if a tenant of mine owns a neighboring house, I will have to give assurances against anticipated injury to him on account of that house. 4. When somebody has put a *superficies* on soil which he has leased, the owner of the soil will not have to give him a *cautio* because injury may occur by defect in the soil, nor will the holder of the right of *superficies* have to give a *cautio* to the owner, since they can employ actions arising respectively from lease and hire. However, only fault comes within the scope of such actions, whereas the scope of a stipulation against anticipated injury is wider by virtue of its inclusion of alleged defect in the property in question. 5. Suppose that someone who owns one house makes a stipulation and then purchases a neighboring house. Does he bind the promisor in respect of the house which he purchased after the making of the stipulation? Julian writes that the *cautio* probably only covers the house which was the original subject of the stipulation between him and the promisor, and that a possible consequence of this seems to be that where two co-owners make a stipulation in respect of a jointly owned house, assurances should apparently only be regarded as covering such injury as is caused to each co-owner individually in his part of the house, since this ensures that if one of them buys the other's portion or had it adjudged to him, the promisor's obligation is not thereby increased. Pomponius, after quoting what Julian wrote on this matter, says that he does not disagree with it. 6. But if a stipulator brings some property into his house after the making of the stipulation and that property is then destroyed by the collapse of the neighboring house, he can bring an action under the stipulation even though the said property was not there when he made the stipulation. 7. If the purchaser of an estate makes a stipulation before delivery, he will get a *cautio* about any injury that may occur after delivery. 8. However, the vendor of a house ought to make a stipulation before delivery of possession since he takes responsibility for this matter as well. 9. But what happens if the vendor, through no fault of his own, was not able to make a stipulation and as a result the purchaser made one? Does he not sustain an injury? Or is it the case that the injury occurred on someone else's property but comes round to the purchaser

since he can bring no action arising from the sale? But in this case, the stipulation is of no value except in reference to something that occurs after delivery since, so long as the vendor has custody, it is he who must make the stipulation and take all precautions in the purchaser's interests; and anything that can be claimed under another sort of action is in no circumstances to be brought within the scope of a stipulation against anticipated injury.   10. But if the vendor makes a stipulation, it will cover such injury as happens to the purchaser after delivery. Aristo says that this is most unfair since, if the purchaser made a stipulation as well, the promisor would be under obligation to two persons with reference to one and the same matter, unless perhaps this consideration tells against such a view, that it is for the amount of the matter in question that the stipulation is made, so that it may be held that the vendor no longer has any interest.   11. Where a stipulation against anticipated injury has been made, the view of Sabinus is correct; he held that if, while building-work is going on during the period covered by the stipulation, a house falls onto my wall and damages it, I can bring an action even if the wall falls down after the time limit of the stipulation, because it was at the moment when the wall became defective that I sustained injury; that there is no obstacle to the bringing of an action even before the wall falls down; and that if the wall is so shaken that it is not feasible for it to be repaired and it has to be taken down, the suit must not be estimated at less than the amount due if the wall had fallen down.   12. If we own neighboring houses and request reciprocal receipt of *cautiones* against anticipated injury, there will be no obstacle to you being granted *missio in possessionem* of my house and my being granted it of yours.   13. It is agreed that if a *pupillus* has prevented someone from entering into possession in a case of anticipated injury, it is not unjust for an action *in factum* to be available against him.   14. If somebody acting on my orders has prevented someone from entering into possession, this action will be available against me.   15. The praetor punishes not only the person who has not permitted someone to be in possession but also the one who has not permitted someone to have possession; since otherwise, if someone who has started to take possession and to acquire ownership through possession is either not admitted to the property or ejected from it, he can get a valid interdict *unde vi* or the Publician action; but if he has brought an action *in factum*, he cannot bring these actions since the praetor acts to stop the plaintiff making a loss not to afford him profit.   16. If a procurator of mine makes a stipulation against anticipated injury, an action arising from that stipulation is available to me subject to investigation of the situation.

19   GAIUS, *Urban Praetor's Edict, Chapter on Anticipated Injury:* The rights of those who are absent in good faith are not prejudiced in a stipulation against anticipated injury; rather, on their return, they have the opportunity of giving a *cautio ex bono et aequo* whether they be owners or have some sort of rights in the matter, for example, as creditor, usufructuary, or holder of a right of *superficies*.   1. The praetor sees to it that a *cautio* is given to a person who fears injury because of defect in a house or defect in work of some sort that is being carried out in a house or in an urban or rural site, whether private or public.

20   GAIUS, *Provincial Edict, book 19:* As between a usufructuary and the owner of a property a *cautio* against anticipated injury is appropriate if the usufructuary requests receipt of a *cautio* about defect in the soil, or if the owner of the property requests receipt of a *cautio* about defect in any building-work that the usufructuary may be carrying out. For neither of them can request receipt of a *cautio* from the other about the collapse of the house, the usufructuary because its repair is part of his obligation, the proprietor because the normal stipulation by which the usufructuary gives a *cautio* for the return of the property at the end of the usufruct extends to these circumstances as well.

21   PAUL, *Plautius, book 8:* Suppose a son-in-power is a tenant. Let us consider whether he should be granted *missio in possessionem* of a neighboring house on account of anticipated injury (for it may be questioned whether the son-in-power, in fact, suffers injury, if the property is part of his *peculium*) and his father can make a stipulation if he sustains any injury. In fact, it is agreed that each of them can be granted *missio in possessionem*, unless the terms of the son's lease are that he is responsible for the house;

for in that case, given that it is only he who is liable under the lease, it is rightly held that it is he who should be granted *missio in possessionem* if no *cautio* is given to him.

22   PAUL, *Plautius, book 10:* If a proprietor has made an undertaking about anticipated injury or, perhaps, has paid something on that account or if (in the contrary case) a usufructuary has paid something, it is unfair that the other should have the use of the house or own it without some cost to himself. If the proprietor has paid something, the usufructuary is not to be allowed to use the property unless he has contributed something to the payment; similarly, the usufructuary is to be benefited to the extent of the proprietor being compelled to contribute something to his payment. Therefore, if the house falls down, the usufructuary will retain the soil as well until the injury he has sustained is made good, so that a usufructuary who has made good injury done to a neighbor may be as well off as a neighbor who has been granted *missio in possessionem*. The same rules will apply even where the injury done is minimal.   1. PLAUTIUS. If I wish to receive security under the proviso, "if he were not the owner," from a person whom I deny to be the owner of the property and just an undertaking from the person whom I assert to be the owner, it is established that I should not succeed in my request, but should choose from which of them I wish to receive assurances.

23   ULPIAN, *Edict, book 63:* In the case of a stipulation against anticipated injury made in reference to a house, *missio in possessionem* is granted unless the *cautio* is given in full.

24   ULPIAN, *Edict, book 81:* The use of public rivers is communal, as is that of public roads and shores. In such places, therefore, anyone at all can carry out building and demolition operations, provided that this is done without inconvenience to anybody. Consequently, it is only with reference to the work, that is, the work that someone is carrying out, that a *cautio* with security is given, and no *cautio* is given with reference to defect of the site. But if it is because of defect of the site that injury is apprehended, it must be in no way held that a stipulation against anticipated injury should be given. For who doubts that there is no one from whom the stipulation can be required, given that, even if no one carries out any work, the public site in question could cause injury by its own nature?   1. Therefore, it is to work that is carried out privately that the stipulation applies. That being so, what are we to do about any defect in work that is being carried out publicly? Clearly, an application must be made to the emperor or, if the work is being done in a province, to the provincial governor. The phrase "defect in work" is to be interpreted as relating not only to the time at which the work is being done but also to anything that may occur later; for what if a building falls down because it was badly built?   1a. The names of the heirs or successors and of those who have an interest are adjoined in this stipulation. In this clause, "successors" means not only those who succeed to the whole estate but also those who succeed just to ownership of the property in question.   2. To prevent the occurrence of any injury because of defect in a house or site or piece of work, a stipulation without payment of security is introduced about such injury. This stipulation applies not only to the whole of a house but also to part of one. Labeo defines a defect in a house or site as anything that arises from outside and makes them less secure. No one has ever held that a stipulation can become operative in reference to a site that is marshy or sandy on the grounds that it has a defect, since the defect in question is inherent in the nature of the site. Hence, a stipulation should not be made in such a case, and, if one is made, it will not become operative.   3. Does this stipulation cover only such injury as arises through illegal actions or any sort of injury originating externally? Labeo, at least, writes that no action can be brought over injury caused, say, by earthquake or the force of a river or any other accidental event.   4. Servius also thinks that if tiles are dislodged by the wind from a promisor's house and cause injury to his neighbor, the former is liable if this occurred because of a defect in the building but not if it occurred because of the violence of the wind or other reason having the character of an act of God. Labeo adjoins a reason for this, that is to say, that it would be unfair not to admit this rule; for what building is so secure that it can stand the shock of a river or the sea

or a storm or collapse or fire or earthquake? 5. The same Servius says that if an onrush of water overwhelms a tenement and the buildings belonging to the stipulator fall down, he will get nothing under the stipulation since it is not because of a defect of work or site that this occurred. But he says that if water damages the foundations and that is why the building fell down, the stipulation does become operative, since it makes a great deal of difference whether it is a case of something which was previously secure and then suddenly collapses under the force of a river or of something that was first damaged and later falls down as a result. Labeo approves this view, pointing out that in relation to the *lex Aquilia* it makes a great deal of difference whether it is a healthy man that one kills or one already somewhat feeble. 6. Although a stipulation becomes operative when injury occurs because of a defect in work, it will not become operative if the work was carried out by someone whom the promisor could not prevent from doing it. Of course, it will become operative if the promisor could prevent it, for example, if the person who carried out the work was doing it in the name of the promisor or of the person on whose behalf the undertaking was made or was someone else who could have been prevented from carrying it out. 7. Furthermore, most authorities hold that if a *cautio* against anticipated injury has been given in relation to an oven and injury is subsequently caused through the fault of the oven-man, the case does not come within the scope of this stipulation. 8. Cassius also writes that the stipulation does not hold when the injury is caused by such violence as could not possibly have been resisted. 9. Again, it is recorded in Vivian that if trees from a neighbor's field are broken by the force of a storm and fall onto my field and by doing so harm my vines or crops or demolish buildings, the stipulation which covers cases where "something occurs because of defect of trees or site" is not available since it is not through a defect in the trees but because of the force of the wind that injury has befallen me. Of course, if the situation arose because of the age of the trees, we can hold that it was through a defect in the trees that I sustained injury. 10. Vivian says that if I have made you an undertaking against anticipated injury with reference to my house and subsequently the said house is caused by the force of a storm to fall on your buildings and destroy them, nothing has to be paid under this stipulation since you have not sustained an injury caused by defect in my house. The exception is if my house was so defective that it would have collapsed in any storm however minor. All this is correct. 11. However, what Labeo thinks is also true, that is to say, that it makes a difference whether a building simply collapses under the force of a river or was first caused to deteriorate and subsequently fell down. 12. Again, let us consider when injury is held to be caused; for the stipulation covers such injury as is caused by defect of house, site, or work. Suppose that I dig a well in my house and by doing so I cut off the sources of your well. Am I liable? Trebatius says that I am not liable on a count of anticipated injury since I am not to be thought of as having caused you injury as a result of any defect in the work that I carried out, seeing that the matter is one in which I was exercising my rights. However, if I dig so deeply on my land that one of your walls cannot stand upright, a stipulation against anticipated injury will become operative.

25   PAUL, *Edict, book 78:* Trebatius says that someone who has the light to his house cut off also sustains injury.

26   ULPIAN, *Edict, book 81:* Proculus says that when somebody carries out work legally on his own property, even if he has made an undertaking to his neighbor against anticipated injury, nonetheless, he is not bound by this stipulation; for example, if you have buildings next to buildings of mine and you increase their height in accordance with your rights or if you divert my water supply by means of a canal, open or closed, on a field of yours, even though in the latter case you deprive me of my water and in the former case you block my light, nonetheless, no action is available to me under this stipulation; the grounds for this are that a person who prevents somebody from enjoying an advantage which he has hitherto enjoyed should not be held to be causing injury, there being a great difference between the causing of injury and the prevention of enjoyment of an advantage previously enjoyed. I consider Proculus's view to be correct.

27   PAUL, *Edict, book 78:* Where there are several owners of a house, they should each make a stipulation individually without adding a statement of the part that they own; for each of them makes his stipulation in reference to the injury that he himself suffers; but the addition of a reference to the part that he owns will subdivide that part. In the opposite case, where a defective house has several owners, each of them must make an undertaking in respect of his personal share in the house, to avoid the possibility of each individual being obligated for the whole sum.

28   ULPIAN, *Edict, book 81:* The amount that the matter at issue is going to be worth is what this stipulation covers. For this reason Cassius writes that if someone who has made a stipulation against anticipated injury props up the buildings in respect of which he has received a *cautio*, because he fears they are going to collapse, he can recover the cost of this operation under the stipulation, and that the same rule applies where someone who has received a *cautio* against anticipated injury on the grounds of a defect in a party-wall shores up those of his buildings which rest on that wall with the aim of relieving the pressure on it. The loss sustained because of removal of tenants is also in the same category, where it results from justified fear. Aristo not improperly adds that just as Cassius demands in this case that it should be justified fear that caused the tenants to move, so he should have added with regard to the person who shores up a building that it was justified fear of collapse that compelled him to do so.

29   GAIUS, *Provincial Edict, book 28:* The same also will have to be held in a case where no one is willing to rent a guest room because of defect in the house.

30   ULPIAN, *Edict, book 81:* The stipulation against anticipated injury also covers any injury I sustain because of defect in work carried out on my land for the purpose of carrying water across it. Work is normally carried out on someone else's property when one carries out work there by virtue of a servitude which one has imposed on the other person's property.   1. Let us consider whether he has to make an undertaking or give security about work of this sort. The influential consideration is that he is carrying out work on someone else's property. Anyone giving a *cautio* about someone else's property has to give security, whereas anyone giving a *cautio* about his own has to give an undertaking. Consequently, Labeo thinks that someone who carries out work for the purpose of making water meters or a channel also has to give security since he is working on someone else's land. But since it is about work that is being done in virtue of a servitude that a stipulation is being demanded, it follows that an undertaking can be held to be sufficient since in a sense the person giving a *cautio* is doing so about his own property.   2. The wording "for the sake of carrying water" is used by way of example; but the stipulation will be adjusted to suit all kinds of work.

31   PAUL, *Edict, book 78:* Those who repair public roads should do so without causing injury to neighbors.   1. If there is a dispute as to whether the person from whom a *cautio* is demanded is or is not the owner, the person in question is directed to give security subject to a proviso.

32   GAIUS, *Provincial Edict, book 28:* Suppose that a house that is jointly mine and yours is next to one that belongs to me and that the former threatens to cause me injury. The question arises of whether you have to give me a *cautio* with reference to any injury done by the jointly owned house to the house that belongs solely to me, a *cautio*, that is, in proportion to the extent of your ownership of the jointly owned house. The opinion of most authorities is that you do. But I am influenced by the fact that I can repair the jointly owned house and recover a proportion of the cost by means of a *judicium* on partnership or one for dividing common property. For if I own just one house in common with you and that house threatens to cause injury and you appear to be in default as far as its repair is concerned, our teachers hold that you do not have to give a *cautio* since I can carry out the repairs myself in the expectation of recovering a proportion of what I spend by means of a *judicium* on partnership or one for dividing common property. It is plainly the view of our teachers that we should consider a stipulation against anticipated injury inapplicable in circumstances in which the injury can be made good by a different sort of action. This rule should be understood as being applicable also in the circumstances stated above.

33   ULPIAN, *Sabinus, book 42:* An action against anticipated injury is not granted to a tenant since he can bring an action under the lease if the owner prevents him from moving out,

34   PAUL, *Sabinus, book 10:* provided that he is prepared to settle any rent that has accrued. Otherwise, the owner may seem entitled to retain the tenant's property as a pledge. But even if he has retained such property as a pledge and it is destroyed by the collapse of a neighboring house, the landlord may be held liable to an action on *pignus* if he could have removed the property to a safer place.

35   ULPIAN, *Sabinus, book 42:* In the case of the demolition of a party-wall, the question whether or not the wall was fit to support the weight put on it must be investigated.

36   PAUL, *Sabinus, book 10:* Most authorities hold that the proper situation is for the party-wall to be capable of bearing the weight legally put on it by the two houses.

37   ULPIAN, *Sabinus, book 42:* For if the wall is not suitable it is necessary to demolish it and if some injury occurs as a result, the person who did the demolition should not be held liable unless he spends too much or does a bad job in building a new wall. If, however, the wall that has been demolished was suitable, the matter comes within the scope of an action against anticipated injury for the amount of the plaintiff's interest in the wall remaining standing. This is as it should be since, if the wall ought not to have been demolished, the person who demolished it should restore it at his own expense. In addition, if there has been any loss of income as a result of the demolition, Sabinus wished that to be restored accordingly; and if the residents moved out or were unable to live as comfortably as before, this can be charged to the responsibility of the builder.

38   PAUL, *Sabinus, book 10:* A stipulation made by the purchaser of a house before delivery of possession has no effect because the vendor must in any case take every precaution on his behalf. Of course, a stipulation made by him is effective when there is no question of fault on the part of the vendor, for example, if he allows the purchaser to be in the house *precario* and delivers custody to him because he himself is about to go away.   1. Where no *cautio* is received in respect of a field, the complainant is to be granted *missio in possessionem* for the part of the field from which danger is apprehended. The reasoning behind this is that whereas in the case of a house the rest of the building may be pulled down by the defective part, the same does not apply in the case of fields. Still it must be said that in the case of larger houses as well the praetor must sometimes, after investigating the case, determine for which part of the house the person who has not received assurances should be granted *missio in possessionem.*   2. Calculations must be made to see whether there is any balance after the deduction of the value of the old wall. And if any material from the old wall is used in constructing the new one, this should be deducted from the calculations.

39   POMPONIUS, *Sabinus, book 21:* Persons who share a party-wall normally make stipulations against anticipated injury in respect of the buildings that each has as his own. But such a *cautio* is necessary only when either it is only one of them who is carrying out building-work and there is a threat of injury from this work or one of them has more valuable buildings than the other and will sustain greater injury should the party-wall fall down. Otherwise, where the risk to each party is equal, the same amount can be claimed from one as he pays to the other.   1. Where a house is the subject of dispute, it must be held that the burden of anticipated injury falls on the person in possession on the grounds that he can charge anything he pays to the owner of the property. But if he fails to give a *cautio*, possession is to be transferred to the petitioner who wants to receive a *cautio* against anticipated injury, since it is unfair for the person making the stipulation to be compelled to leave the property from which he apprehends danger and look for the owner himself.   2. The stipulation against anticipated injury has fairly broad application. Consequently, it is available to the holder of a tenement in *superficies*, if some injury occurs on the *superficies*, and no less available for the owner of the soil, if such injury is caused to the soil that the whole *superficies* is removed, since the owner of the soil will then sustain loss in receipts of rents.   3. It is

possible to make a stipulation in someone else's name such that any injury sustained by the owner is covered by it. But the person making such a stipulation will have to give a *cautio* that the owner will ratify his action and a defense that he is a procurator will have to be inserted into the stipulation, just as in the case of stipulations relating to legacies. But if the procurator does not receive a *cautio*, he must without question be granted *missio in possessionem*, and the defense that he is a procurator is not available against him.   4. In calculating the cost of the new wall, the cost involved in its original ornamentation, provided that that did not exceed a reasonable amount, must be taken into account, though not to the extent of causing us a burden.

40   ULPIAN, *Sabinus, book 43:* The calculation of costs under a stipulation against anticipated injury should not reach huge or immoderate proportions, for example, in respect of plasterwork or pictures. For even if great expenditure was made on such things, nonetheless, the calculation of costs under the stipulation against anticipated injury should be of moderate proportions, because an honorable moderation of behavior is to be preserved and immoderate luxury is not to be condoned on anyone's part.   1. When injury results from a defect in a party-wall, one common owner does not have to pay the other anything since it was through a defect in jointly owned property that injury occurred. But if it was because one of them had put some weight or stress on the wall that the injury occurred, it is logical to hold that he must himself make good damage which arose from an action intended to benefit him. But Sabinus quite correctly wrote that if it was after being put under strain by both of them equally the wall fell down, they are both equally at fault. And even if one of the two has lost more, or more valuable, property, it is better to hold that since both of them put strain on the wall, no action is available to either of them against the other.   2. When several people bring an action against anticipated injury, given that they have sustained injury in the same matter, that is, a house, they should not each bring an action for the whole amount, but should institute proceedings for their share, since an injury sustained by several persons is not all sustained by any one of them, but is held to be sustained by each of them according to his share. Consequently, Julian wrote that an action is available to each of them in respect of his share.   3. Again, suppose that a house which threatens to cause injury belongs to several persons; is an action available against any one of the owners for the whole amount at stake or against each of them for his share? Julian wrote, and Sabinus approves the view, that they must be sued in proportion to their share in ownership.   4. If there are several owners of a house who wish to take precautions against anticipated injury and no one gives them any *cautio*, they must all be granted *missio in possessionem*, and that in equal shares, even if they have different shares in ownership of the house. Pomponius also writes to this effect.

41   POMPONIUS, *Sabinus, book 21:* In the matter of repair to a party-wall, the opportunity to carry out the building-work should be afforded to the person who intends to do the repairs in the most appropriate manner. The same rule applies where there is a question as to which of two or more people should carry out repairs on a given road or bank.

42   JULIAN, *Digest, book 58:* If a jointly owned slave has made a stipulation on anticipated injury, this is considered equivalent to his owners making the stipulation in person and in proportion to their share in ownership.

43   ALFENUS VERUS, *Digest, book 2:* A man had made an undertaking against anticipated injury to his neighbor. Some tiles from his building were blown off by the wind and landed on his neighbor's tiles, breaking them. The question arises of whether any payment has to be made. He replied that if the circumstances arose because of some defect and weakness in the building, then payment has to be made. But if the wind was strong enough to shake even a solid building, payment does not have to be made. In his view, the phrase in the stipulation "if something falls on to it" applies not to material that comes down because of wind or any externally applied force, but to

what collapses for intrinsic reasons.   1. A man wished to build a party-wall together with his neighbor, and before they demolished the existing one, he made an undertaking to his neighbor and had a stipulation made to himself by the latter. After the wall had been removed and the tenants had moved out of the neighbor's upper rooms, the neighbor wanted to claim from the other party the rent which those tenants were not paying. The question arises of whether this claim is legitimate. He replied that when building a party-wall, they ought not to have made mutual undertakings and that neither of them could in any way have been compelled by the other to do so; that granted that they did make undertakings, they ought not to have done so for more than half the value, which is the maximum that anyone would have to undertake even to a third party when building a party-wall; but that since, in fact, they had made undertakings for the whole sum, all loss sustained by the neighbor in the matter of rent would have to be paid.   2. The same individual asked for advice as to whether he could claim back what he paid on this account on the grounds that the stipulation made to him by his neighbor had provided that any loss he might sustain as a result of the carrying out of the building-work should be restored to him and that the money that he paid counted as a loss caused by the carrying out of the work. He replied that such a claim could not be made since it was not because of defect in the work but by virtue of the stipulation that he had sustained the loss in question.

44   AFRICANUS, *Questions, book 9:* When I requested you to make me an undertaking against anticipated injury, you refused to do so, and before application was made to the praetor, your house fell down and caused me injury. He said that the view should rather be taken that the praetor ought to make no decision that would alter the situation and that it was my own fault that I sustained injury seeing that I was rather slow in instituting legal proceedings. However, if the house collapsed after the praetor had decreed that you give an undertaking and, on your failing to do so, had directed that I enter into possession but before I had actually done so, he thought that all those rules should apply which would have applied if the injury had been caused after I entered into possession.   1. After being granted *missio in possessionem* on a count of anticipated injury, I acquired ownership through possession. Subsequently, a creditor wishes to lay claim to the house in question as being under *hypotheca* to him. It will not be unreasonable to hold that he should be restrained from proceeding against me unless he is prepared to pay me back the expenses I incurred for repairs. Why, then, is the same concession not made where somebody buys a tenement that is under *hypotheca*? The two cases cannot be legitimately compared since a purchaser is conducting his business of his own volition and for that reason can and must take care to get assurances from the vendor, whereas the same cannot equally be said of somebody who does not receive an undertaking against anticipated injury.

45   SCAEVOLA, *Questions, book 12: Chapter on the Claim for a Piece of Land from an Unwilling Party:* You have a building. I bring an action to deny your right to it. You fail to defend the case. Possession of it must be transferred to me, not indeed for it to be demolished forthwith (since it is unfair that demolition should occur immediately), but for it to be demolished if, within a fixed period, you do not bring an action to establish your right to have it.

46   PAUL, *Views, book 1:* The functions of the curator of the *respublica* include seeing to it that derelict houses are re-erected by their owners.   1. When a house has been re-erected at public expense, the *respublica* can legally sell it if the owner refuses to return the sum expended plus interest at the proper time.

47   NERATIUS, *Parchments, book 6:* When an owner transfers the use of a lock-up room common to two houses from one house to the other, it will become part of the latter not only if the floorbeams which support it start from the side of the house to whose use it has been transferred but even if the floorbeams rest entirely on the walls of the other house. Labeo also writes in his *Posthumous Works* of a case where the owner of a double house added a portico to both houses, made an entrance into it from one house, and imposed a servitude for the preservation of the portico on the other, and then sold the house. He says that the whole portico was still part of the house that he retained

since it extended the whole length of both houses and was supported by a beam, which rested on both sides on the walls of the house that he had sold. However, it does not follow that the upper part of a house which is not joined to any other construction and has no access from anywhere else can belong to anyone but the owner of the building on which it is superimposed.

48 MARCIAN, *Delatores, sole book:* It is established that where someone is convicted of having sold a house or a part of a house for demolition for the purpose of making a gain by trade, both the purchaser and the vendor should separately pay the sum for which the house was sold. However, it is legal for him to hand over marble or columns for use in public works.

3

WATER AND THE ACTION TO WARD OFF RAINWATER

1 ULPIAN, *Edict, book 53:* If rainwater is going to cause one injury, it can be averted by means of an action to ward off rainwater. We define "rainwater" as water which falls from the sky and is increased in quantity by a rainstorm, whether, as Tubero says, such water from the sky causes damage by itself or in conjunction with some other body of water. 1. This action is appropriate where no injury has yet been caused, but work of some sort has been carried out, that is, work from which injury is apprehended. The action is appropriate whenever water is likely to cause damage to a field as a result of a man-made construction, that is, whenever someone causes water to flow elsewhere than in its normal and natural course, for example, if by letting it in he makes the flow greater or faster or stronger than usual or if by blocking the flow he causes an overflow. But if the water causes damage naturally, the case is not covered by this action. 2. Neratius writes: Where somebody has made a construction to keep out water which normally flows onto his field from an overflowing marsh, if that marsh is increased in size by rainwater and the said water, held back by the construction in question, damages his neighbor's field, he will be compelled to remove it by means of an action to ward off rainwater. 3. Quintus Mucius says that this action is not available with reference to work carried out with a plow for the purpose of cultivating a field. However, Trebatius excludes from the scope of the action not work carried out with a plow for the purpose of cultivating a field but only work carried out with a plow for the purpose of securing a crop. 4. However, Mucius says that the construction of ditches to drain fields counts as something done for the purpose of cultivating the property, but that ditches should not be constructed for the purpose of causing water to flow in one stream since one must only improve one's field in such a way as not to reduce the quality of one's neighbor's field. 5. Mucius says that if someone can plow and sow without making water channels, he is liable should he lay out such channels, even though he may be held to have done so for the purpose of cultivating a field. But if he cannot sow without making water channels, he is not liable. Ofilius, however, says that it is legal to make water channels for the purpose of cultivating a field if they are all made to run in the same direction. 6. It is recorded by the pupils of Servius that if someone plants willows and as a result water overflows, an action to ward off rainwater can be brought, if the said water harms a neighbor. 7. Labeo also writes that anything done for the purpose of gathering crops or fruit falls outside this category of case and that it does not matter what sort of fruits it is whose gathering is the purpose of the performance of the work in question. 8. Again, Sabinus and Cassius say that a man-made construction comes within the scope of this action unless it is made for the purpose of cultivating a field. 9. But anyone who constructs the type of water channels called *elices* is liable to an action to ward off rainwater. 10. The same authorities say that if water flows down naturally, the action to ward off rainwater is not available, but that if, after the carrying out of a piece of work, water is held back in

the upper part of a field or channeled onto the lower part, the action to ward off rainwater lies. 11. The same authorities say that everyone has the right to retain rainwater on his own property and to channel surface rainwater from his neighbor's property onto his own, provided that no work is done on someone else's property, and that no one can be held liable on this account, since no person is forbidden to profit himself as long as he harms nobody else in so doing. 12. Next, Marcellus writes that no action, not even the action for fraud, can be brought against a person who, while digging on his own land, diverts his neighbor's water supply. And of course the latter ought not to have even the action for fraud, assuming that the other person acted not with the intention of harming his neighbor, but with that of improving his own field. 13. Again, it must be understood that this action is available both to the owner of a higher piece of land against the owner of a lower piece to stop the latter carrying out work to prevent naturally flowing water passing down through his own field and to the owner of a lower piece of land against the owner of a higher piece to stop the latter causing the water to flow other than naturally. 14. It must be said in addition that this action is never available when it is the nature of the site that causes the damage, since in that case (to speak accurately) it is not the water, but the nature of the site that causes the damage. 15. In short, I hold that the action to ward off rainwater is available where rainwater, or an existing body of water swollen by rain, causes damage, provided that it does not do so in the nature of things, but because of the carrying out of a piece of work and that work was not carried out for the purpose of cultivating a field. 16. And that a body of water is regarded as being swollen by rain if it changes color when it increases in quantity. 17. Again, it must be understood that this action is not available except when it is a field that is damaged by rainwater. When it is a building or a town that is damaged, this action is not valid, but an action can be brought to deny the right of eavesdrip or the flow of water onto one's property. Consequently, Labeo and Cascellius say that the action to ward off rainwater is of special application, whereas an action on the flow of water and eavesdrip is of general application and can be brought in any circumstances. Thus, it is water that causes damage to a field that is to be controlled by means of the action to ward off rainwater. 18. The question of the source of the water does not have to be raised. For even in cases where water which originated on public or consecrated property flows down onto my neighbor's land and he carries out some work which causes the water to be diverted onto my property, Labeo says that the neighbor is liable to an action to ward off rainwater. 19. Cassius also writes that if water deriving from a town building damages either a field or a rural building, it is an action on a flow of water and eavesdrip that ought to be brought. 20. I find it recorded in Labeo, however, that if water flowing from a field of mine damages a site on the edge of a city, that is, a building, I cannot be sued by the action to ward off rainwater, but that if water flows from the edge of a city onto my field and damages it, the action to ward off rainwater lies. 21. Granted that any piece of work that results in rainwater causing me damage comes within the scope of this action, the contrary question is raised whether an action to ward off rainwater can be brought if my neighbor carries out some work to prevent water which previously flowed onto my land to my advantage affording this benefit. Ofilius and Labeo think that such an action cannot be brought even though it is in my interests for the water to reach my land since the action is appropriate where rainwater causes damage not where it fails to cause benefit. 22. But Labeo considers that even if somebody's neighbor removes a construction and, as a result, water flows naturally onto a lower field and causes damage, an action to ward off rainwater cannot be brought since there is always a servitude applying to lower properties by which they must receive any water that flows onto them naturally. Of course, if the removal of the construction causes the water to flow with a more powerful current or to coalesce with other water, Labeo does allow that an action to ward off rainwater can be brought. 23. Next he says that specific regulations have been imposed by arrangement on certain categories of field, so that, for example, where there are large watercourses in a field I can have dams and ditches, even on your field, but that if no regulation has been imposed affecting a given field, its natural state must be preserved and a lower field must always be under servitude to a higher one, this inconvenience being something that a lower field must suffer vis-à-vis a higher one as a matter of nature and which is compensated by other advantages; for just as all the richness of the soil tends toward the lower field, so does the inconvenience of the downward flow of water. Where, however, no regulation relating to the field in question is to be discovered, he says that established custom takes the place of such regulation. For in the case of servitudes as well, of course, we follow the same rule, that is to say, that where it is discovered that no servitude has been imposed, the person who has for a long time acted as though there were a servitude and has done so neither by force nor *precario* nor secretly, he is regarded as having a servitude imposed quasi-legally by reason of prolonged custom. Consequently, we will not compel the neighbor to construct dams but will construct them ourselves on his land, and this will count as a sort of servitude in respect of which we will have the right to an *actio utilis in rem* or an interdict.

2 PAUL, *Edict, book 49:* In short, there are three ways in which a lower site can become under servitude to a higher one, that is to say, regulation imposed, the nature of the site, and established custom, which last is always regarded as having the force of law, for the purpose, of course, of reducing litigation. 1. In Labeo, the following case is proposed: There was an old ditch constructed for the purpose of draining fields, but no record existed of when the construction occurred. The neighbor occupying the land below us failed to keep it clear. As a consequence, it overflowed, and the water damaged our property. Labeo says that an action to ward off rainwater can be brought against the owner of the lower property to ensure that he either cleans the ditch himself or permits you to restore it to its previous condition. 2. Besides this Labeo says that if a ditch is on a boundary line and the neighbor does not permit the clearing of that part of the ditch which adjoins your land, you can bring an action *in rem* instead of one to ward off rainwater. 3. Cassius writes that work carried out on public authority for the purpose of encouraging water-flow does not come within the scope of the action to ward off rainwater, and that constructions which are too old for there to be a record of their creation are in the same position. 4. It is recorded in Ateius that a neighbor must be compelled to clear a ditch from which water flows down onto a lower property whether or not record of the building of the ditch exists. I, too, think that this view is to be approved. 5. Again, Varus says: Water pressure pushed down a dam in a neighbor's field, and as a result, rainwater caused me damage. Varus says that if the dam was naturally formed, I cannot use the action to ward off rainwater to compel my neighbor to replace the dam or to allow its replacement, and he holds the same to be true even if the dam was man-made but no record of its construction survives. But if such a record does exist he holds that the neighbor is liable to an action to ward off rainwater. Labeo, however, holds that if the dam is man-made and even if no record of its construction survives, an action can be brought to ensure that the neighbor allows its replacement though not one to compel him to replace it. For this action cannot be used to compel anybody to benefit his neighbor, but can be used to stop him damaging his neighbor or interfering with him if the latter is acting legally. However, even though the action to ward off rainwater may be inapplicable, nonetheless, I hold the view that an *actio utilis* or an interdict is available to me against my neighbor if I wish to restore a dam on his land whose construction will be to my advantage and will not harm him in any way. Considerations of fairness support this view even though we may lack a clear legal right. 6. It is recorded in Namusa that if a flow of water gets blocked with dung and as a result of overflow damages a higher field, an action can be brought against the owner of the lower field to ensure that he allows the watercourse to be cleared since this action is valid not only in relation to man-made constructions but also in relation to all changes in the status quo which we do not intend to occur. Labeo approves a view opposite to that of Namusa, saying that the natural condition of a field can change of itself and that, therefore, when this happens, each party must endure the consequences with equanimity whether his individual circumstances are thereby improved or worsened, and that consequently if the character of the soil is altered by an earthquake or by a violent storm, nobody can be compelled to allow the restoration of the site to its former condition. But we allow appeal to considerations of fairness in this case as well. 7. The same Labeo says that if an accumulation of water has hollowed out a site on your land, an action to ward off rainwater cannot be brought against you by your neighbors. Of course, if it destroys a legally constructed ditch, or one a record of whose construction does not exist, an action to ward off rainwater can be brought against you to make you repair it. 8. The same Labeo says that when there is a question as to whether a record of the construction of a piece of work survives the exact date and consular year does not have to be sought out, but that it is sufficient if somebody knows about its construction, that is, if the fact of its construction is not in dispute, and that it is not necessary for there to be still alive people who remember the construction but only people who heard those who remembered it speaking about it. 9. The same Labeo says that if somebody diverts a torrent to stop

the water reaching him and the result of this is to cause damage to his neighbor, an action to ward off rainwater cannot be brought against him since warding off rainwater is seeing to it that it does not flow onto one's property. This view is the more correct one provided that his actions were performed not with the intention of harming you, but of avoiding damage himself.   10. I also hold to be correct what Ofilius writes, that is to say, that if your land is under servitude to the neighboring land and consequently receives water, an action to ward off rainwater is inapplicable so long as the damage caused is not excessive. The consequence of this is the view of Labeo that if someone has conceded to his neighbor the right to cause water to flow onto his land, he cannot bring an action to ward off rainwater.

3   ULPIAN, *Edict, book 53:* It is recorded in Trebatius that someone who had a spring on his land established a fuller's shop at it and began to cause the water there to flow onto his neighbor's property. Trebatius says that he is not liable to an action to ward off rainwater. However, many authorities accept that if he channeled the water into one stream or introduced any dirt into it, he can be restrained.   1. The same Trebatius holds that somebody who sustains harm from a flow of hot water can bring an action to ward off rainwater. This is incorrect since hot water is not rainwater.   2. Ofilius says that if someone who previously watered his field at a fixed time in the year makes a meadow there and starts to cause damage to his neighbor by persistent irrigation of it, he is liable neither to an action against anticipated injury nor to one to ward off rainwater, unless he has leveled the site and, as a result, the water has started to flow more quickly onto the neighbor's property.   3. It is established, and we follow this rule, that only someone who carries out work on his own land is liable to an action to ward off rainwater. Therefore, if someone carries out a piece of work on public property, this action is inapplicable, and anyone who fails to protect himself in advance by means of a *cautio* against anticipated injury has only himself to blame. However, Labeo says that if the work is carried out on private land and some public property intervenes, an action to ward off rainwater can be brought in full.   4. A usufructuary cannot bring an action to ward off rainwater or have one brought against him.

4   ULPIAN, *book 53:* Labeo writes that although an action to ward off rainwater only lies against the owner of a piece of work, nonetheless, if someone has built a tomb and water from it causes damage, despite the fact that the builder has ceased to be the owner because the site has become religious, the view is still to be approved that he is liable to an action to ward off rainwater, since he was the owner at the time the work was carried out, and that if, on a judge's instructions, he restores the site to its previous condition, no action for the violation of a tomb lies.   1. Julian also writes that if, after the institution of a *judicium* to ward off rainwater, the defendant alienates the property, the judge must give the same decision about the existing injury and about restoration as he would have done had no alienation taken place. For, even when the property has been alienated, the grant of a *judicium* remains in force, and the calculation of injury must include any which happened after the alienation.   2. The same Julian writes that an action to ward off rainwater lies only against the owner and that consequently if a tenant farmer carries out some work without the owner's knowledge, the latter only has to allow restoration of previous conditions, whereas the tenant farmer should be compelled by means of the interdict against force or stealth to pay the cost of such restoration and of any injury caused by the work in question. However, if the owner, that is, the person from whose property water is causing damage, wishes to receive a *cautio* against anticipated injury from the person whose property is being damaged, it will be quite fair for such assurances to have to be given to him.   3. Again, if it is not I, but my procurator who has carried out work which results in rainwater harming my neighbor, the action will lie against me to the same extent as it does on account of the actions of a tenant farmer. However, according to Julian's view, the procurator will be able to institute legal proceedings himself under the interdict against force or stealth even after the restoration of the work to previous conditions.

5   PAUL, *Edict, book 49:* Labeo replied that where a tenant farmer has carried out some work without the owner's knowledge and as a result water harms a neighbor, the tenant farmer is liable to the interdict against force or stealth, but the owner is liable to an action to ward off rainwater on the grounds that the latter alone can restore the work to its original condition, but that if he received a *cautio* against anticipated injury, he has only to allow restoration, and he will be able to recover any expense which he incurs in the restoration from the tenant farmer by an action on letting, unless one holds that he should not do so on the grounds that it was not necessary for him to make the restoration. But if the tenant farmer acted on the owner's instructions, Labeo holds that the latter is also liable to the interdict.

6   ULPIAN, *Edict, book 53:* Sabinus says that if my neighbor next-but-one carries out some work and water from it flows down through my immediate neighbor's property and causes me damage, I can bring an action either against the immediate neighbor or, leaving him out of it, against the neighbor next-but-one. This view is correct.   1. Where water flowing from property belonging to several people causes damage, or where damage is caused to property belonging to several people, it is agreed, and we adopt this rule, that if the damaged property has several owners, they may institute legal proceedings individually in proportion to their several shares, and judgment may be rendered proportionately; and if the action is brought against several persons, they may be taken to law individually in proportion to their several shares, and judgment may be rendered proportionately.   2. Hence, there arises this question: If water from a field belonging solely to you causes damage to a field owned jointly by you and me, can an action to ward off rainwater be brought? I would think that it can with the proviso that only part of the injury be paid for by the losing party.   3. In the reverse case also, that is, where it is the jointly owned field that causes damage to the singly owned one, it will be possible to bring an action to ward off rainwater in order to secure damages, but only in part.   4. If someone transfers ownership of a property to another person before bringing an action to ward off rainwater, he ceases to have the right to bring such an action, which passes instead to the person who has just become the owner of the field in question; for, given that the action covers future injury, right to it will start to belong to the person who is going to be the owner in the future even if it was at a time when ownership was vested in the other person that the work was carried out by the neighbor.   5. It must be understood that the action to ward off rainwater is not *in rem* but *in personam.*   6. The duty of the judge will be to order the restoration to its original condition of any work carried out by a neighbor and the making good of any injury which has occurred since the joinder of issue. However, where it is a case of injury which occurred before the joinder of issue, the neighbor will only have to restore the work to its original condition and will not make good the injury.   7. Celsus writes that if I myself carried out some work which results in rainwater causing you injury, I am to be compelled to remove the said work at my own expense, but that if it was somebody else who has no connection with me who did the work it is sufficient for me to permit its removal. But if it was a slave of mine or someone whose heir I am who did the work, then in the case of the slave, I must surrender him noxally, and in the other case, the situation is exactly as if I did the work myself.   8. The judge will assess the damage done on the basis of the truth of the matter, that is, of the injury that appears to have been caused.

7   PAUL, *Edict, book 18:* Somebody against whom an action to ward off rainwater is brought on the grounds that he has carried out some work is compelled to accept the *judicium* even if he is prepared to abandon the site, because he is also being personally sued for removal of the work.   1. It is different in the case of a purchaser in good faith. He only has to permit removal of the work and must consequently be given a hearing if he abandons the property as well, since he is offering to do more than is required.

8   ULPIAN, *Edict, book 53:* In a matter of concession of the right to carry water across land, the consent must be sought not only of those on whose property the water originated but also of those who have a right to use the water, that is, those to whom a servitude on the water is owing. This is not unjustified since, when their rights are being diminished, one must necessarily inquire whether they are agreeable. As a general rule, it is agreed that consideration must be given to the consent of anyone who has an interest in the land itself on which the water originates or in the rights pertaining to that land or in the water itself.

9   PAUL, *Edict, book 49:* Where a property is subject to an *addictio in diem*, the consent of both purchaser and vendor must be sought to ensure that the cession of water rights is made with the owner's consent, whether the property remains with the purchaser or reverts to the vendor.   1. The reason for demanding the owner's consent is to ensure that he does not sustain injury through ignorance. For someone who has once given consent cannot be held to sustain injury.   2. In a case of cession of water rights, the consent is required not only of the person to whom rights over the water belong but also of the owner of the sites involved even if the latter cannot make use of the water, since all rights over the land may revert to him.

10   ULPIAN, *Edict, book 53:* It is not disputed that where the site from which water is led has several owners; it is the consent of all of them that must be respected, since it has been held to be unfair for the consent of one owner, who may have only a modest portion of the whole property, to prejudice his co-owners' interests.   1. Let us consider whether consent can be secured subsequently. It is agreed that it makes no difference whether the consent came before or after the leading of the water since the praetor must uphold even subsequent consent.   2. Labeo says that if a river is navigable, the praetor ought not to allow any leading of water from it which may render it less so. The same rule applies even if another river becomes navigable as a result.

11   PAUL, *Edict, book 49:* An aqueduct cannot legally be constructed over someone else's right of way. Nor can a person who has a right of way in person or with cattle construct a bridge over which to go in person or with cattle. And if he constructs a closed (not an open) channel under a watercourse, the water supply will be damaged because, once the watercourse has been undermined, the water will seep away, and the stream will dry up.   1. Cassius says that if water flowing from or onto a jointly owned piece of land causes damage, an action can be brought either by one owner against another or by one owner against several others individually or by several owners individually against one owner or by several owners against several other owners. Where one owner has brought the action and the restoration of the work and the assessment of damages have been carried out, the others' right to take action is extinguished. Again, if an action has been brought against one of the owners and he has paid, the others are released from liability, and anything given in the name of the co-owners can be recovered through the judge in an action for dividing common property.   2. Proculus says that it is held in Ferox that action does not have to be brought against the particular co-owner who carried out the work and that a co-owner who was not the author of the work is no less bound to restore it to its original condition, and that if an action is brought against one of the owners who did not carry out the work, he has to restore it to its original condition at his own expense, since he can have recourse to an action for dividing common property. But Proculus says that he prefers the view that such an owner only has to permit restoration, it being the plaintiff's fault that he suffers this inconvenience because he failed to bring the action against the person by whom the work was actually done. Indeed, it is unfair that someone who did not carry out the work should have to restore it to its original condition on the grounds that he can bring an action for dividing common property. For what is going to happen if his co-owner is not solvent?   3. Julian says that he is in doubt about the duty of a judge accepted by two parties if it happens that the property damaged by water belongs to one person but the property on which work was carried out belongs to several people and action is being brought against one of them. Should condemnation in full be inflicted with reference to the injury caused after the joinder of issue and the failure to restore the work to its original condition on the analogy of the case where a noxal action relating to a jointly owned slave is brought against one of the owners and condemnation in full is inflicted on the grounds that the defendant can recover what he pays from his co-owner? Or is the defendant to be condemned for injury caused and failure to restore the work to its original condition proportionately to his share of ownership, on the analogy of what happens in an action against anticipated injury where the property from which injury is apprehended belongs to several people and action is brought against one of them? For, when an action against anticipated injury is brought, even though the work which may cause injury is indivisible and the house

itself and the soil cannot cause injury only proportionately, nonetheless, the defendant is condemned proportionately to his share of ownership. Julian prefers the view that the model provided by the action against anticipated injury is the one that should be adhered to in the action to ward off rainwater on the grounds that in both cases the action concerns not existing but future injury. 4. But if the property to which rainwater is causing damage belongs to several people, Julian holds that although they can each individually bring an action, they will each get no more than proportional damages for the injury caused after the joinder of issue, and again that if the work is not restored to its original condition, condemnation ought not to be inflicted for more than the amount of each co-owner's proportional interest in the restoration being done. 5. Ofilius says that if water is introduced into a jointly owned field from a field which is the private property of one co-owner, the other co-owner can bring an action against the latter. 6. Trebatius thinks that where an action is brought in relation to a man-made construction, the latter must certainly be restored to its original condition by the defendant, but that where an embankment has been destroyed by the force of a river or gravel has got in or a ditch has become filled with mud, then the defendant only has to permit the making good of the damage.

12 PAUL, *Sabinus, book 16:* A purchaser (unless the sale is simulated) and the other successors must either restore the work to its original condition, if they so wish, or permit such restoration to be done. For it is clear that his delay must cause harm to the plaintiff. The co-owner of the person who carried out the work is in the same position if he was not himself the author of the work. The same applies in the case of property given as a gift or a legacy.

13 GAIUS, *Urban Praetor's Edict, Chapter on the Action to Ward off Rainwater:* But the vendor or donor will be liable to the interdict against force or stealth in respect of injury and expenses incurred by the plaintiff.

14 PAUL, *Edict, book 49:* Ateius says that if someone who has carried out some work later sells the property to someone more powerful, inasmuch as he has ceased to be its owner, an action against force or stealth is to be brought against him. But if a year has passed, a *judicium* on fraud should be granted. 1. In an action to ward off rainwater, the factual question of what it is that is causing damage arises. Hence, if part of the soil subsides because of a defect of the site, even if the result is that rainwater causes damage to a lower-lying field, no action is available. The same is perhaps to be said where a man-made construction in a field subsides. 2. Future injury comes within the scope of this *judicium*, as it does within that of the *judicium* against anticipated injury, whereas, in almost all other types of *judicium*, payment is made for past injury. 3. With reference to injury caused before the judge's decision is made known, an action against force or stealth should be brought. With reference to injury that is going to occur after the judge's decision has been made known, a *cautio* against anticipated injury should be given or the work should be restored to its original condition in such a way that no danger of injury remains. 4. With reference to work carried out after the joinder of issue, a new action must be brought.

15 PAUL, *Sabinus, book 16:* But sometimes even a construction made after the joinder of issue will be removed, if one that preceded the joinder of issue cannot otherwise be removed.

16 POMPONIUS, *Sabinus, book 20:* Even after sale and delivery claims for any damage done to a property with reference to which a *judicium* to ward off rainwater has been granted can still be pursued by the vendor in that *judicium*, not because the vendor has suffered any damage, but because the property has, and the vendor has to hand over the proceeds to the purchaser. However, if the person who carried out the work sells the property before any damage is done, an action should be brought immediately against the purchaser or, within a year, against the vendor, if he sold the property with a view to evading the *judicium*.

17 PAUL, *Plautius, book 15:* If a servitude for leading water at night has previously been granted to me and then, later and by a separate concession, the right to lead water by day as well is allowed to me but, during the specified period, I only use the right to lead at night, I lose the servitude for leading water by day, because in this

case there are several servitudes with different origins. 1. It is justifiably agreed that water can only be conducted in stone aqueducts if such a provision was included when the servitude was established, since it is not the custom for someone who has the right to conduct water to do so through a stone channel. However, customary procedures such as channeling water through pipes can be carried out even if nothing of the sort was included when the servitude was established, provided that no injury is caused to the owner of the property as a result. 2. It is established that a servitude for drawing water can be established where a public road runs between the two pieces of land involved; and this is correct. But this is so not only if a public road runs between but also if a public river does so, in the same way in which a servitude for right of way by cart or in person or with cattle can be imposed where a public river intervenes, provided, that is, that the size of the river is not such as to impede crossing. 3. Similarly, even if it is not to a field of mine immediately neighboring his property but to one further off that my neighbor owes a servitude, I will be able to bring an action to establish my right of way in person or with cattle to the said more distant property even though I do not have a servitude for passage through my own property, just as in the case where a public road or a fordable public river intervenes. However, no servitude can be imposed where a consecrated, religious, or sanctified piece of land, of the sort that it is wrong to use, intervenes. 4. But if there is a plot lying between you and me and belonging to a third party, I will be able to impose a servitude for drawing water on your plot, provided that the owner of the intermediate plot has granted me right of way in person across his land. In the same way, if I wish to make use of a perpetual right to draw water from a public stream to which a field of yours is adjacent, a right of way in person to the stream can be granted to me.

18   JAVOLENUS, *From Cassius, book 10:* If a piece of work which causes rainwater damage is carried out on public land, no action can be brought. But if the public land intervenes between the site of the work and that of the damage, an action will be possible. The reason for this is that nobody but the owner is liable to this action. 1. Water cannot be led across a public road without the emperor's permission.

19   POMPONIUS, *Quintus Mucius, book 14:* Labeo says that if my neighbor allows me to carry out some work as a result of which rainwater causes him damage, I am not liable to an action to ward off rainwater.

20   POMPONIUS, *Sabinus, book 34:* But this is so only if he was not misled by error or ignorance, since the consent of someone in error is null and void.

21   POMPONIUS, *Quintus Mucius, book 32:* If water which has its sources on your land bursts onto my land and you cut off those sources with the result that the water ceases to reach my land, you will not be considered to have acted with force, provided that no servitude was owed to me in this connection, nor will you be liable to the interdict against force or stealth.

22   POMPONIUS, *Readings, book 10:* If the usufruct of a piece of land is bequeathed as a legacy, the action to ward off rainwater is available to and against the heir of the owner of the property. But if the usufructuary suffers any inconvenience as a result of some construction, he will sometimes be able to institute legal proceedings by means of an interdict against force or stealth. But if this course is not available to him, the question arises of whether an *actio utilis* to ward off rainwater should be granted to him, as though he were the owner, or whether he should also assert his right to usufruct. The preferable opinion is that an *actio utilis* to ward off rainwater should be applied in this case. 1. Somebody who has carried out work is considered to have restored it to its original condition only if he contains the flow of water. 2. But even if it is the usufructuary who has carried out work as a result of which rainwater causes someone damage, a statutory action, in any event, will be available against the owner. However, the question is raised whether an *actio utilis* to ward off rainwater is also to be granted against the usufructuary, and the preferable opinion is that it is.

23   PAUL, *Sabinus, book 16:* Any work carried out either on the orders of the emperor or the senate or by those who first settled the boundaries of fields does not come within the scope of this *judicium.* 1. This action is also appropriate in the case of fields subject to *vectigal.* 2. Dikes built next to rivers on private land come within the scope of the action to ward off rainwater, even if it is on the other side of the river that they cause damage, provided that a record of their construction survives and that they ought not to have been constructed in the way that they were.

24   ALFENUS, *Digest, Epitomized by Paul, book 4:* A man's neighbor, who owned the plot

above him, plowed his meadow in such a way that water passed down through the furrows and ridges onto the lower land. The question arises of whether the neighbor can be compelled by an action to ward off rainwater to low in the other direction, so that the furrows do not point toward the man's field. He replied: The latter can do nothing to prevent his neighbor plowing as he wishes. 1. But if he makes transverse water channels through which water flows down onto another man's field, the arbitrator in an action to ward off rainwater can compel him to fill them up. 2. But even if he makes ditches which may lead to rainwater causing damage, an arbitrator ought to compel him to fill them up, if there seems to be a possibility of rainwater causing damage, and to condemn him if he fails to do so, even if no water has ever flowed down through the ditches in question prior to the arbitrator's passing judgment on the matter. 3. When lakes either increase or diminish in size, it is never permissible for the neighbors to do anything to them to increase or reduce the amount of water.

25 JULIAN, *From Minucius, book 5:* A person to whose land a right of way by cart is owed can bring an action in respect of that land to ward off rainwater from the right of way, since deterioration of the right of way represents damage to the land.

26 SCAEVOLA, *Replies, book 4:* Scaevola replied that those who are responsible for giving judgment normally uphold aqueducts to which antiquity of use gives some authority, even where their legal right to exist is not proved.

4

TAX FARMERS, *VECTIGALIA*, AND CONFISCATIONS

1 ULPIAN, *Edict, book 55:* The praetor says: "If a tax farmer or his *familia* takes anything by force in the name of the public revenue and it is not returned, I will grant a *judicium* against them for double the sum involved, or if the action is brought after the passage of a year, for the sum involved. Similarly, where loss is said to have been wrongfully inflicted or theft is said to have occurred, I shall grant a *judicium*. If the persons whom the matter in hand will concern are not brought before me, I shall grant a *judicium* without possibility of noxal surrender against the owners." 1. The present title related to tax farmers. Tax farmers are those who enjoy the use of public money (whence the name [*publicani*]), whether they pay *vectigal* to the treasury or collect tribute. In fact, all those who lease anything from the imperial treasury are correctly described as *publicani*. 2. Someone may ask why this edict is promulgated, as though the praetor had not elsewhere made provisions about thefts, losses, and robberies. The answer is that having regard to the type of case involved, he thought that he ought to promulgate an edict dealing specifically with tax farmers. 3. This edict is to some degree more lenient in that the penalty laid down is double the sum involved, whereas in the case of robbery of goods, as also in that of manifest theft, the penalty is quadruple. 4. And the tax farmer is given the opportunity of returning that which was taken by force, and if he does so, he is absolved from all obligation and freed from any penal action based on this part of the edict. The question arises, consequently, of whether someone can, if he so wishes, bring an action against a tax farmer on the basis not of this edict, but of the general one relating to robbery of goods, wrongfully inflicted injury, or theft. It is agreed that he can, and Pomponius also

writes that this is so, since it is ridiculous to hold that the legal position of tax farmers has been made better than that of other people. 5. The word *"familia"* in this context we take as referring not only to the slaves of tax farmers but to anyone who is one of their *familiares*; hence, any persons who work for tax farmers in matters of *vectigal*, be they freemen or slaves belonging to someone else, are covered by this edict. It follows, then, that if a slave who belongs to a tax farmer but is not part of the *familia* which works on public *vectigal* robs someone of something, the present edict will be inapplicable. 6. As for what the praetor says at the end, namely, "if they are not brought before me, I will grant a *judicium* without possibility of noxal surrender against the owners," it is a peculiarity of the present edict that if the slaves are not brought before the court, a *judicium* without possibility of noxal surrender is available, whether or not the defendants have the slaves in their power and whether or not they are able to bring them before the court.

2 GAIUS, *Provincial Edict, book 21:* Nor is it permissible for the owner to defend an absent slave.

3 ULPIAN, *Edict, book 55:* Although, if they had produced them, proceedings would have been instituted in a noxal *judicium*. The reason for imposing a condition of this severity is that tax farmers must select good slaves for this type of work. 1. The words "against the owners" should be interpreted as meaning "against the partners in *vectigal*-transactions," even if they are not owners. 2. The plaintiff must state beforehand which person or persons he wishes to be brought before the court so that if they are not brought, he can act accordingly. But if he says, "bring all of them so that I can pick out which one it is," I think that the request must be granted. 3. Where several slaves have committed the theft or caused the loss in question, the rule must be kept that release from liability is granted if that sum is paid which would be paid in the case of a single free man's misdeeds.

4 PAUL, *Edict, book 52:* Labeo says that if a tax farmer who has taken something by force dies, an action should be granted against his heir to the extent that the latter has become richer as a result. 1. On the subject of property which governors direct to be brought to them for their use, the deified Hadrian wrote to governors saying that when a provincial governor or a legionary commander or a procurator of such a person dispatches someone to make a purchase, he should indicate this in a memorandum signed in his own hand and should send this memorandum to a tax farmer so that anything that is brought in excess of what was ordered can be subject to tax. 2. It is normal for customary usage to be taken into account in almost all matters concerning *vectigal*, and this is also assured in imperial *constitutiones*.

5 GAIUS, *Urban Praetor's Edict, Chapter on Tax Farmers:* The present edict provides that if the property in question is returned before the grant of a *judicium* the action lapses, but if it is returned after the grant of a *judicium*, the penalty continues to apply nonetheless. However, someone who is prepared to make restitution after the grant of a *judicium* should also be released from liability. 1. We may ask whether the double damages are purely a matter of penalty with action to recover the property available in addition or whether recovery of the property is included in the double damages, so that the penalty is only single damages. We prefer the view that the property is included in the double damages.

6 MODESTINUS, *Penalties, book 2:* If a number of tax farmers has been involved in making an illegal exaction, the action for double damages is not multiplied; instead, all shall pay their share and anything that one cannot pay will be exacted from another in accordance with a rescript of the deified Severus and Antoninus, who determined that there is a considerable difference between criminal defendants and participants in a fraud.

7 PAPIRIUS JUSTUS, *Constitutions, book 2:* The Emperors Antoninus and Verus stated in a rescript that in matters of *vectigal* it is the estates themselves and not individuals that are the object of legal proceedings and that, consequently, those in possession at

any time have to pay any *vectigal* accumulated in the past, though, if they are ignorant of there being such an accumulation, they will be able to bring an action on sale. 1. They also stated in a rescript that they were waiving the penalty of confiscation against a *pupillus* if the latter paid the *vectigal* within thirty days.

8 PAPINIAN, *Replies, book 13:* The offense of fraud in relation to *vectigal* is transmitted to the heir of the person who committed the fraud on the basis of confiscation. 1. But if there are several heirs and one of them purloins property which is common to them all and is burdened with *vectigal*, the rest do not have their shares taken away.

9 PAUL, *Views, book 5:* Where the heat of competition has led a bidder to offer a contract for *vectigal* above the usual level, this contract should still be allowed, provided the victorious bidder is prepared to offer satisfactory verbal guarantors and a *cautio*. 1. No one is to be compelled against his will to lease collection of *vectigal*; hence, when the time limit on a contract has expired, the *vectigalia* must be leased out afresh. 2. Tax farmers who have failed to produce all the *vectigal* they have contracted for are not to be permitted to make a fresh contract until they have fulfilled the existing one. 3. Debtors of the imperial treasury and similarly of the *respublica* are not allowed to make a contract for collection of *vectigal*; this is to prevent there being an additional cause for their debts to increase. An exception is made if they produce verbal guarantors who are prepared to settle their existing debts. 4. Where partners in *vectigal*-collection administer their shares of the contract separately, one of them can legally petition to have the share of another who is of doubtful solvency transferred to himself. 5. Any illegal exaction, private or public, is paid back to the victims with as much again; but where the extortion was made by force, the restitution is threefold; those responsible are in addition liable to extraordinary criminal punishment. The one measure is demanded by the interests of private individuals, the other by the need for strong public discipline. 6. *Vectigal* cannot be demanded on property on which it has never been paid; but where one tax farmer has carelessly omitted to collect something that is normally paid, another tax farmer is not forbidden to effect the collection. 7. It is established that property provided for the army is not subject to payment of *vectigal*. 8. The imperial treasury is exempt from payment of any sort of *vectigal*. However, merchants who normally deal in treasury property cannot claim any exemption from payment of public *vectigal*.

10 HERMOGENIAN, *Epitome, book 5:* Without imperial instructions neither a governor nor a curator nor a local senate can establish *vectigalia* or modify existing ones either by increase or the reverse. 1. Where payment of *vectigal* has not been completed, the contractors may be expelled even when the period of the contract has not yet expired; or interest can be demanded from them for their delay.

11 PAUL, *Views, book 5:* It is also not permissible to sell flint for striking fire to the enemy, just as it is not permissible to sell them iron, wheat, or salt; and the penalty for doing so is capital. 1. Public lands held under a permanent lease cannot be reclaimed by a curator without imperial authority. 2. If either the owner of a ship or passengers on it bring anything on board illegally, the ship is forfeit to the imperial treasury as well. But if something of the sort is done, in the absence of the owner, by the master or steersman or the pilot or any of the sailors, the latter are liable to capital punishment, and the goods are confiscated, but the ship is returned to its owner. 3. Pursuit of a claim in a matter of illegal merchandise affects an heir as well. 4. The

owner of property which has been confiscated is not forbidden to purchase it either in person or through persons to whom he has given a mandate. 5. Those tax farmers who have made great profits from collection of *vectigal* are to be compelled to take on collection at the previous rate if a contract for the same amount cannot subsequently be placed.

12 ULPIAN, *Edict, book 38:* Nobody is unaware of the extent of the audacity and insolence of cliques of tax farmers. This is the reason why the praetor promulgated this edict to control their audacity. 1. "Where a tax farmer's *familia* is alleged to have committed theft or has caused wrongful injury, if the persons whom the matter in hand will concern are not brought before me, I will grant a *judicium* without possibility of noxal surrender against the owner." 2. It should be understood that in this context the title *"familia"* covers the tax farmer's slaves. However, if somebody else's slave is serving as a slave of a tax farmer in good faith, he is included as well. Perhaps, this is also so if he is serving as his slave in bad faith, since wandering and fugitive slaves are often even knowingly employed in this kind of work. Consequently, even if a freeman is serving as a slave, the present edict will be relevant. 3. The term "tax farmer" is used of those who have contracts for collecting public *vectigal*.

13 GAIUS, *Provincial Edict, book 13:* However, people who have saltworks, chalk-pits, and mines also count as *publicani*. 1. In addition, the present edict is also relevant in the case of someone who has secured a contract for collecting *vectigal* from the public authorities of a municipality. 2. Even if someone sells or manumits a slave or if the slave takes to flight, he will be liable on the slave's account for having such a disorderly *familia*. 3. But what happens if the slave has died? Is the tax farmer liable on account of that slave's actions? I hold that since he has no way of bringing him before the court and since no fraud on his part is involved, the tax farmer should be freed of obligation. 4. We grant this action as a perpetual one, passing to heirs and other successors.

14 ULPIAN, *Disputations, book 8:* Confiscation inflicted in connection with *vectigal* is transmitted to the heir as well. For that which is confiscated immediately ceases to belong to the person who committed the crime, ownership of it being acquired by the treasury. Consequently, the right to execute confiscation is available against an heir just as against any sort of possessor.

15 ALFENUS VARUS, *Digest, book 7:* When Caesar leased the whetstone quarries on the island of Crete, he laid down the following rule: "After the Ides of March, nobody except a lessee is to excavate, remove, or take away any flint from the island of Crete." A ship belonging to a certain individual set out from port in Crete before the Ides of March loaded with flints but was driven back to port by the wind and later set out again after the Ides of March. Advice was sought as to whether the flints should be considered to have been illegally exported after the Ides of March. He replied that although all the ports which are in an island are held also to belong to that island, nonetheless, a person who set out from port before the Ides of March and was carried back to the island by a storm should not be held to have broken the law if he then left again, the grounds being that the flints should be considered to have been exported at the outset, since the ship also left port then.

16 MARCIAN, *Delatores, sole book:* Sometimes a slave who has become subject to confiscation should not be sold, but instead his value as assessed should be paid by his owner. For the deified Severus and Antoninus stated in a rescript that when a slave who is alleged to have carried out a transaction of his owner's has become subject to confiscation, he ought not to be sold, but instead his value as assessed by an honest citizen should be paid. 1. The same emperors directed in the same letter that if a slave has not declared himself and is proved to be subject to confiscation, and if he is alleged to have corrupted his owner's wife or committed some other serious offense, a procurator should investigate the matter; and if the slave is discovered to be in this situation, his value should be assessed, and he should be handed over to his owner for

punishment. 2. The same deified Severus and Antoninus directed in a rescript that when slaves are confiscated the property in their *peculium* is not affected, except for such of it as is involved on its own account in the grounds of confiscation. 3. Where somebody fails to declare slaves in transit for sale or use by someone else, a penalty of confiscation is applicable, provided that they are new slaves, not old ones. Old slaves are defined as those who have been slaves in the city for a year continuously; new slaves are taken to be those who have not yet been slaves for a year. 4. Fugitive slaves do not fall liable to confiscation since they broke bounds without their owner's consent. This provision is made in imperial *constitutiones*, as the deified Pius frequently stated in rescripts, to stop a slave having the power to remove himself from his owner's control by taking to flight without the owner's knowledge or consent. 5. The deified Hadrian determined that even though one alleges ignorance, nonetheless, one is liable to a penalty arising from *vectigal*. 6. The deified Marcus and Commodus also stated in a rescript that a tax farmer should not be blamed for failing to instruct someone who broke the law, but that care should be taken that he does not mislead those who are willing to make a declaration. 7. Types of goods liable to *vectigal*: cinnamon; long pepper; white pepper; pentasphaerum leaf; barbary leaf; costum; costamomum; nard; stachys; Tyrian casia; casia-wood; myrrh; amomum; ginger; malabrathrum; Indic spice; galbanum; asafoetida juice; aloe; lycium; Persian gum; Arabian onyx; cardamonum; cinnamon-wood; cotton goods; Babylonian hides; Persian hides; ivory; Indian iron; linen; all sorts of gem: pearl, sardonyx, ceraunium, hyacinth stone, emerald, diamond, sapphire, turquoise, beryl, tortoise stone; Indian or Assyrian drugs; raw silk; silk or half-silk clothing; embroidered fine linen; silk thread; Indian eununchs; lions; lionesses; pards; leopards; panthers; purple dye; also: Moroccan wool; dye; Indian hair. 8. The deified brothers stated in a rescript that if bad weather necessitated the dumping of a cargo, it should not be claimed in confiscation. 9. The deified Pius also stated in a rescript that when somebody who claimed that he was within the statutory age limits had brought some slaves for his own use and had merely made an error in his declaration, he should be pardoned. 10. The deified brothers also stated in a rescript that where it is through error and not fraud that someone has become liable to confiscation, the tax farmers should be satisfied with double *vectigal* and restore his slaves. 11. But Antoninus the Great stated in a rescript that if a tax farmer or the slaves of a property owner illegally dig for iron on the premises without the owner's knowledge, the owner is not liable to any penalty. 12. The deified Severus and Antoninus stated in a rescript that if someone has made a declaration to a tax farmer but fails to pay the *vectigal* and the tax farmer allows this to pass, as they often do, the property does not become liable to confiscation since, they say, once the declarations are received, the possibility of confiscation lapses because it will be possible to meet the demands of the imperial treasury from the goods of the tax farmers or their verbal guarantors. 13. Penalties cannot be claimed from heirs if the investigation was not started during the lifetime of the person who did wrong. This rule applies to penalties arising from *vectigal* as it does to other types of penalty.   14. The deified Severus and Antoninus stated in a rescript that if an error on the part of the person making payment leads to a tax farmer receiving something that is not due, the latter is obligated to return it.

5

GIFTS

1   JULIAN, *Digest, book 17:* There are several types of gift. When someone makes a gift with the intention that it should immediately become the property of the recipient and will not revert to himself in any circumstances, and when he does this for no other reason than to practice liberality and generosity, this is a gift in the proper sense. When someone makes a gift with the intention that it should become the property of the recipient only after something else has happened, this will not be a gift in the proper sense but an altogether conditional one. Again, when someone makes a gift with the intention that it should immediately become the property of the recipient but that if something else does or does not happen, it should revert to himself, this is not a gift in the proper sense but altogether one made under a resolutive condition. A gift *mortis causa* is of this sort.   1. Therefore, when we say that a gift between betrothed persons is valid, we are using the term in the proper sense and indicating an action proceeding from a party who is making a gift from motives of liberality, intending the gift to become immediately the property of the recipient and not wishing it to revert to himself in any circumstances. But when we say that return of a gift can be requested if it was made between betrothed persons on the understanding that should the marriage not take place, the property would be taken away, we are not contradicting what was said above but allowing that a gift under resolutive conditions can be made between such persons.

2   JULIAN, *Digest, book 60:* If a son-in-power who wishes to make a gift of money undertakes to pay it on his father's instructions, the gift is valid, just as if he had furnished a verbal guarantor.   1. But if a father who intends to give a gift of money to Titius directs his son to undertake to promise it, it can be said to make a difference whether or not the son is in debt to his father, since, if he is in debt to his father for the same amount that he undertakes to give to Titius, the gift is held to be valid, just as if the father had directed any other debtor to undertake to promise the money to Titius.   2. However, if I intend to give a gift of money to Titius and you want to make me a gift of the same size and I direct you to promise the money to Titius, the gift is completed between all the individuals involved.   3. The legal position will be different where, on your instructions, I undertake to give to someone to whom you wish to make a gift money which I thought I owed to you, since I will be able to protect myself by means of a defense of fraud and, in addition, I can use a *condictio incepti* to compel the stipulator to release me from the stipulation.   4. Similarly, if, on your instructions I promise to give to someone whom you think to be your creditor money which I thought I owed you, I will be able to meet the claim of the petitioner by means of a defense of fraud and in addition by bringing an action *incepti* against the stipulator, I will ensure that he formally releases me from the stipulation.   5. If Titius gives me money without any stipulation but on condition that the money becomes mine when Seius is elected consul, then the money will be mine when Seius acquires the consulship, even if the donor is then insane or dead.   6. But if someone who intends to make me a gift of money gives it to somebody to bring to me and then dies before this is done, it is established that the money does not come into my ownership.   7. I gave Titius ten on condition that he use it to buy himself Stichus. I ask: Is there any action by which I can recover the ten if Stichus dies before being purchased? I replied: This is

an issue of fact rather than of law. If I gave Titius the ten for the purpose of buying Stichus and would not otherwise have given them him, I can sue for return of the money by means of *condictio* if Stichus dies. But if I was intending to give Titius the ten in any case and, because, in the meantime, he proposed to purchase Stichus, I then said that I was making the gift to enable him to do so, this will have to be considered rather a reason for the gift than a condition imposed upon the giving of the money and the latter will remain with Titius even in the event of Stichus's death.

3 ULPIAN, *Edict, book 76:* Indeed, in matters of gift, it is as a general rule to be reckoned an issue of great importance whether there is a reason for the making of the gift or a condition imposed upon it. In the former case, suit for recovery is inapplicable; in the latter, it will be in place.

4 POMPONIUS, *Sabinus, book 17:* A gift can be accomplished even through an intermediary.

5 ULPIAN, *Sabinus, book 32:* Neither honorable nor dishonorable gifts are forbidden where they are made on grounds of affection. Honorable gifts are those made to deserving friends and relations; dishonorable ones, those made to prostitutes.

6 ULPIAN, *Sabinus, book 42:* If someone permits me, by way of gift, to remove stone from his property, the stone becomes mine as soon as it is removed, and he cannot stop it becoming mine by preventing me from taking it away since it has become mine in a sense by delivery. Obviously, if a hired employee of mine removes the stone he does so for me. However, if someone purchases or hires from me the right to remove the stone on his own account and I then regret the decision before he has removed it, the stone remains my property; but if I regret the decision after he has removed it, I cannot revoke his action since a sort of delivery is held to have occurred when the stone is removed with its owner's consent. What applies in the case of stone will also apply in cases concerning cut or uprooted trees.

7 ULPIAN, *Sabinus, book 44:* A son-in-power cannot make a gift even if he has the right of free administration of his *peculium* since such a right is not granted for him to dissipate his property.   1. But what happens if he is induced by a good reason to make a gift? Can it be held that such a gift is in place? The preferable view is that it can. 2. Again, let us consider whether a gift is valid if one grants a son-in-power free administration of his *peculium* with the specific provision that the grant is such that he can make gifts as well. I do not doubt that in these circumstances he can make a gift as well.   3. Sometimes this conclusion can be drawn from the type of person involved. Imagine the son of someone of senatorial or other high rank. Why should one not hold that his father has granted him the right to make gifts, unless he specifically excludes such a right, provided that he has granted him free administration of his *peculium*? 4. The same reasoning which forbids a son-in-power to make a gift also forbids him to make a gift *mortis causa*, since, although he can make a gift *mortis causa* as well with his father's consent, where that consent is lacking, such a gift will be barred.   5. For it will have to be remembered that even if someone is permitted to make a gift, he cannot make one *mortis causa* unless the permission to do so has been specifically granted.   6. All these regulations apply to civilians. Those, on the other hand, who have a *castrense peculium* or a quasi-*castrense peculium* are in a position to make gifts both *mortis causa* and otherwise, since they have the right to make a will.

8   PAUL, *Sabinus, book 15:* Dues paid by freedmen which are imposed in order to obtain their freedom do not count as a gift since something substantial is obtained in return for them.

9   POMPONIUS, *Sabinus, book 33:* To live free of charge in someone else's house is considered to be a gift, since a person in this position is held to gain in that he does not pay rent for his right of habitation. A gift can be valid even where it does not involve the giving of a physical object, for example, if, by way of gift, I make a pact with a debtor not to demand payment before a certain date.   1. Income received from property given as a gift is not counted in assessing the size of the gift. But if I give you not a landed estate, but permission to gather the fruits of it, the fruits gathered are counted in assessing the size of the gift.   2. Any gift made by a son-in-power on the instructions of or with the consent of his father has the same standing as if the father made the gift himself or as if you gave some property of mine to Titius in your own name with my consent.   3. A gift cannot be made unless that which is given becomes the property of the recipient.

10   PAUL, *Sabinus, book 15:* A gift can legally be made to an absent party either by sending someone to take him the gift or by instructing him to keep for himself something that he already has. But if he is unaware that the property which is in his possession has been given to him or if he fails to receive something sent to him, he does not become the owner of the gifted property, even if it was sent by the hand of his own slave, unless it was given to the slave on the understanding that it immediately became his.

11   GAIUS, *Urban Praetor's Edict, book 3, Chapter on Legacies:* When a question arises about the size of a gift, no gift is held to have been made in respect of offspring, fruits, rent, or wages.

12   ULPIAN, *Disputations, book 3:* When someone has bound himself to make a gift he can, under a rescript of the deified Pius, be sued for as much as he can afford; for anything that is owed to creditors will have to be subtracted. However, he ought not to subtract anything that he is similarly bound to give to someone else.

13   ULPIAN, *Disputations, book 7:* Somebody who wished to make me a gift handed the property in question to a slave jointly owned by me and Titius. The slave received it, understanding that he was getting it either for my co-owner or for both of us together. The question arose of what the legal result of the transaction was. It is agreed that although the slave received the property on the understanding that he was getting it either for my co-owner or for both of us together, nonetheless, he got it for me; for in the case also in which the donor handed the property to a procurator of mine on the understanding that the latter was getting it for me but the procurator received it as though he were getting it for himself, the latter achieves nothing in his own person but gets the property for me.

14   JULIAN, *Digest, book 17:* Someone who cultivates another person's land by way of gift will have no right of retention on grounds of expense incurred since he causes anything that he introduces onto the land to become immediately the property of its owner.

15   MARCIAN, *Institutes, book 3:* Gifts made after the commission of a capital offense are invalid, under a *constitutio* of the deified Severus and Antoninus, since they are canceled if condemnation results.

16   ULPIAN, *Replies, book 2:* Under the following testamentary provision, "let my heirs know that while alive I have made a gift to my freedmen 'X' and 'Y' of all my wardrobe and such other possessions as I have with me at the time of my death," ownership of the said items, by a liberal interpretation, belongs to the said freedmen.

17   ULPIAN, *Edict, book 58:* If the result of a judicial decision has been incorporated into a stipulation by way of novation and formal release of the stipulation is made by way of gift, it should be held that discharge of the debt has occurred.

18   ULPIAN, *Edict, book 71:* Aristo says that when a business transaction is combined with a gift, no obligation is contracted insofar as a gift is involved. Pomponius also reports that Aristo held this view.   1. Next he quotes Aristo as thinking that if I deliver a slave to you on the understanding that you manumit him after five years have passed, no action can be brought before the five years is up since an element of gift is held to be involved. The situation is different, he says, from the one in which I deliver the slave to you on the understanding that you manumit him immediately since in that case no element of gift comes into it and an obligation exists. But Pomponius says that even in the former case the nature of the act should be investigated since it may be that the five-year period was not imposed with a view to the making of a gift.   2. The same Aristo says that if a slave is delivered by way of gift on the understanding that he be manumitted after five years have elapsed but the slave belongs to someone else, it is doubtful whether he can be acquired by usucapion, since an element of gift is involved. Pomponius says that this type of problem arises in questions of gift *mortis causa* and prefers the view that if the slave is given on the understanding that he be manumitted after five years have elapsed, it can be held that usucapion applies.   3. Labeo says that if someone gives me another person's property and I incur large expenses on its account and it is then recovered from me by judicial process, no action is available to me against the donor, though, of course, I can bring an action of fraud against him if he acted in bad faith.

19   ULPIAN, *Edict, book 76:* We follow the rule that when a question arises about a gift in the context of public affairs, consideration will be given only to whether or not the donor made an undertaking or promise to the *respublica* for good cause; thus, if he did so in order to obtain some office, he is liable, if not, not.   1. Labeo writes that recompense for services of the sort, "if I support you," "if I give security for you," "if in any matter you make use of my services or influence," does not come within the category of gift.   2. A gift given as an act of liberality cannot be acquired by someone who does not want it.   3. If someone lends Titius money to be repaid to Seius to whom he wishes to make a gift, and Titius is then said to have given it to Seius after the donor's death, it follows that one should hold the money to belong to Seius, whether or not Titius knew the donor to be dead, since the money belonged to the transferor. But if, in fact, he did not know that the donor was dead, he is freed from his obligation, whereas if he did know, he is not freed. But if I directed you to give money to Titius to whom I wished to give a gift, and you did so, unaware that I had died, you will be able to bring an action on mandate against my heirs; but if you did so, knowing that I had died, you will not be able to bring such an action.   4. If someone lends money to a slave and the slave then becomes free and undertakes to pay it back, this will be not a gift, but a payment of a debt. The same should be said to apply in the case of a *pupillus* who contracts a debt without his tutor's *auctoritas*, if he later undertakes to repay it with his tutor's *auctoritas*.   5. However, stipulations which are made with some purpose in mind also contain no element of gift.   6. Finally, Pegasus held that if I promise one hundred to you by *sponsio*, on condition that you have sworn to take my name, this is not a gift since it is made for a consideration and that consideration has been obtained.

20   MARCELLUS, *Digest, book 22:* If a patron has been appointed heir in his due share and his freedman directs him by *fideicommissum* to make a gift, even if, in response to the stipulation of the *fideicommissarius*, he undertakes to do so, he will not be compelled to pay, to prevent diminution of the share which is due by statute from respect for one's patron.   1. A doubt may arise about someone who follows a testator's wishes and undertakes to make a gift of something which, under the terms of the *lex Falcidia*, he could have kept for himself. But the preferable opinion is that he cannot go

against his confession. For just as if he had paid he would be held to have accepted the trust of the testator and no suit for recovery would be granted to him, so by allowing the stipulation to stand he is rightly prevented from breaking the trust of the testator which he accepted.

21   CELSUS, *Digest, book 28:* On my delegation, you made an undertaking to a creditor of mine for the purpose of making me a gift. This action is valid, since the creditor receives what is his.   1. But if I have directed a debtor of mine to make an undertaking to you by way of giving you an excessive gift, there will be an issue as to whether or not you can be resisted by means of a defense of gift. My debtor, in any event, cannot successfully resist you by means of a defense, if you bring an action, since I am in the same position as if I had given you a sum of money exacted from my debtor and you had lent the sum to him. However, so long as no money has yet been paid by my debtor, I can bring a rescissory action against him in respect of anything he undertook to give beyond the limit prescribed by law, so that he remains obligated to you only for the balance. But if you have exacted money from my debtor, I can employ a *condictio* against you in respect of anything that exceeds the limit prescribed by law.

22   MODESTINUS, *Distinctions, book 8:* It is entirely fair for someone who undertakes to give money or anything else by way of gift not to owe interest because of any delay in making the payment, especially since the category "gift" is not included in the class of bonae fidei contracts.

23   MODESTINUS, *Replies, book 15:* Modestinus replied that a creditor can remit or reduce by pact the amount of interest owing in the future and that in this sort of gift there can be no question of defect in respect of the size of the amount involved. 1. Modestinus implied that a person mentally afflicted cannot make a gift.

24   JAVOLENUS, *From Cassius, book 14:* The verbal guarantor of someone who has made an undertaking to give money by way of gift in excess of the limit prescribed by law should be granted a defense, even if the defendant is unwilling, to ensure that the former does not lose money if the latter should turn out to be insolvent.

25   JAVOLENUS, *Letters, book 6:* If I have given you some property to give to Titius in my name and you give it to him in your own name, do you think that the property becomes Titius's? He replied that if I have given you some property to give to Titius in my name and you give it to him in your own name, as far as a strict interpretation of law goes, the property does not become the recipient's and you will be liable to a charge of theft. However, the more liberal view is that if I were to bring an action against the recipient, I would be successfully opposed by a defense of fraud.

26   POMPONIUS, *Quintus Mucius, book 4:* A simple statement in an account does not make one a debtor. For example, even if we record in our accounts that we owe something of which we intend to make a gift to a freeman, nonetheless, no gift is considered to have been made.

27   PAPINIAN, *Questions, book 29:* A young man called Aquilius Regulus wrote to the rhetor Nicostratus as follows: "In view of the fact that you were always with my father and that you benefited me by your eloquence and attention, I give and grant to you the right to live in and make use of such and such an apartment." When Regulus died Nicostratus was subjected to a dispute about his right of habitation and when he consulted me on the matter, I said that it was a defensible view that it was not a case of simple gift but that Regulus had rewarded Nicostratus's services as *magister* with a specific recompense and that, consequently, the gift should not be held to be invalid at any future date. But if Nicostratus had been actually expelled and had applied to a judge, he would have had to be defended, on the model of the interdict that is applied to a usufructuary, along the lines that he was in the position of a possessor in that he had received the right to use the apartment.

28   PAPINIAN, *Replies, book 3:* A man made a gift of an inheritance which he had received to his daughter who had been made independent. The daughter has to satisfy any creditors of the estate, or if she completely fails to do so and the creditors bring a suit against her father, she must be compelled by an *actio praescriptis verbis* to defend him against them.

29 PAPINIAN, *Replies, book 12:* Anything that is granted to someone without legal compulsion counts as a gift. 1. While being interrogated in court, a man replied that the heirs of his tutor owed him nothing. I replied that he had lost his right of action of tutelage since, although one might take these words to signify not a *transactio* but a gift, nonetheless, somebody who makes a confession in court cannot annul that confession. 2. It has been established that a gift of part of the goods of one's newest female cognatic relative while she is still alive is invalid. But he replied that actions on the inheritance should be totally denied to anyone who has made such a gift and later succeeds to the estate by praetorian law, since his premature action is against good morals and the law of nations.

30 MARCIAN, *Delatores, sole book:* For the inheritance should be taken away from him on the grounds that he is unfit to have it.

31 PAPINIAN, *Replies, book 12:* It is accepted that gifts made to a concubine cannot be revoked and that if a marriage is later contracted between the same two parties, that which was previously legally valid does not lapse into invalidity. I replied that the question of whether marital honor and affection existed previously should be considered in the light of the persons involved and their union in life, since it is not documents that make a marriage. 1. I replied that goods in addition to dowry given by a woman in her daughter's name to her daughter's husband in her daughter's presence should be considered as having been given to the daughter in person and passed on by her to her husband and that if the mother takes offense, she has no right of recovery and cannot legally make a *vindicatio* of the goods on the grounds that the husband had given a *cautio* that the goods were delivered to him in addition to dowry for the girl's use, since this statement does not amount to a declaration of a limitation on the gift or a separation of ownership from use, but to a distinction between the girl's *peculium* and her dowry. However, if the mother's desire to revoke the gift derives from an offense which justifies the revocation in law, the judge should make a valuation and render a decision appropriate to the respect properly to be felt toward a mother and in accordance with the judgment of a sound citizen. 2. A man who had given some slaves to his daughter-in-power and who did not take away her *peculium* when she was emancipated was held to have completed the gift ex post facto. 3. In a case in which a chest was deposited in a temple on condition that only the depositor or, after the owner's death, Aelius Speratus should remove it, I replied that no gift should be held to have been executed. 4. Gifts made after the commission of an offense of *perduellio* cannot be considered valid even if the defendant dies before being arraigned in court, since such an offense affects the heir as well.

32 SCAEVOLA, *Replies, book 5:* Lucius Titius sent the following letter: "'X' to 'Y,' health. You may use such and such an apartment together with all the rooms above free of charge. This letter is to notify you that you have my consent to do this." Can the heirs prevent the receipient of this letter from enjoying his right of habitation? He replied that given the facts stated above, the heirs can alter Titius's intention.

33 HERMOGENIAN, *Epitome of Law, book 6:* Somebody who has made a *constitutum* to pay what he has undertaken in response to a stipulation made by way of gift can be taken to court in an action on the *constitutum*, not for the whole sum, but for as much as he can pay, since it is agreed that it is the cause and origin of the *constitutum* to pay the money and not the power of the *judicium* that prevails. Someone condemned in an action on judgment arising from a gift can also expect to succeed in a request to be sued only for what he can pay. 1. Where money is paid to Titius by way of gift on condition that it be loaned immediately to the donor, the transfer of ownership is not hindered; consequently, when the money in question has been lent to the donor, it is under new ownership. 2. The mute and deaf are not forbidden to make gifts. 3. When

"A" wishes to make a gift to you and you wish to make a gift to "B," if, with your consent, "A" makes an undertaking in response to a stipulation from "B," the gift is completed; and if "A" fails to give "B" anything and "B" sues him, condemnation can be inflicted on him for the whole sum and not for just as much as he can pay. The same rule is maintained if the circumstances of the donor's undertaking were that the intended recipient delegated the donor to his own creditor, since in this case also the creditor is transacting his own business.

34   PAUL, *Views, book 5:* If a man lends money at interest in the name of his emancipated son with the purpose of making the latter a gift and if the son makes a stipulation regarding the money, there can be no doubt that the gift is legally perfected. 1. If one rescues somebody from robbers or enemies and receives something from him in recognition of this action, this is an irrevocable gift and should not be described as a reward for outstanding service, since it is not accepted that regard for safety be valued at any particular amount.

35   SCAEVOLA, *Digest, book 31:* A man wrote as follows to a slave whom he had manumitted: "Titus to Stichus his freedman, health. This letter, written in my own hand, is to notify you that, in view of the fact that I have manumitted you, I also grant you all such *peculium* as you have in credits, movable property and cash." He also appointed the same freedman in his will as heir to two thirds of the estate, while making Sempronius heir to one third; but he did not bequeath the *peculium* to Stichus, nor did he direct that he be granted the actions arising out of that *peculium*. The question arises whether Stichus should be granted an action for the whole amount of the credits in his *peculium* or whether an action should be granted to both heirs in proportion to their shares of the inheritance. I replied that given the facts as stated above, an action is available to both heirs in proportion to their shares of the inheritance.   1. Lucius Titius gave a piece of land to Maevia. A few days later, and before the delivery, he hypothecated the same piece of land to Seius; then, within thirty days, he gave Maevia vacant possession of it. Is the gift properly completed? He replied that given the facts as stated above, it is, but that the creditor has a secure entitlement to the *hypotheca*.   2. A grandmother lent money under the name of her grandson Labeo and always received the interest on it and got the documents pertaining to the debts from Labeo. These were later found in his inheritance. Is the gift to be held to have been properly completed? He replied that since the debtor was bound to Labeo, the gift was properly completed.

6

GIFTS AND ACQUISITIONS *MORTIS CAUSA*

1   MARCIAN, *Institutes, book 9:* A gift *mortis causa* occurs when one wishes to have the property oneself rather than let the donee have it but even more wishes the donee to have it in preference to one's heir.   1. This is the sort of gift that Telemachus makes to Piraeus in Homer.

2   ULPIAN, *Sabinus, book 32:* Julian, in the seventeenth book of his *Digest,* says that there are three types of gift *mortis causa.* The first is when one makes a gift because of apprehension aroused not by some imminent danger, but simply by reflection on mortality. Another type of gift *mortis causa,* he says, is when, disturbed by imminent danger of some sort, one makes a gift in such a way that it becomes the recipient's property immediately. A third type of gift *mortis causa,* he says, is when, disturbed by imminent danger of some sort, one makes a gift in such a way that it becomes the recipient's property not immediately, but in the event of one's death.

3   PAUL, *Sabinus, book 7:* It is permissible to make a gift *mortis causa* not only on grounds of weak health but also on grounds of impending danger of death due to enemies or robbers or the cruelty or hatred of a powerful man or when about to undertake a sea voyage,

4   GAIUS, *Common Matters or Golden Words, book 1:* or to travel through dangerous places,

5   ULPIAN, *Institutes, book 2:* or when one is worn out by old age,

6   PAUL, *Sabinus, book 7:* since all these circumstances represent impending danger.

7   ULPIAN, *Sabinus, book 32:* If someone makes a gift *mortis causa* and is then condemned to a capital punishment, the gift is set aside as imperfect, even though other gifts made before the suspicion arose of liability to such a punishment are valid.

8   ULPIAN, *Sabinus, book 7:* Anyone who accepts money and passes up an inheritance is held to gain *mortis causa,* whether the estate was going to pass from him to a substitute or he was going to succeed *ab intestato,* since anything that falls to a person because of somebody's death is acquired *mortis causa.* Julian also approves this opinion, and this is the rule that we follow. For even anything received by a *statuliber* for the purpose of fulfilling a condition or by a legatee is an acquisition *mortis causa.* Julian wrote that anything which a father gives on account of the death of his son or a cognatic relative is also acquired *mortis causa.*   1. Finally, he says that a gift can also be made such that if the donor gets better, the gift is taken back.

9   PAUL, *Sabinus, book 3:* Anyone who can accept legacies is allowed to make acquisitions *mortis causa.*

10   ULPIAN, *Sabinus, book 24:* It is established that a substitute can be introduced for someone to whom a gift *mortis causa* has been made by the latter undertaking to give it to someone else if he himself cannot receive it or under some other condition.

11   ULPIAN, *Sabinus, book 33:* A man can legally r   gift *mortis causa* to his daughter-in-law in respect of his son's death even   on's marriage continues.

12   ULPIAN, *Sabinus, book 44:* Julian quite frequent   s that if a woman receives

money to make a fraudulent request for *missio in possessionem* in the name of her unborn child, for example, while she is supporting the claim of a substitute, in order to exclude the appointed heir on some ground or other, she is making an acquisition *mortis causa.*

13 JULIAN, *Digest, book 17:* If I make a gift *mortis causa* of someone else's property and that property is acquired by usucapion, the real owner cannot bring a *condictio* for it, but I can do so in the event of my getting better. 1. MARCELLUS notes: questions of fact can also arise in cases of gift *mortis causa.* For gifts *mortis causa* can be made both such that if the donor dies of his illness, the gift is not to be returned in any circumstances and such that it is to be returned even if the donor dies of the illness in question, provided that he had changed his mind and wished it to be returned to him. A gift *mortis causa* can also be made with the condition that it is to be returned only if the recipient dies first. A gift *mortis causa* can also be made such that there is no right of recovery in any circumstances, that is, not even if the donor gets better.

14 JULIAN, *Digest, book 18:* If a piece of land is given *mortis causa* and necessary and useful expenses are incurred in connection with it, those who make a *vindicatio* of the land can be resisted by means of a defense of fraud, unless they reimburse those expenses.

15 JULIAN, *Digest, book 27:* MARCELLUS notes: Since sons-in-power who are in the army have secured the unrestricted right of willing property to whomsoever they wish, one may believe that any limitations on the making of gifts *mortis causa* are also relaxed. PAUL notes: This has also been decided by imperial constitution, and gifts *mortis causa* have been brought into line with legacies.

16 JULIAN, *Digest, book 29:* A gift *mortis causa* can be revoked even while it is still in the balance whether the donor can get better.

17 JULIAN, *Digest, book 47:* Even where a debtor had no intention of defrauding his creditors, property given by him *mortis causa* must be taken away, since, granted that legacies under the will of someone who is insolvent are quite invalid, it can be held that gifts *mortis causa* ought also to be rescinded, on the grounds that they bear a resemblance to legacies.

18 JULIAN, *Digest, book 60:* We make acquisitions *mortis causa* not only when someone makes a gift on account of his own death but also when he does so on account of someone else's, for example, if someone gives Maevius a gift when his own son or brother is ill on the condition that if either of them gets better, the property is to be returned, but if either dies, it remains with Maevius. 1. If, intending to make me a gift *mortis causa,* you delegate a debtor of yours to a creditor of mine, I shall without question be regarded as receiving as much money as is necessary to free me from my creditor. However, if I make a stipulation for receipt of money from the said debtor, I shall be regarded as receiving a gift only to the extent that the debtor is solvent, since, even if the creditor, who is also the donor, gets better, he will only recover the debtor's obligation by means of a *condictio* or an action *in factum.* 2. Wishing to give her debtors Septicius and Maevius their documents of debt, Titia gave them to Ageria and asked her to give them to Septicius and Maevius in the event of her death but to return them to her in the event of her getting better. After Titia's death Maevia, her daughter, became her heir. But Ageria gave the documents to the above-mentioned Septicius and Maevius, as she had been requested to do. The question arises of whether, if the heiress Maevia seeks to obtain the sum owed under the above-mentioned documents, or the documents themselves, there is any defense by which she can be barred. I replied that Maevia can be resisted by a defense either of pact made or of fraud. 3. Where someone has received *mortis causa* a slave who is liable to noxal surrender or under some other obligation, he is to be taken as having received as much as the slave can be sold for. The same rule can be observed in the case of a piece of land which is encumbered in order to discover the value of the gift.

19 JULIAN, *Digest, book 80:* If property has been given *mortis causa* to a son-in-power and the donor gets better, he can bring an action on *peculium* against the father. But

if the head of a household receives a gift *mortis causa* and then allows himself to be adopted, the property itself can be reclaimed by the donor. The case of someone who receives a gift *mortis causa* and then gives it to somebody else is not similar, since the donor would in that case bring a *condictio* against the latter not for the property, but for its value.

20   JULIAN, *Urseius Ferox, book 1:* A piece of land was left as a legacy to someone who could not receive more than a part of it on the condition that he gave ten to the heir. He does not have to give the whole of that sum in order to get only part of the land, but only a part of it in proportion to the amount of the legacy that he secures.

21   JULIAN, *Urseius Ferox, book 2:* Most authorities, among them Priscus, have replied that someone who has received money to accept an inheritance gets that money *mortis causa*.

22   AFRICANUS, *Questions, book 1:* In cases of gift *mortis causa*, it is not the time of the making of the gift, but that of the death that should be borne in mind in considering whether a person can receive the gift.

23   AFRICANUS, *Questions, book 2:* If a gift *mortis causa* is given to a son-in-power and, while the donor is still alive, the son dies, though his father remains alive, the question arises of what is then the legal position. He replied that a *condictio* is available on the son's death, provided that the intending donor made the gift to the son himself and not to his father. Otherwise, if the father was using his son as a sort of means of acquisition, it is the father's death that must be taken into consideration. The same rule will also apply in the case of questions relating to the person of a slave.

24   AFRICANUS, *Questions, book 9:* Where a debtor has been granted a formal release as a gift *mortis causa*, if the donor gets better, a *condictio* can be made against the debtor even though he has been released by the passage of time, since the occurrence of the formal release means that the creditor has abandoned the right to enforce the previous obligation, which becomes instead a matter for *condictio*.

25   MARCIAN, *Institutes, book 9:* A gift *mortis causa* can be made both by someone who is making a will and by someone who is not.   1. A son-in-power who cannot make a will even with his father's consent can nonetheless make a gift *mortis causa* if his father gives permission.

26   MARCIAN, *Rules, book 2:* If two persons make reciprocal gifts *mortis causa* and then both die at the same time, neither of their heirs can petition to recover the property since neither of them outlived the other. The same rule applies in the case of reciprocal gifts between man and wife.

27   MARCIAN, *Rules, book 5:* Where a gift *mortis causa* is made such that it can in no circumstances be revoked, it is rather the case that death is the reason for the gift than that it is a gift *mortis causa*. Consequently, the gift should be treated exactly like any other gift *inter vivos*. Hence, it is not valid as between man and wife and the *lex Falcidia* is not applicable, as it is in the case of a gift *mortis causa*.

28   MARCELLUS, *Replies, sole book:* Someone who wished to make a gift *mortis causa* to his uncle, who was his debtor, of all that the latter owed him wrote as follows: "Let all the accounts and bonds in existence, wherever they may be, be void," meaning that his uncle did not have to pay. If the heirs claim the money from the deceased's uncle, can he defend himself by means of a defense of fraud? Marcellus replied that he can, since the heir is certainly making a claim against the wishes of the deceased.

29   ULPIAN, *Edict, book 17:* It should be considered whether, if property is given *mortis causa* and the donor then gets better, he can bring an action *in rem*. There is at least no doubt that if someone makes a gift such that the donee gets the property in the event of the donor's death, the latter will be able to make a *vindicatio* of the property, and, if he dies, the donee will be able to do so. However, if the gift is made such that the donee has the property for the moment but must return it in the event of the donor getting better or returning from battle or from a journey abroad, the view can be defended that an action *in rem* is available to the donor if any of these conditions is

fulfilled and is available to the donee in the meantime. But even if the donee is the first to die, then one will still grant an action *in rem* to the donor.

30   ULPIAN, *Edict, book 21:* Anyone who has made a gift *mortis causa* is entitled to a *condictio* or an *actio utilis* on the grounds of change of mind.

31   GAIUS, *Provincial Edict, book 8:* Acquisitions *mortis causa* are made when the opportunity for acquisition arises because of someone's death, except in the case of those types of acquisition that have their own special name. For example, someone who makes an acquisition by virtue of inheritance, legacy, or *fideicommissum* certainly gets the opportunity of making an acquisition as a result of someone's death, but because these types of acquisition have their own special name, they are kept separate from the present definition.   1. Julian holds that a debtor who has been granted a formal release is regarded as having been given a gift *mortis causa* even if he is not solvent.   2. An acquisition *mortis causa* can be made without a gift being involved, for example, money paid by a *statuliber* or a legatee for the purpose of fulfilling a condition, whether the recipient is an outsider or an heir. Money which one receives to accept or not accept an inheritance is in the same class, as also is the person who receives money to pass up a legacy. Again, dowry which one stipulates to receive from a husband in the event of his wife's death is, of course, acquired *mortis causa*. This sort of dowry is called returnable. Again, anything that is given *mortis causa* is given either because one is in danger of death or because one is reflecting on mortality in the knowledge that we will die sometime or other.   3. If, wishing to make me a gift *mortis causa*, you direct a debtor of yours to undertake to pay ten to me or a creditor of mine, the question arises of what is the legal position if the debtor in question is not solvent. Julian says that if I made a stipulation, I am regarded as acquiring as much as the debtor is able to pay, since even if the donor got better he would only be entitled to recover the debtor's obligation. But if my creditor made a stipulation, I am regarded as having received as much as the amount from which I am released from my creditor.   4. A needy debtor freed by the grant of a formal release is considered to have acquired the whole sum from payment of which he has been freed.

32   ULPIAN, *Edict, book 76:* A gift *mortis causa* is not held to have been fully completed until death ensues.

33   PAUL, *Plautius, book 4:* Anyone who acquires by usucapion property belonging to someone else which has been delivered *mortis causa* is considered to have acquired it not from the person whose property it was but from the one who afforded the opportunity of usucapion.

34   MARCELLUS, *Digest, book 28:* A gift *mortis causa* can also arise where someone makes a stipulation for each year of his life, so that collection starts after the death of the promisor.

35   PAUL, *Lex Julia et Papia, book 6:* The senate resolved that gifts *mortis causa* made to persons whom the law forbids to receive them are to be considered in the same situation as testamentary legacies left to persons who cannot legally receive them. There is debate about a great variety of questions arising from this *senatus consultum* on which we may pass some brief comments.   1. "Gift" is derived from "I give" as in "I give a gift" and is taken from the Greek; for the Greeks say δῶρον καὶ δωρεῖσθαι.   2. But a gift *mortis causa* differs considerably from the true and absolute

sort of gift which proceeds in such a way that it can in no circumstances be revoked. In that sort of case, of course, the donor wishes the recipient rather than himself to have the property. But the person who makes a gift *mortis causa* is thinking of himself and, loving life, prefers to receive rather than to give. This is why it is commonly said: "He wishes himself rather than the recipient to have the property, but, that said, wishes the recipient rather than the heir to have it." 3. Consequently, insofar as he is thinking of himself, the person who makes a gift *mortis causa* is making a business transaction, with the purpose, that is, of receiving the property back in the event of his getting better; and the followers of Cassius did not doubt that such property can be reclaimed by a *condictio* on nonreciprocation, the argument being that that *condictio* applies to gifts that are made on condition that you do something or that I do something or that Lucius Titius does something or that some event occurs and the condition is fulfilled. 4. A gift *mortis causa* can be made in many ways. Sometimes there is no suspicion of any danger, and the donor is well and in good health but also reflects on death as part of the human lot; sometimes it is done because of fear of death or because of impending or potential danger, granted that one can fear death in many forms both on land and sea, in peacetime and war, at home and on military service. A gift can also be made both such that the property can in no circumstances be returned even if the donor dies of the illness in question and such that it should be returned even if the donor dies of the illness in question provided that he had changed his mind and wanted it returned to him. A gift can also be made such that it can only be returned in the event of the donee being the first to die. A gift can also be made such that there is no right of reclaim in any circumstances, that is, not even in the event of the donor getting better. 5. It should be stated that if one enters into a partnership by means of a gift *mortis causa*, such a partnership is null and void. 6. If a creditor wishes to make a gift *mortis causa* to two of his debtors and formally releases one of them and then gets better, he can choose against which of the two to bring a *condictio*. 7. But someone who stipulates the payment of money year by year as a gift *mortis causa* is not like someone to whom a legacy payable annually is made, since, whereas they may be many legacies, there is only one stipulation and the circumstances of the person to whom the undertaking has been made have only to be examined once.

36   ULPIAN, *Lex Julia et Papia, book 8:* As for a gift made for the purpose of fulfilling a condition, even if it does not come from the goods of a deceased person, the person whom the law has granted the right of receiving a fixed amount cannot receive more than that amount. Certainly, that which is given by a *statuliber* for the purpose of fulfilling a condition is without doubt counted as part of the amount allowed by law, provided that the slave had it in his *peculium* at the time of death. But if the slave got it after the time of death or again if someone else made the gift on his behalf, what is given will be in the same position as a gift made by a legatee since it was not among the testator's goods at the time of his death.

37   ULPIAN, *Lex Julia et Papia, book 15:* It will be proper to remember as a general rule that gifts made *mortis causa* are comparable with legacies; consequently, any rule that applies to legacies will have to be taken as applying to gifts *mortis causa*. 1. Julian says: If someone sells a slave given to him *mortis causa* and does so while the donor is still alive, the donor will be able to bring a *condictio* for the value of the slave if he gets better and if he chooses to do so. Otherwise, the donee is compelled to return the slave himself.

38   MARCELLUS, *Lex Julia et Papia, book 1:* The difference between a gift *mortis*

causa and other acquisitions *mortis causa* is as follows: A gift *mortis causa* is something given with both parties present, whereas even that which does not fall into the category of gift can be regarded as an acquisition *mortis causa*. For example, when someone directs in his will that his slave Pamphilus is to be free on condition that he pays me ten aurei, he will not be held to have made me a gift, but, nonetheless, it is established that if I receive the ten from the slave, I have made an acquisition *mortis causa*. The same happens when a person is appointed heir on condition of his giving me ten. For in receiving something from an appointed heir for the purpose of fulfilling a condition I make an acquisition *mortis causa*.

39   PAUL, *Plautius, book 17:* If someone who has been given a slave *mortis causa* manumits that slave, he is liable to a *condictio* for the value of the slave, since he knows that a *condictio* can be brought against him in the event of the donor's getting better.

40   PAPINIAN, *Questions, book 29:* A gift *mortis causa* made between man and wife is, in the event of death, referred to the time at which it was made.

41   PAPINIAN, *Replies, book 2:* Anything that a *statuliber* gives to one of the heirs out of his *peculium* is included in calculations under the *lex Falcidia* affecting the recipient, and in an action for the inheritance is to be restored under the *senatus consultum Trebellianum*. Anything that the *statuliber* has received and given as a gift is considered to given out of his *peculium*. Any gift made by someone else but in the name and presence of the *statuliber* is in effect understood as given by the slave himself.

42   PAPINIAN, *Replies, book 13:* Seia made a series of deliveries and ceded her goods by way of gift to Titius, a cognatic relative of hers, but reserved the usufruct for herself, arranging that if Titius predeceased her, ownership of the goods would revert to her and that if she later died while Titius's children were still alive, the goods would then belong to them. Hence, if the heirs of Lucius Titius should make a *vindicatio* of the individual pieces of property, a defense of fraud will be effective against them. However, a *judicium bonae fidei* was brought, and the question was raised whether Seia ought to make an undertaking to restore the goods to Titius's children on her death. There was some hesitation about compelling a gift which had not yet started to take effect with reference to the children. But is it not the case that if a *cautio* is made, it is the first gift, which was already properly completed by the transfer of ownership, which is upheld according to the original terms on which it was made, and not a second gift which has been promised? And so the question is: Was the gift one made on a fixed condition or one having the intention and title of a *mortis causa* gift? In fact, it cannot be denied that it should be regarded as having been made *mortis causa*. It follows that once the first gift was made and given that Seia outlived Titius, it must be held that the second gift can be compelled. Finally, once Seia is dead, if the children of Titius received a *cautio* with her consent, they will be liable on their own account to contribution under the *lex Falcidia*. 1. In a case in which a man, at the very end of his life, made a gift to his emancipated son without imposing any conditions of return and the son's brothers and co-heirs wanted the gift to be attributed to the deceased's goods for the purposes of the *lex Falcidia*, I replied that the old rule should be preserved, since the *constitutio* only applied to things that were given under particular terms and, on death, were in a sense removed from the goods of the deceased in that all hope of retaining them was then removed, whereas the man in question who made an unconditional gift was doing so not so much *mortis causa* as on his deathbed.

43   NERATIUS, *Replies, book 1:* FULCINIUS: A gift *mortis causa* can be made between man and wife if the donor has an entirely justifiable fear of death. NERATIUS: For these purposes the belief of the donor that he is about to die is sufficient. How justifiably or otherwise he has such a belief is not to be investigated. This view is preferable.

44   PAUL, *Handbook, book 1:* If a gift *mortis causa* is made to a slave, let us consider whose death, the owner's or the slave's, is to be regarded as important in determining whether *condictio* is appropriate. It is the death of the donee that is to be so regarded. However, such a gift does not go with the slave if he is manumitted after the owner's death but before the opening of the will.

MANUMISSIONS

1 ULPIAN, *Sabinus, book 6:* It has been approved that a man born on the first of January has the power to manumit after the sixth hour of the night on the previous day, as if he had completed his twentieth year; the fact is that while a man above the age of twenty is not expressly permitted to manumit, one under twenty is forbidden to manumit; however, a man ceases to be under twenty in the last day of his twentieth year.

2 ULPIAN, *Sabinus, book 17:* If an heir has manumitted a slave who has been legated while the legatee is considering [whether to take the legacy] and the legatee has later refused the legacy, it is approved that the slave will be free.

3 PAUL, *Edict, book 39:* A slave in pledge cannot be manumitted, even if the debtor can provide security for repayment.

4 ULPIAN, *Disputations, book 6:* A man who is purchased with his own cash, under a letter of the deified brothers to Urbius Maximus, obtains a status whereby he may secure freedom. 1. Now at first sight the expression "purchased with his own cash" seems improper, since a slave cannot have cash of his own; but we are to close our eyes and suppose him to have been bought with his own cash, when it is not the cash of the purchaser which is used to pay the price. So then whether he has been purchased with his *peculium*, which belongs by right to the vendor, or from profit obtained by chance, or by the kindness or generosity of a friend, or by the slave's carrying a charge to his own account, or giving an undertaking, or accepting a liability or the obligation to pay a debt, we are to suppose that he was purchased with his own cash; it is enough that the nominal purchaser laid out no money of his own. 2. If he was bought by an unknown person, but later tendered his purchase price, it will be right to say that he is not to be heard; for the transaction should from the start have the form of a fictitious sale and of a contract made in good faith between purchaser and slave. 3. If then the transaction did not have this form from the start of purchase with the slave's own cash, or if after its completion the slave did not pay over the cash, his freedom will fail. 4. Perhaps this will raise the question whether, when the transaction took this form from the start, but the purchaser moved fast and paid the price, the slave can avail himself of the constitution after refunding it to him, and in my view he can. 5. So, too, if the purchaser allowed him time for payment, once he has settled the account, he will be able to attain freedom. 6. Whether or not there is an express provision in the contract, as in a sale, that he should be manumitted, it is the more correct view that freedom is his due. 7. Therefore, if by any chance some one has bought a man with his own cash, subject to the covenant that he is not to manumit him, the equitable view is that of those who say that he attains freedom, since the fictitious

purchaser in question has bought him only in name and in addition bears no expense.   8. It is immaterial, moreover, from whom a man is purchased with his own cash, whether it be the imperial treasury, a *civitas*, or a private individual, irrespective of sex. But even if the vendor is under twenty, the constitution will still take effect. Nor is any regard paid to the age of the purchaser; for even if a *pupillus* purchases, it is fair that he should fulfill the trust, inasmuch as this involves him in no loss.   9. So too if he is a slave. In the case of those slaves indeed who are altogether debarred from freedom, the constitution has no effect, for instance, in the case of a slave who should be sent overseas or has been sold under a covenant that he is never to be manumitted or had become subject to this status under a will.   10. Even if a man purchased with his own cash has not paid the full price, provided that a supplement has accrued to complete the payment of the price from his *operae* (days of work) or by his earning something extra, it should be said that freedom is his due.   11. But if the purchaser were to buy shares in the slave with the slave's own cash, when he already possessed the remainder, the transaction will not be relevant to the constitution, no more than the case of the purchaser who held the bare ownership and bought the usufruct.   12. But the fructuary who bought up the ownership [with the slave's own cash] is in such a position that the constitution would apply.   13. But if there are two purchasers, one using his own cash and the other that of the slave, it will have to be said that the constitution has no force, unless perhaps he who used his own cash for the purchase should be prepared to manumit.   14. But if any one purchased a share of the slave [with the slave's own cash] and the remainder accrued to him from a free gift, it will have to be said that the constitution is relevant.

5   MARCIAN, *Institutes*, book 2: If anyone says that he was purchased with his own cash, he can institute proceedings against his master to whose good faith he had recourse and complain on the ground that he is not being manumitted by the master, appearing at Rome before the prefect of the city, but in the provinces before governors, in accordance with the sacred constitutions of the deified brothers, subject, however, to the warning that the slave who has not made good this allegation should be sent to penal labor in the mines unless perchance the master has expressed a preference that he should be handed back to him on the footing that he will not impose any heavier penalty for the offense.   1. But if it has been ordered that he should be free after rendering his accounts, an arbitrator between the slave and the master, that is, the heir, is appointed for the examination of the accounts.

6   ALFENUS VARUS, *Digest*, book 4: A slave had bargained for freedom in return for money and had paid the money to the master; the master had died before manumitting him and had ordered in his will that he should be free and bequeathed him his *peculium*. He inquired whether or not the heirs of his patron were bound to restore to him the money he had paid his master for freedom. [Alfenus] replied that if the master, after receiving the money, had entered it in his accounts as his own, it at once ceased to be part of the *peculium*, but if he had registered it as due to the slave until such time as he manumitted him, then it seemed that it was part of the *peculium* and that the heirs were bound to restore the sum in question to the man manumitted.

7   ALFENUS VARUS, *Digest*, book 7: Two sons-in-power each had slaves belonging to their separate *peculia*; one of them manumitted a little slave belonging to his *peculium* in the lifetime of his father; the father had prelegated the *peculium* in his will to each son. The question arose whether that slave was the freedman of both or of the son by whom he had been manumitted. [Alfenus] replied that if the father had made the will before his son ordered the slave to be free, he was the freedman of the latter alone on the ground that it would seem that he had legated the slave too as part of the *peculium*, but if the father had made the will subsequently, it would not seem to have been his intention to legate the man who had been manumitted, and the slave, since he

had not been prelegated, would have been the slave of both on the death of the father.

8 MARCIAN, *Institutes, book 13:* Persons in penal servitude unquestionably have no power to manumit, since they are slaves themselves. 1. But neither can persons charged with capital crimes manumit their own slaves, as the senate too resolved. 2. Furthermore the deified Pius issued a rescript that grants of freedom made by a man who had already been convicted under the *lex Cornelia* or who expected to be convicted were not valid. 3. But not even those persons who were manumitted in order that they might be removed from the scope of criminal proceedings attain freedom recognized by law, under a rescript of the deified Hadrian.

9 PAUL, *Rules, sole book:* A slave sold subject to the covenant that he should not be manumitted or one debarred from manumission either by a will or by the prefect [of the city] or by a governor on account of some offense cannot attain freedom.

10 PAUL, *Imperial Decisions Made in Judicial Proceedings (six books), book 2:* Aelianus, who was in debt to the imperial treasury, had bought the slave-woman Euemeria many years earlier, subject to the covenant that he was to manumit her, and he had manumitted her; a procurator, finding on investigation that the debtor's assets did not cover his debts, also questioned the status of Euemeria. It was approved that there was no room for the fiscal privilege, whereby all the assets of debtors were treated as pledged to the treasury, since she had been bought subject to the covenant aforesaid, and if she had not been manumitted, she would still have attained freedom under the constitution of the deified Marcus.

11 PAUL, *Edict, book 64:* When a slave had been left to a legatee subject to the fulfillment of a condition, the heir does not make him a freeman by manumitting him in the interval.

12 PAUL, *Edict, book 50:* By the *lex Fabia* the manumission is forbidden within ten years of a slave, who committed the crime of kidnapping, for which the master imposed a penalty. In interpreting this, however, we shall have regard not to the time when the will was made but that of death.

13 POMPONIUS, *From Plautius, book 1:* The slave of the lunatic cannot be manumitted by the agnate curator, since manumission is not included in the management of the patrimony. However, Octavenus says, in order to remove doubt, that if the lunatic owed the man freedom by reason of a *fideicommissum,* the slave should be delivered by the agnate to be manumitted by the person to whom he is delivered.

14 PAUL, *Plautius, book 16:* We cannot manumit before one with *imperium* equal to our own, but a praetor can manumit before a consul. When the emperor manumits a slave, he does not touch him with the wand (*vindicta*), but when he has expressed his will, the man manumitted becomes free in accordance with a law of Augustus.

15 MARCELLUS, *Digest, book 23:* It is not to be doubted that a slave can be manumitted *mortis causa.* But you must not take this to mean that he is ordered to be free on the footing that he would not become free, if the master should recover, but in the same way as if he were to free him by *vindicta,* he would become free unconditionally, evidently because he thinks he will die, so likewise in this type of case freedom is granted with effect on the end of the manumitter's life, provided, of course, (in virtue of the condition implicit in any act *mortis causa*) that the manumitter's intention is unchanged; in the same way, when a man has delivered a thing to become the property of the recipient on his death, it is only alienated if the donor has not altered his intention.

16 MODESTINUS, *Rules, book 1:* If a son under twenty has manumitted his slave with his father's consent, he will make the man a freedman of his father, and the case needs

no scrutiny to justify it because of the father's consent.

17   MODESTINUS, *Rules, book 6:* Slaves acquired by a son-in-power in the army will not be reckoned as part of the father's *familia,* nor in fact will the father have the power to manumit such slaves of the son.

18   GAIUS, *Lex Julia et Papia, book 12:* The vendor can manumit the slave he has sold, as can anyone manumit the slave he has promised to deliver.

19   PAPINIAN, *Questions, book 30:* If anyone has received cash from another person so that he may manumit his slave, the slave's freedom can be wrung even from the unwilling master, although very commonly it is the slave's money that has been paid out, especially if the money has been given by his natural brother or father; in fact, he will resemble the slave who has been purchased with his own cash.

20   PAPINIAN, *Replies, book 10:* A man under twenty who has received the gift of a slave for the purpose of manumission has the most ample justification for manumission since the letter of the deified Marcus to Aufidius Victorinus; in fact, the slave will attain freedom, even if he is not manumitted.   1. The law is not the same in the case of fideicommissary freedom; there the *minor* must justify manumission; for freedom is not due to the slave unless he is thus manumitted.   2. A girl was sold subject to covenant that the purchaser was to manumit her after a year; it was agreed that if he had not done so, the vendor might seize her or that the purchaser should give him ten aurei. [Papinian] replied that if the purchaser had not kept faith, she was nonetheless free in accordance with the sense of the constitution, since seizure generally enters in for the purpose of affording relief; hence, neither will there be a suit for money, since the benefit of the law [the constitution] has fulfilled the vendor's intention.   3. At the time a slave was alienated, it was agreed that the man who had been transferred for the purpose of being freed should be manumitted after five full years and that in the meantime he should make a fixed monthly payment. I replied that this was not to make the payments a condition for freedom but that a limit has been set in advance on the service due during his temporary servitude; nor in fact is it the case that the man transferred for the purpose of being freed is in all points comparable to the *statuliber.*

21   PAPINIAN, *Replies, book 13:* The husband, if solvent, has the power to manumit a dotal slave while the marriage lasts; however, if he is not solvent, although he may have no other creditors [apart from dotal liability], the freedom of the slave will be barred in order that while the marriage lasts, it may be understood that he is liable for the dowry.

22   PAPINIAN, *Definitions, book 2:* A grandson born to his grandfather's son has the power to manumit with the approval of the grandfather, as a son with the approval of his father, but the slave manumitted is the freedman of father or grandfather respectively.

23   PAUL, *Replies, book 15:* Gaius Seius purchased Pamphila subject to covenant that she should be manumitted within a year; then within the year Seius was adjudged a slave; I ask whether in accordance with the terms of sale Pamphila attained freedom at the end of the year.   Paul replied that the slave-woman purchased on those terms had been acquired by the master [of Seius] subject to the terms on which she had been put up for sale.

24   HERMOGENIAN, *Epitome of Law, book 1:* The *lex Junia Petronia* prescribes that if there is a tie in contradictory verdicts between the judges, the decision should go in favor of freedom.   1. But it has also often been laid down by emperors that if as many witnesses have testified for freedom as against it, the decision should go in favor of freedom.

25 GAIUS, *Manumissions, book 1:* The principle of the law qualifies *infantes* too for freedom.

26 JAVOLENUS, *From the Posthumous Works of Labeo, book 4:* In Labeo's opinion, a lunatic slave, manumitted in any way, can attain freedom.

2

MANUMISSIONS *VINDICTA*

1 POMPONIUS, *Sabinus, book 1:* It is settled that a *pupillus* has the power to manumit before a praetor, who is also his tutor, acting with his sanction.

2 ULPIAN, *Sabinus, book 18:* If a fructuary were under twenty, would he have the power to give his consent to freedom? I think that by giving his consent, he has the power to bring the man to freedom.

3 ULPIAN, *Disputations, book 4:* If an heir were to manumit a slave who has been legated and the legatee were later to reject the legacy, the grant of freedom is retroactively valid. It is the same if a slave is unconditionally bequeathed to two legatees, one manumits him and the other rejects the legacy; here too the grant of freedom is retroactively valid.

4 JULIAN, *Digest, book 42:* If a father has given his son permission to manumit a slave and has died in the interval intestate, and the son has then in ignorance of his father's death bestowed freedom, freedom falls to the slave from the principle of favoring freedom (*favore libertatis*), when there is no evidence for a change in the master's wish; if, however, the father without the son's knowledge had sent a message forbidding manumission, and the son had manumitted the slave before receiving the information, the man does not become free. For in order that manumission by the son may convey freedom, the father's wish must remain unchanged; if it has changed, it will cease to be true that the son manumitted by the father's wish. 1. Whenever a master manumits a slave, even though he believes that the slave is owned by someone else, it still remains true that the slave was manumitted by wish of the master, and for this reason he will be free. And conversely, if Stichus supposed that he was not owned by the manumitter, nonetheless, he becomes free. For the facts matter more than what is believed, and in both cases, it is true that Stichus was manumitted by wish of the master. The same rule of law holds even if master and slave erroneously believed, the one that he was not the master, the other that he was not his slave. 2. A master under twenty has no right to manumit even a slave in whom he has a share without sanction of a council. PAUL notes: But if a man under twenty allows the manumission of a slave pledged to him, the manumission is valid, since he is understood not so much to be manumitting him as not to be hindering his manumission.

5 JULIAN, *Digest, book 42:* Whether one may manumit in one's own court, providing a council, is a question often raised. For my part, since I remembered that my teacher, Javolenus, had manumitted his slave both in Africa and in Syria, when providing a council, I followed his example in my own praetorship and consulship and freed some of my own slaves *vindicta* and persuaded some of the praetors who asked my advice to do the same.

6 JULIAN, *Urseius Ferox, book 2:* There is no doubt that masters under twenty can manumit a slave in whom they have a share with the consent of a council, even though only one of the co-owners has approved the grounds.

7 GAIUS, *Common Matters or Golden Words, book 1:* It is not at all necessary to manumit from a tribunal; hence, slaves are very commonly manumitted when [the

magistrate is] moving about, when [for instance] the praetor or proconsul or legate of Caesar has come out to bathe or drive or attend the games.

8   ULPIAN, *Edict, book 5:* When I was at a villa with a praetor, I raised no objection to a manumission before him, although no lictor was present.

9   MARCIAN, *Institutes, book 13:* It is a rightful ground of manumission if a slave has freed the master from danger of death or *infamia*.   1. It should be known that any grounds that have been approved and accepted should bestow freedom; in fact, the deified Pius declared in a rescript that grounds once approved should not be called in question later, provided that no one may manumit someone else's slave; for it is the approval of the grounds that should be challenged, but once they have been approved, manumission is not to be reviewed later.

10   MARCIAN, *Rules, book 3:* The son of a deaf or dumb father can manumit by his command, but the son of a lunatic cannot manumit.

11   ULPIAN, *Duties of Proconsul, book 6:* If a man under twenty manumits, grounds of this kind for manumission are usually accepted: that the slave is his son or daughter, brother or sister by birth,

12   ULPIAN, *Lex Aelia Sentia, book 2:* or that there is a connection by blood (for account is taken of kinship);

13   ULPIAN, *Duties of Proconsul, book 6:* that the slave is his foster brother or foster father or schoolmaster or nurse or son or daughter to any of these or his foster child or *capsarius*, that is, one who carries books, or that he is manumitted for the purpose of being his procurator provided that such a person is not under eighteen. It is a further requirement that the manumitter should not have just one slave. A virgin or woman may also be manumitted for marriage, provided that the master must first swear an oath to take her as his wife within six months; this was resolved by the senate.

14   MARCIAN, *Rules, book 4:* It is more suitable for women to manumit foster children; but it is also sufficiently accepted for men that the manumission of a slave is permitted in whose rearing they have taken a special interest.   1. Some think that even women can manumit for the purpose of marriage, but only if a fellow slave has actually been bequeathed to a woman for the purpose. Even if a man who is impotent should wish to manumit for the purpose of marriage, he can do so; that is not true in the case of an eunuch.

15   PAUL, *Lex Aelia Sentia, book 1:* In addition, men under twenty should be permitted to manumit, to fulfill a condition, for example, if a man has been instituted heir on condition of his effecting the slave's freedom.   1. Past events can provide several grounds for manumission; thus, the slave may have aided the master in battle, protected him against brigands, healed him in sickness, uncovered a plot. And it is a long business, should we wish to make a list, since many services can occur for which it is honorable to grant freedom by a formal decision; the person before whom the procedure takes place will have to evaluate them.   2. Several slaves can be manumitted together by *vindicta*, and the presence of the slaves is enough to allow the manumission of several.   3. A master will also be able to show grounds for manumission in his absence through a procurator.   4. If two persons should manumit for the purpose of marriage, the reason ought not to be accepted.   5. Persons domiciled in Italy or in some province can manumit before the governor of another province with the co-operation of a council.

16   ULPIAN, *Lex Aelia Sentia, book 2:* It is to be borne in mind by judges when approving grounds for manumission that they are to approve grounds that arise not from luxury but from true feeling; for it must be supposed that the *lex Aelia Sentia* granted freedom not for self-indulgence, but for affections recognized by law.   1. If a man

under twenty has alienated a slave either for money received or as a gift subject to the condition that he is to be freed, the recipient can make good grounds for the slave's manumission, adducing the very fact of the condition, and effect his freedom; hence, the original owner is bound to show that this was the agreement between them, so that the matter may be determined in accordance with either the condition attached to the gift or the affection of the donor.

17   PAUL, *Edict, book 50:* We can manumit by *vindicta* before a proconsul after he has left the city, but also before his legate.

18   PAUL, *Plautius, book 16:* A man can be manumitted before a magistrate who is a son-in-power, even though he himself cannot manumit as being a son-in-power.   1. A praetor cannot manumit before his own colleague.   2. A son too can manumit with father's consent before his father.

19   CELSUS, *Digest, book 29:* If a *minor* with a council has manumitted a pregnant woman for the purpose of marriage and she has given birth in the interim, it is not settled whether the child is slave or free.

20   ULPIAN, *Duties of Consul, book 2:* If a man under twenty-five has been requested by *fideicommissum* to manumit, he ought without question to be permitted to do so, unless he was asked to manumit his own slave; in this case, the extent of the gain that he has derived from the judgment of the man who made the request has to be compared with the value of the slaves he has been requested to manumit.   1. But if a slave has been given to him subject to the condition that he be manumitted, he will have due permission to manumit; no need for the further sanction of the constitution of the deified Marcus to dissolve the consul's hesitation.   2. If anyone should wish to manumit for the purpose of marriage, being a person who would receive a wife of this social status without dishonor, this will be duly allowed.   3. Marcellus writes that a woman too, if she wishes, should be permitted to manumit her natural son or anyone for the grounds mentioned above.   4. A consul can manumit in his own court, even if he happens to be under twenty.

21   MODESTINUS, *Encyclopaedia, book 1:* I can manumit a slave before the prefect of Egypt under a constitution of the deified Augustus.

22   PAUL, *Questions, book 12:* A father wrote to his son in the knowledge that he was at Rome, permitting him to free by *vindicta* anyone of his choice among the slaves in his actual service; thereafter the son manumitted Stichus before the praetor; I ask if he thus made him free. I replied: Why should we not think that the father is allowed to permit his son to manumit one of the slaves in his service? In fact, it was only the choice that he allowed to the son, but it is he himself who manumits.

23   HERMOGENIAN, *Epitome of Law, book 1:* Manumission today is customarily effected through the lictors with the master saying nothing, and the formulaic words are deemed to be uttered, even though they are not.

24   PAUL, *Neratius, book 2:* The *pupillus* who is not *infans* has the right to manumit with a council. PAUL: provided of course that the tutor gives his sanction and on condition that the *peculium* does not go to the slave.

25   GAIUS, *Manumissions, book 1:* If a *pupillus* were to manumit for the purpose of obtaining a tutor, Fufidius says that this is a reason for approving the manumission.

Nerva the Younger disagrees with more truth; for it is perfectly ridiculous that the judgment of the *pupillus* should be regarded as strong in the choice of a tutor, when in all matters its supposed weakness requires to be guided by the tutor's sanction.

3

MANUMISSIONS OF SLAVES BELONGING TO A CORPORATION

1   ULPIAN, *Sabinus, book 5:* The deified Marcus gave to all *collegia* which have the right to meet the power to manumit,
2   ULPIAN, *Sabinus, book 14:* in consequence of which they will claim the lawful inheritance of the freedman.
3   PAPINIAN, *Replies, book 14:* The slave of a *civitas* lawfully manumitted retains *peculium*, if not expressly deprived of it, and so a debtor is released on paying the debt to him.

4

TESTAMENTARY MANUMISSIONS

1   ULPIAN, *Sabinus, book 4:* When freedom is given to a slave more than once, it is approved that that grant by which he attained freedom is valid.
2   ULPIAN, *Sabinus, book 5:* If anyone has instituted an heir as follows, "let Titius be heir; if Titius shall not be heir, let Stichus be heir; let Stichus be free," Aristo says that Stichus is not free, if Titius is actually heir. In my view, it can be said that he will be free on the construction that he did not simply receive freedom in the second stage (*gradus*) of the will but twice over; this is the current law.
3   POMPONIUS, *Sabinus, book 1:* Nor is a soldier under twenty permitted on his own authority to manumit a slave by his own will.
4   POMPONIUS, *Sabinus, book 2:* If anyone has written in his will, "let Stichus be free and let my heir give him ten," there is no doubt that the money is due even if the head of the household manumitted him in his own lifetime. 1. Further, if he expressed himself as follows, "let Stichus be free," and then immediately or at a later moment, "and let my heir give him ten, once he is free," the same must be said. 2. This will be accepted: Suppose that after a grant of freedom a bequest shall be made in the form: "If I have freed him *vindicta*, let my heir give him ten"; although a distinction has been made out of undue nicety from testamentary manumission, still out of regard for humanity the bequest will be as valid as if the testator had manumitted him in his lifetime.
5   POMPONIUS, *Sabinus, book 3:* In [direct] grants of freedom the lightest provision [imposing conditions] should be observed, so that if there are several, that is to be regarded as lightest which is easiest for the man manumitted, but in fideicommissary grants, the provision written last is observed.
6   ULPIAN, *Sabinus, book 18:* If the owner of a property has made the fructuary his heir and given conditional freedom to a slave, then since the man becomes the

property in the meantime of the heir as a result of the merger of the usufruct with the title to ownership, he will attain freedom, if the condition is fulfilled.

7   ULPIAN, *Sabinus, book 19:* Neratius writes that if freedom has been given in these terms, "if I have no son at the time of my death, let Stichus be free," the birth of a posthumous son is a bar to his freedom. But while the birth is in prospect, do we say that he remains a slave, or do we rather reply that his freedom takes retroactive effect, if no son is born? I incline to approve the latter view.

8   POMPONIUS, *Sabinus, book 5:* If the will is written in these terms, "let Stichus be free, if he shall appear to have handled the accounts with care," the care to be required is that which will be in the interest of the master and not of the slave, involving good faith, to be shown also in the repayment of sums due.

9   ULPIAN, *Sabinus, book 24:* If anyone has been legated for the purpose of being manumitted, if he has not been manumitted, it should be ordered that he is free and to receive the legacy; that freedom belongs to him, and that the legacy is due has often been stated in responses.   1. As for the rule that a man cannot be manumitted, when his attainment of freedom is forbidden in a will, I consider that this applies to slaves who belonged to testator or heir; it will not be possible to inflict this disability on someone else's slave.

10   PAUL, *Sabinus, book 4:* If the *peculium* has been prelegated and freedom of the *vicarius* has been ordered, it is accepted that he is free. There is a sharp distinction between genus and species; it is approved that an exception can be made for the species within the genus; and this relates to the bequest of *peculium* and manumission of the *vicarius.*   1. If the freedom of a slave who has been legated is ordered, he is free. But if the order for his freedom came first and he was subsequently legated, if the wish of the testator to take away freedom is really manifest, inasmuch as it is now approved that even freedom can be taken away, I consider that he goes with the legacy; but if the testator's wish is uncertain, then it is the kinder response that the man will be free.

11   POMPONIUS, *Sabinus, book 7:* If a slave has been legated but fideicommissary freedom is left to him, the heir or legatee is compelled to manumit him.   1. "If Stichus and Pamphilus have given ten, let them be free"; one of them can be free by giving five, though the other has not given.   2. When the will orders that a slave be free and several heirs have been instituted, he becomes free as soon as even one of them enters on the inheritance.

12   ULPIAN, *Edict, book 50:* If anyone has left a man freedom on condition of his taking an oath, there will be no room for the edict of the praetor waiving the condition of an oath, quite properly; for if anyone waives a condition for freedom, he puts a bar on the grant of freedom itself, which cannot stand if the condition is not observed.   1. Likewise, if anyone has received a legacy along with freedom, he will only get the legacy if he has complied with the condition of the oath.   2. But if he has received freedom unconditionally and a legacy only subject to the condition of an oath, Julian, in the thirty-first book of his *Digest,* considers that the condition of the oath is waived.   3. I consider that this must also be said, if a condition was imposed on his freedom, when in spite of this the testator manumitted him in his lifetime; for here too the condition on the legacy is waived.

13   ULPIAN, *Disputes, book 5:* If freedom has been given to two slaves on condition of their having built a block of apartments or erected a statue, this condition must apply to both. Only one doubt will occur: Suppose only one of them does what is required to meet the testator's wish, will he attain freedom? This is the better view, unless the testator gave express directions to the contrary. However, although by his action he has fulfilled the condition so far as it applies to him and not to the other, the condition is extinguished for the other too; he cannot do anything more to comply with it, once it has been fulfilled.   1. So too can we ask what more was specified in a condition granting freedom to two craftsmen or painters if they had painted a room or built a ship;

was it the testator's wish to make the action of one of them a condition for the freedom of the other? If so, the failure of one may make the other unable to fulfill the condition, when he is prepared to perform. If the testator showed by written or spoken words that he was content for either to perform, there is no difficulty; then by his own performance either of them will advantage both himself and his fellow, or himself alone, in accordance with what appears to have been the wish of the testator. 2. This problem is also discussed in the case where a man has given freedom to two slaves on condition of their rendering accounts. In fact, Julian discusses whether the fact that one is ready to do so and the other not bars the freedom of both; he is perfectly right in saying that if their accounts were separate, the one who renders his accounts does enough to obtain freedom, but if they were jointly responsible, neither seems to have complied with the condition, unless he discharged arrears due from both. In regard to arrears, we ought to take it that the actual account books should be handed over. 3. But also if the freedom of a slave-woman along with her children has been ordered, she will be free, though she has no children; or if she has children and they are debarred from attaining freedom, the same must be said; and if she herself is debarred from freedom, still her children will attain freedom. For the additional words "along with her children" do not constitute a condition, unless you make a case that the testator had a different intention; only then will these words have to be taken as a condition. But that they do not constitute a condition may also be inferred from the edict of the praetor, which provides: "I will order possession of the womb with the children"; for it is approved that even if there are no children, possession can still be taken on behalf of the womb under the edict.

14   ULPIAN, *Disputes, book 8:* When the will makes a slave free unconditionally, and heir subject to a condition, it is approved that though the condition is not fulfilled, he gets freedom.

15   JULIAN, *Digest, book 32:* "I give and bequeath Stichus to Sempronius. If Sempronius has not manumitted Stichus within a year, let Stichus be free." Inquiry was made of the legal position. I replied that when freedom is granted in this way, "if Sempronius has not manumitted Stichus, let Stichus be free," Sempronius will have no rights over Stichus, if he has not manumitted him, but Stichus will be free.

16   JULIAN, *Digest, book 36:* If it has been written in the will, "when Titius reaches the age of thirty, let Stichus be free and let my heir give him a farm," and if Titius has died before reaching his thirtieth year, freedom belongs to Stichus, but the legacy will not be due. For by the principle favoring freedom, it has been accepted that after Titius's death a period of time evidently remained on whose expiry freedom accrued; regarding the legacy, the condition is thought to have failed.

17   JULIAN, *Digest, book 42:* Freedom conferred for the last moment of life, as "when Stichus is dying, let him be free," is to be deemed of no effect. But this provision, "if Stichus has not climbed the Capitol, let him be free," is to be construed as "if Stichus did not climb the Capitol as soon as he had the power to do so"; in this way, Stichus will attain to freedom, if he was given the chance to climb the Capitol and did not take it. 1. If the will has provided, "let Pamphilus be free in such a way that he may render account to my sons," the question was raised if it appeared that freedom had been granted conditionally. I replied that the grant of freedom was unconditional and that the addition, "in such a way that he may render account," did not impose a condition on freedom; however, since it expressed the clear wish of the testator, he should be forced to render account. 2. If freedom is ordered after an unspecified number of years, the slave will be free after two years; this is required by the principle favoring freedom and allowed by the language, unless the person on whom lies the responsibility for granting freedom has proved by the most manifest considerations that the head of the household had a different view.

18   JULIAN, *Urseius Ferox, book 2:* A man instituting two heirs had ordered that a slave should be free on the death of one of them; the man on whose death the freedom depended had died while the testator was alive. Sabinus replied that he would be free.   1. This condition, "when I am dying, let him be free," covers a time when the testator is alive and therefore seems void. But it is better to interpret the words more kindly, so that the testator would seem to have left the man freedom after his own death.   2. Much more clearly, "let him be free in a year" can be construed as "let him be free after a year from the date of my death," and though it may be construed, "let him be free after a year following the making of this will," if the testator should actually die within a year, it will not be void.

19   JULIAN, *Urseius Ferox, book 3:* Someone had requested his heir to manumit a slave and then ordered that if the heir had not manumitted him, he was to be free and had left him a bequest; the heir did manumit him. It is generally considered that the man attains freedom under the will; on this view, the bequest is also due to him.

20   AFRICANUS, *Questions, book 1:* A man legated slaves and made the following stipulation: "If they have deserved well of you, I request you to think them worthy of freedom." It is the office of the praetor to compel the legatee to grant them freedom, unless these slaves have committed some act to make them unworthy of attaining freedom; specific services are not to be required of them by which they have to earn freedom. However, it will be within the discretion of the man requested to free them to do so at what moment he may wish to manumit each person, provided that if he has not manumitted them in his lifetime, his heir should be compelled to grant freedom without delay.

21   AFRICANUS, *Questions, book 4:* "Let Stichus or rather Pamphilus be free." He replied that Pamphilus would be free, since the testator had in a fashion corrected his own mistake. The legal position would be the same if he had written, "let Stichus be free; rather let Pamphilus be free."

22   AFRICANUS, *Questions, book 9:* A man who instituted as heir a son below the age of puberty had ordered that Stichus should be free after rendering account of the silver under his care; the slave removed part of the silver and shared it with the tutor, and in consequence the tutor certified that his account was in balance. On being asked for an opinion whether Stichus was free, he replied that he was not; for whereas in other circumstances it would be approved that a *statuliber* under orders to pay money would attain freedom if he paid the tutor, or if the tutor prevented his compliance with the condition, this must be taken to mean that the transaction should take place in good faith without fraud on the part of the *statuliber* and the tutor in accordance with the regular practice for the alienation of property of a *pupillus.* Hence, if the *statuliber* offers money and the tutor be unwilling to accept it to the detriment of the *pupillus,* freedom only accrues to the slave if his offer is not fraudulent. The same applies in regard to the curator. It has also been asked in what manner a slave ordered to render account of silver should be deemed to have complied with the condition; that is, suppose that some pieces of plate have disappeared through no fault of the slave and he has faithfully handed over the rest to the heir, would he attain freedom? He replied that he would; for it is enough if he renders account on a fair and reasonable basis; then, if his account rendered to the heir is such as a good head of a household would accept, the condition [for his freedom] seems to be fulfilled.

23   MARCIAN, *Institutes, book 1:* A man manumitted by will only becomes free, if the will is valid and the inheritance is accepted under its terms, or if the heir, disregarding his claim under the will, takes possession of the inheritance as on intestacy.   1. Freedom granted without conditions by a will becomes due as soon as the inheritance has been accepted by even one of the heirs, but if freedom has been given as from a certain day or subject to a condition, it becomes due only when the day has arrived or the condition is fulfilled.

24   GAIUS, *Common Matters or Golden Words, book 1:* Slaves ordered to be free are thought to be expressly designated, if they have been unambiguously identified by their craft, office, or in some other way, for example, "my steward," "my butler," "my cook," "the son of my slave Pamphilus."

25   ULPIAN, *Rules, book 4:* A slave ordered to be free in a will becomes free at the moment when the inheritance is entered upon by any of the heirs, provided that it is entered upon by an heir under that stage (*gradus*) of the will in which the man's freedom was ordered and that the manumission was unconditional.

26   MARCIAN, *Rules, book 1:* Under rescripts of the deified Pius and the deified brothers, favorable to freedom, when a legacy had been made to a slave who was to have
freedom as *heres substitutus*, but freedom had not been expressly granted to him unless he were heir, the will was to be construed as if freedom had been expressly
granted to him.

27   PAUL, *Lex Aelia Sentia, book 1:* Persons capable of granting freedom by manumission with a council can also make a *heres necessarius* with the result that the very
obligation imposed on the slave makes his manumission proper for approval.

28   PAUL, *Law of Codicils, sole book:* "Let Stichus be free, unless I shall have forbidden
his freedom by codicils"; this is equivalent to saying: "Let Stichus be free, if I shall not
have climbed the Capitol"; in fact an heir can be instituted in this way.

29   SCAEVOLA, *Digest, book 23:* A man had repudiated his wife when pregnant and
taken another; the first wife gave birth and exposed the son; someone else rescued
him, and he was brought up and always called by his father's name; during his father's
lifetime neither father nor mother knew that he was alive; on the father's death, his
will was read in which he neither disinherited his son nor instituted him as heir; the
son was acknowledged by his mother and paternal grandmother, and took possession
of the father's inheritance as *heres legitimus* succeeding on intestacy. The question
was raised whether those who received freedom under the will were free or slaves. He
replied that the son had certainly suffered no prejudice if the father was unaware of
his existence, and therefore, since he was in the power of the father, though the father
was not aware of this, the will was invalid. However, if the slaves had been manumitted and had enjoyed freedom for five years, the invalidation of freedom already given
is contrary to the principle of favoring freedom.

30   ULPIAN, *Edict, book 19:* Slaves in the hands of the enemy, whose freedom is ordered, attain freedom, although they were not in the possession of the testator, but of
the enemy at the times both of his making the will and of his death.

31   PAUL, *Edict, book 26:* If the freedom of one of several slaves with the same name is
ordered and it is not clear which is meant, none is free.

32   ULPIAN, *Edict, book 65:* It should be known that if there is a *heres necessarius*,
though he may keep himself out of the way, grants of freedom are nonetheless effective, provided that they have not been made in evasion of the *lex Aelia Sentia*.

33   PAUL, *Questions, book 12:* Freedom cannot be given for a period.

34   PAUL, *Edict, book 74:* Hence, if it were provided, "let Stichus be free for ten years,"
the addition of the period serves no purpose.

35   PAUL, *Edict, book 50:* Servius considered that freedom can be given directly by will
to those slaves only who belonged to the testator both at the time of the will and at
that of his death; this opinion is right.

36   PAUL, *Plautius, book 7:* I manumitted a slave by will in these terms: "If he shall
have sworn to give my son Cornelius ten days of labor, let him be free." The question
of the legal position is raised. And it should be known that the slave fulfills the condition by taking the oath, but that he is not bound to the days of labor, since he incurs no
obligation unless he takes the oath after manumission.

37   PAUL, *Plautius, book 9:* A slave is deemed to have been manumitted by name in the
will, when his name is contained in the codicils.

38   PAUL, *Plautius, book 12:* Freedom can be given by will to a slave in these terms:
"Let him be free, when the laws allow."

39   PAUL, *Plautius, book 16:* "Let Stichus, my slave, be free, if the heir alienates him."
The grant of freedom is void, because it is deferred to a time when he will be owned by

someone else. There is no contradiction in the fact that the *statuliber*, even if sold, obtains freedom under the will, inasmuch as a valid grant of freedom is not negated by the action of the heir. Or what shall we say of a legacy made in the same way? There will be no reason for saying anything different; in this regard, there is no difference between freedom and a legacy. Therefore, freedom will not be given rightly in this way: "If he has ceased to be the property of my heir, let him be free," because it has no applicability.

40   POMPONIUS, *From Plautius, book 5:* Julian says that when the same man is given by a *fideicommissum* to someone and ordered to be free, the heir should grant freedom; as Julian states, he will not be compelled to submit to payment of the value on account of the *fideicommissum*, since he will have fulfilled his obligation in granting freedom.   1. But even when conditional freedom is given to the slave under a *fideicommissum* and the slave himself was given [to the fideicommissary] on the appointed day, the heir will not be compelled to hand him over without a proviso for his restoration, once the condition for freedom becomes effective; for in virtually all cases grants of fideicommissary freedom are to be treated like direct grants of freedom. However, Ofilius used to say that if the testator had given fideicommissary freedom for the purpose of revoking a legacy, all this was true, but that if the legatee had shown that the heir was subjected to the burden by the testator, nonetheless, he should furnish the value of the slave to the legatee.

41   POMPONIUS, *From Plautius, book 7:* If freedom has been left to the slave in the following terms, "let Stichus my slave be free in the twelfth year after my death," it is plausible that he is to be free from the beginning of the twelfth year, that being the intention of the deceased. There is a great difference, usually observed in our language, between the phrases "in the twelfth year" and "after twelve years." It is the twelfth year when the smallest part of the twelfth year has come or passed, and if a man's freedom is ordered in the twelfth year, it is ordered for every day of that year. 1. But if the terms of the will have provided, "let Stichus my slave be free, if he has paid or given security for payment of one thousand coins to my heir in one, two, three years after the date of my death," that slave cannot be free until three years are up, unless he should pay or give security for payment of ready cash; in fact, the heir must be compensated for speeding up the man's liberation by an early payment of the moneys.   2. Labeo writes that if freedom has been left in the following terms, "let Stichus be free within a year from the date of my death," he is free at once; for if it were provided, "if he has given ten to my heir within a year, let him be free," it would be the case that he is free without delay, as soon as he made the payment.

42   MARCELLUS, *Digest, book 16:* If anyone has written in his will, "I wish such and such a slave to be the freedman of such and such a man," the slave can seek freedom and the man concerned can demand him as freedman.

43   MODESTINUS, *Manumissions, sole book:* Direct grants of freedom are rightly made by will and codicils confirmed by will, fideicommissary grants can be left by the intestate owner and unconfirmed codicils.

44   MODESTINUS, *Replies, book 10:* Maevia on decease left conditional freedom to her slaves Saccus, Eutychia, and Irene in these words: "Let my slave, Saccus, and my slave-women, Eutychia and Irene, all be free on this condition, that in alternate months they light a torch at my monument and perform the rituals of death"; I ask whether they can be free, given that Saccus, Eutychia, and Irene cannot be continually present at the monument of Maevia. Modestinus replied that neither the verbal context of the whole document nor the intention of the testatrix was such that the freedom granted was suspended by effect of the condition, since she wished them to be free when they were present at the monument; however, it was the task of the judge to compel them to obey the command of the testatrix.

45 MODESTINUS, *Encyclopaedia, book [3]:* As for the common saying that when freedom is granted subject to several conditions, regard should be had only to the lightest,
this is true if the conditions have been separately made; but if they have been made
collectively, the man will not be free unless he has complied with all.

46 POMPONIUS, *Readings, book 7:* Aristo replied to Neratius Priscus that when a man
was ordered by will to be free at the age of thirty and was condemned to penal labor in
the mines before reaching that age and subsequently recalled, a legacy made to him
along with his freedom undoubtedly belonged to him and that his right was not altered
by the penal sentence; so, too, if he had been instituted heir conditionally; for he would
even be the *heres necessarius.*

47 PAPINIAN, *Questions, book 6:* When freedom, though not due, has been erroneously
conferred by the heir as a result of forged codicils, the emperor decided that each person should pay twenty solidi to the heir.   1. But if the heir who has been instituted
has manumitted a slave for the purpose of fulfilling a condition and the son has subsequently won an action invalidating the will as undutiful or the will has been pronounced a forgery, it will be logical that the same rule should apply in this case as has
been decided in that of forged codicils.

48 PAPINIAN, *Questions, book 10:* If a partner gave freedom by will in these terms, "let
Pamphilus be free, if my partner has manumitted him," Servius replied that if the
partner manumitted he would be a common freedman of the households [of the testa-
tor] and of the manumitter; for it is not novel or unfamiliar under various rules of law
that freedom should accrue to a slave owned in common.

49 PAPINIAN, *Replies, book 6:* When a soldier manumits by will in the form, "I have
ordered Samia to be in a state of freedom," it has been approved that she received
direct freedom under military law.

50 PAPINIAN, *Replies, book 9:* The deified Marcus's decision in favor of maintaining
grants of freedom applies when a will has been voided, if the property is to be sold on
bankruptcy; otherwise, if they have been claimed for the imperial treasury as ownerless, it is plainly provided that the constitution does not apply.   1. Furthermore, he
declared that slaves manumitted by will for the purpose of their taking the estate must
offer adequate security not less than other freedmen of the deceased or external heirs;
but when the testamentary heirs are *minores* and request in the usual manner the
assistance prescribed for [management of] the estate, they are not deprived of the
favor.

51 PAPINIAN, *Replies, book 14:* In his will, a centurion forbade the sale of his slaves
and requested their manumission in accordance with their several deserts. He replied
that the grants of freedom were efficacious, since, if none of the slaves has committed
an offense, all can attain freedom; if some of them are excluded for an offense, the
remainder can attain freedom.   1. In regard to a testamentary provision, "let the
slaves who have committed no offense be free," it was approved that a condition was
evidently attached, which was to be construed to mean that he should be deemed not
to have contemplated the grant of freedom to those whom he had punished or removed
from honorific service or from the duty of managing his affairs.

52 PAUL, *Questions, book 12:* The emperors to Missenius Fronto: "A soldier's will contains a grant of freedom in these words: 'I wish' or 'order my slave Stephanus to be
free'; freedom is due to him when the inheritance is entered on, and therefore the
words subjoined, 'so however that he should remain with my heir so long as he is
young; if he has refused or disdained to comply, he should be held in the status of slavery' are not effective to revoke the freedom which is due." The same rule is observed in
the case of civilian wills too.

53 PAUL, *Replies, book 15:* Lucius Titius gave his slave freedom, if he had faithfully
given an account of his administration to his son Gaius Seius; when Gaius Seius had

passed the age of puberty, the slave was sued by the curators of Gaius Seius and gave full satisfaction before a judge; the curators obtained security from him, and it was declared that he was free; now Gaius Seius, the testator's son, claims that he did not make due payment to his curators; was the debt for the sum legally discharged? Paul replied that for a fulfillment of the condition comprised in the will, an account of what was due given merely to the young man's curators did not seem to be a full legal discharge, but that if the money was actually paid over or entered in his accounts as paid, when the young man was present, the condition seemed to be fulfilled, just as if the money had been paid to him personally.

54   SCAEVOLA, *Replies, book 4:* A man who had a slave Cratistus provided in his will: "Let my slave Cratinus be free"; could the slave Cratistus attain freedom, when the testator had not a slave Cratinus but only one called Cratistus? He replied that the mistake of a syllable was no bar.   1. The heirs appointed in a will, before entering on the inheritance, made a pact with the creditors whereby they were to be content with half; this was confirmed by the praetor's decision, and they entered on the inheritance on this footing; were the grants of freedom made in that will valid? He replied that they were, if the testator had not had the design of defrauding the creditors.

55   MARCIAN, *Fideicommissa, book 2:* When a conditional grant of freedom is made, we now have recourse to this rule: If it is the case that the *statuliber* is not responsible for failure to comply with the condition, even though the heir too is not responsible, nonetheless, he attains freedom. In my view, this should be the reply in cases where freedom has been given by *fideicommissum*, at least to slaves of the estate inherited. 1. It will not be absurd to state the same rule for slaves of the heir.   2. But we are right to doubt regarding slaves whom it will be the heir's duty to purchase, since in this case it will be unfair that he should be compelled to purchase them, just as if the condition had been fulfilled, perhaps for the reason that their master forbade them to comply with the condition with a view to obtaining the price for them and avoiding expenditure in regard to the condition.

56   PAUL, *Fideicommissa, book 1:* If anyone has made a grant of freedom to a slave in his will both directly and by *fideicommissum*, it is in the power of the slave to choose whether to attain freedom by direct grant or through the *fideicommissum*, in accordance with a rescript of the deified Marcus.

57   GAIUS, *Manumissions, book 3:* Suppose a needy testator has an affluent heir; would this be of advantage in ensuring that testamentary grants of freedom do not seem to defraud the creditors? And in fact, some have thought that the affluence of the heir creates a situation analogous to that occurring when the resources of the testator had been augmented before his decease. But I was taught that we follow the rule that it was not the affluence or poverty of the heir that was material, but the resources of the testator at his death. Julian carried this view so far as to consider that freedom would not even be secured to the man whose freedom has been ordered by the insolvent testator in the form, "when my debts have been paid, let Stichus be free," but this is not consistent with the view of Sabinus and Cassius, which he seems to follow; for they consider that it is the intention of each manumitter that ought to be examined; in fact, a man who imposes this condition on the freedom of his slave is so far from any fraudulent intention in ordering his freedom that he appears to be taking the most manifest precautions against defrauding his creditors.

58   MAECIAN, *Fideicommissa, book 3:* It is the truth that if a slave whose freedom had

been ordered and who had then been alienated by the testator attains freedom if he once more became a slave of the inheritance before its acceptance and if the heir entered upon it subsequently.

59   SCAEVOLA, *Digest, book 23:* Titia made direct grants of freedom to certain slaves, male and female, by name and then added: "And I wish all my female attendants, whose names are written in my accounts, to be free." The question was raised whether Eutychia, who had received freedom as being one of the female attendants at the time the will was made, but at the time of death was found to have been handed over as a concubine to the bailiff, could obtain freedom under the general heading of female attendants, since she had ceased to be such by the time of death. He replied that it was no bar to the freedom of the female attendant that she had ceased to be such at the time of death.   1. Stichus had received an unconditional and direct grant of freedom by the will of his master and is said to have embezzled much of the inheritance; the question was raised whether he should not postpone his assertion of freedom until he restored to the heirs all that he is proved to have embezzled. He replied that on the facts stated, the man in question was free.   CLAUDIUS: The problem seems to have been solved; the interests of the heirs are sufficiently covered by the edict regarding thefts.   2. Lucius Titius made the following provision in his will: "Onesiphorus is not to be free, unless you have carefully examined his account." Might Onesiphorus claim freedom on the basis of these words? He replied that the words quoted appeared to withhold rather than to grant freedom.

60   SCAEVOLA, *Digest, book 24:* Where there was a testamentary provision, "I wish a thousand aurei to be given to Eudo, since he was born after his mother had been freed," I ask whether Eudo can attain freedom by these words of the will if he fails to prove that he was born after his mother's manumission. He replied that such a statement of the facts should not be prejudicial.

61   POMPONIUS, *Letters, book 11:* I know that some masters who wish to prevent their slaves ever attaining freedom have been accustomed to insert this kind of provision: "Let Stichus be free when dying." But Julian too says that freedom, when its grant is deferred to the end of life has no force, since the testator is understood to have made this provision rather in order to hinder freedom than to grant it; and therefore that even if the provision were to run, "let Stichus be free, if he has not climbed the Capitol," this is of no force, if it is manifest that the testator wished to defer the grant of freedom to the end of life; and that there is no room for the Mucian *cautio*.   1. And, therefore, [he holds] if the provision in the will should have run, "let Stichus be free if he has gone to Capua," he will only be free if he has gone to Capua.   2. In addition, Octavenus used to say that if freedom has been granted to a slave in the will subject to any kind of condition, but with the further provision, "I do not wish the heir to free him until he has fulfilled the conditions," this further provision is void.

5

GRANTS OF FREEDOM BY *FIDEICOMMISSA*

1   ULPIAN, *Edict, book 14:* If of those who may owe fideicommissary freedom, some should be present, others absent for lawful cause, others in hiding, the man to whom

fideicommissary freedom has been left will be just as free, as if only those who were present or absent from lawful cause had been charged to free him; the share [in rights of patronage] of the man in hiding accrues to them.

2   ULPIAN, *Edict, book 60:* If a man dying intestate made grants of freedom by codicils but the intestate heir did not enter on the inheritance, the favor of the *constitutio* of the deified Marcus ought to come in even in this case, which orders that freedom belongs to the slave and the property is addicted to him, provided that he has given adequate security to the creditors for the payment of each in full.

3   ULPIAN, *Edict, book 65:* Against such a person the creditors commonly have *actiones utiles.*

4   ULPIAN, *Edict, book 60:* Hence, so long as it remains uncertain whether or not there will be a successor, the *constitutio* will be in abeyance; it will come in as soon as it becomes certain that there is none.   1. If anyone with a capacity for *restitutio in integrum* has refrained from taking the inheritance, do we consider that so long as such *restitutio* is possible, the *constitutio* is in abeyance, since it is not certain that there is no successor on intestacy? Not so; it is the truer view that the *constitutio* should be applied.   2. What, then, if the man obtains *restitutio* after the property has been addicted for the purpose of maintaining the grants of freedom? Certainly, it will not be right to say that the grants of freedom are canceled; they are valid once and for all.   3. Let us see whether the recipients of freedom ought to be present or not; as the property can be addicted in the interest of freedom, even when they do not assent, it can certainly also be addicted in their absence.   4. What, then, if some be present, some absent? Let us see if freedom is due even to those absent. And it can be said, by analogy with entry on an inheritance, that freedom also belongs to those who are absent.   5. If freedom was granted from a certain date, must that date be awaited? I think that it must; hence, the property will not be addicted until then. What, then, if the grant of freedom was conditional? If, indeed, some grants were unconditional and others conditional, the property can certainly be addicted without delay; but if all were conditional, what will it be logical to say? Should the fulfillment of the condition be awaited, or do we addict the property without delay, though the grant of freedom will not take effect until the condition has been fulfilled? That will be the view that should obtain more approval. When the property has been addicted in this way, direct and unconditional grants of freedom take effect at once, grants due from a certain date on the arrival of that date, conditional grants on fulfillment of the condition; nor will it be untrue to consider that the *constitutio* is relevant, even when the condition for the grants of freedom is unfulfilled, although all grants were conditional; where there is hope of freedom, we should say that the addiction of the property is to be allowed on merely a slight pretext insofar as the creditors are not to sustain any loss.   6. If the grant of freedom was made subject to the condition of the slave giving ten, whether the recipient of freedom was ordered to give to the heir or whether the donee was not specified, it may be asked if he would attain freedom by giving the sum to the addictee. It may be the preferable view that he should give the sum to the addictee so that the condition is deemed to have transferred to the latter's benefit. Of course, if he was ordered to give it to anyone other than the heir, he will give it to the person specified.   7. If any of the slaves have received fideicommissary freedom, they will not be free as soon as the property has been addicted, but they can obtain fideicomissary freedom, that is, they should be manumitted by the addictee.   8. [Marcus's] intention was that the property should only be addicted if sufficient security was given to the creditors for payment of each in full. What is meant by "sufficient?" Giving a surety or pledges will certainly suffice. But if confidence is placed in the man's own undertaking without a surety, the security will seem sufficient.   9. How should security be given to the creditors? To each severally, or to one whom they have appointed to act in the name of all? It is the duty of the judge to bring about an agreement between the

creditors and the appointment of one man to whom security may be given in the name of all. 10. Now consider if security should be given to the creditors first and the property be addicted on that footing or whether the property should be addicted subject to the condition that security is given. In my view, this should be covered by the decision of the judge specifying, "if everything has been done in accordance with the *constitutio* of the deified Marcus." 11. The term "in full" we shall certainly construe to include the capital and interest due. 12. As for those who have received freedom, the *constitutio* shows whose freedmen they become; those who have received fideicommissary freedom should be manumitted by the addictee, whereas those who have received freedom direct will be *liberti orcini*, unless the person who requests the addiction of the property to himself actually wishes it to be a condition of the addiction that even those who have received freedom direct should become his freedmen. 13. As for those who wish to become his freedmen, should they be manumitted by him, or should there be a clause included in the actual addiction, that the property is addicted to him subject to the condition that even the slaves who have received freedom direct should become his freedmen? In my view, the course of introducing a clause into the addiction is to be approved; this is also consonant with the words of the *constitutio*. 14. Further, when a slave has obtained freedom, the addictee will certainly also have his *tutela*. 15. If the deceased has requested the heir to manumit slaves in other ownership, do we say that the *constitutio* applies, or will it have no force? The view that the *constitutio* applies is to be preferred; in fact, after the addiction of the property, the addictee is compelled by the praetor to buy the slaves and free them. 16. If it was not the heir, but a legatee who was requested to manumit, would the *constitutio* have no force, seeing that when legacies are not due, grants of freedom too cannot be due? It is the preferable view that freedom should be favored in the same way; for it was [Marcus's] intention that freedom should be conferred on all alike to whom it would have belonged, if the inheritance had been entered on. 17. The same *constitutio* envisaged that the grants of freedom should be just as effective if the property fell to the imperial treasury; hence, whether the property lies vacant, given that the treasury does not take up its claim, or if the treasury has made its claim, the *constitutio* applies. However, if it should make its claim under a different title, it is evident that the *constitutio* should have no force; hence, the same view must be approved, if an information has been laid that the property escheats to a legion. 18. Further, if a man under twenty has made a grant of freedom, we shall say that it is not effective unless fideicommissary; in that case, it would be effective, provided that a man under twenty could have shown sound cause, if he had been manumitting in his lifetime. 19. Suppose that the deceased was insolvent at time of death and made a grant of freedom to defraud creditors; would it be effective? Provided that the imperial treasury has not claimed the property, perhaps it would, since full security is offered to the creditors; although it would not have been effective, if the inheritance had been entered on. Certainly, if the treasury has claimed the inheritance, it will more easily be established that the grant of freedom fails, unless any one, following the words of the *constitutio*, has argued that the person who wished the property to be addicted to himself under the condition that the grants of freedom should be effective is bound to assume the liability himself. But if anyone should have followed the analogy of a case in which an inheritance has been entered on, direct grants of freedom would not be effective, if their intention and result was to defraud the creditors; nor will fideicommissary grants be honored, if the creditors will be defrauded as a result. 20. If the imperial treasury has not laid claim to the property and it has been addicted for the purpose of maintaining a grant of freedom, may the treasury lay its claim later? It is the preferable view that it may not. We must obviously consider if the *constitutio* would apply, when the property has been addicted for this purpose without notification to the prefects of the imperial treasury. If, in fact, the property was such that it ought to have been claimed, the addiction fails; otherwise, it operates. 21. The addictee ought to be put in the same position as the *bonorum possessor*, and accordingly it will be possible for him to possess sepulchral rights. 22. Further, let us see if he may be sued by the creditors with the actions that can be brought against an heir, or only to the extent of the security he gave. The latter view is to be preferred. 23. If the property has been addicted to two or more persons, they will hold the property and freedmen in common and will resort to the *actio familiae erciscundae*.

5 PAUL, *Edict, book 57:* In fideicommissary grants of freedom, had the praetor, in the absence of the heir, pronounced freedom to be due, the man is free, and a freedman of the deceased, if he was also his slave, or of the heir, if he was the heir's slave. Furthermore, if the heir has died without a successor, the senate resolved in Hadrian's time that the grant of freedom should be maintained.

6 PAUL, *Edict, book 60:* A legatee who had been left a sum of ten was requested to buy and free Stichus; the Falcidian law comes in, and the slave cannot be bought for less; some think that the legatee should take three quarters [of the sum left him in the will] without being compelled to make the purchase. They also think that if he was requested to manumit his own slave and only received three quarters of the legacy, he should not be compelled to manumit. Let us consider this in case something different should be said at least on the latter point. But on the former point some think that the legatee should be compelled to buy the slave, having accepted the liability by taking even three quarters of the legacy. But if he should be prepared to return what he received, we must see if he should be heard. However, the heir should be compelled to pay the whole sum of ten, just as if the testator had added that it should be paid in full.

7 ULPIAN, *Edict, book 63:* If a sum of one hundred has been legated in order that the legatee may purchase and manumit someone else's slave and if, as a result of sale on bankruptcy of the property, he would be entitled to part only of the whole sum, he ought not to obtain the legacy without giving security that he will manumit, though only if the portion he has received is devoted to paying the price of the slave and if the owner is ready to sell at that price; otherwise, the claim of the legatee will properly be met by the defense of fraud.

8 POMPONIUS, *From Plautius, book 7:* It is established that the legatee to whom one thousand coins had been left with a request to manumit a slave at the cost of twenty is not compelled to grant fideicommissary freedom, if he were not to take the legacy.

9 MARCELLUS, *Digest, book 15:* When a testator placed his heir under a *fideicommissum* not to allow a slave to undergo servitude to another, the slave can apply for freedom immediately when he has been alienated. But when the heir does not alienate of his own free will, but is obliged to alienate by reason of the testator's circumstances, one may almost say that the *fideicommissum* should not yet take effect, since it can be deemed that the deceased had not such a contingency of alienation in his mind.

10 POMPONIUS, *Digest, book 16:* A man had written in his will: "I do not wish my slaves 'A' and 'B' to be sold." If it was his intention in making this provision that they should attain freedom if sold, freedom must be given to them; for freedom is evidently left to the slave of whom it was written: "I do not wish him to be a slave of anyone but yourself." Accordingly, if the heir has tried in any way to sell the slave, it will be possible for his freedom to be applied for at once, and the heir will not gain by buying the slave back, to prevent his freedom, since the condition has been once and for all fulfilled. 1. A man to whom freedom was due was sold; if he wishes to be manumitted by the heir, it will not be right to intervene on his behalf if the heir is present and the purchaser not to be found, since he could have availed himself of the *senatus consultum,* so as to attain freedom as if it had been testamentary. 2. A man to whom freedom was due under a *fideicommissum* from a person who was insolvent allowed himself to be transferred to a purchaser in good faith; do you suppose that an action lies against the man manumitted by analogy with the freeman who has deceived the purchaser by pretending to be a slave? I too am inclined to think that an action is properly given against the man sold and that he is rather like the *statuliber* who let the same thing

happen to him the day before he would attain freedom under a will.

11   MODESTINUS, *Distinctions, book 1:* The *pupillus* cannot grant fideicommissary freedom to a slave without the sanction of the tutor.

12   MODESTINUS, *Manumissions, sole book:* When Firmus had legated three tragic actors to Titianus and added, "I entrust them to you, so that they may not be slaves of any one else," the Emperor Antoninus ruled by rescript, on the confiscation of Titianus's property, that they should be manumitted by the state.   1. A legatee can no less than the heir be requested to manumit a slave, and if he should have died before manumitting him, his successors have a duty to manumit.   2. The deified Antoninus and Pertinax ruled by rescript that when an inheritance had been confiscated because of a covert request that the inheritance should be restored to someone incapacitated to receive it, grants of freedom, whether direct or fideicommissary, should be made.

13   MODESTINUS, *Rules, book 9:* If the manumission of a pregnant slave woman should be delayed by chance and not by the intent of the manumitter, her child will not be born free, but should be handed over to the mother by the person bound to manumit, so that it may attain freedom through her agency.

14   MODESTINUS, *Replies, book 10:* In his will, Lucius Titius made his wife Seia and their daughter Titia, heirs with equal shares. He also wrote in another clause: "I wish my slave Eros, also called Psyllus, to be free if my wife should approve." But the wife Seia did not take her portion of the inheritance, and her portion came to her daughter Titia by substitution. Is freedom due to Eros, also called Psyllus, under the words quoted above? Modestinus replied that the fact that the wife did not take her portion of the inheritance ought not to prejudice Eros. But might the wife Seia, who did not take her portion, lawfully object to Eros's request for freedom? Modestinus replied that her dissent was of no weight.

15   MODESTINUS, *Encyclopaedia, book 3:* The man who is to grant fideicommissary freedom cannot in any way make the status of the slave concerned worse; hence, he cannot sell him to any one else in the interim in order that he should be manumitted by the transferee; and if he has transferred him, he is compelled to buy him back and manumit him; for in some circumstances it is in the slave's interest to be manumitted by an old man rather than by a young man.

16   LICINNIUS RUFINUS, *Rules, book 5:* Grants of freedom can also be made by *fideicommissum* and with fewer restrictions than direct grants; for by a *fideicommissum* freedom can be granted not only to one's own slaves but to those of others, provided, however, that the grants are made in words of common use and that they unambiguously express the wish of the testator.

17   SCAEVOLA, *Digest, book 21:* CLAUDIUS: The words "when you think fit to manumit" are an effective grant of fideicommissary freedom.

18   SCAEVOLA, *Digest, book 23:* A will provided: "Let Pamphilus be free, if his management of my accounts has been good." The question was raised whether Pamphilus attained testamentary freedom when the testator died some years later without changing his will and there was no room for any complaint against him regarding his patron's accounts. He replied that on the statement of the facts there was no reason why he should not have obtained it.

19   SCAEVOLA, *Digest, book 24:* A husband was instituted heir and a grant of fideicommissary freedom made to slaves, including Stichus, the husband's steward; in the absence of the owner, they approached the provincial governor with the request that they should be freed on the footing that the heir was absent in a case allowed by the law, and the governor pronounced that freedom was due to them. The question was put whether proceedings could be taken against Stichus to compel him to render an account of his administration; he replied that this was not possible.   1. A man legated

to his wife her dowry and several other things and placed her under a *fideicommissum* to manumit Aquilinus, the woman's own slave, before a council; she says that she has no obligation to comply since the man belonged to her; is freedom due to him? He replied that if the wife wished to receive not only the dowry but the other bequests as well, she should be compelled on the basis of the *fideicommissum* to manumit Aquilinus and that once he was free, it would be for him to sue for the things that had been legated to him.

20 POMPONIUS, *Letters, book 7:* The statement is found in Julian: "If an heir requested to manumit a slave 'restored' the inheritance in accordance with the *senatus consultum Trebellianum*, it will be right that he should be compelled to manumit, and if he hides, or is absent for a reason allowed by law, the praetor shall be bound to hear the case and give judgment in accordance with the relevant *senatus consulta*. If, however, the person to whom the inheritance has been 'restored' has acquired the slave by usucapion, it will be proper for him to manumit and for the same rules to be observed, regarding the slave's person, which are usually followed in the case of purchasers." Do you think this is true? For my part, in my passion for acquiring knowledge, which down to the seventy-eighth year of my life I have accounted as alone the best principle for living, I am mindful of the maxim of him who is reported to have said: "Though I have one foot in the grave, I would desire to learn something new." It was a most elegant opinion of Aristo and Octavenus that the slave in question was not part of the inheritance to be restored by *fideicommissum*, because the testator, in requesting the heir to manumit him, does not seem to have had in mind that he was to be "restored"; however, if the heir gave him in error [to the fideicommissary], what Julian writes is correct.

21 PAPINIAN, *Questions, book 19:* "I request that Stichus should not be in slavery to another"; the emperor decided that fideicommissary freedom is understood to be given by these words; for what is so contrary to slavery as freedom? But the grant will not be deemed to take effect [only] after the death of the heir; this means that if the heir, while living, has alienated him, freedom may be sought at once; nor would it be material to obstructing the suit for freedom, if the heir should have bought him back, since the condition has been fulfilled once and for all. The same view should be approved, even if alienation by the heir was involuntary; nor will it be an objection if the alienation did not take place through his agency. For he has become virtually a *statuliber*, and the condition has been fulfilled in one way or another.

22 PAPINIAN, *Questions, book 22:* If the legatee of a farm has been left a sum of ten as compensation in order that he may manumit his own slave and if, although he has accepted the legacy of the farm, he has not accepted the legacy of the money because of the intervention of the *lex Falcidia*, he should be compelled to take the money, subject to the terms of the *lex Falcidia*, and to grant fideicommissary freedom to the slave, once he has accepted the legacy of the farm. 1. A man who had three slaves asks two heirs to manumit two of their own choice; one of the heirs is in hiding, and the other declares whom he would manumit. It can be said that they become free, so that their freedom would be just as valid as if the heir who was present had had the power to manumit alone. But if one of the slaves should have died, then, whether the heir be absent for cause allowed by law or the heir to whom application has been made is an *infans*, it is proper that the two survivors should become free by the praetor's decision. 2. When the person under obligation to grant fideicommissary freedom is absent for cause allowed by law or in hiding, or when some such persons are present, others absent for cause allowed by law, and others do not make themselves available, in order to frustrate the *fideicommissum*, or if the person who owed a grant of freedom has no heir, or if his heir has failed to take the inheritance, the praetor ought to pronounce that fideicommissary freedom is due under the will of Lucius Titius. This has been made clear by a *senatus consultum*, which includes the provision, to prevent it being doubtful and obscure who is to become patron of the freedman, that the praetor ought to pronounce who is absent for cause allowed by law and who for the purpose of thwarting the grant of freedom.

23 PAPINIAN, *Replies, book 9:* Fideicommissary freedom is not delayed by the plea that the inheritance has been plundered or that accounts have to be rendered. 1. When an heir has not granted fideicommissary freedom, then his own heir, who has "restored" the inheritance in accordance with the *senatus consultum Trebellianum*, should be compelled to

grant it, if the slave to be manumitted should choose him as the person to manumit.   2. In regard to a slave belonging to the *peculium castrense*, whom the father has desired his sons as *heredes legitimi* to free in words expressing a *fideicommissum*, I replied that it is the son who is or has been in military service who should be compelled to manumit, if he has actually inherited from the father, since the deceased supposed that the slave he manumitted was his own, although he had bestowed him by gift on his son; in fact, to avoid infringing the testator's wish, it is not necessary that the brother and co-heir should pay to the brother who owns the slave a proportion of his value. Nor by reason of the same error are the other gifts which the father made to the son who was about to enter the army to accrue to the brother who remained behind, since a son, even when he is among the *heredes legitimi*, keeps his *peculium castrense* over and above his portion of the inheritance. 3. Moreover, fideicommissary freedom, which is due from the son when he reaches a certain age, should be granted as due on the fixed day by the son's heir, if the boy did not live to that age; but this principle is regarded as conveying an exceptional right, and it has been decided that it does not extend to other fideicommissary gifts.   4. A testator desired his son to manumit a slave after five years on condition that he paid the son a daily wage for that period; the man wandered off and had paid nothing for the next two years; he was deemed not to have fulfilled the condition. If, however, the son and heir, or his tutors, preferred to take service from the slave for the two years, it is settled that this circumstance, arising from the past action of the heir, is no hindrance to due fulfillment of the condition.

24   ULPIAN, *Fideicommisa, book 5:* In general terms we shall say that anyone can provide in writing for fideicommissary freedom who can leave a monetary *fideicommissum*.   1. A provision for fideicommissary freedom is valid for the slave of the emperor or of a *municipium* or of any other owner.   2. If provision has been made for fideicommissary freedom for a slave owned by enemies of the state, one can debate whether it is not ineffective. It might perhaps have been said that the slave of enemies is unworthy to be a Roman citizen; but if the bequest is made for the contingency in which he comes to be one of ours, what stops us from saying that his freedom is valid?   3. If provision has been made for the fideicommissary freedom of a freeman and evidence is brought that he has been reduced to slavery, he can apply for freedom, provided that he is found to be a slave at the time of testator's death or of the fulfillment of a condition [to which his manumission is subject].   4. Fideicommissary freedom is properly bequeathed to the slave of one not yet alive.   5. A slave condemned to penal labor in the mines will not be able to entertain hope of freedom. What, then, if fideicommissary freedom has been bequeathed to him and he has been freed from penal labor in the mines by the clemency of the emperor? There is a rescript issued by our emperor that he is not returned to the ownership of his former owner; but it does not specify who his owner is. Certainly, when he becomes the property of the imperial treasury, he can hope for fideicommissary freedom.   6. It will be possible for fideicommissary freedom to be given to a son conceived and borne by a woman condemned to penal labor in the mines; there is nothing odd in this, since the deified Pius laid down by rescript that such a person can actually be sold as if a slave.   7. If the testator requested that Stichus should cease to be a slave, it has been decided that fideicommissary freedom is deemed to have been given; for by requesting that he should cease to be a slave, he seems to be requesting that freedom should be conferred on him.   8. But if he used these terms, "you are not to alienate him" or "you are not to sell him," we shall have to make the same statement, provided that it was the testator's intention in using them to express his desire that the slave should attain to freedom. But if he had other purposes in mind, for example, was advising the heir not to part with the slave in question, or wished him to discipline and torture the slave and give him no hope of finding a better master, or had any other intention and not that of assigning freedom to him, we must say that the grant of freedom fails; so Celsus writes in the twenty-third book of his *Digest*. In fact, it is not the words of a *fideicommissum*, but the mind of the testator that usually assigns fideicommissary freedom. But when there is a presumption that freedom seems to have been conferred, it is the part of the heir to prove that this was not the intention of the testator.   9. If someone has appointed a slave as tutor in his will in the supposition that he was free, it is absolutely certain that there can be no application for freedom and that the tutelage does not serve as

ground for a grant of freedom; Marcellus took this view in the fifteenth book of his *Digest*, and so did our emperor and his father in a rescript.   10. If a direct grant of freedom has been made to a slave in pledge, although the bequest seems to be ineffective by the rigor of the law, nonetheless, just as if there had been a bequest of fideicommissary freedom, the slave can apply to become free by *fideicommissum*; for the principle favoring freedom persuades us to construe the words of the will as authorizing an application for freedom, as if the liberation of the slave had been ordered by *fideicommissum*; in fact, it is well known that many rules have been made in favor of freedom contrary to strict law.   11. It is well enough established that when it has been decided that a will has been avoided by the subsequent birth of a posthumous daughter, direct grants of freedom made therein are not valid and fideicommissary grants are not due, unless the *paterfamilias* made them binding on *heredes legitimi* as well [as on testamentary beneficiaries].   12. Suppose that someone was requested to manumit a slave, belonging to someone else or to himself, and the value of what he received by the judgment of the testator was less than that of the slave; we must see whether he may be compelled to buy the slave from another owner or to manumit his own. Marcellus wrote that on taking the legacy in all circumstances, he should be compelled to manumit his own slave, and, to be sure, we treat it as a substantial difference in law, whether a man is requested to manumit his own slave or someone else's; in the former case, he will be compelled to manumit, even if his legacy was modest; in the latter, it will not be right to compel him, unless he could buy the slave for the sum he obtained by the judgment of the testator.   13. Quite logically, Marcellus says that a man instituted as heir should also be compelled to manumit his own slave, if anything accrued to him from the estate after discharge of liabilities; but if nothing accrued, he should not be compelled.   14. Suppose that the bequest was insufficient but, in fact, the value of the legacy increased from whatever reason; clearly, it will be absolutely fair that he should be compelled to buy the slave for the value that accrued to him; nor should he plead that the bequest was insufficient, inasmuch as his legacy has increased through the contingency of the will; indeed, even if, with the passage of time, fruits or interest accrued to the *fideicommissum*, we should say that freedom should be conferred.   15. So too if the price of the slave has fallen, we should say that he should be compelled to make the purchase.   16. But if the legacy has fallen in value, we should see whether he may be compelled to manumit the slave, when he expected to obtain a richer legacy. And I would think that he should not be compelled, if he be prepared to refund the legacy on the ground that he accepted the legacy without reckoning on its being unexpectedly reduced; if, then, he is ready to withdraw from the legacy, we shall have to permit him, unless it be the case that the residue in the legacy is enough to cover the price.   17. What, then, if a man should have been requested to manumit several slaves, and the sum left be enough to cover the price of some but not of all; should he be compelled to manumit some of them? I would think that he ought to be compelled to manumit at least those whose value is covered. Who, then, will determine which is to be selected for manumission? Should the legatee himself choose whom to manumit, or the heir on whom the legacy is imposed? Perhaps someone has said, quite justly, that the order of names in the will should be followed, but if the order should not be perspicuous, it will either be necessary to choose them by lot, so that the praetor may not fall under any suspicion of graft or bias, or the decision must be taken on representation of the merits of each.   18. A like view must be expressed, if a man should have been ordered to purchase slaves and free them and the money legated be insufficient for the purchase of all to whom freedom has been given; here too the same course will be followed as we have approved above.   19. If a legacy should have been left to someone with a request to manumit his own slave and to present the legacy to him, should the fideicommissary grant of freedom be made? Some are concerned because, if he has been compelled to make the grant of freedom, it will of necessity be right to compel him also to make the grant of the *fideicommissum* [the legacy]; and there are some who think that there should be no compulsion. For if I had been left a legacy and had been requested to hand it over to Titius at once and in addition to make a grant of fideicommissary freedom to my slave, we should undoubtedly have said that I am not to be compelled to make the grant of freedom, since it is apparent that I have received nothing by way of compensation. Obviously, if it so happens that the man has been requested to hand over the legacy left to him after an interval, it can be said that he should be compelled to manumit, having regard to the profit of the intervening period.   20. Just as a man who has been requested to grant a farm to one person, when he dies, and the sum of one hundred to another, should be compelled to comply, if he has acquired from the fruits of the farm the full value of the *fideicommissum*. The result is that a monetary *fideicommissum* and a grant of fideicommissary freedom is each in suspense.   21. But whenever there is an effective bequest of fideicommissary freedom, the position is that it may not be extinguished either by alienation or by usucapion; whoever has acquired the slave, to whom fideicommissary freedom has been left, is compelled to manumit him, according to a very great number of *constitutiones*. Hence, the person who has acquired the slave will be compelled to grant fideicommissary freedom, if the fiduciary preferred this course; in fact, it has been pretty widely accepted that even if the bequest of freedom to him was conditional and he was alienated before fulfillment of the condition, nonetheless, he retains his rights when alienated. But if he should not wish to be manumitted by the new owner, but should wish to receive his freedom from the person requested to manumit him, the deified Hadrian and the deified Pius declared in rescripts that he must be heard. Furthermore, if he has already been manumitted and yet would prefer to become the freedman of the man who had been requested to manumit him, the deified Pius declared in a rescript that he should be heard. But even if the manumitted man can show that his right is being or has actually been impaired by reason of the identity of the manumitter or for any cause whatever, he must receive assistance under these *constitutiones* in order that his circumstances may not be worsened contrary to the intention of the deceased. Obviously, if it were his intention that he should be manumitted no matter by whom, we should say that the aforementioned *constitutiones* do not apply.

25   PAUL, *Fideicommissa, book 3:* If the heir who sold the slave has died without a successor but the purchaser be alive and the slave wish to be freedman of the deceased not of the purchaser, Valens wrote that he should not be heard or else the purchaser would lose both price and freedman.

26   ULPIAN, *Fideicommissa, book 5:* However, when a man requested to manumit a slave, not belonging to someone else, has transferred the slave to another, under the constraint of death or as a result of confiscation of property, I am rather of the opinion that the *constitutiones* apply, to avoid any worsening of the fideicommissary freedom. For even when a man had been requested to manumit a slave on his deathbed and had died without granting him freedom, it has been laid down by *constitutio* that his situation should be just the same as if he had attained freedom from the fiduciary by will, since he can actually make a direct grant of freedom to him by will. The result is that whenever a man has received fideicommissary freedom, if he should be manumitted by anyone but the fiduciary, he has the assistance of the *constitutiones* and is to be regarded as if he had been manumitted by the fiduciary, since favor is shown to grants of fideicommissary freedom, and once the intention to make the grant has been expressed, it does not usually perish; in fact, anyone who has received this gift is deemed to be in provisional possession of freedom.   1. Thus, there is evident assistance to fideicommissary grants of freedom in that delay in giving them effect is deemed to consist in the mere fact and in the case of a slave-woman manumitted in this way the children born to her from the day on which freedom could have been applied for were

to be handed over for manumission to the mother, whereas those born from the day on which application was made are born free. In fact, it is common as a result of lack of initiative or timidity on the part of those to whom fideicommissary freedom has been left, or of the authority and rank of the fiduciaries, that applications for fideicommissary freedom are made too late or not at all; this ought not to prejudice freedom. In our contention, then, a time limit should be imposed with the effect that the children are born free from the moment that there has been delay to the freedom [of the mother]; but it ought to be said that the offspring are manumitted from the moment when an application for freedom could have been made, although it was not made. Certainly, persons under twenty-five should receive assistance with the effect that the delay should be deemed to consist in the mere fact; for the same principle on which the deified Severus decided in court and established by a *constitutio* that "delay" concerning bequests of money made to *minores* by *fideicommissum* should depend on the mere fact should be even more admissible in cases of grants of freedom.   2. A certain Caecilius wished to have a slave-woman manumitted by *fideicommissum*, whom he had assigned as a pledge, after discharge of the debt; the heirs did not discharge the debt, and the children later born to her were sold by the creditor; our emperor with his father ruled by rescript, in accordance with decisions of the deified Pius, that to prevent the boys from being defrauded of free birth as intended by the testator, the price must be repaid to the purchaser and the boys were to be freeborn just as if their mother had been manumitted at the relevant time.   3. Our emperor with his father ruled that if the tablets of the will or the codicils had not been opened until the lapse of five years from testator's death and a child had been born in the interval, to prevent the chance delay inflicting slavery on the child, it should be handed over to the mother, so that she might bring about its freedom.   4. This rescript, and that of the deified Pius we mentioned, show that they did not wish chance delay to harm the child of a mother to whom fideicommissary freedom was given.   5. However, if the woman has received fideicommissary freedom from the substitute heir of one below the age of puberty and has given birth during the latter's lifetime, or if she has received freedom as from a certain date or subject to a condition and has given birth before that date or fulfillment of that condition, the child will not attain freedom; for their circumstances are different; they have suffered delay not by chance but in accordance with the testator's wish.   6. If the legacy has been treated as null or a slave also given fideicommissary freedom, it is a question whether the fideicommissary freedom should fail, or if the slave were to apply for such freedom from the person in whose service he had remained, given the nullity of the legacy bequeathed to the person who has been requested to manumit him, [whether the fideicommissary grant of freedom is safe]. And I would think it right to say that the fideicommissary grant of freedom was safe, although the person requested to manumit the man obtained nothing under the will; the actual recipient of the legacy will then be compelled to grant freedom, since grants of fideicommissary freedom should not be subject to any hindrance.   7. Assistance was given to grants of freedom by a *senatus consultum* passed in the time of the deified Trajan in the consulship of Rubrius Gallus and Caepio Hispo in these terms: "If persons from whom freedom is due on summons by the praetor should have deliberately failed to attend, and if the praetor on hearing the case should have pronounced that freedom was due, the slaves freed are to have the same legal status as if they had been manumitted directly."   8. This *senatus consultum* relates to those to whom freedom is due under a *fideicommissum*. Hence, if it were not due, but the praetor was gulled about their freedom and pronounced judgment [in their favor], freedom does not accrue to them as a result of this *senatus consultum*. This was also ruled in a rescript of our emperor and his father.   9. But it is the praetor's duty to summon the persons bound to grant fideicommissary freedom; if they have not been summoned, the *senatus consultum Rubrianum* does not apply; they must be summoned by announcements, proclamations, and letters.   10. This *senatus consultum* relates to all persons bound to grant fideicommissary freedom who keep under cover. Further, it applies whether the request was enjoined on the heir or on anyone else; all persons without exception on whom the duty might lie to grant fideicommissary freedom are covered by the *senatus consultum*. 11. So if the heir should keep under cover, but the legatee or fiduciary who may have been requested to grant freedom should be present, the *senatus consultum* has no effect, and there will nonetheless be no hindrance to freedom; we have in mind a case when the legatee has not yet acquired ownership of the slave.

27 PAUL, *Fideicommissa, book 3:* So in this case, the emperor should be approached, so that in this case too provision may be made for freedom.

28 ULPIAN, *Fideicommissa, book 5:* If the fiduciary has sold the slave to whom fideicommissary freedom has been left and the purchaser should keep under cover, but the fiduciary should be present, would the *senatus consultum Rubrianum* apply? Marcellus says that it does, because the man bound to manumit is absent.   1. Moreover, the words "deliberately failed to attend" do not imply that the man bound to grant freedom has to be keeping under cover; even if he should merely disdain to appear, the *senatus consultum* will apply.   2. The same practice is followed if several heirs who have been requested to grant fideicommissary freedom should delay the grant by absence without lawful grounds.   3. If it has been pronounced that some are absent with lawful grounds, the man will be the freedman of those absent with lawful grounds and of those present who make no delay to the grant of fideicommissary freedom, just as if they were the only fiduciaries and had lawfully made the man free.   4. In the case of a man who should keep under cover when requested to manumit a slave who is not part of the inheritance, a *senatus consultum* was passed in the consulship of Aemilius Juncus and Julius Severus in these terms: "If it shall be alleged that any of the persons who should owe fideicommissary freedom on whatever grounds to a slave who did not belong to the testator at the time of his death is absent, the praetor should hear the case, and if it shall appear that the circumstances are such that the man should, if present, be compelled to manumit, he should give judgment in this sense; and after judgment the person freed should be in that legal status in which he would have been, if he had been manumitted in accordance with the fideicommissary obligation to manumit." 5. Persons should be said to be absent with lawful grounds quite simply if the reason for their absence is not wrongful, since the fact that they are not absent to evade granting freedom would amply suffice for them to be considered absent with lawful grounds; it is not necessary that they should be absent on public business. Further, if a man should be domiciled in one place and application be made for fideicommissary freedom in another, we should say that it is not necessary to summon the man who, it is claimed, owes fideicommissary freedom, inasmuch as even in his absence, if it has been decided that the freedom is due, it can be pronounced that he is absent for lawful reason, and he does not lose the freedman; for no one will doubt that men are absent for lawful reason who remain in their own seats and domicile.

29 PAUL, *Fideicommissa, book 3:* If anyone should have been alienated, once he was in a situation in which fideicommissary freedom was due to him, the interim owner will be compelled to manumit; but here no distinction is drawn whether he be absent for lawful or unlawful reason; for in all circumstances the man retains his freedman.

30 ULPIAN, *Fideicommissa, book 5:* When a man's absence was alleged and a judicial decision was issued that he was absent for lawful reason, but he was already dead, our

emperor ruled by rescript that the decision should be treated as applying to the heir and that his rights should be such as they would have been if the heir himself had been pronounced absent for the same reason.   1. If an *infans* should be among those from whom manumission is due, the senate decreed that despite the hindrance presented by the age of one fiduciary, the slaves, male and female, should be free to whom freedom must be given by reason of *fideicommissum*.   2. The same will have to be said if an *infans* is the sole heir instituted.   3. But if a *pupillus* has a tutor who refuses his sanction to the grant of freedom, this should not hinder either the *pupillus* from having freedmen or the beneficiaries from obtaining freedom; on the contrary the deified brothers ruled by rescript that fideicommissary freedom should be granted to the slave just as if he had been manumitted by the *pupillus* himself with the tutor's sanction.   4. Hence, in any circumstances in which an *infans* has been made liable to grant fideicommissary freedom, we shall adapt to them the intention of the *senatus consultum*, which must also be extended to the *infans* who is heir of the fiduciary.   5. However, in this case too the praetor is to be approached, especially as a rescript of the deified Pius had the effect that if some of the fiduciaries should be present, others should keep under cover and others should be absent for lawful reason with the complication that one is an *infans*, the man would not be made the freedman of them all, but only of the *infans* and of those absent for lawful reason or actually present.   6. If several heirs have been instituted, including an *infans*, and the latter should not have been requested himself to manumit the slave, the grant of freedom must not fail because of the fact that the *infans* would not be able to sell him to the co-heirs; apart from the *senatus consultum Vitrasianum*, the deified Pius in a rescript to Cassius Dexter explained that the shares of slaves to whom fideicommissary freedom has been given should be equitably valued and that on this basis the slave should be manumitted by those to whom the request was addressed. The manumitters will be liable for the value to their brothers and co-heirs just as if proceedings could be taken against them thereon for a judgment debt.   7. In the case of the lunatic, the deified Pius ruled by rescript that fideicommissary freedom is not hindered by the condition of a testamentary heir who is stated not to be of sound mind. Hence, if it has been established that freedom was due to a man by *fideicommissum*, the praetor will issue a judicial decision embracing this particular point, as in the case of the *infans*.   8. Consequentially, assistance will be given in the cases of the dumb and or the deaf.   9. But even if a man has died without an heir or any other successor who was under obligation to grant fideicommissary freedom, the senate resolved that the praetor was to be approached and freedom granted.   10. But even if a *suus heres* has declined the inheritance, assistance has been given to freedom by means of the *senatus consultum*, even though a man is not without an heir when there is a *suus heres*, albeit one who declines the inheritance.   11. The same is to be said, if a man under twenty-five, after entering on the inheritance of one who owed fideicommissary freedom, has secured *in integrum restitutio* in order that he may decline it.   12. However, we must inquire whose freedman the slave becomes in such circumstances; in fact, under the *constitutio* freedom is due to him just as if he had obtained it by will. So he will be a freedman of the deceased, not a freedman of the person who owed him fideicommissary freedom.   13. If one of the fiduciaries has died without a successor and the other should be absent for lawful reason, there is on record a rescript of the deified Marcus and Verus according to which the man would attain freedom just as if he had obtained it in the proper way both from the person deceased without successor and from the person absent for lawful reason.   14. It is a nice question, given that the heir is deceased without successor, whether one should wait until it be certain that no heir or *bonorum possessor* will appear or whether during this period of uncertainty (caused perhaps by the deliberation of the testamentary heir) the man may attain freedom; and it is the better view that he must wait until it has first become certain that a successor will not appear.   15. The emperor Antoninus issued a rescript that a slave to whom liberty is owed by a *fideicommissum* can, without freedom receive something from the will of the heir.   16. Moreover, the deified Marcus ruled by rescript that neither age nor condition nor delay on the part of those who fail to fulfill grants of fideicommissary freedom or do so too late undoes such grants or impairs the status of the beneficiaries.   17. Although grants of freedom are not due under codicils that are void, nonetheless, if the heir has treated these codicils as valid and has fulfilled some of them and has wished slaves to live in freedom for the purpose of fulfilling the grant of fideicommissary freedom, it is made plain by a rescript of our emperor and his deified father that they have attained lawful freedom.

31   PAUL, *Fideicommissa, book 3:* Freedom can be given by *fideicommissum* to the slave of some other person, provided that there is a community of testamentary rights with that person.   1. When a man about to die intestate laid a *fideicommissum* on his son to manumit a slave and a posthumous son was born to the deceased, the deified brothers ruled by rescript that freedom, being indivisible, was to be granted by both.   2. A man owing fideicommissary freedom will be able to manumit even in the period in which he will be barred from alienating.   3. If a patron has received *bonorum possessio* against the will on the ground that he had been passed over by the freedman, he will not be compelled to sell his own slave whom he had been requested by his freedman to manumit.   4. If the owner of the slave should be unwilling to sell him for the purpose of manumission, the praetor has no role; the same is true, if he should wish to sell him at too high a price. However, if the owner was prepared to sell at a given price, not manifestly unfair, but the fiduciary contends that it is excessive, the praetor should interpose to ensure that a fair price is paid to the owner willing to sell and that freedom is granted by the purchaser. But if the owner should be prepared to sell and the slave should want manumission, the heir must be compelled to buy and manumit, unless the owner should wish to manumit the slave with a view to securing an action for his value against the heir; and this is the course also to be followed, if the heir were to keep under cover; that was also ruled in a rescript of the Emperor Antoninus.

32   MAECIAN, *Fideicommissa, book 15:* But if a man were prepared to alienate but unwilling to do this, until satisfied in regard to the price, it will not be right to compel him to manumit, in case he should manumit the slave and get nothing or too little in return, for example, if the fiduciary were insolvent.   1. However, neither owner nor anyone else should be allowed to carry out this transaction against the will of the slave, since the *fideicommissum* in question is not of the kind that is to enrich the owner; otherwise, the gift would obviously have been made directly to him. That can occur, if the testator expressed the wish that a slave should be bought at more than his value and manumitted; in fact, the owner too then has the right to sue for the *fideicommissum*; for he has an interest in receiving the surplus on the true value, just as the slave has an interest in attaining freedom.   2. This will also be the case if heir or legatee were bidden to buy something belonging to someone else and give it to a third party; for then both the owner concerned and the man who should receive the gift have the right to sue, since both have an interest, the owner in receiving for the thing the price over and above its value at which the testator directed its purchase, and the person to whom the thing was left in obtaining possession of it.

33   PAUL, *Fideicommissa, book 3:* If the son of the deceased should have been requested to manumit his father's slave, we must say that he can take possession of him even against the terms of the will and impose workdays (*operae*); for this he could have done, as son of the patron, even if the man had received freedom direct.   1. The *senatus consultum Rubrianum* will apply even to conditional grants of freedom, provided that the slave himself is not responsible for nonfulfillment of the condition; it makes no difference whether the condition be an obligation to give or to perform or one of any other kind. Furthermore, the heir actually loses his freedman, if he has hindered fulfillment, even if he be son of the deceased, although in that case he would have him as freedman under a different title. On occasion, even the son suffers a penalty; for if he has claimed the man as a slave or accused him of a capital offense, he loses *bonorum possessio* against the will.   2. If the legatee of a slave had been requested to manumit him and should be unwilling to take him, he should be compelled either to take and manumit him or to cede his actions to the nominee of the slave, so that the grant of freedom may not fail.

34   POMPONIUS, *Fideicommissa, book 3:* A man to whom fideicommissary freedom has
been left is not to be transferred against his will to someone else to be manumitted by
him and so become the freedman of someone other than the fiduciary.   1. Campanus
says that if a man under twenty has requested his heir to manumit his own slave, freedom must be granted to him, since here the *lex Aelia Sentia* does not apply.   2. A
slave had been legated to Calpurnius Flaccus with a request to manumit, failing which
the same slave was legated to Titius who was also requested to manumit him; it had
been ordered that if he had not done so, the man was to be free. Sabinus says that the
legacy would be void and that the man would be free at once under the will.

35   MAECIANUS, *Fideicommissa, book 15:* Gaius Cassius thought that on occasion both
heir and legatee should be excused the obligation to free their own slave, if either his
service were so necessary that its loss would be inexpedient, as in the case of an accountant or teacher for the children, or if he had committed an offense so serious that
retribution should not be spared. This opinion has not been accepted. The view has
been taken that they had the slaves in their own power; in fact, they could have dis-
claimed their rights under the will; by taking them, they accepted an obligation to
carry out the wish of the deceased.

36   MAECIANUS, *Fideicommissa, book 16: Infantes,* lunatics, captives of the enemy,
and persons whose delay [in granting freedom] is due to religious scruple or a very
honorable reason or some calamity or a very great risk to estate, civic status or reputation or some like cause, are not within the scope of the *senatus consultum Rubrianum,* nor indeed are *pupilli* without tutors, nor *pupilli* with tutors who are in any of
these situations. However, if tutors do not make themselves available when applied to,
I do not think that *pupilli* are deprived thereby of freedmen, since it is not only unfair
that a *pupillus* should sustain loss from the conduct of a tutor, who may perhaps be
insolvent; and the *senatus consultum* relates only to those who are under obligation to
grant freedom under a *fideicommissum.* And, in fact, they have the assistance of the
senatus consultum Dasumianum which has provided, in the case of persons absent
for lawful reason, that freedom should not be hindered but that those not acting to the
detriment of freedom should not be deprived of a freedman.   1. If anyone is represented by a procurator, his absence is always ascribed to a lawful reason, and he is not
deprived of the freedman.   2. In no case is the jurisdiction of whomever it be who
hears an application for fideicommissary freedom to be obstructed by the privilege of any *civitas,* or corporate body, or by the office that any man holds or by personal status.

37   ULPIAN, *Fideicommissa, book 6:* If fideicommissary freedom should have been
given without condition and it should be alleged that the slave concerned handled accounts, the deified Marcus ruled by rescript that the grant of freedom should not be
subject to delay but that an *arbiter* should at once be appointed to audit them. The
words of the rescript are as follows: "It seems to be the fairer course to confer freedom
on Trophimus in accordance with the *fideicommissum,* as it is established that it was
given to him without a condition that he should render account, nor would it have been
humane to delay his freedom because of a financial investigation. However, once it has
been conferred, the praetor should immediately appoint an *arbiter* before whom he
is to render a faithful account of the administration with which he was evidently
charged." So then he will only be compelled to render account; there is nothing further
to say whether he would be obliged to make good a deficit, nor do I think he should be
compelled to, since a man cannot be sued after he is free on a matter arising from his
conduct in slavery. Clearly, the praetor should compel him to hand back the actual account books and any properties or moneys in his keeping from his administration, and
to provide information on each several matter.

38   PAUL, *Judicial Decisions, book 3:* In a will which had not been duly executed a man
gave freedom and [pecuniary] *fideicommissa* to a woman he had brought up. When
everything had proceeded on the footing of intestacy, the emperor asked whether she

had been manumitted as on the basis of a *fideicommissum*, and issued an interlocutory decision that even if the father had made no request to the intestate heir, nonetheless, dutiful sons werè bound to manumit a woman their father had loved. Therefore, he pronounced that she was rightly manumitted and that consequently the [pecuniary] *fideicommissa* as well were due to her.

39   PAUL, *Replies, book 13:* Paul replied that even if it were found that a slave whom a testator had taken to be his and desired one of his heirs to manumit belonged to someone else, the fiduciary should still be compelled to purchase him and manumit, since he did not think that the case of freedom was like that of a pecuniary *fideicommissum.* 1. Paul replied that the words "believe me, Zoilus, my son Martialis will show his gratitude to you and your children" contain a full indication of the wish of the deceased to benefit Zoilus and the associated persons, and that if they should be slaves, nothing can be given them so welcome to them as freedom, and, therefore, the governor ought to follow the wish of the deceased.

40   PAUL, *Replies, book 15:* Lucius Titius gave his slave-woman, Concordia, to his natural daughter, Septicia; in a subsequent will, he legated the aforementioned woman along with other slave-women to his daughter for the purpose of manumission; could his natural daughter, Septicia, be compelled to manumit the aforementioned slave-woman? Paul replied that if the gift of the woman occurred in the lifetime of the natural father, and the daughter did not accept the judgment of the natural father in regard to the other legacies, she cannot be compelled to manumit her own slave-woman on the footing of a *fideicommissum.* 1. Lucius Titius legated the slave Stichus to Maevius and asked that he should never be manumitted either by Maevius or by his heir. Paul replied that the testator had the power subsequently to make this slave free, since he had bound not himself but the legatee.

41   SCAEVOLA, *Replies, book 4:* "I wish my slave-woman, Thais, to be my freedwoman after she has served my heir for ten years." The question arises, since he wished her to be his freedwoman and this was not in the power of the heir, and since freedom was not given her direct and unconditionally, whether she remained in slavery even after ten years. He replied that the statement of the facts gave no reason why freedom should not be due to Thais.   1. Lucius Titius made the following provision: "My dearest son, Maevius, I request you not to let Stichus, Damas, and Pamphilus be your slaves any longer, if they have deserved well of you and you have discharged your debts"; if it was the heir's responsibility that he did not discharge the debts, could they obtain freedom by *fideicommissum*? He replied that the heir incurred no blame if he was rather slow in discharging his debts for the advantages to be gained in administration of his estate; but if it were proved beyond doubt that his purpose in not making payment was to delay the grants of freedom, the grants should be duly made.   2. A man who had appointed a tutor for his children by will laid him under a *fideicommissum* to manumit slaves of the tutor himself, but the man had been excused from the tutelage; were the tutors appointed to act in his place bound to make the same slaves free? He replied that, on the facts stated, the testamentary heirs seemed responsible for the grants of freedom.   3. "I give Seius three pounds of gold and the shorthand writer Stichus whom I ask you to manumit." Seius who was appointed tutor by the same will excused himself from the tutelage; would the fideicommissary freedom still be due? He replied that the facts stated showed no reason to the contrary.   4. After instituting his sister as heir a man made the following provisions regarding the slaves: "I wish and request you, dearest sister, to treat Stichus and Damas, my stewards, as placed in your trust [deposit]; I did not free them myself until they should have rendered accounts, but if they should also have received your approval, I have indicated to you what I wish." Suppose the stewards are prepared to

render their accounts but the heir should withhold freedom, saying that they do not meet with her approval; should she be heard? He replied that for the purpose of their obtaining freedom it was not what might fail to win the approval of the heirs, but what might win the approval of a good man that was to be examined.   5. Lucia Titia placed her heirs under a *fideicommissum* to purchase Pamphila, the slave-woman of Seia, with her children and manumit them, and the *juridicus* assessed the price to be paid for each; in the interval before payment of the money, Pamphila gave birth; would her child belong to the heirs of Seia or to the heir of Titia? He replied that the child of Pamphila belonged to whomever it was who owned her at the time of birth; but if the heir delayed the fideicommissary grant of freedom, he should be compelled to make the child free as well.   6. Lucius Titius made the following provision in his will: "I commend to you the doctors 'A' and 'B'; it will be for you to judge whether they are to be your good freedmen and doctors. I was afraid that if I had given them freedom they would have acted as the slave doctors of my dearest sister did after she had manumitted them, leaving her at the end of their salaried service." Are the slaves named entitled to fideicommissary freedom? He replied that, on the facts stated, the heirs had no binding obligation but were given discretion.   7. Titius gave his slave Stichus freedom on condition of his rendering accounts; should his liability for his administration be subject to the reservation that fortuitous losses should not be included? He replied that in a business which, on the facts stated, he carried on by the wish of his owner, losses so fortuitous that no blame could attach to the slave should not be included in his liability.   8. I also ask, given that a man has been ordered to hand back the whole *peculium*, whether the *peculium* should be reckoned as restricted to whatever on any ground should [not] accrue to the owner; he replied that in the special case here at issue any debt to the owner should [not] be deducted from the *peculium*.   9. I also ask whether anything appropriated by the slave to his *peculium* from the sums he owes should be deducted from the *peculium* he is to hand back. He replied that if, in the case stated, what he had appropriated to the *peculium* was then paid out under the heading of moneys he owed from his administration, the condition [for manumission] is satisfied if he pays what is left of the *peculium*.   10. The following grant of freedom was made by will: "I wish my slave, Cupitus, to be free after rendering accounts, when my son, Marcianus, has completed sixteen years"; after the testator's death the tutors entrusted Cupitus with the collection of debts; he got in the cash and paid it over to the same tutors; then the son died without reaching the age of puberty, and his mother, who was his heir, secured condemnation of the son's tutor by a judgment on tutelage; Cupitus proclaims his right to freedom at the time at which, if still alive, Marcianus would have been sixteen, furnishing accounts for one year to the date of testator's death, since his other accounts had been certified. The question has been raised whether Cupitus should be compelled to render those accounts too which the tutors had passed at their own risk. He replied that the man in question seems to have complied with the condition that he must render account, if he rendered account in full to the extent that can rightly be required in respect of his administration; in fact, the other condition can be, by a more benign interpretation, accepted as meaning that if the *pupillus* had died, it is enough for him to await the time at which, if he had lived, the *pupillus* would complete his sixteenth year.   11. "Let my slaves Stichus and Damas be free, if they render accounts"; the question was asked whether not only accounts but also the making good of anything removed by their fraud or design be due from them for them to attain their liberty; the reply was that there is inherent in the condition of accounts everything in any way pertaining to the conduct and [good] faith of the slave.   12. They did not prepare the accounts within the period specified in the condition but furnished them later; do they attain liberty? The answer given was that if it was their own fault that they did not prepare them within the time specified in the condition, they will not become free by reason of the fact that they wish to render accounts out of time.   13. "I ask my heirs and commit it to their charge that when my son completes sixteen years of age, they manumit Stichus on his rendering accounts." My question is: Does the testator wish that same slave to continue his activity until the son reaches the age of puberty? The reply was that the testator obviously wished an account to be rendered also of his activities for that period by Stichus.   14. "I direct my slave Stichus to give without dispute so many gold pieces to my heiresses, my wife and daughter, and I charge them to manumit him"; the question was: When the wife would not accept the inheritance, did [Stichus] have to give to both or to the daughter alone? The reply was that all must be given to the daughter who, in such circumstances, becomes sole heiress.   15. A man instituted his son as sole heir and made a grant of freedom in these terms: "My clerk of accounts, Decembrius, my bailiff, Severus, and Victorina, my housekeeper and Severus's *contubernalis*, are to be free after eight years; I wish them to be in the service of my son, but I request you, my dearest son, Severus, to take Decembrius and Severus into your favor, as I have not given them freedom with immediate effect in order that you might have satisfactory services, and I hope that you may also find them satisfactory freedmen." Given that at the time when Titius was making his will, his son had been aged nine and that Titius died two and a half years later, should the term of eight years for which freedom was deferred run from the time that the will was made or from the time of death? He replied that it might appear that the testator had fixed a total period of eight years for the deferment of freedom, which were to be counted from the date of the will, unless it were proved that he had wished something different.   16. "Let Spendophorus be free, after my daughter has married within the family, if he has satisfactorily rendered to her accounts of his administration"; the daughter died without reaching puberty in the father's lifetime, and Seius became the heir by substitution; given that Spendophorus did not administer the affairs of the *pupilla* and ceased to administer the affairs of the head of the household in his own lifetime, and that Titia, if she were alive, would have been over twelve, would he be free under the will? He replied that if he had not administered affairs of which he owed accounts to the heir, he would be free on the facts stated.   17. "I wish Stichus to be free after rendering accounts." Stichus as treasurer lent money with his master's sanction; he produces accounts signed by the master and has made no subsequent loan; if the debtors, with whom other collectors of debts were concerned, were insolvent, would it appear that the condition had not yet been fulfilled? He replied that, on the facts stated, the insolvency of the debtors was immaterial to the man's responsibility for rendering accounts.

42   MAECIAN, *Fideicommissa, book 7:* Our [Emperor] Antoninus Augustus Pius in the desire that the last wishes of his soldiers should invariably be upheld ordered that when the heir whom any of them had instituted and his substitute had died immediately before entering on the inheritance, the slaves to whom the soldier had granted fideicommissary freedom and the inheritance should be free and be his heirs, just as if the grant had been made to them directly. However, in the case of slaves who had received fideicommissary freedom and an inheritance from a civilian, given that the heir instituted and the substitute had similarly died immediately, he held it enough that their freedom should be confirmed.

43   PAUL, *Sabinus, book 4:* Fideicommissary freedom is not due to a slave whom the master later placed in bonds.

44   POMPONIUS, *Sabinus, book 7:* When fideicommissary freedom is due, the slave has a right to bring proceedings against the master.

45   ULPIAN, *Disputations, book 5:* When a debtor has been requested by a creditor to

manumit his own slave-woman pledged to the creditor, it must be said that there is an effective grant of fideicommissary freedom binding on the debtor. For what difference does it make whether he is bound to a particular sum or to make a grant of fideicommissary freedom? And whether or not the cost exceeds the debt, he is compelled to grant freedom, provided only that he has acknowledged the creditor's wish. But we take such acknowledgment to be made, for instance, if when sued by the [creditor's] heir, he has availed himself of an *exceptio* or in some other way has made his willingness [to comply with the creditor's wish] manifest; in fact, if the debtor should be sued by the heir of the creditor, he can avail himself of the defense of fraud to the extent of [the sum that represents] his interest in keeping his own slave-woman. 1. In the case of a fideicommissary grant of freedom, however modest the value of the legacy secured, the legatee is bound to manumit his own slave; in fact, whereas if a fideicommissary liability to pay a sum of money has been shared, . . . it is therefore preferable that there should be a burden on the man who has accepted the legacy than that the grant of freedom should fail. 2. Whenever fideicommissary freedom is left to a slave, man or woman, there is no change in servile status pending manumission; and, indeed, if the person from whom freedom is due has made no delay in the grant, there is no alteration in their status with the consequence that it is agreed that they can be legated for the time being but without derogation from their rights.

46 ULPIAN, *Disputations, book 6:* Fideicommissary freedom can be given in these terms: "My heir, if that should be your wish, I lay upon you a *fideicommissum* to manumit Stichus," even though nothing else in a will can depend for its validity on the nod of the heir. 1. Of course, freedom can also be assigned to a man in the terms: "if this should be the wish of Stichus." 2. But if it should be so drafted, "I wish Stichus to be free, if this should be the wish of Seius," in my view the grant of freedom can be said to be effective, since it is rather a condition analogous to a legacy to me being made conditional on Titius climbing the Capitol. 3. But if the form of words were, "if it should be the wish of the heir," the grant will not be effective, but freedom will only ensue at his pleasure, if testator has made everything turn on the wish of the heir. On the other hand, if he has given him discretion as a good man, we shall not doubt that freedom is due; in fact, it has been decided that freedom is due under the formula: "I request you to manumit if you think fit"; for this is to be taken to mean, "if you, as a good man, think fit." In fact, I also think it due if left in the terms: "if you should approve my wish"; so too in the terms: "if he has earned your favor" or "if he has not offended you," that is, as a good man, or "if you have approved of him" or "if you have not disapproved of him" or "if you have thought him deserving"; indeed, when a testator granted a *fideicommissum* in Greek as follows, "I wish freedom to be given to such and such a man, if this has your sanction," the deified Severus ruled by rescript that the *fideicommissum* might be applied for. 4. But though it cannot be made discretionary for the heir whether freedom is due, it can be made discretionary when it is due. 5. A man, after legating three slaves, made it a *fideicommissum* on his heir to manumit two of his own choice; the fideicommissary grant of freedom will be effective, and the heir will manumit those of his choice; hence, if the legatee were to claim by *vindicatio* those whom the heir wishes to manumit, he will be met by defense of fraud.

47 JULIAN, *Digest, book 42:* If a father has instituted two sons as heirs and the will has been voided by the subsequent birth of a posthumous son, although the inheritance is theirs as to two thirds, nonetheless, they are not under obligation to fulfill fideicommissary grants of freedom, just as they are not compelled to pay even legacies or make fideicommissary gifts. 1. If an heir, who has been requested to manumit a slave in other ownership or one in whom he has a share or one in the usufruct of another person, should keep under cover, it will be equitable under the *senatus consultum* to come to the aid of the grants of freedom. 2. If Stichus has received fideicommissary freedom subject to the condition of his rendering accounts and he is prepared in the absence of the heir to pay all moneys due, it is part of the praetor's function to choose a

good man by whose discretion the accounts may be computed, to put the sum arising from the computation in safekeeping and thereupon to pronounce that freedom in accordance with the *fideicommissum* is due. Still, this procedure will be proper, if the heir is absent for lawful reason; for if he keeps under cover, it will be sufficient that it should be clear to the praetor that the slave is not refusing compliance with the condition, and thereupon it will be his duty to pronounce on his freedom.   3. When fideicommissary and conditional freedom is given to a slave legated, he should not be delivered to the legatee without security that he will be redelivered if the condition is realized.   4. A woman in her last illness, in the presence of several men of good standing and of her mother, who was also her *heres legitima*, said, "I wish my slave-women Maevia and Seia to be free," and died intestate; suppose that the mother did not claim the estate as *heres legitima* under the *senatus consultum* and that it went to the nearest cognate; would fideicommissary freedom be due? I replied that it was due; by saying in her last moments, "I wish such and such slave women to be free," she evidently requested all who were to be *heredes legitimi* or *bonorum possessores* to make this possible.

48   JULIAN, *Digest, book 62:* When it was written in the will, "I legate Stichus to Titius" or "let my heir give Stichus to Titius, in order that Titius may manumit him," I said that if the legatee claims Stichus, a defense of fraud would stand in his way, unless he has given security for granting freedom in accordance with the wish of the deceased.

49   AFRICANUS, *Questions, book 9:* If the legatee of a slave who has been requested to manumit him should keep under cover, he replied that the man becomes a freedman of the deceased; so too if the fideicommissary were not a legatee, but the heir. But even if the *fideicommissum* was laid only on some of the heirs and not on all, it must equally be said that he becomes a freedman of the deceased; however, the co-heirs whose shares had to be bought out should be given on this account an *actio utilis* against the heirs in concealment, or they will also properly proceed with an action for dividing the inheritance.

50   MARCIAN, *Institutes, book 7:* If a slave has been legated and is to be manumitted by *fideicommissum*, Cervidius Scaevola, who was consulted, thought that what was written last was valid, whether it were the grant of freedom or the legacy, inasmuch as it is approved that a grant of freedom may later be canceled, and it is settled that a legacy can effect such a cancellation; but that if it were unclear with what intention the testator legated the slave to whom he had granted freedom, the grant of freedom takes precedence. In my view, too, this opinion is more correct.

51   MARCIAN, *Institutes, book 9:* Not only the man requested to manumit may effect the liberation of the slave but his successors too, whether they have succeeded by purchase or by some other title. But if there proves to be no successor, the man passes to the imperial treasury for the purpose of liberation.   1. Further, a man requested to manumit can manumit even at a time when he is debarred from alienating.   2. If a man should have been requested to manumit someone else's slave, when a specific sum has been legated to him for the purpose of making the purchase and manumitting and the owner is unwilling to sell, he retains the legacy in accordance with the wish of the deceased.   3. A slave to whom fideicommissary freedom is due is in a way in the position of a freeman and secures the status of a *statuliber*, all the more in that he may not be transferred to a third party in such a way as to hinder his freedom or to subject him to more burdensome patronage rights.   4. It has been provided by the *senatus consultum Dasumianum* that if the person from whom fideicommissary freedom is due should be absent for lawful cause and this should have been judicially pronounced, the man obtains freedom just as if he had been duly manumitted in accordance with the *fideicommissum*.   5. A man is taken to be absent, if absent from the court.   6. And since the provision related only to heirs, there has been a supplement to the aforementioned *senatus consultum* that if anyone is under obligation to grant fideicommissary

freedom for whatever reason and it has been judicially pronounced that he or they are absent, the man should be treated as if he had been duly manumitted in accordance with the *fideicommissum*.   7. But it is provided by the *senatus consultum Articuleianum* that in provinces the provincial governors may take cognizance, though the heir is not of that province.   8. But if a man should have been requested to manumit a slave belonging not to the inheritance but to himself, under the *senatus consultum Juncianum*, the man attains freedom after judicial pronouncement.   9. Whether the fiduciary is absent for lawful reason or keeps under cover or is present but unwilling to manumit, he is to be deemed absent by a rescript of the deified Pius.   10. The same *senatus consultum* requires the purchaser too to manumit.   11. And a co-heir who is present may manumit just as if the slave had been delivered to him by the other co-heir; it is reported that the same emperor declared by rescript that this applies to the co-heir who is *impubes* and who had not been requested to manumit.   12. But if a man was requested to manumit a slave-woman for the purpose of marrying her, he should not be compelled to take her as wife; the grant of fideicommissary freedom is enough.

52   ULPIAN, *Replies, book 1:* After a creditor has alienated slaves for whom fideicommissary freedom was provided by the will, no assistance can be given them against the heir except for lawful reason.

53   MARCIAN, *Rules, book 4:* If anyone has delayed in fulfilling a request to manumit a slave-woman and she has given birth in the interim, it has been laid down by *constitutio* that in such circumstances the child is free at birth with the status of a freeborn person. But there are *constitutiones* providing that from the moment at which freedom is first due, a child is born with the status of a freeborn person; and this rule is all the more to be followed without question because freedom is not a private, but a public matter with the effect that the person from whom it is due ought to confer it readily. But if the slave-woman has given birth before the fideicommissary freedom is due and yet it has been the contrivance of the heir that it was not yet due, for example, because he was too slow in entering on the inheritance with the intention that the woman's children should become his slaves, it is approved that they should be manumitted but that they should be delivered to the mother to be manumitted by her and become her freedmen rather than his; in fact, the heir will not even have as freedmen those whom he is not worthy to have as slaves.

54   MAECIAN, *Fideicommissa, book 16:* If, after receiving her son, a mother, or her successor, was unwilling to grant freedom, they are to be compelled; furthermore, if the mother were unwilling to take delivery of her son or if she had ceased to live, it is not false to say that nonetheless the heir liberates children born in these circumstances.

55   MARCIAN, *Rules, book 4:* But even if the heir has been too slow in entering on the inheritance not from intent but while making up his mind whether he should enter on it, the same should be said. Even if he has learned of his institution as heir after the slave-woman has given birth, assistance should be given in this case too; however, in this case, he will have the obligation to manumit himself, not to hand over to the mother.   1. But if there has been a direct grant of freedom and any of these contingencies has arisen, in what way will assistance be given to the children? In the former cases, there is an application for fideicommissary freedom, and the praetor assists the little ones; but when there is a direct grant of freedom, there is no application. Even so, I think that assistance should be given to the child in this case; if approached, the praetor is to award the mother an *actio in rem* on the pattern of fideicommissary freedom. In this sense, indeed, Marcellus, too, in the sixteenth book of his *Digest*, wrote that assistance should also be given to slaves manumitted by will and usucapted before acceptance of the inheritance with effect that their freedom should be secured by agency of the praetor, even though they might be blamed for their usucapion; but in

the case of little children, no fault is to be found.

56   MARCELLUS, *Replies, sole book:* Lucius Titius made the following provisions in his
will: "I wish any codicils I leave to be valid. If Paula who was my wife has given birth
to a son or daughter within ten months, they are to be heirs as to half the inheritance.
Gaius Seius is to be heir as to half the inheritance. I ask my heirs as a *fideicommissum*
to manumit Stichus and Pamphilus, my slaves, and Eros and Diphilus, when my children have reached puberty." Then in a final part he provided: "But if children have not
been born to me or have died before puberty, then Mucius and Maevius are to be heirs
with equal shares. I wish the legacies which I bequeathed in my former will wherein I
made my sons and Seius heirs, to be discharged, that is, by the subsequent heirs."
Then in codicils he provided: "Lucius Titius greeting to his first and substitute heirs; I
ask you to discharge the provisions and legacies of my will and those made by codicils."
Given that Lucius Titius had no children, are Stichus, Pamphilus, Eros, and Diphilus
entitled to fideicommissary freedom without delay? Marcellus replied that the condition attached to the freedom of the persons in question, if the sons had proved to be
heirs, had apparently not been repeated and that therefore freedom was due without
delay from the first and substitute heirs; for, as stated above, he asked the provisions
in his will be discharged, and one provision concerned the freedom of those slaves.
True, the provision was subject to a condition, and if the condition had been of another
kind, its fulfillment should have been awaited, but it is not plausible that he had this in
mind in regard to the condition, when he laid a *fideicommissum* on substitute heirs,
who could not have been admitted to the inheritance, if the condition had been
fulfilled.

6

REVOCATION OF FREEDOM

1   TERENTIUS CLEMENS, *Lex Julia et Papia, book 18:* When freedom is revoked by
law, it must be either deemed not to have been given or certainly treated as if it had
been revoked by the testator.

7

STATULIBERI

1   PAUL, *Sabinus, book 5:* The *statuliber* is one who has freedom arranged to take
effect on completion of a period or fulfillment of a condition. Men become *statuliberi* as
a result of an express condition, or by the very nature of the case. The meaning of
"express condition" presents no problem. The status arises from the very nature of
the case when men are manumitted for the purpose of defrauding a creditor; for so
long as it is uncertain whether the creditor will use his right, the men remain *statuliberi*, since fraud is taken in the *lex Aelia Sentia* to involve actual damage.

2   ULPIAN, *Sabinus, book 4:* A man who acquires the status of a *statuliber* is so cir-
cumstanced that if he transferred to another owner, his hope of freedom is not affected
by the alienation; if he be usucapted, he retains his status, and if he be manumitted, he
does not lose the hope of becoming freedman of the deceased testator. But a slave does
not obtain this status unless at least one of the heirs instituted has entered on the
inheritance; if he is alienated or usucapted or manumitted at an earlier stage, his hope

of the freedom arranged lapses.   1. But if freedom should have been provided for a slave in the testament made for an *impubes*, would he be *statuliber* in the lifetime of the *pupillus*, of course, after acceptance of the father's inheritance? Cassius says: "No"; Julian takes the contrary opinion, which is held to be more correct.   2. Julian went further, saying that even when the slave had been legated away from the father's heir, if his liberation were ordered in the testament made for the *pupillus*, the grant of freedom prevails.   3. If in the first will a slave should be conditionally freed and instituted heir as to half the estate, would he obtain the status of a *statuliber* with effect that on entry by the heir he would be usucapted retaining his status? Inasmuch as he would have received freedom from himself, he cannot obtain the status of a *statuliber*. If, indeed, the conditional institution should fail in which case according to Julian he secures freedom at least, it must be said that he obtains the status of a *statuliber*, since he is thought to have received freedom not from himself, but from the co-heir.   4. Whatever the stage in which a slave is substituted with freedom for a *pupillus* he obtains the status of a *necessarius heres*; this view has been adopted for the sake of utility and has our approval. Celsus also thinks in his fifteenth book that a slave made substitute heir with freedom obtains the status of a *statuliber*.

3   ULPIAN, *Sabinus, book 27:* Statuliberi must comply with the condition [for freedom], assuming that no one hinders them and the condition is capable of fulfillment.   1. But if he should have been directed to comply with the condition with heir in the role of beneficiary, what should be said? If, in fact, he has complied, the man is free at once, even against the heir's wish. But if the heir does not allow compliance, for example, on the slave offering ten, as directed, the slave is unquestionably free, since the heir is evidently responsible for his not fulfilling the condition. It matters little whether he offers the money from his *peculium* or a sum received from a third party; it is accepted that the slave attains to freedom by giving money from his *peculium*, whether he was directed to give it to the heir himself or to a third party.   2. What if money is owed to the slave either by the heir, as a result of his having overspent on his owner's account, or by a third party, and the heir is unwilling to sue the debtor or to repay the *statuliber*; should he attain freedom on the ground that the heir is responsible for the delay? Now the *peculium* was either legated to the *statuliber* or it was not; in the former case, Servius writes that he has been subjected to delay in obtaining freedom, inasmuch as money was due to him from the owner's account and not repaid by the heir; this view is also approved by Labeo. Servius also takes the same view, if the heir were responsible for delay by unwillingness to collect from the debtors; in fact, he says that the man would attain freedom. I too regard Servius's opinion as correct. Now, given that we think Servius's view correct, should the same be said, even if the *peculium* were not legated to the slave; in fact, it is settled that the slave can make the payment ordered from his *peculium* either to the heir himself or to a third party, and if the heir should hinder him, the *statuliber* will attain freedom. And then too a sort of remedy is suggested to the owner of the *statuliber*; he may forbid him to give what he was directed to give to a third party, so as to avoid losing both the cash and the *statuliber*. Accordingly, it can be maintained that if he is unwilling to collect the debt or make payment himself to provide the slave with the means to comply with the condition, freedom is due; and Cassius too writes in this sense.   3. The *statuliber* attains freedom not only if he is prevented from giving what he was ordered to give but also if he is forbidden to carry out an order to climb the Capitol or prevented from going to Capua when ordered to give what was due at Capua; for a man who prevents the slave from setting forth must be understood to be intent on obstructing his freedom rather than on availing himself of his services.   4. But if one of the heirs should not let him give what he was ordered to a co-heir, he will equally be free, but the heir to whom he had been ordered to give and so to become free, by bringing an action *familiae erciscundae*, will obtain from the co-heir who causes the obstruction the sum representing his interest in the *statuliber* not being prevented [from doing what was required].   5. If a man's freedom is ordered on his giving ten and he gives five, he does not attain freedom unless he gives the whole sum; in the meantime, then, the owner of the five coins can claim them by *vindicatio*. But if the balance has been paid, the sum first paid, the ownership of which had not previously been transferred, then is alienated. So the alienation of this sum will be in suspense but with the effect that the coins do not become

retroactively the property of the recipient, who becomes their owner only from the time when the balance has been paid in full.   6. If the *statuliber* has given more than he was ordered to give, for example, twenty instead of ten, whether he counted them out or gave them in a purse, he attains freedom and can sue for return of the excess.   7. If a slave ordered to give ten and so to be free has been sold without his *peculium*, does he become free at once on the basis that he would seem to have been prevented from giving the sum from his *peculium* by the mere fact of his being sold without it, or not until he is prevented from touching the *peculium*? In my opinion, he will be free only when he wishes to give and is prevented and not immediately on sale.   8. If a slave ordered to give ten and so to be free should be prevented from working for hire, or if the heir has taken away his wages, or if he has given the heir what he amassed from his wages, would he attain freedom? In my opinion, he would attain freedom, if, in fact, he has given the sum [to the heir] from his wage-labor or from any other source, but not if he be prevented from working for wages, since he is under obligation to work for his owner. Clearly, if the money amassed from his wage-labor has been taken away, I think he would be free, since he is then being prevented from giving out of his *peculium*. To be sure, if the testator ordered him to give from the product of his labor and he is prevented from working, I do not doubt that he would attain freedom.   9. But even if the coins he has given have been scraped together by stealing plate or embezzling other property, he will attain freedom, although he would not have done so if the actual coins were stolen; in that case, it is evident that he did not give them, but rather gave them back. He would not even attain freedom if he had stolen the coins from a third party and given them to the heir, as the coins can be recovered from the recipient, though, of course, if they have been spent, so that there is no possibility of their recovery, freedom would be due.   10. We shall say that freedom is due if delay is caused not only by the heir but by a tutor, curator, procurator, and anyone else in the role of beneficiary of the condition. In fact, the principle of law that we apply to the *statuliber* is that it should be enough that he is not responsible for failure to comply with the condition.   11. Suppose that a man has been ordered to give to the heir within thirty days from the testator's death and that the heir was rather slow in entering on the inheritance; Trebatius and Labeo say that if his slowness was not fraudulent, the slave attains freedom by giving within thirty days from his entry; this opinion is correct. But suppose that he delayed deliberately; would the man on that account attain freedom as soon as the inheritance was entered on? What if he has the money at the time and no longer after the entry? But in this case, too, the condition seems to have been fulfilled, since it was not his responsibility that he did not meet it.   12. Suppose a man to have received freedom in these terms: "Let him be free when he is able to give ten." Trebatius says that although he has come into possession of ten or has the resources to acquire and keep a *peculium* of that value, he will still not attain freedom unless he has given the sum or the responsibility for his failure to give it is not his; this opinion is correct.   13. Stichus was ordered to be free if he gave the heir ten aurei on a specified day in three successive years. If the heir was responsible for his not accepting ten at the first payment, it is approved that the third payment must be awaited, since the grant of freedom depended partly on the lapse of time and two payments still remain to be made. But if he should only have the same ten aurei which he offered for the first payment, would that serve him for the subsequent payment, too, if he were to offer them, and again for the third, if the second payment were not accepted? In my view, the very same coins are enough, and there is no room for the heir to change his mind. Pomponius too approves this view.   14. What if a slave has been ordered to give ten on a specified day in three successive years and should offer the whole sum at once to the heir without awaiting the day, or if he gave ten in the first year and offered twenty in the second? It is the more benevolent view that he attains freedom, since both parties show their ability to look ahead, the slave in attaining freedom earlier and the heir in cutting the delay and accepting at once what he could have obtained later.   15. If freedom has been given to a slave on condition of his serving the heir as a slave for five years and the heir has then manumitted him, he becomes free at once on the footing that it is the heir's doing that the man ceases to serve him, although if he [simply] refused his service, he would only attain freedom after the passage of five years. The principle here is manifest; once a man has been manumitted, he cannot continue to serve as a slave, but if the heir [simply] refuses such service, he can still accept it at any time within the five years. It is true that the man can no longer serve him for a quinquennium, but he can still serve for a shorter time. 16. Further, Julian, in the sixteenth book of his *Digest*, wrote that if Arethusa was given freedom subject to the condition of her bearing three children and the heir was responsible for her not giving birth, for example, by the administration of a contraceptive, she would be free at once; for what is the point of waiting? So, too, if the heir had procured an abortion; for she might have born triplets. 17. Further, if the heir sold and transferred a *statuliber*, who was ordered to serve him as a slave, I believe that the man attains freedom at once.

4 PAUL, *Sabinus, book 5:* When the heir was absent on public business, the *statuliber* with the cash must wait until the return of the person to whom the money is to be given, or deposit it in a temple under seal, whereupon he attains freedom at once. 1. A man is not *statuliber* whose freedom is deferred to a time so distant that the person to be manumitted could not survive until then, or if [the testator] added a condition so difficult, or rather virtually impossible, that his freedom could not accrue, for example, that he should have given the heir one thousand, or that his freedom was ordered only on his deathbed; such a grant of freedom is ineffective, as Julian too writes, since there is not even an intention that it should be given. 2. If a man's freedom is ordered after he has served Titius as a slave for a year, he will not become free immediately on Titius's death but only after passage of the year, since the grant seems to be not merely conditional but subject to a time clause, and it is actually absurd that he should become free when he is not fulfilling the condition, earlier than he would have been, had he fulfilled it. 3. If a man's freedom has been ordered on condition of his giving ten to two persons and one has refused to accept five, it is better to say that he can attain freedom by offering the same five to the other person. 4. "Let Stichus be free if he has served Titius as a slave for three years" or "if he has given him one hundred workdays (*operae*)." It is settled that freedom can effectively be given in this form; for even someone else's slave can serve us, as can a freeman, and *a fortiori* give workdays, unless in writing of service the testator had in mind ownership rather than work (*operam*). Hence, if the heir prevents him serving Titius, he attains freedom. 5. "Let Stichus be free, if he has served my heir as a slave for a year"; we must ask how "year" is to be interpreted; would it consist simply of three hundred sixty-five days or must they be continuous? But Pomponius writes that the second interpretation must be adopted. If, however, ill-health or any other just impediment prevents the man serving on certain days, they too are to be reckoned part of the year; for persons whom we care for in illness are also understood to be in our service, when they wish to serve us and are hindered by ill-health. 6. Further, if a man has been ordered to give ten to the heir, the heir must be compelled by the principle favoring freedom to accept them in part payments. 7. Suppose a man's freedom has been ordered "if Titius has climbed the Capitol," and Titius refuses, the freedom will be barred. The same principle applies in like cases and conditions. 8. Further, Cassius says that if a man is ordered to serve for a year, the period during which he is in flight or is suing for his freedom does not count.

5 POMPONIUS, *Sabinus, book 8:* A *statuliber* ordered to render accounts paid the balance clearly due and was prepared to give security for that on which his liability was less plain. Neratius and Aristo rightly think that he would be free; otherwise, many would not attain freedom, given the uncertainty of accounting and this type of

business. 1. A *statuliber* who was ordered not to render accounts but to give cash is bound to pay, not to provide a surety (*fideiussor*).

6   ULPIAN, *Sabinus, book 27:* If a *statulibera* has been sentenced to penal servitude and after her conviction the condition attached to her freedom has been realized, though this is of no benefit to the *statulibera* herself, it must be of benefit to a child she bears; he will be born free just as if the mother had not been convicted. 1. But what if she conceived the child in servitude and then gave birth after being captured by the enemy, when the condition had been realized; there is indeed not the slightest doubt that the child is a slave of the enemy for the time being, but it is the more correct view that he becomes free by *postliminium*, since he would have been born free, if his mother had been on Roman territory. 2. Clearly, if she had conceived him when with the enemy and given birth after the condition had been realized, it will be the more benevolent thing to say that *postliminium* is due to him and that he is free. 3. By complying with a condition with the purchaser in the role of beneficiary, a *statuliber* attains freedom; it should be known that this applies to *statuliberi* of each sex. It is not only in the case of sale that the condition is transferred to the purchaser; it is also transferred to all who have in any way acquired rightful ownership over the *statuliber.* Hence, whether the *statuliber* has been legated to you by the heir or assigned by court order or usucapted by you or alienated to you by *traditio* or made your property by any course of law, we shall say without hesitation that he can comply with the condition to your benefit. The same applies to purchaser's heir. 4. If a son-in-power was instituted as heir and the *statuliber* was ordered to give to him and so to be free, he attains freedom by giving to either son or father, since the benefit of the inheritance accrues to the father. But he will also be free if after the son's death he has paid the father as heir of the heir; in fact, if a man has been ordered to give to an *extraneus* and so to be free and the *extraneus* subsequently becomes heir to the heir, he will comply with the condition by paying him not qua *extraneus* but qua heir. 5. A *statuliber* ordered to give ten and so to be free gives five and is then sold; the other five he will give to the purchaser. 6. Your slave has bought a *statuliber;* what he was ordered to give to the heirs is given to you. But suppose that he has paid your slave; provided that the slave bought him from the account of his *peculium* and you have not taken his *peculium* away, I think he would be free, that is, on the basis that he is understood to have paid you, just as if he had paid any other slave of yours with your consent. 7. Suppose a man's freedom was ordered, subject to the condition not of his giving ten, but of his rendering accounts, would this condition pass to the purchaser? It is certain in other cases that only those conditions pass to the purchaser which consist in giving, not in doing, for example, teaching a boy his letters; conditions of the latter sort are tied indissolubly to the particular persons named; but a condition that accounts are to be rendered insofar as it involves payment of sums due, consists in giving money, though insofar as it involves handing over the actual books of accounts, elucidating them by questions, balancing, and then checking and scrutinizing them, it means having done something. Would the man not then attain freedom by actually giving to the purchaser any sums due, whereas the other actions concern the heirs? So in my opinion, it remains for the heir to require rendering of the accounts and the sums due are to be paid over to the purchaser with effect that the condition is divided; so too Pomponius writes in the eighth book of *Sabinus.*

7   PAUL, *Sabinus, book 5:* Alienation of usufruct does not carry with it the condition whereby the *statuliber* becomes free.

8   POMPONIUS, *Sabinus, book 8:* Suppose the freedom of a man has been ordered in the terms: "If he has given ten, let him be free"; he is bound to give to the heir; for when the recipient is not named, the man attains freedom by giving to the heir. 1. If each heir has sold his portion of the inheritance to different purchasers, the *statuliber* will give to the purchasers the same proportions that he owed the heirs. But Labeo says that if the heirs are actually mentioned by name in the will, they are to receive

equal amounts, but that if the will uses the terms, "if he has given to the heirs," they get amounts proportioned to their shares in the inheritance.

9   ULPIAN, *Sabinus, book 28:* No one should be ignorant that the *statuliber* is in the intervening time the slave of the heir; on that account, it will be possible to surrender him noxally. But he will still be able to hope for freedom after surrender, nor does surrender deprive him of hope of freedom. 1. If the heir should sell a *statuliber* and impose a different condition on his liberation, his status is not subject to change, and he will be able to discharge himself from the purchaser in like manner as from the heir. What if the heir has concealed the condition? He is then at least liable to action on sale, but those who take a harsher view also involve the man who knowingly concealed the condition under which freedom was prescribed and sold him without specifying it in the criminal charge of cheating (*stellionatus*). 2. The question has been discussed whether a man is acquitted of his obligation when he has noxally surrendered the *statuliber*; Octavenus thought that he was, and he took the same view if a man on stipulation was obliged to transfer Stichus and fulfilled his obligation when Stichus was a *statuliber*; in fact, if Stichus had previously attained freedom, the whole obligation would have been extinguished, for obligations can be discharged and met by payment of cash, but freedom cannot be compensated or made good by such payment. I think this view correct. 3. The condition of a *statuliber* only becomes final if the inheritance has been entered on, but until then usucapion affects the man's own status as a slave and his hope of freedom is diminished; but once the inheritance has been entered on later, his hope of freedom will be renewed in accordance with the principle favoring it.

10   PAUL, *Sabinus, book 5:* Suppose that a man was ordered to give ten and that the heir has sold him and given delivery and said that it was a condition of his freedom that he should have given twenty; an action on sale will lie against the seller, or to be more precise, if double the price has been promised, there will be a claim for double simply for eviction, and by action on sale on the score of deception.

11   POMPONIUS, *Sabinus, book 14:* If the heir had made a gift of money to the *statuliber* to enable him to give it to him and become free, Aristo says that he does not become free; he becomes free only if the gift had been unconditional.

12   JULIAN, *Digest, book 7:* If a man had received freedom by will subject to the condition of rendering accounts and has complied with the condition, he should pay sums due to [all] the heirs in proportion to their shares in the inheritance, even if the names of [only] certain heirs have been specified in the condition.

13   JULIAN, *Digest, book 43:* If someone had given freedom in the terms, "let Stichus be free, if my heir should not have manumitted him by his own will," this seems to mean in accordance with the wish of the deceased, "if in his own will the heir should not have assigned freedom to him." Hence, if the heir has actually given freedom to the slave in his will, the condition seems to be ineffective; if not, it has been fulfilled, and the man will attain freedom at the last moment of the heir's life. 1. When the freedom of a slave owned by more than one person has been ordered, "if he has given ten," he can give the money from his *peculium* in whatever way it has been acquired; it makes no difference whether it is in the custody of the heir or a partner or whether he was ordered to give to the heir or an *extraneus*. For in all cases, there is a reference to the legal status of the *statuliber* who can alienate the cash in his *peculium* for the purpose of fulfilling the condition. 2. If the freedom of two slaves has been ordered subject to their rendering accounts and they handled the accounts separately, beyond question they will also be able to comply with the condition separately, but if they were in management together and their affairs inextricably connected, it is inevitable that the failure of one to render accounts will hinder the freedom of the other. Nor will the condition appear to have been fulfilled on the part of one unless any sum due on reckoning up the accounts is discharged in full either by both or by one of them. 3. A man whose freedom has been ordered, "if he has sworn to climb the Capitol," will

become free as soon as he has taken the oath, although he has not climbed the Capitol. 4. A slave of the heir, whose freedom is ordered after he has given the heir a thing that belongs to the heir will attain freedom, since the testator can order the manumission of the heir's slave without any condition that he should give anything.   5. The words, "let Stichus be free on reaching the age of thirty; Stichus is not to be free if he has not given ten," have the following effect: "Stichus is to be free, if he has given ten and reached the age of thirty"; for the revocation of a grant of freedom or of a legacy made subject to condition has automatically imposed a condition detrimental to the legacy or grant of freedom previously made.

14   ALFENUS VARUS, *Digest, book 4:* A slave whose freedom had been ordered by his master's will, once he had given ten to the heir, was accustomed to transmit to the heir the wage he received for his days of work; the slave would say that he was free once the heir had received more than ten from his wage; he was consulted on the point. He replied that the man did not appear to be free; he had given the sum in question not for his freedom, but in respect of his workdays, and he was no more free on that account than if he had leased a farm from the master and given money in respect of its fruits.   1. The freedom of a slave had been ordered, once he had given the heir work-days for seven years; the slave had run away and spent a year in flight. He replied that the man was not free at the expiry of the seven years; for as a fugitive he had not given workdays to the master, and so he would not be free, unless he has served for as many days as he had been absent. But if it had been provided in express terms in the will that he was to be free after he had served as a slave for seven years, he could have secured freedom by so serving after his return for the period of his flight.

15   AFRICANUS, *Questions, book 9:* If on the death of the heir the *statuliber* had enriched the inheritance with as large a sum as he had been ordered to give, for example, by paying creditors or providing maintenance for the household, he thought that the man would come to freedom without delay.   1. The heir, in selling a *statuliber* who had been ordered to give ten, declared it to be a condition and made it a clause of the contract at delivery that the same sum of ten was to be given to him rather than to the purchaser; it was asked whether the *statuliber* obtained freedom by giving the money to either of them. He replied that he was bound to give to the heir. But also if he had put a clause in the contract to the effect that the *statuliber* was to give the money to any third party, he replied that in that case too the agreement was binding, since the man is deemed to pay the heir when he pays some one else by the heir's wish.

16   ULPIAN, *Rules, book 4:* The offspring of a *statulibera* is the heir's slave.

17   NERATIUS, *Parchments, book 3:* The freedom of a slave was ordered, if he had given the heir ten; he has ten but owes that sum to the master; he will not be freed on giving him this ten. For we must not interpret the concession made to the slave, whereby he can give the sum from his *peculium* for the purpose of fulfilling the condition, to mean that he can also give out of moneys which are outside the *peculium*. It does not escape me that these coins can be said to belong to the *peculium*, but if the slave has nothing else, his *peculium* is worthless. But it should not be put in doubt that it was the intention of persons making this disposition to enable the slave to give, as it were, from his own patrimony, under the head of *peculium*, since this was the concession that appeared to do least injury to masters; if you go any further, you will not be far from thinking that the *statuliber* would satisfy the condition by giving coins stolen from the master.

18   PAUL, *Grants of Freedom, sole book:* If a man ordered to give ten a year for three years offered twenty in the first year and the heir refused it, he does not become free at once, since he would not yet have been free, even if the heir had accepted.

19 ULPIAN, *Edict, book 14:* If the freedom of a slave should have been ordered and a legacy given him on the son completing his fourteenth year and the son died earlier, by the principle favoring freedom it becomes his due when the day comes, but the condition for the legacy fails.

20 PAUL, *Plautius, book 16:* Suppose that his *peculium* was legated to a slave, who was ordered to give ten to someone else and thus be free, and that the heir prevented him giving the money and that after subsequent manumission he sues on the legacy for *peculium*; may the heir employ a defense of fraud and deduct the sum he was to have given, so that he and not the freedman may profit from its not having been given? Or would the heir really be unworthy of the profit, as he acted against the wish of the deceased? Since the slave has lost nothing and obtained freedom, it is invidious for the heir to be defrauded. 1. Suppose he gives against the wish of the heir or without his knowledge; would he give title to the recipient? Julian actually thinks that in this case *statuliberi* are apparently allowed to alienate the coins, even against the wish of the heir, and thereby to give title to the recipients. 2. But if he was ordered to give ten to the heir and the heir should owe that sum to the slave, the slave will be free, should he wish to set off one sum against the other. 3. A slave was ordered to give ten in order that he should be free, and the recipient designated died. In Sabinus's view, he will be free, if he had the cash ready to give, since it was not his fault that he did not give it. But Julian says that in accordance with the principle favoring freedom, he would rightly attain freedom, even if he did not have the sum till later. However, he attains freedom by a rule of the law rather than under the will; hence, if a legacy were also made to him and the recipient designated dies, he will indeed attain freedom, but he would not get the legacy as well; this is also Julian's opinion, to put him in the same situation as other legatees. 4. A man ordered to pay the heir can also pay the heir's heir by a rescript of the deified Hadrian; and if this was in the mind of the testator, the same view can be taken in the case of a legatee. 5. Some conditions cannot in their nature be fulfilled at the same time; any period of time is necessarily divided into parts, for instance, when a man is ordered to give ten workdays (*operae*); for *operae* are given one day at a time. By this reasoning if a *statuliber* gives aurei one at a time, it can be said that he has fulfilled the condition. This case is different from that of *operae*, since they must of necessity be given one at a time. But if the heir has refused to accept *operae*, the man will not be free at once, but only at the expiry of the period in which the number of *operae* would be complete. So, too, if a man were ordered to go to Capua and be free and the heir prevents his going, he will be free at the time when he could have reached Capua; in fact, the element of time is deemed to be inherent in both the provision of *operae* and in a journey. 6. If freedom has been granted on the terms, "let Stichus be free, if the heir has not manumitted him," it will also be possible for the heir to manumit him; in fact, it would be contrary to the wish of the testator that he should lose a freedman; but no such immediacy must be required as to compel the heir to act in undue haste, to return too quickly from foreign parts to manumit, or to interrupt his management of necessary business, nor, on the other hand, must postponement be so long that manumission is deferred for his lifetime; a modest interval is allowed for the heir to manumit as soon as he can without suffering great inconvenience. However, if a period of time has been specified, this will be respected.

21 POMPONIUS, *From Plautius, book 7:* In a book of his *Posthumous Works* Labeo cites the case: "Let my steward (*dispensator*) Calenus be free and have all that belongs to him plus one hundred, if it shall appear that he handled my accounts with care." The care we should require is that which will have been in the master's interest,

not the slave's. This care will be accompanied with good faith not only in the presentation of the accounts but in the payment of any balance due. The phrase "shall appear" should be construed to mean "shall be capable of appearing"; so too the old authorities interpreted the words of the *Twelve Tables* "if damage is done by rainwater" to mean "if damage could have been done." And if the question were put, who should certify the care, we shall be bound to follow the arbitration of the heirs acting as a good man would; similarly, if the freedom of a slave was ordered on his giving a specified sum, and there was no further statement naming the recipient, it will be possible for the man to be free in the same way as he could have been free, if the will had specified that he should give to the heir. 1. Pactumerus Clemens used to say that if a *fideicommissum* were left in the form, "I ask you to make over to whichever of them you please," without choosing which, the Emperor Antoninus decided by *constitutio* that all were entitled.

22   PAUL, *Vitellius, book 3:* A man ordered to give money with the recipient unspecified should give it to the heirs in proportion to their shares in the inheritance; each should receive according to his share in the ownership. 1. If certain heirs to whom he should give are named, he will give to them in proportion to their shares in the inheritance. 2. If an *extraneus* is joined with the heirs named, the *extraneus* should receive an arithmetic share, the others that appropriate to their share in the inheritance; Julian also writes that if he had not only added Titius but other *extranei* too, they will get arithmetic shares and the co-heirs shares proportionate to their shares in the inheritance.

23   CELSUS, *Digest, book 22:* "If Stichus has given one hundred within a quinquennium, let him be free"; he will not give to a third party or to the heir or the purchaser after the quinquennium. 1. A man whose freedom was ordered on condition of his rendering accounts is not allowed by the heir to sell the things in his *peculium* and pay the balance due; he is just as free as if he had complied with the condition.

24   MARCELLUS, *Digest, book 16:* "Let Stichus be free, if he has promised ten to my heir or sworn to give him workdays." The condition can be fulfilled by his promise; for it can be said that his undertaking had some meaning, even though no legal obligation followed on it.

25   MODESTINUS, *Distinctions, book 9:* The possibility of selling *statuliberi* was assumed in the *Law of the Twelve Tables*, but it is not at all right to burden them with harsh conditions in the sale, for example, forbidding them to serve within certain areas or to be manumitted at any time.

26   MODESTINUS, *Rules, book 9:* Freedom has been given to a slave by will subject to his rendering accounts; the heir not only requires the written accounts but also an account of what he administered without making entries in the ledger. 1. If it was ordered that a slave should attain freedom on rendering accounts, he will still be free, even though he had no accounts of his administration to render.

27   MODESTINUS, *Encyclopaedia, book 1:* If the *statuliber* was bought by the person whom he was ordered to pay and then sold by him to a third party, he will pay the last purchaser; it was in fact Julian's view that when ownership of the slave passed to the designated recipient, the condition was also transferred by him to the purchaser on alienation.

28   JAVOLENUS, *From Cassius, book 6:* If the inheritance of a man who had ordered the freedom of a slave to be granted within thirty days of his death on his rendering accounts was entered on after thirty days, in strict law the man manumitted on these terms cannot be free, since the condition is not met; but the principle favoring freedom has been taken so far that one may reply that the condition has been fulfilled if its nonfulfillment is not due to the beneficiary. 1. It is stated in the books of Gaius Cassius that any acquisition made by the *statuliber* before the condition for his freedom

has been realized would not go to the *peculium* legated to him unless the legacy had been made operative at the moment of liberation; but since *peculium* can be increased and decreased, may it not be that an accession to the *peculium*, provided that it has not been taken away from the man by the heir, would also adhere to the legacy; and this is the rule we are apt to use.

29   POMPONIUS, *Quintus Mucius, book 18: Statuliberi* hardly differ at all from the rest of our slaves. Hence, in regard to actions arising from delict, unauthorized administration or contract, *statuliberi* have the same status as the rest. Hence, too, in public trials they undergo the same penalties as the other slaves.   1. Quintus Mucius writes that the head of the household had written in his will: "Let my slave Andronicus be free on giving ten to my heir." A dispute had then arisen about the property of the heir; the man who claimed to be his legal heir [on intestacy] asserted that the inheritance belonged to him, while the man in possession of the inheritance claimed to be the testamentary heir. Judgment was given against the man who claimed to be the testamentary heir. Then, Andronicus put the question: On the footing that he had given twenty to that claimant, inasmuch as he would have been free if judgment had been given in the latter's favor, would the decision be deemed to have no effect determining on his freedom? He roundly replied that the decision did have determining effect. In consequence, if he had given twenty to the testamentary heir and the judgment had gone against the possessor, he would remain in slavery. Labeo thinks that Quintus Mucius's statement is true on the basis that the successful claimant really was in law the heir under intestacy; but if the true, testamentary heir had been defeated by a wrongful decision of the judge, the slave, nonetheless, had complied with the condition by paying him and would be free. But the real truth is, as Aristo wrote in reply to Celsus, that the money can be paid to the intestate heir, in whose favor judgment was given, since the *Law of the Twelve Tables* would seem to have included every kind of alienation under the term "sale"; it makes no difference in what category anyone had become the man's owner, and, therefore, the law also includes the person in whose favor judgment was given, and the man would be free who had made payment to him; further that the man to whom the sum had been paid, that is, the possessor of the inheritance, if defeated in his claim to the inheritance, is bound to make over this money too along with the remaining assets to the successful party.

30   JAVOLENUS, *Readings, book 7:* If a man's freedom should be ordered in the terms, "let Stichus be free, if the heir has not alienated him," he can still be alienated, even though a *statuliber*.

31   GAIUS, *Lex Julia et Papia, book 13:* Suppose a slave has been given a legacy on condition of his presenting accounts; there is no doubt that thereby he is required to pay any money owing, if he is to take the legacy.   1. And for that reason, when the question was raised, given that freedom was left on these terms, "let Stichus be free, after giving accounts, along with his *contubernalis*," and that he died before fulfilling the condition, whether she could be free, Julian said that the question was of the same kind raised in regard to legacies of the form: "I give to 'X' together with 'Y'"; if "X" fails to take, is "Y" to be admitted to the legacy? He inclined to think so, just as if the legacy had been expressly given to "X" and "Y." He also thought that there was a further question: would the condition apply to the *contubernalis* too? That was the better view; hence, if Stichus had no arrears to pay, she was free at once; if there were any arrears, she was bound to count out the money; and yet she would not be allowed

to pay from her own *peculium*, since that was permitted only to those who are ordered to give money as principals for their own freedom.

32   LICINNIUS RUFINUS, *Rules, book 1:* Suppose that two heirs are instituted and the
freedom of a slave is ordered on his giving ten to the heirs, but that one of them has
then sold him and given delivery; he will be free on making part payment to the purchaser and part payment to the heir who did not sell him.

33   PAPINIAN, *Questions, book 2:* The heir cannot impair the rights of *statuliberi.*

34   PAPINIAN, *Questions, book 21:* The freedom of a slave was ordered on his giving ten
to the heir; the heir manumitted the *statuliber* and later died. No payment is due to
the heir of the heir; you will recall that the rule that payment must be made to the heir
of the heir is only in place when the previous heir would have received the payment as
owner. In this case, there is what I might call a transferable condition; in fact, there
are two titles for fulfillment of the condition in regard to the original heir qua heir; he
is entitled as owner and as the designated beneficiary; the former title passes to every
successive owner into whose ownership the slave has been transferred in unbroken
line, whereas the second title belongs only to the person designated as beneficiary.
1. By a rescript of the Emperor Antoninus, a man whose freedom has been ordered on
his rendering accounts is nonetheless to be free, if the heir objects to receiving the
accounts. This should be taken to mean that he is free, if he does not drag out paying
the arrears; in that case he is only to be free, if he has fairly and truly offered the sum
which should be refunded; for it is not enough for his freedom that the heir should have
made delays, unless the *statuliber* does not perform what would give him access to
freedom if no such delay had occurred. What if a man has been manumitted in these
terms, "let Dama be free, if he has set off for Spain next year and collected the fruits,"
and the heir should detain him at Rome and not let him set off? Surely, we are not to
say that he would be free at once before the fruits have been collected? For when a
stipulation is expressed in the terms, "do you undertake to give one hundred in
Spain," the lapse of time required for a journey to Spain is implicit in the stipulation,
and it has been decided that there can be no legal action at an earlier date. But suppose that the accounts have been rendered and the arrears reckoned up, and the heir
then enters a record that he is making a gift of the sum to the *statuliber* who has not
the means to pay, or even makes his intention plain in a letter to him, the condition for
freedom will be deemed to have been fulfilled. What, then, if the *statuliber* denies that
he has dragged out paying the arrears and claims that he has become free, since it was
the responsibility of the heir to receive the accounts, whereas the heir contends that
he made no delay and the *statuliber* owes arrears? It will be for whoever decides suits
for freedom to determine if the condition has been fulfilled, and it will be part of his
task to examine the point concerning delay and equally to reckon up the accounts and,
if he has ascertained that the man is dragging out the arrears, to pronounce that he is
not free. But if the man never denied that arrears were owing and had promised on
meeting the heir and offering the accounts to refund whatever was found to be due,
and had offered a man of substance who was ready to assume the obligation for the
sum concerned and to pay, and the heir made delays, the judgment will then be given
for freedom.

35   PAPINIAN, *Replies, book 9:* The *statuliber* will not be deemed free of responsibility
for a condition not being realized, if he be unable to offer the money required by the
condition out of the *peculium* which he had as a slave with the vendor; for the wish of
the deceased [that is to say, that he should pay out of *peculium*] could not have extended to *peculium* from another source. This will also apply if the slave has been sold
with his *peculium* and the vendor has broken faith and retained the *peculium*; although an action on sale would arise, it is still true that the slave did not possess *peculium* with the purchaser.

36   PAPINIAN, *Definitions, book 2:* If a slave has been substituted for the son in the
second stage of the will with a grant of freedom, jurists have secured to him the right

of a *statuliber*; this is regarded as useful to ensure that he should only be alienated with his rights intact, so that the son, while still a boy, may not avoid the father's will. Juristic authority has extended this to the second or third *heres substitutus* without regard to stages in the will.

37 GAIUS, *Problems, sole book:* If the will says, "I give Stichus to Titius in order that he may manumit him; if he has not manumitted him, let him be free," Stichus is free at once.

38 PAUL, *Neratius, book 1:* It is not every hindrance put in the way of the *statuliber* from the heir's side that counts as fulfillment of a condition, but only such as have been designed to hinder freedom.

39 JAVOLENUS, *From the Posthumous Works of Labeo, book 4:* "I give and legate Stichus to Attius, and if he has given him one hundred coins, let him be free." If the slave had given the coins to Attius under the will, Labeo thinks that the heir cannot reclaim them, since Attius received them from his own slave and not from the slave of the heir. Quintus Mucius, Gallus, and Labeo himself think that the man is a *statuliber*; not so Servius and Ofilius. I endorse the former opinion, but only on the footing that he is the slave of the heir, not of the legatee, inasmuch as the legacy is extinguished by his being a *statuliber*. 1. "Let Stichus be free, once my debt is paid and my creditors satisfied." Labeo and Ofilius replied that although the heir had ample assets, Stichus would not be free before the creditors had received money or satisfaction or had taken some other security for the debt. 2. Labeo and Trebatius replied that if the heir had given a slave money for business, the *statuliber* was not free under the will on counting out that very money, since he would be deemed to be returning it rather than giving it. In my own view, he would be free under the will if the coins he gave came from his *peculium*. 3. "Let the slave Dama be free when he has discharged an obligation of workdays for seven years for my heir." Within this period the slave was involved in a criminal case and the seventh year expired; Servius says that he should not be freed, Labeo that he would be free, if he later discharged the obligation of workdays for seven years, which is right. 4. "If Stichus has given one thousand coins to Attia, let him be free." Attia died in the testator's lifetime. Labeo and Ofilius replied that Stichus could not be free. Trebatius took the same view if she died before the will was made; if later, he would be free. There is reason in the opinion of Labeo and Ofilius, but under the law now in force, the slave is free under the will. 5. If a slave had been ordered to give workdays, no third party can release him by giving workdays himself in the slave's name; the rule concerning money is different; by giving money on his behalf, a third party would release the slave.

40 SCAEVOLA, *Digest, book 24:* Freedom was given to Stichus thus: "I ask my heirs, and commit it to their good faith, to manumit Stichus after he has rendered accounts." A large sum was due from the chest entrusted to the man after the testator's death; he had not entered in the accounts certain moneys collected from the tenants; he had despoiled the inheritance by secretly opening the barns, removing furniture and clothing, and emptying the stores. Would fideicommissary freedom be due to him only when he had restored the sums he had embezzled and all the things he had stolen? He replied

that he should not be given fideicommissary freedom before he had made good the arrears and the losses for which he was responsible.   1. "Let Pamphilus be free on faithfully giving his *peculium* to the heirs." Would freedom be due to him under the will, when he owed his master more than he had in his *peculium* and had given all of that in good faith to the heirs? He replied that on the facts stated, there was no ground to refuse it.   2. A man had prelegated the slave Stichus to his freedman and part heir Pamphilus and had given him freedom in these terms: "in such manner that if he has paid you sixty a month for five successive years from the day of my death, you are then to manumit him." Pamphilus, dying before the end of the five years, in instituting his son and wife as heirs, inserted this provision regarding the same Stichus: "I order that the slave Stichus, who was bequeathed to me by the will of my patron subject to a condition, should give and provide to my son and wife without dispute and that at the end of the period they should manumit him." If Stichus had not provided sixty coins a month, would fideicommissary freedom be due to him at the end of five years? He replied that on this basis, it would not.   3. A slave was manumitted by will in these terms: "Let my slave and steward Stichus be free if he has rendered a complete account to my heir of his administration and given satisfaction for it, and I wish him, when he is free, to be given twenty and his *peculium*." If he is ready to render to the heir accounts of which he was in charge for many years without a signature by the testator [certifying that they were correct], would he be free under the will, considering that because of ill health the testator was unable to sign the accounts, though he did sign the will? He replied that if the accounts were rendered honestly and any sums due paid in, he would be free.   4. Suppose that moneys collected by his assistants were not entered in the ledger or were fraudulently treated, could he be held responsible for the sums, since he was in charge of the assistants? He replied that anything that should be attributed to his fault was relevant to his obligation to render accounts.   5. Should account also be taken of installments not collected from lessees of farms or from farm bailiffs, which he had in addition actually treated as loans to them? He gave the aforementioned reply.   6. Would he be liable for having removed all his own belongings, that is, his *peculium*, before rendering accounts? He replied that that was no bar to the condition, provided that he did render account.   7. Titius legated by will his slave stewards, each to a different person, subject to their rendering accounts to the heir and then wrote in a special clause: "I wish all the stewards whom I have legated or manumitted to render accounts within the fourth month from my death and to do so to the owners to whom I have legated them"; then, later in the will, he ordered the freedom of other stewards subject to their rendering accounts to the heir. Given that the heir is not responsible for their failure to render accounts, do they cease to be *statuliberi*, or can they, nonetheless, at any time secure freedom under the will after rendering accounts and bringing in what is due? He replied that the legacies and grants of freedom do not take effect unless the accounts had been rendered or the heir prevented this, but that the future judge would have to determine whether a time limit appeared to be attached to the condition on which the legacies and grants of freedom were made or whether, given that the slaves were willing to repay sums due in their own free time, the four months represented a condition imposed on the heirs, resulting from the testator's anxiety to fix a limit on their hesitation. It is, however, the better view that they should be presumed *statuliberi*.   8. A banker, almost all whose assets consisted in debts due to him, gave freedom to his slave stewards in these terms: "Whoever is my heir, if my slave Dama has rendered accounts to my heir for administration of the affairs carried on in his name and that of his fellow slave Pamphilus and has squared them within the sixth month from my death, he is to be free." Does the phrase "squared them" refer to all debts, except when the debtors are bankrupt, with the meaning that they must collect all money due from all debtors and pay the heir or give him security therefor with the effect that they would not be entitled to freedom, if they had failed to collect from the debtors within six months? He replied that the condition expressed in the words quoted from the will was perfectly plain; so they would only be free, if they complied with it or were prevented by the heir.

41   LABEO, *Plausible Views Epitomized by Paul, book 1:* If you wish to leave your slave a *statuliber* with freedom at the end of a specific time, it makes no difference whether you provide "let him be free, if he has served [for three years]" or "if he has given workdays for three years." 1. PAUL. If the freedom of a man has been ordered subject to his having promised ten to the heir, although his promise would have no force, he will still be freed on giving it.

42   LABEO, *Plausible Views, book 3:* If a man has legated a slave to his wife and ordered that he should be free on her marriage, and she has married legally, the man will become free.

8

PERSONS WHO OBTAIN FREEDOM WITHOUT MANUMISSION

1   PAUL, *Plautius, book 5:* If a slave has been sold with a covenant for manumission within a fixed time, even if seller and purchaser should have died without heirs, freedom is due to the slave, as the deified Marcus also ruled in a rescript. But even if the seller has changed his mind, freedom is still due.

2   MODESTINUS, *Rules, book 6:* Under an edict of the deified Claudius, freedom is due to the slave whom the owner treated as abandoned because of grave bodily weakness.

3   CALLISTRATUS, *Judicial Examinations, book 3:* By a rescript of the deified Marcus and his son, a slave sold with a covenant for his manumission within a given time, once the day for the grant of freedom has come with the seller alive and his wish unchanged, is to be treated as if he had been manumitted by the man bound to manumit; but if the seller is dead, the wishes of his heirs are not to be ascertained.

4   ULPIAN, *Sabinus, book 3:* A man purchased under covenant that he is to be manumitted by the purchaser in his lifetime is entitled to freedom at once on the purchaser's death.

5   MARCIAN, *Rules, book 5:* A man who obtains freedom as a reward for discovering his master's murder becomes a *libertus orcinus.*

6   MARCIAN, *Action on a Mortgage, sole book:* If anyone has purchased a slave subject to a covenant to manumit him, freedom is due to him under the *constitutio* of the deified Marcus, though the purchaser may have pledged all his possessions present or future. The same must be said if the covenant debars him from prostituting a slave-woman, and he has done so.

7   PAUL, *Gifts of Freedom, sole book:* In the case of a man who, having the power to carry off a slave-woman who had been prostituted, bartered his right to seizure for cash, our emperor and his father decided that she should be free on the basis that it makes no difference whether you yourself carry off a woman and prostitute her or allow her prostitution, which you might prevent, for a consideration in money.

8   PAPINIAN, *Replies, book 9:* A mother had given slaves to her daughter on the terms that the daughter was to provide for their liberation after her own death; when the terms of the gift had not been observed, I replied that in accordance with the spirit of the *constitutio* of the deified Marcus freedom accrued to the slaves with the mother's consent, and if the mother predeceased the daughter, it accrued absolutely.

9   PAUL, *Problems, book 5:* Latinus Largus sold a slave-woman with a covenant for her manumission without specifying the time; under the *constitutio* when does freedom begin to be due to her, if the purchaser fails to manumit? I replied that we must

examine what the aim had been; was the purchaser to manumit as soon as he had the power, or was he empowered to choose when to manumit? In the former case, it will be easy to determine the time; in the latter, freedom is due at least on the purchaser's death. If it should not be apparent what has been agreed, the principle of favoring freedom will lead to the former opinion, that is, that the slave should be manumitted within two months, if both slave and purchaser are present; for if the slave is absent and the purchaser has not set him free within four months, he is free in accordance with the *constitutiones* and snatched from the owner.

9

MANUMITTED PERSONS NOT FREE
AND THE *LEX AELIA SENTIA*

1   ULPIAN, *Sabinus, book 1:* In the twelfth book of his *Digest*, Celsus, in the interest of utility, says that a man deaf from birth can manumit.

2   ULPIAN, *Sabinus, book 3:* A slave cannot be entitled to freedom if he lives in the city after relegation.

3   GAIUS, *Legacies in the Urban Edict, book 2:* If a legatee has been given a choice of a man or if a man has been legated without clear identification, the heir cannot impair or subvert the right of choice by manumitting some or all of the slaves; for when the choice or selection of a slave is given, each of the slaves seems in a manner to have been conditionally legated.

4   ULPIAN, *Disputations, book 3:* We cannot manumit a slave given in pledge.

5   JULIAN, *Digest, book 64:* When an inheritance is insolvent, though the heir may have ample resources, freedom is not due under the will.   1. However, if an insolvent testator has given freedom in the form, "if my creditors have been paid in full, let Stichus be free," he cannot be deemed to have ordered liberation to the detriment of creditors.   2. If Titius should have no possessions but Stichus and Pamphilus and has promised them to Maevius stipulating in the form, "do you undertake to give Stichus or Pamphilus," and has then, having no other creditor, manumitted Stichus, his freedom is annulled by the *lex Aelia Sentia*. For though it was within the power of Titius to give Pamphilus, nonetheless, so long as he did not give him, seeing that he might die in the interval, his manumission of Stichus was detrimental to the other party to the bargain. But if he had promised to give Pamphilus alone, I would not doubt that Stichus could attain freedom, although as in the other case Pamphilus might die; for it makes a great difference whether the man manumitted is included in the stipulation itself or is not covered by the contractual liability. So, too, if he has pledged Stichus and Pamphilus to any one for five gold pieces, although each be worth that sum, neither can be manumitted; but if he has only pledged Stichus, his manumission of Pamphilus is not held detrimental to the creditor.

6   SCAEVOLA, *Problems, book 16:* Julian is speaking of the man who may have no other assets; for if he should have any, why shall we not say that he can manumit one of the slaves; he is solvent if one is dead and solvent if one is manumitted, and we should not

reckon with incalculable eventualities; otherwise, anyone who has promised an unspecified slave from his household will manumit none of his slaves.

7   JULIAN, *Urseius Ferox, book 2:* If anyone ratified codicils when his resources were unimpaired but later, when planning to defraud his creditors, made grants of freedom by codicils, there is no way of preventing the grants from being legally hindered; for the fraudulent intent of the testator operates not at the time when the codicils are ratified, but at that at which freedom is granted by codicils.   1. A man under twenty wishing to manumit a slave, after failing to produce a reason recognized by law to a council, gave the slave to you with a view to your manumitting him; Proculus said that he was not free, since the law had been evaded.

8   AFRICANUS, *Problems, book 3:* When a person with a conditional debt manumits for the purpose of defrauding creditors, the *lex Aelia Sentia* applies.   1. If a soldier has made a will under military law and made grants of freedom to the detriment of creditors and dies insolvent, the grants are stopped.

9   MARCIAN, *Institutes, book 1:* A man will not be free who has used violence to compel his owner to manumit him, even if under terror he has given him freedom in his will.   1. No more can the man be free whom his owner did not defend on a capital charge and who was subsequently acquitted.   2. Slaves sold subject to a covenant that they should not be manumitted or slaves whose manumission may have been forbidden by will or command of a provincial governor, do not attain freedom, even if manumitted.

10   GAIUS, *Common Matters, book 1:* It is deemed that a man manumits to the detriment of creditors if he is insolvent at the time of manumission or would become insolvent after the grants of freedom; for men often hope that their assets are greater than they actually are. This frequently happens to persons who carry on business through slaves and freedmen beyond the sea or in regions where they are not living themselves; they are often ignorant of losses incurred over a long period and bestow the favor of freedom on their slaves, manumitting without fraudulent intent.

11   MARCIAN, *Institutes, book 13:* Slaves manumitted to the detriment of a *civitas* do not attain freedom by resolution of the senate.   1. But it is also provided by imperial *constitutiones* that grants of freedom to the detriment of the imperial treasury do not succeed, although as the deified brothers ruled by rescript, such grants are not stopped in all cases, but only if the owner was insolvent at the time and manumitted fraudulently.

12   ULPIAN, *Adulteries, book 4:* The legislator took care to prevent slaves being withdrawn by manumission from judicial examination [under torture] and therefore forbade their manumission and fixed a period within which manumission would not be allowed.   1. In fact, the woman leaving the matrimonial state is forbidden herself to manumit or alienate any of her slaves in any circumstances, since the language of the law debars her from manumitting or alienating even a slave employed on an estate or in a province and not in her personal service; this is indeed very harsh, but it is the express provision of the law.   2. But even if the woman has bought or otherwise acquired a slave after the divorce, she will not be able to manumit him, as Sextus

Caecilius also remarks.   3. However, if she is a daughter-in-power, her father is only forbidden to manumit or alienate those slaves whom he had allowed his daughter for her personal service.   4. The law also forbade the mother to manumit or alienate those slaves she had allowed her daughter for that purpose.   5. And likewise, the grandfather and grandmother, since it was the purpose of the law that their slaves too could be demanded for judicial examination.   6. Sextus Caecilius rightly says that the law fixed an extremely narrow limit of time regarding the manumission or alienation of slaves. Suppose, he says, that a woman is accused of adultery within sixty days; what trial has it been possible to conduct so expeditiously that it would be completed within sixty days? And yet a woman already on a charge of adultery is allowed to manumit a slave suspected in regard to the crime or indispensable to the judicial examination, so far as the words of the law go. Certainly, in such a case the remedy must be adopted of denying manumission before completion of the trial to slaves designated for judicial examination as privy to or guilty of the crime.   7. Father or mother of the woman, if they should die within sixty days, will not be able [by will] to manumit or alienate any of the slaves they gave the daughter for personal service.

13   PAUL, *Adulteries, book 3:* But if they have manumitted within sixty days, the slave will be a *statuliber*.

14   ULPIAN, *Adulteries, book 4:* But if the husband should have died within sixty days, let us see if any of the aforementioned persons may then manumit or alienate. And in my belief, they cannot, although the woman no longer has an accuser in her husband, since her father may accuse her.   1. And, in fact, the law forbade the woman without qualification to manumit within sixty days of divorce.   2. Manumission will be barred whether she divorced or was put away by a deed of repudiation by her husband.   3. Though not if the marriage has been ended by his death or by some punishment imposed on him.   4. But if he has ended the marriage amicably, it will be said that there is no bar to manumission or alienation.   5. But if, while the marriage is in being, the woman meditating divorce should manumit or alienate and if this has been proved beyond doubt, the alienation or manumission ought not to be valid on the footing that it constitutes an evasion of the law.   6. We should take alienation to include every type.

15   PAUL, *Lex Julia, book 1:* The question has been raised whether a man accused of *maiestas* may manumit, since he is owner prior to condemnation. And the Emperor Antoninus ruled in a rescript to Calpurnius Cato that once a man could be certain of his punishment from reflection on his own crimes, he had lost the right of granting freedom from consciousness of his guilt long before his condemnation.   1. Julian says that if a son, after receiving permission from his father to manumit, subsequently manumitted *vindicta* in ignorance that his father was deceased, the man is not freed. But even if the father is alive but has changed his wish, the son is deemed not to have manumitted with father's consent.

16   PAUL, *Lex Aelia Sentia, book 3:* If a man under twenty should sell a slave with a covenant that he be manumitted, because fideicommissary freedom is due to him or because he had bought him subject to this covenant, there will be no hindrance to alienation.   1. Delivery for purpose of manumission by a man under twenty of his share in a common slave will be void; but no evasion of the law will be imputed, if the delivery occurred when he could have shown lawful grounds.   2. This law provides that no one should manumit a slave to detriment of creditors; creditors include all who would be

entitled to take proceedings on any grounds against the person acting to their detriment. 3. Aristo replied that a man manumitted by an insolvent debtor of the imperial treasury should be re-enslaved, provided that he had not been in freedom for long, that is, for less than ten years; of course, whatever he had pocketed to the detriment of the treasury was to be recovered. 4. If money should be conditionally due to anyone, the slave manumitted by the debtor will be a sort of *statuliber,* his freedom depending on the condition. 5. If a son has manumitted by wish of his father, whether father or son know that the father is insolvent, there will be a bar to freedom.

17   PAUL, *Grants of Freedom, sole book:* If a private person has manumitted a slave under popular pressure, even if he has lent his consent, the man will still not be free; in fact, the deified Marcus also forbade manumissions arising from popular clamor. 1. A man is also not freed, if his owner mendaciously said that he was free, to prevent his being flogged by the magistrates, if it was not his wish to manumit. 2. In the case of slaves whom it is not permitted to manumit within fixed periods, if they have received testamentary freedom, it is not the date of the will but that on which freedom falls due that should be looked into.

18   PAUL, *Plautius, book 16:* If an inheritance should be solvent at the the time of death, but no longer at the time of acceptance, freedom bequeathed by the testator to the detriment of creditors will not be due; for just as the growth of the inheritance benefits grants of freedom, its diminution does them damage. 1. Let us see if there is already detriment to creditors if the man to whom freedom has been left should be ordered to pay his value to the heir and be free, seeing that the heir would receive this anyhow as a result of the testator's death, or whether there is no detriment, if the payment be made by someone else on his behalf or by the slave himself from *peculium.* But if the heir's resources do not assist in making a grant of freedom good, neither can a gift of money.

19   MODESTINUS, *Rules, book 1:* No grant of freedom is valid if made by one who has subsequently been judicially declared to be a slave himself.

20   MODESTINUS, *Problems Solved, sole book:* If freedom has been given to someone else's slave without consent of the owner, the grant can have no legal force, even though the manumitter later turns out to be the owner's heir; for though he turns out to be his heir by right of kinship, his entry on the inheritance does not confirm the grant of freedom.

21   MODESTINUS, *Encyclopaedia, book 1:* A slave-woman can be manumitted for the purpose of marriage only by the man who is to take her as his wife. But if one man has manumitted her for that purpose and another take her as his wife, she will not be free; even if the husband has put her away within six months and the manumitter has later taken her as wife, Julian replied that she is not freed on the basis that the senate had in mind only marriages which occurred after manumission with none taking place in between.

22   POMPONIUS, *Quintus Mucius, book 25:* The curator of a lunatic cannot manumit the latter's slave.

23   POMPONIUS, *Readings, book 4:* Every grant of freedom by a man who knew that he was insolvent is detrimental to creditors, even though the gift was made honorably and deserved.

24   TERENTIUS CLEMENS, *Lex Julia et Papia, book 9:* If a man with creditors has manumitted several slaves, there will be no bar on the freedom of all; the first manumitted will be free so long as the creditors are paid. On this principle, Julian would say that to take the case of two manumissions, if the creditors would suffer detriment by the freedom of one but not of both, then there is a bar to the freedom of one or other, generally of the second to be named, unless the first named be the more valuable, and it

would not be enough to deny freedom to the second, while the first would be enough; in that case, only the man mentioned second would attain freedom.

25   PAPINIAN, *Replies, book 5:* Grants of freedom by will to the detriment of creditors are voided, after settlement with old creditors, by the appearance of new creditors.

26   SCAEVOLA, *Replies, book 4:* An heir manumitted the pledged slave of a man in debt; was he free? He replied that, on the facts stated, he had not been freed by the manumission, if the money were still due. PAUL. So, when the money has been paid, he is freed in accordance with the manumitter's wish.

27   HERMOGENIAN, *Epitome of Law, book 1:* A man is manumitted to the detriment of creditors and his freedom is then forbidden, whether the day for repayment has already passed or whether repayment is postponed or conditional. The case of a conditional legacy is different; for until the condition has been satisfied, the legatee concerned is not counted among the creditors. The *lex Aelia Sentia* in this part protected creditors of every kind, and it has been decided that the fideicommissary should also be included among them. 1. A pledged slave cannot be manumitted without creditors' consent before security be given for the debt. But if a *pupillus* is creditor, his consent without the tutor's sanction, is of no avail for freedom, just as it is of no avail if a *pupillus* as fructuary were similarly to give his consent to manumission.

28   PAUL, *Views, book 3:* The manumission by an heir of his own slave legated by the testator [to a third party] is of no effect, since it has been decided that no account should be taken of his knowing or not knowing [of the legacy].

29   GAIUS, *Manumissions, book 1:* It is in general beyond doubt that a slave pledged is in law fully the property of the debtor and can obtain lawful freedom from him, if the *lex Aelia Sentia* should not bar freedom, that is, if the debtor be solvent and no evident detriment to the creditors should result. 1. A slave conditionally legated is in law fully the property of the heir, so long as the condition is unsatisfied, but cannot obtain freedom from him, lest wrong be done to the legatee.

30   ULPIAN, *Lex Aelia Sentia, book 4:* If anyone has bought a slave subject to covenant to manumit and, as a result of his failure to manumit, the slave has attained freedom under the *constitutio* of the deified Marcus, let us see if he can charge him [the freedman] as ungrateful. And it can be said that as he is not the manumitter, he does not have this right. 1. If my son has manumitted in accordance with my wish, it will be possible to doubt whether I have the right of charging him as ungrateful, since I did not manumit him; however, I am to be treated as if I had manumitted. 2. But if my son should manumit a slave belonging to his *peculium castrense*, I shall certainly not have this right, since I did not manumit myself; clearly, the son will himself be able to prosecute. 3. But anyone will be able to prosecute so long as he remains patron. 4. But whenever several patrons wish to charge a freedman, we should see whether the agreement of all is required or whether one alone may act. And it is the truer view that if he has committed an offense only against one, that man may accuse him as ungrateful, but that the agreement of all is required, if they are in the same position. 5. If a father has assigned a freedman to one of his sons, Julian wrote that he alone can proceed, since he alone is the patron.

31   TERENTIUS CLEMENS, *Lex Julia et Papia, book 5:* The question was raised what was the legal position if a patron had bound a freedwoman by oath not to marry so long as she had children below the age of puberty. Julian says that since he had not enjoined perpetual widowhood on her, he is not deemed to have contravened the *lex Aelia Sentia*.

32   TERENTIUS CLEMENS, *Lex Julia et Papia, book 8:* If without consent of a patron a man in his power bound a freedwoman by oath or stipulation not to marry, unless the

patron should remit the obligation, he will come under the law; for it will be deemed that he was acting in bad faith.   1. Patrons are not forbidden by the *lex Aelia Sentia* to receive regular payments from freedmen but only to bind them [to make such payments]; so if the freedman has made such a payment voluntarily to a patron, he will obtain no advantage from this law.   2. It is not relevant to this law if a man has promised workdays or a fixed sum in lieu of each workday, since he can be free of liability by providing the workdays. Octavenus approves this view and adds: A man is understood to be binding the freedman to pay him for the workdays, if his only aim is to obtain the payment, even though he has stipulated for it under the guise of workdays.

10

THE RIGHT TO GOLD RINGS

1   PAPINIAN, *Replies, book 1:* It is not the case that a bequest of maintenance made to a particular freedman among others is not due for the reason that the freedman has received the right to gold rings from the emperor.   1. A different view is approved in the case of the freedman who has been adjudged to be freeborn by collusion, which has been discovered by the agency of another patron, and who has been restored to his proper status and desires to receive the maintenance which a third patron has left him. In fact, it has been decided that he should also lose the privilege of the rings.

2   PAPINIAN, *Replies, book 15:* A verdict given in favor of free birth had been rescinded within five years; I replied that the man who lost the case ceased to possess the privilege of gold rings which he had received before the verdict was given in favor of free birth and which he then laid down.

3   MARCIAN, *Institutes, book 1:* The deified Commodus took away even the right to rings from those who had accepted it against the wishes or without the knowledge of their patrons.

4   ULPIAN, *Lex Julia et Papia, book 3:* Even women will be able to seek and obtain the right to gold rings and restitution of their birth rights.

5   PAUL, *Lex Julia et Papia, book 9:* A man who has sought and obtained the right to rings is deemed to be of free birth, although the patron is not debarred from his rights in regard to the inheritance.

6   ULPIAN, *Lex Julia et Papia, book 1:* If a freedman has sought and obtained the right to rings, although he has secured the rights of a freeborn man subject to his patron's right, nonetheless, he is understood to be freeborn; and the deified Hadrian so ruled by rescript.

11

THE RESTITUTION OF BIRTHRIGHTS

1   ULPIAN, *Replies, book 2:* A man restored by the emperor to his birthrights on making a declaration to the emperor that he was of free birth is deemed to have failed in his plea, if he was actually born to a slave-woman.

2   MARCIAN, *Institutes, book 1:* On occasion, even slaves by birth become freeborn persons by the retroactive intervention of the law, for example, if a freedman should have been restored to his birthrights by the emperor. For he is restored to those birth rights at least which all men once enjoyed, not to those of his own actual birth, seeing that he had been born a slave. In fact, this man is treated in regard to his entire legal status as if he had been born free, nor can his patron enter on the succession. For this very reason the emperors are generally reluctant to restore anyone to his birthrights without the patron's consent.

3   SCAEVOLA, *Replies, book 6:* You ask if a man whom the most sacred and noble emperor restored to his birthrights enjoys the legal status of a freeborn man. But this is

a question on which there neither is nor ever has been any doubt; it is fully established that anyone who enjoys this privilege from the emperor is entirely restored to the status of a freeborn man.

4   PAUL, *Views, book 4:* Nor can a freedman be restored to his birthrights without the consent of the patron's son; for what difference does it make whether a wrong were done to the patron himself or to his sons?

5   MODESTINUS, *Rules, book 7:* The patron's consent is necessary to the restoration of birthrights by the emperor to a freedman; for if the freedman seeks and obtains this grant, the patron loses his right.   1. A freedman who has been restored to his birthrights is treated as if he had been born free and not been besmirched by slavery in the intervening time.

12

THE SUIT FOR FREEDOM

1   ULPIAN, *Edict, book 54:* If ever a person who is in *de facto* slavery does not allow a suit concerning his status, I suppose because he wished to inflict a kind of outrage on himself and his line, in this case it is fair that certain persons should be authorized to bring the suit on his behalf, for example, a parent who claims him as son-in-power; for he will bring the suit on the son's behalf, even against his will. But even if he be not a son-in-power, this right will be given to the parent, since it is always in a parent's interest that his son should not be subject to slavery.   1. Conversely, we shall say that sons are empowered in the same way to act for parents, even without their consent; for the disgrace suffered by a son, if his parent should be a slave, is substantial.   2. On this account, it has been thought fit that kinsmen too should be given this right,

2   GAIUS, *Urban Praetor's Edict, Chapter on Suits for Freedom:* since the slavery of kinsmen affects us, causing us pain and and outrage.

3   ULPIAN, *Edict, book 54:* Furthermore, I think that this same right should be available to natural connections too with the effect that a parent may claim freedom for a [natural] son who has been discovered in slavery and manumitted.   1. A soldier too is allowed to sue for freedom on behalf of his *necessarii.*   2. But when there is no such male person to sue on a man's behalf, then his mother, daughters or sisters, and other kinswomen, and his wife too, must also be empowered to approach the praetor and to provide information, so that the case may be heard and aid brought to him even against his wishes.   3. But even if I should claim the person as my freedman or freedwoman, we shall have to state the same view.

4   GAIUS, *Urban Praetor's Edict, Chapter on Suits for Freedom:* However, a patron is only allowed to sue for the freedom of a freedman, if the freedman let himself be sold into slavery without his knowledge.

5   ULPIAN, *Edict, book 54:* For it is in our interest to have freedmen and freedwomen.   1. But if there are several who wish to sue on behalf of the aforementioned persons, it should be the role of the praetor to intervene; it is for him to choose the person most suitable for the purpose in his judgment. This should also be the practice where there are several patrons.

6   GAIUS, *Urban Praetor's Edict, [Chapter on Suits for Freedom]:* But it is the more kindly course which should be followed, if the person being enslaved is a lunatic and *infans,* that this authority should be given not only to *necessarii* but even to *extranei.*

7   ULPIAN, *Edict, book 54:* Freemen too, if in particular, being over twenty they allowed themselves to be sold or to pass by any procedure into slavery, are not barred from proclaiming freedom, unless they shared in the price.   1. If anyone under twenty allowed himself to be sold with a view to sharing in the price, this will not prejudice him even after he becomes twenty. But if he sold himself before then, but shared in the price after his twentieth year, it will be possible for freedom to be denied him.   2. If anyone has bought a freeman in knowledge of his freedom, a proclamation

of freedom against the purchaser is not denied to the man sold, whatever his age, on the ground that the purchaser deserves no favor, even if the man he bought knew the position and was of sound mind. However, if subsequently another person, in ignorance of his status, bought him from the purchaser, freedom should be denied to him.   3. If two persons have bought shares [in the man], one in knowledge of the position, the other without, we shall have to see whether it can really be that the former by his knowledge ought not to prejudice the latter; indeed, this is the view to be preferred. But then the question will arise whether the purchaser without knowledge is to have only a share in the whole. And what shall we say of the other share? Would it belong to the purchaser who knew the facts? Yet he does not deserve to have anything, since he made the purchase in knowledge. On the other hand, the purchaser without knowledge cannot have a larger share in the property than he bought. So it comes about that the ignorance of the one is beneficial to the other who bought the man in knowledge of his status.   4. There are other grounds too on which a proclamation of freedom is denied, for example, when a man is said to be free by the terms of a will, the opening of which is forbidden by the praetor because the testator has allegedly been murdered by his household; for when the man is in a position in which he may be liable to punishment, a suit for freedom ought not to be granted to him. But even if freedom has been given him [by the will], on account of the doubt whether he is guilty or innocent, the suit for freedom is postponed until the death of the murdered man has been cleared up; it will then be evident whether he should be punished or not.   5. If a man in slavery proclaims freedom, he has the role of plaintiff; but if a man in freedom is claimed as a slave, the claimant takes on the role of plaintiff. So when there is uncertainty on this point, in order that the trial may take a regular course, there is a preliminary hearing before whomever it is who is to decide on the issue of freedom to determine whether the proceedings concern the passage from freedom to slavery or the reverse. And in case it has become evident that the man whose freedom is at stake was in nonfraudulent enjoyment of freedom, the person who claims to be his owner will assume the role of plaintiff and will be obliged to prove the man his slave; but if it has been declared in the preliminary proceedings that he was not in enjoyment or not in nonfraudulent enjoyment of the freedom, the man whose freedom is at stake must himself prove that he is free.

8   ULPIAN, *Edict, book 55:* The fructuary can take proceedings in a case of freedom, even if the owner, that is, the professed owner, should also wish to raise the question of status.   1. If several persons claim ownership of a slave, alleging that he is their common property, they will have to be sent to the same judge; this was also decreed by the senate. But if each should allege that he is sole and not part owner, the decree of the senate does not apply; nor in fact are conflicting judgments to be feared, when each and all claim sole ownership for himself.   2. But even if one man claims only the usufruct and another the ownership of the slave, and also if one man claims to be owner and another to be pledgee, the judge will be the same; and it makes little difference whether the man was given him in pledge by the professed owner or by someone else.

9   GAIUS, *Urban Praetor's Edict, Chapter on Suits for Freedom:* If both fructuary and proprietor should be joined in the proceedings against the man engaged in a lawsuit for freedom, it may be that one or the other is absent; in this case, there may be doubt whether the praetor is to permit the one who is present to proceed against him, since the right of either ought not to be damaged by the collusion or ineffectiveness of the other. But it is more correct to say that either should be allowed to proceed but without prejudice to the other's right. If the latter should have come on the scene before conclusion of the trial, he will be sent to the same judge, unless he should show good reason to the contrary, for example, if he should affirm that the judge concerned was his personal enemy.   1. We shall state the same view if two or more persons should be said to be owners, and some should be available, others absent.   2. Hence, in both cases we should examine whether, the first litigant having failed, the success of the later litigant may accrue to his benefit or the reverse, that is, whether the success of either, irrespective of order, would also accrue to the other's benefit, as it benefits the heir of a freedman that slaves were manumitted to defraud the patron. Anyone who should take this view ought to infer that when the man renews the suit he has lost, the defense of *res judicata* may be met by *replicatio*, but anyone who

should take the contrary view will be faced with the consequential question whether the property [the share of the slave] on which he lost his claim will not belong to anyone or should belong to the person against whom he took proceedings [the slave himself] or rather to the successful litigant, presumably on the footing that an *actio utilis* may be given to the successful litigant; the praetor could not possibly allow any one to be partly a slave.

10   ULPIAN, *Edict, book 55:* Our expression "in enjoyment of freedom" should not be taken to mean that the man subject to a trial for freedom is not to show that he is free, but only that he was in enjoyment of freedom without fraud. But let us consider what "without fraud" means. For Julian says that all who think themselves free have been in enjoyment of freedom without fraud, provided that they behave as freemen, even though they are slaves, but Varus writes that a man who knows himself to be free is, while a fugitive, not deemed to be in enjoyment of freedom without fraud but that, as soon as he has ceased to hide like a fugitive and to act as a freeman, he begins from that moment to be in enjoyment of freedom without fraud; in fact, he says that the man who knows himself to be free but acts as a fugitive is acting as a slave simply by being in flight,

11   GAIUS, *Urban Praetor's Edict, Chapter on Suits for Freedom:* although in the period of flight he conducted himself as a freeman; for we shall say that he is in the same case.

12   ULPIAN, *Edict, book 55:* It should then be known that a free man can be in fraudulent enjoyment of freedom and a slave can be in nonfraudulent enjoyment of freedom.   1. An *infans* who had been kidnapped was in slavery in good faith, although he was free, and then, while ignorant of his status, ran away and began to live in hiding as a freeman; he is undoubtedly living fraudulently in freedom.   2. It is also possible for a slave to live in freedom without fraud; for example, he has accepted freedom under a will without knowing that it has no validity, or he has been freed by *vindicta* by someone whom he mistakenly supposed to be his owner, or he has been brought up as a freeman, although a slave.   3. And in general, whenever a man for reasons good or bad has genuinely supposed himself to be free and has lived in freedom, we are bound to say that he is in the situation of enjoying nonfraudulent freedom and has the advantage of being the possessor [of freedom].   4. But the burden of proof whether a man was in nonfraudulent enjoyment of freedom will be related to the time at which legal proceedings began.   5. If anyone has workdays due to him, he too can get a decision on this at a trial of freedom.   6. If the person proclaiming freedom caused me loss at the time when he was in slavery to me in good faith, for instance, if as his owner in good faith I was sued on a noxal action and condemned and offered compensation on his account, a sum will be awarded to me for this.

13   GAIUS, *Urban Praetor's Edict, Chapter on Suits for Freedom:* This is certain that the only loss included in this *actio in factum* is that due to malice (*dolus*) and not to negligence (*culpa*) as well. Hence, though he has been acquitted from liability on this action, nonetheless, it will remain possible to take proceedings against him under the *lex Aquilia*, since under that law there is liability for negligence too.   1. Further, it is certain that not only our own property but that of others which is at our risk, for example, that which has been lent to us for use or leased, is included in this action; certainly, property deposited with us, since it is not at our risk, does not come within its scope.

14   ULPIAN, *Edict, book 55:* The praetor is absolutely right to check the craft of those who, knowing themselves to be free, have fraudulently permitted themselves to be sold as slaves.   1. For he has given an action against them which applies whenever the man who permitted his own sale is not in a situation in which he would be denied a claim to freedom.   2. We take fraud to have been shown not when a man failed to volunteer information to the purchaser but when he deceived him,

15 PAUL, *Edict, book 51:* (that is, if, whether male or female, the person was of age to
practice fraud),

16 ULPIAN, *Edict, book 55:* especially when he made himself out to be a slave and so
procured his sale with the purpose of deceiving the purchaser. 1. However, if the
man sold was under the compulsion of force or fear, we shall say that he was innocent
of fraud. 2. The purchaser has this action only when he did not know that the man
was free; for if he knows him to be free and still buys him, he is cheating himself. 3. So if the purchaser is a son-in-power who knows the facts himself, he does
not obtain the action for his father who was in ignorance; I mean, if he has made the
purchase for account of his *peculium.* But if the father mandates, the question arises
whether he would be prejudiced by the son's knowledge; I still think that he is, just as
by the knowledge of a procurator. 4. Obviously, if the father knows and the son did
not, I still say that the father should be refused in the same way, even if the son made
the purchase for account of his *peculium,* provided that the father was present and
could have stopped the son buying.

17 PAUL, *Edict, book 51:* In the case of a slave and of a person who makes a purchase
by our mandate, the position is that if I have mandated the purchase of a particular
individual in the knowledge that he is free, and he has made the purchase, the action
would not be available to him; on the other hand, if I did not know, though the procurator does, it is not to be denied to me.

18 ULPIAN, *Edict, book 55:* A freeman who has been sold as a slave with his knowledge is therefore liable to the purchaser on the sum he gave or was under obligation to
give, in fact, for double the sum. 1. But let us see whether it is only the price that is
doubled or anything accessory to the price as well; I would think that the whole cost
without any exception, which was given in consideration of the purchase

19 PAUL, *Edict, book 51:* or exchanged or provided in compensation on that account
(since all this must be taken to have been given)

20 ULPIAN, *Edict, book 55:* or incurred as an obligation, ought to be doubled. 1. So,
too, if a legitimate gift was made to anyone on account of this acquisition, this too must
be said to come under this edict and to be doubled. 2. An obligation we should take
to be one incurred to the vendor himself or to a third party; it will include anything
given to the vendor himself or to a third party on his instruction by the purchaser
himself or by anyone else. 3. We should take a man to be under obligation, if he cannot protect himself by a defense (*exceptio*); but if he can, we must say that he is not
under obligation. 4. It happens on occasion that the purchaser may have an action
for fourfold compensation; for he has an action for double compensation against the
man himself who was knowingly sold as a slave, and in addition, an action for double
compensation lies against the vendor and the man who promised double compensation,

21 MODESTINUS, *Penalties, book 1:* that is, double the sum he gave or was under obligation to give for the purchase. Accordingly, what one of them has paid will not
contribute to relieving the other of liability, since it has been decided that this action is
penal. As a result, it is not given after lapse of a year, nor will proceedings be taken
against successors, since it is penal. 1. It will be absolutely right to say that the action arising from this edict is not extinguished by manumission, although it is true that
the vendor cannot be sued after recourse to the man who has proclaimed his freedom.

22 ULPIAN, *Edict, book 55:* But not only the purchaser but his successors too will be
able to take proceedings by this *actio in factum.* 1. Purchase we shall take to include
purchase through a third party such as a procurator. 2. But further, if there are several purchasers, they will all have this action, subject to the proviso that the purchaser of a share has the action for his share, but each member of a consortium for the
whole price. Nor will any be prejudiced by another's knowledge of the facts nor assisted by his ignorance. 3. If the purchaser knew that the man was free only at a

later stage, this will not prejudice him, since he was ignorant at the time of purchase. But if he knew at the time, the fact that he later conceived doubts will be of no assistance to him. 4. His knowledge does not prejudice and his ignorance does not assist his heir or other successors. 5. But if the procurator through whom he made the purchase possessed the knowledge, he is prejudiced, just as in Labeo's view he is prejudiced by knowledge of his tutor. 6. This action is not given after lapse of a year, since it is praetorian; it is in addition penal.

23   PAUL, *Edict, book 50:* If I have sold you usufruct of a freeman sharing in the price and performed *in jure cessio,* Quintus Mucius used to say that he is made a slave but that I become his owner only if I had bought him in good faith and that otherwise he would be a slave without an owner. 1. To summarize, it should be known that what has been said of the denial of proclamation of freedom to slaves sold applies to those given away as presents and as parts of a dowry, and also to those who have allowed themselves to be pledged. 2. If mother and son are engaged in legal proceedings for freedom, the cases of both should be joined together, or the case of the son deferred until that of the mother is settled, as the deified Hadrian also decided. In fact, when mother and son are engaged in proceedings before different judges, Augustus said that the case of the mother should be settled first, and a decision taken on the son later.

24   PAUL, *Edict, book 51:* When a suit for freedom has been instituted, the person whose status is the subject of proceedings is treated as free to the extent that actions of any kind he may wish to bring are not denied him even against the person who claims to be his owner; what, then, if any of them be such as lapse with time or death? Why should he not be allowed to secure his right to bring them by joinder of issue? 1. Indeed, Servius says that in actions that lapse after a year, the year runs from the time when the suit was instituted. 2. But if he should wish to go to law with third parties, we are not to examine whether the suit had been instituted, lest a procedure may be devised whereby actions may be barred for the time being by putting someone up to question a man's freedom; the judgment of the suit for freedom will, of course, in itself make the man's action effective or void. 3. But if the owner should bring actions against him, it is a question whether he should be compelled to accept trial. On the general view, if the action is personal, he should accept to the point of joinder of issue, but the judgment must await that on the suit for freedom, nor is it deemed that there is any prejudgment on his freedom or that he remains in freedom by the owner's wish; in fact, once a suit for freedom has been instituted, he is treated as free for the time being, and just as he can bring actions, so can actions be brought against him. But according to the issue [of that suit] if it goes in his favor, the action will be effective, but null if the verdict is given against freedom. 4. If the man proclaiming freedom should be impleaded for theft or wrongful damage by anyone, Mela says that for the time being he should give security for appearance in a court, so that a person whose free status is in doubt should not be in a better position than one whose status is certain, but the trial should be postponed, so that there may be no prejudgment on the issue of freedom. Equally, if proceedings for theft have begun with a man's possessor and the man on whose account the proceedings were instituted has subsequently proclaimed freedom, the trial should be postponed, so that if he has been adjudged free, the suit may be brought against him instead; or, if condemnation has already occurred [in the former proceedings], the action on judgment should be granted against him rather [than against the former possessor].

25   GAIUS, *Urban Praetor's Edict, Chapter on Suits for Freedom:* If an option has been legated to anyone engaged in litigation about his freedom, whatever is said in reference to an inheritance left him can be applied to the option. 1. On occasions, a second proclamation of freedom is granted, for example, in the case of the man who affirms that he was defeated at the first trial only because a condition for his freedom had not yet taken effect, which he alleges has now taken effect. 2. Although it is commonly said that once a suit for freedom has been instituted, the man whose status is at issue is treated as free, nonetheless, if he should be a slave, it is certain in spite of this that

he acquires for the owner what comes to him by delivery or stipulation just as if his freedom was not the subject of inquiry. We shall consider only the matter of possession, since the owner ceases to possess the man himself after institution of the suit, but it is the better view that the owner acquires, though he does not have possession of the man. And since it has been approved that we can acquire possession even through a runaway slave, it is not surprising that we can do so through the man in question.

26   GAIUS, *Provincial Edict, book 20:* A person who claims that a "freeman" is his slave is not liable to the action for insults if he takes proceedings against the man's freedom for the purpose of keeping his right to sue for eviction.

27   ULPIAN, *Duties of Consul, book 2:* The deified brothers sent this rescript to Proculus and Munatius: "Inasmuch as Romulus, whose status is at issue, is a *pupillus* in age, and his mother, Varia Hedo, with the agreement of his tutor, Varius Hermes, demands that the case be deferred until he reaches puberty, it is a matter for your responsible judgment to decide the question in accordance with the honor of the persons and the interest of the *pupillus*." 1. If the person who raised the issue of someone's status should fail to appear at trial, the man whose freedom is the subject of the proceedings is in the same position as before his freedom was at issue with indeed this advantage that the person who raised the issue loses his case. Not that this makes him free by birth, if he was not, nor, in fact, does want of a contestant usually confer freeborn status. I think the judges will act correctly and properly if, in the event of failure to appear by the plaintiff claiming a "freeman" as his slave, they should have followed the procedure of allowing the other party to choose whether he would prefer the trial to be canceled or the case to be heard and judgment pronounced. If they should have tried the case, they will be bound to pronounce that he does not appear to be a slave; there is no quibble here, since the judgment is not that he is freeborn, but that he does not appear to be a slave. But if the man is in slavery and claiming to be freeborn, they will have done better to cancel the trial, so as not to give judgment that he appears to be freeborn without a contestant present, unless strong reason were to influence them and manifest proofs suggest that they should give judgment in favor of freedom, a matter also covered in a rescript of Hadrian. 2. But if the man pleading for his freedom should fail to appear but his opponent should be present, it will be better for the latter's case to prevail and a verdict given, if the matter is clear, against freedom; however, it is possible for a man to win even in absence, and in fact a verdict can actually be given in favor of his freedom.

28   POMPONIUS, *Quintus Mucius, book 12:* A slave is not deemed to enjoy freedom by the wish of his owner, when the owner had not known that the man was his; that is right; for a man only enjoys freedom by the wish of the owner, when he obtains the possession of freedom in accordance with that wish.

29   ARRIUS MENANDER, *Military Law, book 1:* A man pleading for his own freedom who enlists in the army before judgment is given, if condemned, is to be treated like other slaves, and it is no mitigation that in some points he was being treated as free. And though his freedom has been proved, he will be discharged, that is, banned from military service, and expelled from the camp, at least if the suit should have been one to raise him from slavery to freedom or if he lived fraudulently as a freeman; if there was a malicious suit to reduce him to slavery, he will be kept in service. 1. If a man who enlisted was declared freeborn but the verdict was reversed within five years, he should be handed back to his new owner.

30   JULIAN, *From Minicius, book 5:* If two persons in separate suits claim a man [who purports to be free] as a slave, each as to a half-share, and he is adjudged free in one trial and a slave in the other, it is most convenient that pressure should be brought on the judges until they agree; if this does not happen, Sabinus is reported to have thought that the successful claimant should lead him away as a slave; Cassius too and I are of the same opinion. And it is perfectly absurd to suppose that he is half a slave and half free. However, it is more convenient under the principle favoring freedom

that he should be free and yet be compelled to pay half his value to the successful claimant, as assessed by a good man.

31   ULPIAN, *Replies, book 1:* He replied that a son on account of his being heir to his father is forbidden by his father to claim as a slave one whom his father has manumitted.

32   PAUL, *Rules, book 6:* In regard to the property of those who had made good a claim to be freeborn, when reputed slaves or freedmen, the senate passed a decree which provides in the case of those whose claim had been made when they were in reputed slavery, that they should take only what they had brought into the household concerned; as to the property of those who had wished to reclaim their original status after manumission, it added that they were to take with them what they had also acquired after manumission but not from the assets of the manumitter, and to leave other property to the person whose household they had left.

33   PAUL, *Suits for Freedom, sole book:* Anyone who has knowingly bought a freeman, even though the man permitted his own sale, nonetheless, is unable to contest his proclamation of freedom; but if he has sold the man to a third party ignorant of the facts, proclamation will be denied.

34   ULPIAN, *Encyclopaedia, sole book:* By a *constitutio* of the Emperor Antoninus no man is to be allowed to proclaim freedom without having rendered an account of his administration in the time when he was in slavery.

35   PAPINIAN, *Replies, book 9:* It has been settled that slaves designated for custody of a temple which Titia wished to have built and not manumitted belong to the heir.

36   PAPINIAN, *Replies, book 12:* The owner who has won his case will not be compelled to take monetary compensation for his own slave, if he should wish to take him away.

37   CALLISTRATUS, *Questions, book 2:* A private pact cannot make a man anyone's slave or freedman.

38   PAUL, *Replies, book 15:* Paul replied that if the facts were as stated and if after completion of an unconditional sale the purchaser had freely sent off a letter, professing that he would after a given time manumit the man he had bought, the letter did not seem relevant to the *constitutio* of the deified Marcus. 1. He also replied that that *constitutio* actually applied to the freedom of slaves sold subject to the condition that they should be manumitted after a time, but that the same favor was also due, for the purpose of securing freedom, to the woman for whom the owner received a price that he might manumit his own slave-woman, inasmuch as he was also to have her as his freedwoman. 2. The question was raised whether the purchaser did right to give freedom before the price was paid. Paul replied that the slave whom the vendor has delivered to the purchaser has become part of the purchaser's property, even though the price has not been paid, provided that security has been given for payment. 3. Gaius Seius sold the slave Stichus to Lucius Titius with the proviso that Titius was to manumit him if he had served continuously for three years; before the term was over, Stichus ran away and returned after some time had elapsed when Titius was deceased; I ask if Stichus would be hindered in obtaining freedom under the sale because he left before the end of the three year term. Paul replied that on the facts stated, freedom was available to him on completion of the period after which Stichus's manumission was due.

39   PAUL, *Views, book 5:* A man who is not under the burden of proving his free birth is to be heard, if he himself wishes to volunteer proof. 1. On a question of free birth, judges can pass sentence as heavy as exile on anyone who has maliciously raised the question. 2. Tutors or curators of *pupilli*, after exercising *tutela* and administering their property, cannot raise the issue of their status. 3. A husband is not forbidden to raise the status of a wife who is also his freedwoman.

40   HERMOGENIAN, *Epitome of Law, book 5:* A man over twenty who has put himself up for sale with an agreement to share the price cannot even after manumission proclaim his free birth.

41   PAUL, *Suits for Freedom, sole book:* If the situation of a person engaged in proceedings for his freedom is obscure, a hearing must first be given to his wish to prove that he is in actual possession of freedom.   1. Furthermore, the judge who tries the issue of freedom should also try suits for removal of goods and fraudulent damage; for it may be that in reliance on his freedom he may have ventured to purloin, spoil, and consume some of the goods of his master.

42   LABEO, *Posthumous Works, book 4:* If a slave whom you had bought in good faith proclaimed freedom and the judge wrongly decided in his favor and the owner of that slave after the verdict against you made you his heir or he came to be yours under any other title, you will be able to claim him as yours without hindrance from a demurrer (*praescriptio*) of *res judicata.*

43   POMPONIUS, *Senatus Consulta, book 3:* Those who appropriated the goods of their masters and then proclaimed their freedom were the subject of a rescript of the deified Hadrian in these terms: "Just as it is not fair in reliance on the freedom due under a *fideicommissum* to appropriate money in the inheritance, so too it is not right to seek pretexts for delay in making grants of freedom that are due. It was then your duty to appoint an *arbiter* without delay who should settle what can be kept for the heir before he should be compelled to manumit the slave."

44   VENULEIUS, *Actions, book 7:* Though it was formerly doubted whether a man was bound to a patron in respect of the burdens imposed as a condition of freedom by oath taken as a slave or on his becoming a freedman, still it is the truer opinion that he can only be bound when free. But for this very reason men usually exact an oath from slaves in order that a religious bond might compel them, once they had become their own masters, to take a [second] oath, provided that the oath or promise be given immediately after manumission.   1. It is also permissible to include women in provisions for gifts, services, and workdays.   2. An *actio utilis* under the heading of workdays is to be given against the man who took the oath before reaching puberty, provided that he was capable of taking an oath, but only after he has reached the age of puberty. Still even before that age he can give days of service, for example, as an attendant who informed his master of the names of persons he met or stage actor.

13

MEN DEBARRED FROM PROCLAIMING FREEDOM

1   ULPIAN, *Duties of Proconsul, book 2:* Men over twenty are only debarred from proclaiming freedom, if they received the price of their sale, but in other circumstances, even if a man over twenty allowed himself to be sold, he may proclaim his freedom.   1. But a man under twenty must not be denied proclamation of freedom even on the ground mentioned above, and though he remained in slavery after the age of twenty, unless thereafter he shared in the price; for then we shall have to say that proclamation of freedom ought to be denied him.

2   MARCELLUS, *Digest, book 24:* A man took a slave from Titius by force and ordered him to be free in his will; although he was solvent at death, the slave will not be free; otherwise, Titius will be defrauded, since if the grant of freedom does not proceed, he

can take proceedings against the heir, but if the slave has attained to freedom, he would have no action, since the heir will be deemed to have had no benefit from the delict (*dolus*) of the deceased.

3 POMPONIUS, *Letters and Readings, book 11:* Given that men who have let themselves be sold are denied the right of proclaiming their freedom, do the relevant *senatus consulta* also apply to women who have let themselves be sold and to their offspring? It cannot be doubted that the right to proclaim freedom should also be denied to a woman over twenty who has let herself be sold; it is also not to be given to her children born while she is in slavery.

4 PAUL, *Questions, book 12:* Licinnius Rufus wrote to Julius Paulus [Paul]: "A man to whom fideicommissary freedom was due after his twentieth year let himself be sold; I am asking if he should be denied the right to proclaim freedom. My doubt arises from the pattern case of any freeman; one who had obtained freedom and sold himself would have been denied the right, and we ought not to take a man as being in a better position because he was in a condition of slavery when he let himself be sold than if he obtained freedom. But a doubt arises on the other side, because with the man in question the sale has occurred, and there is a person to be sold, whereas in the case of a freeman, there is no sale and nothing to be sold. So I am asking for a comprehensive exposition." He replied: "There can be a contract of sale for both a slave and a freeman with a stipulation regarding eviction; of course, we are not speaking of the purchaser who knows the man to be free; for proclamation of freedom is not denied against him to the freeman who let himself be sold. But the man still in slavery can be sold even against his will, although he himself is at fault in that he conceals his situation, when it is within his power to attain freedom immediately indeed, that cannot be imputed to the slave to whom freedom is not yet due. Suppose a *statuliber* let himself be sold; no one would say that a suit for freedom should be denied him, when the condition takes effect which it was not in his power to make effective. However, on the facts stated, it is the better view that a suit for freedom should be denied to the man who could have applied for freedom and preferred to let himself be sold, since he does not deserve assistance from the praetor responsible for *fideicommissa*."

5 PAUL, *Senatus Consultum Claudianum, sole book:* If two of us have bought a freeman over twenty, one in knowledge of his status, the other without, the knowledge of the one does not entitle him to proclaim his freedom; the ignorance of the other will make him his slave; the purchaser who knows the facts will not have a share.

14

CLAIMS TO FREE BIRTH

1 MARCELLUS, *Digest, book 7:* If it should be alleged that one man's freedman has been pronounced freeborn on the action of a third party, the patron of the man can normally bring the matter to court without any limit of time.

2 SATURNINUS, *Duties of a Proconsul, book 1:* By a *constitutio* of the deified Hadrian, a man who let himself be sold after reaching his majority, that is, for the purpose of obtaining the price, is to be forbidden to take proceedings for his freedom, though Hadrian permitted this on occasion, provided that he had paid the price back. 1. Freedmen who may claim free birth will not be heard after five years have lapsed from their manumission. 2. Those who assert that they have discovered evidence of their free birth after five years must approach the emperors themselves on the matter, and they will try the claim.

3 POMPONIUS, *Senatus Consulta, book 5:* By using the phrase "recognition of birth rights" the senate must be understood to have had only persons of free birth in

mind.   1. The word "leave" must be understood to mean that they are to restore whatever they may have acquired from the property of the manumitter. But we must see how this is to be interpreted; should they restore what they had taken away without the knowledge of the owners plus resulting acquisitions, or does it also include what the manumitters freely gave them? The second view is the better.

4   PAPINIAN, *Questions, book 22:* The imperial speech which forbids consuls or provincial governors to hear proclamations of free birth after the lapse of five years from manumission makes no exception of circumstances or persons.

5   PAPINIAN, *Replies, book 10:* When a verdict has been given for free birth but the matter was decided without the patron's knowledge, I replied that the patron was not to be nonsuited after five years by a demurrer (*praescriptio*) of lapse of time.

6   ULPIAN, *Edict, book 38:* Whenever a man's status as freedman is at issue, there is a preliminary inquiry before hearing of a suit for workdays or *obsequium* or before an *actio famosa* be brought or summons issued against the self-styled patron or if no case is actually pending. Furthermore, whenever a man admits his status as a freedman but denies that he is the freedman of Gaius Seius, there is also a preliminary inquiry. The trial takes place at the instance of either party, but the self-styled patron always has the role of plaintiff, and the burden of proving that the man is his freedman; if he does not prove it, he fails.

15

STATUS OF DECEASED NOT TO BE QUESTIONED
AFTER FIVE YEARS

1   MARCIAN, *Delators, sole book:* No inquiry into the status of deceased persons is permitted after five years either at the instance of a private individual or on behalf of the imperial treasury.   1. But neither must the status of a man be called in question who died within the term of five years, if the inquiry would be prejudicial to a man who died before that term.   2. Furthermore, even the status of a living person is not to be questioned, if that is prejudicial to one who died more than five years before; this is also stated in a *constitutio* of the deified Hadrian.   3. But on occasion, it is also forbidden to rule on the status of a person deceased within the five-year period; for the speech of the deified Marcus provides that if anyone has been pronounced a man of free birth, the verdict may be reviewed only during his life, but not after his death; this goes so far that even a review that has been initiated is extinguished by his death, as the same speech provides.   4. What I have said must govern a case when the review was to depreciate the man's status, but what if it was to improve it? Suppose he is alleged to be a freedman and not a slave; why should that not be admitted? What if a man should be alleged to be a slave on the basis that his mother, deceased more than five years before, was a slave-woman? Why should he be debarred from proving that she was free? This is for the benefit of the deceased woman. Marcellus wrote in the fifth book of his *Duties of Consul* that this was possible, and I too have followed the same view in the public hearing of a case.

2   PAPINIAN, *Replies, book 14:* It is agreed that the freedom of sons should not be questioned for the sake of the posthumous repute of mother or father, when that has not been reviewed for five years from death.   1. And as this is a case which has been thought worthy of public protection, the remedy of *restitutio in integrum* is not to be granted when *pupilli* take proceedings on the ground that the term of five years ran

out when they had no tutors. 2. The demurrer of five years which protects the status of persons deceased is not voided on the pretext that a suit was instituted before their death, if it should be proved that the old suit ended in a long silence owing to the plaintiff's failure to attend.

3 HERMOGENIAN, *Epitome of Law, book 6:* It is not forbidden to prove that the status of a person deceased more than five years before was more honorable than was believed at the time of death. Hence, if anyone should die in slavery, it can be proved after five years that he was a freeman at death.

4 CALLISTRATUS, *Rights of the Imperial Treasury, book 1:* The deified Nerva was the very first to forbid by edict any inquiry into the status of a man five years after death. But there is also a rescript of the deified Claudius to Claudianus that a pecuniary inquiry has no effect if it will evidently prejudice a man's status.

16

DISCOVERY OF COLLUSION

1 GAIUS, *Urban Praetor's Edict, Chapter on Suits for Freedom, book 2:* To prevent the undue indulgence of certain owners to their slaves sullying the most distinguished order [that is, the senate], by their allowing their own slaves to proclaim their free birth and obtain judgment of freedom, the senate passed a decree in Domitian's time, wherein it was provided that if anyone had proved that there had been any collusion in ending the man's status as a slave, he should become the slave of whoever had discovered the collusion.

2 ULPIAN, *Duties of Consul, book 2:* By a *constitutio* of the deified Marcus it is possible to discover collusion in regard to free birth within five years after judgment. 1. We shall certainly take the period of five years to run without a break. 2. Obviously, as the age of the person in whose case collusion is reviewed may be a reason for postponing review until he reaches the age of puberty or even beyond, we must say that the period of five years [then] ceases to run. 3. But in my view, the limit of the period is set not by the time when the review is to be completed, but by that when it is to be initiated; this is reversed in the case of anyone claiming to be freeborn, when reputed a freedman. 4. The speech of the deified Marcus provides that even *extranei* who had the right of taking proceedings on behalf of a third party should be permitted to discover collusion.

3 CALLISTRATUS, *Judicial Examinations, book 4:* When anyone has been pronounced of free birth in the absence of the person with a right to contest the suit, the decision is just as ineffective as if there had been no judgment in the case at all; and this is provided in imperial *constitutiones*.

4 ULPIAN, *Lex Julia et Papia, book 1:* If a freedman has been collusively pronounced of free birth and the collusion has been discovered, from that time he is treated as a freedman in all respects, but in the intervening time after the judgment for free birth and before discovery of the collusion, he is certainly taken to be of free birth.

5 HERMOGENIAN, *Epitome of Law, book 5:* A judgment in favor of free birth may be reviewed once on the plea of collusion. 1. If several persons should apply at the same time to discover collusion, there must be a hearing to decide which should be admitted, after comparison of the characters and ages of all and their respective interests.

Printed in the United States
215004BV00001B/2/P

9 780812 2203